A BIRDER'S GUIDE TO

THE UNIVERSITY OF NORT

COASTAL NORTH CAROLINA

AROLINA PRESS | CHAPEL HILL & LONDON

JOHN O. FUSSELL III

Maps © 1994 The University of North Carolina Press
Manufactured in the United States of America
The paper in this book meets the guidelines for permanence and durability of the
Committee on Production Guidelines for Book Longevity of the Council on
Library Resources.
All photographs courtesy of Jack Dermid

Library of Congress Cataloging-in-Publication Data
Fussell, John O.
    A birder's guide to coastal North Carolina / by John O. Fussell III.
        p. cm.
    Includes bibliographical references and indexes.
    ISBN 0-8078-2146-2 (cloth : alk. paper). — ISBN 0-8078-4453-5 (pbk. : alk.
paper)
    1. Bird watching—North Carolina—Atlantic Coast—Guidebooks. 2. Birds—
North Carolina—Atlantic Coast. 3. Atlantic Coast (N.C.)—Guidebooks. I. Title.
QL684.N8F87 1994
598.29756—dc20   93-32475
                                                                      CIP

98 97 96 95 94   5 4 3 2 1

QL
684
N8
F87
1994

THIS BOOK IS DEDICATED first and foremost to my parents, who introduced me to a wonderful, exciting world: my father taught me the joy of seeing a thrasher, a catbird, a towhee, when I was five or so—my mother ferried me around on many expeditions and on trips to the library in Beaufort to borrow the old copy of *Birds of North Carolina*, which fueled my imagination—and both parents entrusted a pair of binoculars to me when I was only ten.

And to all those adults who took time to help out this boy with a passion for bird-watching, especially to Harry Davis of the State Museum of Natural History (now the North Carolina Museum of Natural Sciences), John Thompson, and the other men who were willing to put up with a thirteen-year-old for a several-day-long banding expedition.

And to T. L. Quay at North Carolina State University and all the birding students of the bird and mammal range at State in the late 1960s and early 1970s. It was a very special time.

And to all those who share with me their enthusiasm about birding, including every backyard birder who calls to excitedly report her first close-up sighting of a chickadee, a titmouse.

CONTENTS

Overview maps of the five coastal sections can be found on pages 62, 90, 134, 212, and 314.

ACKNOWLEDGMENTS

Although I would like to think that this guide contains a few original bird-finding ideas, it is in fact largely a compilation of previously existing bird-finding knowledge, which I have gleaned from many sources and innumerable conversations. To anyone from whom I have learned the slightest tidbit of information, I offer my appreciation. This is your book as well as mine.

Many people associated with federal, state, and other agencies were very helpful to me while I was collecting information for this guide. Appreciation is extended to the following: Walker Golder, National Audubon Society; Merrill Lynch, North Carolina Nature Conservancy; Alan Olmstead, North Carolina Wildlife Resources Commission; Ben Nottingham, Mackay Island NWR; Teresa Cherry, Great Dismal Swamp NWR; Floyd Williams, Merchants Millpond SP; Bob Noffsinger and Bonnie Strawser, Alligator River NWR and Pea Island NWR; John Smith, Tidewater Research Station; Kelly Davis, Mattamuskeet NWR; Lauris Joyner, Goose Creek SP; Jeff Smith, Nags Head Woods Ecological Preserve; Marcia Lyons, Cape Hatteras NS; Bill Harris and Michael Rikard, Cape Lookout NS; Joyce Bland, Rachel Carson Estuarine Research Reserve; Jody Merritt and Randall Newman, Fort Macon SP; Holly Jenkins and Pam Robinson, Croatan NF; Sam Bland, Hammocks Beach SP; Vic French, Holly Shelter Game Land; John Ruble, Carolina Power and Light's L. V. Sutton Electric Plant; and Don Cooke, Carolina Power and Light's Brunswick Plant. Bonnie Strawser, Kelly Davis, and Marcia Lyons were especially helpful and encouraging, and each of them reviewed one or more site guides. (Kelly even filled in some of the mileages.)

Other individuals that have contributed useful information to this project, if only through a brief conversation, are Rich Boyd, Allen Bryan, Sam Cooper, Larry Crawford, Ricky Davis, Steve Dinsmore, Jack Fennell, Wade Fuller, Buddy Garrett, Gil Grant, Bob Hader, Bob Holmes, Jeannie Kraus, Harry Le-Grand, Greg Massey, Nell Moore, Jeremy Nance, James Parnell, JoAnne Powell, T. L. Quay, Paul Spitzer, Deb Squires, John Taggart, Michael Tove, John Wright, and Paula Wright. Special thanks are extended to Allen Bryan, Sam Cooper, Steve Dinsmore, Bob Holmes, Harry LeGrand, and Jeremy Nance, all of whom answered several questions about certain sites or provided information about birds of special interest. Steve did his best to keep my interest level high in 1993 by calling in reports of rarities almost every week, although I began to fear that he might make this book out-of-date before its publication!

Appreciation is also extended to David Perry, Christi Stanforth, and Heidi Perov of the University of North Carolina Press. David has been supportive and unbelievably patient during the course of this project. Christi is to be commended for remaining organized despite receiving the manuscript in bits and pieces. And if the instructions in this guide prove to be unambiguous, she should get most of the credit.

FSR	U.S. Forest Service road
NA	Natural Area
NC	North Carolina route
NF	National Forest
NHS	National Historic Site
NS	National Seashore
NWR	National Wildlife Refuge
ORV	Off-road vehicle
SHS	State Historic Site
SP	State Park
SR	North Carolina secondary road
US	U.S. route
VA	Virginia route

PART 1

INTRODUCTION

Bird-watching is one of the most popular hobbies in the United States, and its popularity increases yearly. Birding undoubtedly appeals to people for numerous reasons. Perhaps the most basic one is that most of us feel some kinship with nature, and bird-watching can give us an excuse to leave our increasingly manmade surroundings for a while, to go out and enjoy the natural world. Another reason for birding's popularity is that it can be enjoyed at many levels of activity and intensity. Many backyard birders dearly love their chickadees and titmice but would never dream of heading off on a field trip to see new species. At the other extreme, some birders fly frequently to the far corners of the globe to add new species to their life lists.

Coastal North Carolina provides wonderful opportunities for bird-watching. The region contains an excellent variety of habitat, and over four hundred species have been identified in the area, although the region only has a handful of active birders and is actually not birded very heavily. New species are found almost every year.

In many ways, north and south come together in coastal North Carolina. Several species reach their southern breeding limit here, and in winter there are vast flocks of waterfowl in some areas; you can often find species such as Iceland and Glaucous gulls, eiders, and Harlequin Duck. On the other hand, species typically associated with the Deep South, like the Anhinga, Wilson's Plover, Red-cockaded Woodpecker, Painted Bunting, and Bachman's Sparrow can also be found.

One reason for the birding potential of the region is the presence of the tropics and subtropics just offshore. The Gulf Stream edge, which sometimes lies only a few miles off Cape Hatteras, provides excellent pelagic birding. And the relative proximity of deep water to Oregon and Hatteras inlets offers birders the chance to find Black-capped Petrels and Band-rumped Storm-Petrels regularly. In fact, no area of the United States is better for finding these species and the White-tailed Tropicbird. Even better, during recent trips off these inlets birders have found that even more "exotic" species, such as Herald and Soft-plumaged petrels, may be regular in these waters.

Probably no one area typifies the appeal of the region so much as the Outer Banks, particularly the Pea Island National Wildlife Refuge (NWR) and Bodie

Island area. At the ponds and impoundments here, a long list of water birds can be found in the course of a year. Many species are found far more easily here than anywhere else in the state. This area is especially exciting during the autumn migration, when passerines pour through, leaving the observer delightfully frustrated, not knowing which site to go to next. And on the Outer Banks, rarities are the norm rather than the exception.

As in most coastal areas of the nation, habitat loss is rampant in coastal North Carolina. On the positive side, though, much critical habitat is being preserved in public lands—national seashores, national wildlife refuges, national forests, state parks, state estuarine reserves, and state game lands. Also, the Nature Conservancy and National Audubon Society are protecting some special natural areas in the region. Thus, in the future there will still be numerous sites for bird-watching and enjoying nature.

Although coastal North Carolina is one of the better birding areas in the nation, there has not previously been a comprehensive guide to the region's birding sites. This book is an attempt to fill that void. The meat of the book presents site guides to all major birding areas in the region, an annotated list of all birds, and bar graphs showing the seasonal occurrence for all regularly occurring species. Furthermore, the Birds of Special Interest section (part 3) gives detailed bird-finding information for 141 of the most frequently sought-after species.

While compiling this book, I have become even more intrigued by the major birding areas of our coastal area. However, I have perhaps been most impressed by all the minor off-the-beaten-path birding areas, each with its own unique character. The discoveries that I made in such areas were often more gratifying than the things I learned about the major areas. Even as I was finishing up this book, I was finding new information that I would have liked to include in the book but couldn't. I definitely plan to update this book; indeed, I will certainly have recorded numerous tentative changes and additions before this first edition is printed. I would greatly appreciate any suggestions.

THIS BOOK IS of course not a field guide. Its basic purpose is to describe the better birding sites in the coastal area so that the reader will know when and how to visit these areas, as well as what to look for. It follows the basic format of most bird-finding guides.

The names used in this book and the sequence followed in chapter 3, in part 3, and in the appendix follow the American Ornithologists' Union Checklist of North American Birds (sixth edition, 1983), including more recent addenda. This is basically the same sequence you will see in most field guides.

Chapter 1 includes a brief description of the physiography, vegetation, and climate of the region. A basic knowledge of the plant communities mentioned here would be helpful to the reader but is not essential. Elsewhere in the book, descriptions of habitat are quite simple (for instance, "a wet shrubby area"). Birds respond primarily to the structure of a habitat, and attempting to describe where they occur in terms of a particular plant community is often difficult and misleading.

Chapter 2 provides basic advice for the birder and traveler in the region, including discussions of hazards and travel as well as some basic birding tips.

Chapter 3 gives a brief summary of abundance, seasonal occurrence, and habitat for all species (except accidentals) occurring in the area. It also includes a listing of all accidentals that have been recorded.

Part 2 contains the site guides, which are arranged from north to south in five chapters (4 through 8): North Coast, Albemarle-Pamlico, Outer Banks, Central Coast, and South Coast. Chapter 9, the last chapter in part 2, contains information on pelagic trips.

Part 3—Birds of Special Interest—provides detailed information about where, when, and how to find 141 species that are frequently sought by birders. Especially important is the information about how to look for these birds: the best weather conditions, tide conditions, etc.

The appendix presents bar graphs showing seasonal abundance for all species except extremely rare or accidental ones.

Some readers may initially be confused about the overlapping information provided in chapter 3 (the annotated list), part 3 (the Birds of Special Interest section), and the appendix. Again, the basic purpose of chapter 3 is to give a summary of status and habitat for virtually all species occurring in the area. This chapter also describes important regional differences in status. For most species, a reader interested in the abundance level at a particular date should then refer to the frequency graphs. These bar graphs are particularly helpful for showing changing levels of abundance during arrival/departure periods.

Each of the species accounts in part 3 includes a brief summary of seasonal status. Here readers should focus on the peak times for finding a particular species, referring also to the corresponding bar graph. In general, references to seasonal occurrence in the site guides (part 2) are often very general, like "breeding season" and "autumn migration," to avoid being repetitive. To find out when the breeding season or the autumn migration period is for a certain species, refer to the bar graphs. Note that the peak of the "autumn migration period" for some species may actually occur during the summer. Occasionally, the status given in the site guides (part 2) for some species may be slightly different from that given in the bar graphs, because the descriptions in part 2 indicate species' status for the actual site, while the bar graphs show the average for the region.

Virtually all areas discussed in this book are public lands—national seashores, national wildlife refuges, state parks, state game lands, etc. However, in some cases I describe roadside birding through lands that I clearly identify as private. In these cases you will have to stick to the road and find the birds from its shoulder.

A less clear-cut situation involves ocean fishing piers. These sites are privately owned, but the parking areas are often used for public parking, at least seasonally. Most of the piers sell refreshments and actually want more potential customers, as long as there is enough parking for fishermen. Any pier discussed in this book is commonly used by the general public (at least seasonally). However, pier management and policies can change; be alert to any such changes. (Hint: buy a snack before you ask whether it's all right to park.)

The book also includes a few estuarine access points that may be privately owned (ownership is in many cases contested) but have been used as public access for decades. I included these sites if it was clearly unlikely that this policy would change. Nevertheless, if you see any No Trespassing signs in such areas, stay out.

Highway distances between different points in the site guides were checked carefully. Nevertheless, readers should be aware that odometers vary from one vehicle to another. To be on the safe side, begin looking for a turn a little before your odometer indicates that you should have gotten to it.

In the past, secondary roads in North Carolina have typically been identified only by four-digit numbers. In recent years, some counties have added signs with road names. Thus, the book might give a name, number, or both for a particular road. If you do not see a street sign at an intersection, look for the four-digit road number on the support posts for any stop signs and/or directional signs there.

In order to keep the site-guide maps relatively uncluttered, many of the smaller roadways were left out, although of course each map shows all roads needed to get to a site. If in driving to a site you see a road that does not appear on the map, do not be concerned.

It is also worth mentioning that many small bridges are being replaced by culverts. If instructions for a particular site say to pull off at the bridge after a certain distance, but you don't see a bridge, then look for a culvert.

CHAPTER 1

BRIEF SURVEY OF
THE COASTAL AREA

The inland boundary of the area covered by this guide is somewhat arbitrary; it was actually determined largely by the distribution of the better birding spots along and near the coast. Coincidentally, the defined area corresponds rather closely to the area typically referred to as "Tidewater" or "outer coastal plain." The inland boundary lies just west of the limits of tidal influence (including wind tides) along the rivers and estuaries. For instance, the boundary lies approximately where the Pamlico (Tar) and Neuse rivers change from narrow, flowing, true rivers to wide estuaries.

The delineation of the different sections—North Coast, Albemarle-Pamlico, Outer Banks, Central Coast, and South Coast—was based in part on well-defined geographical divisions but is also to some extent arbitrary. For example, many people like to argue over what should or should not be considered the Outer Banks. The boundary in this book basically follows what seems to be the most widely held definition. I grouped Portsmouth Island with the Outer Banks partly because visitors usually reach it by way of Ocracoke to the north.

CLIMATE

Coastal North Carolina has a temperate climate. The mean temperature is in the low sixties. The January mean is about forty-five degrees; the July mean is about eighty. For most of the area, the daily high and low can differ by roughly twenty degrees. Thus, on an "average" day in January, the temperature can rise from a low of thirty-five to a high of fifty-five. The daily range is somewhat less on the Outer Banks and many of the other barrier islands, especially during the warmer months.

The average annual rainfall is about fifty inches. Most of this rain falls during the warmer months, although it seems the other way around. That is, a summer day may be clear except for a brief thunderstorm that produces an inch of rain, while a few days' worth of rain in winter may produce the same amount of rainfall.

Of course, with weather, averages tell little of the whole story. Winter is particularly variable. In the last decade, there have been winters with day after day of what many would consider to be almost perfect weather—calm, no clouds in the sky all day, with a seventy-degree high. The last decade has also produced zero-degree cold as well as a sixteen-inch snow with near-blizzard conditions, which left many of the smaller estuaries completely frozen. Coastal North Carolina's weather typically lies between these two extremes. Unfortunately, milder periods in winter also tend to be rainy.

On average, winter is especially nice at South Coast sites away from the water. Here windchill values are seldom of concern. Ironically, the Outer Banks area in a way has both the mildest and the coldest weather. Overnight lows here usually do not reach freezing; the first freeze of the winter often does not occur until Christmas and, indeed, has even been as late as February. On the other hand, windchill values can be particularly raw. This area can be one of the coldest places anywhere when it's fifty degrees. And on those occasions when the temperature itself is cold, you'll probably prefer to do your birding from inside a car, no matter where you're from. To a lesser extent, such cold windchill values also affect other parts of the immediate coast—barrier islands and sound-side areas.

Spring is overall quite pleasant, and April and May usually have little rain. Southward and inland, April is the most comfortable month. In May, daytime highs may approach summertime levels, and searches for land birds become more and more limited to early mornings. By the water from the Central Coast north, many days in April can actually be rather chilly, and May is the most pleasant month. Springtime can offer some of the most striking north-to-south temperature differences across the region because of the strong "backdoor" cold fronts with brisk northeasterly winds that occasionally push halfway down the coast. It is not too unusual for an April day in Elizabeth City to be fifty-five degrees and drizzling, due to a raw northeaster, while it's sunny and eighty-five degrees at Wilmington.

Temperature-wise, summers in coastal North Carolina are really not too extreme. However, the humidity levels and heat indices can wither the interests of even the most intense birders. Along the inland fringe of the region, almost any day that is clear is also hot, with a high of ninety degrees or above. Early morning birding is a must. From the barrier islands of the Central Coast north, especially on the Outer Banks, June is usually rather comfortable. Even in July and August, temperatures usually stay below ninety degrees, but the air is usually almost dripping with humidity, and overnight lows may not get below eighty. But sometimes within this period—especially in late August—northeasters can drastically lower temperatures and humidity levels.

Many would argue that autumn tends to offer the most pleasant weather of the year. In September, especially early September, daytime highs often reach summertime levels, but humidity levels are a bit lower and early mornings have at least a hint of autumn, especially inland. Beginning about late September or early October, stronger cold fronts begin to pass through the region, lowering temperatures and humidities and sweeping passerines to the coast. October is arguably the most pleasant month of the year. Temperatures range from mild to pleasantly brisk, and rainfall is a rarity: on most October days, there's nothing but blue overhead. November can be almost as nice, although a bit cooler. However, cloudy rainy weather is a bit more likely, especially toward the end of the month.

PHYSIOGRAPHY AND HABITAT

North Coast Section
The barrier islands of this section have historically been open and windswept, with numerous mobile dunes, some quite high, like Luark (or Penny's) Hill north of Corolla. These barrier islands definitely seem like they should belong to a state farther north; the dominant grasses of the dunes are American beach grass and tall bitter panic grass. The northern bayberry is also common.

Only a few years ago, much of this strand was virtually untouched. But a staggering degree of beach development has since occurred and continues to occur. Fortunately, some sections of this strand are being preserved in the Currituck NWR and the Currituck Banks Estuarine Research Reserve, as well as on land owned by the Nature Conservancy.

The waters of Currituck Sound are brackish, and the Albemarle Sound is fresh to brackish. Water levels in these sounds are determined by wind tides. Over most of the area, water levels are lowest during northerly winds and up to two feet higher during southwesterly winds, which force water up from the Pamlico Sound.

The marshes along Currituck Sound are brackish, vegetated with a mixture of species like black needlerush, saltmeadow cordgrass, bulrushes, and cattails. The best example of this type of marsh is the Great Marsh, which can be seen along the causeway to Knotts Island. This marsh has resident King Rails and Marsh Wrens, and Least Bitterns are common here in summer.

The waters of Currituck Sound harbored vast numbers of waterfowl earlier in the century, but today there are very few waterfowl on the open waters of the sound. However, numerous waterfowl still use the brackish marshes of

Currituck Banks and Knotts Island, including the impoundments at Mackay Island NWR.

The mainland of this section is mostly low and flat. Much of the area has been converted to farmland. The Great Dismal Swamp NWR preserves a vast area of the Great Dismal. Of the several swamp forest habitats, the most interesting are the tupelo gum–bald cypress and Atlantic white cedar communities. The Great Dismal has an excellent variety of breeding warblers and is an excellent place to find Swainson's Warblers.

Albemarle-Pamlico Section

The waters of the Pamlico Sound and lower Pamlico River adjacent to this section have some of the best populations of diving ducks in the state. Lesser Scaup, Buffleheads, Black and Surf scoters, and Canvasbacks are common. Especially interesting are the sound waters near Swan Quarter, where numerous Oldsquaws overwinter each year. The best way to see these birds is by way of the Swan Quarter–Ocracoke ferry.

The Albemarle-Pamlico peninsula is low and flat, especially Tyrrell, Hyde, and Dare counties, which lie only a few feet above sea level and get progressively lower as sea level rises and the land subsides. This section contains some of the most expansive farmlands in the coastal area. On the farmlands west of Lake Phelps, Lapland Longspurs have been regular in recent years.

Curiously, two of the better waterfowl spots in the region—Mattamuskeet NWR and the Pungo unit of Pocosin Lakes NWR—are located on the sites of failed agricultural operations. Both sites harbor impressive numbers of swans, geese, and dabbling ducks each winter.

In contrast with most of the peninsula, the eastern tip, in Dare County, is largely covered with native vegetation of swamp forest and pocosins. Preserved as part of Alligator NWR and other federal lands, this area has a good variety of breeding land birds and is another good spot for finding Swainson's Warblers.

Outer Banks

From the air, the Outer Banks, which separate the Atlantic Ocean and Pamlico Sound, strike viewers as an especially narrow and fragile strip. These barrier islands are very unstable and geologically active. They have been migrating landward for thousands of years and continue to do so. At several sites on the Banks, portions of NC 12 have had to be relocated landward in recent years, and more relocations are in the planning stages.

The profile of most of the Banks is actually quite unnatural, the result of constant human efforts to protect the highway. Broad overwash flats and temporary inlets were once common along much of the Banks; the narrow steep dune line that lies between NC 12 and the ocean today is a manmade feature, a vain effort to hold back the sea.

Perhaps the most distinctive feature of the Outer Banks is Cape Hatteras, which extends to within a few miles of the Gulf Stream. Because of its proximity to the Gulf Stream, numerous pelagic birds pass by the cape each spring.

The physiography of Portsmouth Island and the south end of Ocracoke Island is especially distinctive. There are extensive flats seaward of the main portion of both islands, and these flats are separated from the ocean by a narrow beach or dune line. At Ocracoke, these flats, which were once barren, have become vegetated with salt meadows (with species like black needlerush, salt-meadow cordgrass, and marsh fimbry) and salt marshes. At Portsmouth, the flats are still largely barren, but marsh vegetation has begun to invade in recent years, and in the future the area may grow up in salt meadows and salt marshes.

Some portions of the Outer Banks are wider, somewhat more stable, and forested. Kitty Hawk Woods, at the northern end of the Banks, is actually a relict mainland area that the migrating barrier island strand ran into. On the other hand, the Buxton Woods area at Cape Hatteras is a section of the actual barrier island that has widened and stabilized. Each of the ridges in the woods represents a different shoreline that existed during this widening process. Most of the ridges of Buxton Woods are several hundred years old.

Vegetation of the Outer Banks primarily consists of southern species, although mid-Atlantic species are also prominent on the northern Outer Banks.

Most of the Banks are dunes and open, sandy areas vegetated with herbaceous vegetation, especially sea oats and saltmeadow cordgrass. However, the more northerly American beach grass is also common, especially on the northern Outer Banks.

Scattered low shrub thickets are dominated by species like red cedar, yaupon, wax myrtle, and groundsel-tree. As you go north from Cape Hatteras, northern bayberry becomes increasingly common.

Just as the vegetation exhibits some north-to-south variation along the Banks, there is also some variation in birdlife. Field Sparrows breed in low shrub vegetation south to Bodie Island but no farther. Portsmouth Island represents the southern breeding limit of the Song Sparrow.

The maritime forest areas of Kitty Hawk Woods, Nags Head Woods, and Buxton Woods are especially interesting. The first two sites have an interesting mixture of northern (or inland) and southern species. However, they are generally dominated by deciduous species. The Buxton Woods area is dominated by more southern species, many of which are broadleaf evergreens. Dominant vegetation there includes loblolly pine, laurel oak, live oak, red bay, and yaupon. Dwarf palmettos are common at many sites.

The sounds adjacent to the Outer Banks have virtually no lunar tide, except immediately adjacent to the inlets, where tides range from about one to two feet. Far more important in this area are wind tides. During brisk southwest winds, the sound waters adjacent to the northern Outer Banks may be two to three feet higher than during northeast winds. Adjacent to the southern Outer Banks, the opposite is true.

At the extreme north end of the area, the water in these sounds is brackish; farther south, it becomes saline. Submerged aquatic vegetation like eel-grass, shoal-grass, and wigeon-grass are common, and this area supports a good population of wintering waterfowl, including Brants at Hatteras and Ocracoke inlets.

Regularly flooded salt marshes occur only immediately adjacent to the inlets. These marshes are flooded daily by lunar tides and are dominated by saltmarsh cordgrass. Along the Outer Banks, saltmarsh cordgrass generally grows to be only two to three feet high and does not form thick stands. These regularly flooded salt marshes provide good year-round habitat for Clapper Rails and seasonal habitat for migrant and wintering Marsh Wrens and Sharp-tailed and Seaside sparrows.

Most of the marshes along the Outer Banks are irregularly flooded salt marshes, which are flooded only by wind tides. Dominant species of these marshes are black needlerush, saltmeadow cordgrass, salt grass, and saltmarsh cordgrass. The numbers of breeding marsh birds in such marshes is largely related to how extensive the marsh is. Small marshes may have no breeding birds. Extensive marshes, such as the Roanoke Island Marshes, have breeding Virginia and Black rails, Marsh Wrens, and Seaside Sparrows.

Historically, many such marshes were diked to improve habitat for waterfowl, especially at Bodie Island. Today the impoundments at Pea Island NWR provide winter habitat for numerous waterfowl.

Central Coast Section

The barrier islands of this section vary considerably from north to south. To the north, Core Banks lies about three miles from the mainland. However, the barrier islands of Camp Lejeune Marine Corps Base almost touch the mainland.

The Core Banks area (part of the Cape Lookout National Seashore [NS]) is also geologically active, under constant assault from the waters of the Atlantic. However, in contrast with the Outer Banks, no highway runs through here, and the barrier island profile is natural, with low dunes and numerous overwash deposits. Sea oats and saltmeadow cordgrass are the dominant dune plants on Core Banks, although American beach grass also occurs.

A notable feature of the north end of Core Banks and south end of Portsmouth Island is the frequent presence of temporary inlets—low sites where the waters of ocean and sound often meet during extreme tides. These sites are created when sound waters piled up during storm-force winds from the north and northeast seek an outlet through the barrier islands. These sites are important nesting areas for Piping Plovers.

Cape Lookout does not project as far toward the Gulf Stream as Cape Hatteras. Yet it is more likely to be bathed in Gulf Stream waters, courtesy of occasional eddies that break off from the Gulf Stream and move inshore. Several species of tropical fish show up at the jetty there each summer.

South-facing Shackleford Banks (also part of the Cape Lookout NS) was almost covered with maritime forests until the mid-1800s. Thereafter, most of the forest disappeared as settlers and their livestock increased in numbers. Today a remnant of the forest stands at the west end of the island, but the rest of the island is open dunes, grasslands, and marshes.

Until the mid-twentieth century, Bogue Banks was also almost covered with maritime forests, but virtually all of this forest has succumbed to bulldozers in recent years. Fortunately, a small area of maritime forest is being preserved within the Theodore Roosevelt Natural Area (NA). This forest is also dominated by southern species, many of which are broadleaf evergreens. Common species include loblolly pine, laurel oak, live oak, wild olive, and red bay. Farther south, the barrier islands become increasingly smaller, narrower, and less stable.

Most of the estuarine waters of this section are saline, but the Neuse River is brackish. The Neuse River, Pamlico Sound, and much of Core Sound are characterized by wind tides, lowest during southwest winds and up to three feet higher during strong northeast winds. However, from Cape Lookout southward, water levels in the estuaries are determined largely by lunar tides, which average about three feet in the lower parts of the estuaries.

Large numbers of rafting ducks overwinter in the more open portions of the estuaries to the north and east. On Pamlico Sound and the lower Neuse River, there are often large numbers of scoters and other species. Farther up the Neuse River, Ruddy Ducks are usually common. Large flocks of Redheads often overwinter on the upper portion of Core Sound.

In eastern Pamlico County and eastern Carteret County, there are a few extensive irregularly flooded marshes that provide nesting habitat for Seaside Sparrows, Marsh Wrens, and Clapper, Virginia, and Black rails. The vast Cedar Island Marshes, part of Cedar Island NWR, are an excellent example of this type of marsh. The marshes at Cedar Island are also the southernmost nesting site of the Northern Harriers. In eastern Pamlico County, many of these marshes have been enclosed to create waterfowl impoundments, some of which harbor impressive winter concentrations. However, most of these are private, and the public Pamlico Point Impoundment is rather inaccessible.

Most of the mainland of the Central Coast is flat, although the relief is somewhat more varied toward the west and southwest. Southeastern Beaufort County, eastern Carteret County, and most of Pamlico County are reminiscent of the North Coast and Albemarle-Pamlico sections: flat and low in elevation, only a few feet above sea level.

A large part of the mainland is devoted to agriculture or intensive sylviculture (e.g., loblolly pine plantations). The Croatan National Forest (NF) contains many of the best remaining examples of natural habitats. Much of the central part of this forest is dominated by pocosin vegetation—primarily low pocosin, in which pond pines are only a few feet high, and the mass of broadleaf evergreen shrubs is only a few feet high. Such low pocosins harbor only a few bird species. Much more interesting are the borders of the pocosins—high pocosin and, especially, pond pine woodland. In such areas, pond pines are often forty feet and higher, and many of the broadleaf evergreen species reach tree height. Such areas harbor many breeding warblers, including Black-and-white, Worm-eating, Black-throated Green, and a few Swainson's.

The Croatan also has several types of longleaf pine–dominated habitats, such as wet pine flatwoods, pine/scrub oak sandhill, and xeric sandhill scrub. Red-cockaded Woodpeckers are found in such areas if trees are mature and occur in open stands with little understory vegetation. (This habitat structure is maintained by periodic burning.) Open examples of wet pine flatwoods, such as the Millis Road Savanna, are especially interesting. These areas have a dense ground cover of wiregrass, which attracts Bachman's Sparrows.

Streamside swamps in the Croatan are usually dominated by bald cypress, swamp tupelo, and other hardwoods. Even more noteworthy are those swamp forests that lie on upland flats, such as the Great Lake Sweet Gum Forest and the Gum Swamp Bottomland Forest. Along the northern edge of the Croatan, there are a few upland hardwood forests. The most special example of this type of forest is along the Island Creek Forest Walk, where there are numerous plant species that are found primarily in the Piedmont.

South Coast Section

The barrier islands are narrow, separated from the mainland by extensive salt marshes rather than open water sounds. Most of these islands have been developed for residential use. However, Masonboro Island and part of the barrier strand between Fort Fisher and Bald Head Island have been acquired for public protection as part of the Masonboro Island and Zeke's Island estuarine research reserves. At two areas within this section—Carolina Beach–Fort Fisher and Caswell Beach–Long Beach—there are no barrier islands; the ocean beats directly against the mainland.

The only natural rock beach in the state is at Fort Fisher. This outcrop of coquina rock covers less than an acre; however, more important, a larger outcrop of the rock lies underwater just offshore, and this habitat is undoubtedly part of the reason that these waters support such large numbers of loons, gannets, and other species in winter.

The only significant maritime forest on the South Coast barrier islands is at Bald Head Island. Most of this forest is being developed for residential use, but a tract at the southeast end of the island is being preserved. This maritime forest resembles the southern maritime forests described above but is even more strongly dominated by broadleaf evergreen species; cabbage palmettos are also common, and this site represents their northern limit.

The narrow estuaries lying between the barrier islands and the mainland have lunar tides that vary from about three feet in the north to four or five feet at the South Carolina line. The regularly flooded salt marshes in this area are especially tall and lush; at some sites the grasses reach six feet. Clapper Rails are common throughout the year, and Seaside and Sharp-tailed sparrows are common in the cooler months.

The Cape Fear River is the only river in North Carolina that flows directly into the ocean. The Cape Fear also has a lunar tide upriver, where the water is fresh. Consequently, the marshes at Wilmington provide good habitat for King Rails.

Two areas where significant tracts of natural habitats are being preserved are Holly Shelter Game Land and Green Swamp Ecological Preserve. Much of the game land consists of low- and medium-height pocosin. However, there are extensive areas of wet pine flatwoods and pine savannas, especially near US 17. Pine savannas are similar to wet pine flatwoods but are wetter and more open, with an especially rich variety of herbaceous species. In the flatwoods and savannas, birders can easily find Red-cockaded Woodpeckers and Bachman's Sparrows. The game land also includes swamp forests along the Northeast Cape Fear River.

The Green Swamp Ecological Preserve contains extensive areas of wet pine flatwoods, pine savannas, and pocosin habitats. These are the most exemplary examples of pine savannas in North Carolina. The flatwoods and savannas support an excellent population of breeding Bachman's Sparrows, and Red-cockaded Woodpeckers are easy to find throughout the year.

CHAPTER 2

GENERAL ADVICE AND BIRDING TIPS

HAZARDS

When visiting a new area, one of course wonders what sorts of unfamiliar beasties are out there. Poison ivy, poison oak, and bees and similar insects are widespread and do not merit any special comment. Some critters that do warrant mention are listed below, in descending order of concern.

Ticks
Tick-carried diseases like Rocky Mountain spotted fever and Lyme disease are now widespread across the United States. Most people are aware of these potential problems, but readers should note that both diseases have been reported in eastern North Carolina, although both are quite infrequent. Keep your pants cuffs tucked into your socks and wear insect repellent. Even more important, check yourself carefully for ticks a few times during the day. Don't panic when you do find ticks; reportedly a tick must remain attached for several hours before it can transmit the organisms that carry the above diseases. Ticks may be disgustingly common in some areas (usually sites on the mainland where deer are common) and almost absent in other areas, especially on the barrier islands.

Fire Ants
You are far more likely to have an unfortunate encounter with these pests than with any other species listed here. It is very easy to overlook a small mound and stand on it. Within seconds, numerous ants can crawl between your sock and pants cuff and begin biting you all at once. Even if you don't suffer allergies, you will probably receive many small but painful welts.

Fire ants have spread as far north as the Alligator River NWR, although they have not yet colonized the Outer Banks. They inhabit disturbed ground, especially roadsides, dikes, and similar areas. Larger mounds, up to a foot high in coastal North Carolina, are quite distinctive, but new, smaller mounds are similar to those of other ants. Learn what these ants and their mounds look like and avoid them.

Fire ants are actually small and unimpressive in appearance. They are reddish brown and can be identified easily by their behavior. If you disturb a mound with a stick, almost instantly there will be dozens of ants moving about very actively, weaving from side to side like they want to bite something.

Other Insects
While mosquitoes and similar biting insects are perhaps not quite as hazardous as ticks and fire ants, they can be even more annoying and harder to avoid. During the warmer months, you should always carry insect repellent just in case, although at many sites you won't often have to use it. Mosquitoes are usually worst in the vicinity of the larger marshes bordering Pamlico Sound and at Bodie and Pea islands, but populations vary considerably depending on how wet or dry it has been. In many areas, biting flies can be annoying—or worse—in May and June. The greenheads of Portsmouth Island can be unbelievably vicious in June and July. Anyone planning to camp out during the warmer months on the barrier islands should be prepared for onslaughts of "no-see-ums" or "sand gnats," although these insects are not a problem unless it is calm.

Poisonous Snakes
Undoubtedly some visitors from the North envision coastal North Carolina as the sort of place where poisonous snakes are lurking behind every shrub. In reality, one can easily spend an entire summer in the field and never see a poisonous snake.

Six species of poisonous snakes occur in coastal North Carolina: eastern coral snake, copperhead, cottonmouth, eastern diamondback rattlesnake, timber (canebrake) rattlesnake, and pigmy rattlesnake. However, two of these—the diamondback and the coral snake—are limited to the southern third of the area and are extremely scarce. In all upland areas, you are very unlikely to come across a poisonous snake. Cottonmouths are fairly common along streams in some areas, though, and if you spend a morning in such habitat you may well see one. They are most evident during drought conditions, when they often collect around drying-up pools.

Be aware that although many barrier islands do not have any poisonous snakes, others do. The Buxton Woods at Cape Hatteras has numerous cottonmouths; the Theodore Roosevelt NA on Bogue Banks has copperheads and a few timber rattlesnakes.

The best rule regarding poisonous snakes is simply to always look where you step. In wilder areas, it is best not to walk too far from your car if you're alone. Don't forget that snakes can be active as late as December if the weather is warm.

Bears

The black bear is fairly common in some of the wilder areas, especially in the Albemarle-Pamlico section. In our area, bears are quite shy and generally move away quickly as soon as they see you. Probably the only potential danger is from a mother with a cub. If you see a cub while in the woods, move away from the area as quickly as possible.

Alligators

The American alligator is found as far north as the Alligator River NWR. However, you're likely to see one only in the South Coast section. In North Carolina, these creatures are quite shy; most of those seen in this area are also small—only a few feet long.

Although these animals probably don't represent much danger, you shouldn't wade around during the warmer months in areas where they occur. You probably wouldn't do this anyway; most sites with alligators also have cottonmouths.

TRAVEL AND PLANNING TIPS

Most of the region has a typical scattering of motels. However, there are few motels in much of the Albemarle-Pamlico section. In the eastern part of this section, the only motels are in Fairfield and Columbia (and nearby in Manteo).

Motels along the immediate coast are often filled up on weekends from late spring through autumn. Major holidays are especially bad. You will want to make reservations well in advance. If you get into a scrape, you can sometimes find vacant rooms by driving several miles inland.

You can easily find all the areas discussed in the site guides (part 2) by using this book's maps in conjunction with a good highway map. I would recommend the official state highway map prepared by the North Carolina Department of Transportation. This map can be obtained free of charge at numerous locations—welcome centers (local as well as state), ferry terminals, etc. You can also order one by writing the North Carolina Department of Transportation, Public Affairs Division, P.O. Box 25201, Raleigh, NC 27611, or by calling 919-733-7600 (from within North Carolina) or 800-VISIT NC (from outside the state). This map includes the most up-to-date ferry fees and schedules.

A special map book that I also recommend highly is the *North Carolina Atlas and Gazetteer*, by DeLorme Mapping. This atlas is available at many bookstores, outdoor supply stores, visitors centers, etc., and can also be ordered from De-

Lorme Mapping, P.O. Box 298, Freeport, ME 04032 (phone 800-227-1656). This atlas has a very useful scale and shows all types of roads. However, it does have some shortcomings. For example, it lists names rather than state road numbers for secondary roads. Yet in many areas, local governments have not yet put up road signs identifying the names of roads; signs show only the state numbers. Also, the atlas has listed some names incorrectly. In spite of these problems, using this atlas shouldn't give you any problems if you pay attention.

The book *North Carolina Beaches* (University of North Carolina Press, 1993) is also an excellent complement to this bird-finding guide. It describes access to and background information about sites on all the barrier islands and some of the adjacent mainland.

When traveling, it is often difficult to obtain accurate and up-to-date weather forecasts, but a weather radio can remedy this situation. A weather radio is particularly helpful if you're trying to find particular species that are easiest to find during certain unusual types of weather. The Weather Channel is now available at many motels, decreasing most people's need for weather radios. The visitors center at the ferry terminal in Hatteras keeps its television tuned to the Weather Channel throughout the day.

Information about times of lunar tides at a particular site always refers to the tides at the oceanfront. The weather radio broadcasts out of Cape Hatteras and Wilmington both give tide times for oceanfront locations. If you use news-papers or tide tables to get tidal information, be sure to look for oceanfront sites—Cape Hatteras, Cape Lookout, Atlantic Beach, Wilmington Beach, Cape Fear, etc. Tide times listed for inlet locations may lag an hour behind those for oceanfront locations. Because the exact time of high or low tide may be influenced by several factors, you should always get to a site an hour or two earlier than the desired time, just to be safe—especially if you're planning to wade a tidal creek. Also remember that the farther up an estuary you go, the more difficult it is to accurately predict the time of high and low tides. For instance, if high tide at a site is said to lag about one hour behind that on the oceanfront, then the actual time of high tide at the site will almost always be within thirty minutes of the predicted time. However, for sites where high tide lags about three hours behind that on the oceanfront, you should expect more variability—up to one to two hours from the predicted tide time.

Some of the roads discussed in the site guides may periodically be flooded during storms; the individual tours point out those roads where flooding is more likely. Keep in mind that for sites near the coast, the water remaining on some roads after storm flooding will be primarily salt water, which (as you probably know) will cause rusting on automobiles.

Some refuges have many roads that are open to foot traffic but not auto-mobiles. Bicycles are allowed on these roads. Needless to say, you will be able to cover much more territory on a bike than on foot.

BIRDING TIPS

Birders who have bought a copy of this book probably own a field guide and a pair of binoculars already. However, as they improve in ability, many birders begin to inquire about improved optics and better birding guides.

Information about binoculars and scopes lies outside the scope of this book, but some advice about field guides is in order. Most birders start out with Roger Tory Peterson's *A Field Guide to the Birds* or Chandler Robbins's *Birds of North America*. Both of these books are simple and straightforward and are the best field guides for beginners. Indeed, these are the only guides many birders will ever need. Peterson's book is perhaps preferable: because it is limited to eastern birds, there are fewer species to sort through. Even as birders improve in ability and acquire some of the more advanced field guides, they might do well to use Peterson as their main reference and then refer to the other books after making a tentative identification.

This book contains occasional references to "more advanced field guides" and "newer field guides." These terms primarily refer to the National Geographic Society's *Field Guide to the Birds of North America*. This guide is an excellent distillation of the most up-to-date field identification knowledge. It is worth the price just for its plates of shorebirds, gulls, and terns. The Audubon Society's *Master Guide to Birding* is also good, although limited, I think, by its use of photographs alone. The compilation of photographs is excellent, though, and makes the book a good supplement for your field identification library. Other good advanced guides are *A Field Guide to Seabirds of the World* and *Seabirds: An Identification Guide*, by Peter Harrison; *Shorebirds: An Identification Guide*, by Peter Hayman, John Marchant, and Tony Prater; *Advanced Birding*, by Kenn Kaufman; and *Hawks in Flight*, by Pete Dunne, David Sibley, and Clay Sutton.

Of course, the best way to learn about bird identification is from experienced birders. Birders from the Carolinas and adjacent states should join the Carolina Bird Club (P.O. Box 29555, Raleigh, NC 27626). This organization holds general meetings three times a year, usually in areas that offer excellent birding. The meetings include numerous field trips with experienced leaders. In recent years, the club has begun to organize smaller field trips not associated with the general meetings. The club also operates a hotline that gives information about unusual sightings in the Carolinas; call 704-332-2473. The club also publishes records of interest in a quarterly journal called *Chat*. (North Carolina records are also included in the national journal *Audubon Field Notes*, published by the National Audubon Society.)

Local bird clubs, which were almost nonexistent for several years, seem to be making a comeback. There are now local clubs at Cape Hatteras, New Bern, Jacksonville, Wilmington, and perhaps elsewhere.

Many bookstores carry a good selection of bird books, but an especially good selection is available at two new birding specialty stores, Wild Birds Unlimited and Wild Bird World. These stores carry tapes of bird songs, binoculars, and other useful supplies, and they are also excellent places to talk with others about birds and find out about local sightings of unusual species. There are Wild Birds Unlimited stores at Cedar Point (near Swansboro) and Wilmington and a Wild Bird World store at New Bern. The store at Cedar Point has several bird feeders just outside the windows where several species can be seen at close range. Occasionally an unusual species shows up here.

This book makes occasional references to "squeaking" or "squeaking up" birds. To squeak up a bird is to make a squeaking or hissing sound—like that of a bird in distress—with your mouth, often with the mouth on the back of the hand. This method can be an effective way to draw small land birds in close for good views, although some species largely ignore it.

Many birders use the taped calls of a screech-owl, which can be even more effective. However, this practice can also be counterproductive. When you're playing a tape all the time, you have effectively subtracted much of your hearing ability. Furthermore, some secretive species never come in to squeaking or a tape; you are most likely to see or hear them when you just sit quietly for several minutes.

Birders also frequently use taped songs to draw birds of that species in close during the breeding season. This method can be extremely effective but is also potentially damaging. When the same bird is subjected to frequent disturbance of this type, it may abandon its territory, resulting in a failed nesting attempt. If you do use this technique, use it seldom and for a short period only, and avoid sites where birds are likely to be subjected to the same type of disturbance from others.

BIRDS OF COASTAL
NORTH CAROLINA
AN ANNOTATED LIST

Four hundred and one species, not including extinct or extirpated species, have been well documented as occurring in coastal North Carolina. Of these, forty-one are accidentals—that is, species for which there are five or fewer records, or species that are usually found at greater than ten-year intervals.

The statuses of all regularly occurring (i.e., nonaccidental) species are discussed briefly in the species accounts below. These accounts are to be used in conjunction with the frequency graphs. For species of special interest, which are marked with asterisks, more detailed bird-finding information is given in the Birds of Special Interest section. Accidentals are listed at the end of the species accounts.

The frequency graphs are intended primarily to give a detailed picture of the changing abundance of species during the course of a year. The species accounts complement the bar graphs by giving habitat information and other important modifying comments.

In the species accounts, the term "resident" means that a species is present continuously throughout a designated period. The term "visitor" is used for species that may not be present throughout the designated period. When the term "migrant" is used in conjunction with the term "resident" (e.g., summer resident and fall migrant), this means that the species' migration period stands out as separate from its residence period, through different numbers, appearance at different sites, etc.

I use the following frequency-level designations: common, fairly common, uncommon, occasional, rare, very rare, extremely rare, and accidental. "Common" species are ones that are certain to be found, at least in most areas. Common water birds will usually be found in large numbers. "Fairly common" species will usually be found, generally in low numbers, although some water birds in this category occur in widely variable numbers. "Fairly common" species are not as widespread as "common" species. It will generally require a few visits to find an "uncommon" species and several visits to find an "occasional" species. In situations where a bird's frequency level lies somewhere between "uncommon" and "occasional," "uncommon" is favored for resident species that are continuously present, and "occasional" is favored for migrants and visitors that are not continuously present.

A "rare" species will usually be missed during a year (or season) by an active birder; however, such species can often be found in a year (or season) after a determined effort—by making many visits to prime sites during the best conditions, etc. All birders' sightings, taken collectively, usually include rare species each year; "very rare" species at about two- to five-year intervals; and "extremely rare" species at about six- to ten-year intervals. The terms "regular," "scarce," and "frequent" are deliberately generic terms, used so as not to imply any of the specific categories defined above. The frequency level given for a season refers to the peak frequency during that season; see the bar graphs for more specific information.

The information given in each species account is a brief generalization. The status of many birds will vary locally and regionally, but only the most dramatic regional differences are cited. Of course, one should search for a bird in the proper habitat. In some cases the habitat requirements of a species can be very strict. For example, some shorebirds—like Long-billed Dowitcher and Stilt Sandpiper—are found in shallow, fresh to brackish pools, like those at impoundments and dredged-material deposition areas. You might spend weeks on nearby intertidal flats and never see these birds. In general, the larger an expanse of habitat, the better. Fragments of habitat—for instance, a forest on a barrier island, or a small agricultural area in a sea of suburbia—will often lack species that you would expect them to have. I should also stress that the fall statuses given for many land birds refer to their statuses at the better migrant traps, on the barrier islands and at a few other choice spots. And many land birds that can easily be found early in the breeding season, when they are singing, may become almost impossible to find later in the summer, even though they are still present in similar numbers.

Keep in mind that the information in the species accounts and bar graphs pertains to an average year. Statuses for many species can vary considerably from year to year depending on weather. Severe winters will have more waterfowl, but wading birds, shorebirds, and small land birds will be scarcer. The abundance of many fall migrants along the coast can also vary greatly from year to year. Some years have numerous fronts with northwesterly winds that push birds to the coast. Unfortunately, in coastal North Carolina, some years have almost no such fronts until after the bulk of migration is over.

Most of the habitat information given in this list is very general, but more detailed information is given here for some species and in the Birds of Special Interest section for others. For species that occur both as summer residents and migrants, the habitat information given pertains to nesting habitat unless stated otherwise.

*RED-THROATED LOON. Common winter resident in most areas, although scarcer at a few sites; very rare in summer. Ocean, larger saline estuaries (especially Pamlico Sound).

PACIFIC LOON. Very rare winter visitor. Ocean.

COMMON LOON. Common winter resident; occasional in summer. Ocean, estuaries. Frequently migrate over land in April and early May.

PIED-BILLED GREBE. Common winter resident; uncommon and very local during the breeding season. Fresh water, sheltered portions of estuaries. Most breeding season records are at impoundments.

HORNED GREBE. Winter resident. In most areas, uncommon in early winter, but common in late winter and early spring. Ocean, estuaries.

*RED-NECKED GREBE. Rare winter visitor at better sites. Ocean, sometimes inside inlets; Pamlico Sound.

*EARED GREBE. Rare winter visitor/resident. Have been found on ocean, sheltered portions of estuaries, and fresh water.

*NORTHERN FULMAR. Apparently occur primarily in migration. Most common off the northern Outer Banks, where they are uncommon in fall and fairly common in spring. Apparently occasional in spring off Central Coast and perhaps off North Coast, although there are few non–Outer Banks records. Offshore.

*SOFT-PLUMAGED PETREL. Very rare late spring/early summer visitor. Offshore, over and near Gulf Stream, usually over water one hundred fathoms and deeper.

*HERALD PETREL. Very rare late spring/early summer visitor; occasional late summer visitor. Offshore, over and near Gulf Stream, usually over water one hundred fathoms and deeper. Lack of midsummer records may reflect actual absence/near absence or may merely reflect fewer offshore birding trips at that time.

*BLACK-CAPPED PETREL. Fairly common permanent resident. Offshore, over and near Gulf Stream, usually over water one hundred fathoms and deeper.

*CORY'S SHEARWATER. Common summer resident. Offshore. Often occur within a few miles of land, and sometimes seen from shore.

*GREATER SHEARWATER. Summer resident. Common in early summer off the Outer Banks. Less common off other sections of the coast, especially after

July. Offshore. Sometimes seen from shore, especially after easterly winds in June.

*Sooty Shearwater. Fairly common at Cape Hatteras and uncommon elsewhere as a spring migrant, then gradually decreasing during the summer. Spring peak status varies greatly according to weather and (apparently) other factors. Normally a pelagic species, but during spring migration most likely to be seen just beyond the surf. Mid- and late summer records are mostly for the offshore waters.

*Manx Shearwater. Occasional to uncommon winter resident/spring migrant; apparently most common and widespread in late winter/early spring. Offshore.

*Audubon's Shearwater. Common summer resident; rare in midwinter. Offshore, especially along edge of Gulf Stream. Sometimes seen from shore, especially from late July to early August.

*Wilson's Storm-Petrel. Common summer resident. Offshore. Often occur within a few miles of land, and sometimes seen from shore, especially after easterly winds from mid-May to mid-June.

*White-faced Storm-Petrel. Rare late summer/early autumn visitor. Offshore (usually over water one hundred fathoms and deeper), northern Outer Banks.

*Leach's Storm-Petrel. Uncommon summer resident, at least from Cape Hatteras north. Offshore, over deeper waters; found over Gulf Stream but also farther north. Often found in loose association with large numbers of Wilson's Storm-Petrels. In late summer, perhaps most likely to be found northeast of Oregon Inlet.

*Band-rumped Storm-Petrel. Uncommon summer resident. Offshore, over the Gulf Stream, over water one hundred fathoms and deeper.

*White-tailed Tropicbird. Rare to occasional summer visitor. Offshore, most records over and near the Gulf Stream.

*Masked Booby. Rare summer visitor. Offshore, mostly near the edge of the Gulf Stream.

*Northern Gannet. Common winter resident; very rare in late summer. Ocean, sometimes entering the inlets. Regular but uncommon on deeper portions of Pamlico Sound.

*American White Pelican. Occasional year-round visitor on the Outer Banks; elsewhere, rare, except occasional in fall. Increasing. May be found at impoundments, at inlets with flocks of Brown Pelicans, or, in fall, in migratory flight along the coastline.

Brown Pelican. Common permanent resident, except uncommon in North Coast section in midwinter. Increasing. Ocean, especially around inlets, and salt-water estuaries. Erratic and less common in the western portions of the Pamlico and Neuse River estuaries.

*GREAT CORMORANT. Generally uncommon winter resident, varying from fairly common at a few favored localities to occasional at most sites; one or two immatures sometimes linger throughout the summer at favored sites. Increasing. Ocean, inlets. Favor hard-bottom areas, including old shipwrecks, for feeding. Prefer high perches for roosting.

DOUBLE-CRESTED CORMORANT. Common winter resident; in midsummer, vary from occasional at most sites to fairly common at a few sites. Ocean, estuaries. In winter, found primarily around inlets. In midsummer, found primarily in less saline sections of the estuaries.

*ANHINGA. Occur primarily in South Coast section, where they are permanent residents, varying from fairly common in late summer to rare in midwinter. Farther north, uncommon and very local in spring and summer and generally absent in winter. Occur primarily at extensive areas of fresh-water marshes and swamps with some open water.

*MAGNIFICENT FRIGATEBIRD. Rare summer visitor; most records are from Cape Lookout south. Most often seen in flight along barrier island beaches or over the adjacent sounds. Multiple sightings sometimes occur in conjunction with hurricanes or tropical storms.

*AMERICAN BITTERN. Uncommon migrant; occasional winter resident; generally rare in early summer, although they occasionally breed locally. Decreasing. In winter, may be scarce after extreme cold. Occur in fresh, brackish, and salt marshes. In salt marshes, most frequent in upper section of marsh, in thick grass along tidal guts.

*LEAST BITTERN. Fairly common (locally common) summer resident; extremely rare in midwinter. Apparently decreasing. Fresh, brackish, and salt marshes. Found primarily where thick and tall grass cover stands immediately next to water.

GREAT BLUE HERON. Permanent resident. Common, except uncommon in May and June. Associated with both fresh water and estuarine waters. In North Carolina, virtually all nesting is in fresh-water swamps.

GREAT EGRET. Permanent resident. Common during warmer months; fairly common in winter. Occur commonly in fresh- and salt-water habitats. In winter, more restricted to salt water, and found primarily near immediate coast.

SNOWY EGRET. Permanent resident. Common during warmer months, decreasing to uncommon in most areas (but fairly common around the more southern inlets) in midwinter. Estuaries and adjacent fresh-water sites. In winter, restricted to the immediate coast, primarily near inlets.

LITTLE BLUE HERON. Permanent resident. Locally common during warmer months, decreasing to uncommon in most areas (but fairly common in South Coast section) in winter. Most common at fresh-water sites.

TRICOLORED HERON. Permanent resident. Common during warmer months, decreasing to uncommon in most areas (but fairly common near the more southern inlets) in midwinter. Estuaries; not usually found far from salt water.

*REDDISH EGRET. Rare summer visitor/resident; occasional at a few sites. Formerly extremely rare, but now being found with increasing frequency. Most records are associated with sand flats at inlets.

CATTLE EGRET. Common summer resident, although local, largely restricted to the vicinity of breeding colonies. Very rare in midwinter (but occasional at a few favored sites during milder years). Agricultural areas, especially with livestock or where fields are being plowed.

GREEN HERON. Fairly common (locally common) summer resident; very rare in midwinter, but occasional in South Coast section during most years. Fresh water, sheltered portions of estuaries.

*BLACK-CROWNED NIGHT-HERON. Permanent resident. Generally fairly common, but common in some areas and scarce in others. More common and widespread in winter. Most common near inlets. In winter, often common in the vicinity of fish houses, where they scavenge.

*YELLOW-CROWNED NIGHT-HERON. Generally uncommon summer resident, although fairly common at a few sites; generally absent in winter, although very rare in South Coast section. Occur in both fresh- and salt-water wetlands.

*WHITE IBIS. Locally common permanent resident at many sites near inlets from Bodie Island south. Increasing. Feed in both salt marshes and freshwater areas.

GLOSSY IBIS. In general, uncommon summer resident near a few breeding colonies; rare to very rare in winter. Most common on the Outer Banks, where they are locally fairly common during the warmer months and occasional in winter. Decreasing. Seldom feed in intertidal areas, preferring brackish nontidal pools, impoundments, and similar sites.

ROSEATE SPOONBILL. Very rare summer visitor. Most records are for salt-water flats.

*WOOD STORK. Uncommon late summer/early fall resident at Twin Lakes, Sunset Beach. Otherwise very rare to rare summer/early fall visitor. Extremely rare in winter. At Twin Lakes, storks feed in the adjacent salt marshes and roost at the lakes. Elsewhere, records are for tidal flats and impoundments.

*FULVOUS WHISTLING-DUCK. Irruptive species. Occasional at impoundments and ponds in refuges during invasion years. Most records are for late fall/early winter and April.

TUNDRA SWAN. Common winter resident in North Coast and Albemarle-Pamlico sections, and on the northern Outer Banks. Uncommon to occasional farther south, but increasing. Lakes, impoundments, fields. A few birds may be found throughout summer at refuges.

MUTE SWAN. Very rare winter visitor, although an increase in population may be anticipated. Most likely to be found at refuges.

*GREATER WHITE-FRONTED GOOSE. Very rare winter visitor/resident at Pea Island NWR and Lake Mattamuskeet area. Extremely rare elsewhere. Most often found with Canada Geese.

SNOW GOOSE (light morph). Common winter resident at refuges from Cape Hatteras and Lake Mattamuskeet north. Rare farther south. Departure dates in spring vary greatly from north to south. Birds may leave Cape Hatteras by late January but remain at Knotts Island until late April. Very rare in summer.

SNOW GOOSE (dark morph, or "Blue Goose"). Common winter resident at Lake Mattamuskeet. Less common at other refuges. Rare in Central Coast and South Coast sections.

*ROSS' GOOSE. In recent years, a Ross' Goose has been found almost annually at Pea Island NWR, in flocks of Snow Geese, from mid-October to early February. Accidental elsewhere.

*BRANT. Fairly common winter resident at Hatteras and Ocracoke inlets. Much less common elsewhere; generally rare south of Cape Lookout. Numbers vary greatly from year to year; may be widespread after extreme and prolonged cold. Usually found over sea-grass beds.

CANADA GOOSE. Common winter resident at refuges; less common elsewhere; occasional to uncommon in Central Coast and South Coast sections. Summering birds consist primarily of introduced feral birds.

WOOD DUCK. Overall, fairly common permanent resident, but rather local. Primarily associated with areas that have extensive fresh-water swamps.

GREEN-WINGED TEAL. Common winter resident. Impoundments, ponds, sheltered portions of estuaries.

"COMMON TEAL." Rare winter visitor at Pea Island NWR and Bodie Island. A drake of this Eurasian race of the Green-winged Teal can often be found in these areas by scoping through the flocks of Green-wings carefully and patiently. Elsewhere, apparently extremely rare. But of course "Common Teals" are easily overlooked, and because they are not considered a separate species, birders don't spend much time looking for them.

AMERICAN BLACK DUCK. Primarily a winter resident. Range from common on the Outer Banks to uncommon in South Coast section. Present in summer from Beaufort north; fairly common on the Outer Banks and occasional to uncommon elsewhere. Impoundments, ponds, estuaries.

MALLARD. Common winter resident south to Pamlico County; fairly common farther south; uncommon and local in breeding season, but increasing. Impoundments, ponds, sheltered portions of estuaries.

NORTHERN PINTAIL. Common winter resident south to Pamlico County and Ocracoke Inlet; fairly common farther south. Impoundments, ponds, estuaries.

BLUE-WINGED TEAL. Common during migrations; occasional in winter (but uncommon in South Coast section); rare in June (but occasional on the Outer Banks). Impoundments, ponds. During migrations, frequently found in salt marshes.

CINNAMON TEAL. Extremely rare, recorded from late December to late April; most of the handful of records are for March and April. (Of course, any peak in fall would likely go undetected, as males are then in eclipse plumage.) Most likely to be found at impoundments and other sites having large numbers of puddle ducks.

NORTHERN SHOVELER. Fairly common (locally common) winter resident. Most likely to be found at impoundments and ponds in refuges.

GADWALL. Common winter resident south to Pamlico County; fairly common farther south. In the breeding season, found from Cedar Island north; fairly common on the Outer Banks and uncommon to occasional elsewhere. Impoundments, ponds, estuaries.

*EURASIAN WIGEON. Winter visitor/resident. Rare to uncommon at Pea Island NWR and Bodie Island. Very rare elsewhere, except rare at a few favored sites. Impoundments, ponds; usually found with American Wigeons.

AMERICAN WIGEON. Common winter resident south to Pamlico County; fairly common farther south. Impoundments, ponds, estuaries.

CANVASBACK. Locally fairly common (sometimes common) winter resident south to the Neuse River; uncommon to occasional farther south. Open water impoundments, locally on estuaries. Often common on the lower Pamlico River.

REDHEAD. Locally fairly common (sometimes common) winter resident south to Core Sound; uncommon to occasional farther south. Very rare in summer. Open water impoundments, locally on estuaries. Often common on Core Sound.

RING-NECKED DUCK. Fairly common to common winter resident, but rather local. Scarce in many areas because of lack of habitat. Very rare in summer. Fresh water, impoundments, and some brackish estuaries.

*GREATER SCAUP. Uncommon winter resident. Primarily ocean and larger estuaries.

LESSER SCAUP. Common winter resident. Impoundments, some estuaries, ocean (mostly in migration). Very rare in summer.

*COMMON EIDER. Occasional winter visitor/resident on the Outer Banks; rare elsewhere. Extremely rare in summer. Ocean, inlets. Most likely to be found near rock jetties and similar structures.

*KING EIDER. Occasional winter visitor/resident on the Outer Banks; rare elsewhere. Ocean, inlets. Most likely to be found near rock jetties and similar structures.

*HARLEQUIN DUCK. Occasional winter visitor/resident on the Outer Banks;

rare elsewhere. Ocean, inlets; very rare on Pamlico Sound. Most likely to be found near rock jetties and similar structures.

*OLDSQUAW. In most areas, occasional winter visitor/resident. Ocean and inlets, often near piers and jetties; larger salt-water sounds. Uncommon in a few areas, and common from December to March on the sound near Swan Quarter.

*BLACK SCOTER. Fairly common winter resident; common during the migrations. Ocean, Pamlico Sound, and the lower Pamlico and Neuse rivers. Sometimes common throughout winter on western Pamlico Sound, particularly near Swan Quarter. Rare to very rare in summer.

*SURF SCOTER. Fairly common winter resident; often common during fall migration. Ocean, Pamlico Sound, and the lower Pamlico and Neuse rivers. Common throughout winter on western Pamlico Sound and the lower Neuse and Pamlico rivers. Very rare in summer.

*WHITE-WINGED SCOTER. Uncommon winter visitor/resident from Cape Hatteras north; occasional farther south. May be fairly common during severe winters. Ocean. Occasional on western Pamlico Sound and lower Pamlico River.

*COMMON GOLDENEYE. Local and uncommon winter resident. Estuaries. Often found at sites favored by Buffleheads.

BUFFLEHEAD. Common winter resident. Estuaries. Also occur on ocean from Topsail Island south.

HOODED MERGANSER. Common winter resident. Fresh water, sheltered portions of estuaries.

*COMMON MERGANSER. Rare winter visitor. May be occasional after extremely severe cold. Most likely to be found on fresh water, but there are several records for brackish and even salt water.

RED-BREASTED MERGANSER. Common winter resident; rare in late summer. Estuaries, ocean.

RUDDY DUCK. Locally common winter resident. Estuaries, impoundments. Occasional in summer at impoundments.

*BLACK VULTURE. Overall, uncommon permanent resident. Fairly common in a few areas, but almost absent in many areas. Most typical in areas that have a mix of forest and open habitats. Seem to be most common in areas with large deer populations.

TURKEY VULTURE. Common permanent resident in most areas, but less common locally. Most common in areas that have a mix of forest and open habitats.

OSPREY. Fairly common to common summer resident; in midwinter, rare in most areas, but occasional from Wilmington south. Increasing. Feed in fresh, brackish, and salt water. Nest in tall dead trees and on various types of manmade structures, such as towers, channel markers, etc.

*AMERICAN SWALLOW-TAILED KITE. Very rare to rare spring/summer visitor in most areas; occasional on southern Outer Banks from mid-April through May. Most likely to be seen in flight along the barrier islands or shorelines of nearby mainland.

*MISSISSIPPI KITE. Rare spring migrant; very rare fall migrant. Increasing. Most likely to be seen in flight along the barrier islands or shorelines of nearby mainland.

*BALD EAGLE. Uncommon and very local permanent resident. Most frequent in the Lake Mattamuskeet area. Eagles are somewhat more widespread in summer, when immatures sometimes show up around nesting sites of colonial waterbirds.

NORTHERN HARRIER. Occur primarily as a common winter resident; mostly absent in early summer, but uncommon on the Outer Banks and at Cedar Island NWR. Marshes, fields.

SHARP-SHINNED HAWK. Fairly common winter resident, except common during fall migration. Woods/field borders, shrub thickets. In fall, most common on barrier islands.

*COOPER'S HAWK. Permanent resident. Uncommon in fall migration; occasional in winter; rare and local in summer. Increasing. Wooded habitats, especially along woods/field borders, often near water. In fall, found mostly on barrier islands.

NORTHERN GOSHAWK. Extremely rare fall migrant and winter visitor. Perhaps most likely to be found along the immediate coast in November.

RED-SHOULDERED HAWK. Permanent resident. Most typical in bottomlands, especially along rivers and streams. Fairly common where suitable habitat is extensive; uncommon where bottomlands are narrow and limited in extent.

BROAD-WINGED HAWK. Rare to occasional migrant and summer resident. Apparently increasing during the breeding season. Most breeding season records are for dry pine or pine-oak areas.

RED-TAILED HAWK. Permanent resident. Common in winter; fairly common rest of year, except uncommon in summer toward south. Open and semiopen country, such as agricultural lands, clearings.

ROUGH-LEGGED HAWK. Very rare winter visitor. Most sightings have been in the Bodie Island–Pea Island area. Also occur over the expansive agricultural lands of the Albemarle-Pamlico section.

*GOLDEN EAGLE. Very rare winter visitor/resident in the Lake Mattamuskeet–Pungo NWR area. Extremely rare elsewhere.

AMERICAN KESTREL. Common winter resident; apparently decreasing. Open habitats—fields, clearings, roadsides. Extremely rare in midsummer.

*MERLIN. Fairly common fall migrant and uncommon winter resident along the barrier islands and adjacent mainland; less common farther inland. Open habitats, especially sites with large concentrations of smaller birds.

*PEREGRINE FALCON. Uncommon fall migrant and occasional winter resident along the barrier islands and adjacent mainland; generally rare farther inland. Fairly common on the Outer Banks during fall migration peak and uncommon at a few sites in winter. Extremely rare in midsummer.

*RING-NECKED PHEASANT. Very local permanent resident at Cape Hatteras NS and Cape Lookout NS. Decreasing at some sites and increasing at others. Currently uncommon at the following sites, where they are found most frequently: Pea Island NWR, Ocracoke Island, Portsmouth Island, and Core Banks. Occur in grasslands and shrub thickets.

*WILD TURKEY. Very local and uncommon permanent resident. Hardwoods and mixed woods. Most common in Camp Lejeune Marine Corps Base.

*NORTHERN BOBWHITE. Fairly common permanent resident, but common in many areas. Decreasing. Rather secretive and hard to find outside the breeding season. Grown-up fields and clearings, some agricultural areas, wood/field borders.

*YELLOW RAIL. Status uncertain because they are extremely secretive. Probably occasional to uncommon winter resident. May be most common and widespread during fall migration, about October. Have been recorded in irregularly flooded salt marshes, brackish marshes, and clear-cuts with thick herbaceous cover. In fall migration, have also been found at edges of regularly flooded salt marshes.

*BLACK RAIL. Permanent resident. Uncommon in spring and summer; occasional in winter. Very local. Fairly common at a few sites during warmer months and common at the Cedar Island NWR. Found primarily in irregularly flooded salt marshes, typically where there is black needlerush intermixed with varying amounts of fine grasses, usually saltmeadow cordgrass or salt grass.

*CLAPPER RAIL. Permanent resident. Common from Morehead City south throughout the year. Farther north, uncommon in winter. Most common in regularly flooded salt marshes. Less common in irregularly flooded salt marshes, especially in winter.

*KING RAIL. Permanent resident. Generally uncommon, but fairly common at a few sites. May be more widespread in winter. Fresh marshes, some brackish marshes (especially in winter).

*VIRGINIA RAIL. Common winter resident; as a summer resident, uncommon (fairly common locally) north of the North River, in Carteret County, and generally rare farther south. Found primarily in irregularly flooded salt marshes and brackish marshes.

*SORA. Fairly common migrant; uncommon and local winter resident; extremely rare in midsummer. Fresh and brackish marshes. Frequently occur at the edges of salt marshes during the migrations.

*PURPLE GALLINULE. Found primarily in South Coast section, where they are apparently decreasing; in that area, occasional spring visitor and rare summer resident or visitor. Farther north, rare spring visitor and very rare summer visitor. Fresh-water ponds and fresh marshes with some open water.

*COMMON MOORHEN. Permanent resident. In summer, fairly common; in winter, uncommon, except fairly common in South Coast section. Fresh-water ponds and lakes, brackish impoundments.

AMERICAN COOT. Primarily a common winter resident; occasional and local in summer. Fresh-water ponds and lakes, brackish impoundments; less frequent on brackish estuaries.

SANDHILL CRANE. Very rare migrant and winter resident. May be increasing. Migrant birds are perhaps most likely to be seen following shorelines. Wintering birds have been found primarily on extensive agricultural lands.

BLACK-BELLIED PLOVER. Common most of year, but becoming uncommon in early summer. Most common on sand flats and mud flats near inlets, but commonly occur elsewhere—ocean beaches, wet fields, etc.

*AMERICAN GOLDEN-PLOVER. Occasional fall migrant on the Outer Banks; rare elsewhere. Very rare spring migrant in all sections. Very rare early summer visitor on the Outer Banks. Most likely to be found at relatively dry, short-grass sites; less likely on wetter flats.

*WILSON'S PLOVER. Summer resident. Fairly common from Portsmouth Island south; uncommon from Hatteras Inlet to Ocracoke Inlet. Extremely rare in winter, except at the Rachel Carson Research Reserve, where they are rare. Found primarily on sand flats and mud flats at inlets, especially where the end of an island is accreting. Large groups may form at a few favored sites from August to early September.

SEMIPALMATED PLOVER. Common migrant; uncommon winter resident, except fairly common from Beaufort Inlet south; occasional in early summer. In migration, occur in most shorebird habitats, including ocean beaches; in winter, occur mainly on intertidal flats near inlets.

*PIPING PLOVER. In general, uncommon all year, but locally fairly common during the migrations—from mid-March to mid-April and August to October. In the breeding season, mostly restricted to Cape Hatteras NS and Cape Lookout NS. In winter, occur mainly from Beaufort Inlet south. Primarily sand flats near inlets. More widespread in migration, when they regularly occur along ocean beaches.

KILLDEER. In most areas, fairly common to common most of the year, but becoming uncommon and local during the breeding season. Agricultural areas and other short-grass habitats.

AMERICAN OYSTERCATCHER. From Beaufort Inlet south, fairly common, but locally common, especially during fall and winter. Farther north, fairly common during warmer months, but uncommon in winter. In winter, primarily found at sites with numerous oyster rocks, mostly near inlets. More widespread during the breeding season.

*BLACK-NECKED STILT. Fairly common summer resident at Pea Island NWR and Bodie Island; elsewhere, uncommon and very local. Occur at impoundments and other similar nontidal habitats.

*AMERICAN AVOCET. Largely restricted to Pea Island NWR and Bodie Island, where they are fairly common in fall and uncommon during the rest of the year, although they may be scarce during extreme winters. Elsewhere, occasional during fall migration and rare at other times. Largely restricted to impoundments and similar nontidal habitats.

GREATER YELLOWLEGS. Common migrant; fairly common to common winter resident; uncommon during June. Commonly found in intertidal habitats and at impoundments and similar areas.

LESSER YELLOWLEGS. Locally common migrant; local and uncommon winter resident; rare during June. Largely shun intertidal habitats; found primarily at impoundments and similar sites.

SOLITARY SANDPIPER. Uncommon migrant, except fairly common in South Coast section. Primarily fresh water, but also occur at brackish impoundments and similar sites.

WILLET. From Beaufort Inlet south, common all year. Farther north, common at least during the warmer months, but numbers may be quite variable in winter. Found primarily around inlets, but usually common along ocean beaches. More widespread during the breeding season, when they also occur farther up the estuaries, even along the western shores of Pamlico Sound.

SPOTTED SANDPIPER. Fairly common migrant (common in some areas during migration peaks); rare in mid-June; very rare in most areas during midwinter, but occasional most years in South Coast section. Found along most nonocean shorelines.

*UPLAND SANDPIPER. Very rare spring migrant; occasional fall migrant (uncommon at a few sites). Found primarily on upland short-grass habitats, such as airports and campgrounds.

WHIMBREL. Common migrant; generally rare winter resident, but occasional at Rachel Carson Research Reserve, Masonboro Island, Fort Fisher, and perhaps elsewhere; occasional in early summer. Ocean beaches and intertidal flats near inlets. In winter, often occur near oyster rocks.

*LONG-BILLED CURLEW. Occasional winter resident at a few favored sites; very rare to rare at most locations. Very rare in all areas in early summer. Intertidal flats near inlets, usually in association with large flocks of Marbled Godwits. Seem to be increasing.

*HUDSONIAN GODWIT. Fall migrant. Uncommon at Pea Island NWR and Bodie

Island; rare from Cape Hatteras to Portsmouth Island; very rare to extremely rare elsewhere. Extremely rare spring migrant (late May) at Bodie Island. Impoundments and similar nontidal habitats.

*MARBLED GODWIT. In most areas, uncommon fall migrant, occasional in winter, and rare in early summer. However, flocks of one hundred to more than two hundred birds winter at a handful of sites, where a few are occasionally seen throughout the summer. Intertidal flats.

RUDDY TURNSTONE. Primarily a migrant and winter resident. Common during the migrations. In winter, vary from common in South Coast section to uncommon north of Beaufort Inlet. Intertidal habitats. Most common at rock jetties, oyster rocks, and along rocky or shelly shores.

*RED KNOT. Occur primarily in migrations—common in spring, uncommon to fairly common in fall; winter status rather variable, ranging from occasional to fairly common; occasional in midsummer. Ocean beaches and sand flats at inlets. At least locally, they occur on rock jetties.

SANDERLING. Common most of the year, but decreasing to uncommon in early summer. Primarily ocean beaches and sand flats near inlets. In early summer, found primarily on sand flats near inlets.

SEMIPALMATED SANDPIPER. Migrant. In spring, common; in fall, common on the Outer Banks and very locally elsewhere. In spring, widespread, occurring in many shorebird habitats; in fall, largely restricted to brackish pools and similar sites, mostly shunning intertidal habitats.

WESTERN SANDPIPER. Common fall migrant. In winter, usually common from Beaufort Inlet south; often uncommon north, especially after severe weather. In early summer, occasional south and rare north. Associated with intertidal flats and with brackish pools and similar sites.

LEAST SANDPIPER. Common migrant; generally uncommon and very local winter resident. Found primarily at brackish pools and similar sites, although common in intertidal habitats during migration peaks. In winter, usually fairly common on the rock jetties at Masonboro Inlet and the rock breakwater at Fort Fisher.

*WHITE-RUMPED SANDPIPER. Migrant. On the Outer Banks, fairly common in spring and uncommon in fall; elsewhere, uncommon in spring and occasional in fall. Primarily brackish pools and similar sites; in spring migration, occasional on intertidal flats.

*BAIRD'S SANDPIPER. Fall migrant. Occasional on the Outer Banks; elsewhere, very rare to rare at favored sites. Sparsely vegetated sand flats, brackish pools, and similar sites.

PECTORAL SANDPIPER. Migrant. Uncommon in spring and fairly common in fall on the Outer Banks and locally elsewhere. Short-grass marshes, brackish pools, and similar sites.

*PURPLE SANDPIPER. Very local winter resident. Fairly common on the jetties at Oregon Inlet and Wrightsville Beach. Occasional on the jetties at Fort Macon SP. Rare elsewhere.

DUNLIN. Common migrant and winter resident; occasional in summer. Most typical on intertidal flats. The most abundant shorebird in winter.

*CURLEW SANDPIPER. Migrant. On the Outer Banks, rare in spring and occasional in late summer (at least at Portsmouth Island, and at Pea Island NWR during low-water levels). Elsewhere, very rare in spring and late summer at favored sites. Favor brackish pools and similar sites.

STILT SANDPIPER. Migrant. At Pea Island NWR and Bodie Island, uncommon in spring and fairly common in fall. Elsewhere, occasional in spring and uncommon in fall, although they may be locally uncommon in spring and fairly common in fall if conditions are suitable. Brackish pools and similar sites.

*BUFF-BREASTED SANDPIPER. Fall migrant. Occasional on the Outer Banks; rare elsewhere. Sparsely vegetated sand flats, drawn-down impoundments.

*RUFF. Migrant. Very rare in spring; rare in summer. Brackish pools and similar sites.

SHORT-BILLED DOWITCHER. Common migrant; uncommon in early summer. In winter, locally fairly common from Beaufort Inlet south; less common farther north. This is *the* dowitcher of intertidal flats, although it is commonly found at brackish pools and similar sites as well.

*LONG-BILLED DOWITCHER. Regular at Pea Island NWR and Bodie Island, where they are fairly common in fall and uncommon in winter and spring. Elsewhere, primarily uncommon (sometimes fairly common) and very local fall migrant; occasional in winter and spring. Impoundments and similar nontidal habitats. Generally shun intertidal habitats.

COMMON SNIPE. Fairly common (locally common) winter resident. Wet short-grass areas.

AMERICAN WOODCOCK. Fairly common winter resident; occasional summer visitor/resident. Moist bottomlands, especially those adjacent to fields and clearings.

*WILSON'S PHALAROPE. Migrant. Very rare in spring. In fall, uncommon on the Outer Banks, and occasional elsewhere. Brackish pools and similar sites.

*RED-NECKED PHALAROPE. Common migrant. Offshore; found primarily along Gulf Stream edge and over shoals off the capes. Occasional at brackish pools and similar sites, especially on the Outer Banks, from early May to early June. Rare at such sites from late August to early October.

*RED PHALAROPE. Fairly common to common migrant and winter resident. Offshore; found primarily over shoals off the capes, and perhaps along edge of the Gulf Stream. Very rare on land.

*POMARINE JAEGER. Present all year. Fairly common migrant; occasional in early summer; rare in midwinter. Offshore, especially along edge of the Gulf Stream and over other productive waters. Sometimes seen from the beaches, especially along the Outer Banks, where they are uncommon during peaks of migration.

*PARASITIC JAEGER. Fairly common spring migrant; uncommon fall migrant; rare winter visitor/resident. Ocean; apparently occur mostly within a few miles of land; seen much less frequently than Pomarine Jaeger on Gulf Stream pelagic trips. Sometimes seen from the beaches, especially along the Outer Banks, where they are uncommon during peaks of migration.

*LONG-TAILED JAEGER. Migrant. Uncommon in spring; apparently rare (may be occasional) in fall. Offshore, mostly along edge of the Gulf Stream. On rare occasions, seen from Cape Hatteras Point in late May.

*GREAT SKUA. Assumed to be a rare winter visitor from the Central Coast north. Offshore.

*SOUTH POLAR SKUA. Uncommon spring migrant; occasional summer resident. Offshore, mostly along edge of the Gulf Stream. During mid- and late May, sometimes seen over near-shore waters, very rarely from land.

LAUGHING GULL. Common summer resident. Occasional in midwinter from Cape Hatteras south, although status varies depending on weather; may be virtually absent at that season during some years. Ocean, estuaries.

*FRANKLIN'S GULL. Very rare fall migrant on the Outer Banks. Accidental in spring (Currituck County) and summer (Outer Banks). Impoundments, brackish pools.

*LITTLE GULL. Winter resident. Uncommon on the Outer Banks and in North Coast section; rare in Central Coast section. Apparently increasing. Ocean, usually in flocks of Bonaparte's Gulls.

*COMMON BLACK-HEADED GULL. Rare winter visitor/resident. Apparently increasing. Most records are for the barrier islands and immediate coast. Many records are at pools at dredging sites, ponds at sewage treatment plants, impoundments, and similar areas.

BONAPARTE'S GULL. Common winter resident, although toward the south they may not become common until late winter. Immature birds sometimes linger into summer. Most common over the ocean and inlets. Late spring and summer birds are most likely to be found at brackish pools, especially at dredging sites.

RING-BILLED GULL. Common permanent resident, except fairly common and local in summer. Ocean, estuaries, fields, and sites where scavenging is productive, such as fishing piers and picnicking areas. Summer birds are primarily immatures, found mostly at scavenging sites.

HERRING GULL. Common permanent resident, except somewhat less common southward during the breeding season. Ocean, estuaries, and, in winter, landfills and fish houses. Increasing during the breeding season, although most summer birds are immatures and subadults.

*THAYER'S GULL. Very rare winter visitor, although may be rare at Cape Hatteras Point. Probably increasing; however, birders are becoming more adept at picking out this species. Will probably be considered conspecific with Iceland Gull in the future.

*ICELAND GULL. Occasional winter visitor/resident from Morehead City north; rare farther south. Increasing. Most likely to be found at sites where large numbers of gulls congregate, like Cape Hatteras Point, and at landfills and fish houses.

*LESSER BLACK-BACKED GULL. Uncommon winter resident on the Outer Banks (fairly common at Cape Hatteras Point); occasional elsewhere. Increasing. Generally found where Herring Gulls congregate—along ocean beaches, at inlets, and at landfills and fish houses.

*GLAUCOUS GULL. Occasional winter visitor/resident from Morehead City north; rare farther south. Extremely rare in summer. Most likely to be found where gulls congregate—at inlets, fish houses, landfills.

GREAT BLACK-BACKED GULL. Common permanent resident, except in summer, when fairly common from Morehead City north, and uncommon farther south. Increasing. Ocean, estuaries.

*BLACK-LEGGED KITTIWAKE. Fairly common winter resident off the North Coast and Outer Banks; uncommon farther south. Offshore. Rarely seen from land, except at Cape Hatteras, where they are occasional in early winter.

*SABINE'S GULL. Very rare migrant, although perhaps not as rare as the records indicate. Offshore, especially along the edge of the Gulf Stream.

*GULL-BILLED TERN. Fairly common summer resident. Rather local, largely restricted to the vicinity of nesting colonies. Occur mostly from Bodie Island south. Feed primarily over beaches, intertidal flats, marshes, and shrub thickets.

CASPIAN TERN. Common and widespread fall migrant. In spring and early summer, very local, mostly near nesting sites on the Outer Banks. In midwinter, restricted to South Coast section, from Masonboro Inlet south. Feed primarily in tidal creeks and other sheltered sites.

ROYAL TERN. Common permanent resident, except less common in winter (ranging from occasional in North Coast section to fairly common in South Coast section). May be scarce in winter after extreme cold. Ocean; estuaries, especially near inlets. In warmer months, often range far up the estuaries, to New Bern and Washington.

*SANDWICH TERN. Common migrant and fairly common (locally common) summer resident. Very local while nesting, from mid-May to early July. Accidental in midwinter. Ocean, primarily at capes and inlets; estuaries beside the ocean.

*ROSEATE TERN. Migrant and summer visitor. Most likely to be found on the Outer Banks from Cape Hatteras south, where they are occasional in spring migration and in mid- to late summer. Elsewhere, very rare to rare migrant and summer visitor, most likely to be found at Cape Lookout and Cape Fear. Apparently increasing. Many of the records have been at Common Tern colonies at capes and inlets, immediately adjacent to the ocean.

COMMON TERN. Common summer resident. In fall, birds linger latest at the capes and a few other favored roosting areas. At this season most feeding is done offshore. Ocean, primarily at capes and inlets; estuaries adjacent to ocean.

*ARCTIC TERN. Migrant. In spring, uncommon in offshore waters—Gulf Stream edge and farther offshore—east of the Outer Banks and North Coast section, and probably occasional in offshore waters farther south. In fall, may be very rare in offshore waters, but there are no definitive records, and the exact status at this season is open to question. During the spring migration, they have been recorded on land at Cape Hatteras and Cape Lookout.

FORSTER'S TERN. Common permanent resident, except fairly common in summer. Uncommon in North Coast section in midwinter; uncommon south of Beaufort Inlet during the breeding season. From fall to early spring, occur over inshore ocean and saline estuaries; in breeding season, generally restricted to estuaries.

LEAST TERN. Common summer resident. Occur primarily along ocean beaches and around inlets, especially in the vicinity of nesting colonies. Recent records of rooftop nesting at a shopping center. Most widespread in late summer, when they often occur farther up the estuaries.

*BRIDLED TERN. Fairly common summer resident in offshore waters, particularly along the edge of the Gulf Stream. Numbers quite variable; often common in late summer. Virtually never seen from land except in connection with hurricanes.

*SOOTY TERN. Occasional (uncommon at Cape Hatteras) summer visitor/resident at tern colonies. Have nested, but never successfully. Also, uncommon summer resident in offshore waters near and over the Gulf Stream, increasing to fairly common in late summer. Increasing at tern colonies.

BLACK TERN. Fairly common fall migrant; rare to occasional spring migrant/early summer visitor. Found along the oceanfront—especially at capes and inlets, over offshore waters, and at impoundments and similar sites.

BROWN NODDY. Extremely rare summer visitor. Offshore, along the edge of the Gulf Stream. Have also been seen along the coast in connection with hurricanes.

BLACK SKIMMER. Common summer resident, although usually local, especially in fall. In midwinter, occasional in South Coast section; less frequent farther north. In fall, often gather into large flocks at a few favored inlets. During the cooler months, feed almost exclusively at twilight and night.

*DOVEKIE. Rare winter visitor. May be occasional off North Coast section. Ocean, primarily in offshore waters. In North Carolina, there have been no major invasions of this species for more than twenty-five years.

*RAZORBILL. Rare winter visitor. May be occasional off North Coast and northern Outer Banks. Ocean, primarily in offshore waters.

ROCK DOVE. Common permanent resident. Most frequent in cities and towns and in some agricultural areas.

WHITE-WINGED DOVE. Very rare fall migrant. All records have been on the barrier islands between Pea Island and Cape Lookout.

MOURNING DOVE. Common permanent resident. Agricultural lands and many open and semiopen habitats.

*COMMON GROUND-DOVE. Rare to occasional year-round visitor on the barrier islands of south Brunswick County. Most likely to be found in late summer and fall. Decreasing. (In the 1970s they were resident from Brunswick County north to Fort Macon SP.) Found primarily in dunes and along the borders between dunes and shrub thickets. Very rare farther north and inland, mostly in late summer and fall.

BLACK-BILLED CUCKOO. Rare migrant, except occasional on the Outer Banks and North Coast barrier islands in early June and late August. Found primarily in shrub thickets on the barrier islands. In fall, immature Yellow-billeds have dusky bills and are sometimes misidentified as Black-billeds.

YELLOW-BILLED CUCKOO. Summer resident, usually common, although abundance is variable. Primarily in moist and thick broadleaf forests.

*BARN OWL. Decreasing. Primarily an uncommon winter resident, mostly on the barrier islands. Less frequent farther inland. Very local breeder. In winter, feed primarily over dunes and marshes.

EASTERN SCREECH-OWL. Common permanent resident. Most wooded habitats. Most common where fields and clearings alternate with wooded areas.

GREAT HORNED OWL. Fairly common permanent resident. Most common where pine or mixed woods lie adjacent to extensive marshes, fields, or clearings.

SNOWY OWL. Extremely rare winter visitor. All records have been on the barrier islands between Kill Devil Hills and Core Banks.

*BARRED OWL. Fairly common permanent resident in most areas. Bottomland forests, especially along rivers and larger streams. Where habitat is extensive, often common; uncommon in many areas where habitat is fragmented.

*SHORT-EARED OWL. Occasional winter resident/visitor, locally uncommon. Various open habitats—abandoned grown-up fields and clearings, marshes, dune areas; many records are on dredged-material islands. To be looked for wherever Northern Harriers are common.

*NORTHERN SAW-WHET OWL. Winter visitor/resident. Rare on the barrier islands from Cape Hatteras north; very rare farther south and inland. This species may be more common than the records indicate, especially on the Outer Banks.

COMMON NIGHTHAWK. Overall, fairly common summer resident. Primarily around towns and open areas, such as clear-cuts and recently burned-over woods. Common in some areas, but scarce in others because of lack of habitat.

*CHUCK-WILL'S-WIDOW. Summer resident, common over most of the region. In open woods and along borders of woods and fields. In South Coast section, especially common in upland areas with broadleaf vegetation; farther north, most common in thickets along edges of marshes. Extremely rare on barrier islands until early winter.

*WHIP-POOR-WILL. Formerly known primarily as a fall migrant; now locally fairly common during the breeding season, and increasing. Uncommon in fall migration, mostly on barrier islands and adjacent mainland. Very rare in midwinter in South Coast section. In the breeding season, found primarily in pine plantations. In fall and early winter, found primarily in thick woods and shrub thickets adjacent to extensive marshes.

CHIMNEY SWIFT. Common summer resident. Primarily around towns and communities.

RUBY-THROATED HUMMINGBIRD. Fairly common to common summer resident. Most widespread and noticeable in late summer. Feeders, residential areas with flowers, wood margins, bottomlands. Rare during milder winters at feeders. Some reports of wintering "Ruby-throateds" are undoubtedly other species, but there are also some definitive winter records of Ruby-throateds.

RUFOUS HUMMINGBIRD. Very rare to rare fall migrant and winter visitor/resident. Increasing or being detected more readily. All records have been at feeders.

BELTED KINGFISHER. Permanent resident. Common, except scarce in many areas during the breeding season. Fresh water, sheltered portions of estuaries. In breeding season, largely restricted to areas with steep banks.

RED-HEADED WOODPECKER. Primarily a fairly common summer resident, common in some areas. In winter, occasional in most areas, although they may be uncommon locally. In summer, found in many wooded habitats, but especially in open pine woods or in clear-cuts with scattered dead trees. In winter, may be found in orchards, wooded residential areas, and hardwood swamps.

RED-BELLIED WOODPECKER. Common permanent resident. Hardwood and mixed forests; most common in bottomlands.

YELLOW-BELLIED SAPSUCKER. Common winter resident. Most common in somewhat open stands of hardwoods; frequent in residential areas.

DOWNY WOODPECKER. Common permanent resident. Most wooded habitats.

HAIRY WOODPECKER. Uncommon permanent resident. Most often found where forests are extensive and woods mature. Found in pine, mixed, and hardwood forests.

*RED-COCKADED WOODPECKER. Uncommon and very local permanent resident. Open stands of pines, especially longleaf pines, with at least some mature trees.

NORTHERN FLICKER. Common permanent resident, except fairly common in most areas during the breeding season. Most common in open stands of trees and along wood margins.

PILEATED WOODPECKER. Fairly common (locally common) permanent resident. Most common in bottomland forests, especially along rivers and larger streams.

OLIVE-SIDED FLYCATCHER. Very rare fall migrant; accidental in spring (late May). Most records have been along the barrier islands from Pea Island north.

EASTERN WOOD-PEWEE. Common summer resident. Open woods, especially open pine woods.

YELLOW-BELLIED FLYCATCHER. Rare fall migrant; accidental in spring. Most records have been in woods and shrub thickets on the barrier islands.

ACADIAN FLYCATCHER. Common summer resident. Bottomlands and other moist deciduous forests.

ALDER FLYCATCHER. Assumed to be a fall migrant, but there are no definitive records for this species, which is difficult to identify visually. Probably most likely to be found in woods and shrub thickets on the barrier islands.

WILLOW FLYCATCHER. Perhaps an occasional fall migrant, although this assigned status is largely conjectural—there are few definitive fall records for this species, which is difficult to identify visually. Very rare spring migrant. Probably most likely to be found in woods and shrub thickets on the barrier islands.

LEAST FLYCATCHER. Fall migrant. Occasional, except uncommon on the Outer Banks and North Coast barrier islands. Most likely to be found in woods and shrub thickets on the barrier islands. Extremely rare as late as early winter.

EASTERN PHOEBE. Fairly common winter resident, except common toward south. Open woods, woods/field borders. Uncommon summer resident along the western border of the North Coast section.

GREAT CRESTED FLYCATCHER. Common summer resident, especially in somewhat open pine and mixed woods, including wooded residential areas. Extremely rare as late as December.

*WESTERN KINGBIRD. Fall migrant. Uncommon on the Outer Banks; occasional elsewhere. Found in open habitats, primarily on the barrier islands. Accidental in June.

EASTERN KINGBIRD. Common summer resident and fall migrant. Open areas with scattered trees or shrubs.

*GRAY KINGBIRD. Rare spring migrant; very rare summer visitor and fall migrant. Most records are in open habitats on the barrier islands, or sometimes the adjacent mainland, from Bodie Island south.

*SCISSOR-TAILED FLYCATCHER. Very rare spring migrant, summer visitor, and fall migrant. Perhaps most likely to be found in June and October. Most records are in open habitats on the barrier islands—especially the Outer Banks—or adjacent mainland.

HORNED LARK. Rare winter visitor, except occasional in the Albemarle-Pamlico section. Found in barren fields, bare flats on barrier islands, and other open habitats. Might turn up during any month along the western border of the region.

PURPLE MARTIN. Common summer resident, found in open areas wherever nesting structures are available. Extremely rare as late as mid-November.

TREE SWALLOW. Common migrant and fairly common winter resident at many sites, especially in eastern part of North Coast section and along western border of the region farther south. On the Outer Banks, and toward the immediate coast in Central Coast section, they are much less common in spring and the early part of fall migration. In winter, numbers often vary greatly. Occasional throughout June in North Coast section and locally elsewhere. There is one recent breeding record, and they may breed occasionally in the region, especially in North Coast section. Found in open areas, usually near water.

NORTHERN ROUGH-WINGED SWALLOW. Fairly common, but local, summer resident. Scarce in many areas because of lack of habitat. Found primarily near banks and similar sites that provide nesting habitat. Accidental in winter.

BANK SWALLOW. Over most of region, uncommon spring migrant and fairly common fall migrant; more common locally. Fairly common in spring along western border of the region. Open areas, often near water. There is one record of possible nesting in the region.

CLIFF SWALLOW. In most areas, occasional spring migrant and uncommon fall migrant. Have been found nesting at two sites in the region—Oregon Inlet and Oriental. Nesting was still taking place at Oriental in 1993.

BARN SWALLOW. Common summer resident. Open country, especially near bridges, docks, and other structures that provide nesting sites. Extremely rare until late December, and accidental in midwinter.

BLUE JAY. Common permanent resident. Most wooded habitats.

American Crow. Common permanent resident. Primarily associated with agricultural lands.

Fish Crow. Common permanent resident. Most common on the barrier islands and along the borders of estuaries, but occur throughout the region, at least in the breeding season. Inland habitats include agricultural lands, urban areas, and pine woods.

Carolina Chickadee. Common permanent resident. Most wooded habitats. Virtually absent from many barrier island sites—notably Hatteras Island—in spite of adequate habitat.

Tufted Titmouse. Common permanent resident. Most wooded habitats. Virtually absent from most barrier islands.

Red-breasted Nuthatch. Irruptive species. During invasion years, fairly common fall migrant and uncommon winter resident. During other years, uncommon in fall and rare to occasional in winter. Found primarily in pines; in coastal North Carolina, seem to prefer longleaf pines.

White-breasted Nuthatch. Uncommon and very local permanent resident over most of region. In general, more common toward north and west. Fairly common in the Great Dismal Swamp. Mature hardwoods and mixed woods.

*Brown-headed Nuthatch. Fairly common permanent resident over most of the region. More common toward south; less common toward north. Pine woods. Absent on the barrier islands.

Brown Creeper. Uncommon winter resident. Found mostly in mixed woods, usually in flocks of chickadees and kinglets. Fairly common on the Outer Banks in October.

Carolina Wren. Common permanent resident. Most wooded habitats. Very widespread.

House Wren. Common winter resident over most of region, except somewhat less common inland and toward north. Less common during severe winters. Thick brushy areas. Local breeder, uncommon to fairly common; most breeding records have been at pocosin sites that have recently experienced severe fires.

Winter Wren. Common winter resident. Most common along streams in forested areas, especially where there are numerous logs, low thick ground cover, etc.

*Sedge Wren. Common winter resident. Irregularly flooded salt marshes, especially along landward borders where a few shrubs are present, and wet grassy clear-cuts and abandoned fields, especially toward south.

*Marsh Wren. Common, but rather local, permanent resident. Irregularly flooded salt marshes, brackish marshes, fresh marshes. In breeding season, largely limited to areas where marshes are extensive. More widespread in winter.

GOLDEN-CROWNED KINGLET. Common winter resident. Pine and mixed woods. In October, most common on barrier islands.

RUBY-CROWNED KINGLET. Common winter resident. Various wooded habitats; most common in moist woods with understory of broadleaf evergreens.

BLUE-GRAY GNATCATCHER. Common summer resident. Absent in winter in most areas, but occasional throughout milder years in South Coast section, as well as a few favored sites elsewhere. Primarily swamps and moist deciduous woods; wintering birds are usually associated with live oaks.

EASTERN BLUEBIRD. Common permanent resident. Open and semiopen country.

VEERY. Migrant. Occasional in spring; in fall, occasional in most of region, but uncommon in South Coast section. Most likely to be found in woods and shrub thickets on the barrier islands and immediate coast.

GRAY-CHEEKED THRUSH. Migrant. Rare in spring; occasional in fall. Most likely to be found in woods and shrub thickets on the barrier islands and immediate coast.

SWAINSON'S THRUSH. Migrant. Occasional in spring; uncommon in fall. Most likely to be found in woods and shrub thickets on the barrier islands and immediate coast.

HERMIT THRUSH. Common winter resident. Most common in moist thickets and in moist woods with thick undergrowth of broadleaf evergreens.

WOOD THRUSH. Common summer resident, although scarce in some areas because of lack of habitat. Most common in deciduous woods near and along streams, and in wooded residential areas.

AMERICAN ROBIN. Common permanent resident, although restricted in range in the breeding season. Widespread from early November to spring in most wooded habitats. In the breeding season, mostly restricted to wooded suburban habitats, and absent from many areas, especially near the immediate coast.

GRAY CATBIRD. Common permanent resident, except somewhat less common toward south in breeding season. Most common in moist areas with dense shrub cover, especially of broadleaf evergreens. In breeding season, often common in wooded residential areas.

NORTHERN MOCKINGBIRD. Common permanent resident. Open country with scattered trees and shrubs. Most common around towns and communities.

BROWN THRASHER. Comm.n permanent resident. Found in various habitats with thick shrub cover, including residential areas; especially typical in dry sites with a thick shrub cover of live oaks and other broadleaf evergreens.

AMERICAN PIPIT. Fairly common winter resident. Most common in areas with extensive bare fields. Heard flying overhead far more frequently than they are seen. In October, heard mostly over the barrier islands and immediate coast.

CEDAR WAXWING. Common winter resident; very rare over most of the area in midsummer, but occasional throughout the summer in North Coast section. May be increasing in summer in all sections. Various habitats, but usually associated with berry-bearing trees and shrubs, especially red cedar.

LOGGERHEAD SHRIKE. Continue to decrease. In most of the region, very rare in fall and winter, except rare in South Coast section. A few permanent resident birds may persist along the immediate western border of the region, especially in South Coast section.

EUROPEAN STARLING. Common permanent resident. Primarily in cities, towns, and agricultural areas.

WHITE-EYED VIREO. Common summer resident. In winter, rare in most areas, but occasional throughout milder years in South Coast section and a few favored sites farther north. Dense shrub vegetation, especially where moist.

SOLITARY VIREO. Uncommon winter resident from Central Coast section and Cape Hatteras south; fairly common locally, especially during milder winters. Less common toward north. Found primarily in pine and mixed woods with moderate to thick broadleaf evergreen vegetation.

YELLOW-THROATED VIREO. Fairly common (locally common) summer resident from the western Croatan NF south. Less common toward north and east. Often most common in somewhat open mixed forests on drier sites. However, also frequent in taller trees along streams.

PHILADELPHIA VIREO. Occasional fall migrant at better sites—North Coast barrier islands, Outer Banks, and Fort Fisher. Most likely to be found in wood margins and shrub thickets.

RED-EYED VIREO. Common summer resident. Occur primarily in wet to moist deciduous forests.

BLUE-WINGED WARBLER. Migrant. Rare in spring; occasional in fall. In spring, wood margins throughout region. In fall, most likely to be found in wood margins and shrub thickets on barrier islands.

GOLDEN-WINGED WARBLER. Rare fall migrant. Most likely to be found in wood margins and shrub thickets on barrier islands.

TENNESSEE WARBLER. Occasional fall migrant. Most likely to be found in wood margins and shrub thickets on barrier islands.

*ORANGE-CROWNED WARBLER. Uncommon winter resident, although locally fairly common on the barrier islands and adjacent mainland from Cape Hatteras south. Found primarily in shrub thickets with broadleaf evergreens, or in woods having shrub layer of broadleaf evergreens, especially where moist or wet.

NASHVILLE WARBLER. Occasional fall migrant. Most likely to be found in wood margins and shrub thickets on barrier islands.

NORTHERN PARULA. Common summer resident. Swamps, moist deciduous forests. Most common in areas with an abundance of Spanish moss; in such areas, often occur in dry habitats.

YELLOW WARBLER. Fairly common migrant. Breed locally and sporadically on the barrier islands from Cape Hatteras north. In spring migration, found most readily in wooded residential areas. Breeders are found at wet sites with willows. Fall migrants are found primarily in wood margins and shrub thickets on barrier islands.

CHESTNUT-SIDED WARBLER. Migrant. Very rare in spring; rare in fall. In spring, have been found in wood margins widely dispersed throughout the region. In fall, most likely to be found in wood margins and shrub thickets on barrier islands.

MAGNOLIA WARBLER. Migrant. Very rare in spring; fairly common in fall. In spring, most likely to be found in wood margins scattered throughout the region. In fall, most likely to be found in wood margins and shrub thickets on barrier islands.

CAPE MAY WARBLER. Migrant. Rare in spring; common in fall on barrier islands from Ocracoke Island north, uncommon to fairly common elsewhere. In spring, often found in well-wooded residential areas. In fall, most likely to be found in wood margins and shrub thickets on barrier islands. Extremely rare until December.

BLACK-THROATED BLUE WARBLER. Migrant. Uncommon in spring; fairly common in fall. In spring, mixed woods. In fall, most likely to be found in wood margins and shrub thickets on barrier islands. Extremely rare until December.

YELLOW-RUMPED WARBLER. Common winter resident. Most wooded habitats, especially abundant in shrub thickets near the immediate coast.

BLACK-THROATED GREEN WARBLER. Fairly common, but very local, summer resident; uncommon fall migrant. Breeding birds occur in nonriverine swamp forests, typically where a few coniferous trees—pines, white cedars, bald cypresses—are present. Fall migrants are most likely to be found in wood margins and shrub thickets on barrier islands.

BLACKBURNIAN WARBLER. Migrant. Rare in spring (mostly along barrier islands from Ocracoke north); occasional in fall. Most likely to be found in wood margins and shrub thickets on barrier islands.

YELLOW-THROATED WARBLER. Common summer resident. Generally absent in midwinter, except rare in South Coast section. Mixed and deciduous forests, especially along streams. Often associated with sites that have a few tall pines; most common in areas with an abundance of Spanish moss. Wintering birds are often associated with live oaks.

PINE WARBLER. Permanent resident. Common most of the year, except fairly common in early winter in most areas. Mature pine forests and woodlands. Common all winter in longleaf pine areas from the Croatan NF south.

PRAIRIE WARBLER. Common summer resident; rare in winter in South Coast section and locally farther north. Found primarily at sites with young pines and dense shrub cover.

PALM WARBLER. Common fall migrant; uncommon winter resident. Open habitats—field edges, open pine woods, edges of marshes, dunes. During fall migration, most common on barrier islands. In winter, especially likely to be found around areas with livestock. Winter abundance quite variable; may become scarce after extreme weather.

BAY-BREASTED WARBLER. Migrant. Very rare in spring on the Outer Banks; occasional in fall. Most likely to be found in wood margins and shrub thickets on barrier islands.

BLACKPOLL WARBLER. Migrant. Fairly common in spring; fairly common in fall on North Coast barrier islands and Outer Banks, but uncommon farther south and inland. In spring, widespread in pine and mixed woods; perhaps most likely to be found in well-wooded residential areas. In fall, most likely to be found in wood margins and shrub thickets on barrier islands.

CERULEAN WARBLER. Migrant. Very rare in spring; rare in fall. Spring records are for wood margins throughout region. In fall, most likely to be found in wood margins and shrub thickets on barrier islands.

BLACK-AND-WHITE WARBLER. Summer resident and migrant. Most widespread during migration, when they are fairly common. As a summer resident, vary from fairly common toward north to occasional in South Coast section. Rare in winter, except occasional in South Coast section. Breeding birds occur in mixed woods in moist areas. During migration, widespread in most wooded habitats. Wintering birds are often found where pines and broadleaf evergreens are intermixed.

AMERICAN REDSTART. Summer resident and fall migrant. As a summer resident, uncommon and local over much of the area, varying from fairly common in the Great Dismal Swamp area to rare in South Coast section. In fall, common and widespread. Breeding birds occur in hardwood swamps, at sites grown up in vines and tangles. In fall, occur in most wooded habitats, but most common in woods and shrub thickets on barrier islands.

*PROTHONOTARY WARBLER. Common summer resident. Found in many types of moist to wet wooded habitats.

*WORM-EATING WARBLER. Fairly common (locally common) summer resident. Most common at moist sites that have somewhat open growth of pine trees with thick understory or shrub layer of broadleaf evergreens.

*SWAINSON'S WARBLER. Uncommon and local summer resident. Virtually absent in some areas because of lack of habitat; fairly common in a few areas. Found primarily in wet areas with thick growth of cane or broadleaf evergreens.

OVENBIRD. Summer resident. Abundance varies from common in most of area to occasional in South Coast section. Primarily in moist broadleaf or mixed woods. Generally absent in winter, but occasional in maritime forests at Cape Hatteras.

NORTHERN WATERTHRUSH. Migrant. Occasional in spring; fairly common in fall. Occur primarily along swamp edges and in wet thickets.

***LOUISIANA WATERTHRUSH.** Summer resident. Fairly common in western portion of North Coast section; farther south, uncommon and local, occurring mostly along western border of region. Found primarily along flowing streams with steep banks, although in the North Coast section, also occur along stagnant streams and canals.

KENTUCKY WARBLER. Uncommon summer resident, mostly along western border of region. Rare in many areas. Moist rich deciduous woods.

CONNECTICUT WARBLER. Rare fall migrant, except occasional on the Outer Banks. Moist shrub thickets.

MOURNING WARBLER. Very rare fall migrant. Most likely to be found in shrub thickets on barrier islands.

COMMON YELLOWTHROAT. Permanent resident. Common during the warmer months, decreasing to uncommon in winter in most areas, although fairly common locally and toward south. Fresh and brackish marshes, wet shrub thickets, pocosins.

HOODED WARBLER. Common summer resident. Moist broadleaf and mixed woods.

WILSON'S WARBLER. Occasional fall migrant. Most likely to be found in wood margins and shrub thickets on barrier islands. Extremely rare until December.

CANADA WARBLER. Rare fall migrant. Most likely to be found in wood margins and shrub thickets on barrier islands.

YELLOW-BREASTED CHAT. Fairly common summer resident; rare in winter, although often occasional at a few sites during milder years. In breeding season, occur in areas with thick growth of shrubs and vines, especially blackberries. In winter, most likely to be found in similar areas with some broadleaf evergreen cover.

***SUMMER TANAGER.** Summer resident. Common from the Croatan NF south; less common farther north. Mixed and pine woods; most common on drier sites with a mixture of pines and oaks.

SCARLET TANAGER. Occasional migrant throughout most of the region; uncommon summer resident along western border of North Coast section. Mixed woods. Fall migrants are most likely to be found in wood margins and shrub thickets on barrier islands.

WESTERN TANAGER. Very rare winter visitor/resident. Most records have been at feeders, but some birds have also been found in mixed woods.

NORTHERN CARDINAL. Common and widespread permanent resident. Most wooded habitats.

ROSE-BREASTED GROSBEAK. Occasional migrant. Mixed woods. Fall migrants are most likely to be found in wood margins and shrub thickets on barrier islands. Extremely rare in winter.

*BLUE GROSBEAK. Summer resident; common in most areas, but locally less common. Thick, overgrown abandoned fields and clearings, open pine and mixed woods. Usually on dry sites.

INDIGO BUNTING. Common summer resident. Thick, overgrown abandoned fields and clearings, wood margins, thickets within openings in woods. Extremely rare in midwinter.

*PAINTED BUNTING. Summer resident. Fairly common but local on the barrier islands and adjacent mainland from Marshallberg, in Carteret County, south; rare farther north on the barrier islands to Cape Hatteras; extremely rare farther north and inland. Found primarily in dense shrub thickets; occur in some residential areas, but usually in the vicinity of some shrub-thicket vegetation. Rare in winter, usually at feeders.

DICKCISSEL. Primarily a fall migrant, rare in most areas, but occasional on the Outer Banks and at Fort Fisher. Very rare winter resident/visitor in all sections; extremely rare in summer. Most fall records are flyovers, heard calling overhead. Many winter and early spring records are of individuals at feeders, often with House Sparrows, although they have also been found in weedy areas with other sparrows. A small group of Dickcissels may have nested at Alligator River NWR in Dare County in 1988.

RUFOUS-SIDED TOWHEE. Common permanent resident. Thick shrubby areas, especially shrub thickets on barrier islands, overgrown abandoned fields and clearings, some pocosins.

*BACHMAN'S SPARROW. Extremely local. Fairly common summer resident at a handful of sites from Croatan NF south; rare elsewhere within this range. No recent records north of the Croatan NF. Open to moderately open stands of pine (usually longleaf) with thick grass ground cover and little or no understory and shrub vegetation. In winter, rare to occasional at breeding sites in South Coast section. Farther north, absent to occasional, depending on suitability of habitat. Wintering birds are found primarily at sites that were burned over during the previous growing season and thus have especially thick ground cover and an abundance of seeds.

CHIPPING SPARROW. Over most of the region, primarily a common winter resident. Generally uncommon and local in summer, but fairly common in North Coast section and along the western border of the region farther south. In winter, common in a variety of habitats. In summer, occur mostly in wooded residential areas and at golf courses.

*CLAY-COLORED SPARROW. Primarily a fall migrant. Generally rare, but occasional on the Outer Banks and at Fort Fisher. Very rare in winter. Along the borders of shrub thickets, usually on the barrier islands.

FIELD SPARROW. Common winter resident. In summer, absent in many areas, but fairly common on barrier islands from Bodie Island north, uncommon on North Coast mainland, and occasional along western border of the region farther south. Abandoned overgrown fields and clearings. On Outer Banks and North Coast barrier islands, breeding birds are found in dunes with scattered shrubs.

VESPER SPARROW. Winter resident. Uncommon in South Coast section, occasional in Central Coast section, and rare farther north, except occasional on Outer Banks in fall (mid-October to early November). Fields, especially partially harvested fields that have a mixture of bare and vegetated areas.

*LARK SPARROW. Primarily a fall migrant. Occasional on the Outer Banks; rare elsewhere. Very rare winter visitor/resident and spring migrant. Most likely to be found in borders of shrub thickets on barrier islands. Wintering birds are sometimes found at feeders.

"IPSWICH SPARROW." Occasional winter resident. Dunes on the barrier islands. Other races of Savannah Sparrow can be quite pale and are frequently misidentified as this subspecies.

SAVANNAH SPARROW. Common winter resident. Open bare or short-grass habitats, including fields, dunes, and some short-grass marshes.

GRASSHOPPER SPARROW. Primarily a rare winter resident/visitor. Abandoned fields and clearings with very thick grass cover. Apparently breeds at the New Hanover County airport in Wilmington.

*HENSLOW'S SPARROW. Primarily a winter resident, generally rare. However, sometimes occasional in abandoned fields and clearings that are moist and have thick grass cover, and sometimes uncommon in pine savannas that have been burned over during the previous summer, from the Croatan NF south. Occasionally, a few birds breed in clear-cuts in pocosin areas along the western border of the region.

LE CONTE'S SPARROW. Very rare winter resident/visitor. Wet overgrown fields with very thick grass cover.

*SHARP-TAILED SPARROW. Winter resident. Common from Beaufort Inlet south; fairly common around inlets farther north. Regularly flooded salt marshes. Most widespread in fall.

*SEASIDE SPARROW. Permanent resident. Common breeder in certain irregularly flooded salt marshes, mostly in Central Coast section, less common elsewhere. Common from fall to spring in regularly flooded salt marshes in South Coast section; less common farther north. Most widespread from late August to October.

FOX SPARROW. Fairly common winter resident. Seem to favor rather open woods with moderately thick cover of broadleaf evergreen shrubs. Frequent at feeders after snows and severe cold.

SONG SPARROW. Common winter resident. Grown-up fields and clearings;

variety of shrubby habitats. In the breeding season, locally fairly common on the barrier islands from Portsmouth Island north. Breeding birds are found in shrub thickets either within dunes or bordering marshes.

*LINCOLN'S SPARROW. Rare winter resident/visitor over most of the region. However, occasional in Albemarle-Pamlico section. Found most often in brush piles in large cut-over areas, especially where wet. Also, occasional on the Outer Banks and at Fort Fisher during fall migration (October).

SWAMP SPARROW. Common winter resident. Fresh marshes, some brackish marshes, wet shrubby areas.

WHITE-THROATED SPARROW. Common winter resident. Thick shrubby areas in both open and wooded landscapes. Common in wooded residential areas.

*WHITE-CROWNED SPARROW. Primarily a fall migrant. Occasional in most areas, but uncommon to fairly common on the Outer Banks. Also, a rare winter resident, except uncommon in farmland near Lake Phelps. Fall migrants are most likely to be found along borders of shrub thickets on barrier islands. Wintering birds are also found in thickets and brush piles in open areas.

DARK-EYED JUNCO. Over most of the region, common winter resident. Fairly common toward south and toward immediate coast, except common on barrier islands north of Cape Hatteras during fall migration (mid-October through November). Wintering birds are found along wood/field borders and in wooded residential areas. Fall migrants on barrier islands occur along borders of shrub thickets.

*LAPLAND LONGSPUR. Winter resident/visitor. Occasional at a few sites on the Outer Banks—Oregon Inlet, Cape Hatteras Point, Hatteras Inlet. Uncommon (at least during some years) in farmland near Lake Phelps. Very rare elsewhere. On barrier islands, birds are found mostly on expansive, dry, sparsely vegetated sand flats. Inland, found in expansive barren fields.

*SNOW BUNTING. Winter resident. Occasional from Cape Lookout north; farther south, generally rare, but may be occasional early in season (mid-November to mid-December), at least during some years. Virtually all records are on the barrier islands. Expansive, dry, sparsely vegetated sand flats, such as those that occur next to inlets.

BOBOLINK. Migrant. Uncommon in spring; fairly common in fall. Fields, marshes, and other open habitats. In fall, they can be heard on most nights as they migrate overhead.

RED-WINGED BLACKBIRD. Common permanent resident. Breeding birds are found mostly in and along borders of marshes. In winter, found in many habitats, including suburban and agricultural areas.

EASTERN MEADOWLARK. Common permanent resident. Fields and other open habitats.

*YELLOW-HEADED BLACKBIRD. Primarily a fall migrant. Occasional on the Outer Banks; rare elsewhere. Very rare in winter and spring. Fall migrants are found primarily in open habitats on the barrier islands. Wintering birds are found mostly with other blackbirds in extensive agricultural areas, often at feedlots.

*RUSTY BLACKBIRD. Uncommon winter resident, but fairly common locally. Bottomland forests and adjacent areas, including wet fields. Often found at feedlots in wet areas. Sometimes found on lawns in wetter regions, such as around Lake Mattamuskeet and in eastern Pamlico County.

BREWER'S BLACKBIRD. Overall, a very rare winter resident/visitor. However, a small flock is present every year at a "superfarm" in Carteret County, and small flocks may winter at a few similar sites.

BOAT-TAILED GRACKLE. Common permanent resident. Barrier islands and nearby mainland, usually adjacent to salt water. Salt marshes and along shorelines of estuaries. Often move into adjacent agricultural lands in winter. Less common along western shores of Pamlico Sound.

COMMON GRACKLE. Common permanent resident, although may be local in fall and early winter, when they gather into large flocks. Many wooded habitats, agricultural lands, residential areas.

*SHINY COWBIRD. Currently rare year-round visitor, although expected to increase. Found wherever Brown-headed Cowbirds congregate.

BROWN-HEADED COWBIRD. Common permanent resident, although may be local in fall and early winter. Occur in most open and semiopen habitats.

ORCHARD ORIOLE. Common summer resident. Semiopen areas with deciduous trees or shrubs. Common in many wooded residential areas.

NORTHERN (BALTIMORE) ORIOLE. Primarily a common fall migrant. Occasional and very local winter resident, mostly at feeders. Fall migrants are most likely to be found in wood margins and shrub thickets on barrier islands.

PURPLE FINCH. Irruptive species; decreasing. Formerly common winter resident during most years; now fairly common winter resident during invasion years, which are becoming more and more infrequent; uncommon during noninvasion winters. Deciduous and mixed woods, residential areas with feeders.

HOUSE FINCH. Common permanent resident, except less common toward south during the breeding season, although increasing. Found primarily in urban and suburban areas, although increasingly common in rural areas, especially in winter.

RED CROSSBILL. Very rare winter visitor. Most of the few winter records are for the Bodie Island–Pea Island area and South Coast section. Usually associated with pines.

COMMON REDPOLL. Very rare winter visitor on the barrier islands from Fort

Macon SP north. Accidental elsewhere. Most records are for semiopen habitats along the barrier islands.

PINE SISKIN. Irruptive species; decreasing. Formerly common winter resident during invasion years; now fairly common winter resident during invasion years, which are becoming more and more infrequent; rare visitor during noninvasion years, except occasional on the Outer Banks in fall. Most frequent in hardwood forests (especially sweet gum), residential areas with feeders.

AMERICAN GOLDFINCH. Common winter resident; in summer, generally rare, but uncommon north and inland, and apparently increasing. Deciduous and mixed woods, weedy fields, residential areas with feeders.

EVENING GROSBEAK. Irruptive species; decreasing. Formerly common winter resident during invasion years; now fairly common winter resident during invasion years, which are becoming more and more infrequent; rare visitor during noninvasion years. Found primarily at feeders in residential areas; in fall and early winter, most frequent in bottomlands.

HOUSE SPARROW. Common permanent resident. Urban and some agricultural areas; less common in suburban areas.

ACCIDENTALS

Western Grebe
Albatross (species undetermined)
Bermuda Petrel
Bulwer's Petrel
Red-billed Tropicbird
Brown Booby
"Great White Heron"
"Black Brant"
Masked Duck
White-tailed Kite
Swainson's Hawk
Gyrfalcon
Spotted Redshank
"Eurasian Whimbrel"
Black-tailed Godwit
Bar-tailed Godwit
Little Stint
Common/Mew Gull
California Gull
"Cayenne Tern"

Thick-billed Murre
Black Guillemot
Atlantic Puffin
Smooth-billed Ani
Burrowing Owl
Long-eared Owl
Say's Phoebe
Vermilion Flycatcher
Tropical Kingbird
Fork-tailed Flycatcher
Cave Swallow
Bewick's Wren
Northern Wheatear
Black-backed Wagtail
Sage Thrasher
Sprague's Pipit
Northern Shrike
Warbling Vireo
Black-whiskered Vireo
"Brewster's Warbler"
"Lawrence's Warbler"

"Audubon's Warbler"
Black-throated Gray Warbler
Townsend's Warbler
Black-headed Grosbeak

American Tree Sparrow
Lark Bunting
Western Meadowlark
"Bullock's Oriole"

ASSUMED ESCAPES

Chilean Flamingo
Black-bellied Whistling-Duck
    (might be wild)
Barnacle Goose (might be wild)
Ruddy Shelduck
Common Shelduck

Baikal Teal
Falcated Teal
Mandarin Duck
Garganey (might be wild)
Prairie Falcon (might be wild)

PART 2

GUIDES TO
BIRD-FINDING
SITES

CHAPTER 4

The North Coast Section

Mackay Island National Wildlife Refuge, Knotts Island
MAP 1

Mackay Island NWR receives little attention from birders because it definitely lies off the beaten path. It is also not one of the better coastal spots for seeing rarities, and during much of the year only a small part of the refuge is open. However, birding can be plenty entertaining here. The Great Marsh, which you can see from the NC 615 causeway, harbors a good variety of marsh birds. King Rails and Marsh Wrens are common throughout the year. Virginia Rails are common from autumn to spring, and they may breed here as well. American Bitterns are seen regularly in the migrations and winter and may sometimes breed here. In winter Snow Geese and a variety of other waterfowl can often be seen from the causeway.

From March 15 to October 15 the trails around the three impoundments in the refuge's southwestern section (the East, Middle, and West pools) are open to the public, at least to those who are willing to walk a mile or more. These impoundments host several Wood Ducks throughout the year, and you may see a variety of dabbling ducks just after the impoundments are opened in the spring and just before they are closed in autumn. Common Moorhens are easy to find in the impoundments during the period that they're open, and a few Least Bitterns also breed here.

The refuge also has resident Brown-headed Nuthatches. In the breeding season Prothonotary Warblers are common and there are a few Chuck-will's-widows. Black Vultures are occasional throughout the year.

In the future, this area's birding possibilities may increase somewhat. There is

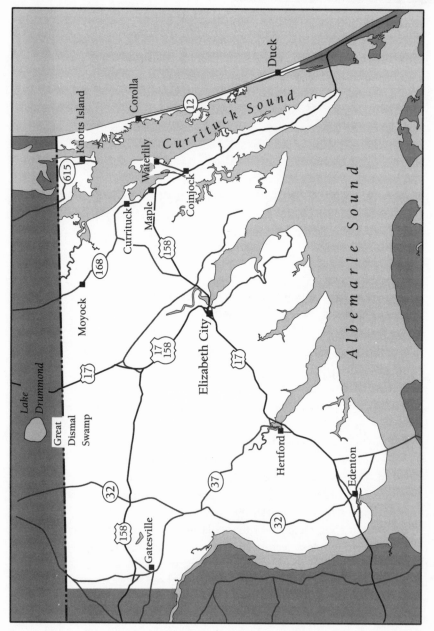

THE NORTH COAST SECTION

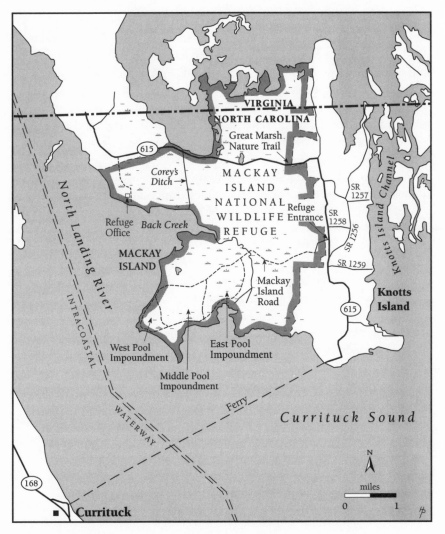

On map:
VIRGINIA
NORTH CAROLINA

Great Marsh
Nature Trail

615

Corey's
Ditch →

MACKAY
ISLAND
NATIONAL
WILDLIFE
REFUGE

Refuge
Entrance

SR 1257
SR 1258
SR 1256
SR 1259

Knotts Island Channel

Refuge
Office   Back Creek

MACKAY
ISLAND

North Landing River

INTRACOASTAL

Mackay
Island
Road

Knotts
Island

615

West Pool
Impoundment

East Pool
Impoundment

Middle Pool
Impoundment

Ferry

WATERWAY

Currituck Sound

N

miles
0   1

168

Currituck

1. MACKAY ISLAND NATIONAL WILDLIFE REFUGE, KNOTTS ISLAND

a small impoundment near the refuge office, and the refuge managers plan to open the dike around it to the public during the warmer months, perhaps during the same period as the other impoundments. Call the refuge for the latest information. By walking the dike around this impoundment you would be able to look for marsh birds within the Great Marsh without having to contend with any highway traffic and noise.

LOGISTICS. The most scenic way to get to Mackay Island NWR and Knotts Island (although it's usually not that good for birding) is by taking the ferry from the Currituck community. (See the end of this site guide for more information.) From Virginia Beach, access is via VA/NC 615. If you decide to drive around from the Currituck mainland rather than wait for the ferry, take NC/VA 168 north into Virginia. At 1.8 miles past the state line, turn right onto Galbush Road. This ends at 1.6 miles; here, turn right onto Indian River Road and go 5.6 miles, until the road ends at Blackwater Road. Turn left, drive 1.8 miles, then turn right on Pungo Ferry Road. Shortly after crossing the Intracoastal Waterway, this road will end on VA/NC 615. (In Virginia this road is called Princess Anne Road; in North Carolina it has various names.) Turn right and drive about 5 miles to the North Carolina line. About a mile past the state line you will see the road to the refuge office on your right.

The refuge office/visitors center is open from 8 A.M. to 4 P.M. weekdays throughout the year. Here you can see mounted specimens and photographs of several bird species found in the refuge. The site also affords a scenic view of the North Landing River.

THE MILE-LONG ROAD to the office is bordered by swamps and fields. Listen for Prothonotary Warblers in the swamps during the nesting season. In winter the fields may have a few Tundra Swans and Snow Geese.

If you're visiting between spring and autumn, be sure to ask whether the dike around the nearby impoundment is open to the public. This impoundment could be a good place to see Least Bitterns, Wood Ducks, and Common Moorhens, and the marshes outside the impoundment should harbor Least Bitterns and King Rails. Other dabbling ducks might join the Wood Ducks in early spring and autumn.

Usually the refuge's primary birding attraction is the 3-mile-long **causeway across Great Marsh** on NC 615. These vast brackish marshes are the year-round home of large numbers of King Rails and Marsh Wrens; you'll also find many Least Bitterns in summer and Snow Geese in late winter. This may be the state's best place for seeing King Rail and Least Bittern.

You may prefer to do most of your birding here from your car, by slowly driving up and down the causeway. This is a good way to look for rails, but be careful: this road is curvy, with limited visibility, and the locals drive it fast. On weekdays the worst traffic is about 6:30 A.M. and 5 P.M., when local people are headed to and from work. In many places the road shoulders are wide enough for you to park safely, but watch out for soggy spots after rainy weather.

At dawn during the breeding season—especially from about May 1 to mid-June—the causeway can be a lot of fun. In this open environment a calm morning is highly desirable. The combined vocal efforts of several species will produce quite a din. Listen for the loud "kak-kak-kak" of the King Rails, the cooing of the Least Bitterns, and the almost omnipresent gurgling of the Marsh Wrens. Also common are Red-winged Blackbirds and Common Yellowthroats. The Marsh Wrens are easy to see, and with a little patience you can also see King

Rails and Least Bitterns. You may see bitterns making occasional short flights; to see King Rails, watch the edges of the little pools and other openings.

During the breeding season these marshes might harbor some supposedly extralimital and poorly known species, including American Bittern, Virginia and Black rails, Sora, and Sedge Wren. This area is at least marginal habitat for Black Rails—some probably breed here at least occasionally. A few Virginia Rails should nest here; even Soras might sometimes nest here. The western edge of the marshes (south of the highway), where they grade into the pine woods, looks like suitable nesting habitat for Sedge Wrens, especially after managed burns.

A late-night listen from the causeway might be rewarding, especially if it's calm and there's a full moon. In addition to the marsh birds, listen for Chuck-will's-widows at the two ends of the causeway.

In addition to the breeding species, you can also expect some shorebirds along the causeway from April through May. Check any openings in the marsh.

Winter can also be entertaining. Look for Tundra Swans, Snow Geese, and a few dabbling ducks. Late winter is often best; there are often more geese and ducks then. There are always a few Northern Harriers, and often one or two Red-tailed Hawks, in sight over the marshes. From November to March a Rough-legged Hawk would be a very rare possibility. A calm sunrise is the best time to be here, but sunset can also be nice; King and Virginia rails will be calling, and Snow Geese will be flying overhead. You should have little trouble spotting Marsh Wrens and Swamp Sparrows. As the light fades, watch for owls—Great Horned, Barn, and Short-eared are all possible.

In autumn, after cold fronts with west to northwest winds, check the shrub-thicket vegetation along the causeway for migrant passerines. On some mornings displaced migrants no doubt use the causeway as a corridor as they make their way back westward.

Watch for one special weather event: when severe low-pressure storms with strong south to southwest winds pass by. This situation could happen at any season but is most likely to happen in winter and early spring. I've witnessed this sort of weather on one occasion, and the marshes were completely flooded, forcing King Rails, Virginia Rails, and Soras up onto the causeway. During such conditions a Black or Yellow rail would be possible. Don't expect such water levels during every strong southerly wind—the barometer has got to be way down there, to 29.70 inches or so.

At the east end of the causeway you will see the **Great Marsh Trail**, a 0.3-mile loop. The trail doesn't offer any additional water bird possibilities, but it does get you away from the highway and annoying traffic noise and gives you a chance to see Carolina Chickadees, Brown-headed Nuthatches, and other land birds. Near the end of the trail, where it runs beside a small pool, watch carefully for King Rails.

Look for the beginning of **Mackay Island Road** on NC 615, just south of SR 1258. The first 1.4 miles of the road is open to automobiles at all seasons. At first the road passes through fields. Farther along, it is bordered by a variety of habitats—upland pine woods, pine and hardwood swamps, and brackish marshes. Watch for Wood Ducks in the roadside canal. You might see a Pileated Woodpecker in any of the wooded areas. Brown-headed Nuthatches live in the pines year-round. In the hardwood swamps, listen for Prothonotary Warblers from late April into July. These marshes are also good for King Rails, and you might see a Least Bittern in the breeding season.

At 1.4 miles you will come to a gate. The road and trails beyond this gate—including the trails around the East Pool, Middle Pool, and West Pool impoundments—are open to pedestrian (and bicycle) travel from March 15 to October 15. To circle the East Pool is a fair hike (about 4 miles), and to walk all the way around all of the impoundments is a 6.5-mile hike. However, most of the area around the impoundments is wooded, with few openings where you can see much. One of the best vantage points is near the northeastern end of East Pool (from where the trees begin on the north dike, and from the east dike/trail). Checking these sites will require a hike of 2 miles or less. You can walk on the north dike—the No Entry signs pertain to the impoundment itself.

East Pool has several Wood Duck boxes; you should have no trouble getting good looks at some Woodies. Common Yellowthroats and Marsh Wrens also breed here and will be easy to see. At the openings look carefully for Common Moorhens. Watch for Least Bitterns both within the impoundment and in the marshes outside the impoundment.

Along the road at the north side of the impoundment, look and listen for Pileated Woodpeckers and other land birds. If you hear hysterical crows, check them out—you might see a Great Horned Owl being mobbed. Turkey Vultures are common in the area, and Black Vultures show up occasionally.

In late March to early April and in early October, look for American Black Ducks, Blue-winged and Green-winged teal, and other dabblers. American Coots are usually common, and Tree Swallows are frequent. If there are many Blue-winged Teal, look carefully—one April the impoundment hosted a drake Cinnamon Teal.

Outside the refuge, birding possibilities on Knotts Island are rather limited. An estuary abuts the island, and at any season you might want to check it at three points: the end of SR 1257 (Cason Point Road), the end of SR 1259 (Brumley Road), and the ferry terminal at the end of NC 615. You might see a few waterfowl in winter, and Ospreys and a few gulls and terns in summer. During April and May the end of SR 1257 should be a strategic spot to set up watch. Quite a few migrating gulls, terns, and shorebirds get funneled up Currituck Sound during their northward flight, and many of those that don't "escape" to the ocean will fly up the Knotts Island channel. Morning will offer the most birds, afternoon the best light.

The island also has many fields and small woodlots and is well situated to attract rare migrants occasionally, so you might want to drive many of its roads, especially during the spring and fall migrations. There is an autumn record of a Scissor-tailed Flycatcher, and a Sandhill Crane turned up one winter.

The **ferry from Currituck Village** to Knotts Island makes several runs throughout the day. (See an official North Carolina transportation map or a roadside ferry schedule sign for the exact schedule.) Unfortunately, in summer you can't get to Knotts Island until well after sunrise. The ferry run takes about forty minutes. In summer you will want to get in line early to be certain of getting on; during the rest of the year, especially on weekdays, you can often arrive at the last minute.

The ride is pleasant but usually not too exciting in terms of birds. In winter there may be several waterfowl in sight—there are usually more birds toward the Currituck Village end—but in summer, don't expect much more than a few gulls.

For further information: For information about Mackay Island NWR, contact Mackay Island NWR, P.O. Box 39, Knotts Island, NC 27950; phone 919-429-3100. For information about the ferry schedule, call the Currituck terminal at 919-232-2683.

CURRITUCK BANKS, NORTH DARE BANKS
MAP 2

It is an understatement to say that no section of the North Carolina coast has changed more drastically in as short a period of time as this area has. In the mid-1980s there were only a few small outposts of development north of Duck; otherwise, all you saw between the ocean and Currituck Sound were dunes and shrub thickets. But within just a few years much of this wild area was transformed into civilization. Today development continues at a rapid pace. If you don't visit this area quite frequently, you are likely to become disoriented here. What was an expanse of sand dunes one year may well be a shopping center the next.

Fortunately, some important sections of this barrier strand are being preserved by public ownership. However, these areas—Currituck NWR and Currituck Banks Estuarine Research Reserve—are on the roadless portion of the barrier strand north of Corolla and are inaccessible without a four-wheel-drive vehicle.

Along the portion of this barrier strand that is accessible by highway there are some protected sites that can offer very good birding during the migrations. The area around the lighthouse at Corolla can be one of the state's best areas for

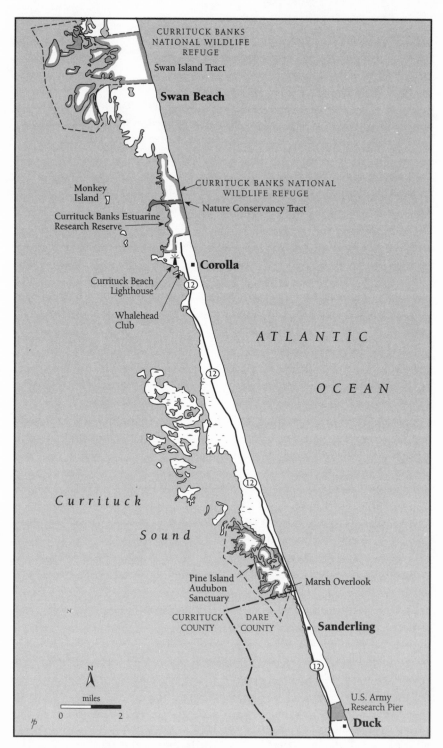

2. CURRITUCK BANKS, NORTH DARE BANKS

migrant land birds in both autumn and spring. A boardwalk through the nearby swamp forest and marsh can provide views of a few King Rails at all seasons and Prothonotary Warblers in the breeding season.

The observation deck at the south end of the Pine Island Audubon Sanctuary can be one of the North Carolina coast's most exciting spots in spring, when a variety of migrants pass by, many of them at very close range. This site can also be good in autumn, when the nearby shrub thickets may host rare sparrows. The observation deck can also be a good place to see King Rails and Marsh Wrens at any season, wading birds during the warmer months, and a few ducks from autumn to spring.

Most nature-oriented people will appreciate the scenery and vegetation of the remaining natural sites on Currituck Banks. The vegetation here is a mixture of northern and southern species, often growing side by side: tall bitter panic grass, American beach grass, sea oats, northern bayberry, wax-myrtle, and live oak. Most southerners will immediately feel like they're in the mid-Atlantic region when they look out over the landscape—especially in winter, when the bayberries are mostly leafless. Northerners, however, will probably focus on the live oaks and decide that they're definitely in the Deep South.

Parking is limited in this area during the summer months; fortunately, though, the best birding by far takes place during the quieter months, from autumn to spring, when parking is not generally a problem.

Your opinion about this section of the coast is likely to be somewhat more positive if you have a four-wheel-drive vehicle. By driving up the beach north of Corolla you can appreciate the relatively large expanses of natural vegetation within the research reserve and the wildlife refuge. This drive is especially worthwhile in winter, when this section of coast can be alive with loons, gannets, and mergansers. In late winter Little Gulls are regular and a Red-necked Grebe is possible. Snow Buntings are occasional on the area's berms.

FOR THOSE WITH ONLY two-wheel-drive vehicles, this tour begins at the lighthouse at Corolla, described several paragraphs below. But if you have a four-wheel-drive vehicle, you might want to drive the 12-plus-mile stretch of beach from here to the Virginia line, at least in winter and during the migrations when the weather conditions are suitable for good birding.

This stretch of barrier beach includes the **Currituck Banks Estuarine Research Reserve** and two sections of the **Currituck Banks NWR**. You will see boundary signs for these lands as you drive up the beach. All three places include maritime shrub thickets and brackish marshes. These habitats are easily accessible from NC 12 farther south on the island, so this drive up the beach is recommended primarily for its ocean-birding potential in winter and early spring.

To get to the beach access, continue straight ahead through the Ocean Hill development when you get to the end of NC 12. Be sure to read the county regulations regarding driving on the beach, which are posted at the access point. Be sure to stay on the beach. The Swan Island tract—the northernmost tract of wildlife refuge—begins about 5 miles north of the beach access point and has a very wide berm with scattered dunes. Do not drive up into this area. Beach driving is easiest at low tide, of course, but in this area, wind direction is almost as important. Avoid strong north and northeast winds, which drive water far up the beach. Winds from a westerly direction are best.

The ocean along this section of barrier beach is typically most interesting from January to early April. Some birders might assume that birding could be good during strong northeasters, but that is definitely not the case. During such conditions the beaches may have hardly a gull, and in the ocean all you'll see is white water. Most of the seabirds actually move farther offshore during northeasters. Luckily, the best conditions for driving are also the best for birding. After westerly winds, which smooth the water and create some upwelling, you may see large numbers of loons, Northern Gannets, and mergansers just off the shore from January through March. The light is best in the afternoon. Slowly work your way up the beach, checking through the various flocks. Many birds will be so close to shore that you will be able to see a lot without getting out of your vehicle.

In addition to the more common species, you may see an occasional Common Goldeneye, Oldsquaw, or scoter. If you're really lucky you might see an alcid. On some days there are many small flocks of gulls on the beaches. Look for a Lesser Black-backed, or maybe a Glaucous or Iceland.

Horned Grebes are usually most common around March; also look carefully for a Red-necked Grebe then. From around late January to early April there are often large numbers of Bonaparte's Gulls. If you sort through enough of these birds, you are almost certain to find one or more Little Gulls. At the wide berm about 5 to 7 miles north of the access point at Corolla, you may want to get out of your car and do some walking. From late autumn through winter, Snow Buntings are seen in this area occasionally, and Horned Larks and Lapland Longspurs are also possible.

During the migrations the shrub thickets of the Currituck Banks Estuarine Research Reserve and the two sections of Currituck Banks NWR can attract many land bird migrants. In autumn this section of the coast is no better than other more accessible sites farther south, but in spring it surpasses other sites. At that season this northern extremity of the state's coastline is the very best place for a variety of warblers and other land birds, probably because it lies the closest to the major migration routes of some of the "trans-Gulf migrants." (Nearby Corolla and the Pine Island Sanctuary are almost as good.) In late May you might even hope for something like an Olive-sided Flycatcher or Mourning Warbler. If you venture into the shrub thickets, be advised that some wooded areas along this section of barrier island have an appalling tick population, probably because of the large numbers of deer and livestock in the area.

About 3 miles north of the beach access site you will see the most prominent landmark of the area—a dune over fifty feet high named **Luark Hill** (often erroneously called Penny's Hill). The barrier island is narrow here, and from the top of the dune you will have an excellent view of both the sound and ocean. During the autumn migration this is a good place to watch for swallows and hawks, and a few hawks migrate past here in spring as well. This site is private land but has been used by the public for many years and has never been posted.

During the migrations these beaches often attract many shorebirds and terns as well, at least when there is little traffic. In a vehicle you can get very close to many birds, so you may get excellent views. Rare migrants do not often show up along these beaches, but if you sort through every bird along the whole stretch from Corolla north, you might see something unusual. Around late May and late July to August, if there are large numbers of terns, look carefully for a Roseate.

From April to August you might see a few Piping Plovers on the beaches. One or two pairs sometimes nest on the wide berm within the Swan Island tract of the Currituck NWR, as do colonies of Least Terns. (*Do not* walk into this area between April and July, whether or not it is posted.)

The area around the lighthouse at Corolla, the **Currituck Beach Lighthouse**, can be a very good magnet for land bird migrants during the autumn migration. In fact, this area can sometimes be almost as good as the best migrant traps on the Outer Banks. You'll find the best variety of birds, including many warblers, after cold fronts with northwest winds in September and early October. The spring migration isn't nearly as good as the autumn migration, but it can be entertaining, especially in early May. Again, the northern section of Currituck Banks is the best area along the state's coastline for land bird migrants in spring. Watch then for this particular weather pattern: a backdoor cold front that moves south to this area during the night, producing northeast winds and foggy conditions here while there are clear skies and southwest winds just to the south. At such times you may see a good fallout of migrants. This sort of weather pattern usually happens a few times each spring.

To get to the parking area for the lighthouse, drive south on NC 12 and turn right onto Corolla Village Road (SR 1185), the first street past the lighthouse. First, thoroughly check the trees and shrubs on the lighthouse grounds; often this is the best area for migrants in both autumn and spring. Resident birds include Eastern Bluebird. Currituck Banks is one of the few areas along the state's barrier islands where this species occurs. This site may offer the coastal area's earliest-arriving and latest-departing Golden-crowned Kinglets. During cold years you might find one until late April.

After you've looked around the lighthouse, walk down Corolla Village Road past the turn; you will see a swamp forest on the left. In the breeding season listen here for Prothonotary Warblers and a Yellow-billed Cuckoo. At the turn in the road you will see the beginning of a 300-yard-long boardwalk out to the sound. At first the boardwalk is bordered by swamp forest on the right and shrubs on the left. Farther along, it runs through brackish marsh before it reaches the sound.

During the migrations the beginning of the boardwalk can offer good looks at a variety of species. Just watch quietly as the birds flit across the boardwalk, from the vegetation on one side to the other. Around late September you have a reasonable chance of spotting two species that are scarce in coastal North Carolina—a Yellow-bellied Flycatcher or Philadelphia Vireo. This is one of the coast's best areas for these species.

In the marshes near the end of the trail you might hear a King Rail at any season. Virginia Rails are possible from late summer to spring. Soras are most likely during the migrations. The end of the boardwalk overlooks the sound, where you may see a few swans and dabbling ducks in winter. During low water levels, which are most likely during northerly winds, scan the edges of the nearby marshes for a rail.

During the winter you should walk to the ocean near the lighthouse, especially when winds are westerly. Look for loons, Horned Grebes, Northern Gannets, Red-breasted Mergansers, and maybe a Red-necked Grebe or other rarity.

From the lighthouse, return to NC 12 and turn right. Immediately turn right again, onto the road to the **Whalehead Club**, the clubhouse for one of the many hunt clubs that dominated this region back in the days when waterfowl blanketed the waters of Currituck Sound. The building has been purchased by the county and is to become the Currituck Wildlife Museum. Its open lawns, scattered live oaks, and shrub border near the sound offer some additional habitat possibilities; and you should definitely check this site during the migrations.

From the Whalehead Club, return to NC 12, turn right, and set your odometer to zero. The **Pine Island Sanctuary**, owned by the National Audubon Society, lies on the right between about 6 and 7 miles. Despite all the No Trespassing signs in this area, the walking/jogging trail here is open to the public. Parking is a problem, though.

At 7.1 miles, just before the county line, pull over on the paved shoulder and walk south along the road until you get to the sign that says "Sanderling." Here the trail runs beside the highway. (Do not try to cut through the ornamental vegetation that has been planted along the roadside before this point.) When you get on the trail, turn right (north).

After a short hike, look for a path to the left that runs to a ten-foot-high observation deck overlooking the sound. During the spring migration this deck can be one of the most entertaining spots on the North Carolina coast. Right at this point many of the diurnal migrants heading northward over Currituck Sound shift their flight line over to the ocean beach. On a good morning you can see a good variety of water birds—loons, wading birds, shorebirds, gulls, and terns—and often several land birds, including hawks, swallows, and finches. This is one of those special places where you don't just witness migration—you also feel that you may get swept along with it. The island is so narrow at this site that in addition to birds flying north over the sound, you can see northbound gannets and other ocean birds over the surf.

The best flights occur on mornings with light southerly winds when a cold front is approaching. You may see good flights anytime from early April to mid-May, although the species composing the flights will vary somewhat during that period. About May 1 you might be able to pick out all of the swallows that regularly occur in the state. The spring flight of hawks along the North Carolina coast is almost nonexistent in most areas, but here on spring mornings you will often see a few hawks fly over—Northern Harriers, Sharp-shinned Hawks, and American Kestrels are most likely, you may also see a Cooper's Hawk, Merlin, or Peregrine Falcon.

In addition to the daytime migrants, on many mornings you will detect movements of warblers and other birds that are primarily nocturnal migrants. One moment there may be a Blackpoll Warbler in the shrubs next to the plat-form; the next, a Cape May.

Fall flights can also be quite good, although not as good as at many other sites, especially those on the Outer Banks. Westerly winds and clear skies in late September and early October can be especially good; with such winds many of these southbound birds will pass by very close to the platform, so you can get some very close looks at fly-bys. About August 1 look for a good variety of swallows. In October you may see thousands of Tree Swallows.

Even outside of the migration periods, birding from this nifty perch can be entertaining. From autumn to spring you will usually see Pied-billed Grebes, a few species of dabbling ducks, and American Coots, and in winter there may be a few Tundra Swans. During the warmer months look for several herons and egrets.

During low water levels at any time of year, check the marsh edges across the little bay for a King Rail. In fact, if you're really quiet, you might spot one along the marsh edge right next to the observation deck. Look for Marsh Wrens here too. When water levels are low during the migrations, you may also see several shorebirds, especially Greater Yellowlegs.

At any season you may want to walk north along the hiking/jogging trail for a half-mile or so. You will notice a gradual transition in the vegetation—toward the north, the low growth of young pines and live oaks becomes somewhat taller and more continuous in cover. Species you should find along the trail at any season include Gray Catbird, Northern Cardinal, Rufous-sided Towhee, and Field Sparrow. In the breeding season you will also hear Prairie Warblers, Common Yellowthroats, and Indigo Buntings.

In the autumn migration check through the flocks of Field Sparrows for White-crowned Sparrows, and maybe a Lark or Clay-colored. White-crowneds and a Clay-colored have showed up here in winter as well.

At the county line, reset your odometer to zero and continue south. At 0.5 miles you will see a seafood store and boat ramp on your right. Low water levels will expose a sandbar just off the shore here. In the spring migration, during uncrowded periods (or whenever there is a brisk northeast wind during cool weather), check here for a few gulls, Forster's Terns, and often a Caspian.

At 3.5 miles you will see on the left the entrance road into the Field Research Facility of the U.S. **Army Corps of Engineers Coastal Engineering Research Center**. This facility has a long concrete pier that you should check from late autumn to early spring. Despite the imposing signs, this site is open to the public from 9 A.M. to 4:30 P.M. on weekdays (and at least occasionally on weekends).

Follow the road in and park in the public parking lot (on the left). Across the road you will see a jeep trail that goes around the facility to the shore. The pier is not open to the public, but you can scan it from the shore. It is the longest (over one-third mile) and northernmost ocean pier on the North Carolina coast and probably attracts something of interest occasionally. On calm days you will see numerous Herring Gulls feeding on the barnacle-encrusted pilings, and you might spot a Harlequin Duck or eider.

When you get back to NC 12, reset your odometer to zero and turn left. Just south of here lies the original community of Duck. A maritime forest here, the Duck Woods, has long been known as an excellent area for land bird migrants in autumn; unfortunately, though, development is rapidly whittling away this forest. But there are still two little patches of woods right next to the highway. Both are very good magnets for migrants, and they should persist because they are swamps. At 0.8 miles, pull off beside the water tower and walk around to the back of it; you can check the margins of the little swamp there. At 1.0 miles, pull into the Methodist church parking lot. This fragment of woods can also be quite good in autumn, and a boardwalk runs into and along the edge of the swamp, enabling you to bird this area more thoroughly.

For further information: For information about the Currituck NWR, contact Mackay Island NWR, P.O. Box 39, Knotts Island, NC 27950; phone 919-429-3100. For information about the Currituck Banks Estuarine Research Reserve, contact Coastal Reserve Coordinator, North Carolina National Estuarine Research Reserve, 7205 Wrightsville Avenue, Wilmington, NC 28403; phone 910-256-3721. For information about the Pine Island Audubon Sanctuary, call the site manager at 919-453-8430. For information about the U.S. Army Corps of Engineers research pier, call the facility at 919-261-3511.

BELLS ISLAND, CHURCH ISLAND (WATERLILY)
MAP 3

If you're driving through the mainland of Currituck County on NC 168 and US 158, you might want to consider a couple of very short side trips, to Bells Island and to Church Island. In both cases it is not the islands themselves that are interesting but the marshes along the way.

The Bells Island marshes have some open areas that host a few waterfowl in winter. A few shorebirds and wading birds may occur at any season, although shorebirds are most frequent during the migrations and waders during the warmer months. King Rails are sometimes seen here. Overall, the Church Island route is less interesting but is very reliable for King Rails.

Bells Island Road (SR 1245) begins on NC 168 about 1 mile south of the village of Currituck (so you might have time to check out these marshes while waiting for the Knotts Island ferry). After you have driven 1.5 miles down the road, you will see some open areas in the marshes on the left. These areas will be water or exposed mud, depending on the water level. The number of birds varies widely. Sometimes you may see an entertaining variety, sometimes almost nothing. In general, low water levels, which occur during northerly winds, are best.

At all seasons this is a good place to see Boat-tailed Grackles and a few Marsh Wrens. In winter you can expect two or three species of waterfowl, and often a few snipe and Greater Yellowlegs. You might spot several species of shorebirds during the migrations, although you will never see many individuals. During the warmer months you will see a few wading birds, and you might spot a Common Moorhen at the edge of the open areas.

During low water levels at all seasons, watch the edges of the open areas carefully, especially early and late in the day. You might spot a King Rail—a few live here year-round. You might also see a Virginia Rail at any season, and Soras are possible during the migrations.

To get to the Church Island area, begin at the US 158 bridge across the Intracoastal Waterway, near Coinjock. Drive south. After you get off the bridge, take the first road to your left, Old US 158. Then turn right onto **Waterlily Road** (SR 1142), which crosses the marshes and ends on Church Island. From this road you will also see **Piney Island Road** (SR 1145) on your left. This road, 0.5 miles long, is bordered by marshes and by wet fields.

This is an excellent place to see King Rails in "classic" plumage. Furthermore, you should be able to see these rails from your car, during either high or low water levels. It is best to look for the birds at dawn or dusk, but you should be able to spot one at any time of day. During low water levels, which occur primarily during northerly winds, watch for birds along the borders of the canals along Waterlily Road. Along Piney Island Road watch for birds in the

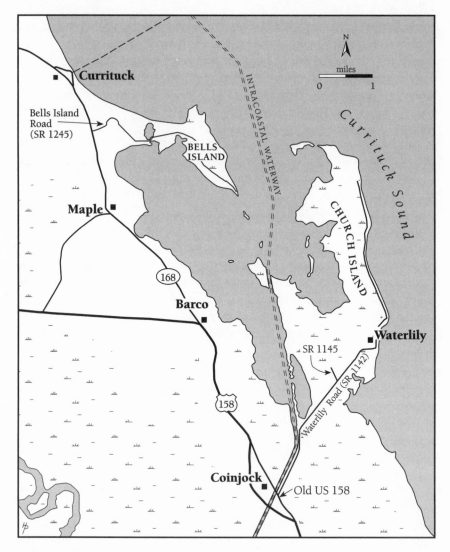

3. BELLS ISLAND, CHURCH ISLAND (WATERLILY)

ditches that run perpendicular to the road or at several openings in the marshes. During high water levels, which occur primarily during southerly winds, you might spot birds on the shoulders of Piney Island Road. Virginia Rails and Soras are also possible.

Drive on to the end of Waterlily Road just to appreciate the scenery. The road lies several feet above the Currituck Sound, and on clear days the view is spectacular. Early morning is especially nice, but late afternoon, with the sunlight shining on the Currituck Beach Lighthouse in the distance, isn't bad either.

The many roadside lawns on Church Island might attract certain species of migrants after autumn cold fronts. The area looks especially good for Western Kingbirds. Nowadays the sound is virtually birdless, but you can at least dream of those winter days earlier in the century when the waters before you were virtually covered with waterfowl.

GREAT DISMAL SWAMP NATIONAL WILDLIFE REFUGE

MAP 4

The present-day Great Dismal Swamp is much smaller than and quite different from the Great Dismal Swamp that the first European colonists encountered. The hydrology of the swamp has been altered considerably by extensive ditching, and the forests have been logged repeatedly. The plant communities have changed considerably: much of the original bald cypress and Atlantic white cedar forests have been replaced by other species, especially red maple. Nevertheless, the Great Dismal is still a vast and impressive tract of wilderness. Over 100,000 acres are protected as part of the Great Dismal Swamp NWR. The Great Dismal is the northernmost of the great swamp forests that characterize the South.

Virtually the whole refuge is off-limits to automobiles. To appreciate this area for all that it is, you will have to do some long-distance hiking. For instance, to get to Lake Drummond in the center of the refuge requires a hike (or bicycle trip) of almost 5 miles one-way. Fortunately, most of the bird species in the refuge—including the ones frequently sought by birders—can be found at easily accessible sites along the refuge's northwestern border.

I included the Great Dismal Swamp NWR in this book because it lies partly in North Carolina, and the North Carolina portion of the refuge has basically the same birdlife as the rest of the refuge. However, the most accessible sites in the refuge are in Virginia, so this tour emphasizes the Virginia sites.

During the breeding season the refuge is a paradise for songbirds, including an excellent variety of breeding warblers. Prothonotary Warblers are abundant. Although this site lies close to its northern limit, the Swainson's Warbler is perhaps as common here as anywhere. Another noteworthy species is the Black-throated Green Warbler; this is the northernmost location for the population that breeds in the Southeast's coastal plain—the "Wayne's Black-throated Green Warbler"—yet the birds are common here.

Other breeding species here include Acadian Flycatcher, Yellow-throated Vireo, and Yellow-throated and Hooded warblers. In upland woods along the western border of the refuge, you should find a few Brown-headed Nuthatches at all seasons, and Chuck-will's-widows, Whip-poor-wills, and Summer Tanagers in the breeding season. A few Summer Tanagers may occur in the swampy

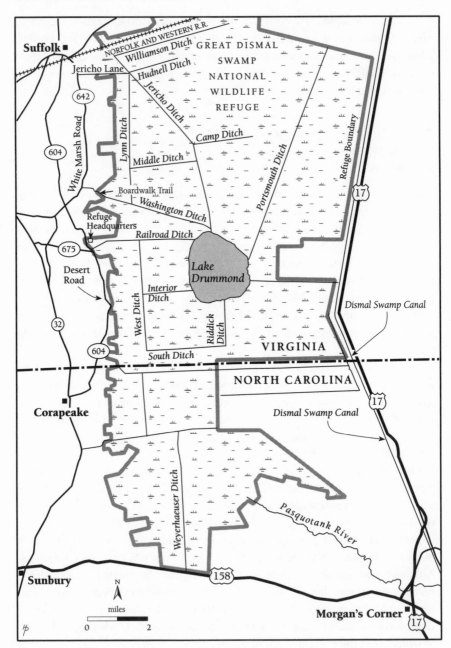

4. GREAT DISMAL SWAMP NATIONAL WILDLIFE REFUGE

areas; the Great Dismal is one of those places where Scarlet and Summer tanagers sometimes breed next to each other. Along the refuge's western border are open farmlands, where you can see Blue Grosbeaks in the breeding season and Turkey Vultures and occasional Black Vultures throughout the year.

Wood Ducks are easy to find year-round in the roadside canals. Barred Owls are common and are frequently spotted during the daytime. Although they are currently rather scarce, Wild Turkeys are increasing; in the future they may not be too difficult to see, at least in the breeding season.

The early part of the breeding season is an especially nice time to visit, because then a variety of passerine migrants join the summer resident species. The autumn migration can also be quite good. Winter doesn't offer as much variety as the other seasons but can still be entertaining; many of the resident species are easier to see then. The refuge often attracts large numbers of robins, and it can be good for winter finches.

The cooler months can be a good time for some long-distance hiking (or biking), especially if you would like to see Lake Drummond or some of the more exemplary stands of Atlantic white cedar. One of the best stands of white cedar is on the north side of South Ditch, between one-half and one mile east of West Ditch. (Call the refuge at 804-986-3705 for further information.) Lake Drummond is worth a visit for its scenic appeal; however, its acidic waters tend not to attract birds, although a few waterfowl often stop here during the migrations.

LOGISTICS. The refuge office is open from 8 A.M. to 4:30 P.M. The refuge is open from one-half hour before sunrise to one hour after sunset. Jericho Lane is usually open to automobiles. The first mile of Washington Ditch Road is open to automobiles from 6:30 A.M. until 8 P.M. between April 1 and September 30. During the rest of the year it is open from 6:30 A.M. to 5 P.M. Do not attempt to park at the beginning of this road and walk in before 6:30 A.M., because there just isn't enough room to park. You can park outside the gates at the entrances to Railroad Ditch and Weyerhaeuser Ditch roads, but please pull over as far as you can and do not park right in front of the gates.

The majority of the refuge is closed during a management hunt for deer in October and November. You should call the refuge office if you are considering a trip to the refuge at that time of year.

Again, bring a bicycle if you want to do some exploring. Many of the roads are soft, so a mountain bike is best. Washington Ditch Road is more compacted and is good for all types of bicycles.

The Jericho Lane has become a very popular spot for birders searching for Swainson's Warblers—so popular, in fact, that there is a real danger that the repeated use of tape-recorded calls may disrupt the birds' nesting. I would ask birders to refrain from using taped calls in this area. With a little patience, you should be able to spot a singing Swainson's without them.

The best time to find the breeding species of the Great Dismal is from late

April to about June 15. All of the nesting species will be singing during this period. Mid-April is actually the peak singing time for several species; however, Swainson's Warblers are not reliable until about April 20, and Acadian Flycatchers and Yellow-billed Cuckoos may not show up until almost the end of the month. The very best time to visit here is the last few days of April and the first week of May, when all the summer resident species have arrived, singing intensity is at or near peak levels for all species, and several species of migrants are passing through.

JERICHO LANE SHOULD be your first priority during the nesting season. After you leave White Marsh Road, set your odometer to zero. Make several stops along Jericho Lane between 0.7 miles and the gate at 2.0 miles. You may also want to park at this gate and walk one-half mile or so down the Hudnell and Jericho ditches. Covering these areas may allow you to hear all the warblers that breed in the refuge.

If you start out at dawn, you might hear a Barred Owl as well as Great Horned Owls and Eastern Screech-Owls. Prothonotary Warblers are abundant—you will probably see several. Hooded Warblers are also common but are a bit harder to see. The patches of thick undergrowth on the north side of the road are very attractive to Swainson's Warblers, which are perhaps as common in this part of the Great Dismal as they are anywhere. You might hear as many as ten in a morning from the road. At this location they sing regularly as late as mid-July, and later on rare occasions.

This is a good area for comparing the song of the Swainson's with that of the Louisiana Waterthrush. Some species whose singing peaks in April are Northern Parula and Black-throated Green, Yellow-throated, and Prairie warblers. Both the Northern Parula and Yellow-throated Warbler are less common in the Great Dismal than one might expect, although you should be able to hear a few in April and May. The song of the Black-throated Green is one of the most prevalent sounds in the swamp in April, but by mid-June these birds sing only occasionally. If you walk down the Hudnell or Jericho ditches, you might hear the dry buzzy song of a Worm-eating Warbler.

Other species you should having little trouble seeing or hearing include Yellow-billed Cuckoo, Acadian Flycatcher, Wood Thrush, Ovenbird, Common Yellowthroat, and American Redstart. In addition to Red-eyed and White-eyed vireos, listen for one or two Yellow-throated Vireos. You're sure to hear the screams of a Red-shouldered Hawk.

After 6:30 A.M. you should check out the **Washington Ditch Road** area. Drive in 1 mile, park at the parking area for the Dismal Town Boardwalk Trail, and walk down the road (past a gate) for half a mile or so.

You may not find any additional species in this area, but it is worth checking anyway. The trees are larger and better for woodpeckers. Pileateds are common, and this is a fairly good area for seeing a Hairy. Watch for Wood Ducks in the roadside canal and for Louisiana Waterthrushes along the canal's edges. In this area you might hear both Summer and Scarlet tanagers. If you are squeamish about walking through wooded areas in summer, you will appreciate the several-hundred-yard-long boardwalk trail, which can provide good looks at Acadian Flycatchers and Prothonotary Warblers.

You may also want to bird around the **refuge office**, along the beginning of **Railroad Ditch Road**, and along the nearby portions of **Desert Road**. A few Brown-headed Nuthatches and Pine Warblers are permanent residents in this area's mixed woods. In the breeding season listen for Summer Tanagers. If you stop along the road at dawn, you might hear both Chuck-will's-widows and Whip-poor-wills.

The **Weyerhaeuser Ditch Road**, which begins on US 158, leads into the North Carolina portion of the refuge. You may want to walk down this road a mile or so; this area hosts the same swamp forest species that you can find along Jericho Lane and Washington Ditch Road, including Swainson's Warbler. Don't be surprised if you see a bear crossing the road.

Driving **White Marsh and Desert roads** can be a good complement to birding in the refuge. In the breeding season check the field edges along the roads for Eastern Kingbirds, Blue Grosbeaks, and Indigo Buntings. At all seasons watch for Turkey Vultures, an occasional Black Vulture, and Red-tailed and Red-shouldered hawks.

As summer progresses the refuge gradually becomes less and less interesting. In late June some of the breeding species will have stopped singing altogether, and you may have trouble finding species like Yellow-throated and Black-throated Green warblers. But some others, like Acadian Flycatcher and Prothonotary Warbler, are easy to find throughout the summer.

Again, birding in the refuge can be especially good in late April and early May because a good variety of migrants passes through the area, especially in comparison with sites on North Carolina's lower coastal plain. Species that are much easier to find here than they are farther south include Swainson's Thrush; Veery; and a long list of warblers, including Golden-winged, Blue-winged, Tennessee, Nashville, Magnolia, Blackburnian, Chestnut-sided, and Bay-breasted.

In autumn, too, this area is better than "inland" coastal plain sites farther south, but it is not as exciting as sites on the barrier islands. As in spring, there are relatively good numbers of "trans-Gulf migrants." You'll see the most birds, and the greatest variety, after cold fronts in September and early October.

Winter can be a nice time to visit, although there is less variety then. You can cover ground more easily in winter, and the lack of leafy vegetation makes many of the permanent resident species—like Red-shouldered Hawk, Barred Owl, and

Pileated Woodpecker—easier to see. Together, Jericho Lane (where there is more shrub-level vegetation), Washington Ditch Road, and the area around the refuge office should supply you with a good variety of species.

At Jericho Lane, look and listen for Winter Wren and Hermit Thrush. On Washington Ditch Road, look for six species of woodpeckers—Pileated, Red-bellied, Hairy, and Downy, plus Northern Flicker and Yellow-bellied Sapsucker. You might spot an American Woodcock from the Dismal Town Boardwalk Trail.

Large flocks of American Robins usually inhabit the refuge, and small flocks of Cedar Waxwings often associate with them. Also look for a few Rusty Black-birds, although you will probably see only Red-wingeds. Check the treetops for flocks of American Goldfinches and Purple Finches. During finch winters—winters when large numbers of finches come south—you should also be able to spot Pine Siskins and Evening Grosbeaks.

For further information: Contact Great Dismal Swamp NWR, P.O. Box 349, Suffolk, VA 23439; phone 804-986-3705. A seasonal checklist of the refuge's birds is available.

MERCHANTS MILLPOND STATE PARK
MAP 5

Ironically, this site—located just a few miles from the Virginia line—has the look most people visualize when they hear the term "Deep South." Many people would consider Merchants Millpond, which was created in 1811, one of the most beautiful areas in coastal North Carolina. With its towering bald cypresses and tupelo gums and garlands of Spanish moss, the millpond is the sort of place you'll thoroughly enjoy even when the birding is slow. It seldom is, though. Species found in the park throughout the year include Red-shouldered Hawk, Barred Owl, Pileated Woodpecker, and Brown-headed Nuthatch. There are even a few Wild Turkeys.

The breeding season is especially nice. Among the easiest-to-find birds then are Acadian Flycatcher, Blue-gray Gnatcatcher, Northern Parula, and Yellow-throated and Prothonotary warblers. Chuck-will's-widows and Whip-poor-wills can be heard then, as can Summer and Scarlet tanagers. The presence of the Scarlet Tanager reflects this site's northerly location. Similarly, Louisiana Waterthrushes are more common here than at sites farther south and east. This site's location makes it better for migrant land birds than most of the coastal plain (i.e., non–barrier island) sites covered in this book.

Wood Ducks live on the pond year-round, and there are often other ducks in winter. Great Blue Herons are always present, Green Herons are summer residents, and a few other wading birds often show up in late summer.

A canoe trip toward the upper end of the millpond can be especially pleasant

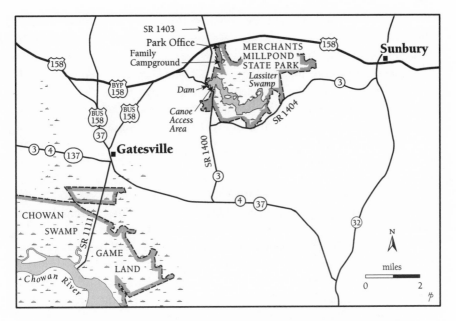

SR 1403 →
Park Office
Family
Campground

MERCHANTS
MILLPOND
STATE PARK

*Lassiter
Swamp*

Dam

Canoe
Access
Area

158

BYP
158

BUS
158

BUS
158

37

158

3

SR 1404

SR 1400

3

Gatesville

3 — 4 — 137

3

4 — 37

32

158

Sunbury

N

miles

0   2

CHOWAN

SWAMP

SR 1111

GAME

LAND

Chowan River

5. MERCHANTS MILLPOND STATE PARK, CHOWAN SWAMP GAME LAND

and can increase your chances of seeing waterfowl and other water birds—maybe a rarity. Within the Lassiter Swamp, upstream of the pond, there is a stand of old-growth bald cypresses and the largest tupelo gum tree that has been documented in North Carolina. The park also contains a climax beech slope. Not surprisingly, the park, with its special habitats, harbors several rare plant species.

If you would like to visit the park just to view its scenery and varied habitats, you might consider hiking its several miles of trails on a crisp, calm winter day, or going canoeing on one of the fine days when spring is first coming alive, in March or early April.

LOGISTICS. The park opens at 8 A.M.; closing time varies seasonally. Some of the best birding is along the dam on SR 1400, and you can park here on the road shoulder as early in the morning as you like. You can also launch a canoe as early as you like. Canoe rentals are available, beginning at 8 A.M. daily, at the Canoe Access Area. Call the park office at 919-357-1191 for more information.

Several types of camping are available in the park, and you might want to consider camping in order to be on the park's trails before 8 A.M. The family campground is a good spot to hear Eastern Screech-Owls, Chuck-will's-widows, and Whip-poor-wills.

Unfortunately, this park does have one major detraction: during the warmer months the tick population can be appalling. Check yourself frequently during the day. Actually, you can have a very productive day of birding without walking any of the trails of the park; most species found in the park can be seen from SR 1400 around the dam and from the nearby Canoe Access Area.

To find the park's breeding birds, try to visit here between late April and mid-June, when the best variety is present, active, and easy to find. Warm days in mid-April can also be very nice. Northern Parulas, Yellow-throated Warblers, and Louisiana Waterthrushes sing more actively then, but other summer residents have not yet arrived. Early May is perhaps the very best time to visit; in addition to the summer resident species, you should see a few migrants then.

AGAIN, YOU CAN FIND most of the park's bird species from SR 1400, at the **dam and nearby areas**. You can park along the road shoulder. During the peak period—late April to mid-June—you should definitely start your day here, as early as possible. If you get here early enough, you may well hear one or more Barred Owls. Blue-gray Gnatcatchers, Northern Parulas, and Yellow-throated and Prothonotary warblers will be easy to find. You should also hear the hiccuping of several Acadian Flycatchers. Listen for the loud, ringing song of a Louisiana Waterthrush along the stream below the dam.

You may hear the screaming of a Red-shouldered Hawk, and you might also see one fly over. You should see several woodpeckers, perhaps including a Pileated. Other species you should hear and/or see include Yellow-billed Cuckoo, Great Crested Flycatcher, Wood Thrush, Red-eyed and Yellow-throated vireos, Common Yellowthroat, Hooded Warbler, and Indigo Bunting.

On the pond you might see a few Wood Ducks, although you are perhaps most likely to spot these birds as they fly over at dawn. You should also see one or two Great Blue and Green herons.

Be sure to walk up the road in both directions so that you can check both the upland hardwoods and mixed woods. Listen for White-breasted and Brown-headed nuthatches, Ovenbirds, and Summer and Scarlet tanagers.

After the park opens you will want to work the grounds around the **Canoe Access Area**, including the nearby loop trail (picnic area) that runs out on a peninsula, giving you a view of other sections of the pond. You might also want to walk the first 0.8 miles of the **Lassiter Trail**. (Look for the beginning of the trail just north of the dam, directly opposite the junction of SR 1400 and SR 1403. When you get to the first fork in the trail, take the trail on the right; the one on the left goes to the campground/park office. At the second fork you will have gone 0.8 miles.) This section of the trail takes you along some steep slopes covered with tall hardwoods and mixed woods. You should hear Ovenbirds here, and maybe a Kentucky Warbler.

If you stay at the **family campground** you are likely to hear Eastern Screech-Owls year-round, and Chuck-will's-widows and Whip-poor-wills during the breeding season. The Chucks start calling around mid-April, Whips in early

April. Campers are allowed to be on the trails before 8 A.M. You could bird along the nearby portion of the Lassiter Trail at dawn, then head to the dam.

The scenery along the 5-mile-long **loop portion** of the Lassiter Trail is quite pretty, but you may not see any additional birds here. A possible exception is the Wild Turkey: if you walk the whole trail during the nesting season, you might spot a few of these birds. Otherwise, you might want to forgo walking this section trail until winter or early spring, when ticks are not a problem.

Likewise, a canoe trip during the nesting season can be pleasant, but you probably won't find any birds by canoe that you can't find by foot. However, you are more likely to see Wood Ducks this way, and you might get good views of a Barred Owl. There have been a handful of sightings of both Anhinga and Purple Gallinule in spring.

Although the breeding season is generally the most entertaining time of year here, any season can be pretty good. Late summer is probably the dullest time—many of the breeding species become increasingly difficult to find as summer progresses. However, Acadian Flycatchers and Prothonotary Warblers can be found easily throughout the summer.

This site can be rather good during the migration periods. The best place to look for migrants is, again, around the dam. The best time for spring migrants is around early May; for fall migrants, after cold fronts in September and early October.

Calm mornings in winter can also be very nice. Many birds, like Red-shouldered Hawks, Barred Owls, and Pileated Woodpeckers, will be easier to see then. The dam area is good in winter, but you will also want to hike a good portion of the Lassiter Trail. The bands of small land birds can feature a nice variety: look for chickadees; titmice; both kinglets; Brown Creepers; White-breasted, Brown-headed, and Red-breasted nuthatches; and Pine and Yellow-rumped warblers. Near thick patches of ground cover, listen for a Winter Wren. This area is also good for finches; check the tops of the sweet gums and yellow poplars for American Goldfinches and Purple Finches. During finch winters you are also likely to see Pine Siskins and Evening Grosbeaks.

In winter look for other waterfowl in addition to the permanent resident Wood Ducks. There are often a few Mallards, American Wigeons, and other dabblers, as well as Canada Geese and Hooded Mergansers.

For further information: Contact Merchants Millpond SP, Route 1, Box 141-A, Gatesville, NC 27938; phone 919-357-1191. A checklist of the park's birds is available.

CHOWAN SWAMP GAME LAND
MAP 5

This vast tract of swamp forest—over 10,000 acres—lies on the north side of the Chowan River, near the town of Gatesville. The game land is administered by the North Carolina Wildlife Resources Commission, and much of it is inaccessible except by small boat; fortunately, though, SR 1111 runs from Gatesville down to the Chowan River, providing a convenient way to bird along a roughly 2-mile cross section of the swamp.

Except for its size, the swamp forest is not impressive, having been cut over several times earlier in this century. Most of the area is dominated by young red maples and swamp tupelos. But the area attracts a good variety of swamp forest land birds in the breeding season. Prothonotary Warblers are abundant; Acadian Flycatchers, Northern Parulas, and Hooded Warblers are easy to find; and a few Yellow-throated Warblers breed along the river. Perhaps because this area is rather scruffy, it is also good for Swainson's Warblers. Before it reaches the swamp forest, SR 1111 passes an expanse of fields that host Blue Grosbeaks in the breeding season.

You can find Red-shouldered Hawks and Barred Owls in the area throughout the year, and occasionally you may see Wood Ducks in the roadside canals. The area is also good for woodpeckers. Pileateds are easy to find, and there are a few Hairy Woodpeckers as well.

LOGISTICS. This area is most interesting during the breeding season, from late April to mid-June, and the description below refers to this period unless otherwise indicated. Early May is the best time to be here; then you can see a few migrants in addition to the breeding species. Along most of its 3.2 miles SR 1111 is a dirt road and is bordered by canals on both sides; it is fairly quiet, so you can bird from the road. There is a boat ramp at the end of the road, and traffic gets a little more distracting on weekends.

To get to SR 1111, begin at the intersection of NC 37/NC 137 in Gatesville. From here, take NC 137 (Court Street) west. The first road you see on the left, across from the courthouse, is SR 1111 (New Road Street).

From 0.3 to 0.8 miles down the road you will see fields on your right. Look and listen here for Eastern Kingbirds, Blue Grosbeaks, Indigo Buntings, and Orchard Orioles. Around midmorning this could be a good place to see a Red-shouldered Hawk in flight.

Beyond these fields, the swamp forest/game land begins. From this point on, make several stops along the road. There are two areas without roadside canals, so if you want you can get off the road and into the swamp. (Remember to watch your step.) These two places are at the old road on your left at 1.8 miles and at the end of SR 1111 on the right.

You will have little trouble finding Prothonotary Warblers; they are almost everywhere. This is the sort of place where Prothonotary Warblers can be found late in the season, probably through August. Acadian Flycatchers are easy to hear, although sometimes it takes a while before one comes into view. Listen for one or two Yellow-throated Warblers in the tall bald cypresses at the end of the road. This is also a good area for Northern Parulas, and you might hear a Yellow-throated Vireo as well.

You are most likely to hear Hooded and Swainson's warblers between the little roadway on the left at 1.8 miles and the end of the road, because this section has the thickest undergrowth. Summer resident species that you might hear almost anywhere past the fields include Yellow-billed Cuckoo, Great Crested Flycatcher, Blue-gray Gnatcatcher, Wood Thrush, Gray Catbird, White-eyed and Red-eyed vireos, and American Redstart.

If you drive the road at dawn, you are almost certain to hear one or more Barred Owls. Around midmorning listen for the screams of a Red-shouldered Hawk. On mornings with little traffic, watch for Wood Ducks in the roadside canals.

You should also find Red-bellied and Downy Woodpeckers. You'll probably hear a Pileated Woodpecker, and one might fly across the road. As you might expect in a forest this large, a Hairy Woodpecker is possible here.

This area is much less interesting at other times of the year, although it can still be entertaining. In autumn the passerine migrants are often more diverse than in most of the coastal plain areas covered in this book, because this site is so far to the northwest. Calm mornings in winter can also be pleasant, and this could be a good time for beginning birders to visit: once the deciduous trees are bare, many birds will be far easier to see, including Red-shouldered Hawk, Barred Owl, and Pileated Woodpecker. Among the flocks of chickadees, titmice, and White-breasted Nuthatches, look for a Brown Creeper. Among the thicker patches of ground cover, listen for the double call-note of a Winter Wren. Wood Ducks are more likely to occur during the cooler months, and if you are here at dusk, you might see a woodcock.

For further information: Call the North Carolina Wildlife Resources Commission at 919-733-7291.

CHAPTER 5

The Albemarle-Pamlico Section

Alligator River National Wildlife Refuge (North Section)
MAP 6

One aspect of Dare County probably seems remarkable to visitors: the great majority of the county's residents live on the Outer Banks or Roanoke Island, while the vast mainland is very sparsely populated. But this situation is quite understandable. The highest points on mainland Dare are only a few feet above sea level, and most of the area is made up of expansive swamp forests and vast impenetrable pocosins (pond pines with an understory of broadleaf evergreens).

Fortunately, most of this mainland wilderness has been acquired for permanent protection as the Alligator River NWR. This refuge is home to a substantial population of black bears; if you spend a little time here, you are almost certain to see a bear. Two other noteworthy species, but ones you are unlikely to see, are the endangered red wolf and the American alligator. A small number of the wolves have been reintroduced to the wild here, and the refuge represents the northern limit of the alligators' range.

So far, the Alligator River NWR has attracted very little birding activity, partly because most of the refuge is inaccessible—most roads are passable only during the driest times of the year. And of course, when most birders are in this area they are itching to get to the Outer Banks. Finally, the truth is that during much of the year the refuge doesn't offer much of birding interest.

However, the refuge does have a fairly good variety of resident and breeding land birds. Especially in the breeding season, the birdlife here complements that

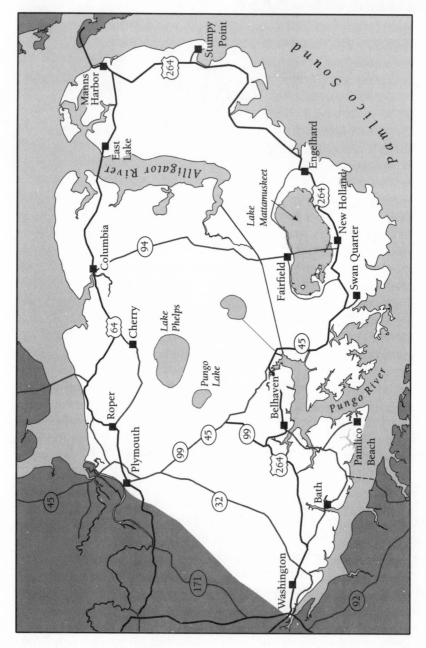

THE ALBEMARLE-PAMLICO SECTION

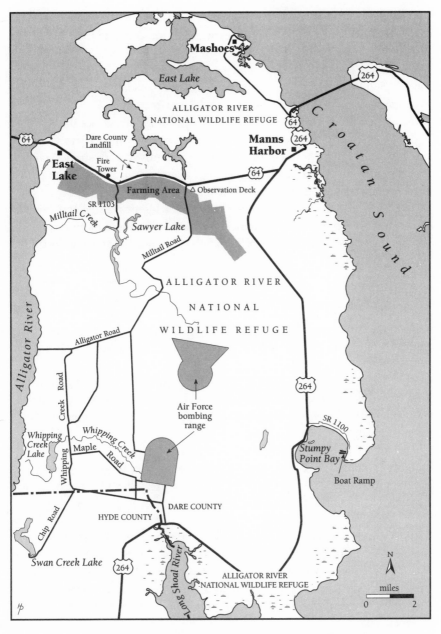

Mashoes

East Lake

ALLIGATOR RIVER
NATIONAL WILDLIFE REFUGE

264

64

C r o a t a n

Dare County
Landfill

64

Manns
Harbor

264

East
Lake

Fire
Tower

64

S o u n d

Farming Area

△ Observation Deck

SR 1103

Milltail Creek

Sawyer Lake

Milltail Road

ALLIGATOR RIVER

NATIONAL

WILDLIFE REFUGE

Alligator River

Alligator Road

Creek Road

Air Force
bombing
range

SR 1100

Whipping Creek

Whipping
Creek
Lake

Whipping Creek Road

Maple

Road

Stumpy
Point Bay

Boat Ramp

Whipping

Chip Road

DARE COUNTY

HYDE COUNTY

Swan Creek Lake

264

Long Shoal River

ALLIGATOR RIVER
NATIONAL WILDLIFE REFUGE

N

miles

0   2

6. ALLIGATOR RIVER NATIONAL WILDLIFE REFUGE, STUMPY POINT AREA

of the nearby Outer Banks. Prothonotary Warblers are abundant then, and Black-throated Green and Worm-eating warblers are also easy to find. You can also find Yellow-throated Warblers, at least early in the season, and Swainson's Warblers, at a few sites. Other breeding and permanent resident species here include Wood Duck, Northern Bobwhite, Chuck-will's-widow, Barred Owl, Hairy Woodpecker, Brown-headed Nuthatch, and Blue Grosbeak.

Two especially noteworthy species that occur in the refuge are the Anhinga and the Red-cockaded Woodpecker, but you're extremely unlikely to see either one here. The refuge lies near the northeastern limits of both species' ranges. (See the Alligator River National Wildlife Refuge (South Section) site guide; these species occur in that section of the refuge.)

The refuge also includes a farming area where fields are planted with grain to attract feeding waterfowl in winter. These fields offer the opportunity to see raptors (mostly in winter) and Northern Bobwhites and Blue Grosbeaks (in the breeding season).

LOGISTICS. Keep in mind that many of the refuge's roads are impassable most of the year to two-wheel-drive vehicles. In some areas not even four-wheel-drive cars are adequate. The two site guides describing the refuge rely on some of the better roads and will give you access to the best birding spots. (The Stumpy Point Area site guide also includes fragments of the Alligator River NWR.)

This site guide covers sites that, in combination, can produce a good list of land birds in the breeding season. It also includes the farming area, which is most interesting in winter. This section of the refuge is convenient to those passing through the area on US 64.

The refuge is open to deer hunting; the season runs from around mid-October to January 1. During this time you may prefer to visit the refuge on Sundays or to restrict your visit to the farming area after October 31, when hunting becomes off-limits there.

THIS TOUR BEGINS at the fire tower on US 64 just west of the US 64/SR 1103 intersection. In the breeding season check the tall pines here for an Eastern Wood-Pewee and a Pine Warbler; a few Brown-headed Nuthatches should be present all year. Some years you may hear a Yellow-throated Warbler. Behind the tower, at a trail that runs back into the woods, listen for a Worm-eating Warbler.

Just east of the fire tower you will see SR 1103 (**Buffalo City Road**), which runs southward about 2 miles to the scenic Milltail Creek. This road is good and can be traveled throughout the year. Most of the breeding land bird species of the refuge can be found here from the end of April to early June. Early and mid-April are also pleasant and birdy, but there is less diversity then.

You will want to make several stops from about 0.8 miles to the end of the road. This section combines an extensive swamp forest (across the canal to your left) and a moist mixed woods (on your right), providing habitat for a good variety of species.

Throughout the nesting season Prothonotary Warblers are very common and much in evidence. Prairie Warblers are also common, although around late May they begin to sing much less frequently. Black-throated Green Warblers sing most vigorously in April, although you can hear a few until around early June. One or two Prairie Warblers might sing songs patterned somewhat like those of Black-throated Greens. You might hear an occasional Yellow-throated Warbler, usually in April and early May.

In the woods on the right, listen for one or two Wood Thrushes, Worm-eating and Hooded warblers, and Ovenbirds. Listen for thrushes especially near the cottages. You might hear Worm-eatings anywhere, but listen especially where a small trail runs into the woods past the cottages.

Other species to look and listen for are Wood Duck (in the canal), Red-shouldered Hawk, Yellow-billed Cuckoo, and Pileated Woodpecker. If you are here at dawn or dusk, you might hear a Barred Owl or even see one feeding along the road. At the end of the road, in the swampy woods on your right, one or two Swainson's Warblers can be heard during most years; listen from about April 20 to mid-June.

At the end of the road an observation tower affords a nice view of **Milltail Creek**. You may also want to walk across the footbridge over the canal and down the trail (Sandy Ridge Trail) for at least a few hundred yards, to a stand of Atlantic white cedars. You probably won't find any additional species, but you'll certainly gain more of a feel for the swamp, and you might get better looks at some birds. Swainson's Warblers have been heard in this area. (Bring insect repellent: deerflies may be horrible along this trail in summer, especially early summer.)

By the way, a canoe would allow you to explore much more of this area. A display at the end of the road identifies potential canoe routes. However, you probably wouldn't see any species by canoe that can't be found from the road.

The Buffalo City Road is much less interesting at other seasons. Although it can probably be at least mildly entertaining for migrants after autumn cold fronts, on such days you will probably want to be at some of the better migrant traps on the nearby Outer Banks. Mild days in winter can also be pleasant. Yellow-rumped Warblers and American Robins may be everywhere. Pileated Woodpeckers and Barred Owls may be more in evidence then.

Return to US 64 and reset your odometer to zero. Turn right and go 2.1 miles; here you will see the **Dare County Landfill** on your left. This relatively small landfill is open from Monday through Friday. It is worth checking at least in midwinter, when there may be one or two thousand gulls—on these days you have a fair chance of seeing a Lesser Black-backed Gull, and the possibility of seeing one of the rarer species. Birders don't often visit this site, so landfill managers may be a bit befuddled when you ask for permission to enter. However, they will usually let you in. If not, look over part of the landfill from the highway shoulder. Turkey Vultures occasionally fly overhead here, and you might see a Black on rare occasions.

Go another 1.1 miles and turn right onto **Milltail Road**. Here you will see a kiosk with a large display map of the refuge and a dispenser containing free maps. Set your odometer at zero here. Just beyond this kiosk you will see the farming area. On both sides of the road the fields are shallowly flooded in winter to attract waterfowl. From around November to at least February, watch for Tundra Swans, several species of dabbling ducks, and Ring-necked Ducks. In the near future an observation deck will be constructed overlooking the fields at the end of a nature trail (Creef Cut Trail) that will begin near the intersection of Milltail Road and US 64.

In winter the farming area is also worth checking for raptors. Watch for American Kestrels, Northern Harriers, Turkey Vultures, and Red-tailed, Red-shouldered, and Sharp-shinned hawks. This is the sort of place where Cooper's Hawks and Merlins might occur with some regularity. An occasional Bald Eagle or Black Vulture is also possible; even a Rough-legged Hawk has been reported. At dusk, watch for Short-eared Owls.

In the breeding season Indigo Buntings and Blue Grosbeaks are easy to find in the shrubs along the ditch banks. Northern Bobwhites are common and are often seen on the road—early in the morning, in particular. Occasionally rails have been seen running across the road at dawn and dusk; King Rails have been spotted in summer and Virginia Rails in winter.

The farming area is likely to be interesting during autumn, when migrant species typical of open habitats should be drawn to it readily. Bobolinks are probably regular around September, and this could be a good spot for Dickcissels and other western rarities. All the fields are open to public access in September and October. (They are off-limits the rest of the year.)

At 2.2 miles the farming area ends on your left, and Milltail Road bends to the right. Outside the nesting season you may not want to drive any farther than this; the road gradually gets worse as you proceed farther south. It is a pretty good road overall during dry periods but can be slick and muddy during wet weather, although improvements are being made. If you do proceed farther, be alert to changing road conditions and take note of potential turnarounds.

At any season you are almost certain to see one or more black bears along the road south of this point, at least if you drive it at dawn. If road conditions permit, you will probably want to drive at least as far as the bridge across the upper portion of Milltail Creek, a pleasantly scenic spot.

During the nesting season you will definitely want to drive on as far as

Milltail Creek. Late April to mid-June is the best period for variety, although April may offer the most singing activity. (Roads may still be muddy in April.) From late May to mid-June it is very important to get here early in the morning.

You will want to make several stops all the way from where the fields end to Milltail Creek. Along this stretch you will find a very good variety of warblers and other land birds. Prairie and Prothonotary warblers are common. You should hear several Black-throated Green Warblers as well, but they sing much less frequently after mid-May. Although most of this area is not prime habitat for Swainson's Warblers, you might hear one anywhere.

From 2.3 to 3.5 miles, the taller pocosin vegetation on the right is a good area for Black-throated Green and Worm-eating warblers. Listen for Brown-headed Nuthatches also.

You may want to park in the pulloff on the right at 5.9 miles and walk on to the bridge, especially if the road is getting bad. Tall Atlantic white cedars are common along this stretch of road, which is an excellent area for Black-throated Green Warblers. Also listen for Northern Parulas.

At 6.6 miles you will see the bridge over the quietly flowing, tea-colored water of Milltail Creek. You may want to walk another half mile beyond the bridge. In the low woods on both sides of the road you should hear Hooded and Worm-eating warblers. Swainson's Warblers are also heard occasionally along this stretch.

Again, the southern portion of Milltail Road is much less interesting outside the nesting season and is actually rather dull most of the year. From November to March the higher pocosin vegetation is probably worth checking on calm mornings. Look for Brown-headed Nuthatches and check through the flocks of chickadees and kinglets. A Solitary Vireo or Orange-crowned Warbler is a possibility, especially during warm winters.

For further information: Contact Alligator River NWR, P.O. Box 1969, Manteo, NC 27954; phone 919-473-1131. The street address is 708 West US 64. Maps of the refuge are available here.

STUMPY POINT AREA
MAP 6

If you're driving down US 264 to or from the Outer Banks, you might want to stop and briefly investigate this area—especially from around January to March, when you might see several diving ducks on Stumpy Point Bay. For those with botanical inclinations, a good and easily accessible example of a bay forest stands immediately next to the highway north of the Stumpy Point community.

This brief tour starts at the end of the secondary road (1100) at the south tip of the community of Stumpy Point. You will probably be impressed by the narrowness of this community, which is essentially limited to the shoreline of the bay. Stumpy Point Bay is actually a Carolina Bay that was invaded by the waters of Pamlico Sound as sea level rose, and the community is restricted to the narrow rim of this Carolina Bay. (The prominent levee along the immediate shore is of course a manmade feature.)

At the end of the road is a Wildlife Resources Commission **boat ramp and parking area**. This is a good site for surveying the lower bay. In winter and early spring look for loons, sometimes including Red-throated; Horned Grebes; Buffleheads; Red-breasted Mergansers; and, often, rafts of scaup and Canvasbacks. Just off the shore there are several pilings that are usually topped with gulls in winter and terns in summer.

In the breeding season the wet shrubby areas bordering the road host Gray Catbirds and Common Yellowthroats, and you should also see a few Boat-tailed Grackles and Eastern Kingbirds. In mid- and late summer you might see congregations of Purple Martins, swallows, and Eastern Kingbirds. During the migrations it is likely that all the roadsides of this community attract land bird migrants. For certain species this area would probably stand out as an island of favorable habitat. This might be a very good area to look for a Western Kingbird after an October cold front.

From the boat ramp, head back toward US 264. After 0.9 miles you will see the **community center** on your left—another good place to survey the bay for loons, grebes, and ducks in winter. There are also several pilings here that attract a few gulls and terns.

When you get to US 264, reset your odometer to zero and turn left. After 0.8 miles, just past the little bridge, pull off on the right. This is a good spot to listen for Chuck-will's-widows at dawn or dusk in summer. You might find Brown-headed Nuthatches here at any season. Walk across the road for another good spot from which to survey the bay. The shrubs here usually have several Boat-tailed Grackles.

If you see any ducks off to the right, you can drive another 0.8 miles down the highway for another good vantage point. By the way, the habitat on the western side of the highway—a mixture of pines, shrubs, and invading marsh—looks interesting, and its potential would increase after fire. (Wildfires occur rather frequently in this area.) Perhaps this is where a singing Henslow's Sparrow was recorded one summer in the early 1930s.

Turn around and head back up US 264. At the intersection with SR 1100 reset your odometer to zero. After 1.0 miles, park on the shoulder, pulling as far off the road as possible. The woods on the right (part of Alligator River NWR) are an excellent example of a bay forest—a forest in which the canopy is dominated by one or more broadleaf evergreen species (in this case, loblolly bay). If you're willing to wade across the ditch and work your way through the thick but

narrow border of shrubbery, you'll find that the forest beyond this border is very easy to walk through. There is little understory and ground-cover vegetation, partly because little sunlight can pass through the canopy at any season.

Walking through this forest will be most comfortable during the cooler months. Don't expect to see many birds here at any season; in fact, you may find the area almost birdless outside the nesting season. Some species you should find during the nesting season are Prothonotary, Prairie, and Black-throated Green warblers. Ovenbirds, Hooded Warblers, and Acadian Flycatchers are also possible.

ALLIGATOR RIVER NATIONAL WILDLIFE REFUGE (SOUTH SECTION)
MAP 6

This area is definitely worth visiting in the nesting season, when there is an excellent variety of land birds. In fact, along one particular mile-long section of Maple Road you can find virtually all the land birds that breed in the Alligator River NWR, including a nice assortment of warblers. This site is excellent for Swainson's Warblers, and other species you may see here include Wood Duck, Yellow-billed Cuckoo, Barred Owl, Hairy and Pileated woodpeckers, and Black-throated Green and Worm-eating warblers. Brown-headed Nuthatches are also regular around here. In springtime this southern section of the Alligator River NWR provides an excellent complement to an Outer Banks birding trip; from south Nags Head to this site is about a one-hour drive.

There are also colonies of Red-cockaded Woodpeckers in the vicinity, although you will almost certainly not see any. Even Anhingas breed some years in this area, but you are not likely to see these birds either.

LOGISTICS. Much of this birding route lies on Air Force land, but on roads open to the public by agreement with the Fish and Wildlife Service. Furthermore, this route lies right beside an Air Force bombing range. Safety is not an issue, but the noise can be terrific at times—definitely not conducive to birding by ear. However, the Air Force doesn't often use the range early in the morning (before about 9 A.M.) or on weekends. You might do well to visit here on a Sunday morning.

Also, many of the roadways in this area get very muddy and slick after even a little bit of wet weather. The road into the main birding site is good, passable in all weather, but Whipping Creek Road and much of Maple Road can be terrible (although they are gradually being improved). If you decide to drive these roads, be alert to changing conditions so that you can turn around before you enter a risky section. (These roads are not identified with signs—pay attention to your map.)

On an early morning visit you will almost certainly see one or more bears.

These bears are quite shy and tend to move away as quickly as possible. However, if you see a cub, or a mother and a cub, you should stay away.

MOST OF THIS TOUR will be of interest primarily during the nesting season. You will find the most species from late April to mid-June. Early and mid-April offer lots of singing activity but not as much variety. From late May to mid-June you will definitely want to visit first thing in the morning. The following descriptions refer to the nesting period, unless otherwise indicated.

This tour begins at the US 264 bridge on the Dare County–Hyde County line. The marshes here—the **Long Shoal River Marshes**—are worth checking at any season, not just during the nesting period. From the bridge, drive 0.3 miles west and park on the shoulder. In the marshes on your left you will usually hear only Common Yellowthroats and Red-winged Blackbirds. However, Marsh Wrens are possible, and "Cling Rails" have been heard as well. The habitat looks adequate for Virginia and Black rails, although there are no records for them. In the shrubs along the edges of the marsh, watch for Eastern Kingbirds. From autumn until spring these marshes harbor Marsh and Sedge wrens and Swamp Sparrows. Virginia Rails are also likely.

Turn around and head east on US 264. Just past the bridge, turn left on the road that leads to the Air Force bombing range, setting your odometer to zero at the turn.

Along the first 0.9 miles of the road (before you reach a bombing range entrance road) you will hear and see numerous Gray Catbirds, Prairie Warblers, Common Yellowthroats, and Rufous-sided Towhees. In the taller vegetation on the left, just before the bombing range road, listen for Brown-headed Nuthatches and Worm-eating Warblers. And you might see a bobwhite running across the road here.

Keep following the main road, which bends to the left. Here the road passes through low shrub growth, with more Gray Catbirds and Common Yellowthroats. Eastern Kingbirds also occur here regularly.

At 2.1 miles you will see a dispenser that usually has maps of the refuge. The road straight ahead is Whipping Creek Road; turn right here onto **Maple Road**. For the next mile, in the dense woods on both sides of the road, you will hear numerous Prothonotary Warblers. Also listen for Worm-eating and Hooded warblers, and maybe a Swainson's.

At 3.0 miles you may want to park opposite the next bombing range entrance road and walk farther down Maple Road. From the left bend in the road to the right turn at 3.9 miles is the refuge's "superspot." Here, tall bald cypresses and hardwoods combined with patches of thick understory and shrub-layer growth provide habitat for numerous species. You will want to walk this section of road or at least make numerous stops along it. At the beginning of this section the road is good, but it begins to deteriorate slightly toward the end. However, if you visit after a dry spell, or if you have a four-wheel-drive vehicle, you won't have any problem. Your birding here is basically limited to what you can see from the road. On the right is a deep canal, and most people would consider the vegetation on the left side impenetrable.

You should have no trouble finding Northern Parulas and Black-throated Green, Prairie, Prothonotary, Worm-eating, Swainson's, Ovenbird, Common Yellowthroat, and Hooded warblers. (Most of these birds arrive in early to mid-April.) You might also spot one or two Yellow-throateds, especially in April and early May. (Strangely, this species is much less common in the Alligator River NWR than in areas to the west and southwest.) Swainson's Warblers are quite easy to find here; you will usually hear five or more. These birds are reliable after about April 20; if you visit first thing in the morning, you should be able to hear one or two until at least early July.

If you arrive early enough, you might hear a Barred Owl. As you walk along, watch for Wood Ducks flushing from the canals and look and listen for Pileated and Hairy woodpeckers. This site can provide you with good looks at Pileateds. One or two Red-shouldered Hawks live here. You might see an Acadian Fly-catcher or two, although they are relatively scarce in this refuge.

At the bend in the road at 3.9 miles, you may want to turn around. The habitat remains almost as good for another half mile or so, though, and at 4.6 miles there is another good spot to turn around.

If you have a four-wheel-drive vehicle, you may want to drive on to **Whipping Creek Road**, about 2 miles farther. Vehicles are not permitted on Whipping Creek Road north of this intersection, but the hike to the bridge across Whipping Creek is less than a mile long. As you walk, you might see Great Blue Herons flying to and from a nesting colony at Whipping Creek Lake, about a mile to the west and southwest. It is possible, although extremely unlikely, that you might see an Anhinga; they sometimes nest at the lake as well. This corner of the refuge seems to have more Turkey Vultures than farther north and east, and you might see a Black too.

If you have a four-wheel-drive vehicle, you may want to return to US 264 by turning left onto Whipping Creek Road, which is discussed below. If you have come this far in a regular vehicle, you should probably return the way you came; there are a couple of bad spots along this portion of Whipping Creek Road.

On Maple Road head back all the way to the intersection with Whipping Creek Road (where the map dispenser is located) and turn right.

At first the land on the road's south (left) side is covered with low shrubs and scattered pines. Gray Catbirds, White-eyed Vireos, Prairie Warblers, Common Yellowthroats, and Rufous-sided Towhees are common. Gradually (after about a mile) the pines become larger and less scattered. In this area listen for an Eastern Wood-Pewee and Brown-headed Nuthatches. On the north side of the road the vegetation is higher, with more deciduous plants, and you should hear a few Worm-eating Warblers, and maybe a Swainson's or two.

There are colonies of Red-cockaded Woodpeckers in the pocosins a half mile or more southwest of Whipping Creek Road. The intervening area is virtually impenetrable and, perhaps just as important, featureless. Woodpeckers have actually been spotted along the road on a couple of occasions, but the chances that you'll see one here are virtually nil.

You will probably want to end your tour at the intersection with Chip Road (about 2.5 miles from the map dispenser site), which is a good turnaround site. Beyond this point Whipping Creek Road gradually gets less and less passable.

For further information: Contact Alligator River NWR, P.O. Box 1969, Manteo, NC 27954; phone 919-473-1131. The street address is 708 West US 64. Maps of the refuge are available here.

PETTIGREW STATE PARK, SOMERSET PLACE STATE HISTORIC SITE
MAP 7

Although it lies next to the vast Lake Phelps, this area is actually most noteworthy for its land birds. Permanent resident species include Red-shouldered Hawk, Barred Owl, and Pileated and Hairy woodpeckers. The breeding season is especially interesting. Summer resident species that are easy to find include Yellow-billed Cuckoo, Acadian Flycatcher, Wood Thrush, Northern Parula, Prothonotary Warbler, and Ovenbird. Winter also offers a nice variety of woodland birds. Species like Red-shouldered Hawk, Barred Owl, and woodpeckers are often more in evidence then, and you will have little trouble finding Hermit Thrushes and one or two Winter Wrens. The park is basically a fringe of trees surrounded by the lake and by farmlands, so it probably stands out as an island to migrating land birds; both the spring and autumn migration periods are likely to be relatively good here.

The lake is not particularly attractive to water birds, but a few Wood Ducks live there. In winter large flocks of swans use the lake for roosting, so a sunset visit then can be really pleasing. During extreme cold weather Common Mergansers have been seen on the lake.

Because of the adjacent farmlands, this area can be rather good for raptors in the winter months. Occasionally a Bald Eagle shows up here.

Aside from its birding appeal, this is a nice place to visit, very peaceful and quiet and off the beaten path. The fringe of lakeside forest, which is dominated by deciduous hardwoods with numerous bald cypresses, has many trees with impressively large trunks; indeed, this park has five state-record-sized trees. A park trail follows the forest fringe for several miles, and a couple of overlooks on the lake shore offer very scenic views, especially at sunset in winter.

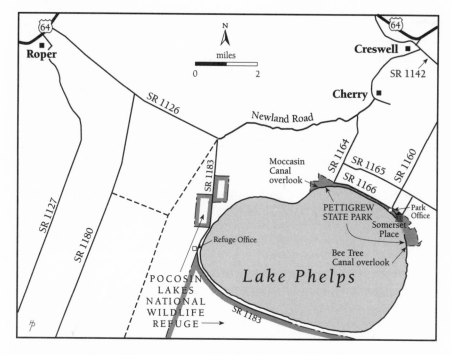

7. Pettigrew State Park, Somerset Place, Pocosin Lakes National
Wildlife Refuge (Lake Phelps Area)

This site is also historically interesting. Within the park is the eight-acre Somerset Place State Historic Site (SHS), which centers around a plantation house that dates to the 1700s. During the eighteenth century a 6-mile-long canal was dug to the Scuppernong River in order to manipulate the lake's water levels for agricultural purposes. Rice was one of the crops these farmers grew. Next to the boat ramp near the park office there is also a display of Indian artifacts found in the area. Several dugout canoes have been recovered from the lake, some of them over four thousand years old.

Logistics. The park opens at 8 a.m., but fishermen are frequently at the Moccasin Canal overlook at dawn, and rangers don't seem to object. Park closing time varies seasonally; it is around sunset.

The park has a family campground. You might consider camping here so that you can be on the park's trails at dawn. This area is not very wild-looking, but cottonmouths are fairly common, so be careful where you step.

To reach this park from US 64, drive to Creswell and then watch for signs directing you to the park. Follow these signs for 7 miles, along Sixth Street, Main Street, SR 1142, SR 1160, and SR 1168, until you reach the park office. (If you continue down SR 1168, you will come to the parking area for Somerset

Place.) Beyond the park office you will see the picnic area, the boat ramp to your right, and the family campground to your left.

At any season you will want to check out the picnic and campground areas and follow the eastern portion of the hiking trail (which begins at the campground) about a mile, to the **Bee Tree Canal overlook**. You can usually see all of the park's bird species in this area.

This area has a good variety of woodpeckers year-round. Red-bellied and Downy woodpeckers are common, and you will usually see one or two Pileateds as well. This is also a relatively good area for Hairy Woodpeckers—listen for their sharp "peek." A few Red-shouldered Hawks live here; listen for their screaming, especially in late winter and early spring. If you visit at dawn or camp out, you are likely to hear a Barred Owl.

For a really pleasant time, walk this area early on a calm morning between late April and mid-June. Beginning birders will appreciate the fact that many birds here are rather easy to see. Breeding species that are common and easy to find include Yellow-billed Cuckoo, Acadian Flycatcher, Wood Thrush, White-eyed and Red-eyed vireos, Northern Parula, Prothonotary Warbler, Ovenbird, and Indigo Bunting. Yellow-throated Warblers are most likely to be heard in April and May. In April and early May listen for a few Black-throated Green Warblers, especially near the Bee Tree Canal overlook.

You will definitely want to spend some time looking around the grounds of **Somerset Place**, with its lawns and scattered large trees. Look and listen for Eastern Wood-Pewees and Chipping Sparrows throughout the grounds, and for Blue Grosbeaks, Indigo Buntings, and Orchard Orioles along their borders.

Around the first week of May, be especially alert to the possibility of a few migrants. In the trees at Somerset Place listen for possible Blackpoll and Yellow warblers. In September and October, mornings after cold fronts can also be good for passerines; again, the trees around Somerset Place are perhaps your best bet.

Winter also provides a good variety of land birds. Calm mornings are best then; late afternoons can also be good. You will want to avoid days with strong south, southwest, or west winds, which blow off the lake and greatly inhibit bird activity. Once the deciduous trees have lost their leaves, it is easy to get good looks at woodpeckers. The numerous sweet gums can attract a lot of goldfinches; also watch for Pine Siskins and Purple Finches. On many days robins are everywhere, and a few Rusty Blackbirds may join them.

The chickadee-kinglet flocks often include a White-breasted Nuthatch and a Brown Creeper. Orange-crowned Warblers are seen with some regularity, although this spot is rather far north and inland. In the thick ground cover of honeysuckle and periwinkle, White-throated Sparrows are abundant. Hermit Thrushes are also easy to find here; listen for the double call-note of a Winter Wren as well. And don't be surprised if you flush a woodcock. Around sunset, listen for the calls of a Barred Owl.

At all seasons you will want to check out the lake from the boat ramp, from Somerset Place, and from the Bee Tree Canal overlook. Even if you don't see any water birds, you'll enjoy the scenery. In winter a view of the lake is especially nice at sunset, when flocks of Tundra Swans may be seen heading to roost. You might see a few Wood Ducks year-round, especially at the Bee Tree Canal overlook, and there are sometimes a few other ducks as well, especially after cold weather. During extremely cold winters a few Common Mergansers have been sighted here. You will also want to scan the trees around the lake for a Bald Eagle.

From the park office the western portion of the hiking trail extends about 3.5 miles, to the Moccasin Canal overlook. However, for the first 3 miles the trail actually runs right next to the road (SR 1166, or Lake Shore Drive), so you may choose to bird from your car along Lake Shore Drive—perhaps at dawn, before the park opens. The species in these woods are the same as those farther east. Barred and Great Horned owls and Eastern Screech-Owls can all be heard along this 3-mile section. Throughout the year check the skies above the fields on the road's north side for Turkey Vultures, Red-tailed Hawks, and maybe a Black Vulture. In winter watch for American Kestrels, Northern Harriers, and maybe a Cooper's Hawk. Near the west end of Lake Shore Drive there are woods on both sides of the road, and you will want to make several stops here in the breeding season.

About 3 miles from the park office, the road bends away from the lake and becomes SR 1164. At the turn pull over as far as you can and look for the access to the last section of the hiking trail, which continues another one-half mile to the **Moccasin Canal overlook**. This is another nice spot to be at sunset, especially in winter. You might spot Wood Ducks here at any season. Again, this site is regularly used by the public before 8 A.M., so during the breeding season you may want to visit well before that time. Overall, the birdlife here is about the same as that in the eastern part of the park, but the end of the trail seems to be especially good for Prothonotary Warblers. Louisiana Waterthrushes may be regular along the beginning of the trail; they are most likely to be heard in April. This area also looks at least marginally suitable for Swainson's Warblers. Barred Owls have been heard along this trail in midafternoon.

For further information: Contact Pettigrew SP, Route 1, Box 336, Creswell, NC 27928; phone 919-797-4475.

Pocosin Lakes National Wildlife Refuge (Lake Phelps Area) and Adjacent Farmlands
MAP 7

The farmlands and newly cleared lands of this area have long been popular with North Carolina birders as a good winter site for certain specialties. The farmlands attract occasional flocks of Horned Larks and Lapland Longspurs, and Short-eared Owls are regularly seen at dusk. And the brush piles associated with the conversion of land from forests to fields have been the coastal region's best area for Lincoln's and White-crowned sparrows.

However, birding in this area will inevitably change in the future. Some of the brush piles are now almost gone; other sites have become less attractive to sparrows as vegetation has grown up in surrounding areas. And the creation of this habitat has ceased here. The open fields may become less attractive to Short-eared Owls as adjacent old-field habitat becomes increasingly vegetated. Horned Larks and Lapland Longspurs will probably remain regular, but there is no assurance that the road from which they are seen—a private road—will remain open.

Much of the area's old-field habitat (the result of failed farming operations) has been acquired for the new Pocosin Lakes NWR, and the Fish and Wildlife Service has begun some habitat alterations, such as the disking of certain sites. The area has not attracted much waterfowl in the past, but it will probably begin to attract more. In short, you should regard much of the following description as subject to change, although I have tried to focus on the habitats and birdlife that should be around for several years.

Whatever happens in the future, this area will certainly remain of interest primarily during the winter months, from about November to March. Currently the waterfowl that you're most likely to see are Tundra Swans, either in the fields or flying to the lake at sunset. In the future there will probably be a greater variety of waterfowl. You may want to call the refuge office (919-797-4431) to inquire about any changes in habitat and waterfowl populations.

The winter months also offer a nice assortment of raptors. In addition to the Short-eared Owls, you can hear Barred and Great Horned owls and Eastern Screech-Owls. Red-shouldered Hawks and Black Vultures are seen regularly, and this is a pretty good site for Cooper's Hawks.

Habitat will decline for both Lincoln's and White-crowned sparrows; although both species will probably still occur here, finding them will take more effort. And habitat will remain good for a variety of sparrows.

LOGISTICS. This tour of the area focuses on the state road (SR 1183, or Shore Drive) that runs through refuge land along the west and south sides of Lake Phelps. This road is passable during all conditions. The tour also includes the main road through adjacent private farmlands—a road that will probably (but not necessarily) remain open in the future. Unless otherwise indicated, these descriptions refer to the winter season.

TO REACH THIS AREA, take SR 1126 from US 64 at Roper. (You will see signs directing you to the refuge.) Continue 6.7 miles, then turn right onto SR 1183 and set your odometer to zero.

At the beginning of SR 1183 there is a large grain elevator. If there are many blackbirds, check through them—Brewer's Blackbirds have been seen here at least once.

At 1.6 miles one of many refuge boundaries begins. The government has bought the many small sections of land that were available, but the sections that have not been available remain private. From here on, you should assume that land is public only where you see refuge signs.

At 2.4 miles you will see a gated trail on the right. This trail can be good for a nice variety of small land birds, including Eastern Phoebes, House Wrens, Common Yellowthroats, and sparrows—mostly Fields, Savannahs, Songs, Swamps, and White-throateds. This is old-field habitat and will probably become less attractive to birds in a few years.

At 2.7 miles you will see a pulloff on the left, where you can walk down to a fringe of swamp forest (part of Pettigrew SP). You might see Pileated Woodpeckers here at any season, and one or two Prothonotaries in the nesting season.

At 2.9 miles there is a gated roadway on the right that runs about one-quarter mile before it comes to private land. Along this road you will see fields on the left (private land) and old-field habitat on the right. This old-field habitat is more open in aspect than that mentioned above, and it should remain good for sparrows for several years. A few White-crowned Sparrows can usually be found here, and a Lincoln's is possible.

The refuge office is on the left at 3.2 miles. Here you can check the lake, although you probably won't see much except at sunset, when the swans are flying in to roost. You might see a few Wood Ducks, and if the weather is really cold, other ducks are possible. Common Mergansers have been seen here after extreme cold. A Great Cormorant showed up here one March, producing one of North Carolina's most bizarre records.

As you continue along the road, watch the skies for Turkey and Black vultures and Red-tailed Hawks. Over the adjacent fields and old-field habitat, you will see several harriers. Watch the roadsides for a Red-shouldered Hawk and hope for a glimpse of a Cooper's. If you make several stops along the road at dusk during calm conditions, you should hear Great Horned and Barred owls, Eastern Screech-Owls, and American Woodcocks. If the private road on the adjacent farmlands is closed to the public in the future, you can still watch for Short-eared Owls along this road. Barn Owls are also possible.

At 4.5 miles, on the right, a strip of wet marshy habitat begins. This marsh has been disked in places. Where marsh vegetation remains, look for Common Yellowthroats. A few Virginia and King rails are possible in these areas.

From here to the end of the road, about 5 miles away, the habitat remains largely the same. There are a few places where you can walk down to the lake. Be sure to walk down roads/paths only where there are refuge signs.

To check the road through the private farmlands (currently Tyson Farms), return to the beginning of SR 1183. Just before you come to the stop sign, look for a dirt road toward your left. If road conditions are good, you might want to drive in for 2 or 3 miles. (This road can sometimes be bad after rainy weather.) Since this is private land, you are limited to what you can see from the main road. Do not drive onto any side roads. When you park, pull over as far as possible in order not to block any farm machinery. It is probably best not to walk too far from your car. This farm is a big operation, and it often seems that farm equipment is on the move from dawn to dusk Monday through Saturday. If you can, try to visit on a Sunday.

Check all the bare fields, especially newly plowed ones, for American Pipits, Horned Larks, and Lapland Longspurs. This area is also very good for hawks and vultures. All the species mentioned earlier can be seen here. Rough-legged Hawks have also occurred on a couple of occasions.

To look for Short-eared Owls, watch just above the fields at dusk or, perhaps even better, before sunrise. Even when the birds are seen at a distance you can pick them out by their distinctive nighthawklike flight. In late autumn and early winter you should focus your attention on any fields that haven't been plowed yet (especially when most of the fields have). If you see any sites that attract harriers in the daytime, check these sites at dusk for owls.

For further information: Contact Pocosin Lakes NWR, Route 1, Box 195-B, Creswell, NC 27928; phone 919-797-4431.

TIDEWATER RESEARCH STATION

Birders heading to or from the Outer Banks on US 64 should always keep this spot in mind. It is not a major birding area, but it lies right next to the highway, usually provides at least mild entertainment, and has the potential to attract something unusual.

Located just south of US 64 between Plymouth and Roper, the Tidewater Research Station is an agricultural research station administered by the North Carolina Department of Agriculture. The researchers grow various crops here, and there are often fallow fields in addition to pastures and livestock; thus, a variety of common species can usually be found. Habitat is always changing here, so you never know exactly what you might find.

The research station is easy to find. About halfway between Plymouth and Roper (3.7 miles from the state rest stop on the east side of Plymouth), watch for signs that say "Tidewater Research Station" and "Vernon G. James Research and Extension Center." At these signs turn south onto SR 1119. You will see the research center building on the left. Beyond this building, the research station grounds lie on both sides of SR 1119. After about 2 miles, SR 1119 makes a ninety-degree turn to the left. About three-quarters of a mile past this turn, you will see a boundary marker on the left that marks the end of the research station.

You can bird the area adequately from SR 1119. If you see any areas that seem to merit a closer look (like fallow fields), during business hours you can go to the research center and get permission to walk the grounds. The center is closed on weekends, but you might find a station employee around the barns.

At all seasons you can expect to see a fair variety of birds, especially open-country species like Turkey Vulture, Red-tailed Hawk, Eastern Bluebird, and Eastern Meadowlark. A drive through the station will probably be most entertaining during the breeding season and in winter. Species you can find in the breeding season include Eastern Kingbird, Blue Grosbeak, and Indigo Bunting. Listen for Chipping Sparrows in the trees beside the barns. Winter is potentially the most interesting season to check this site. If there are any blackbirds and grackles feeding around the livestock, check them carefully for a rarity like a Brewer's Blackbird. American Pipits have been seen feeding right next to the roadsides, and Horned Larks are possible. Fallow fields can provide a good variety of sparrows, such as Savannahs and Fields. A Le Conte's was found one winter.

If you're ever driving through this area after there has been snow—enough to just cover the ground—you will definitely want to pull into the station and check the cattle pens. During such conditions, sites with livestock (and hence open ground) can attract many types of birds. You might get very close views of blackbirds, sparrows, pipits, and maybe something unusual.

The fields along SR 1119 beyond the research station are often also good for birds. Especially if you are traveling east on US 64, you may wish to continue on 1119 into Roper, where you can turn on Main Street, which will take you back to US 64. (A right turn will take you to US 64 east of Roper, a left turn to the west.)

For further information: Contact Tidewater Research Station, Route 2, Box 141, Plymouth, NC 27962; phone 919-793-4118.

POCOSIN LAKES NATIONAL WILDLIFE
REFUGE (PUNGO UNIT)
MAP 8

The Pungo unit of the Pocosin Lakes NWR (formerly Pungo NWR) is definitely worth visiting in winter, from November to early March. Pungo Lake serves as an important roosting site for vast numbers of Tundra Swans, Snow Geese, Canada Geese, and dabbling ducks, and large flocks of swans and geese feed on the managed agricultural fields during the day. Wood Ducks are common residents on the refuge's canals.

Much of the Pungo unit of the refuge consists of old-field habitats, the result of unsuccessful attempts during earlier years to convert natural pocosin vegetation to agricultural lands, and this vast area of old-field habitat attracts a large

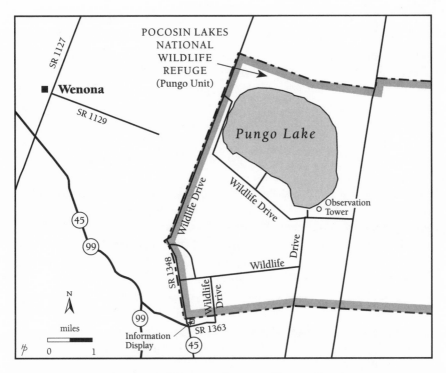

POCOSIN LAKES
NATIONAL
WILDLIFE
REFUGE
(Pungo Unit)

SR 1127

■ **Wenona**

SR 1129

Pungo Lake

Wildlife Drive

Wildlife Drive

○ Observation
Tower

45

99

SR 1348

Wildlife   Drive

N

miles

99

Wildlife
Drive

Information
Display   SR 1363

45

0   1

8. Pocosin Lakes National Wildlife Refuge (Pungo Unit)

number of species. Raptors are especially common, and in winter this is one of the best spots in North Carolina for finding Cooper's Hawks. Black Vultures and one or two Bald Eagles are also seen here regularly. A Golden Eagle has sometimes overwintered.

The Fish and Wildlife Service has recently begun to construct impoundments, so birding should be even better in the future. You are also likely to see other wildlife here. Deer are common, and you might spot a river otter or black bear as well.

Logistics. This area's roads can be terrible after rainy weather. Try to schedule a visit after a dry spell, unless you own a four-wheel-drive vehicle.

This wintertime tour of the Pungo Lake area follows the **Wildlife Drive**, which runs along the south and west sides of the lake. The Wildlife Drive begins at NC 45. Just east of the Hyde/Beaufort boundary, and 1.1 miles east of the NC 99/NC 45 intersection, NC 45 makes an abrupt turn, and SR 1363 cuts off to the left/right. The first part of the Wildlife Drive follows SR 1363.

Immediately after you turn onto SR 1363, you will see a Fish and Wildlife Service information display on your left. Farther along, you will see a cattle pen on your right. Among the Red-winged Blackbirds, Common Grackles, and

Brown-headed Cowbirds at the pen, check for Rusty Blackbirds and hope for a Yellow-headed. In the pines across the road, listen for chickadees and Brown-headed Nuthatches.

At 0.6 miles the Wildlife Drive turns left off the state road. Soon you will see extensive fields on your left, which often attract swans and Canada and Snow geese. Light here is best early in the morning. Look carefully—a Ross' Goose has been seen in the Pungo Lake area twice, and a Greater White-fronted would also be possible here. Almost all the Snow Geese here are white morphs; at Matta-muskeet NWR, on the other hand, up to half of the birds are dark morphs ("Blue Geese").

At 1.6 miles the Wildlife Drive turns right. On your left is an impounded area that usually attracts a few Wood Ducks and other dabblers. Beyond this im-poundment there is old-field habitat on both sides of the road, with open grass and sedge areas gradually being invaded by shrub vegetation. Raptors are com-mon in this area; Northern Harriers, Red-tailed Hawks, and Turkey Vultures occur most frequently, but several species are possible. Watch for Black Vul-tures, Red-shouldered Hawks (especially as you get closer to the lake), and one or two Sharp-shinned and Cooper's hawks. A Merlin or Peregrine Falcon is also possible, and Rough-legged Hawks have been been sighted here. If you make several stops along this road at dusk, you might hear a woodcock or see a Barn or Short-eared owl.

Sparrows, especially Song and Swamp sparrows, are common along this sec-tion of road. And watch carefully—this road's borders are a good area to find the rapidly declining Northern Bobwhite, even in winter.

At 3.6 miles the Wildlife Drive turns to the left. The road to the right is closed to vehicular traffic, but you may want to walk a portion of it if you see ducks, swans, or geese in the fields in the distance.

After this turn you may want to make a few stops to check the open marshy strip that parallels the road on your left. Common Yellowthroats are common here, and a rail, Common Snipe, or Sedge Wren is possible. In the canal on your right an otter might swim up to check you out, especially if you're here early or late.

At 4.7 miles you will come to a crossroads and see the **observation tower** up ahead. This is a great place to check out the lake, and the light is very good most of the day, but most of the waterfowl will typically be too distant for good views (although you might have Wood Ducks land in the canal right next to you). Aesthetically, though, this is a nice spot at sunset, when thousands of swans and geese fly to the lake from the fields.

This is also a great place to watch for raptors. Check carefully for a Bald Eagle, or perhaps even a Golden Eagle—Goldens have overwintered on at least a couple of occasions. Watch for vultures coming in to roost; Turkeys predominate, but you might see a few Blacks. Especially on calm evenings during mild winters, listen for a King or Virginia rail in the marshy area in front of the tower.

Go back to the crossroads, reset your odometer to zero, and turn right. (If you want to check out more of the marshy old-field habitat that characterizes much of the refuge—to look for more raptors, perhaps—you can make a side trip down the mile-long road to the left.) After 0.8 miles there is more woody vegetation, including small trees. American Robins are usually everywhere.

At 2.1 miles you will see a gated roadway on your right. From here to the lake is a half-mile hike. This road is sometimes closed to entry (e.g., during banding operations). When it is open, walk down to the lake; here you can get much closer views of waterfowl, especially dabbling ducks, than from the observation tower. At the beginning of your walk—on your left, in the open, flooded area—listen for King and Virginia rails.

At 2.6 miles, where the Wildlife Drive makes a sharp turn to the right, you will see an impounded area in front of you. You can also reach another impounded area by walking to your left, following the dike. At these sites you should see additional dabbling ducks, coots, Great Blue Herons, and maybe other wading birds.

The Wildlife Drive runs near the northwestern margin of the lake; it turns left once at 3.8 miles, and again at 4.1 miles. At 5.4 miles you will see extensive fields on your left. Blackbirds frequently blanket these fields, and geese and swans often congregate here late in the day before heading to roost. (The sun will be at your back then, providing good viewing conditions.)

Within these fields, at 6.4 miles, a road on your left offers access to a brush line and brush piles, which can be good for the common sparrows. A White-crowned or Lincoln's is also possible here; however, the site's productiveness will probably decline in the future.

At 7.6 miles you will come to paved SR 1348, which leads back to the beginning of the Wildlife Drive.

During rainy weather these dirt roads may become impassable; if so, you may wish to reverse the above route and begin along SR 1348. From the end of SR 1348, it is only about a mile to the fields where the geese and swans frequently congregate at sunset.

The Pungo Lake area is much less interesting at other seasons, although the introduction of new impoundments may make birding increasingly productive at other seasons. In the many shrubby old-field areas watch for Northern Bobwhites, Eastern Kingbirds, Indigo Buntings, and maybe a few Blue Grosbeaks. In the wooded areas near the lake, Prothonotary Warblers are common. This vast open area is the kind of place that could attract rarities during migrations.

For further information: Contact Pocosin Lakes NWR, Route 1, Box 195-B, Creswell, NC 27928; phone 919-797-4431.

MATTAMUSKEET NATIONAL WILDLIFE REFUGE,
GULL ROCK GAME LAND, SWANQUARTER NATIONAL
WILDLIFE REFUGE
MAP 9

In winter—especially early winter—Mattamuskeet NWR is one of the premier birding spots in coastal North Carolina. The refuge, which includes most of Lake Mattamuskeet and its margins, harbors an excellent variety of waterfowl, and you can watch many of these birds at very close range. Many waterfowl can be seen from your car, so a birding weekend can be quite successful even during rainy weather.

The refuge hosts good numbers and a diverse selection of raptors. Bald Eagles are easy to find from late October through February; you might also see a Merlin or Peregrine Falcon and hear a Barred Owl.

At all seasons you might see marsh birds, including Least and American bitterns, Common Moorhen, King and Virginia rails, and Sora. In late summer and early autumn low water levels in some of the impoundments often produce good shorebirding.

The refuge has a good variety of land birds both in the breeding season and in winter. The causeway can be excellent for migrant passerines in autumn, but it is more noteworthy as a magnet for lingering passerines in early winter.

Not surprisingly, the refuge and surrounding areas regularly attract rare species. Eurasian Wigeons occur here regularly, and Greater White-fronted Geese and Fulvous Whistling-Ducks are found during some winters. Eared Grebes are showing up with increasing frequency, and American White Pelicans are also possible. Sandhill Cranes have overwintered in this area, and on one Christmas Bird Count a Tropical Kingbird put in an appearance at a nearby pig farm.

Even the most avicentric birders will probably find themselves distracted by other wildlife at Mattamuskeet. If you're out early in the morning or late in the afternoon, you're sure to get some great views of several mammals, including deer, muskrats, raccoons, and otters.

The Gull Rock Game Land and the portion of Swanquarter NWR that is accessible by car are not major birding areas, but they complement Mattamuskeet NWR. During the breeding season a drive down SR 1164 through the game land can be good for Chuck-will's-widows and Swainson's Warblers. The marshes at the end of the road harbor at least a few Clapper Rails, Marsh Wrens, and Seaside Sparrows. In winter this is also a good site to scope the Pamlico Sound for Red-throated Loons and Surf and Black scoters. At Swanquarter NWR the fishing pier overlooking Rose Bay can be worth checking in late winter, when you should see several diving ducks.

LOGISTICS. The Mattamuskeet refuge office is located approximately 2 miles off the causeway that crosses the lake (NC 94). On the gravel road to the of-

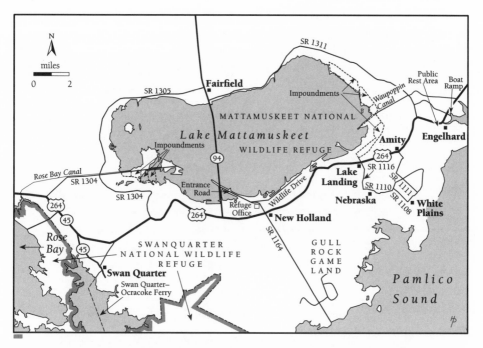

9. MATTAMUSKEET NATIONAL WILDLIFE REFUGE, GULL ROCK GAME LAND, SWANQUARTER NATIONAL WILDLIFE REFUGE

fice (Entrance Road) you will see a display case that holds maps of the refuge, refuge information, and checklists of the area's birds, amphibians, reptiles, and mammals.

Birdlife at the various impoundments varies according to management (which varies from year to year) and other factors, so you will want to check at the office (919-926-4021) for the latest information about which areas are best for certain species—especially before heading for sites that involve long hikes, such as the west and east ends of the lake. A bicycle, especially a mountain bike, will allow you to cover much more area than you could on foot.

If you're organizing a visit for a group, you should know the locations of the few public restrooms in this area. There is a restroom at the refuge office, but the office is usually closed on weekends. Otherwise, the nearest public restrooms are at the ferry terminal south of Swan Quarter and at a public rest stop on US 264 in Engelhard. If you're driving here from the west on US 264 on a weekend, you will definitely want to stop at the Hardee's in Belhaven.

THE MATTAMUSKEET NWR and adjacent lands can be divided into five general tours: the causeway; the Entrance Road and Wildlife Drive on the south side of the lake; the fields and impoundments at the eastern end of the lake; the woods and impoundments along the Rose Bay Canal, at the western end of the refuge; and a highway drive around the eastern half of the lake, from Fairfield to New Holland.

At times some of the best birding in the refuge takes place along the **cause-way across the lake**. This causeway, part of NC 94, is over 5 miles long. The southern part of the causeway, which lies adjacent to impoundments, can be entertaining at any season; but if you really want to see Lake Mattamuskeet at its best, plan a birding trip along the causeway from about mid-November to the first week in December, when you can see excellent numbers of Tundra Swans, Canada Geese, dabbling ducks, and diving ducks, many at very close range. Make sure that you stay here until sunset for a truly unforgettable experience.

During roughly the same period the shrubs along the causeway can offer an excellent assortment of passerines, although you should avoid windy days. Easy-to-find species include House Wren, Solitary Vireo, Common Yellow-throat, and Palm Warbler; also, Orange-crowned Warblers often occur in surprisingly large numbers. The causeway obviously serves as a magnet for lingering birds, and in December gnatcatchers and Prairie Warblers are almost easy to find. Amazingly, Yellow Warblers—birds that tend to be virtually gone from North Carolina by mid-October—have been found along the causeway three times in winter. One year some really unusual vagrant is going to turn up here.

Numbers of waterfowl on the lake gradually decline after early December. Late December and January are typically still entertaining, but by February you may see virtually no waterfowl on the lake.

The causeway certainly has the potential to be interesting after cold fronts on September and October mornings; hundreds of warblers and other passerines have been seen then, working their way northward along the causeway. It is unfortunate that the refuge receives little birding activity at this season, because the causeway is the sort of place that could attract something really interesting.

This tour along the causeway begins at the intersection of NC 94 and US 264. In the pines at the refuge boundary, at 0.5 miles, look for Brown-headed Nuthatches and Pine Warblers year-round and for Yellow-throated Warblers in spring and early summer.

On the right at 0.6 miles you will see a gated roadway that runs along the south dike of an impoundment. From autumn through spring you will want to walk down this road for a few hundred yards, especially during calm conditions at sunset. You can usually find Swamp Sparrows and Marsh and Sedge wrens, and you might hear or see a King Rail, Virginia Rail, or Sora.

On the left at 0.7 miles, across the little bridge, is an impoundment that is usually flooded. In winter look for Wood Ducks and other dabblers, several Ring-necked Ducks, and Hooded Mergansers. This is a good place to see muskrats and perhaps an otter. In summer Wood Ducks nest here, and you might get to see a hen with her brood. Prothonotary Warblers are common, and you should see a few Eastern Kingbirds as well.

At 1.0 miles you can look over the impoundment to the right or the lake to the left. In winter the impoundment hosts many dabbling ducks (but the best viewing is usually from the Entrance Road). You should find a few Great Blue Herons and Great Egrets here, and during the warmer months other wading birds are likely. If water levels are low, there may be several shorebirds, and this spot can attract Long-billed Dowitchers in autumn and early winter.

At 1.5 miles you will see the beginning of the Entrance Road. The shrubs along this section of the causeway usually have the area's most diverse assortment of land birds in early winter; search carefully through all the chickadee-kinglet flocks. This also seems to be the best area during autumn migration. In the breeding season you should see Orchard Orioles along this section, and you might spot a Yellow-billed Cuckoo.

From this point on, birding along the causeway is generally interesting only during the winter; you will want to make numerous stops from the Entrance Road to the north end of the causeway to sort through all the winter waterfowl. During early winter—the peak period—you will see all or almost all of the dabblers (Blue-winged Teal may be absent) and several species of divers. Ring-necked Ducks, Lesser Scaup, Canvasbacks, and Ruddy Ducks can always be found, and you might also see Greater Scaup, Redheads, and a few Surf and Black scoters. Even Oldsquaws are occasionally spotted in the early winter.

At the first culvert, at 1.9 miles, scope the treetops along the lake shore to the southeast; you should see one or more Bald Eagles. There are four more culverts between here and the north side of the lake. Typically there is a noticeable current underneath each culvert, and the outflow attracts Double-crested Cormorants, Ring-billed Gulls, and often a few Bonaparte's Gulls and Forster's Terns. These sites might occasionally attract something like a rare gull, although there are no such records.

From spring to early autumn this portion of the causeway tends to be quite dull in terms of birding, but it's always a pleasant, scenic drive. In the breeding season you will see numerous Fish Crows, Common Grackles, and Red-winged Blackbirds.

The 2.2-mile-long **Entrance Road/Wildlife Drive** can be productive at any season. The Entrance Road begins on the lake causeway, 1.5 miles north of the NC 94/US 264 intersection and runs beside a waterfowl impoundment to the refuge headquarters. The Wildlife Drive starts at the headquarters and runs for 3.6 miles near the south side of the lake. The Wildlife Drive is closed three or four mornings a week during the waterfowl hunting season, around late November through January.

Just at the beginning of the Entrance Road you will see an impoundment on your right. Throughout the winter you will be able to find most species of dabblers here, plus coots and Pied-billed Grebes. Look carefully—Eared Grebes have been seen here. This impoundment also tends to be rather entertaining during the nonwinter months, when you may see several wading birds and perhaps a few shorebirds. During low water levels in summer—especially late summer—look for a few terns, especially Forster's, Caspian, and Black.

At 0.7 miles is a pulloff. From here for the next three hundred yards or so, check the little openings in the marsh carefully. One or more Common Moorhens may occur here at any season. This is also a good area for Northern Shovelers during the winter.

On the left side of the road, opposite the impoundment, there is woody vegetation along the canal—mostly shrubs at first, with increasing numbers of trees farther along. This shrub/tree line can be good at any season. In the breeding season watch for Eastern Kingbirds and Orchard Orioles. In winter and during the fall migration these shrubs can be nearly as good as those along the causeway, and you should find many of the same species.

Just after the impoundment ends, at 1.7 miles, an extensive wooded area begins on the right. From here to the old lodge—about one-half mile—there is a variety of habitat for land birds: wet mixed pine and hardwoods, slightly drier pine woods, and the open areas with scattered trees near the lodge. Park and walk this area; a good variety of species can be found at any time.

Throughout the year you will find several species of woodpeckers; Pileateds are frequent. Brown-headed Nuthatches can always be found, and you might also see bobwhites or a Red-shouldered Hawk. This is a great area for Eastern Screech-Owls; if you stay here until dusk you should be able to call one up. A Barred Owl is also possible.

This area is especially fun during the breeding season, from about late April to June. Some species that are almost automatic here are Yellow-billed Cuckoo, Eastern Wood-Pewee, Acadian Flycatcher, Wood Thrush, Prothonotary and Yellow-throated warblers, Northern Parula, Indigo Bunting, and Blue Grosbeak. Barn Swallows nest around the old lodge, and you should also see one or more Ruby-throated Hummingbirds. If you are here at dusk, you may hear a Chuck-will's-widow or Whip-poor-will.

Winter can be almost as good. The chickadee-kinglet flocks may include Solitary Vireos, a Brown Creeper, and maybe a lingering Black-and-white or Yellow-throated warbler. If you walk back into the woods a little ways, you should find Hermit Thrushes and a Winter Wren.

Cross the Main Canal bridge and turn right. At this point the **Wildlife Drive** begins. Reset your odometer to zero and continue.

Before you get to the next bridge, you will pass through an area with a thick cover of privet (an evergreen or semievergreen shrub); this area attracts Gray Catbirds and Brown Thrashers year-round. In winter you will see White-throated Sparrows, and maybe a Hermit Thrush or Fox Sparrow.

At the bridge at 0.2 miles, look north along the canal—in winter you might see an eagle or two. The three-quarter-mile walk on the dike to the lake is most worthwhile in winter, when eagles and more waterfowl may be present.

For the next 1.5 miles you are very likely to see bobwhites, especially if you're driving. In the breeding season this section also offers many of the same species as the lodge area, including Eastern Wood-Pewee, Brown-headed Nuthatch, Yellow-throated Warbler, and Blue Grosbeak.

At 0.8 miles you should walk out the dikes to the marshes beside the lake. Common Yellowthroats frequent these marshes throughout the year, and you should find Marsh Wrens at least from autumn to spring. Listen for King Rails at any season and for Virginia Rails and Soras from August to spring. (Soras are most likely during the migrations.)

For the next mile there is an impoundment on your left that usually attracts a few dabbling ducks in winter.

From 1.9 miles to the end of Wildlife Drive, hardwoods and bald cypresses dominate. Prothonotary Warblers are abundant here in spring and early summer, and you might see a Barred Owl at any season. In late autumn and early winter this is a good area for Rusty Blackbirds, but by late winter you may find only Common Grackles.

At 1.9 miles a trail goes down to the lake. The view is not very good here, but this trail can be good for small land birds. Near its end, Wildlife Drive runs along near the lake, and at the end of the road a short boardwalk allows you to survey more of the lake area.

The fields and impoundments at the **east end of the refuge**, north of Lake Landing, are best in winter, when they may be covered with swans, Canada Geese, Snow Geese (both white and dark morphs), and ducks. This is also a good area for raptors; Bald Eagles are regular, and you might spot a Merlin or Peregrine Falcon as well. During some years a Golden Eagle has been found. Shorebirding is unpredictable but occasionally good—sometimes even in winter, when the fields may be good after rainy weather. A Ruff was once seen here on a Christmas Bird Count!

The breeding season can also be entertaining. You can compile a good list of land birds by checking both the field edges and the woods beside the impoundments northwest of Waupoppin Canal. Along the edges of the lake there are King Rails and Least Bitterns. The most distant impoundment—still called "the wooded impoundment" despite the recent spread of marsh vegetation—holds nesting Wood Ducks, and sometimes Least Bitterns and Common Moorhens. And if the refuge managers keep any of the other impoundments flooded throughout the summer, you will have the chance to find Common Moorhens, an American Bittern or two, and more Least Bitterns.

Covering this area requires a lot of walking, though. From November through February, when the road to the Waupoppin Canal is closed to vehicles, you would have to walk about 12 miles round-trip to check all the impound-ments, including the most distant wooded impoundment, and you might have to walk at least 3 miles in (one-way) before you get to sites with many water-fowl. From March to October you can drive to the Waupoppin Canal; from here it is a 7-mile hike around the wooded impoundment, which may be the only interesting area in summer. At all seasons you should call the refuge office and see which areas are productive before you start out. Also, keep in mind that the refuge may permit organized tour groups accompanied by refuge personnel to drive in to the area. (This policy may be discontinued in the future if not enough refuge personnel are available.)

This tour of the east end begins on US 264 at Lake Landing. From the highway you can see the gravel road leading to the refuge. At the end of the road is a parking area. In winter, park here, walk around the gate to the right, and start hiking. From March through October turn right and continue.

In winter the fields and the moist soil impoundments from here to the Wau-poppin Canal, about 3 miles away, may be covered with Tundra Swans, Canada Geese, and Snow Geese, including many dark-morph "Blue Geese." Snow Geese comprise two populations—the Greater Snow Geese and the Lesser. The Great-ers are almost all white-morph individuals, while a large percentage of the Lessers are dark morphs. Look carefully for a rarity such as a Greater White-fronted Goose.

If the fields are wet, look for Common Snipes and other shorebirds. When the lake is high and these fields are wet, you might find Least Sandpipers, Greater and Lesser yellowlegs, and maybe Long-billed Dowitchers.

In winter you will probably see several raptors. Red-tailed Hawks and Turkey Vultures are common, and you should see a few Black Vultures and a Red-shouldered Hawk. If you're lucky you might have a Merlin or Peregrine Falcon zip by. A Golden Eagle has been seen here during some winters.

During the warmer months these fields are much less interesting. Look for Eastern Meadowlarks, Indigo Buntings, and Blue Grosbeaks; you might also spot a bobwhite. If any wet spots linger in the fields, they may attract a few shorebirds during the spring migration.

In winter, as you get closer to the Waupoppin Canal, you will see numerous dabbling ducks. If many American Wigeons are present, look carefully for a Eurasian Wigeon. Fulvous Whistling-Ducks have been seen here during some winters. Tree Swallows may number in the thousands; during mild winters a Barn Swallow may show up.

At the Waupoppin Canal take the road to the left, which runs down to the lake and can be good at any season. As you drive or walk along you might spot a King Rail on the dike. At the end, on your left, look for waterfowl in winter. This area can be especially good about November, when the birds prefer to feed here rather than in the fields. Look for swans, Canada Geese, Snow Geese, and many dabbling ducks. During low water levels at any season you may see a few wading birds, shorebirds, and terns, although these birds are more likely during the warmer months and migrations. In summer you may see a few Boat-tailed Grackles, notably far "inland," and beside fresh water.

Return to the bridge across the Waupoppin Canal. Beyond the bridge you will see two open impoundments and, beyond them, the wooded impoundment.

To walk around just the open impoundments is about a 3-mile hike. These impoundments can host many dabbling ducks in winter. In the breeding season, if they are kept flooded, they may have a few Pied-billed Grebes, Common Moorhens, and Least and American bitterns. In the breeding season the west side of the impoundments is often best. Listen for Yellow-billed Cuckoos and Prothonotary Warblers in the woods to your left. You may hear a Least Bittern calling from the marshes of the lake, but getting down to the lake here is quite laborious (and there are many cottonmouths here).

About 2 miles from the Waupoppin Canal bridge is the beginning of the wooded impoundment. In winter this isn't worth the long hike (4 miles around), but it can be worthwhile during the breeding season if the day isn't too warm. Despite its name, this impoundment has many open marshy areas. There are also many dead hardwoods and some live bald cypresses. Wood Ducks nest here, and you might see a Least Bittern or Common Moorhen. Many vultures roost here, including a few Blacks. You should see several woodpeckers; this is a great place for Pileateds. Common Yellowthroats and Prothonotary Warblers are abundant, and you will see several Great Crested Flycatchers and Eastern Kingbirds. In the swamp forest along the southwest dike you might add a few species of land birds. Watch for a Yellow-billed Cuckoo.

The western end of the refuge, along the **Rose Bay Canal**, is accessible only by foot; this section of road is closed to vehicles throughout the year. Fortunately, the mature woodland (Salyer's Ridge Natural Area), which is usually the prime attraction, begins at the gate, and you can check out part of it by walking a mile or less. An 8-mile walk will take you around all the impoundments, and the first impoundment is only a mile away. Some of these impoundments may be good for Least Bitterns in the breeding season and for shorebirds on occasion. Call the refuge office for the current situation before you plan a long hike.

To reach this area, begin at the NC 94/US 264 intersection. Take US 264 west for 4.6 miles and turn right onto SR 1304 at Swindell Fork. After 4.7 miles, on your right, you will see the road into the refuge. Just down the road you will see a small parking area and gate.

The woodland here, with its mature pines and hardwood understory, can be good year-round for a long list of species, but the breeding season is especially good. You may want to explore the footpath that runs to the right. You can also walk down the road to the first impoundment; as you approach it, the woods gradually get wetter, and eventually red maples become dominant.

Woodpeckers are common in this area. You should see Pileateds, and you have a fair chance of spotting a Hairy. Red-shouldered Hawks are frequently seen here, and you might hear a Barred Owl, even in midmorning. If you're lucky, you might see a Wild Turkey.

For a really good morning, visit this area between late April and June. Some of the species you should find include Yellow-billed Cuckoo, Acadian Flycatcher, Wood Thrush, Red-eyed Vireo, Northern Parula, Ovenbird, and Yellow-throated and Prothonotary warblers. This is one of the best places in the refuge to find one or more Yellow-throated Vireos; listen for them in the tall pines next to the road.

These woods can also be quite productive in winter. Look for a Solitary Vireo in the flocks of chickadees, titmice, Brown-headed Nuthatches, and kinglets. Check the pine trunks for a Brown Creeper, and listen for the call notes of a Winter Wren. This area is also good for Hermit Thrushes and Fox Sparrows.

There are three open impoundments and one wooded impoundment in this area. The three open impoundments can be good for swans and dabbling ducks in winter, and for shorebirds during low water levels. If water levels are kept high during the breeding season, these impoundments may attract Least Bitterns and Common Moorhens.

By the way, Least Bitterns are often common in summer at the marshy edges of some of the small islands at the lake's west end. You could explore these areas by means of canoe or boat. You can put in at the parking lot, and from there to the lake is about 2 miles down the canal.

From November to February a tour around the eastern half of the lake from **Fairfield to New Holland** by way of SR 1311 and US 264 can be a fine complement to birding on the refuge. This trip, which is about 28 miles long—a little more if you make a couple of suggested side trips—can be an excellent activity on a rainy or bitter cold day. All the land along these roads is private land, but you can see a very good variety from your car.

The first section of this tour follows SR 1311 from Fairfield to US 264 just west of Engelhard. This roughly 14-mile stretch often provides the best birding, so if you don't have time for the whole tour, consider doing just this section.

Near the beginning the road runs along close to the lake in many places, and you will usually see many waterfowl. There are also swamp forests on the right; extensive fields (usually wet); yards, often with pecan trees; and frequent marshy weedy spots, so there is habitat for a nice variety of species. The fields may have swans, geese, pipits, and large flocks of blackbirds. In wet spots Common Snipes are frequent. The weedy spots are often loaded with sparrows.

If you see any sites with domestic waterfowl or livestock, stop and check carefully for Rusty Blackbirds; Brewer's and Yellow-headeds are also possible. These types of sites are often good for Palm Warblers. Next to the Pleasant Grove Church, about 10 miles from Fairfield, you may spot a few Cattle Egrets; in winter this is one of the state's most reliable sites for finding this species.

This whole route is very good for raptors, including Red-tailed Hawks, Red-shouldered Hawks, kestrels, and Turkey Vultures; you might even get to see a Merlin. About 8 to 10 miles from Fairfield, watch for a few Black Vultures.

If you see any sites beside the highway where wood from timbering operations has been piled up and become overgrown with weeds, check them for sparrows. Lincoln's Sparrows are often seen in this area when such habitat is available.

When you reach US 264, you may want to make a side trip into Engelhard, 1 mile away; on US 264 there is a state rest stop with restrooms. (This community also has a hamburger stand that is open most of the time.) If you drive another mile east on US 264, you will see a Wildlife Resources Commission boat ramp and parking lot, where you can glimpse the estuary. Here you will see pelicans, gulls, Forster's Terns, and maybe a few ducks.

The last half of the tour, to New Holland, is generally less interesting but can also be good. Between Lake Landing and New Holland you will see many sites with a thick growth of privet. These sites have many Gray Catbirds, Brown Thrashers, and Hermit Thrushes and are good places to look for Orange-crowned Warblers.

If you're feeling lucky, you might consider taking an 8-mile detour between Amity and Lake Landing, by way of the **White Plains and Nebraska communities**. Along this side trip you will have more opportunities to see raptors, including Northern Harriers; blackbird flocks; shorebirds in the fields; and maybe pipits. To take this route, turn left onto SR 1111 at the Amity United Methodist Church, 2.2 miles west of the US 264/SR 1311 intersection. Where SR 1111 ends, turn right onto SR 1108 and continue to the stop sign (at SR 1110). Then turn left and drive along SR 1110 until you come to SR 1116; turn right on this road and return to US 264.

Along SR 1111 and SR 1108 check the fields very carefully—a Sandhill Crane has overwintered here during two recent years. The cattle pasture at the 1108/1110 intersection is often loaded with grackles, blackbirds, and cowbirds, which you can study from your car. This is a good place for seeing Common and Boat-tailed grackles together. You also might see Rusty Blackbirds, and perhaps a Brewer's or Yellow-headed.

THE 7-MILE DRIVE down SR 1164 from New Holland to the **Gull Rock Game Land** and Pamlico Sound is usually worthwhile only in winter and during the breeding season, from late April to June. After rainy periods in winter this dirt road can become almost impassable unless you have a four-wheel-drive vehicle.

This road begins at the signpost for New Holland on US 264. After driving SR 1164 for 1.3 miles you will see an area of extensive fields on your right. Along this roadside you can usually find Indigo Buntings and Blue Grosbeaks in late spring and summer. Check the skies year-round for both vultures and Red-tailed Hawks.

From the end of these fields (at 2.3 miles) to the end of the road, you can hear several Chuck-will's-widows at dusk from late April to July.

The section of road from the fields to the crossroads at 5.5 miles can be productive at dawn from late April to June. Common species include Gray Catbird, White-eyed Vireo, Prairie and Prothonotary warbler, Common Yellow-throat, and Rufous-sided Towhee. You might get to see a Yellow-billed Cuckoo and a Yellow-breasted Chat. Bobwhites are seen on this road rather frequently. From about 4.4 miles to the crossroads you are likely to hear one or two Swainson's Warblers.

The game land boundary is at 4.3 miles. Just beyond this boundary you will see a gated roadway on your right. By walking this road you might add a couple of species to your morning list; a Worm-eating Warbler is a possibility.

When you reach the crossroads, you will see a gated roadway to your left, which leads to an impoundment a little over one-half mile away. This impoundment is not very productive, but in winter you should find a few dabbling ducks. In the breeding season there may be a pair of Red-headed Woodpeckers in the numerous dead trees, and you may also want to hike another mile to a small tract of red maples and other hardwoods. Stay on the main road that runs past the impoundment. Just after this road turns sharply to your right, check the wooded area on your right, listening for Yellow-billed Cuckoos and Acadian Flycatchers.

At the end of SR 1164, on the shores of Pamlico Sound, you should find Boat-tailed Grackles during the nesting season. This can also be a good place to set up watch in winter. Look for Red-throated and Common loons, Horned Grebes, and a few diving ducks, sometimes including Surf and Black scoters. On rare occasions a Northern Gannet may show up.

On your right there is an area of dense shrubs. If you crawl through these for a short distance, you will see on your right an extensive brackish marsh where a few Clapper Rails and Marsh Wrens can be found throughout the year. Virginia Rails are usually present but might be harder to find from April to July. From April to July there are also a few Willets and Seaside Sparrows. The wrens and sparrows are few and widely scattered. The habitat here is at least marginally suitable for Black Rails, although it may be a little too wet.

THE SWANQUARTER NWR complements the Mattamuskeet refuge quite nicely. Much of the refuge consists of open water (part of Pamlico Sound, plus associated bays) harboring an impressive number of diving ducks in winter.

(Technically these state-owned waters are not part of the refuge, but they lie within a presidential proclamation boundary where hunting is prohibited.) Most of these birds can be seen only by boat; the best way to see them is by taking the ferry from Swan Quarter to Ocracoke (see "Ferries to Ocracoke Island" in chapter 6).

But you can see at least a few waterfowl by taking the refuge's only road, which leads to a fishing pier on Rose Bay. From the intersection of US 264 and NC 45 (northwest of Swan Quarter), drive west on US 264/NC 45 for about 1.5 miles. Here you will see a refuge sign and the road to the bay on your left.

It is about 2 miles from the turnoff to the pier. Birding possibilities along the road are rather limited, but you might want to make a stop or two. In winter Yellow-rumped Warblers are common, and you might also see an Orange-crowned or two. You might see a few Brown-headed Nuthatches at any season. You will notice that in many areas, the pine trees have marsh vegetation growing beneath them—evidence of the area's rising sea level.

The pier is quite long; from the end you can easily check out any waterfowl on the upper portion of Rose Bay. The lighting here is best early in the morning; it is generally terrible in the middle of the day.

The number of ducks here varies rather widely. In general, more birds occur here in late winter—February and early March. You should at least see Buffleheads, and you might see Lesser Scaup, Canvasbacks, and Hooded and Red-breasted mergansers as well. Sort through any Buffleheads carefully—a Harlequin Duck was seen here one year in early March.

The pier often attracts several gulls and terns. In the marshy area around the parking lot you may find a wintering Swamp Sparrow or Sedge Wren. Strangely, a Snow Bunting showed up along the shore here one November.

For further information: For information about Mattamuskeet NWR or Swanquarter NWR, contact Mattamuskeet NWR, Route 1, Box N-2, Swan Quarter, NC 27885; phone 919-926-4021. For information about Gull Rock Game Land, call the North Carolina Wildlife Resources Commission at 919-733-7291.

BELHAVEN, PAMLICO BEACH–WADES POINT, PUNGO RIVER MARSHES
MAP 10

Birders rushing to or from Mattamuskeet NWR or the Pungo Lake area would often do well to slow down and check out these sites. It is only a short detour to the Belhaven waterfront, which can have several diving ducks in winter. The Pamlico Beach–Wades Point area is a bit farther out of the way but can be excellent for diving ducks. Both areas are best in late winter, around February to mid-March, when numbers peak here and when numbers of diving ducks along the Mattamuskeet causeway have waned considerably. The Pungo River

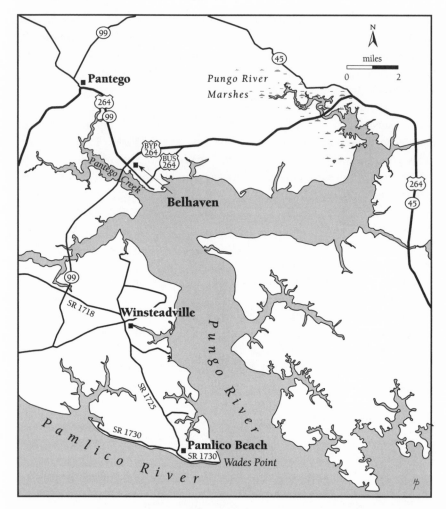

10. BELHAVEN, PAMLICO BEACH—WADES POINT, PUNGO RIVER MARSHES

Marshes have King (or "Cling") and Virginia rails year-round and a few Black Rails in summer.

For a tour of the **Belhaven waterfront**, begin on the town's northwest side at the intersection of the US 264 bypass and business routes. Drive southeast into the downtown area on Main Street (Business 264). At the beginning of the downtown area, turn right onto Haslin Street, then left onto Front Street. Just before you come to a small bridge, look for a **Wildlife Resources Commission boat ramp** and parking area on your right. From here you can check out the bay and sort through the gulls that congregate on the lawn of the hospital next door. This is a good spot to bird from your car.

In winter—especially late winter—look for a flock of Lesser Scaup. There are several fish houses here, so sort through the gulls carefully. One block farther southeast, at the waterfront, there are fish houses on both sides of the road.

Continue down Front Street, which becomes Riverside Drive, and check out the bay at the L-intersection of Riverside Drive and Riverside Street, next to the River Forest Manor.

Next, continue on Riverside Street, turn right onto Main Street, and go one block. Look for the **Charlie Smith Community House** on your right. This site has a gate that unfortunately is sometimes locked in winter, but it is usually open on weekdays. From the shore you can scope the mouth of Pantego Creek and the Pungo River. Look for numerous Canvasbacks, Lesser Scaup, and Buffleheads.

Despite its excellent birding potential, North Carolina birders virtually never check the **Pamlico Beach–Wades Point** area. To get here, take NC 99 south out of Belhaven. At 5.6 miles past the NC 99/US 264 intersection, turn left onto SR 1718. At 2.5 miles, continue straight through the intersection onto SR 1725. After 5.3 miles, at the Life Gate Free Will Baptist Church, turn left onto SR 1730. After 0.7 miles the road runs right next to the Pamlico River. You can bird from your car, and this could be a good spot during a rainy northeaster. Look for Common Loons, Horned Grebes, Lesser Scaup, Canvasbacks, Buffleheads, Surf Scoters, and Red-breasted Mergansers. In late winter the numbers of birds may be impressive. In the little marsh across the road look for Common Yellowthroats, Sedge Wrens, and maybe a Marsh Wren.

Continue on down SR 1730 through Pamlico Beach toward Wades Point. If it's not too windy, check the pines on your left for Brown-headed Nuthatches and Pine Warblers.

The road ends at Wades Point. The view here is exceptional, with water almost all around you. A winter sunrise here can be spectacular. And you can bird from your car here, so this could be an excellent spot to check in rainy or windy weather. The lighting here is best in the afternoon, especially late afternoon.

You can expect to see all the waterfowl species listed just above, but in greater numbers, and here you're more likely to see less common species—look for Greater Scaup, Black Scoters, Common Goldeneyes, Oldsquaws, and maybe a White-winged Scoter. This site is especially interesting in late winter, from February to mid-March. Numbers of birds are typically higher then, and chances of a rarity are better. This would seem to be the sort of place where a Red-necked or Western grebe might show up. Also, keep this site in mind during a severe southwester, when ducks likely move into the Pungo River, in the lee of the point.

On calm mornings you might want to work the wooded areas on the north side of the road. The habitat here is good for Orange-crowned Warblers.

If the waterfowl are plentiful and you would like to check out another nearby location, go back to the intersection at the church and turn left onto SR 1730. A short distance down the road you will see the **Pamlico Marina**. You can walk down to the shore here and survey a different portion of the Pamlico River. This shore is a lee shore during a northeast to north wind.

Outside the winter months the drive down to Pamlico Beach and Wades Point may not be worth the effort, at least in terms of birding. However, the view from Wades Point would make the trip worthwhile at any season, and this is the sort of place where a rarity could turn up anytime. During the spring migration it is likely that water birds regularly migrate northward up the Pungo River. And in the breeding season the road to Wades Point is probably excellent for Chuck-will's-widows.

The **Pungo River Marshes** lie beside US 264 in Hyde County, just inside the Beaufort-Hyde boundary. If you're traveling east on US 264, you will see the marshes on your right after you cross the bridge across the Pungo River. Just past the bridge, pull off on your right; this is the best place to park.

Although they lie right next to the highway, these marshes have received very little attention from birders. In the breeding season "Cling Rails," Virginia Rails, and Black Rails have been heard here. The "Clings" are presumably King Rails, but they might be King-Clapper hybrids. (If you get to see any of these birds, please report your findings to *Audubon Field Notes* or *Chat*.)

The "Clings" and Virginias probably occur here throughout the winter. Black Rails have been heard here only sporadically, but this situation is typical at sites with only a few birds. A few Black Rails are probably present every summer; however, this site is probably too wet for them to overwinter.

Marsh Wrens can be found here throughout the year. At least in the breeding season you may see a few Boat-tailed Grackles; here this species is close to its inland limit.

PAMLICO RIVER FERRY

Birding from this ferry can be quite entertaining in winter—from about Thanksgiving to March—when several species of diving ducks, including Canvasback, can often be seen. Many birders schedule a ride on this ferry as part of a trip to Mattamuskeet NWR. This ride can also be a good rainy-day activity, although the enclosed passenger sections are not elevated, so your view from inside is somewhat limited. There are elevated decks, but these are exposed.

The northern ferry terminal is near Bayview, the southern terminal near Aurora. The run takes about thirty minutes. Unfortunately, this ferry runs only at intervals of about two hours for most of the day; for the exact schedule, check roadside schedule signs in the area, call the Bayview terminal at 919-964-4521, or check the latest North Carolina State Transportation Map. This ferry is usually not crowded, but at certain hours it can be crowded with workers going to and from the Texas Gulf facility near Aurora, so you should get in line early.

You'll have the best lighting if you make this run from south to north. Most waterfowl tend to be to the east, so the light is generally best in the afternoon. And, if possible, try to take this ferry when the water is slick calm.

Numbers of waterfowl visible from the ferry will vary greatly. On a slow day you should see at least a few dozen birds. Occasionally there may be rafts of thousands of ducks, although most of these birds will be downriver and outside of a good viewing distance. On most days you will see Common Loons, Horned Grebes, Lesser Scaup, Canvasbacks, Buffleheads, Surf Scoters, and Red-breasted Mergansers. You may also see Ruddy Ducks. Species that occur less frequently include Greater Scaup, Ring-necked Duck, Black Scoter, and Common Golden-eye. Oldsquaws and White-winged Scoters have been spotted on rare occasions.

Check out the gulls carefully. Ferries and ferry terminals seem to attract rare species, and both Glaucous and Common Black-headed gulls have made appearances at the south terminal.

During the rest of the year birding from the ferry is much less interesting. Ospreys nest along the ferry route, and you will also see Brown Pelicans, gulls, and a few terns.

At the south terminal, birding can be rewarding much of the year. There is a dredge spoil site beside the terminal; depending on how recently it has been used, it may be either birdless or quite productive. Wood Ducks have bred here, and a few shorebirds are possible during the migrations. Even Black-necked Stilts have been found here in late summer. In the breeding season, land birds you may find near the terminal include Yellow-throated Warbler, Blue Grosbeak, and Indigo Bunting. Considering the small amount of habitat available, the north terminal can be surprisingly entertaining at times; while you wait in line you may see bluebirds, Chipping Sparrows, Pine Warblers, and other species feeding on the lawn.

For further information: Call the Bayview terminal at 919-964-4521.

BATH WATERFRONT

This is not a major birding site, but it can be mildly entertaining, at least in winter and during the migrations. Bath is North Carolina's oldest town; if you're planning to visit the town for its historical attractions, keep the waterfront in mind. A few minutes here can provide a pleasant diversion for a birder who is visiting the town with a historically oriented spouse or family.

Coming into Bath from the west, on NC 92, turn right onto the first street (Main Street). You will want to check out the creek from the Hardings Landing State Dock on your right, from Bonner Point Park at the end of Main Street, and from the end of King Street. At the last two sites you can check out the creek from your car. At the first site the light is best in the morning; at the other two, early morning and late afternoon are best.

In winter look for Pied-billed Grebes, gulls, a few Forster's Terns, American Coots, and maybe a few ducks, including Lesser Scaup and Canvasbacks. Frequently many Tree Swallows will be flitting around above the water. In the migration periods you should see a good variety of swallows over the creek, possibly including Banks and perhaps a Cliff or two.

GOOSE CREEK STATE PARK
MAP 11

This park offers a good to very good variety of woodland birds throughout the year. Permanent resident species include Red-shouldered Hawk, Barred Owl, Hairy and Pileated woodpeckers, and Brown-headed Nuthatch. The breeding season, from around late April to June, is especially entertaining; Blue-gray Gnatcatchers, Northern Parulas, and Yellow-throated and Prothonotary warblers are common then. Other nesters include Chuck-will's-widow, Whip-poor-will, Acadian Flycatcher, Yellow-throated Vireo, and Summer Tanager. Early May is a good time to see a few migrants, and the park can also be fairly good for migrants after cold fronts in September and October. Even winter days can offer a nice variety of land birds, often including Solitary Vireo and Orange-crowned Warbler.

Birding aside, this can be a very pleasant spot to visit. The park protects several types of habitats, including hardwood and bald cypress–hardwood swamps, shrub swamps, and upland pine-oak woods. Spanish moss drapes several spots, and there are some very scenic vistas. Several miles of hiking trails, including boardwalks through wetland habitats, add to the park's appeal. Finally, the park tends to be surprisingly uncrowded.

LOGISTICS. Unfortunately, the tick population here is quite bad; you will want to check yourself frequently. If you're squeamish about these pests, you'll be happy to know that you can see or hear most of the park's breeding bird species from the roads, without taking a step on the trails. This description of the park will emphasize birding from the roadsides, picnic areas, and campground.

The park opens at 8 A.M. throughout the year; closing time varies seasonally. You might consider camping in the park's primitive family campground so that you can both bird at dawn and listen for nocturnal species.

THE PARK IS easy to get to. From Washington take US 264 east. About 10 miles from Washington, watch for signs directing you to the park, and turn right onto SR 1334. After 2.2 miles you will see the park entrance sign on your right.

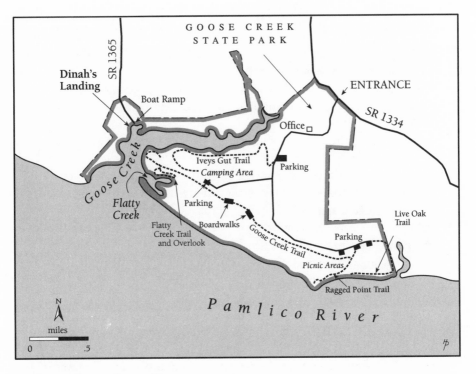

GOOSE CREEK
STATE PARK

SR 1365

Dinah's
Landing

Boat Ramp

ENTRANCE

SR 1334

Office

Iveys Gut Trail
Camping Area

Parking

Goose Creek

*Flatty
Creek*

Parking

Live Oak
Trail

Flatty
Creek Trail
and Overlook

Boardwalks

Goose Creek Trail

Parking

Picnic Areas

Ragged Point Trail

N

miles

0   .5

P a m l i c o   R i v e r

11. GOOSE CREEK STATE PARK

At the far end of the parking lot at the park office, set your odometer to zero. After 0.6 miles you will see a little parking area (for Iveys Gut Trail) on your left. During the breeding season you will want to park here or nearby along the dirt road to the campground and spend some time in this area. If you walk a little ways in both directions along the main road, and a short distance down the campground road, you will have access to hardwood swamps, upland pine-hardwood forests, and pine plantations. In the swamp areas listen for Yellow-billed Cuckoo, Pileated Woodpecker, Acadian Flycatcher, and Prothonotary Warbler. In the upland habitats look and listen for Brown-headed Nuthatch, Ovenbird, and Summer Tanager. Listen for the screams of a Red-shouldered Hawk at any season. If you are here at twilight, you might hear a Whip-poor-will in the breeding season, or a Barred Owl year-round. In late autumn and early winter, by the park's closing time it is often dark enough for Barred Owls to call.

Check the woods around the **picnic areas** next to the first two parking lots (both on the right). All year you can find Brown-headed and White-breasted nuthatches and Pine Warblers. Red-cockaded Woodpeckers were once resident here but are now apparently extirpated due to the deterioration of the site's habitat. Springtime begins in earnest here in early April; gnatcatchers may be everywhere, and the songs of Yellow-throated Warblers and Northern Parulas fill the air. Beginning around late April this is a good area for Summer Tanagers. At dawn from about mid-April to early July you can probably hear both Chuck-will's-widows and Whip-poor-wills.

Around early May look and listen for a few migrant species, like Black-throated Blue and Blackpoll warblers, Scarlet Tanager, and Rose-breasted Grosbeak.

This area can also be fun in winter, from about November to March, although you will want to avoid days with strong southerly winds. Yellow-rumped Warblers may be everywhere. Among the chickadees and kinglets look for a Brown Creeper and a Solitary Vireo. This is the sort of place where you might even find a wintering Black-and-white or Yellow-throated warbler.

From the second parking lot there is a short footpath to the Pamlico River shore. This view of the river is nice, but there are usually few water birds. Until the 1970s large rafts of waterfowl were frequent here; apparently their numbers have diminished because a decline in water quality has caused a drastic decrease in aquatic vegetation in this portion of the river.

Along the trail to the river you will see the beginnings of two hiking trails— the **Goose Creek Trail**, which runs 2.9 miles to the campground, and the **Ragged Point Trail**, which runs one-quarter mile down to the river. The Goose Creek Trail is pretty, with boardwalks across a couple of swamp forest areas, but the birds you are likely to see along it can usually be found from the park's roads. However, you will want to walk the Ragged Point Trail even when birding is slow. The trail becomes a boardwalk across a shrub swamp (which is being invaded by brackish marsh) and ends at an elevated observation deck overlooking the river.

Species along this trail in the breeding season include Green Heron, Prairie Warbler, Common Yellowthroat, and Red-winged Blackbird. In winter the swamp/marsh area has numerous Swamp Sparrows. In this area watch the shrubs for Ruby-crowned Kinglets and an occasional Orange-crowned Warbler. In autumn Virginia Rails are sometimes heard in this area; they may overwinter here, at least during milder years.

This trail could be a very good area to visit after cold fronts in autumn, as migrating passerines work their way along the river shore. This site can be especially good for beginning birders, because migrants here are not way up in the trees but are flitting around in the shrubs at eye level. The boardwalk can be a very good spot to stand quietly and wait for something to move in close. If you stand quietly watching an opening in the marsh, you might see a Sora or Northern Waterthrush walking by.

You will also want to check out the park's campground area. Drive back up the main road, turn left on the road to the campground, and park near the campground's beginning. Here you will see the ends of three trails—Goose

Creek, Iveys Gut, and a trail that leads to the Flatty Creek Trail. You can even put together a good list of birds simply by walking back a little ways along the road you drove in on, walking the road through the campground, or walking the Iveys Gut Trail a few hundred yards.

At all seasons look and listen for Pileated Woodpeckers, White-breasted and Brown-headed nuthatches, and Pine Warblers. Often one or two Hairy Wood-peckers can be found. Like the picnic areas, this is an area where Red-cockaded Woodpeckers were once present but are apparently now extirpated.

You will definitely want to bird this area during the breeding season, about late April to late June. In the campground area listen for Eastern Wood-Pewees, Yellow-throated Vireos, and Summer Tanagers. In the nearby swamps you should find Acadian Flycatchers, Red-eyed Vireos, and Prothonotary and Hooded warblers. Portions of the trail to the Flatty Creek Trail look suitable for Swainson's Warblers.

If you camp out you will have the opportunity to listen for nocturnal species. From mid-April to early July you are very likely to hear Chuck-will's-widows. A few screech-owls may call year-round near the campground, and a Barred or Great Horned owl is also possible.

The **Flatty Creek Trail** (about 0.7 miles long) is similar to the Ragged Point Trail. It becomes a boardwalk that crosses a shrub swamp/brackish marsh, and it ends at an elevated observation deck that overlooks Flatty Creek. Birdlife along this trail is very similar to that along the Ragged Point Trail.

The 2.1-mile **Iveys Gut Trail** might not offer any different species, but you might want to walk it anyway, at least the first half mile or so. There are some very scenic views of Goose Creek here, and you might see Wood Ducks.

For further information: Contact Goose Creek SP, Route 2, Box 372, Washington, NC 27889; phone 919-923-2191.

CHAPTER 6

THE OUTER BANKS

KITTY HAWK–KILL DEVIL HILLS–
NAGS HEAD BEACHES

This almost 20-mile stretch of beaches can be good for ocean birding, at least between late October and March. The period from late October to December, when large numbers of ocean birds are southbound, can be especially fun. Later in winter, from January to March, is more variable, but birding will usually be good somewhere along this stretch.

This area has five ocean fishing piers and several beach access points, so you will be able to check out the ocean at numerous sites. The abundance of sites will be particularly helpful in late winter, when bird activity may be spotty: the more sites you check, the more likely you are to find large numbers of birds and something interesting.

The piers and beach access points are all located along NC 12/US 158 Business, which is informally called "the Beach Road," though the particular street names differ from one community to the next. On the highway you will notice mileposts, numbered from north to south. The Kitty Hawk Fishing Pier is located opposite the intersection of US 158 Bypass and US 158 Business. The other four fishing piers are located at the following milepost locations: Avalon Fishing Pier, milepost 6.2; Nags Head Fishing Pier, milepost 11.6; Jennette's Fishing Pier, milepost 16.5; Outer Banks Fishing Pier, milepost 18.3.

From the ends of these piers you can often get much better looks at birds than you can from shore. Most of the piers are open from about late March to early December, and the Nags Head Fishing Pier is open all year. Unfortunately, none of the piers have rain or wind shelters. The piers all charge a slight fee for nonfishermen; the passes are good for a day.

After a cold front from late October to December, setting up watch on a pier end can be great fun: you can see a good variety of southbound birds, many flying just past the pier end. Early morning has the most birds, but afternoon has the best light. During this time of year what you see from all the piers will be about the same, although numbers of birds are presumably better farther south. The Outer Banks Fishing Pier may be your best bet.

By late October you should see numerous southbound Northern Gannets in addition to the gulls and terns. The scoter migration peaks during late October and early November. On some days there will be long strings of Black and Surf scoters. Afternoons will offer the best light for picking out the white on the heads of drake Surfs. If you're lucky, you might see a few White-winged Scoters as well.

Generally, the most impressive movements of birds will be from about mid-November into December. Gulls and terns will be everywhere, and there will be an endless southbound procession of Red-throated and Common loons, Double-crested Cormorants, scoters, and Red-breasted Mergansers, along with occasional Horned Grebes. Watch carefully for something like an Oldsquaw, eider, or Black-legged Kittiwake. A jaeger may occur anytime in autumn and early winter.

In mid- to late winter you will often see more birds when the weather is calm or when winds are westerly. At this time of year you will want to make several stops in the area to search out the best activity. If you're lucky, you might encounter a lot of activity at the Nags Head Fishing Pier, the only one that stays open all winter.

On a good day you will see waters dotted with Red-throated and Common loons and varying numbers of Horned Grebes. These grebes are typically most common in late winter. Look hard for a Red-necked Grebe as well; they've been seen on a few occasions. At times gannets may be seen feeding just past the surf. Watch for passing flocks of Red-breasted Mergansers and scoters, and maybe an Oldsquaw.

In mid- to late winter, on days with brisk southwest or west winds, make several stops until you find a spot with hundreds of Bonaparte's Gulls. Search through these birds patiently for a possible Little Gull. Throughout the winter, when it is calm or when winds are offshore, you might want to check beside all the piers' pilings for a scoter and maybe an eider or Harlequin Duck.

Some mornings in March and April may have a good variety of northbound birds—loons, Horned Grebes, gannets, mergansers, scoters, and other ducks, in addition to gulls and terns. During such flights the southernmost pier, the Outer Banks Fishing Pier, is probably the best location.

Late spring and summer are typically much less interesting. The Outer Banks Fishing Pier is also best then, because it is closest to Oregon Inlet and the birds that nest there. Watch for Sandwich Terns and other species. This pier is also a little farther east than those to the north, so pelagic species are slightly more

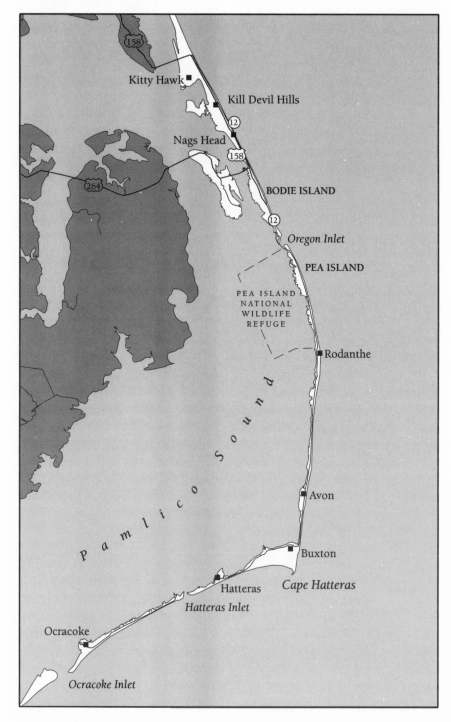

THE OUTER BANKS

likely. In April and May, watch for Pomarine and Parasitic jaegers; in late May, hope for a Sooty Shearwater.

WRIGHT BROTHERS NATIONAL MEMORIAL

With its large expanse of short-grass habitat, this historically significant spot has long been known to birders as a site that regularly attracts scarce open-country species like Buff-breasted and Baird's sandpipers and Lapland Longspurs. However, in recent years this reputation has become less and less deserved: sightings of such species are increasingly infrequent. Each year the site becomes less open as trees next to it grow higher, and it has probably become much less conspicuous to migrants. Also, this site is often almost covered with people, especially during late summer and early autumn, when most "grasspipers" would be expected.

Nevertheless, such open-country species still show up from time to time, so you should watch for them, especially during severe weather. In addition, the autumn migration period is at least mildly interesting overall; species like Lark Sparrow turn up fairly regularly.

Of course, virtually everyone will enjoy a visit here whether they see any birds or not. The talks and exhibits at the visitors center will take you back to the days when the Wright brothers made their short but monumental flights from Big Kill Devil Hill. And the view from the top of the monument is great.

LOGISTICS. This site, which is administered by the National Park Service, is located right next to the US 158 bypass in Kill Devil Hills at milepost 7.7. The site does not officially open until 9 A.M., but visitors frequently walk to the memorial grounds earlier in the morning, parking on nearby roads or at the adjacent airport. (The airport is located off Ocean Bay Boulevard, which intersects the bypass just south of the memorial.) These early morning visits are apparently condoned by the Park Service. During the summer the park charges an admission fee—$4 per car or $2 for walk-ins. Each admission pass is good for seven days.

AS YOU DRIVE into the memorial, you will see the visitors center and parking area on your right, but you can stay on the road that circles the monument. Stretching from the visitors center to the monument is a wide expanse of sandy, frequently mowed short-grass habitat. Most birders' attention focuses on this area. To find any grasspipers, your best bet is to look during really intense northeasters in September and early October. The conditions should involve not only high winds but also rain—a lot of it; apparently there is more food for the birds during wet conditions. This type of weather brings an added reward: the grounds are not covered with people. You will want to get here first thing in the morning.

During such stormy conditions you can hope that the resident Killdeers will be joined by species like American Golden-Plover, Baird's Sandpiper, and Buff-breasted Sandpiper. Golden-Plovers are possible into November. If any of these specialties appear, you can often get really good looks at them from your car. If an Eskimo Curlew is ever seen in North Carolina again, perhaps it will be at this site during such weather conditions. Upland Sandpipers have also been seen here, but since their peak is in August, they are especially unlikely to be found, because the area is so crowded then and stormy weather is unlikely.

During severe autumn northeasters you're actually far more likely to see shorebirds that have been forced off the ocean beaches by the tides and weather—species like Sanderling, Black-bellied Plover, and Red Knot—than grasspipers. Many beginning birders may have no idea what they're looking at when they see winter-plumaged Red Knots in this unlikely habitat. Sanderlings are almost as surprising, especially on the slopes of Monument Hill. If the weather is wet enough to create pools, you may see several gulls; check them for something unusual.

Open-country birds like larks and longspurs are even more unlikely to be seen nowadays, but you might look for them after really strong cold fronts in November and early December. You will occasionally see a few American Pipits then, but you'll have to be very lucky to find any Horned Larks or Lapland Longspurs.

Even if you don't see any of these specialties, this site can be at least mildly entertaining after cold fronts in September and October. You will want to check the shrub thickets on the left as you enter, the taller pines on the west side of the memorial, and all along the margins of the grounds. Along the grounds' margins Palm Warblers are often abundant. In the shrub thickets and along the grounds' margins, check through the Field Sparrows for something unusual. Look for Lark Sparrows, especially in September, and for White-crowned and Clay-colored sparrows in October. In the pines search through flocks of chickadees for migrant passerines. After October cold fronts the pines often host Brown Creepers and Red-breasted Nuthatches.

The spring migration period can also be a better-than-average time to go birding here. The best time is probably from late April to mid-May. Thanks to the combination of habitats, you should be able to find at least a few migrants in addition to permanent resident and summer resident species.

Beginning birders may enjoy a visit here at any season. Permanent residents include catbirds, thrashers, cardinals, and towhees, and always several Field Sparrows. A few bobwhites are still hanging on here, and you might have the opportunity to compare Common and Boat-tailed grackles and the calls of the two crow species.

For further information: Call the visitors center at 919-441-7430, or contact the Wright Brothers National Memorial, c/o Cape Hatteras NS, Route 1, Box 675, Manteo, NC 27954.

Nags Head Woods Ecological Preserve

The Nags Head Woods contrasts greatly with most nearby areas. When you stand in this ancient maritime forest, it is easy to forget that you're just a short distance from the ocean and a major resort area. Although the birding here is rather slow during parts of the year, at times it can be quite good, offering a few species that are scarce or absent at more popular birding areas nearby.

Most birders will probably like this site best during the early part of the nesting season, when singing is at its peak and a few migrants often show up. Breeding species include Northern Parula and Prothonotary Warbler. Actually, the birding here is often better during the fall migration; however, at this season the area's appeal is overshadowed by nearby areas that are much more interesting, like Pea Island NWR and Bodie Island. Some species are easier to find at Nags Head Woods, however, and birders often visit here in the afternoon to pad their lists. In winter the adjacent Fresh Pond often has a few ducks and occasionally offers something unusual.

Even when birding is slow, you'll probably enjoy a visit to this area. This forest is unique both geologically and botanically and harbors several plant species that are rare or near the limits of their ranges. You will immediately notice the area's striking Piedmont-like relief. The vegetation differs from that of maritime forests to the north and south—especially from those farther south, because most of the hardwoods here are deciduous.

Logistics. Most of the Nags Head Woods is being protected as part of the Nags Head Woods Ecological Preserve, lands owned and leased by the Nature Conservancy. Please remember that this land is *not a public park*. The Nature Conservancy has acquired or leased the land in order to protect its unique, fragile plant communities and rare plant species. Nevertheless, the preserve has a couple of nature trails that are open to the public.

These trails are open to the public just a few hours a day on selected days of the week; for exact schedule information call the visitors center at 919-441-2525. The trails are open most of the time for Nature Conservancy members. If you're not a Nature Conservancy member, join now! Anyone interested in birds really should support an organization that has done so much to protect key natural areas.

To get to the ecological preserve, turn west onto Ocean Acres Drive from the US 158 bypass in Kill Devil Hills. On the bypass, at milepost 9.5, look for the sign that says "Nature Conservancy." Continue down Ocean Acres Drive, which becomes unpaved, until you see the visitors center on your left. The nature trails—one a quarter mile long, the other two and a quarter—begin at the center.

Actually, the best way to see birds in this area is from the south part of the **Nags Head Woods Road**. Anything you might see along the trails, you are as likely or more likely to see from this road. If possible, work this road first thing in the morning, then stop at the visitors center later in the day to get interpretive information and, if you like, to walk the trails.

To get to Nags Head Woods Road, continue past the visitors center down Ocean Acres Drive. Where this road ends, turn left, or south, onto Nags Head Woods Road. This stretch dead-ends after about 2 miles. Remember to stay on the road. Some of the adjacent land is part of the ecological preserve; some of it is privately owned. This road is narrow and winding, so park along the straighter stretches and pull over as far as you can.

Along this road you can get a good feel for the varied relief of this area. The forested slopes are reminiscent of the Piedmont. Most of the habitat along the road is an upland pine-hardwood forest; in places, though, you will be looking into the canopy of an adjacent swamp forest. You will want to make several stops all along the road.

Birding along the road is especially nice at sunrise on calm mornings during the early part of the nesting season, from about late April to early June. Among the breeding species that you should find are Yellow-billed Cuckoo, Great Crested Flycatcher, White-eyed and Red-eyed vireos, Northern Parula, and Prothonotary Warbler. Acadian Flycatcher and Summer Tanager are possible. The period from about May 1 to May 15 can be especially nice because a few migrant species will usually be mixed in with the others. Look and listen for Black-throated Blue and Blackpoll warblers, and maybe a Rose-breasted Grosbeak or Scarlet Tanager. You might hear the spiraling song of a Veery in early to mid-May.

In mid- to late summer, the woods are typically hot, dry, and virtually birdless. However, activity picks up again in autumn, and birding can be fun after cold fronts during the peak of the autumn migration, about mid-September to early October. A late afternoon tour here can be a nice complement to a morning at the migrant traps of Pea Island. Look for Red-shouldered Hawks and Pileated Woodpeckers; both species are resident.

Calm mornings in late autumn and winter can be at least mildly entertaining. Yellow-rumped Warblers are common, and you will also see chickadees, Pine Warblers, both kinglets, and maybe an Orange-crowned Warbler.

From about Thanksgiving to March you will also want to check the **Fresh Pond**, on the east side of Nags Head Woods. To get here, return to the 158 bypass and turn right. After going 0.3 miles, turn right on West Eighth Street, which ends at the Kill Devil Hills water treatment plant. Ask for permission to scan the pond from the treatment plant parking lot. There are usually many gulls here and often a few diving ducks. Likely species are Ring-necked Duck, Lesser Scaup, Hooded Merganser, and Ruddy Duck. Common Mergansers have been seen here at least once, and a Bald Eagle overwintered one year.

For further information: Contact Nags Head Woods Ecological Preserve, Visitors Center, 701 West Ocean Acres Drive, Kill Devil Hills, NC 27948; 919-441-2525.

JOCKEY'S RIDGE STATE PARK

This state park consists largely of a massive sand dune ridge—Jockey's Ridge—plus a fringe of shrub-thicket vegetation. Birdwise, the park is largely overshadowed by Bodie Island and Pea Island NWR, super birding areas just down the road; birders virtually never visit this park.

However, the western side of the ridge, beside Roanoke Sound, can be a pretty good hawk-watching spot during the autumn migration. On good days you may see numerous hawks of different species, and many of them pass by almost at eye level. A few hawks may also fly over during the spring migration.

Whether you see any birds or not, you're sure to appreciate the fantastic views from the top of the ridge. Jockey's Ridge is the highest sand dune on the East Coast, about 125 feet high. If you have young children, this is a good place to kill two birds with one stone: you can watch for hawks or just appreciate the scenery while the kids happily exhaust themselves running up and down the dune slopes.

LOGISTICS. The state park lies on the west side of the US 158 bypass at Nags Head. As you drive by, you can't miss seeing the vast dune. The roadway into the park is located just north of the dune at milepost 11.9. The park opens at 8 A.M.; closing time varies seasonally. To get to the west side of the ridge, you will have to walk about one-third mile, one-way. Needless to say, a hike of this distance in deep sand takes a bit of effort, especially given that you'll have to ascend about a hundred feet.

SHRUB THICKETS of live oak and other species grow around the parking area. At all seasons you should see thrashers and towhees here, and in winter Yellow-rumped Warblers are common. After autumn cold fronts, look for a few migrant passerines.

Begin by taking the nature trail from the parking area. Then branch off and continue across the dune crest, heading southwest toward the sound.

After a pretty good cardiovascular workout, you will come to the western slope of the ridge, which presents a great view of the sound. On clear days in autumn, about midmorning, when winds are westerly, this can be a good spot to watch migrating hawks. Most of them pass close by, at or below eye level.

Sometimes these migrating birds follow the sound shoreline; in this case you will want to move down the slope for a better view.

When the migration peaks—about the first week of October—you may see numerous Sharp-shinned Hawks, a few American Kestrels, and one or two Peregrine Falcons, Merlins, and Cooper's Hawks. This is a good spot for a beginning birder to learn the differences between Sharp-shinned and Cooper's hawks and to get familiar with the Cooper's Hawk's long-tailed silhouette. In addition to hawks, you should see other diurnal migrants, like Tree Swallows, Northern Flickers, and Blue Jays.

In springtime, from about late March to mid-May, you might also want to set up watch here about midmorning on clear days with southwest winds. Admittedly, at this season few hawks migrate through the area, but on a good day you might get good looks at a handful of them. A Peregrine Falcon or a Merlin is a possibility. If you're really lucky, you might see a Swallow-tailed or Mississippi kite, although these birds don't usually get this far up the Banks.

During the autumn migration period you will want to check the low shrubs between the slope and the sound shore. A few warblers are possible, and sometimes there's something of interest with the Field Sparrows. Look for a Lark or White-crowned sparrow. These shrubs have produced an entertaining variety of species as late as early December.

Just to the south, during low water levels, you may see a little exposed sandbar; it is most likely to appear during northerly winds. When this sandbar is exposed it often hosts several gulls, terns, and shorebirds. Forster's Terns may occur here at any time. A few Royal Terns are often present, except in midwinter, and Caspians are regular in autumn. In winter look for Sanderlings, Black-bellied Plovers, and Dunlins. Other shorebirds are possible during the migrations.

For further information: Contact Jockey's Ridge SP, P.O. Box 592, Nags Head, NC 27959; phone 919-441-7132.

ROANOKE ISLAND

This island, home of the first English settlement in the New World, has resisted clutter and still retains its charm. Entering the island from the west, on US 64, is especially impressive: after you cross the bridge you see vegetation, not strip development. This is indeed a special place, in a very quiet unassuming sort of way.

Roanoke Island is not a major birding area, but it can supplement or complement the nearby Outer Banks. The woods, lawns, and gardens of the Fort Raleigh National Historic Site (NHS) can provide some very pleasant land birding at any season, especially during the autumn migration and the early part of the breeding season. Brown-headed Nuthatches may be found throughout the year, and Chuck-will's-widows can be found in the nesting season. Although autumn migration is not as impressive here as on the Outer Banks, a few species are often easier to find on Roanoke.

In winter the sound beside the Fort Raleigh NHS is a good area for Common Goldeneyes. The Roanoke Island Marshes, near Wanchese, are quite good for several species of marsh birds, including the Black Rail. This is one of the few areas in the state where the Black Rail can be found reliably in winter. The harbor at nearby Wanchese sometimes has large aggregations of gulls in winter. Lesser Black-backeds are regular, and Iceland, Glaucous, and Common Black-headed gulls have also been found.

THIS TOUR OF Roanoke Island begins at the northwest end of the island, at the US 64 bridge across Croatan Sound. Immediately after you come off the bridge onto the island, you will see a paved side road on your right; this road leads to the sound shore beside the bridge. Most birders would probably want to stop here only during the autumn migration. Drive to the end of the road and walk up the beach to the left. After a hundred yards you will see a small thicket of shrubby live oaks. After cold fronts in September and early October, migrant warblers sometimes collect here, probably hesitant to fly west across the sound until nightfall. Although you should never expect more than a handful of birds, you may find almost as many species as individuals. During the breeding season—at least the early part—you might hear one or two Prothonotary Warblers in the swamp next to the side road.

Just up the highway on the right you will see a welcome center, which has public restrooms and picnic areas. Brown-headed Nuthatches occur here occasionally.

Less than a mile farther down US 64 you will see the entrance to the **Fort Raleigh NHS** on your left. This area has a pretty good variety of land birds throughout the year but is especially worth checking during the breeding season and the autumn migration.

Even when the birding is slow, this area is worth a visit. The first English colony in the New World was established here in the late sixteenth century. As most students of American history know, this ill-fated colony failed: the colonists disappeared and were never heard from again.

The grounds here include a visitors center (open year-round), an exhibit featuring the restored fort, a nature trail, the Elizabethan Gardens, and the Cape Hatteras NS administrative offices, as well as an outdoor theater where "The Lost Colony" is presented during the summer. This area can be great for a group that includes both birders and nonbirders.

The property encompasses a good variety of habitats, including open lawns; wooded areas in which the undergrowth has been cleared or partially cleared; and the maintained Elizabethan Gardens, which have patches of thick vegetation. Uncleared woodlands of pines and hardwoods surround the developed areas. You will want to explore along all the trails. During every season but winter there is a fee for access into the gardens, which most deserve a visit during the migrations.

During the summer tourist season you will want to get here early in the day; you can bird along the main road at dawn. However, late afternoon can be a really pleasant time here in autumn, and the area is usually rather uncrowded on weekdays in spring and autumn. If you plan to walk through the gardens, you will want to get in first thing, right at 9 A.M. (sometimes the gates open a few minutes earlier). In addition to beating the crowds, you will be there right after the sprinklers have been turned off, and the dripping leaves can be very attractive to migrants.

A few of the commonplace species that you can find at Fort Raleigh all year are Red-bellied Woodpecker, Brown Thrasher, and Pine Warbler. If you're in the area at dusk, you might hear a screech-owl. A few Brown-headed Nuthatches often make appearances, and occasionally you might see a Red-shouldered Hawk or Pileated Woodpecker. You may notice the lack of Tufted Titmice; this species is apparently not resident on the island.

Some breeding species that are fairly easy to find are Yellow-billed Cuckoo, Ruby-throated Hummingbird, Great Crested Flycatcher, White-eyed and Red-eyed vireos, and Northern Parula. At dusk you should hear Chuck-will's-widows along the entrance road from about late April to July. Yellow-throated Warblers have been heard here some years; they are most likely in April and May. Around late April and early May you should also find several migrant species. Birders have found Yellow-throated Vireos at this time of year.

This area is best for autumn migrants from September to mid-October, on mornings after cold fronts with northwest winds. Admittedly, during such conditions most avid birders will want to be at the Outer Banks' better migrant traps. Thus, you might want to visit this site on a less-than-prime morning. Or during prime conditions you might want to visit here late in the afternoon after a day on the Banks. You are likely to add to your daily list, because some species—like thrushes—may be easier to find here. Furthermore, birds seen at this site late in the day (and on slower mornings) are typically not restless, so you can study them leisurely—a plus for beginning birders.

During the peak autumn migration you should look for several warblers and for flycatchers, thrushes (Swainson's is most likely, but Veery and Gray-cheeked are possible), Scarlet Tanager, Rose-breasted Grosbeak, and Northern Oriole. There is some dense undergrowth in the woods just west of the gardens. This undergrowth can be good for thrushes. And if you're here in the morning, you definitely will want to go to the Overlook Terrace in the Elizabethan Gardens. A bench on this terrace sits a few feet from a live oak; here you may study warblers at close range, with perfect light.

In winter walk to the back of the **Waterside Theatre**, where you can look over the sound. Your views will be best when the waters are smooth—when winds are calm or from a southerly quadrant. You should see Buffleheads and Red-breasted Mergansers and maybe a few Horned Grebes or a flock of scaup. Look among the net stakes carefully; there is often a Common Goldeneye here.

From Fort Raleigh, return to US 64 and turn left. After 0.4 miles, turn left onto Morrison Grove Road. In winter this is a reliable site for Common Goldeneye—better than the Fort Raleigh area. Drive to the end of the road and park in the first parking lot, which is nearly empty in winter. The sound lies just beyond this lot, and the site is protected from southwest winds. When the waters are smooth, you should be able to find at least one Common Goldeneye (but probably not an adult male) among the net stakes offshore. You should at least see numerous Buffleheads.

Continue east on US 64. After one-half mile you will see Airport Road on your right. This road leads to the **North Carolina Aquarium** and, next door, **Dare County Airport**. This area has little of interest birdwise, but is mentioned in case birders find themselves here as part of a family visit.

In the breeding season a few Northern Rough-winged Swallows nest in the eroding banks just northwest of the aquarium (i.e., to your right as you face the sound). You can also look over the edge of the air field. In mid- to late summer large aggregations of martins and swallows are frequent. In late summer you might check for an Upland Sandpiper. For a better chance of seeing this species, return to US 64, turn right and go 0.3 miles, then turn right onto **Etheridge Road**. From the end of this road there is an unobstructed view of the air field, and if the area has been mowed recently, you have a pretty good chance of seeing Uplands from mid-July through August.

Continue driving east on US 64 through Manteo. Just before the highway reaches an extensive tract of marshes, turn right onto NC 345. At several sites along the highway from here to Wanchese, you may hear Chuck-will's-widows from late April to July.

At 1.2 miles from the US 64/NC 345 intersection, a road that leads to a well site heads off to the left. Here you will see a portion of the **Roanoke Island Marshes**. You can easily find Virginia Rails and Marsh Wrens here throughout the year, although both species are most common from autumn to early spring. You should also hear "Cling Rails," although these birds are usually in the distance, closer to the bay. This area may be an especially appropriate place to use the term "Cling Rail." Some road-kills found on the highway were intermediate between Clapper Rails and King Rails, although typical examples of both species may also be found. Most years a few Seaside Sparrows show up from April to July or August. This is also a very reliable spot for the Black Rail. They call mostly from April into summer, but you might hear them here in winter as well. From autumn to spring look for Sedge Wrens along the upper edge of the marsh.

From this road continue down NC 345 another 1.4 miles. Here, just before a grocery store and other businesses, you will see a road to your left. Park at the gate and walk from there. This road leads to another well site and gives access to another portion of the Roanoke Island Marshes, an area that is more distant from highway noise and somewhat wind-sheltered during west and southwest winds.

This road is presumably public, since it leads to a public well site. Birders have used it for years. However, on a couple of occasions in recent summers, birders coming out of the marsh after dark have been questioned by a deputy sheriff (undoubtedly because the gate is right next to a business where several boats are kept outside). When these birders explained what they were doing, there was no problem, but you may feel more comfortable getting out of the marsh before dark. There's really no reason to stay later, because on average Black Rails actually call less frequently after dark.

The well site is a couple hundred yards from the gate. Just before the site, look on the left for a little path through a thick growth of low shrubs and vines (including much poison ivy). The marsh just beyond the well site is another very reliable site for Black Rails. Again, April into summer is best, and this can be a good place to listen for these birds when the wind is from a westerly direction and not too strong. This can be important in winter, when frequency of Black Rail calling seems to be especially susceptible to wind and microclimate. In winter Black Rails call as readily here as anywhere in the state. This site is very exposed to north and northeast winds, though, and you would probably be wasting your time to listen for these birds during brisk winds from these directions.

The marshes beside the well site are very good for Virginia Rails at all seasons and for Sedge Wrens during the cooler months. In the marshes about a hundred yards to your right, closer to the sound, you can find Marsh Wrens at all seasons. Still closer to the sound, listen for "Cling Rails" at all seasons and for Seaside Sparrows from April to late summer.

Continue south on NC 345 (Mill Landing Road). Near the end of the road you will see the **Wanchese Harbor** on your left. Check here for gulls from about late December into March. Numbers of birds will vary considerably. You will see far more of them when fishing boats are being unloaded. You're also likely to see more birds after long periods of severe cold.

Unfortunately, there are no vantage points for surveying large portions of the harbor. If possible, get down to the docks where you see bird activity, staying away from posted areas. Be careful not to interfere with any work activity.

On most days you can find at least one Lesser Black-backed Gull. During prime conditions in mid- to late winter you definitely have a chance of finding an Iceland or Glaucous gull. Common Black-headed Gulls have been seen here once or twice.

Just past the end of NC 345, turn left onto SR 1141. The marshy little pasture on your right is often worth checking. Don't expect much, but there are often a few shorebirds or a wading bird that you can watch at close range from your car.

For further information: For information about the Fort Raleigh NHS, contact Cape Hatteras NS, Route 1, Box 675, Manteo, NC 27954; phone 919-473-2111.

BODIE ISLAND
MAP 12

Bodie Island—the northern tip of Cape Hatteras NS—and Pea Island NWR, just to the south, together provide a wonderful variety of good birding sites. Many birders would consider it unthinkable to visit one of these areas and not the other; indeed, birders often refer not just to one or the other but to "Bodie–Pea Island," which is also the name of the local Audubon Christmas bird count. Pea Island NWR is generally better for birding than its northern neighbor and usually is better for rarities, but Bodie Island is an excellent complement to the refuge. The extensive flats at Bodie's south end provide habitat that is not available on Pea Island. These flats can be good for intertidal shorebirds, such as Piping Plover. On the drier portions of these flats Lapland Longspurs and Snow Buntings are sometimes seen in late autumn and winter.

Regardless of the area's water levels, the shorebirding will probably be good in at least a few places. The Bodie Island Lighthouse Pond can be very attractive to pool-type shorebirds—species generally found in nontidal habitats—although its water levels are determined largely by wind tides. In contrast with Pea Island NWR, where at most sites you have to scope shorebirds from a distance and where some good sites are completely off-limits, all of Bodie's sites are open to the public. You can wade around anywhere you want, getting up close to shorebirds for good views.

Like Pea Island, Bodie Island can offer excellent ocean birding from autumn to spring. At Coquina Beach you can actually survey the ocean from your car (although this situation may change in the future due to erosion), and several rarities have been spotted here over the years.

Bodie Island has an excellent variety of wading birds in the warmer months; most winters are also good. White Ibises and Black-crowned Night-Herons are always easy to find; Glossy Ibises and Yellow-crowned Night-Herons occur in the warmer months, and a few Glossies overwinter. The Bodie–Pea Island area is the state's most reliable area for American Bitterns. One or two of these bitterns can usually be found from autumn to spring; they are sometimes sighted even in summer. This is also an excellent area for rails—Kings, Clappers, and Virginias occur throughout the year, and Soras are fairly common in migration. Black Rails have been heard sporadically at all seasons, and there have even been a few sightings of Yellow Rails.

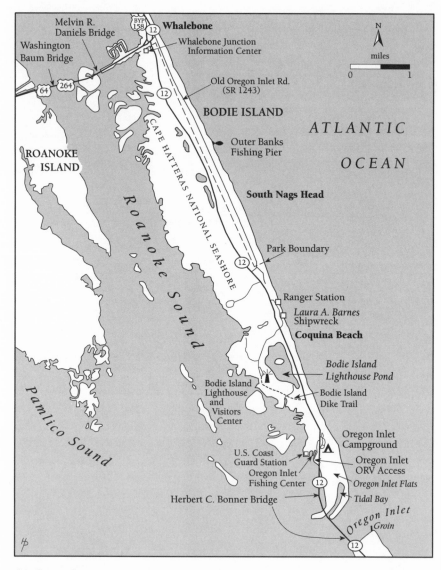

12. BODIE ISLAND

American Black Ducks, Gadwalls, and (on occasion) Blue-winged Teal breed at Bodie Island, and usually there are good numbers of wintering Tundra Swans, Canada and Snow geese, and dabbling ducks. Eurasian Wigeons show up regularly in late autumn and early winter.

During the cooler months this area is rich in raptors. Peregrine Falcons and Merlins are easy to find during the peak of the autumn migration, and usually some individuals stay here throughout the winter. Sightings of Bald Eagles are becoming more frequent, and Rough-legged Hawks have been seen on a few occasions. Traditionally birders have considered this a good spot for Barn and Short-eared owls. Both species have decreased appreciably but are still seen on occasion.

Bodie Island Lighthouse Pond is perhaps the state's best place for Long-billed Dowitchers. Black-necked Stilts breed here, and you can find American Avocets much of the year. Hudsonian Godwits are regular in autumn.

The flats at Oregon Inlet and the island's many ponds and pools allow birders to see most of the state's terns at close range during the warmer months. This is a very good area for Gull-billed Terns. In winter the Oregon Inlet flats can also be good for gulls.

During the autumn migration Bodie Island is typically not quite as exciting as Pea Island for passerines, but some species are seen more easily here. Many birders like to work Pea Island first thing in the morning and then work Bodie Island's pine groves later in the morning or in the afternoon. Although Pea Island is better on average for finding rarities, Bodie Island also hosts rare species each autumn, and a long list of goodies has been compiled here over the years. Some land birds found here during the fall migration period include Northern Saw-whet Owl, Olive-sided Flycatcher, Connecticut and Mourning warblers, Lark Bunting, and Le Conte's Sparrow.

Some species that breed on Bodie Island do not occur on Pea Island—for example, Yellow-breasted Chat and Field Sparrow—and Blue Grosbeaks are easier to find on Bodie. In late spring and early summer you can often find Chuck-will's-widows near the Bodie Island Lighthouse.

In short, the birding at Bodie Island is generally very good to excellent at all seasons. During really cold years the variety may decrease in midwinter, and many of the waterfowl may move out. However, such conditions may also result in the presence of some exciting rarities, like white-winged gulls. Once even a Snowy Owl was seen here.

By the way, the name of this "island" is pronounced "BAHD i." Like Pea Island, this area has a name that no longer applies to a geographic entity: Bodie Island's northern limit was once defined by an inlet in the present-day Kitty Hawk area, but that inlet filled in long ago. Today the name refers to the barrier strand between Whalebone Junction (the intersection just north of the National Seashore entrance) and Oregon Inlet. "North Bodie," a vague term used only by birders, refers to the northernmost 2 or 3 miles of Bodie Island.

Several hunting clubs made up of wealthy northern sportsmen were located here in the early part of the century. Much of the area's current waterfowl habitat is not natural. The hunt clubs impounded portions of the natural marshes and ponds, manipulating water levels in order to increase production of certain plant species. Shrubs are growing up in many of these areas, but the Park Service has begun some fire management to reverse this trend. Many of the pine groves here are also "unnatural"; they were planted at various times earlier in the century, and many of them are nonnative slash pines.

LOGISTICS. Be prepared for mosquitoes—they are usually terrible in this area, and typically they remain bad into November (until Christmastime if the weather is warm). Also, be prepared to wade if you want to cover this area thoroughly, although in most places the water will be only an inch or two deep. In many areas the mud is sticky enough that you may want to wade in old tennis shoes rather than boots, at least during the warmer months.

When birding along NC 12, it is easy to get distracted by the birds and forget that you're on a major highway. Cars frequently zip along here at sixty-five miles an hour and faster; be very careful when pulling on or off the highway. There are few paved pulloffs. If you're parking on the road shoulder, pull off as far as possible. (Most shoulders here are grass-covered and fine for parking.)

At North Bodie the Park Service allows waterfowl hunting from certain designated blinds. You will see signs along NC 12 identifying the paths to these blinds. You may want to avoid these areas during the waterfowl season. Hunting is not allowed on Sundays, and the waterfowl season gets shorter each year; call the Park Service at 919-473-2111 for more information.

THIS TOUR STARTS at the **Whalebone Junction Information Center** on NC 12, just south of the entrance to the Cape Hatteras NS. From around late April to July you may want to cross the road and explore the shrub thickets and pine groves. Breeding species here include Great Crested Flycatcher, Prairie Warbler, Yellow-breasted Chat, Indigo Bunting, and Field Sparrow. Listen for a Blue Grosbeak; if you find one, don't be surprised if it's a one-year-old male. Many of the less common land birds sighted during breeding season on the Outer Banks are first-year birds.

From the parking lot, head south on NC 12. Set your odometer to zero at the stop sign at the information center exit.

At first wet shrub thickets will line the road. At 0.9 miles, on the right, the habitat becomes more open and marshy; in the breeding season listen here for Common Yellowthroats and Red-winged Blackbirds. Common species in the cooler months include Sedge Wren, Common Yellowthroat, and Swamp Sparrow.

In places where the vegetation on the right is low enough for good visibility, watch for raptors during the cooler months. Northern Harriers and Red-tailed Hawks are frequent, and sightings of Bald Eagles are becoming less remarkable. Especially from around mid-November into December, keep your eyes peeled for a Rough-legged Hawk.

Along North Bodie, during the cooler months—from about November to March—it can be pleasant (although not always productive) to watch the western horizon on clear evenings after sunset. Try any sites from 0.9 miles to 1.4

miles with unobstructed views toward the west. As it gets darker, use your binoculars to search the skies for the silhouette of a Short-eared or Barn owl. Both species are decreasing here but are still seen occasionally. You should at least see the silhouettes of and hear Black-crowned Night-Herons and American Woodcocks. You might also hear a Great Horned Owl. (These owls were formerly quite scarce here; their increase may be one reason behind the decrease of the Short-eareds and Barns.)

At 1.6 miles you will see a sign on the right that says "Blinds 1, 2, 3, 4." Here there is a short footpath (usually wet) through the shrub vegetation. Beyond this path are extensive marshes, ponds to the left and right, and some shallow pools straight ahead. During the shorebird migrations this spot is worth checking, because the ponds can be productive during dry conditions, and the pools can be good when water levels are high. Virginia and King rails can be heard here year-round. Black Rails have been heard here a few times; even in January they have responded to tape-recorded calls.

At 2.6 miles is another wet footpath on the right, to hunting blinds 5 through 7. After a few feet along this path you will see large ponds to your right and left that can have a fair variety of waterfowl in the cooler months. If you see several American Wigeons, check for a possible Eurasian. These marshes are also good for rails. In the cooler months listen for Sedge Wrens and Swamp Sparrows.

During calm conditions in the cooler months, a sunset walk across the marshes toward the sound (a quarter mile or so) can be fun. The Sedge Wrens will be vocal then; if you go far enough, you should also hear Marsh Wrens. Around dusk watch for Barn and Short-eared owls. (If you stay out late and get off the path, be sure to note landmarks—such as the grove of pines—so that you can be sure to find your way out.)

At 2.9 miles there is an observation deck overlooking one of the ponds. At any season, but especially from autumn to spring, search the margins of this pond for an American Bittern.

At 3.3 miles you will have a good unobstructed view toward the west; this is a good spot to watch for owls after sunset. On the right at 3.5 miles there is another short footpath to some shallow pools that can be good for shorebirds.

At 4.2 miles there is another observation deck that overlooks an extensive pond. During the cooler months this pond can have good numbers of waterfowl and/or gulls. Lesser Black-backed Gulls have occurred here, and this is the sort of spot where a Franklin's Gull might be found in autumn. In summer, during dry weather and falling water levels, this pond can have many diverse wading birds—one year a Wood Stork visited for several days. During such conditions look for a good variety of terns. This pond can be excellent for shorebirds during the migrations. Sometimes in late summer and early autumn this pond dries up completely; at such times you may see American Golden-Plover and Buff-breasted and Baird's sandpipers.

At 4.4 miles, turn left onto Old Oregon Inlet Road and then right onto the road that runs through the **Park Service maintenance area**. The power lines here should be checked for Western Kingbirds in autumn. In winter White-crowned and even Clay-colored sparrows have been found in the shrub thickets in this area.

Return to NC 12, reset your odometer to zero, and turn left. At 1.2 miles you will see the road to Coquina Beach on your left and the road to the Bodie Island Lighthouse on your right. During the cooler months **Coquina Beach** is a very popular spot for ocean birding. Currently you can see the ocean from your car, so it's a good spot on a rainy day; if the weather is rough, though, you won't be able to see much, because you're right at sea level. There's no assurance that this convenient spot will be available in the future; erosion has destroyed many of the structures here, and the parking lot may not last much longer.

In any case, the birding here should remain good. In late October and early November look for frequent long strings of scoters. On many days in November and December vast numbers of loons, grebes, gannets, ducks, and gulls will be heading south. On many winter days you will be able to get good looks at loons and Horned Grebes on the water, and Northern Gannets frequently plunge just offshore. Numerous sightings of uncommon to rare species have been recorded here. Jaegers are most likely during stormy weather in autumn but might occur at almost any time of year. Red-necked Grebes have been spotted a few times in winter; even Manx Shearwaters have been spotted from shore here.

The pine groves and shrub thickets along the mile-long road into the **Bodie Island Lighthouse** can be good in the breeding season, during the autumn migration, and in winter. Because this site contains the biggest "island" of woody vegetation in the Bodie Island–Pea Island area, it also has the best variety of breeding land birds. Try to be here at dawn when winds are light. The best period is from late April to late June. In addition to the main roadway, check the gated roadway on the right (you'll see an Authorized Vehicles Only sign, but pedestrian access is permitted) and the grounds around the lighthouse. Gray Catbirds, Prairie Warblers, Common Yellowthroats, and Rufous-sided Towhees are common. Other species you should find include Yellow-billed Cuckoo, Eastern Wood-Pewee, Great Crested Flycatcher, Eastern Kingbird, White-eyed Vireo, Pine Warbler, Yellow-breasted Chat, and Indigo Bunting. A few Northern Bobwhites seem to be hanging on here, and you might find one or two Blue Grosbeaks (one-year-old males are most likely). This area has chickadees, but there are no titmice or Brown-headed Nuthatches. If you drive along this road at dusk, you may hear Chuck-will's-widows—they are present here at least some years.

After fall cold fronts the pine groves here can complement Pea Island nicely. Pea Island is typically more exciting—the birds there are funneled into a few patches of shrubs and rarities are easier to find—but most of the birds there typically will have moved on by midmorning. At Bodie Island migrants are a bit more likely to linger, so you might want to bird this area later in the day, perhaps about sunset. After fronts in September and early October look for Veeries and for Gray-cheeked and Swainson's thrushes. Bodie Island's pines seem to be especially attractive to migrant woodpeckers. Pileated Woodpeckers don't get out here very often, but those that do may linger for several days or even weeks. After October cold fronts Golden-crowned Kinglets are often common, and one or two Brown Creepers and Red-breasted Nuthatches often show up.

This area can often be fairly entertaining in winter; a calm morning is best then (although this area has precious few of those). Yellow-rumped Warblers are everywhere, and along with the chickadees you may find Yellow-bellied Sapsucker, Downy Woodpecker, Brown Creeper, Hermit Thrush, and both kinglets. If you walk the road at dusk, you might see one or more American Woodcocks. If you drive the road after dark, watch for the eyes of an owl—a Saw-whet would be possible. Strangely, a Chuck-will's-widow was once found here on the Christmas Bird Count. At night you'll at least see a few mammals; gray foxes are surprisingly common.

Behind the lighthouse is the **Bodie Island Lighthouse Pond**, which is typically the most exciting birding spot on Bodie Island. Hunting is off-limits here, so waterfowl are never chased away from this spot as they are at North Bodie. From the parking lot, walk east, past the visitors center and lighthouse. At the far end of the grounds you will see a trail to the left. Here two observation decks overlook the pond. The first deck you come to is eight feet high and offers an unobstructed view of most of the pond. The second deck is right at the edge of the pond but is lower. You will probably want to check out the view from both sites. Most of the water birds here are typically rather distant; you will need a scope. The lighting is terrible early in the morning—you look directly into the sun then—but it is passable by midday and gradually improves during the afternoon. This is a great place to be at sunset, especially when it is nearly calm. If you stand long enough and quietly enough at the pondside deck, a rail may walk right in front of you.

American Black Ducks and Gadwalls breed around the edges of the pond, and during the cooler months there is almost always an excellent variety of puddle ducks. Beginning birders are usually surprised to find that most species of non-breeding puddle ducks will have arrived by early or mid-September. Around Thanksgiving look for Eurasian Wigeons. Fulvous Whistling-Ducks have also shown up here a few times.

During the warmer months this site is excellent for wading birds, in terms of both numbers and variety. Winter has far fewer birds, but you can often find almost as many species. White Ibises are almost always present. A few Glossies are usually around from spring into autumn; one or two may be seen even in midwinter. At dusk you can usually see Black-crowned Night-Herons at any season. Look for one or two Yellow-crowned Night-Herons from about May 1 until mid-October; they are most likely to occur in late summer. From autumn to spring watch for an American Bittern skulking along the marsh edges.

Water levels at this pond are typically a bit high, but suitable for the longer-legged shorebirds. This is probably the state's most reliable spot for Long-billed Dowitchers. Look (and listen) for them from early August to early May. (Short-billed Dowitchers also occur, often outnumbering the Long-billeds during the migration periods. From around November through March most dowitchers seen here are Long-billeds.) Look for several Black-necked Stilts during the breeding season. A few American Avocets may be seen year-round but are most likely in autumn. This is also one of the state's best sites for Hudsonian Godwit; look for one or two especially in September and October.

This site can be an excellent place to find pool-type shorebirds and, possibly, rare shorebirds, but often the water is too high to attract most shorebirds. In contrast with most ponds at Bodie Island (and the impoundments at Pea Island), water levels here are primarily determined not by rainfall but by tidal conditions in the sound (to which the pond is connected by a canal). During southwest winds the lighthouse pond is typically high. But after a few days of northeast winds, especially during dry weather, the pond may be at its best for shorebirds. Birders who like to see their shorebirds up close will be delighted to know that there are no restrictions on wading out into the pond. However, if you come near any Black-necked Stilts or ducks that are obviously nesting, stay away. (In general it is best to stay out in the more open areas.) The bottom of the pond is quite sticky. Boots can be quite tiring; during the warmer months you will probably prefer to wear old tennis shoes and get your feet wet.

When water levels are low during the migration periods, this pond can be very good for species like White-rumped, Pectoral, and Stilt sandpipers. Other uncommon to rare species that can occur during good conditions are Curlew Sandpiper, Ruff, and Wilson's and Red-necked phalaropes. This pond boasts one of North Carolina's most exciting shorebird records: one year birders on the local Christmas Bird Count found a Black-tailed Godwit.

If water levels are low enough, in late summer the pond can attract a good variety of terns, including Gull-billed, Black, and Caspian. One year a White-winged Tern is bound to show up here. In autumn this would be a good spot to look for a Franklin's Gull with the Laughings.

You can get really good looks at rails here. Low water levels are best, because the birds are more likely to come to the marsh edges then. Again, your best bet is to stand here quietly at sunset. King, Clapper, and Virginia rails may be seen year-round. The Virginias are seen most frequently from autumn to spring, although adults followed by strings of chicks have even paraded past the observation deck in summer. You may see "good Kings," "good Clappers," or perhaps birds that look a bit intermediate. Soras are most likely to show up during the

migrations. If you are really lucky, you might spot a Black or Yellow rail, particularly in autumn.

During the cooler months the marshes beside the boardwalk to the more
distant observation deck always host numerous Sedge Wrens and Swamp Sparrows. The observation decks can be pretty good hawk-watching platforms during the autumn migration, although the light is poor during midmorning, when
most hawks are moving. It seems that many of the hawks moving through this
area can't resist altering their route a little in order to check out the pond's
birdlife, so you might have a Peregrine, Merlin, or Cooper's Hawk fly right past
you.

The road to the lighthouse makes a loop in front of the visitors center. At the
far end of this loop a short gated roadway leads to the floodgate for the pond.
When water levels are changing, wading birds attracted to this site can be
absurdly tame. Black-crowned Night-Herons are frequent here at dusk. The
road continues a short distance past the floodgate to the sound. On the left at
the floodgate you will see the beginning of the **Bodie Island Dike Trail**, which
runs almost a mile to NC 12 and follows the dike built by a gun club in the early
1900s. This trail is worth hiking primarily during the autumn migration. (Don't
forget the insect repellent!) At this season you will want to walk at least to the
pine grove; this grove is a good magnet for passerines after autumn cold fronts,
because it is the first tree-covered area that migrants flying north along the
Outer Banks come to. The tidal creek about halfway down the trail (at trail stop
number 7) may harbor wading birds, including Black-crowned Night-Herons,
during cold windy days in autumn and winter. Close to NC 12, woody vegetation along the trail is limited to low shrubs along the dike. This could be a good
area during the autumn migration. From this point you will probably want to
retrace your steps, but you can also return to the lighthouse by following the
power line north and then walking the paved lighthouse road (a hike of 2.5
miles). During the autumn migration the strips of shrub vegetation bordering
the power line are probably very good.

Return to NC 12, reset your odometer to zero, and turn right. After 2.1 miles
you will see the Oregon Inlet Campground on your left. This site used to be
worth checking for longspurs, but now you are more likely to see these birds on
the extensive sandy flats created by the southward migration of the inlet. Just
past the campground, turn right onto the entrance road to the **Oregon Inlet
Fishing Center**. On the small lawn here, look for a flock of Brown-headed
Cowbirds in autumn and winter; if you see these birds in autumn, sort through
them for a possible Yellow-headed Blackbird. Shiny Cowbirds may show up
here in the future. After making the right turn, then turn left. The marina will be
on your right as you continue through this parking lot. (At dusk you may see
Black-crowned Night-Herons on the marina's pilings.) At the end of the parking
lot you will see an eleven-ton propeller on your left.

Just a few feet away there is often a little mud flat with a nice variety of shorebirds and terns; this can be a good spot to check on a rainy or stormy day. However, the water level has to be just right—if it's too high, the flat may be submerged, and if it's too low, the birds may scatter out to the flats in the inlet. Perhaps the best times to come here are during either a low lunar tide when the wind is southwest or a high lunar tide when winds are light or northerly. The lunar tide here lags about two hours after that on the oceanfront.

When conditions are right, look for a good variety of terns during the warmer months. Oystercatchers occur here year-round. During the migrations, and to lesser extent in winter, look for shorebirds like Semipalmated and Piping plovers, Marbled Godwits, Dunlins, and Short-billed Dowitchers. This isn't the best habitat for rare shorebirds; nevertheless, one May a Curlew Sandpiper in breeding plumage showed up right here, just a few feet from the parking lot.

In winter, on the open water to the right, check for a few ducks, especially Red-breasted and Hooded mergansers and Buffleheads. If you're lucky, you might spot an Oldsquaw or a Common Goldeneye. In late summer scope the more distant flats for a possible Reddish Egret.

You may want to wade through the water and kick through these marshes. Clapper Rails live here all year, and Marsh Wrens and Seaside and Sharp-tailed sparrows can be found from autumn to winter, although the Seaside Sparrows decrease in midwinter. (A few Seasides breed in the more distant portion of the marshes, closer to the inlet.) Concentrate on areas along the shore where the grasses are slightly taller and thicker, and on little grassy peninsulas where you are more likely to flush rails.

In the breeding season check for Cliff Swallows nesting with the Barns under the bridge, although none have been found in recent years. In autumn and winter check the bridge supports for a Peregrine Falcon.

Toward your left, under the bridge, the open flats narrow into a couple of tidal guts. During the cooler months an American Bittern can sometimes be found along these guts.

Opposite the parking lot is the four-wheel-drive access from NC 12 to the **Oregon Inlet flats**. (Don't even think about trying to drive out here in a two-wheel-drive car.) Each year this site becomes more inaccessible to pedestrians. It is now almost 2 miles from the highway to the inlet, and it gets farther every year as the inlet migrates south. If you don't have a four-wheel-drive vehicle, you may still want to walk to the head of the large tidal bay, about a mile from the highway.

The first one-quarter mile of the four-wheel-drive trail runs through the dunes. Open flats lie beyond the dunes, both straight ahead and to the right, and to the left (north) you will see a more narrow strip of flats. In late autumn and winter you may want to start out toward the north. In the widely spaced, sparsely vegetated low dunes between the open flats and higher dunes, Lapland

Longspurs and Snow Buntings are occasional. Horned Larks have also been seen a few times. However, sightings may decline here and become more frequent farther south as the inlet and habitats shift southward.

A hike southward, toward the inlet, is most worthwhile during the migration periods, when there are likely to be several shorebirds. The fewer vehicles the better—weekends can be really crowded. Higher water levels are best. During strong southwest winds, especially during a high lunar tide in the sound, there are likely to be more gulls, terns, and shorebirds, because the high water forces them off the shoals inside the inlet. The lunar tide in the sound lags about two hours after that on the oceanfront.

This particular area's geography has changed drastically in recent years, and it continues to change. Take this into account when reading the following description; what you see may not be the same as what you read about! However, birding should remain good at least for the next several years, and it could even improve.

For example, the tidal bay was formed in 1987 when the inlet shifted markedly southward (and began threatening the south end of the bridge). During its first winter the bay harbored several Common and King eiders. Recently the ducks here have been more mundane—usually Red-breasted and Hooded mergansers and Buffleheads—although occasionally an Oldsquaw or scoter makes an appearance. Accretion is about to close this bay's connection with the inlet; in the future the bay may become a nontidal pond, attractive to a different assortment of interesting species.

Look around the bay's edges during the migrations for a good variety of intertidal shorebirds—species like Semipalmated and Piping plovers, Red Knot, Western Sandpiper, Dunlin, and Short-billed Dowitcher. Winter offers fewer birds, but you may be able to find most of these species.

During the warmer months you can often see a good variety of terns along this bay. Look for Sandwich Terns from about early April to early November. If you're here (with a four-wheel-drive vehicle) during a strong northeaster in August or September, drive slowly through the area and carefully sort through the Common Terns for a possible Roseate. (An Arctic might also be a possibility, but you should get a photograph of one before you report it.) During stormy weather in winter there may also be large aggregations of gulls. Lesser Black-backeds can often be found, and Iceland and Glaucous gulls are possible.

The sand spit east and south of the bay is now becoming more extensive, and a few low dunes are developing. Snow Buntings have been seen here recently, and in the future this may become the best area for buntings and longspurs.

If you have a four-wheel-drive vehicle, you might also want to check out the spit (beach and dune line) on the west side of the bay. (This spit roughly follows the inlet shoreline of the 1970s.) A few Seaside Sparrows breed in the extensive salt marshes on the spit's west side. During extremely high tides in autumn (a high lunar tide plus strong southwest winds), the sand beach and marsh border could be a good area for rails. In such conditions you might even flush a Yellow Rail.

For further information: Contact Cape Hatteras NS, Route 1, Box 675, Manteo, NC 27954; phone 919-473-2111. The nearest visitors center is at the Bodie Island Lighthouse; it is usually open only during the peak tourist months.

Pea Island National Wildlife Refuge
MAP 13

Most birders can fondly recall the time and place when they first caught the birding bug, and perhaps another time or two when the bug really flared up and they became irreversibly hooked. For many North Carolina birders, and several from nearby states as well, such memories often involve autumn trips to Bodie Island and Pea Island NWR. If you are susceptible to the birding bug, it'll definitely hit you on a trip to this area during the peak autumn migration, when migrant passerines fill the bushes, Peregrines zip by, and most of the shorebirds known to occur in North Carolina can be seen in a single day.

When casual birders think of Pea Island they think of waterfowl, and indeed

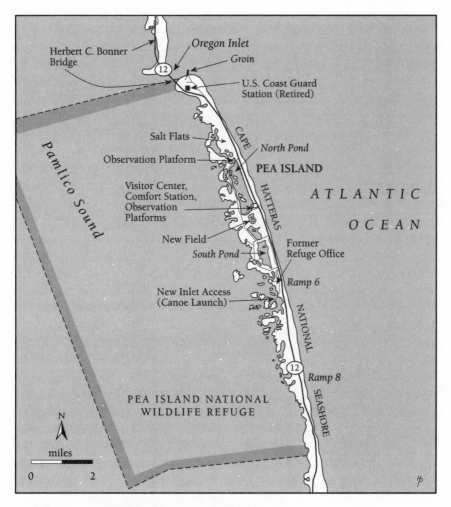

Herbert C. Bonner
Bridge

Oregon Inlet

Groin

12

U.S. Coast Guard
Station (Retired)

Pamlico Sound

Salt Flats

Observation Platform

CAPE

North Pond

PEA ISLAND

Visitor Center,
Comfort Station,
Observation
Platforms

HATTERAS

A T L A N T I C

O C E A N

New Field

South Pond

Former
Refuge Office

Ramp 6

New Inlet Access
(Canoe Launch)

NATIONAL

12

Ramp 8

PEA ISLAND NATIONAL
WILDLIFE REFUGE

SEASHORE

N

miles

0   2

13. PEA ISLAND NATIONAL WILDLIFE REFUGE

there are large numbers of these birds, and an excellent variety, from autumn into at least the early part of the winter. Beginning birders will appreciate how close you can get to a lot of the waterfowl. Ducks frequently swim right next to the highway in the northeast corner of North Pond, and geese often feed next to the highway at New Field and elsewhere.

Thanks to the large numbers of birds, sightings of rarities are the rule here rather than the exception. In late autumn, when the population of American Wigeons peaks, one or more Eurasian Wigeons can usually be found. Similarly, (Eurasian) Green-winged Teal are sighted a couple of times a winter, and there would undoubtedly be more records for these birds if they were considered a different species from our Green-winged Teal. Two especially noteworthy species are Ross' and Greater White-fronted geese. This is virtually the only location in the state where the Ross' Goose has been found, yet in recent years one has been seen almost annually. White-fronted Geese are rarer, seen at intervals of a few years. When these geese make appearances, birders are often able to see them very closely, because they frequently feed next to the highway at New Field.

To the most avid birders, Pea Island is perhaps most noteworthy for its migration of land birds in autumn. Many casual birders might find this fact strange, given the refuge's scarcity of woody vegetation. But the very facts that vegetation is scarce and that water surrounds most of the area combine to make the area a birder's paradise after autumn cold fronts. Especially at the north end of the island and along the dikes at North Pond, the shrubs may swarm with warblers and other species. Some generally rare species, such as Lark and Clay-colored sparrows, Western Kingbird, and Dickcissel, are found here quite regularly. Some of the rarest migrants that have been seen include White-winged Dove, Vermilion and Scissor-tailed flycatchers, Tropical/Couch's Kingbird, Sprague's Pipit, and Townsend's Warbler.

Pea Island NWR is still the best area in North Carolina for shorebirds, despite the fact that South Pond and New Field are now off-limits to birders throughout the year in order to prevent disturbance to waterfowl. (In fact, New Field is often the state's best single site for shorebirds.) Nevertheless, an impressive variety of species can still be found in the refuge during the autumn migration period. One very positive feature of the refuge and neighboring Bodie Island is that no matter how wet or dry the weather is, some place in the area will still be good for shorebirds. Two shorebirds that many birders associate with Pea Island are the Black-necked Stilt and the American Avocet. The stilt is a common breeder, and at least a few avocets can be found most of the year. The refuge even attracts those shorebird species that are rarely found on intertidal flats in the state—species like American Golden-Plover, Hudsonian Godwit, Baird's Sandpiper, and Buff-breasted Sandpiper.

Even if this area were not attractive to any of the above birds, it would still attract birders, because ocean birding can be quite productive from autumn to early spring. Pomarine and Parasitic jaegers are seen quite regularly here. Occasionally a very well-defined tide line forms just off the beaches; such tide lines can attract rarer species. A recently constructed groin now attracts Purple Sandpipers; if there is some erosion, this site will develop the potential to attract many sea ducks.

In autumn the hawk migration can keep many birders occupied for hours. During the migration's peak you may get to see several Peregrines go by in a morning. Even in winter birders can almost always find one or two Peregrines and Merlins.

Beginning birders may not need to find any of the above specialties to be content. They will probably be delighted by the variety and approachability of many of the more commonplace species. The refuge has an excellent variety of wading birds; it is a good area for Glossy and White ibises and both night-herons, and American Bitterns are seen as frequently here as anywhere in the state. This is also a good place to study several species of terns, including Gull-billed, at close range.

LOGISTICS. Administered by the Fish and Wildlife Service, Pea Island NWR consists primarily of impoundments, marshes, dunes, and the adjacent waters of Pamlico Sound. The refuge office is actually located at Manteo. (The former refuge office, located south of the South Pond impoundment, is still used as an office, but it is usually not staffed.) The visitors center and a comfort station are located at the southeast corner of North Pond; the restrooms here are open throughout the year. At the visitors center you will find a clipboard where rarities are logged in.

Mosquitoes can be terrible along the dikes of the impoundments from May through November, sometimes later. Although birding from the highway shoulder can allow great views of waterfowl, it definitely presents a risk. Be very careful when pulling on and off the highway, and pull off the highway as far as possible. Don't forget that the highway here has a speed limit of fifty-five miles an hour and that people frequently drive sixty-five (and faster).

Please remember that South Pond and New Field are off-limits to general birding. However, when a refuge volunteer is available to escort them in, groups may be allowed along the dike of South Pond. Call the refuge office (919-473-1131) for more information.

Some visitors may wonder why this area, which appears to be part of Hatteras Island, is named as if it were separate. The reason is that Pea and Hatteras were once different islands, separated by the New Inlet. The inlet filled in earlier this century, but the name Pea Island has persisted.

This rich area has generally excellent birding almost all year, but birding can sometimes be slow. Typically, numbers of waterfowl peak in late autumn and gradually decline during the winter. Sometimes mid- and late winter can be rather dull. The worst conditions follow severe extended cold, when most waterfowl pull out of the impoundments and move elsewhere. Even during this worst-case scenario, though, you're still likely to find something exciting. Mid-June is also relatively slow, with the birdlife mostly limited to summer resident species. However, the area has enough of these to keep most birders happily entertained.

THIS TOUR OF the refuge begins at the south end of the **Oregon Inlet bridge**. Just past the bridge, pull into the parking area on the road's east side. From about November to April you will want to walk back over to the bridge. On the bases of the first couple of supports you may see Purple Sandpipers. However, they often stay out of sight behind the supports, and you can wait several minutes before they put in an appearance. Harlequin Ducks have also been seen swimming next to the supports, but they are unlikely to appear when people are fishing from the bridge above. The bay here deserves close attention during severe northeasters. Look for scoters, an Oldsquaw, or something more unusual. Even a Razorbill has been spotted.

Cross the highway and go out to the end of the fishermen's walkway. Out in the sound, toward the northwest, you will see some range markers. These markers are often topped with one or two Great Cormorants from October to April.

After autumn cold fronts you may see several migrants in the shrubs around the parking lot, but for the best birding you will want to go out on the little spit of land across the bay. This spit projects farther north. However, if further erosion causes the parking lot to become the most northerly point, then in the future it will probably be the best site for pile-ups.

Just south on NC 12 you will see a road to the left that leads back up to the north tip of the island. Drive as far as you can, then walk past the **old coast guard station**. At the very end is a groin that was constructed in 1989. The groin is likely to be covered both with No Trespassing signs and with fishermen. Each winter the groin has a few Purple Sandpipers, and sometimes a Great Cor-·morant shows up. Initially it attracted a few sea ducks, but recent accretion has resulted in shoaling almost to the end of the groin, so these species do not often appear anymore. However, this is the only groin for miles, so if erosion resumes, this site will certainly start to attract sea ducks again. Eiders could become regular here, and something more unusual—like a Razorbill—would be possible, especially during severe weather.

Northern Section of Pea Island

The area north of the old coast guard station is hallowed ground to birders, offering some of the state's most exciting birding for land bird migrants. Some birders will probably wonder why it is the south side of the inlet, not the north, that attracts birds during the autumn migration. The reason is essentially that most land birds are nocturnal migrants. During northwest winds associated with cold fronts, many of these night-flying birds are swept southeast of where they want to be. When morning comes, these birds return northwestward, attempting to get back on track. However, if land is in the vicinity when day comes, the birds head toward it, and if it runs in the general direction they wish to go, they follow it. So on the morning following a cold front, there may be thousands of small land birds winging their way north along this portion of the Outer Banks. When they get to the inlet, many birds are obviously hesitant about crossing all that water (especially with a headwind), so they pile up just before the inlet, here on the south side. Birds may also be hesitant about crossing other open types of habitats, and smaller pile-ups occur on the impoundment dikes just south of here.

This area is constantly changing due to erosion; however, the important thing is to locate the last patch of shrubs the birds come to before they confront the inlet. Just watch the birds and go where they go. Sometimes you may be able to identify a patch of shrubs, maybe even a particular shrub, where many birds perch for varying lengths of time before taking off across the inlet. If so, stand back far enough from the site that birds will land there, but close enough that you can get good looks. Although you will want to focus your activity on the best pile-up point, you will also want to move around some. Carefully check the coast guard station lawn, especially its borders, and the wires around the station.

Typically the best pile-ups occur following a cold front, on the morning after a clear night with brisk northwest winds. West and north winds can also be good. (If these conditions follow a hurricane or tropical storm, the numbers of birds can be phenomenal.) Very modest pile-ups may be seen during winds from other directions.

Flights here, although impressive, are generally less exciting than those at prime spots in the mid-Atlantic states and the Northeast, partly because prime weather conditions here are infrequent until after the migration peak for many species, including warblers. Nevertheless, this area has certainly seen its share of rarities.

"Autumn" migration may be discerned here from at least late July through December. In the early part of the migration period—through August—you will usually see no more than a handful of migrants, and on some mornings there will be none. Some frequent species during this period are Eastern Kingbird, Yellow Warbler, Northern Waterthrush, and American Redstart. Despite the general scarcity of birds then, a rarity is possible. An Olive-sided Flycatcher was seen here one August. At this time of year, when cold fronts are feeble and infrequent, the best potential for a good flight is after the passage of a hurricane or tropical storm (either through the area or just offshore). Frequently, just after tropical systems have passed, birders head to the coast and spend their time looking for pelagic birds. But if the area never experienced any strong onshore winds and in fact has had offshore winds for at least several hours, searching for land bird migrants would be more rewarding.

You are indeed lucky if you happen to be here during prime conditions in late September and early October. (Mid-September is potentially just as good, but the few fronts that pass through this early are almost always followed by unfavorable northeast winds.) This is the peak time for warblers, and you can compile a long list. On ideal pile-up days you should see one or two of the less common species, like Wilson's and Nashville.

During the middle of October, fronts with favorable winds become more likely, but the diversity of birds (especially warblers) drops off. Sparrows are more common then; watch for Clay-colored, Lincoln's, and White-crowned. This period is the peak time for sightings of Western Kingbird and Dickcissel. Birdlife also begins to take on a more wintertime flavor. Yellow-rumped Warblers begin to dominate the flights, and you are more likely to see species like Brown Creeper, Winter Wren, Golden-crowned Kinglet, Hermit Thrush, Dark-eyed Junco and, if it's a finch winter, Red-breasted Nuthatch.

In late October and November diversity drops off even more, although flights can still be impressive. Wintering species now strongly dominate; by the end of November sightings of nonwintering warblers are exceptional. From late October through early November, watch for a few Vesper Sparrows and Rusty Blackbirds. Although flights are generally less interesting in November, some rare to accidental species are more likely then. A Townsend's Warbler and a Tropical/Couch's Kingbird have been sighted then, and November would also be a good time to hope for a Black-throated Gray Warbler.

Even in late December flights can be impressive, at least in terms of numbers. Thousands of robins and Yellow-rumped Warblers, with smaller numbers of goldfinches and winter finches, have been seen streaming north at this time. The flights of winter finches deserve close scrutiny; species like Red Crossbill and Common Redpoll are possible. Unfortunately, such flights are becoming increasingly rare.

Although impressive flights of land bird migrants are limited to the autumn migration period, the smattering of migrants coming through in springtime can be plenty entertaining. There may even be pile-ups, albeit smaller than autumn pile-ups, here at the island's northern tip. Most sightings occur during clear skies and winds from the southwest, west, and northwest. Brisk west and northwest winds after cold fronts are probably best, but this situation becomes increasingly rare as spring progresses.

You should never expect more than a few birds in spring, but you might get excellent close-up views of birds in breeding plumage—species like Scarlet Tanager, Rose-breasted Grosbeak, Blue Grosbeak, and Northern Oriole. This area deserves careful scrutiny in late May and the first couple of days of June. Migrants are quite infrequent at this time, but some of the rarest springtime sightings show up then. Most of these birds are one-year males. Blackburnian and Bay-breasted warblers have been sighted at this time. From Late May to early June you should also check the wires around the old coast guard station for a possible Gray Kingbird.

The Salt Flats
This half-mile-long expanse is made up primarily of flats sparsely vegetated with marsh grasses and other herbaceous species. The area probably remains

only sparsely vegetated because of high levels of salt in the soil, the result of frequent wind tides.

This area can be excellent for shorebirds during the migrations, late April to May and July to October. It is also a favored loafing spot for terns from April through October. Wading birds are also common during the warmer months. Winter is much less interesting, and it is best to avoid walking through the area then so as not to disturb waterfowl. The north end of the area can be scoped from the observation deck on the north dike of North Pond.

For shorebirding, this site is often best when nearby impoundments and ponds are worst—after wet weather. Rainy weather dampens these flats without flooding them, because they are not impounded. The flats can also be suitably wet for shorebirds during strong southwest winds, which push an inch or two of water onto the flats (and drive wading birds and terns to the flats from adjacent areas).

This is the best site on Bodie and Pea islands for American Golden-Plover and Buff-breasted Sandpiper. Baird's Sandpipers have also been seen here regularly, and there are a few sightings of Long-billed Curlews.

LOGISTICS. To reach the salt flats, continue south on NC 12. Just ahead, on the right, you will see an interpretive display with a large map of the refuge. At 1.6 miles past the display, you will see a small parking area on your left. (There is another parking area farther down on the right.) Across the road is a sand track that leads to the salt flats.

Because this site is usually not flooded and involves a long hike, you will probably prefer wearing tennis shoes rather than boots. Also, the following description pertains to the warmer months.

WALK DOWN THE sand track to a borrow-pit pond, then follow the edge of the pond away from the highway. There are usually a few American Black Ducks and Gadwalls. (*Note:* If you encounter any birds that are obviously nesting, move away as quickly as possible.)

Beyond the pond you will see a portion of the flats that is usually flooded. This area can be good for Black-necked Stilts during the nesting season and for Wilson's Phalaropes during the autumn migration. Wading birds are also frequent. White Ibises are becoming increasingly common. Also look for Glossy Ibises and a Yellow-crowned Night-Heron.

From here work northward across the main portion of the flats. Although this unique area attracts grasspipers and pool-type species, it is also favored by typical intertidal species. Whimbrels peak in May and about early August; they are most common when high tide forces them off the nearby ocean beaches. Look carefully—a Whimbrel of the Eurasian race was spotted here once, quite conspicuous with its white back and rump.

During all the warmer months this is a good place for terns. From late April to early September you should see Gull-billeds. Around August, Blacks are frequent. Sandwich Terns are most common in late summer and early autumn but may be seen as early as April.

A few Seaside Sparrows often breed here, but they may not show up until about June, when there is enough vegetation cover. Occasionally a Black Rail is heard here in July and August.

To get back to your car you may have to walk back toward the sand track. Each year it becomes more difficult to walk straight back out to the highway, because the vegetation next to the highway becomes increasingly dense.

CONTINUE SOUTH on NC 12 to the little parking lot just ahead on the right, where you will see the **north dike** of the **North Pond impoundment**. A walk around the whole impoundment can be enjoyable; however, it is about 4 miles. If you're part of a group with at least two cars, you might consider walking from here to the south parking lot via the west dike, which is about 2.5 miles long. Most birders simply work the north dike, then drive down and work the south dike, and the description here follows this approach.

From the parking lot it is just a short hike to the north dike observation deck. The dikes can also attract small land birds during the autumn migration, and after cold fronts you may see several warblers and/or sparrows between the parking lot and the overlook.

This observation deck is usually terrible for checking the impoundment, because the light is always poor except in late afternoon. In autumn and winter, however, flocks of Snow Geese often congregate on the adjacent salt flats, and the light is excellent most of the day for sorting through these birds for a possible Ross' Goose. Look especially in late October and November.

The deck is also a great hawk-watching site in autumn. Sharp-shinneds may stream by on good days in October, and sightings of Cooper's Hawks are becoming more frequent. The migration of Peregrine Falcons and Merlins peaks around the first week in October, and on a good day you may see several of each; some birds are likely to fly right over the platform. Pea Island is also the best spot in the state for seeing a Peregrine or Merlin in winter. Birders who live north and west of North Carolina will be impressed by the near absence of Broad-winged Hawks here.

Continue walking west along the dike. On your left you will see some long narrow islands, attractive roosting sites for wading birds. This area may host lots of Pied-billed Grebes in autumn. If you see a "Horned Grebe," look again—it might be an Eared.

Just beyond this point, on the right, is the tallest, most extensive area of woody vegetation on the north dike, and this area can be the best place to look for warblers and other small land birds in autumn. During the warmer months check the borders of the impoundment's marshy islands for Common Moorhens. Listen for the "coo-coo-coo" of a Black-billed Cuckoo around the first week in June, which seems to be the best time to find this species in coastal North Carolina.

Where the dike begins to straighten out generally north to south, check the wooded islands to the left. Roosting Black-crowned Night-Herons may be seen here at any season, and Yellow-crowneds are frequent from about early May to early October. In winter you can usually find a Cooper's Hawk in this area.

You may want to check out the salt marshes just to the west of the dike. (Look for openings through the shrub vegetation on your right.) These marshes have Marsh Wrens all year. In the breeding season a few Seaside Sparrows and a Yellow-crowned Night-Heron are possible. In autumn and winter look for Sharp-tailed Sparrows and occasionally a Seaside Sparrow.

Walk back to your car and continue south on NC 12, with **North Pond** to your right. At the north end of the impoundment you can park on the road shoulder and look over the water from there. From autumn to spring this is a great place to bird from your car in rainy or severely windy weather; you can often see a good variety of waterfowl at very close range. The lighting is excellent in the early morning but horrible in the afternoon. You're actually most likely to see a good variety of ducks in this corner of the impoundment early in the season, especially from October to December. In fact, there may be numerous ducks even in early September.

During low water levels in late summer and autumn you will probably see several shorebirds and a flock of gulls and terns on a little point in the impoundment. Baird's and Curlew sandpipers have been sighted here. In October and early November carefully check through the immature Laughing Gulls for a possible Franklin's. You should definitely check this impoundment from the road shoulders during fierce autumn northeasters, when shorebirds may move in especially close to the road; you might get to see something like a Baird's Sandpiper just outside your car window. Toward the south the impoundment is difficult to see from the highway. From autumn to spring, watch for American Bitterns wherever you see openings in the marsh.

The visitors center and comfort station are located at the southeast corner of North Pond. Be sure to check the list of rarities and record any that you have seen. Next to the restrooms you will see a service road that runs out onto the dike. After autumn cold fronts you will want to check the beginning of this road, which is a good site for Lark and Clay-colored sparrows. Then return to the front of the restrooms, where the marked trail begins. When the trail reaches the dike, it turns right and runs beneath a canopy of low-growing live oaks. Gray Catbirds, Rufous-sided Towhees, and Boat-tailed Grackles can be found here throughout the year, but this site is most interesting after autumn cold fronts. What makes it especially appealing is that you are within the vegetation; by being quiet and still you can get great looks at warblers.

Just beyond the live oaks is an observation deck that is arguably the best single birding spot in the state. On a good day in autumn a sharp birder could undoubtedly tally a hundred species without ever leaving this platform. Lighting here is best during the morning.

Waterfowl watching is great from autumn into winter. Dabbling ducks actually peak in November, and during this month you should see all species found in the state except for Wood Duck. Especially around late October and November, in any large flocks of American Wigeons you should be able to pick out a Eurasian. (Eurasians are undoubtedly regular before late October but are seldom reported earlier, because males in eclipse plumage are much less conspicuous, and the females are rather difficult to tell from American Wigeons.)

Most of the swans, Canada Geese, and Snow Geese begin to arrive during the October full moon. This impoundment is too shallow for most diving ducks, but beginning in November you should look for Ring-necked and Ruddy ducks, Buffleheads, and usually a few other species.

Although numbers vary according to water levels, a good variety of shorebirds can usually be seen here from midsummer through autumn, and often in May as well. In September and October check carefully for suspicious-looking "Willets": this is the best area in the state for Hudsonian Godwits, which birders may overlook by assuming they are Willets.

During the warmer months check the edges of the marshes to your right (as you face the impoundment) for Common Moorhens. Often you may see several chicks. In autumn you might spot a Sora here. At any season, a King Rail is possible.

Behind you, in the marshes just out from the dike, you may hear Clapper Rails (or "Cling Rails") at any season and Seaside Sparrows in summer. Marsh and Sedge wrens live in these marshes from autumn to spring. In April and the first few days of May, listen for the Sedge Wren's chattering song.

Continue westward on the dike. In autumn and winter watch for an American White Pelican in the impoundment. Although these pelicans are still scarce, they are on the increase. You are most likely to see them in October and November.

You will see a couple of small breaks in the vegetation that you can squeeze through for a peek at the New Field. This effort is especially worthwhile in the warmer months. During the migrations this site has excellent shorebirding potential. You should see Black-necked Stilts from mid-April to early September. American Avocets are most frequent from about August to November but might be spotted at any season. This is also an excellent area for wading birds. White Ibises are likely at any season. Glossy Ibises are common here during the warmer months, and you might see one or two throughout the winter.

At the southwest corner of North Pond is another observation deck. This deck is elevated several feet and provides a nice view of the impoundment, the adjacent salt marshes, and Pamlico Sound. For viewing the impoundment, the light here is best in the afternoon.

The marshes beyond the overlook are good for Marsh Wrens all year. You can find a few Seaside Sparrows here during the warmer months and sometimes in winter, and Sharp-taileds are regular from late September to early May. This is also a good spot for Yellow-crowned Night-Heron, from early May to early October.

The ocean off Pea Island can be plenty entertaining from late October through March, and often later as well. Traditionally, most birders choose to watch ocean birds from the dunes just across the highway from the parking area at the North Pond's southeast corner. Although activity is usually greatest in the early morning, afternoons definitely provide the best light along this stretch of coast.

In autumn this is a very likely spot for finding Pomarine and Parasitic jaegers. The autumn scoter migration peaks in late October and early November. Especially after cold fronts watch for long strings of Blacks and Surfs coming by every few minutes. Occasionally you will see one or two White-wingeds.

Actually, some of the most impressive southbound migration often takes place in December. After cold fronts watch for impressive flights that include loons, Horned Grebes, cormorants, gannets, gulls, Red-breasted Mergansers, and a few scoters. During these flights watch for an Oldsquaw or maybe an eider.

Just offshore you will see a partially exposed shipwreck. A Great Cormorant can often be seen here from October to April.

If you're ever in this area between December and March during really calm conditions, you may want to devote some time to searching for a tide line that often develops in the Pea Island area. The line might appear anywhere off Pea Island; you will want to check the ocean from as many spots as possible.

When this tide line is extremely well defined, it attracts impressive concentrations of birds—loons, grebes, gannets, cormorants, mergansers, gulls, and terns. If you're lucky enough to witness this phenomenon, especially if the line extends right up to the beach, you can easily devote an hour or more to enjoying the spectacle and searching for something unusual. Red-necked Grebes and Razorbills have been spotted along these tide lines; even a Great Skua was once seen. You might even stand a chance of seeing a Manx Shearwater.

In mid- to late winter, from January to March, Little Gulls are seen regularly off Pea Island. During brisk southwest winds check the ocean at as many sites as possible. If you find a flock of a thousand or more Bonaparte's Gulls, you should be able to find a Little.

From the parking lot at the southeast corner of North Pond, continue south on NC 12. **New Field** lies just past North Pond, on the right. Grain is planted here each year, so in late autumn and early winter this is a good place to watch grazing geese from your car and to study the two color morphs (light and dark) of Snow Geese. The light birds have always been called Snow Geese, but formerly the darker birds were thought to be a different species and were called Blue Geese.

If you see any Snow Geese here in late October and November, sort through them very carefully—this is the best time of year to find a Ross' Goose. Ross' Geese have also been seen several times in December. Later in winter your chances of finding one drop to almost nil. If you see a roadside flock of Canada Geese, check through them for a Greater White-fronted Goose. One of these is found here every few years; a sighting is most likely in late autumn and early winter.

New Field and South Pond are off-limits to birders. However, tours along the South Pond dike can sometimes be arranged if a refuge volunteer is available to lead the group, so a few comments about this area are in order.

South Pond is the deepest impoundment and attracts the most diving ducks. These ducks do not usually show up until November, and this impoundment is often at its best in December. Ring-necked Ducks, Lesser Scaup, and Ruddy Ducks are common. Also look for Canvasbacks, maybe a few Redheads, and sometimes a Greater Scaup. In winter South Pond is often the refuge's best site for wading birds. White Ibises are often common then, and there are usually a few Glossy Ibises as well.

In recent years South Pond has often been drawn down in summer, resulting in excellent aggregations of shorebirds in mid- to late summer. During such aggregations Curlew Sandpipers are occasionally sighted; most records have been in July.

From the impoundment's west dike Common Moorhens can always be seen in the warmer months. Look for them around the little marsh islands within the impoundment. Near the pump house you can usually find one or two Yellow-crowned Night-Herons during the warmer months, either in the impoundment or in the adjacent salt marshes. From the dike Marsh Wrens and Seaside Sparrows can be heard singing in the marshes during the breeding season.

South of South Pond are the old refuge office and its parking areas. The beach is just a short walk away, so this is another good site from which to check the ocean.

For further information: Contact Pea Island NWR, P.O. Box 1969, Manteo, NC 27954; phone 919-473-1131. The street address is 708 North US 64. No check-list of birds of the refuge itself is available; refer to the Park Service's checklist for Cape Hatteras NS.

RODANTHE AREA TO BUXTON

Birders have long regarded the 30-mile stretch of barrier island between the former refuge office at Pea Island NWR and Cape Hatteras as nearly birdless—a section of highway to be covered as quickly as possible when driving to and from the bird-rich areas of Pea Island NWR and Cape Hatteras. But we are now learning that, at least during certain seasons, a few stops are warranted. The prominent tide line discussed in the Pea Island NWR section sometimes shifts as far south as the fishing pier at Rodanthe, providing exceptional ocean birding in winter. Even during normal conditions, birding from this pier can be excellent from late autumn to early spring. This section of island also contains several Park Service parking areas and walkways that provide easy access to the ocean. In winter, bird activity in and over the ocean along the Outer Banks tends to be quite impressive but typically patchy and always shifting. The more sites you check, the better your chances for finding large numbers of birds. For example, if you are hunting for a Little Gull, you will want to find large flocks of Bonaparte's Gulls, which are constantly moving from site to site. The more places you check, the more likely you are to find them.

Along this section of barrier island the highway is susceptible to flooding during severe northeasters. The two areas with the worst potential for flooding are just north of Rodanthe and between Avon and Buxton. During such weather stay tuned to your weather radio for information about road closings. Keep in mind that the water remaining on the highway after storm flooding is primarily salt water.

This tour actually starts at the former refuge office at Pea Island NWR. From the office, head south toward Rodanthe on NC 12. The south end of the refuge—from here to the village of Rodanthe—has no impoundments, and there is usually no need to even slow down. But along much of this section you can gauge bird activity over the nearby ocean, and if it is impressive you can park on the road shoulder and walk across the dunes to check it out. Especially in winter, you may want to look for the tide line and the bird activity associated with it. (Parking along this stretch of highway has typically been impossible for regular vehicles, but the state has recently been planting grass along the highway shoulders. Nevertheless, look over any site carefully before parking.)

At 0.6 miles south of the refuge office, you will see a pulloff on your right where a bay lies beside the highway. This is the location of the **former New Inlet**, which used to separate Pea Island from Hatteras Island. Typically this site is not worth stopping for. However, during severe northeasters, when the waters of the sound are forced southwestward, a small area of exposed flats may attract several gulls and terns.

Rodanthe begins at 5.4 miles. In autumn check the transmission lines from Rodanthe south for a possible Western Kingbird, or maybe something even more unusual, like the Northern Wheatear that was seen one year.

At 6.9 miles, turn left onto SR 1247, which runs to the **Hatteras Island Fishing Pier**. This pier can be worth checking at any season but especially merits a visit from about late October to April. The pier is officially open from about early April to early December. Nonfishermen usually have to pay a nominal fee; the pass is good for a day. In winter, when the pierhouse is closed, entry to the pier is blocked during some years but not during others. You should always check, because this pier can be a truly excellent lookout point in the winter months.

The prominent tide line that sometimes forms in the Pea Island–Rodanthe area can sometimes be seen from the pier. You are most likely to see it when the ocean is nearly calm. If it appears between December and March—especially if it extends close to the shore—you will probably want to settle in for some very persistent scoping. You should see large numbers of Red-throated and Common loons, Northern Gannets, and Red-breasted Mergansers. You may also see several Horned Grebes, especially in mid- to late winter. A Red-necked Grebe has been seen from the pier along one of these tide lines. Look hard for a Razorbill, and hope for something really exciting, like a Great Skua. Even without a prominent tide line, ocean birding here can be quite exciting.

This pier is actually located at the easternmost point on the Outer Banks, and both the late autumn and late winter–spring migration periods can offer an almost endless procession of loons, gannets, cormorants, scoters, Red-breasted Mergansers, gulls, and terns. During these migrations Pomarine and Parasitic jaegers are seen regularly. In late May this area doesn't have nearly as much potential for pelagic species as Cape Hatteras to the south; nevertheless, large numbers of Wilson's Storm-Petrels and Sooty Shearwaters have been seen on occasion, and rarer species are possible.

In winter ocean birding tends to be best during calm conditions or winds from a generally westerly direction (which smooth the surface of the ocean, allowing greater visibility). A shipwreck lies off the end of the pier; you can find it by looking for the water swirling around it at low tide. From about November to April watch for one or two Great Cormorants feeding around this wreck. Harlequin Ducks and both eiders have also been sighted from the pier. Scoters frequently fly by, and you might spot an Oldsquaw or Greater Scaup. During brisk west to southwest winds in mid- to late winter you may see flocks of Bonaparte's Gulls numbering in the thousands. If so, you should be able to find a Little Gull.

Return to NC 12, reset your odometer to zero, and continue south. At 3.7 miles, after you pass through Salvo, you will see the Salvo Campground on your right and a parking area on your left; a path leads from this parking area to the ocean. During the winter you will want to check out the ocean here and at the next three parking areas between here and Avon.

Because it has the largest extent of open short-grass habitat for miles, the **Salvo Campground** always deserves a check from the beginning of the autumn migration, around July, through winter. If you get off the pavement, though, beware! The prickly-pear cacti are thick and vicious, although they can be inconspicuous.

In all honesty, this site usually does not offer anything interesting. However, goodies show up often enough that you should always pull in here, if only for a minute. From about mid-July to early September look for one or two Upland Sandpipers. They do not show up every year, but when one does appear you may be able to study it at really close range from your car. Buff-breasted Sandpipers are also possible. In late autumn and winter look for Lapland Longspurs, which have been seen here on a couple of occasions.

The pine plantation south of the campground is the biggest patch of woods for quite some ways and can serve as a magnet for passerine migrants after autumn cold fronts. At times, especially during north and northwest winds, there may be pile-ups in the shrubs right next to the campground. Lark Sparrows have been seen here a few times. The pines can attract Golden-crowned Kinglets and Brown Creepers (and Red-breasted Nuthatches during some years) after cold fronts in October and November.

Continue south on NC 12. Note other parking areas and ocean access points at 8.0, 10.1, and 14.4 miles. At 16.6 miles you will see the **Avon Fishing Pier** on your left. This pier is open from about early April to early December. Nonfishermen must pay a nominal fee. Some years the pier is gated in winter, but other years it is not.

This pier can be especially good in late autumn and early winter, when loons, gannets, mergansers, scoters, gulls, and terns are southbound. Jaegers are seen here regularly then, and this would probably be a good spot to look for a kittiwake as well. These waters can also be quite good in winter. After strong west and southwest winds there are often large flocks of Bonaparte's Gulls, which may contain one or more Little Gulls.

At 3.3 miles south of the pier you will see a parking area on the right side of the highway. If you're here at sunset from autumn to early spring, you should see streams of gulls and terns headed west to a roosting area (Clam Shoals). From here to Buxton, between October and March, watch the roadsides carefully at dusk; Barn Owls are seen here occasionally.

For further information: Contact Cape Hatteras NS, Route 1, Box 675, Manteo, NC 27954; phone 919-473-2111. The administrative office is located at the Fort Raleigh NHS, near Manteo. The nearest visitors centers are located at the Cape Hatteras lighthouse and at North Pond in Pea Island NWR. Both visitors centers are open all year, and a checklist of the seashore's birds is available.

CAPE HATTERAS AREA
MAP 14

You are birding the Cape Hatteras area in late December. It's a cold, raw day, with a biting north wind. That night you're awakened briefly by a terrific thunderstorm. The next morning, before dawn, you head outside and are shocked by

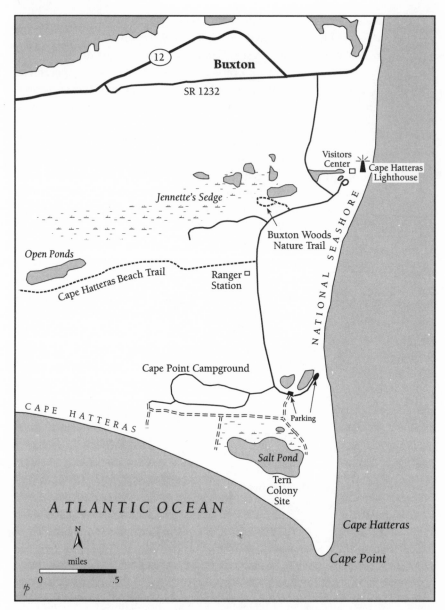

14. CAPE HATTERAS AREA

how balmy it is—the temperature has climbed to seventy degrees during the night, thanks to a brisk southeaster blowing in off the Gulf Stream, only a few miles offshore.

If you spend a little time here in winter, you will understand that this area is indeed quite special. Only perhaps in the highest mountains can you appreciate weather so much as here: cold fronts are not merely lines on maps, but strong shifting winds and lines of seething clouds; low pressure storms are not just two-dimensional circles, but huge swirling masses of clouds you can look up and see. Because it projects so far southeast and so close to the Gulf Stream, Cape Hatteras is often the only point on the entire East Coast that lies on the east side of the tract of storms sweeping up the coast. At such times temperatures at the cape may reach balmy levels while snow is falling on the adjacent mainland.

Not surprisingly, this special area—part of Cape Hatteras NS—often provides some very special birding. No other location in the state has produced as many exciting finds per acre as the Cape Point portion of Cape Hatteras, from the campground seaward. A discussion of this area often dwells on the rarest species, because so many of them have been sighted. Perhaps the only negative thing to say about this area is that it can get quite crowded on weekends in summer and autumn; holiday weekends are especially bad. Even during crowded conditions, though, the birding can be good.

Birding here is usually at its best during bad weather. When weather systems are very stagnant, birding can occasionally be slow. However, in this sort of place, even when things are slow you might have one sighting that makes the day worthwhile.

At Cape Point pelagic birds are sighted with noteworthy frequency. Most of these sightings take place around late May, when many species are moving northward. Typically the flights contain only a few dozen birds, but occasionally hundreds may be seen, and once in 1970 there were thousands. During these late May flights South Polar Skuas and Long-tailed Jaegers have been seen flying directly over the point. Pelagic species sometimes occur during the other seasons as well, although such sightings are less common. Perhaps the most unusual pelagic species that have been seen from the point are Masked Booby, White-tailed Tropicbird, and Leach's Storm-Petrel.

The point is also renowned for its wintering gull flocks. During stormy weather thousands of birds may congregate here, providing birders with a good opportunity to find white-winged gulls and other rarities. Every gull species that has been found in North Carolina has been observed at Cape Point.

Each spring and summer the point hosts a colony of nesting terns and skimmers. The presence of this colony allows birders to get good looks at several of the regular breeding species. In addition, Sooty and Roseate terns are seen here every year, and Sooties sometimes nest. Piping Plovers nest within the colony each year; a Wilson's is spotted very rarely.

Although shorebirds do not appear in great numbers here, the area has excellent potential for the rarer species. During the autumn migration period the tern colony area is perhaps the best site in the state for Buff-breasted and Baird's sandpipers and American Golden-Plovers. And the margins of the nearby Salt

Pond have hosted species like Spotted Redshank, Little Stint, Ruff, and Curlew Sandpiper. In late autumn the tern colony area is a good spot to check for Lapland Longspurs and Snow Buntings.

Even if Cape Point didn't exist, the Cape Hatteras area would still merit a birding trip. The area is not one of the Outer Banks' better spots for land bird migrants (because birds are not funneled into small patches of vegetation), but it can still be interesting. Connecticut Warblers are found as regularly here as anywhere in the state, and rarities like White-winged Dove and Scissor-tailed Flycatcher have also been spotted. Breeding birds include Chuck-will's-widows and Prothonotary Warblers, and birders find American Swallow-tailed Kites each spring.

THIS TOUR OF the Cape Hatteras area begins in Buxton at the intersection of NC 12 with the Park Service road to the lighthouse and the point. If you're driving in from the north, the highway curves to the right after you enter Buxton. After the highway straightens out, look for the road and Park Service signs on your left.

During the early part of the breeding season—from late April to at least early June—you will want to make several stops along this road to look for resident land birds and maybe a few migrants. Dawn is certainly best; the traffic gets noisy soon thereafter. If you start out early enough, you should hear one or more Chuck-will's-widows.

From NC 12 to the intersection near the lighthouse (at 0.9 miles) the Park Service road crosses several low ridges and swales, and you will see fresh-water marshes and shrub swamps as well as upland woods. Breeding species you should find include Yellow-billed Cuckoo, Great Crested Flycatcher, Gray Catbird, White-eyed Vireo, Prothonotary Warbler, and Common Yellowthroat. Along this stretch of road, about midmorning, look up frequently. American Swallow-tailed Kites are seen here every year; Mississippi Kites are seen almost every year and are increasing. You can find an entertaining variety of migrating land birds here after autumn cold fronts. In winter sort through the flocks of Yellow-rumped Warblers and kinglets (you may be surprised by the lack of chickadees and titmice) for Solitary Vireos and Orange-crowned Warblers—both are rather easy to find. White-eyed Vireos are also regular in winter, and you might spot a lingering Black-and-white or Prairie warbler; something even more unusual is sighted on rare occasions. Although you're not likely to see one from the road, Ovenbirds overwinter each year in the vicinity. In fact, this is the only site north of Florida where this species is regularly reported on Christmas Bird Counts.

At 0.5 miles there is a scenic little pond on your left. It is sometimes birdless but is always worth checking. There are often a few wading birds, and in winter you should look for a few Pied-billed Grebes, coots, and ducks. A few Common

Moorhens are present here virtually every year, from about November to March, but you may have to wait several minutes for one to swim into the open. Fulvous Whistling-Ducks have been found here.

The shrub thickets at the intersection 0.9 miles from NC 12 have numerous Brown Thrashers at all seasons. Check the thicket borders in autumn for Lark and White-crowned sparrows. The latter is sometimes seen in winter.

Turn left into the **Cape Hatteras Lighthouse** parking lot; here you will find a visitors center, bookstore, and restrooms. Next to the parking lot there is a small pond. In winter this pond usually has Pied-billed Grebes and American Coots, and occasionally a duck or two.

Recently the lighthouse has been reopened to the public during the warmer months. It will remain open if volunteers are available to conduct tours. If you have the time, on a day with good visibility you will definitely want to make the long climb; the view out toward Diamond Shoals can be fantastic. In spring this might be a great spot to look over the adjacent woods for kites. By the way, if you're ever in the area during a foggy night, be sure to pull into the parking lot for the impressive sight of the lighthouse beam in the fog.

On the beach near the lighthouse there are three groins. These groins are quite short, but they occasionally attract a Purple Sandpiper, Harlequin Duck, or eider, perhaps because they're the only groins around. These birds tend not to linger at this location, though. Here ocean birding is most interesting in autumn and winter. In autumn watch for southbound gannets and scoters. In winter the ocean may be alive with loons, gannets, mergansers, gulls, and terns. Some goodies seen from here include Red-necked Grebe, Razorbill, Dovekie, and Little Gull. You are most likely to find Little Gulls when large numbers of Bonaparte's are present; at this site, strong southwest or west winds are best.

Incidentally, on clear days you may be able to see a tower on the horizon toward the east-southeast. This is the Diamond Shoals Light Tower, located 12 miles away. The base of this tower is occasionally bathed in Gulf Stream water, and on a day in January the water temperature there may be seventy degrees, while the water here along shore is fifty or lower.

Continue south toward the point on the Park Service road, resetting your odometer at the stop sign when you leave the lighthouse. Just beyond this sign, at 0.3 miles, you will see the parking lot for the **Buxton Woods Nature Trail** on your right. During much of the year you're not too likely to find anything on the trail that can't be found on the roadsides. However, this pleasant trail takes you away from traffic noise and runs into an area that is somewhat wind-sheltered. This loop trail is about three-quarters of a mile long. The trail perhaps most deserves a hike in autumn and winter. Connecticut Warblers have been seen along the trail (near the boardwalk) a few times in late September. The trail runs along next to a large fresh-water marsh (Jennette's Sedge). Common Yellow-throats can be found here all year, and Marsh Wrens and Swamp Sparrows can be found from autumn to spring. During the cooler months, if the water level is not too high, listen for Soras and Virginia Rails.

At 0.7 miles, on your right, you will see the **Cape Hatteras Beach Trail**. Again, this trail doesn't offer much potential for seeing something new, but you might consider hiking in as far as the Open Ponds (about 1.5 miles away), at least during the breeding season. (Do not park in front of the gate, but off to one side.) Along the beginning of the trail there are pine stands where you might find an Eastern Wood-Pewee or Summer Tanager in the breeding season, and Brown Creepers and Yellow-bellied Sapsuckers in winter. At the Open Ponds look for Wood Ducks at any season. Birders have seen American Swallow-tailed and Mississippi kites overhead here in late spring.

At 0.9 miles you will see the **Cape Hatteras Ranger Station** (a former coast guard station) on your right. In future years Shiny Cowbirds might be sighted in this sort of place. A small structure next to the parking lot houses a clipboard where rarities can be logged in. In summer, if you're headed to the point, don't forget to see whether any Sooty and Roseate terns have been seen in the tern colony and, if so, in what part of the colony they were sighted. Don't forget to report sightings of any species that are locally scarce—for instance, Carolina Chickadee. The Park Service is interested in all such records.

From the ranger station to the Cape Point parking lot, at 1.6 miles, the road is bordered by shrub thickets, both dry and wet. In the breeding season this is a good area for Eastern Kingbirds. In winter look for American Woodcocks along the road at dusk. If you're really lucky, you might spot a Saw-whet Owl.

When the weather is nasty and you don't have a four-wheel-drive vehicle, or if you're not up for the mile-long hike out to the point, then drive on to the parking lot at the end of the road. This parking lot is right next to the ocean and provides an easily accessible ocean-birding spot. In rainy weather you can view the pond next to the parking lot from your car. It usually has a few ducks, and there are often a few shorebirds when water levels are low. A pond this close to the ocean could host something rare during severe weather.

From the **Cape Point parking area** (located next to the fish cleaning tables and across from Ramp 44) to the point is a hike of about a mile. In summer, when the sand is soft and often deeply rutted from off-road vehicle (ORV) traffic, it is a long mile indeed.

Four-wheel-drive vehicles can be rented in the Buxton area; if you don't own one, during stormy weather in winter you might strongly consider renting one. The primary reason is not creature comfort. During severe weather, the point may be blanketed with gulls; these birds may be skittish about pedestrians, but if it is very windy, they will allow vehicles to approach very closely.

Head south on the ORV trail (Ramp 44) toward the point. After a couple hundred yards you will cross a prominent manmade berm (dune line). As you cross the berm, note a large pond—the Salt Pond—up ahead. When you come down off the berm and approach the pond, look for a small pool on your right that is nearly hidden by the surrounding marsh. This pool almost always has a few Gadwalls. The short marsh walk to get to it is most worthwhile when water levels are low during the migration periods. A Spotted Redshank put on a well-attended performance here one May.

The **Salt Pond** is actually a borrow-pit pond, created in the early 1970s when sand was dredged from the site and pumped to the lighthouse to protect it from erosion. The pond is over ten feet deep in the middle and is usually nontidal. However, the sea occasionally breaks through to it from the south (most likely in autumn), and the connection may persist for several weeks.

In winter the pond hosts a small flock of Snow Geese. Also look for American Black Ducks, Gadwalls, Buffleheads, Red-breasted Mergansers, and other ducks. Look carefully for a Common Merganser; these birds have been found here on a few occasions. In autumn and winter, look for an Eared Grebe. Peregrine Falcons are seen here often in autumn, and one overwinters every year. If all the birds in the area flush for no apparent reason, check the sky for a Peregrine. Sometimes a Peregrine may be spotted on the radio tower to the north.

During the migrations shorebirding can be quite entertaining, especially when water levels are low. (Even when the tern colony area is posted, you can walk along the pond's north shore.) Typically the two ends of the pond are best. The easier way to get to the west end is from the campground (see the description below). You are not likely to see large numbers of shorebirds here, but you can often see a pretty good variety, including pool-type species rarely found on intertidal flats. Species that can be found each year include American Golden-Plover, Lesser Yellowlegs, Wilson's Phalarope, and White-rumped, Baird's, Pectoral, Stilt, and Buff-breasted sandpipers. (Of these, the golden-plovers and Baird's and Buff-breasted sandpipers are more likely to be seen on the tern colony site described below.) Long-billed Dowitchers should occur regularly. Black-necked Stilts show up here some years (although they haven't nested), and Hudsonian Godwits and Upland Sandpipers have been seen here a few times. Overall, the autumn migration period (July to October) has the most potential, although water levels may get too high in October. On the other hand, once in mid-May a Spotted Redshank, a Curlew Sandpiper, and a Ruff were all seen here on the same day.

The east end of the pond usually has numerous loafing gulls and terns, and they are usually rather tame. During the nesting season several birds from the adjacent colony—Gull-billed and Common terns and Black Skimmers—will show up here, and there might be a few Royal and Sandwich terns. In late summer, less often in spring, there may be a few Black Terns. From April to October one or two Piping Plovers often appear here. From autumn to spring check through any gull flocks for a Lesser Black-backed.

In autumn check through the Laughing Gulls for two potential rarities—Sabine's Gull and Franklin's Gull. Sabine's is most likely from late August to early October, Franklin's from early October to early November.

From April through August your trek from the Salt Pond to the point will follow the eastern boundary of the posted **tern colony**. In recent years Sooty Terns have nested in this colony almost annually, although so far apparently every nesting has been unsuccessful. Sometimes the nesting site is close enough to the colony boundary signs that you can see the adult on the nest. However, looking for a Sooty here can be frustrating because of all the skimmers. Remember that Sooty Terns nest in the vegetation, while skimmers nest in the open. If you can't spot a Sooty on the ground, you might get lucky and see one flying to or from or over the colony.

When the signs prohibiting entrance to the tern colony area are taken down—around September 1—you can walk through this area in search of Upland, Buff-breasted, and Baird's sandpipers and American Golden-Plovers, in addition to more common shorebirds. The Upland Sandpiper passes through mostly before September, but you might also spot one in early September. You are most likely to find golden-plovers from late September through October, particularly after strong northeast winds. Baird's Sandpipers are occasional and are most likely to show up between early September and early October. Buff-breasteds are occasional from mid-August to mid-October.

Later in autumn and during the winter, check this area for Lapland Longspurs and Snow Buntings as well. Both species are occasional. The longspurs seem to be most likely from mid-October through November. Most sightings of buntings have taken place between early November and mid-December.

During many years one or more small tidal pools or damp depressions develop near the southeastern corner of the colony. These pools may lie outside or just inside the roped-off area. You would do well to watch any such sites for several minutes (or, if you have a four-wheel-drive vehicle, to check them periodically over several hours). These pools often attract loafing terns, and this seems to be the best area for finding a Roseate Tern. Look from late spring through summer, especially in late May and from late June to mid-August.

In winter, even on slow days, you have a reasonable chance of finding a rare gull at the cape. Lesser Black-backed Gulls are now almost routine. From early November through March you can usually find at least one bird on the slowest of days. The birds are still increasing; in the future they will probably be reliable earlier in autumn and later in spring.

During really nasty weather from about late December to mid-March, Cape Point can be an avid gull-watcher's heaven. On some days you may see more gulls than sand, stretching all the way from the Salt Pond to the tip of the point. Such occurrences are most likely during winds of thirty-plus miles an hour and low barometric pressures, especially when such conditions persist for several days. Numbers of gulls may be similarly impressive after major fish die-offs, but these are rare events.

Again, you can exploit such opportunities most fully by using a four-wheel-drive vehicle. In really windy conditions you don't even need a scope. You can drive right up to the birds and examine them closely with binoculars—a great way to identify problem species, like Thayer's Gull.

On the really prime days you should see several Lesser Black-backed Gulls, and you have a reasonable chance of seeing an Iceland or Glaucous. Although there are still only a few records of Thayer's Gulls, sightings have been increasing in recent years, so you should definitely be on the lookout for one. During vicious weather late in winter Ring-billed Gulls may be by far the dominant species on the point. If such an aggregation occurs, sort through the birds very carefully. Mew/Common Gulls have been seen at the point twice.

Little Gulls are most likely to make appearances from late January to early March. Look for them out over the water except during the most severe conditions. During north and northeast winds watch for them off the south beach; during west or southwest winds, off the east beach (or, better, farther up the island). During strong north and northeast winds look for a vast flock of Bonaparte's Gulls on the water off the south beach. When the flock takes wing, you might be able to spot a Little. When Littles do come ashore, they are most likely to show up near the tip of the point, especially around tide pools.

Even on the slowest birding day you will want to press on to the very tip of Cape Point, although it may be covered with fishermen's vehicles. The point is the sort of place where something really exciting might fly by any day of the year. Part of the point's allure is its constantly changing nature. Sometimes the point is a simple ninety-degree bend of the coastline; often, though, a narrow spit extends southward for a few hundred yards, enhancing the birding possibilities. Occasionally one or two sand islands will build up just off the point and attract resting gulls and terns. Also, tidal pools frequently form at the base of Cape Point's tip.

The waters and birdlife just off the cape are most frenzied from around November through March. You may see thousands of gannets, many plunging into the waters just a few feet away, and the sky is constantly filled with cormorants streaming to and from these waters. Common and Red-throated loons are common. Look for several Horned Grebes just off the south beach in late winter. Pacific Loon, Red-necked Grebe, and Eared Grebe have all been seen in this area. Black-legged Kittiwakes make occasional appearances off the point in late November and December, sometimes earlier and later.

Flocks of scoters, which sometimes pass directly over the point, are most likely from late October to early November and from mid-March to early April, but a few are sighted throughout the winter. Pomarine and Parasitic jaegers occur regularly during the migrations, especially from late April to late May.

However, you might spot either species at virtually any time of year, except perhaps midsummer.

The point is an especially good spot for Royal and Sandwich terns. Royals can always be found, except sometimes in the dead of winter, and Sandwiches are reliable from early or mid-April to mid-November. These birds like to roost on any small islands that form off the point.

Occasionally a bay or one or more tidal pools develop at the base of the point. These protected waters, which offer close-up views, may well attract something interesting. At a bay you can often get close looks at Horned Grebes in winter, and you might even see a Common Eider. If there are tidal pools, look for Red-necked Phalaropes during stormy weather from around mid-May to early June and mid-August to early September. Red Phalaropes have been seen here during a severe northeaster in late April.

Late May is by far the best time to see large numbers of pelagic species moving past the point. A few Wilson's Storm-Petrels and Sooty Shearwaters may occur about May 15, but the largest numbers and the widest variety should fly by from about May 20 through the first couple of days of June. Even during this period, numbers are extremely variable from day to day and year to year. Some years may not have any good flights; you might see only a few Wilson's Storm-Petrels and Sooty Shearwaters. Larger numbers of birds are typically associated with a couple of days of strong northeast or easterly winds (especially when such conditions extend far south of the state). However, more subtle factors also seem to come into play, probably including the locations of Gulf Stream eddies. It has been suggested that the best flights happen on the first day with south winds following a period of brisk northeast and east winds. This does seem to be the case. The weather associated with the "superflight" of 1970 is worth mentioning. On May 31 and June 1, 1970, several thousand pelagic birds were observed moving up the coast past Cape Hatteras. Just before this flight, a tropical storm had moved north into the Gulf of Mexico, creating strong easterly winds over the Atlantic east of Florida.

Typically, you're most likely to see good numbers early in the morning. Smaller flights may be over by 9 A.M. However, birds are sometimes sighted throughout the day, and flights may pick up again around 4 P.M.

The pelagic birds you see at the cape in spring are migrating individuals that have "collided" with the cape and are trying to get around it. Thus, you will be looking for birds flying in from the west or southwest. You will get better views if the point extends out in a narrow spit, because many birds fly closer to shore when confronted with a shoreline that actually bends back southward. Some birds, especially jaegers, may fly directly across the base of the spit, allowing great views.

On a good day you should see these species: Cory's, Greater, and Sooty shearwaters; Wilson's Storm-Petrel; Pomarine and Parasitic jaegers; and one or two Audubon's Shearwaters. If you're really lucky, you might see a Long-tailed Jaeger or a South Polar Skua. On one exceptional morning, a birder counted at least twelve Long-taileds; some of these birds flew directly over the point. Strangely, one or two Manx Shearwaters and Leach's Storm-Petrels have also been observed in these late May flights.

After early June, flights of pelagics become increasingly infrequent. Wilson's Storm-Petrels are occasionally sighted as late as August, and Cory's Shearwaters are sometimes seen into autumn. Until early July, after northeast and east winds, watch for Greater Shearwaters. Audubon's Shearwaters are most likely to be seen from mid-July to early August; sightings are possible, but quite unusual, in autumn and winter. A White-tailed Tropicbird once flew past the point on a calm midsummer day, and a Masked Booby was once spotted just off the point in early September.

Autumn sightings of pelagics (other than jaegers and kittiwakes) are quite exceptional, but Cory's and Audubon's shearwaters are possible. Winter sightings are also quite exceptional. Dovekies and Razorbills have been spotted from the point at this time of year, and at least one Manx Shearwater and one Audubon's Shearwater have been seen. Birders looking for Manx Shearwaters in winter should remember that Audubon's Shearwaters are perhaps about as likely—maybe more so, with the Gulf Stream just offshore.

In the nesting season you may want to continue westward along the south side of the tern colony, especially if you're still looking for a Sooty Tern or Piping Plover. If you have a four-wheel-drive vehicle, in winter you will probably want to work west a mile or two to check for additional gulls (there are often several near a little "inlet"—a manmade fresh-water outflow). The following paragraphs begin with the nearby campground and proceed along the west side of the Salt Pond. You can cover these places in reverse by continuing along the south side of the colony.

Near the Cape Point parking area you will see the entrance to the **Cape Point Campground**. The campground itself is usually not too interesting, but you should definitely check it during wet, stormy weather. Short-eared and Barn owls are sometimes spotted here in winter. The annual closing time for the campground varies from year to year. It may close from early to late autumn. You can drive through it most of the time, even when it is closed; however, in summer you will have to get permission at the gate to drive around. Your primary interest in summer will probably be to use the campground roads to reach the western part of the Salt Pond, and you can park at the campground gate if you have to.

The campground is not very good for "grasspipers"; typically, these birds are more likely to head for the nearby tern colony area. However, they may be forced out of the tern colony area during really nasty weather—heavy rains and/or extreme tides. During such conditions check the campground for American Golden-Plover and Upland, Baird's, and Buff-breasted sandpipers. Of course, it is also better if the campground is closed. In addition to the seasonal closing, the campground sometimes closes during unusually wet weather due to flooding. During severe weather in winter, gulls spill over into the campground, and you can check them from your car (a good activity on a rainy day if you don't have a four-wheel-drive vehicle).

This is a traditional spot for Short-eared Owl in late autumn and winter. Birders are more likely to miss these owls than to see them, but there are a few sightings every year. Watch for the owls after sunset. Evening provides better light than morning, because the birds are usually seen to the west. A Barn Owl is also possible. You should at least hear the "peenting" of woodcocks. A Chuck-will's-widow was once seen here in late December—further evidence of how mild this area can be in autumn and early winter.

The owls are seen less frequently now than in former years, probably because the vegetation around the campground is shifting from primarily herbaceous vegetation to primarily woody vegetation. You would probably be more likely to spot an owl by walking over to the west end of the Salt Pond.

In case you don't have a four-wheel-drive vehicle and don't feel up to the mile-long hike to the point, a quarter-mile hike from the campground to the ocean will take you past the Salt Pond and beside the southwest end of the tern colony. From this ocean beach you can also watch for pelagic species in the spring, but you won't be able to see them as closely here as at the point.

The shortest route to the Salt Pond begins between the third and fourth rows in the campground (rows "C" and "D"). Look for a footpath that runs over the prominent berm. As soon as you cross the berm, you will see the Salt Pond and the ocean.

The west end of the Salt Pond is often the best area for shorebirds, unless water levels are high, and typically this area lies outside the roped-off tern colony boundary. The light here is best in the afternoon. Look for all of the species mentioned above. A Little Stint showed up here one July.

In the salt meadows beside the pond you can usually find a few Bobolinks from late August to at least mid-October. During high water levels in autumn kick through these areas for a Sora or other rail. You might even kick up a Yellow Rail. On one Christmas Bird Count birders clicked rocks together here late at night, and a Yellow came into view! During the cooler months there should be several Sedge Wrens.

Closer to the beach you will see the tern colony on your left. Very rarely, a Wilson's Plover or two show up in the tern colony during the nesting season. You are most likely to see these plovers near this end of the colony.

Keep in mind that this description of Cape Point may not always be strictly applicable in the future. For instance, the location of the tern/skimmer colony could easily shift. More important, this area is very much subject to natural forces; geological change will inevitably occur. The Salt Pond could easily disappear in a hurricane. However, there should still be habitat in the future for most of the bird species listed above, and the Park Service is dedicated to maintaining the nesting colony here.

For further information: Contact Cape Hatteras NS, Route 1, Box 675, Manteo, NC 27954; phone 919-473-2111. The administrative office is located at the Fort Raleigh NHS, near Manteo. The visitors center at the Cape Hatteras Lighthouse is open all year. A checklist of the seashore's birds is available.

FRISCO, HATTERAS VILLAGE, HATTERAS SPIT
MAP 15

In terms of birding, this section of Hatteras Island is somewhat overshadowed by nearby Cape Hatteras Point. Nevertheless, this area has several sites worth checking, and it complements the nearby point. The Hatteras Village area is much better than the Cape Hatteras area for migrant land birds in autumn, because there is much less woody vegetation. The woods at Frisco can be good for land birds during the breeding season and in winter, and the dunes at the Frisco Campground provide a good vantage point for surveying the adjacent sky above the island's maritime forest. The Cape Hatteras Fishing Pier is an easily accessible site that can provide good ocean birding. In winter the harbor at Hatteras, which can be excellent for gulls, is a good spot to check on a rainy day. If you have a four-wheel-drive vehicle or if you are willing to make a long hike, you can also check out the Hatteras Spit. Here you can see Piping Plovers, and sometimes Wilson's Plovers, during the breeding season. The spit also has a nice marsh, with Clapper Rails year-round, Yellow-crowned Night-Herons in summer, and marsh sparrows and wrens in the cooler months.

THIS TOUR BEGINS in Frisco at the intersection of NC 12 and the **Water Association Road**, 2.9 miles north of the Frisco post office. Drive down the Water Association Road one-quarter mile until you see the treatment plant on your left. During the breeding season and in winter you will want to walk down this road for at least one-half mile (to the turn) past the plant. The woods can be decent after autumn cold fronts, but they are dull compared to the better migrant traps on the Outer Banks. (*Note*: This area is not Park Service land; stay on the road.)

The early part of the breeding season is best: visit from about late April to early June. If you get here at dawn, you should hear Eastern Screech-Owls and Chuck-will's-widows. Other breeding species you should see and hear include Yellow-billed Cuckoo (may not be present until early May), White-eyed Vireo, Northern Parula, Indigo Bunting, and Prairie, Pine, and Prothonotary warblers. Usually you will hear the screams of at least one Red-shouldered Hawk and the

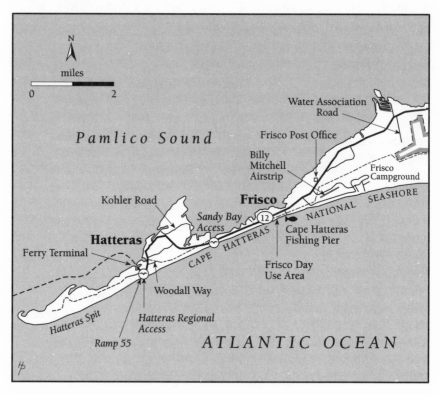

N

miles

0   2

Pamlico Sound

Water Association
Road

Frisco Post Office

Billy
Mitchell
Airstrip

Frisco
Campground

Kohler Road

Frisco

NATIONAL   SEASHORE

Sandy Bay
Access

12

Cape Hatteras
Fishing Pier

Hatteras

CAPE   HATTERAS

Ferry Terminal

Frisco Day
Use Area

Woodall Way

Hatteras Spit

Hatteras Regional
Access

Ramp 55

ATLANTIC OCEAN

15. FRISCO, HATTERAS VILLAGE, HATTERAS SPIT

calls of both American and Fish crows. If you find a Summer Tanager, it will most likely be a one-year-old male, not in full breeding plumage.

This section of road can also be quite enjoyable in late autumn and in winter. Try to visit early in the morning when winds are light. If you're here at dawn, listen for screech-owls and a Great Horned Owl, and watch and listen for woodcocks. Until December, especially during warm weather, a Whip-poor-will might come and flutter around you if you mimic its call. The woods here are excellent for both kinglets. Among the Yellow-rumped Warbler and kinglet flocks, watch for a few Pine Warblers. Listen for the distinctive scolding call of a Solitary Vireo and the chip-note of an Orange-crowned Warbler; both species are easy to find here. If you are really lucky, while squeaking for birds you might hear the loud call-note of an Ovenbird; a few overwinter each year. You will no doubt be impressed by the scarcity of woodpeckers on the island. During most winters you should find one or two Red-bellieds (they don't summer here), and a Pileated Woodpecker is also possible.

From the Water Association Road return to NC 12 and turn left. After 2.9 miles, turn left onto the Park Service road that runs by the Billy Mitchell Airport to the **Frisco Campground**. From about mid-April through May this site is a good place for watching the skies over the adjacent maritime forest for a possible American Swallow-tailed Kite. Mid- to late morning on clear days is the best time to look. Park at the campground entrance and walk to the left, where you can observe the forest. You might want to climb up on one of the dunes for an especially good view. Even if you don't see a kite, you should at least see Ospreys, a Red-shouldered Hawk, Chimney Swifts, Purple Martins, and Barn Swallows, as well as wading birds flying to and from their nesting colonies.

Return to NC 12 and turn left. After 0.8 miles, turn left onto the road to the **Cape Hatteras Fishing Pier**. The pier is open from about early April through November. There is an admission fee for nonfishermen; the pass is good for a day. The parking lot is open throughout the winter.

In winter you can often get close looks at Red-throated and Common loons here, and the pier might also attract a scoter, eider, or Harlequin Duck. During April the end of the pier can be great for getting good looks at migrating loons, gannets, scoters, and other species. This section of beach seems to be very attractive to Whimbrels; they can virtually always be seen here during the migration peaks.

Because it lies on the south side of the cape, this site can sometimes be good in late May for pelagic birds migrating north. (See the Cape Hatteras site guide for a list of species you might find.) This site, which is over 6 miles west of Cape Hatteras Point, has much less potential than the point for large numbers of pelagics, but the pier is much more accessible, and from its end you might actually get better views of the birds that do fly by. The pier also has a little wind shelter (but no rain protection) at the end, so you should definitely keep this site in mind if you're in the area during strong northeasters in late autumn or spring. During such conditions large numbers of birds may move into the lee of the cape. In November such weather might bring a Black-legged Kittiwake; you might even spot a fulmar. The end of the pier could be especially interesting during a severe northeaster in April. Birds migrating north are especially prone to being deflected to the west by northeast winds, and April could be an especially good time to strain your eyes in search of a fulmar or Manx Shearwater.

Return to NC 12 and turn left. For the next 2 miles the island is rather narrow and can be good for finding hawks and swallows during the autumn migration. In winter birders sometimes spot Barn Owls feeding next to the road at dusk. This section also has three parking areas—two for ocean beach access and one for sound shore access. From late September into October any of these areas might provide good lookout points for migrating hawks. Northwest winds following cold fronts are best. Next to the soundside access point, there is a little marsh where you might find a few Sharp-tailed Sparrows, and maybe a rail, in autumn. Strangely, one February a Northern Saw-whet Owl was heard calling in the shrubs here during the daytime.

At 3.2 miles from the road to the Cape Hatteras Fishing Pier, you will see a road to the right (Kohler Road) in **Hatteras Village**. After autumn cold fronts the first half-mile of this road, through the village's main residential area, can be as good for migrants as any place in the village. A Gray Kingbird once showed up here in late May. After three-quarters of a mile, you will see the sound on your left. This is a good spot for seeing Horned Grebes and Buffleheads in winter. If you're ever in the area during a fierce southwest or west wind, you might want to check this spot, because the waters here are somewhat protected. Beyond this point the road crosses a marsh, and you might see a Clapper or Virginia rail run across the road in autumn.

Return to NC 12 and turn right. After 0.1 miles the **Hatteras Harbor** begins on your right. In winter you should check this harbor for gulls. On most days you will only see a few, but when fish are being brought in there may be several hundred birds. During these times you should find one or more Lesser Black-backeds, and an Iceland or Glaucous gull is quite possible. In fact, when fish are being unloaded, this harbor may be the best place in the state to find an Iceland.

Unfortunately, no one site provides a really good view of the whole harbor. You'll get the best view by taking the road that runs around to the back of the harbor. This road leaves NC 12 0.2 miles past the beginning of the harbor. You may want to throw some bread out to attract gulls. Do not throw bread right next to any of the boats, though; boat owners do not like to have gull flocks directly overhead, for obvious reasons. From this road you can also look out over the sound. Brant can sometimes be seen here in winter.

One-half mile up NC 12, on the right, there is another marina that you should check in winter. It usually has fewer gulls than the Hatteras Harbor, but occasionally it has more. Birders have seen Lesser Black-backed, Iceland, and Glaucous gulls here.

From NC 12 just past the marina, look for **Woodall Way** on your left. A few hundred yards down this road you will see **Isaac Pond** on your left. This pond is worth checking year-round for wading birds, but it is most interesting in winter. Look for Pied-billed Grebes, coots, and a few ducks. One or two Common Moorhens are present virtually every winter, and one year a Fulvous Whistling-Duck made an appearance. You can see the pond from the road, but you can observe it best by walking to it across a marshy vacant lot.

From here continue south on NC 12. Just before the ferry terminal, bear left to avoid getting into the line for the ferry. Restrooms are available at the terminal. The television in the visitors center is tuned to the Weather Channel throughout the day. Just past the ferry terminal, opposite the coast station entrance, you will see another good ocean access point.

The area west of this access point is called **Hatteras Spit**. Unless you own a four-wheel-drive vehicle or are ready for a good hike, you have reached the end of the road. It is about 3 miles from here to Hatteras Inlet, and it gets farther every year as the inlet migrates west. The flats beside the inlet usually have a few shorebirds, although this is certainly not a major shorebird area. And in winter there are sometimes large gull flocks, but this area is typically not nearly as good as Cape Hatteras Point. In summer there is usually a tern colony, which has a few Piping Plovers each year, and one or two pairs of Wilson's Plovers during some years.

The best way to continue down the Hatteras Spit is by way of the ORV trail. For the first mile and a half you will see extensive shrub thickets on your right. In the breeding season you'll definitely see land birds like Fish Crows, Gray Catbirds, Prairie Warblers, Common Yellowthroats, Rufous-sided Towhees, Boat-tailed Grackles, and Red-winged Blackbirds. After autumn cold fronts with brisk northwest winds, some passerine migrants may pile up where the shrub thickets end.

About a mile from the end of the pavement you will see a side trail to your right. This is where the main ORV trail closely approaches the sound. Follow the side trail to the sound shore and walk to the left. About one-third mile up the shore you will see an extensive salt marsh that often has several wading birds during the warmer months, including White and Glossy ibises and both night-herons. This is a very reliable spot for the Yellow-crowned, which apparently nests in the adjacent shrub thickets. This marsh has a few resident Clapper Rails. From autumn to spring look for Sharp-tailed Sparrows, Marsh Wrens, and a few Seaside Sparrows. Along the upper borders of the marshes you can also find Sedge Wrens.

Sparsely vegetated flats begin at about 2 miles—probably farther in the future, because the flats are becoming increasingly vegetated. The flats closer to the inlet are more barren.

Each year there is a nesting colony here, made up mostly of Least Terns; Common and Gull-billed terns and Black Skimmers may occur as well. Piping Plovers can usually be seen from the edge of the colony. American Oystercatchers also nest nearby. (Do not go into any roped-off areas!)

Again, these flats are normally not that great for shorebirds, but you can usually find most of the regular intertidal species during the migrations. Red Knots are often common in May. Occasionally Marbled Godwits make appearances here, and Long-billed Curlews have been spotted a couple of times. In winter the flats typically have very few shorebirds. One or two Piping Plovers will occasionally overwinter here. In late autumn and winter check the drier portions of the flats for possible Lapland Longspurs and Snow Buntings.

If you have a four-wheel-drive vehicle, you may want to check through the gull flocks here in winter. Numbers are usually less impressive than at Cape Hatteras Point, but exceptions are possible. Once in late December, following a fish kill, the spit was virtually covered with gulls, including Iceland, Thayer's, Glaucous, and Common/Mew gulls and Black-legged Kittiwake. If you happen to pick a slow day, you still may be able to find a Lesser Black-backed Gull.

For further information: Contact Cape Hatteras NS, Route 1, Box 675, Manteo, NC 27954; phone 919-473-2111. The administrative office is located at the Fort Raleigh NHS, near Manteo. The nearest visitors center, located at the Cape Hatteras Lighthouse, is open all year. A checklist of the seashore's birds is available.

OCRACOKE ISLAND
MAP 16

Of the Outer Banks islands connected by NC 12, Ocracoke Island is visited the least by birdwatchers, partly because from any direction, getting there requires at least a short ferry ride. The island also lacks the habitat diversity of some of the more accessible parts of the Banks, and the chances of finding rare species are admittedly not as good on Ocracoke.

Nevertheless, birding on the island can be enjoyable. Land bird migration can be exceptional after autumn cold fronts, and the island offers a fairly long list of frequently sought-after species—like Yellow-crowned Night-Heron, White Ibis, Brant, Clapper Rail, Black Rail, Long-billed Curlew, Marsh and Sedge wrens, and Seaside and Sharp-tailed sparrows.

The late summer shorebird migration period (July and August) can also provide rewarding birding, especially if combined with a trip to nearby Portsmouth Island; so can winter, especially if combined with a ferry trip to or from Cedar Island or, even better, Swan Quarter.

BECAUSE MOST PEOPLE reach Ocracoke Island by way of the Hatteras Inlet ferry from Hatteras Village, this site guide begins at the ferry terminal. Specifically, the mileage figures begin at the stop sign you come to immediately after driving off the ferry; set your trip odometer to zero here. Note that sections of highway are sometimes relocated because of erosion; such changes could alter mileage figures slightly.

If you want to see shorebirds and you're in the mood to do some hiking, turn left at the stop sign, as if you were going to take the ferry back to Hatteras. Park in one of the spaces for waiting ferry traffic and survey the nearby bay and shoreline. During low water levels there may be a few shorebirds close by. More important, from here you can judge whether it is worth the mile-plus hike out to the flats beside Hatteras Inlet. This hike is most likely to be worthwhile from late April to early June and from July through October.

If the water level is low or you don't mind wading, you can walk from here (there's a parking lot just across from the ferry terminal). If you want a higher, drier route, drive down to the parking area at 0.6 miles and walk north along the ocean beach. For those with four-wheel-drive vehicles there's a beach access point just before the parking lot (at 0.5 miles).

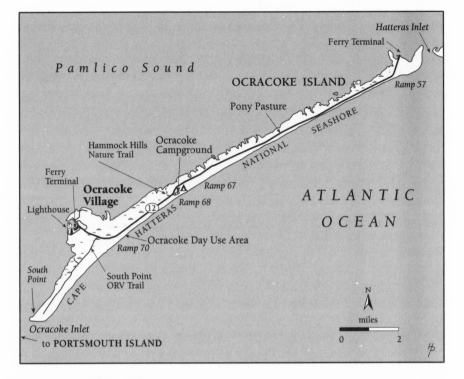

Pamlico Sound

OCRACOKE ISLAND

Hatteras Inlet

Ferry Terminal

Ramp 57

Pony Pasture

NATIONAL SEASHORE

Ocracoke Campground

Hammock Hills Nature Trail

Ferry Terminal

Ocracoke Village

Lighthouse

Ramp 67

Ramp 68

HATTERAS

ATLANTIC OCEAN

Ocracoke Day Use Area

Ramp 70

South Point

CAPE

South Point ORV Trail

N

miles

0   2

Ocracoke Inlet

to PORTSMOUTH ISLAND

16. OCRACOKE ISLAND

During the migration periods a good list of shorebirds is possible. In May look for breeding-plumaged Dunlins, Short-billed Dowitchers, and Red Knots. In autumn there may be several Marbled Godwits.

From about late April to July you can expect to see nesting Common and Least terns, Black Skimmers, American Oystercatchers, and maybe a couple of pairs of Wilson's and/or Piping plovers. (Stay out of any roped-off areas!) Forster's Terns sometimes nest in the adjacent marshes, and there are also Clapper Rails and sometimes Seaside Sparrows.

In winter the walk out to the flats is generally not worth the effort unless large numbers of gulls are present. If you are really lucky you might find a situation like the one that developed here in late December 1983. A die-off of menhaden had attracted thousands and thousands of gulls. The ground was almost literally covered by the feasting birds, including Glaucous, Iceland, Thayer's, Common Black-headed, and Mew gulls.

Other sites worth checking near the ferry terminal are a sand track to the right (at 0.1 miles) and, just beyond the sand track, a pond to the left of the highway.

Most of the time a regular car can easily handle the sand track, but you might prefer to walk it. The road runs along the edge of a dredged spoil area that is typically of no interest to the birder. However, any shallow pools that have been created by recent dredging can be very attractive to shorebirds. The track ends at a point on the sound—a good place to scope for waterfowl in winter, including Brant. During migrations, if the water level is low, there may be a few shorebirds.

Next to the sand track on the south lies a salt marsh that is small but usually worth checking. Clapper Rails and Seaside Sparrows breed in this marsh. Listen for the sparrows' wheezy songs from April into July. The habitat looks great for Black Rails, but I don't know anyone who has heard them here. The marsh has several shallow pools that often host a few shorebirds in spring and in late summer.

Autumn (especially September and October) brings high water levels. If the tide is extremely high during your visit to this marsh, wade out to some of the slightly higher sites—ones that haven't been submerged—and kick around. Hope for a Yellow Rail, although you are more likely to see Clapper Rail, Sora, and Virginia Rail. You may also see Seaside and Sharp-tailed sparrows and Marsh and Sedge wrens. (The Sharp-tailed Sparrows and Sedge Wrens are more likely in October.) In winter, calm sunrises and sunsets are the best times to go marsh-tromping. Squeaking should get you good looks at Sharp-tailed Sparrows and Sedge Wrens. At sunset listen for the low call-note of the Sedge Wren, which has the quality of two rocks being hit together.

Just past the sand track, a pond about eight hundred feet long lies right next to the highway. The road shoulders here are adequate for parking. Sometimes the pond is almost empty of birds, but typically it hosts a surprisingly diverse selection. In winter there are often several gulls—more in stormy weather—and dabbling ducks, up to four or five species at times. During the warmer months, particularly during the migrations and when the water level is low, there may be several wading birds, shorebirds, and terns. Shorebirds here include the pool-type species, like Stilt Sandpiper, Lesser Yellowlegs, and Long-billed Dowitcher. Black-necked Stilts show up occasionally. Over the years several goodies have been found here, including Eared Grebe, Fulvous Whistling-Duck, and Yellow-headed Blackbird.

At 4.5 miles from the ferry terminal, on the right you will see a four-wheel-drive sand track that runs one-half mile to the sound. In winter you might walk this track to look for waterfowl in the sound; and during the fall migration you might find migrant passerines in the shrub thickets. Most important, this site provides an adequate parking spot close to a couple of good hawk-watching dunes.

These dunes are located to your right as you begin down the track. Set up watch after a cold front in October, if the winds are west to northwest and the skies clear. Some days you may see hundreds of hawks—mostly Sharp-shinneds and American Kestrels, but also Cooper's Hawks, Merlins, and Peregrine Falcons. Springtime generally offers no notable hawk migration along the Outer Banks, but you might sometimes see a few. In April and May, hope for an American Swallow-tailed Kite.

The next paved parking area you will come to is on the ocean side of the highway, at 5.3 miles. Park here, cross the road, and take a short path that ends at the fence enclosing the **Pony Pasture**. (The pasture is off-limits; keep out.) Wide and grassy, this end of the pasture is worth checking from July to October for species like Upland Sandpiper and American Golden-Plover.

A short walk from the parking lot takes you to the ocean. Look for terns in summer and for Common Loons, Double-crested Cormorants, Northern Gannets, and gulls in winter. Wintertime ocean birding on Ocracoke Island is almost always productive, nice and birdy, with frequent close views of loons and gannets. (If you're hoping for species like jaegers and Black-legged Kittiwake, though, you're more likely to be successful at Cape Hatteras.) If you don't see many birds at this site, check some of the other ocean access points on the island.

The primary viewing area for the Pony Pasture is at 6.0 miles; you will see paved parking on both sides of the highway and an observation platform. Especially if you're in a lazy mood, the observation platform is a great place to loiter and hope for something of interest to show up. This end of the pasture has scattered shrubs that may attract a few passerines during the fall migration. The horse feed regularly attracts large numbers of blackbirds and Fish Crows. Around early September check the blackbirds carefully—a Yellow-headed is quite possible here. And check the doves also—one recent August a White-winged Dove flew by here. During the fall migration the observation platform also serves as a good hawk-watching station.

Incidentally, the whole island is very good for Barn Owls, at least from October to March. In fact, this seems to be the best location on the North Carolina coast for seeing this species. For some reason they come out relatively early in the evening here, sometimes as early as sunset. Generally the best strategy for finding them is to ride slowly along the highway at dawn or dusk. It is best if the sky is clear and you are driving toward the light; the silhouette of a feeding owl will be especially easy to pick out then. Owls are also relatively easy to see during a full moon. During a really dark night you might be lucky and glimpse one in your headlights. If possible, pull off on the shoulder, get out, and "squeak" loudly. Often an owl will come in and hover right above your head. A Short-eared Owl is also a possibility.

An area we'll call **The Pines** stretches from 8.6 to 9.2 miles. This area includes several stands of slash pines planted during the 1950s. These trees stand out as taller and more luxuriant than those in adjacent areas, and they must look that way to migrant passerines too, because at times after fall cold fronts these trees swarm with birds. There are places along this stretch where you can safely park a regular vehicle; however, beware of places where a thin carpet of pine needles presents an illusion of terra firma. During most of the warmer months, and sometimes into December, you will need lots of insect repellent.

This area offers a fairly wide variety of breeding land birds. From mid-April into June you will find Prairie Warblers, Common Yellowthroats, Carolina Wrens, Northern Cardinals, Great Crested Flycatchers, and others. If you get back into the pines watch carefully for Yellow-crowned Night-Herons—they nest here regularly.

About the same time—from mid-April to early June—watch for a few migrant passerines, especially during brisk winds from the southwest, west, or northwest. Don't expect more than a few birds, but several species are possible. The latest migrants pass through here in late May and early June; virtually no migrants can be found this late on the mainland. It is among these latest migrants that you are most likely to find a rare species. One recent year, on May 30, I found several migrants here, including Blackburnian and Bay-breasted warblers, which are very rare in spring on the adjacent mainland.

Of course, the best time to be here is after fall cold fronts with brisk west to northwest winds, especially in September and early October. You are sure to get delightfully frustrated trying to identify each warbler before it moves out of sight. Check the edges of the power-line clearing where it runs through thick undergrowth. Also, a marshy swale southeast of the highway and a few hundred yards northeast of the Island Creek bridge is usually very good (but the mosquitoes are terrible). During your frenzy remember that most of the birds will clearly be moving in a definite direction, and you might be able to anticipate where a pile-up will occur. If the birds are moving toward the west, you might check for concentrations at the nearby Hammock Hills Nature Trail, or you might consider heading for the island's other major autumn land bird spot—Ocracoke Village.

These pines are usually rather dull in winter, but if you walk quietly and look down frequently, you may see owl pellets that mark the location of a Barn Owl roosting in the trees above. Red-breasted Nuthatches can often be found here—interestingly, even during winters when they are scarce along most of the coast. I have a suspicion that a rare northern finch—like a White-winged Crossbill or Pine Grosbeak—has rested in these pines at least once.

Just beyond the pines is the bridge across Island Creek and then, on the left (at 9.4 miles), a paved parking area and the entrance to the Park Service campground. On the right is another small paved parking area and the beginning of the Hammock Hills Nature Trail.

Island Creek often hosts a coot or moorhen and, during the warmer months, a wading bird or two. Look for them swimming near the bridge. You can park on the road shoulder and often get great views, and photographs, of any birds here.

During rainy and stormy weather in autumn look over the campground for shorebirds. If you see any, beg the park attendant for permission to drive through the campground.

The **Hammock Hills Nature Trail** is one-quarter mile long and runs through the edge of the pines and through dense shrub-thicket vegetation. Part of it overlooks a little bay on the sound. Although the trail is pretty enough, you will usually have more birding success from the highway. However, on autumn days after cold fronts, migrants may pile up near the trail. One advantage of the trail is that it allows you to walk through thick vegetation relatively quietly, enabling you to see secretive species. (Wouldn't a Connecticut Warbler be nice?)

Just south of the nature trail parking lot is a sand track that runs down to the sound shore, about one-third mile away. During most of the year a regular car can handle this road. From the end of the road you will have a good view of a wide portion of the sound. During low water levels—usually during south to southwest winds—there are often a few shorebirds. This is a nice spot to be at sunset.

At 11.5 and 11.9 miles you will see paved parking areas for ocean access. At the latter site there is a small airfield; it is too small and too similar to nearby areas to offer much birding potential but may be worth checking nonetheless.

At 12.4 miles, just before the first stores on the edge of Ocracoke Village, a turnoff on the left leads to the sand track that runs to **South Point**, the island's south tip, almost 4 miles away at Ocracoke Inlet. Generally only four-wheel drive vehicles should use this track; but during wet weather in the cooler months, when the sand becomes more solid, you can often drive it in a regular vehicle. However, if you drive in a long distance then reach an impassable section, you could be in trouble, because you might not be able to turn around. Also, remember that any water on the road may be primarily salt water.

For roughly the first 2 miles the track runs through a vast salt meadow. (Many birders still call this area "**the Flats**," because until the 1970s it was indeed unvegetated sand flats.) In the breeding season listen for Eastern Meadowlarks and a few Seaside Sparrows. In recent years birders have also heard a few Black Rails. In winter Savannah Sparrows are common, and if you are here during a calm sunset you are sure to hear several Sedge Wrens.

A special weather possibility: sometimes in autumn during extremely high tides, the marshes and meadows are flooded, creating conditions in which you might see rails. Clappers, Virginias, and Soras are quite possible, and maybe, just maybe, a Black or Yellow will appear. The water must be high enough to cover the sand track, so of course you will not want to drive a car out. Not just any higher-than-average autumn tide will do; the weather must be stormy, with a very low barometric pressure.

At 1.0 miles down the track, another track forks off to the right and runs a short distance to the sound shoreline. In spring and summer there is usually a heronry in one of the shrub hammocks to the south, and this area can be very good for White and Glossy ibises and Black-crowned and Yellow-crowned night-herons. During low water levels a few shorebirds are possible.

Back on the main track, about 2 miles from the highway, you will begin to pass through areas of sparser vegetation. Each year a few birds nest on the dry shelly sites to the left. Look for oystercatchers, terns, skimmers, and (rarely) Piping and Wilson's plovers. On the right, on the moister flats, there may be flocks of gulls, terns, and shorebirds in autumn, especially during wet weather. From July to November look for Long-billed Curlews. They are regular here, although birders miss them more often than see them.

The end of the road gives a good view of the inlet. During the fall migration hawks and swallows flying south may circle around the area as they ponder whether to cross the inlet. Check the adjacent marshes this time of year, especially during high tides, for Seaside and Sharp-tailed sparrows. Over the turbulent waters of the inlet you will see several terns (including Sandwich) in summer, and both gulls and terns in winter.

Within **Ocracoke Village** you may want to walk all the streets and check the lawns and patches of shrub thickets, especially during the fall migration. You'll also want to check around the harbor (Silver Lake). In winter the shoreline and sound near the ferry terminal are often productive. Many of the village's stores offer a detailed street map, either free or at nominal cost.

Breeding birds in the village include Northern Cardinals, Carolina Wrens, Prairie Warblers, Gray Catbirds, Brown Thrashers, and other common species. Look for, but don't expect, a Painted Bunting; they have occurred in the village but are very rare. During the spring, after westerly winds, look for a few spring migrants—the same species listed above in the description of The Pines.

The best time to bird the village is after autumn cold fronts with west to northwest winds. Remember that "backdoor" cold fronts, with northeast winds, tend to be unproductive. There are good spots for misplaced passerines—patches of shrub thickets—throughout the village. Look for any dominant movement by the birds during the morning. If the birds are moving toward the northwest, check the shrubs near the ferry terminal: an impressive pile-up might occur there. If the birds are moving toward the west, walk the streets west of the harbor, along the western edge of the village. In this area the grounds of the old **Ocracoke Lighthouse** are worth checking. Next to the lighthouse is a large marshy area that could serve as a magnet to certain species.

To whet your appetite I'll mention that Western Kingbirds occur regularly on the island each fall. Other rarities that have been found include Scissor-tailed Flycatcher, Connecticut Warbler, Mourning Warbler, Clay-colored Sparrow, and Dickcissel.

Even if you see few birds, a walk around **Silver Lake** can be pleasant, especially at sunset. In summer you can expect to find Laughing Gulls, a few terns, and wading birds. Winter is usually much more interesting. If the weather is stormy, or if there has been recent fishing activity, check the gulls carefully. Sometimes large numbers are present, and Glaucous, Iceland, and Common Black-headed have all been found here. Also, look around all the pier ends and pilings. Scoters are occasional within the harbor, and both Common and King eiders have shown up.

While you're touring the village or waiting in line for the ferry, explore the shore near the ferry terminal. In winter check the flocks of Buffleheads near the shore—a Harlequin Duck was seen here once. Also, check the nearby pilings and range markers for a Great Cormorant or two.

Especially if the water level is low, go down to the shore next to the large parking lot just northeast of the ferry terminal office and scope toward the north. You will see a large sand shoal—called **The Reef** or **Howard's Reef**—about a mile away. In winter this shoal may be covered by Double-crested Cormorants, and you may just be able to identify the flocks of Brant that are frequent here. During much of the year you may sight some large shorebirds of a rich, warm reddish-brown color, but from this distance you probably can't tell what they are. What they are is Marbled Godwits; the shoal frequently hosts a large flock, up to two hundred birds.

During dry weather with southwest winds and low water levels, you might want to ride out to Howard's Reef; you could probably hire a local fisherman to take you. The Marbled Godwit flock often has one or two Long-billed Curlews, and in July and August you should see Sanderlings, Western Sandpipers, Semi-palmated Plovers, Short-billed Dowitchers, and other birds. During high water levels (usually associated with north to northeast winds) you will not want to go to the reef; it will be submerged, and birds will have gone elsewhere, mainly to Portsmouth Island.

For further information: Contact Cape Hatteras NS, Route 1, Box 675, Manteo, NC 27954; phone 919-473-2111. The administrative office is located at the Fort Raleigh NHS, near Manteo. The visitors center in Ocracoke Village, located next to the ferry terminal, is open most of the year; phone 919-928-4531.

FERRIES TO OCRACOKE ISLAND

One of Ocracoke's charming qualities is its relative inaccessibility; you don't reach this island quickly or incidentally. For most visitors the only way to get here is by ferry, from either Hatteras, Cedar Island, or Swan Quarter. Fortunately, all of these ferry trips can provide excellent birding, at least seasonally. The relatively short Hatteras Inlet run is free and does not require much planning. The other two are toll ferries that take longer and require a bit of planning.

Hatteras Inlet Ferry

This ferry trip has a lot going for it: it's free and short and offers productive birding most of the time. Keep this trip in mind as an excellent alternate activity on stormy, rainy winter days. The elevated passenger lounge provides excellent visibility—and it's dry and warm.

The ferry departs from the terminal at the end of NC 12, just southwest of Hatteras Village. The ferry crossing takes about forty minutes. Ferries run from before sunrise until about midnight. Most of the day, ferry runs are scheduled at intervals of an hour or less. A state highway map or roadside ferry information sign will give the exact schedule; when traffic is heavy, though, the ferries may run continuously rather than adhering to the set schedule. Usually you will not have to wait in line long. However, in summertime long lines may develop from midmorning to early afternoon—especially on weekends—and the wait can be long. You can also expect long lines at the Ocracoke terminal in mid- to late afternoon. The Hatteras Inlet ferry runs in all but the most severe weather.

Generally, the migration periods are best. Winter can also be good, especially when gulls are abundant. Early morning and late afternoon often have the largest numbers of birds; and late afternoon light is best for seeing birds on Hatteras and Ocracoke islands.

Water levels along the ferry route are influenced partly by lunar tides flowing in and out of the inlet and partly by the direction of the winds across Pamlico Sound. The lunar tide's influence is greatest right beside the inlet; as far "inland" as the Hatteras ferry terminal, its influence is almost nil. Water levels in the area are highest during winds from a northerly direction and lowest during winds from a southerly direction.

As soon as you board the ferry, you should decide whether you're going to bird from the bow or from the elevated passenger lounge. In nice weather the bow is preferable—the visibility is better and you can move around. During rainy and windy weather, though, head for the lounge: it's small, and passengers often ignore it, so you may have it all to yourself. If so, you should lower one of the windows for better visibility.

As the ferry pulls out from the harbor, check the adjacent shorelines. In winter there may be several gulls; Glaucous and Common Black-headed have both been seen here. In the warmer months there may also be a few wading birds.

Just out from the harbor the channel runs by numerous shoals and eel-grass beds. In winter watch for Brant, which are regular here. During low water levels, when the shoals are exposed, you may see gulls, terns, and shorebirds.

The channel swings out farther from Hatteras Island, then runs along next to a dredged-material island, where many water birds usually nest. The species of birds nesting from year to year may vary according to what habitats are present (which depends on the frequency of spoil deposition), but you might see anything from Brown Pelicans to wading birds to gulls and terns. During much of the year this island is a favorite loafing and roosting spot for Brown Pelicans. Look through them carefully—an American White Pelican has been an almost annual visitor in recent years.

Just past this island the channel turns back toward Hatteras Island, and you should get on the left side of the ferry. Near channel marker 16, look for a little tidal creek that runs up into the marsh. During the warmer months this creek often has a few herons, egrets, and ibises when water levels are low. This is a very good spot to look for Yellow-crowned Night-Herons, and late in the day you might see Black-crowneds as well. There may be a few shorebirds. Watch for a Clapper Rail skulking along the edge of the marsh.

For the next one-half mile the adjacent shoreline becomes less interesting; take this time to check out the gulls behind the ferry. In winter birders have spotted Lesser Black-backed, Glaucous, and Iceland gulls among the more common species.

The channel also lies close to the island, near the Hatteras Inlet flats. At peak fishing times the shore here may be almost covered by human beings and their vehicles, but at other times you should see at least a few shorebirds, gulls, and terns. During the migrations there may be several shorebirds—look for Marbled Godwits and, at times in winter, large flocks of gulls.

The remnants of ocean swells are often noticeable in the inlet gorge, and you may feel like you're on a pelagic trip for a couple of minutes as the ferry moves through this area. In fact, you might see a Northern Gannet flying past in winter. Even Black-legged Kittiwakes have been seen here, and northbound jaegers have entered the inlet in spring. (After all, Pamlico Sound does look like an ocean.) On the right is a large dredged-material island that harbors nesting gulls, terns, and skimmers. In winter this island is a major roost for cormorants, pelicans, and gulls.

Just beyond the inlet is the northeast end of Ocracoke Island. The ferry passes within a short distance of a narrow sand spit; the area protected by this spit becomes a shallow bay during high water levels and exposed mud flats during low water levels. In the warmer months, especially during the migrations, there may be several birds here. Look for wading birds, shorebirds (including Marbled Godwits), and gulls and terns. If there are enough birds, you might consider walking out to the area after you get off the ferry. (See the first site discussed under "Ocracoke Island.")

Between the spit and the Ocracoke Island terminal, watch for ducks in winter. Buffleheads are frequent, Common Goldeneyes occasional. Birders have also seen Harlequin Ducks and Common Eiders in this area.

Cedar Island–Ocracoke Ferry
For predictably good birding you should take this trip only during the winter months, but occasionally the birding can also be good at other seasons. The

Cedar Island ferry terminal is located at the end of the mainland portion of NC 12. In planning your drive to the site, avoid a tight schedule—US 70 and NC 12 in eastern Carteret County are curvy roads that frequently run through residential areas.

This is a heavily used ferry, and you will usually need to make a reservation in advance. Call 919-225-3551 between 6 A.M. and 6 P.M. for reservations and schedule information. (For an Ocracoke to Cedar Island run, call 919-928-3841.) The schedule is also listed on a state highway map. The ferries run much less frequently during the winter months.

This run takes about two hours and fifteen minutes. Ferry rates (one-way) are currently $10 for a regular car, $2 for a bicycle and rider, and $1 for a pedestrian. If the trip itself is your primary object in terms of birding, you really should consider going as a pedestrian, perhaps taking a bicycle so that you can bird much of Ocracoke Island. If you do go as a pedestrian, however, keep in mind that on rare occasions ferry runs may be canceled due to gale or storm warnings or extremely dense fog. When forecasts indicate that the weather is about to change, ask ferry personnel whether the return trip might be canceled.

You will definitely want to wait for the right weather, because you will not be able to bird from the passenger lounge. The only suitable birding spots are on the bow and the upper deck. Neither spot shields you from rain, so avoid this ferry run during rainy weather.

Also avoid days with strong winds, especially headwinds or winds blowing perpendicular to the ferry's path. Tailwinds aren't so bad; actually, a tailwind of about ten miles per hour produces nearly calm conditions on deck.

Although the early morning run usually has the most birds, the afternoon ferry during a light southwest wind provides the most comfort and best views. The wind and water will seem relatively calm, and the light will be excellent. Also, the southwest wind will cause many of the birds to take off so that they fly back toward or by the ferry.

The "Carteret" is rarely used in the winter season, but when you call for reservations, you might ask whether this newer ferry is available. It is great for bad weather, because it has a passenger lounge up front on the upper level. Visibility through the front window is excellent. If you do have the good fortune to schedule this ferry, you will want to claim this perch as soon as you can after boarding the ferry.

AGAIN, THE BEST TIME of year is winter—specifically, late November through March. The following description applies to this period.

As soon as you have boarded the ferry, get up on the upper deck to scan the nearby shorelines and harbor and rock jetties while the ferry is pulling out. Look carefully—Common Eiders have wintered in the harbor, a Purple Sandpiper was once seen on the rock jetty, and on rare occasions Great Cormorants perch on the pilings.

Once the ferry has cleared the harbor, get down to the bow as quickly as you can. The first thirty minutes of the trip will be the best time for seeing loons, grebes, cormorants, and scoters. The first loons you see will probably be Commons; you will notice a shift toward Red-throateds as the ferry continues toward deeper water. You will also see scoters—Surf Scoters are the most common, but you may see Blacks as well. There may be huge flocks of Red-breasted Mergansers and at least a few Horned Grebes.

In addition to these common species, you might see something unusual. Oldsquaws and White-winged Scoters are occasionally seen here, and a Red-necked Grebe is also possible.

Farther out, the variety of waterfowl usually drops off noticeably, but you should continue to see Red-throated Loons and flocks of Red-breasted Mergansers. By the way, Northern Gannets occur regularly on the sound, and even jaegers are seen occasionally.

About one hour after you've left Cedar Island (or one hour and fifteen minutes out of Ocracoke), look for channel marker SRS on your right; you can often see several Great Cormorants here. Sometimes the ferry passes close enough to the marker for reasonably good views.

If watching from the bow gets boring, check out the gulls behind the ferry. They often fly in close, enabling one to get good photographs and study plumage differences. Birders have spotted Lesser Black-backed, Glaucous, and Iceland gulls following this ferry.

About forty minutes from Ocracoke, your interest level should rise again. This final leg of the trip offers at least as many birds as the beginning, and you will see some additional species.

Watch on your right for two smokestacks of a submerged boat, where one or two Great Cormorants often perch. Across the channel from these stacks there may be a dredged-material island (unless it has washed away). Check here for roosting Brown Pelicans (and rarely an American White), cormorants, and gulls. This channel, by the way, is called Big Foot Slough.

Farther on you will see many Double-crested Cormorants (and maybe a Great Cormorant) on the channel markers and net stakes. Over the shoals you should see Canada Geese and Brant, and maybe American Wigeons and Northern Pintails. Along the channel there will be Red-breasted Mergansers and Buffleheads, and occasionally a Common Goldeneye or a rarity like a Harlequin Duck.

On your left, a particularly large shoal (marked by numerous duck blinds) is often exposed. Here you may see large flocks of cormorants, and maybe geese, Brant, and Marbled Godwits as well. This shoal, called Howard's Reef or The Reef, is discussed in more detail in the Ocracoke Island site guide.

As the ferry makes its final turn into the harbor, you may want to get back up on the upper deck for a quick survey of the jetties at the harbor entrance (there may be oystercatchers here) and the harbor itself. (See the description of Silver Lake in the Ocracoke Island site guide.)

During the nonwinter months this ferry is usually much less interesting and, except for the final run into Ocracoke, can be almost boring. However, you could possibly see something exciting during the migrations, and in autumn, if large numbers of gulls are over the sound, you have some chance of seeing a jaeger.

If you begin the run at Ocracoke instead of Cedar Island, early morning will provide the best light. Calm conditions or a light northeast wind would be best.

Swan Quarter–Ocracoke Ferry

This ferry run has many similarities to the Cedar Island–Ocracoke run. They're good at the same seasons; they're about the same length; they cost the same. However, the Swan Quarter run usually offers many more birds than the Cedar Island–Ocracoke ferry—especially ducks—and boasts very impressive numbers of Oldsquaws, for North Carolina. Considering how productive this ferry ride is, the fact that birders seldom take it is unfortunate.

The Swan Quarter terminal is located just south of the community of Swan Quarter at the end of NC 45. The ferry schedule stays the same throughout the year, with only two round-trips available each day. See a state highway map or call the Swan Quarter terminal (919-926-1111) for the exact schedule. This ferry is often not heavily used, but you might want to make a reservation just in case, particularly on weekends and holidays. (If you plan to take the ferry from Ocracoke to Swan Quarter, call the Ocracoke ferry terminal at 919-928-3841.)

The ferry run takes about two hours and thirty minutes. Rates (one-way) are currently $10 for a regular car, $2 for a bicycle and rider, and $1 for a pedestrian. This is another ferry that you might consider taking as a pedestrian.

The best birding spot is from the ferry's bow. However, the bow provides no protection from wind or rain. For the most enjoyable trip, avoid days with rain and a strong headwind or side wind. A tailwind (west to northwest) is fine if it is not too strong. During most of the winter you should take only the morning run, because the afternoon run takes place mostly in the dark or near dark. In March and early April, however, the light will be better during the afternoon run. The best time of year is winter—specifically, late November to early April—and the following description covers this period.

As soon as you get on the ferry, head for the bow. The run's first hour is the best; you'll see large numbers of loons, grebes, and ducks almost constantly.

As the ferry heads out of the narrow channel onto Swan Quarter Bay, look for a large raft of diving ducks. This raft usually consists primarily of Canvasbacks and scaup but may also contain Ruddy Ducks and other species.

For about forty-five minutes after the ferry departs, you will be thoroughly entertained watching Red-throated and Common loons, Horned Grebes, Double-crested Cormorants, Red-breasted Mergansers, Oldsquaws, Buffleheads, and Surf and Black scoters. For North Carolina the number of Oldsquaws here is impressive, probably outnumbering the combined numbers of birds elsewhere in the state. This is a good place to look for a rarity. A Western Grebe has been identified here, and the area might well attract Red-necked Grebes too.

As the ferry continues to deeper water, you will notice a gradual decline in the variety of waterfowl; eventually you begin to see little more than Red-throated Loons and flocks of Red-breasted Mergansers. As on the Cedar Island–Ocracoke ferry, you may see one or two Northern Gannets.

The final leg of the trip follows Big Foot Slough, the same channel described for the Cedar Island–Ocracoke ferry run. You will know that you have entered this channel when you see the two smokestacks of the submerged boat on your right.

For the very best birding, head the other direction: take the early morning run *from* Ocracoke when it is calm or when there is a light southeast to south wind. The light will be excellent; it should be comfortable, because there will be relatively little windchill; birds near Ocracoke Inlet will be especially active; and the waterfowl at the Swan Quarter end of the run are more likely to be in the channel right in the ferry's path. (The birds are flushed by the first ferry run, and they may not have come back to the channel by the time the ferry returns a short time later.)

The Swan Quarter to Ocracoke ferry can be rather dull in the warmer months. Then the most interesting section of the run is along the channel just outside Ocracoke, where you should see Brown Pelicans and terns. An American White Pelican is sometimes seen around here throughout the summer.

For information and reservations: For information call the Cedar Island ferry terminal (919-225-3551), the Swan Quarter ferry terminal (919-926-1111), or the Ocracoke ferry terminal (919-928-3841). For reservations call the ferry terminal from which you plan to leave.

PORTSMOUTH ISLAND
MAP 17

This fascinating island is quite difficult to get to, but visiting here can certainly be worth the effort at times. This island is quite distinctive: a vast expanse of barren flats (the Portsmouth Flats) lies in the middle of the island, between the ocean beach and the more stable soundside land, which is covered with shrub-thicket vegetation.

During suitable conditions—that is, when the flats are wet—this area can be superlative for shorebirds. Large flocks of Marbled Godwits are frequent, and

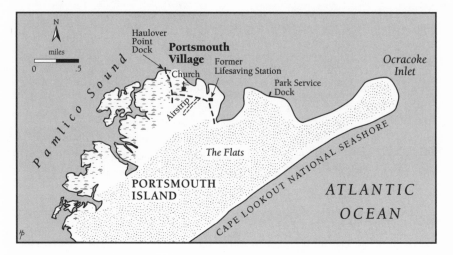

17. PORTSMOUTH ISLAND

this is traditionally one of the best spots in the state for Long-billed Curlews. Each year, around late July, Curlew Sandpipers occur almost routinely. Although birders visit this site very infrequently, Bar-tailed Godwits have been found here three times. If this site was birded regularly, it would no doubt boast of other super-rarities.

Outside of the peak shorebird periods or during unsuitable conditions, jaded longtime birders will probably not be willing to invest the effort it takes to get to Portsmouth. Nevertheless, the island is always at least mildly interesting. Both Wilson's and Piping plovers nest here and are easy to find during the breeding season, and the island is a major feeding area for migrating Piping Plovers. During the warmer months this area hosts a variety of wading birds. White Ibises are fairly common, and you can often find a few Black-crowned and Yellow-crowned night-herons in the village. In recent years Reddish Egrets have been spotted occasionally in late summer.

Most of the tern species that occur in North Carolina can usually be found beside the inlet. Seaside Sparrows nest in the salt marshes and meadows next to the dunes near the inlet, and Clapper Rails frequently show up in the village's salt marshes.

The shrub thickets of the village can be excellent for migrant land birds in autumn. However, the island is not usually as good as some of the more accessible spots on the Outer Banks—such as Pea Island and Ocracoke Island—so birders virtually never come to Portsmouth in search of these migrants. Portsmouth is a wonderful place to visit, though, especially if you like to get away from everything and can savor a view of sky, water, and flats that stretches forever. On the most crowded days you probably won't see more than a dozen people here.

Portsmouth can be a fun trip for a couple or group that includes both birders and nonbirders. The ocean beach can often be excellent for shelling, and most visitors will find a walk through the old ghost village intriguing. During the 1700s and early 1800s Portsmouth Village was a thriving commercial center where oceangoing ships transferred their cargoes to smaller craft that then sailed to the port cities along the western shores of the sounds. In the mid-1800s a storm opened up Hatteras and Oregon inlets and made Ocracoke Inlet shallower; from that point on Portsmouth's commercial importance diminished drastically, and the population began a steady decline. The last two residents of the village moved to the mainland in 1971.

Today Portsmouth is part of the Cape Lookout NS. Many of the old buildings, including the old lifesaving station and the old church, are maintained by the Park Service. Others are leased and maintained by individuals.

As you stroll along the lanes through the village, it is difficult to imagine the bustling activity that once took place here. Epitaphs on the tombstones in the numerous small graveyards reveal how harsh life could be on the Outer Banks well into this century. Especially if you come during high water levels, you are sure to be impressed by how low the village is—it lies virtually at sea level. One bit of lore associated with Portsmouth is truly amazing: legend has it that no one ever drowned here during a hurricane.

LOGISTICS. Most visitors can get to Portsmouth only by boat from Ocracoke Village. There is no regularly scheduled ferry service, but a few people licensed by the Park Service can be hired to take you to Portsmouth in small open boats. Call the Cape Lookout NS Visitors Center (919-728-2250) for a list of these licensees. In the summer you can also call the Ocracoke Island Visitors Center (919-928-4531). You can expect a transportation fee of about $40 for one or two people, $15 per person for a group of three or more.

During windy conditions you should be prepared for lots of spray on the trip over to the island. Bring some sort of waterproof bag for binoculars and anything else you want to keep dry. In cooler weather you should also bring rain gear and a change of clothes.

Fortunately, the best shorebirding spot is usually just a few yards from the Park Service dock at the inlet (the primary docking area), so you can have a rewarding day with little walking. However, to check Portsmouth's other birding attractions—the nearby dunes and developing marsh areas, the ocean beach, and the inlet side of the spit at the island's northeast end—will require a hike of about 2 miles. To explore Portsmouth Village you will have to hike another mile. You can often get by without having to get your feet wet, but you should be prepared to wade through ankle-deep water. If you can tolerate wet feet and if you plan to walk a lot, wear tennis shoes or some other sort of light, comfortable footwear.

There is no drinking water on the island; during warm weather bring plenty to drink and plenty of heavy-duty sunscreen. Insects are not usually a problem on the flats. However, during June and July greenheads (biting flies) can be appallingly ferocious and persistent; you'll needs lots of repellent to deter these pests. In Portsmouth Village mosquitoes may be only mildly annoying after dry weather, but after extended wet periods they're impossible, and they can be bad into December.

If you have a four-wheel-drive vehicle, you might consider taking the small private ferry (Park Service concession) from Atlantic to Core Banks, then driving up the barrier strand—about 15 miles—to Portsmouth. (There are currently no inlets between Core Banks and Portsmouth Island.) This alternative is expensive and requires a lot of planning, but it will enable you to cover a lot more area, including the flats where the Kathryn Jane and Whalebone inlets used to be (about 5 miles southwest of Portsmouth Village and Ocracoke Inlet). Occasionally, this area can be as good for shorebirds as the Portsmouth Flats.

The ferry is run by a concessionaire called Morris Marina, Kabin Kamps, and Ferry Service (919-225-4261). Transporting a vehicle to the island costs $60 (round-trip), plus $12 per person. Anyone taking a vehicle to the island should call the Cape Lookout NS Visitors Center (919-728-2250) for the latest regulations and cautions regarding the use of vehicles in the national seashore.

Camping is allowed in the national seashore. Call the Cape Lookout NS Visitors Center for more information. Those with four-wheel-drive vehicles might want to consider renting one of the primitive cabins at the ferry terminal on Core Banks. These cabins are least expensive and most likely to be available outside the fall fishing season, which lasts from October to early December.

Again, for the best birding you've got to visit during the right times and conditions. The best times are during the migration periods, from late April to late May and early July to October. For your very best chances to see something unusual, visit around mid-May or late July. These expansive flats are not regularly flooded by lunar tides. Most of the time they are actually quite dry; but they are subject to occasional wetting and flooding by heavy rains and wind tides associated with strong winds out of the northwest, north, or northeast (and sometimes, in autumn, by abnormally high lunar tides). During high wind tides the flats may be flooded with up to a foot of water—more on rare occasions. However, you are not likely ever to see such water levels: you wouldn't want to make a boat ride to the island during the wind conditions required to create such flooding.

When the flats are dry, they are often almost birdless, but when they are wet, this area can be a shorebirder's heaven. If possible, try to visit here just after a really strong northerly wind (at least twenty-five miles per hour) has just subsided—the sooner after the wind dies down, the better. Also, the periods just after heavy rainfall (two or more inches) may be just as good, and they are much easier to plan for. In July and August the shorebird numbers will probably be impressive only after heavy rains, because strong northerly winds are so rare in those months. Again, you will want to get to the island as soon as possible after the rains, at least within twenty-four hours. Consider planning your visit to coincide with the high tide in the adjacent sound, which lags about two hours after that on the ocean beach; high tide in the sound will reduce the available habitat there and force more birds onto the Portsmouth flats.

Although you should definitely make an attempt to visit Portsmouth during these prime conditions, a birding trip during less-than-prime conditions is not necessarily doomed to failure. Even rarities may still show up; Long-billed Curlews, Bar-tailed Godwits, and Curlew Sandpipers have been spotted during dry conditions when very few birds were present.

THIS TOUR OF the island focuses on the period from April through October, when the island is most accessible.

When arranging your trip, be sure to specify that you want to go to the Park Service dock on the inlet shore (the Wallace Channel dock). Also, *before you confirm* your intention to charter a particular boat you may want to ask two questions that could lead you to an American White Pelican. Some summers an American White frequently rests at a Brown Pelican nesting colony on an island inside the inlet near Portsmouth Village. This site is not along the regular boat route; but you can ask the boat captain if he has seen "the white pelican" at one of the islands lately and, if so, whether he would alter the trip slightly so you can see it.

When you arrive at the Park Service dock, you will see the **Portsmouth Flats** ahead, stretching off toward the southwest. Again, the area of the flats that tends to be the best (particularly during dry conditions) is the area just ahead. East and southeast of the Park Service dock, look for several tidal pools between the flats and the inlet shore. In this area, storms periodically create small, narrow inlets that later become isolated as pools, flooded only by the highest tides. Such pools can provide your best chance for rarities—especially Curlew Sandpiper—and they attract birds particularly well during dry weather.

During really wet conditions you may become a bit frustrated, because shorebirds will be scattered across the flats as far as you can see. Fortunately, even during these prime conditions most birds will be concentrated in the northeastern portion of the flats, within a mile of the Park Service dock.

You will probably also want to walk about half a mile from the Park Service dock to check out the spit at the island's northeastern corner. The flats on the inland side of this spit usually attract shorebirds. Lunar tides affect this site more strongly than the Portsmouth Flats, so you may find birds here even during dry conditions. By the way, this spit was formed quite recently—about

1990—when an island in the inlet migrated westward and collided with what was then the end of Portsmouth Island. The spit is constantly changing size and shape, and it could easily disappear in a severe storm.

If you happen to visit the island during really dry conditions, when you have to struggle for every shorebird, you might want to hike southwest over the flats and head down the island (past the village) for a mile and a half. Here you will see a series of small inlets connecting the flats to the sound. The flats at these inlets are always wet and often harbor a few shorebirds even during dry conditions.

During good conditions in the migration periods, the Portsmouth Flats will always produce a long list of shorebirds typical of intertidal habitats—species like Semipalmated Plover, Willet, Whimbrel, Western Sandpiper, Dunlin, and Short-billed Dowitcher. Even during shorebirds' seasonal low point (in mid- to late June) birders can usually find several species here, including birds that nest far to the north, like Red Knot, Short-billed Dowitcher, and Dunlin. Most such birds found in mid- to late June are one-year-old birds, which do not acquire full breeding plumage.

Each year up to two hundred Marbled Godwits overwinter in the Ocracoke Inlet area. Peak numbers occur from about late August to early April, but several of these godwits are usually present as early as mid-July and as late as late April, and you can often find a few through early summer. Typically you will see just a handful of godwits during low water levels, when they feed on shoals in Pamlico Sound—especially Howard's Reef, northwest of Ocracoke Village. During high water levels, however, the entire flock may come to Portsmouth Island. The godwit flock often includes a Long-billed Curlew (sometimes as many as three). You are most likely to see a Long-billed from about mid-July to mid-April, but you might see one in early summer.

The Portsmouth Flats are especially attractive to Red Knots. These birds are often common in winter as well as during the migrations, and at least a few of them can be found throughout the early summer.

Perhaps because rain regularly wets them, the flats tend to attract many types of shorebirds that typically shun intertidal flats. During the migrations, especially after heavy rains, you may see species like Lesser Yellowlegs and White-rumped, Pectoral, and Stilt sandpipers. Wilson's Phalaropes are seen occasionally in July and August, and American Avocets and Hudsonian Godwits sometimes show up during the fall migration. You are most likely to find such pool-type shorebirds at any tide pools near the boat dock.

The Red-necked Phalarope, which is primarily pelagic, also makes somewhat regular appearances at Portsmouth. These birds are probably occasional here in late May and early June.

When many birders hear "Portsmouth Island," they immediately think of the Curlew Sandpiper. Many birders have added this predominantly Eurasian species to their life lists by visiting Portsmouth. Indeed, this island is apparently one of North America's most reliable sites for this bird. Most recorded sightings have taken place between mid-July and early August. You're most likely to find a bird during the last few days of July; you have at least a fairly good chance then of finding one (or more), especially during wet conditions. Any tide pools near the inlet deserve special scrutiny if you're looking for this species. Though birders have long considered the Curlew Sandpiper primarily an autumn migrant, recent records suggest that birds may also be occasional here in May, especially mid-May.

Portsmouth Island has actually had little birding activity, almost all of which has focused on the period between mid-July and early August. Despite this sparse coverage, Bar-tailed Godwits have been seen here three times—twice in spring and once in autumn. This total equals the number of records elsewhere in the state, all from the much more heavily birded Bodie Island–Pea Island area. If they birded Portsmouth more heavily, birders might find this species to be almost annual here. Indeed, Portsmouth would seem to be the sort of place where super-rarities like stints, Black-tailed Godwit, and Sharp-tailed Sandpiper might occur.

However, I should add a cautionary note: it is possible that this excellent shorebird area may actually disappear in the future. The flats have been a permanent feature of the island for decades, even centuries; for some reason the area was never invaded by vegetation. In recent years, though, marsh vegetation has colonized some of the edges of the flats, and it is rapidly spreading. This thought is sobering to anyone who remembers the extreme transformation of Ocracoke's flats, which were similar to Portsmouth's, in the 1970s. But it seems likely that the great expanse of still-barren flats at Portsmouth, combined with the unaltered geology of the area (there is no highway to keep salt-laden sound water from flooding the flats) will combine to maintain a large expanse of good shorebird habitat through at least the rest of the decade. Stay tuned.

Two shorebirds that should be easy to find during the breeding season, regardless of the water level, are the Wilson's and Piping plovers. Both species feed on the flats and nest along their edges. (Piping Plover nesting areas are often posted. In nonposted areas, if you encounter any birds that are obviously nesting, stay away.) This is the state's northernmost site where Wilson's Plovers are easy to find. Look for them from early April to about mid-September; they are often most common in August. Piping Plovers are most common during the migrations—March through April and August through September. A few often stay throughout the winter.

In addition to shorebirds, the flats can be quite good for a variety of other water birds. During the warmer months you can expect a good variety of terns, including Sandwich and Gull-billed. This is one of the state's better areas for Black Terns, a few of which usually make appearances from early July to early

September. Look carefully through all the flocks of gulls and terns: Roseate Terns have been spotted here in late May and Sooty Terns in summer. One July, after stormy weather, even a Sabine's Gull was spotted.

Wading birds—including White Ibises—are also frequent along the edges of the flats during the warmer months. In late summer watch for Reddish Egrets, which have been seen a few times.

You should also check the developing salt marshes and meadows along the ocean side of the flats. A few Seaside Sparrows breed here, and both Seaside and Sharp-tailed sparrows occur during the autumn migration. Small isolated patches of marsh allow you to flush rails in autumn; Clapper Rails will probably become regular here in the near future.

At all seasons you should check the skies periodically. In April and May birders have seen Swallow-tailed Kites following the barrier islands up and down the coast, and Magnificent Frigatebirds have been seen overhead in summer. In autumn this is a good spot for both Merlins and Peregrine Falcons.

During the migrations, especially after cold fronts in September and October, you should make at least a quick check of **Portsmouth Village**. You might be able to arrange to be put off or picked up on the village's sound side (Haulover Point dock) to reduce the amount of walking. It is easy to find your way through the village. One main roadway runs through it, and there are several good landmarks—the old lifesaving station, the old airstrip, and the church. Don't be surprised if you see a Ring-necked Pheasant along the stretch of road between the village and the flats.

If you have the good fortune to be in the village after a good autumn cold front, you will want to explore all the trails and work along the edges of the old airstrip. Western Kingbirds are regular in October. Cold fronts from late April through May typically produce just a handful of birds; nevertheless, they offer the possibility of something unusual. For example, Gray Kingbirds have been spotted around late May. Along some of the more distant trails on the west side of the village, look for Black-crowned Night-Herons at any season and a few Yellow-crowneds from early May to late September. Along the little tide creeks at the lifesaving station and near the church, look for a Clapper Rail.

Birders seldom visit Portsmouth Island in winter, although a Christmas Bird Count has been held here for several years. The Christmas counts and other winter visits have revealed that wintertime birding here generally offers little variety, but an occasional exciting record makes the trip worthwhile. The Christmas counts have turned up a Red Phalarope, a Northern Saw-whet Owl, and a Western Kingbird. The large numbers of Marbled Godwits that occasionally show up in winter are sometimes accompanied by a Long-billed Curlew. Typically, in winter the shorebirds are sparse and not very diverse, except during wet and mild years. One of the state's most bizarre bird records occurred here: a Curlew Sandpiper showed up one winter.

Anyone with a four-wheel-drive vehicle should consider visiting another good shorebirding area nearby. The flats at the southwestern end of Portsmouth Island (about 5 miles from Ocracoke Inlet), which mark the locations of the former **Kathryn Jane and Whalebone inlets**, can attract many of the same species found on the Portsmouth Flats. A Long-billed Curlew sometimes appears here. You'll spot this area easily from the ocean beach, because it is so open—you can see Pamlico Sound in the background. In the middle of the open expanse look for three prominent soundside shrub-thicket islands, a very good landmark.

For further information: Contact Cape Lookout NS, 131 Charles Street, Harkers Island, NC 28531; phone 919-728-2250. A checklist of the seashore's birds and a detailed map of Portsmouth Village are available.

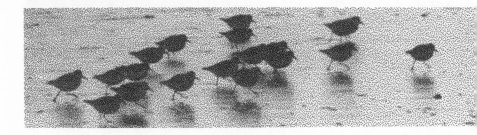

CHAPTER 7

THE CENTRAL COAST SECTION

PAMLICO POINT IMPOUNDMENT
MAP 18

Tucked away at the northeast corner of Pamlico County (some would say at the end of the earth), this area offers the potential for good to excellent birding during most of the year. Unfortunately, though, this site is very inaccessible. Indeed, during most years birders don't even visit it.

Part of the Goose Creek Game Land, which is administered by the North Carolina Wildlife Resources Commission, the Pamlico Point Impoundment is excellent for waterfowl in autumn and winter. Dabbling ducks predominate, but several diving ducks may also be seen on the impoundment itself, and large rafts are sometimes present on the adjacent river. This is also a good place to look for the rarer species: Eurasian Wigeons undoubtedly occur here regularly, and Fulvous Whistling-Ducks have been found during some years.

Unlike some other impoundments, this one is frequently interesting during the warmer months. A few ducks breed here, as do Common Moorhens and Black-necked Stilts. During most years all four subimpoundments are drawn down slightly in late spring and summer, so wading birds are usually common, especially in late summer. Occasionally one of the subimpoundments is completely drawn down; in this case shorebirds can be common in July and August. Marsh Wrens and Seaside Sparrows are common breeders in the marshes around the impoundment. There are also a few rails and Least Bitterns.

The impoundment is well situated for attracting rare species of all sorts, not just waterfowl. It is located at the northeastern tip of the Pamlico County land mass, where the Pamlico River meets the Pamlico Sound. For many migrating water and land birds this is a natural stopping point.

Access to Pamlico Point is by private boat only, and a vessel with a shallow draft is required. On days with near-calm conditions or light southerly winds, you could canoe to the impoundment, but it would be a long paddle indeed.

You can put a boat in at the Oyster Creek boat ramp. To reach this point from NC 33 at Hobucken, turn left onto Lowland Road. Continue 4.2 miles, until you come to the community of Lowland. Here, turn right onto Horne Road. After 0.8 miles turn right on Oyster Creek Road. Shortly before this road ends at some fish houses, you will see the boat ramp on your right.

From the ramp it is about 2 miles to the northwest corner of the impoundment, and about 3 miles to the center, by way of Boat Creek. If you have a motorboat, go slow—the waters are often almost covered with crab pots and nets. The best strategy is to go up Boat Creek and take the canal to the center of the impoundment. From here you can judge which subimpoundments are best that day and decide where to direct your efforts. (It is about 5 miles around the impoundment's perimeter.)

The impoundment generally has large numbers of dabbling ducks from October to March, although it can be good as early as September and as late as early April. Try to avoid the hunting season (these dates vary from year to year), plus a couple of weeks after the season, perhaps. Northern Pintails and American Wigeons are usually the most common ducks, but you should also be able to find most of the dabblers. Considering the abundance of American Wigeons, it shouldn't be too difficult to find a Eurasian Wigeon in late October or November. And during invasion years this is probably one of the better spots in North Carolina for Fulvous Whistling-Ducks.

Several diving ducks can usually be found here. Look for Ring-neckeds, scaup, Canvasbacks, and Ruddy Ducks, which generally arrive about Thanksgiving. Occasionally large rafts of divers may be seen on the adjacent river. The species may include Greater Scaup, Surf and Black scoters, Common Goldeneye, and Oldsquaw.

In addition to waterfowl, you should see a good variety of other species. Bald Eagles are seen here occasionally. Also watch for a Peregrine Falcon and Merlin and, in the marshes, for Marsh Wrens, Common Yellowthroats, and Swamp Sparrows. Vegetation along the dikes is likely to attract small land birds during the autumn migration.

During the breeding season this is one of the most interesting impoundments in the state. American Black Ducks and Gadwalls are common, and you might also see Mallards and Blue-winged Teal. Ruddy Ducks have nested here on at least one occasion. Black-necked Stilts are common here during many years, and you should see a few Common Moorhens. With luck you might spot a Least Bittern or Virginia Rail. In the salt marshes around the impoundment, listen for Seaside Sparrows and Marsh Wrens. You might also hear Clapper Rails and Virginia Rails. Black Rails have never been recorded here, but they undoubtedly occur occasionally, especially in the marshes on the east side of the impoundment.

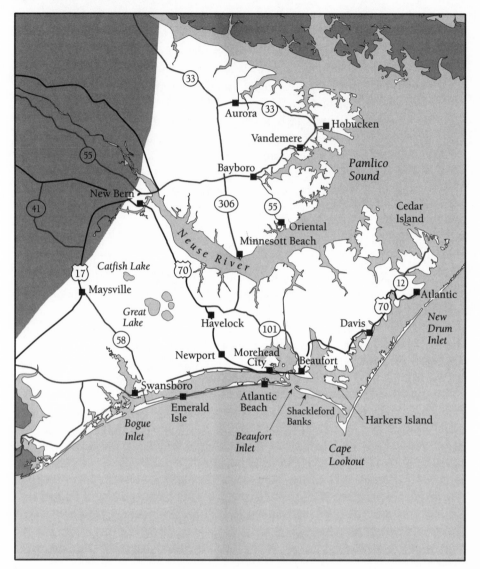

THE CENTRAL COAST SECTION

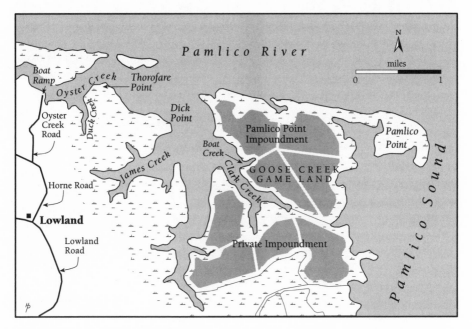

18. PAMLICO POINT IMPOUNDMENT

The dikes are not mowed during the warmer months, so as summer progresses it becomes increasingly difficult to walk along them. At this time of year you will definitely want to take your boat up to the center of the impoundment so that you can find the best areas with the least amount of effort.

In mid- to late summer, low water levels can offer some productive birding. Among the numerous wading birds, you may see a Wood Stork or other rarity. Gulls and terns also congregate here; look for Black Terns and Caspian Terns in late summer. Migrant shorebirds are often common in July and August, and later if water levels remain low. Species in this category will include those that generally shun intertidal habitats, such as Lesser Yellowlegs, Stilt Sandpiper, and Long-billed Dowitcher. A few Wilson's Phalaropes are possible, and this would be a good spot for an American Avocet.

It is unfortunate that this site is visited so infrequently, because it has the potential to produce exciting birding during the migration periods, and rare birds certainly occur here regularly. After severe storms in autumn and winter, more diving ducks are likely to move into the impoundment. This looks like a great place to find Eared Grebe and Red-necked Grebe (on the adjacent river) and possibly even a Western Grebe. During spring migration, vagrant Swallow-tailed and Mississippi kites have undoubtedly tarried overhead here as they pondered whether to cross the river or head northwest. And who knows what rare land birds may have stopped here in autumn.

From spring through summer, on your way over to the impoundment you will want to check the edges of the marshes from Duck Creek to Thorofare Point to Dick Point. If your boat is small enough, you may want to travel up one of the canals a little ways. This area is good for Marsh Wrens and Seaside Sparrows, and you should see a few Least Bitterns. Clapper and Virginia rails are also possible.

For further information: Call the North Carolina Wildlife Resources Commission Work Center in New Bern; phone 919-638-3000.

VANDEMERE, HOBUCKEN AREA, GOOSE CREEK GAME LAND, AURORA AREA
MAP 19

This route, which is about 40 miles long, can be very productive in winter and during the breeding season. At Vandemere and along the Pamlico River and South Creek northeast of Aurora, you can see large numbers and a good variety of diving ducks. Adjacent to the highway there are two small impoundments in Goose Creek Game Land. These are largely overgrown and thus not good for waterfowl, but they do have a few Wood Ducks and possibly a few other water birds. An easily accessible salt marsh just east of Hobucken has a few rails and Marsh Wrens throughout the year and Seaside Sparrows in the breeding season. And the woods along NC 33 northwest of Hobucken—part of Goose Creek Game Land—offer an excellent variety of resident and breeding birds, including Chuck-will's-widow, Barred Owl, Brown-headed Nuthatch, several warblers (including an occasional Swainson's), Blue Grosbeak, and Summer Tanager.

THIS TOUR BEGINS on NC 304 opposite the community of **Vandemere** (about 5 miles northeast of Bayboro). Take NC 307 into Vandemere and continue down to the bay. At the end of the road, check the pilings at the fish house for gulls and terns. In winter, look over the bay for diving ducks. Usually most ducks are toward your right, and you can get the best view by taking First Street over to Main Street and then walking to the water. From here you can usually see Horned Grebes, Lesser Scaup, Canvasbacks, and Buffleheads.

Return to NC 304 and continue northeast toward Hobucken. After 7.1 miles, just before the bridge, look for a little pulloff on your right, with a gate. The small impoundment here is too overgrown with vegetation to be productive but is worth a brief check—it is less than a mile around. In winter you can expect a few Wood Ducks and occasionally other ducks. In the marshes look for Marsh Wrens, Common Yellowthroats, and Swamp Sparrows. The breeding season is somewhat more interesting. Ospreys and Wood Ducks nest here, and you should see several species of land birds. Along the dikes watch for Northern Bobwhites, Eastern Kingbirds, Prairie Warblers, and Orchard Orioles. In the

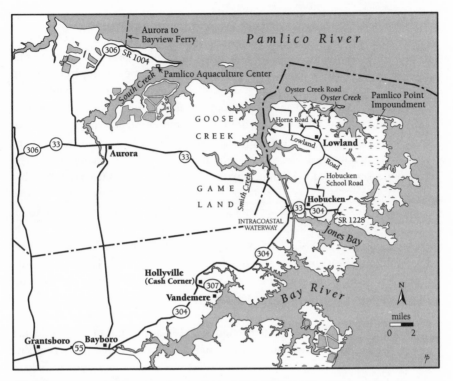

Pamlico River

Aurora to Bayview Ferry

306 SR 1004

South Creek

Pamlico Aquaculture Center

Oyster Creek Road
Oyster Creek   Pamlico Point Impoundment

GOOSE

CREEK

Horne Road

306   33

Aurora   33

Lowland   **Lowland**

Road

GAME

LAND

Smith Creek

Hobucken School Road

INTRACOASTAL WATERWAY

Hobucken
33 304   SR 1228

Jones Bay

304

Hollyville
(Cash Corner)   307

Vandemere
304

Bay River

N

miles
0   2

Grantsboro   **Bayboro**
55

19. VANDEMERE, HOBUCKEN AREA, GOOSE CREEK GAME LAND, AURORA AREA

wet woods on the south side of the impoundment, look for White-eyed Vireos, Prothonotary Warblers, and maybe an Acadian Flycatcher, and listen for Red-shouldered Hawk. The pine grove on the east side of the impoundment, next to the inland waterway, is of at least slight ornithological interest: one year two participants in the local Christmas Bird Count actually got married in this grove on the day of the count!

Continue on NC 304 and NC 304/33 toward Hobucken. Just before the bridge across the inland waterway, there is a roadway to the right that goes by several fish houses. In winter you may want to drive this road and check the pilings for gulls.

In **Hobucken**, where NC 304/33 ends, continue straight on to SR 1228. At the edge of the community the road becomes unpaved, and beyond this point you will see an extensive area of salt marsh on your right. From late April into June, birding along this quiet road at dawn can be productive. Before daylight you can hear several Chuck-will's-widows. No doubt Chucks rest on this dirt road regularly. At dawn, on the left side of the road, just out from the village, look and listen for Eastern Kingbirds, Blue Grosbeaks, and Orchard Orioles. In the vicinity of the two bridges you should hear and see a few Seaside Sparrows and Marsh Wrens. There are a few rails in these marshes, but they do not usually occur close to the road during the nesting season. You might hear a Clapper or Virginia, though. There are also a few Black Rails, but you're likely to hear one only on a dead calm night, when you might hear one calling from several hundred yards away.

This area is also worth checking at other seasons, during calm conditions at sunrise and sunset. Virginia Rails are more common outside the breeding season; they are likely to be heard from late August to early April. At the western end of the marsh—near the village, where there are shrubs mixed in with the marsh grasses—look for Swamp Sparrows and Sedge Wrens from late October through April.

Because this road is not separated from the marshes by major canals, it could be a good place to check during high wind tides from autumn to early spring. Such conditions occur only rarely, but if you're ever in this area during strong northeast, east, or southeast winds (especially the last), you should check out this site. You might get lucky and see a rail darting across the road. In autumn and spring you might get really lucky and see a Black or Yellow rail.

Return to the NC 304/33 intersection and stop at the pulloff next to the fire tower. Brown-headed Nuthatches can usually be found here; in the breeding season, listen for Pine and Yellow-throated warblers, and maybe a Yellow-throated Vireo.

Set your odometer at zero here. From this point west along NC 33 to the parking area and boat ramp at Smith Creek (2.9 miles away), there is a variety of wooded habitats. Here you should be able to find a long list of land birds, including almost all of the warblers that breed in coastal North Carolina. This area is part of the Goose Creek Game Land, administered by the North Carolina Wildlife Resources Commission.

At the beginning of this stretch, on the left, there is an extensive hardwood bottomland area. From 0.6 to 2.9 miles, a wet pine woodland with an understory of broadleaf evergreen vegetation lies on the left, while on the right there are open stands of pine trees. On your left at 0.6 miles, a roadside canal begins, limiting your birding in this area to what you can see from the road shoulder. Fortunately, though, traffic is usually light.

Resident birds along this section include chickadees, titmice, bluebirds, and several species of woodpeckers. You should have little trouble spotting a Pileated, and the open pine woods on the right usually have a Hairy or two. Listen for the screaming of a Red-shouldered Hawk, especially on warm mornings in late winter and early spring. This section is also good for Barred Owls. Turkey Vultures are common, and you often can spot a Black as well.

For a really good list of land birds, work along this road at dawn from late

April to early June. Start your day by making several stops along the road at first light—you should hear one or more Chuck-will's-widows, and you might also hear a Whip-poor-will. In the hardwoods on your left, near the coast guard station, listen for Yellow-billed Cuckoos, Wood Thrushes, Red-eyed Vireos, Acadian Flycatchers, Prothonotary Warblers, and Ovenbirds. (*Note*: Personnel at this coast guard station are *not* accustomed to seeing birders. Don't look toward the station, especially in early morning, with binoculars—you might get questioned.)

Past the coast guard station, on your right, you will see an area that is periodically used for disposal of dredge spoil from the inland waterway. Habitat here varies according to how recently the site has been used. If water and spoil have recently been pumped into the site, check for a few shorebirds. If the site is inactive and overgrown with shrubs, look for Indigo Buntings, Blue Grosbeaks, and Orchard Orioles. In the pines that lie between the spoil area and the high-way, listen for Eastern Wood-Pewees and Pine and Yellow-throated warblers. If you walk over to the inland waterway, you may find a few Rough-winged Swallow nesting burrows.

On your left at 0.6 miles you will see a short trail to a field. Walk this trail to find more hardwood bottomland birds. This is a good site for finding a Worm-eating Warbler or two, and you might also hear a Black-throated Green Warbler (more likely in April than later).

From the trail to the boat ramp, check the open stands of mature pines on your right for Eastern Wood-Pewees, Great Crested Flycatchers, Brown-headed Nuthatches, Yellow-throated Warblers, and Rufous-sided Towhees. You will hear a few Northern Bobwhites, and with a little effort you ought to see Summer Tanagers and Blue Grosbeaks.

In the wet pine woodland on the left side of the road, White-eyed Vireos and Prothonotary Warblers are abundant. At the beginning of this area—from about 0.6 miles to 1.2 miles—you should hear Worm-eating and Hooded warblers. Occasionally birders find a Swainson's Warbler here.

At 2.1 miles you will see a pulloff on your right. Here is another small waterfowl impoundment, less than a mile around. It is overgrown with reeds and usually has almost no water birds but is at least worth checking. You should at least see nesting Wood Ducks and Ospreys, and you might add some land birds to your list. Along the dikes, watch for Eastern Kingbirds.

Although this section of game land is most interesting during the breeding season, roadside birding here can also be quite good in winter. In addition to the permanent resident birds mentioned above, there will be swarms of Yellow-rumped Warblers, plenty of Golden-crowned and Ruby-crowned Kinglets, and several other species, including Winter Wren, Hermit Thrush, and several spar-rows (including Fox Sparrow). In the understory on the left side of the road, after 0.6 miles, look for Orange-crowned Warblers. In winter the impoundment is still rather dull, but it might attract a few American Black Ducks and other dabblers, in addition to the resident Wood Ducks, and you might see a Bald Eagle soaring over the inland waterway.

Continue west on NC 33 to the town of Aurora. Here, turn north on NC 306, and at the turn reset your odometer to zero. At 1.8 miles on your right you will see a little pond right beside the road. In winter check this pond for Pied-billed Grebes and a few coots and dabbling ducks. Beyond this point, you can't miss the vast moonscape on your left—a phosphate mining operation. This expansive open area certainly has the potential to attract rare species, especially during migrations, but you are limited to what you can see from the highway. In winter watch carefully for raptors—a Rough-legged Hawk has been seen on at least one occasion. From 2.4 to 5.5 miles the shrub line on your left probably can be interesting during migrations, although noisy highway traffic to and from the mining operation never ceases.

At 7.0 miles, at the end of NC 306, you will see the **Pamlico River ferry terminal** on your left. (See the Pamlico River Ferry site guide for more information.) From about Thanksgiving to March, check the river here for flocks of diving ducks, including Lesser Scaup, Canvasbacks, Buffleheads, and Red-breasted Mergansers.

Usually more ducks can be seen from the river shore farther east. Continue down the highway (which becomes SR 1004). At 1.2 miles from the ferry terminal, turn left onto an unnamed dirt road, just past a small store. At the end of this road you can walk down to the shore. Look for large flocks of Lesser Scaup, Canvasbacks, and Ruddy Ducks; you should also see Buffleheads, Surf Scoters, and Red-breasted Mergansers. On better days you might find Ring-necked Ducks, Greater Scaup, and Black Scoters.

Return to SR 1004 and turn left. After 0.7 miles you will see the driveway into the state-owned **Pamlico Aquaculture Center**. Drive to the office and ask for permission to bird the grounds. In winter there are usually many ducks on South Creek just out from the center, and this can be a good area to check from your car on a rainy day. Look for Ruddy Ducks, Canvasbacks, and Ring-necked Ducks. The ponds may have a few wading birds during the warmer months, and perhaps Pied-billed Grebes and a duck or two in winter. Occasionally a few gulls are attracted to the ponds. If you see any, check them—this would seem to be a spot with potential for a Common Black-headed or even a Franklin's. During the migrations a few shorebirds are seen around the ponds, and swallows are often abundant.

For further information: For information about Goose Creek Game Land, call the North Carolina Wildlife Resources Commission Work Center at New Bern; phone 919-638-3000.

ORIENTAL TO MINNESOTT BEACH AREA
MAP 20

Birding along this route is most interesting in winter, from about Thanksgiving to March, when numerous diving ducks can usually be seen on the Neuse River. At several stops you can bird from your car, so this is a tour worth considering on a rainy day. Furthermore, all these stops are along shorelines that face southward, so this route can be good during strong northeast to north winds, when the waters just off the beaches will be smooth and the waterfowl easy to see.

Although this route is most likely to be productive in winter, it is certainly scenic and thoroughly enjoyable anytime. Wilkinson Point at Minnesott Beach is the sort of place where a rarity can turn up at any season, and the area around Minnesott Beach can be good for a variety of breeding species, including Summer Tanager.

UNLESS OTHERWISE indicated, the following site descriptions refer to the winter season, from about Thanksgiving to early March.

This tour begins at the bridge just southwest of **Oriental**, at the beginning of NC 55. From here drive into town and take the first right, onto New Street. Where this street ends, turn right on South Water Street and continue to the sharp bend to the right, where you can overlook the bay and the rock breakwater beyond. In the bay there may be a few ducks, and the breakwater is often covered with cormorants, Brown Pelicans, and gulls. Check carefully—a Glaucous Gull has been seen here.

Return up South Water Street to Hodges Street and turn right. On your left look for a display with a large map of the town. A dispenser at this display contains small free maps for the public.

Continue down Hodges Street and Wall Street and turn left on South Avenue. After a few blocks the street will run along next to the river; this is a great place to look for waterfowl and other species. On most days you will see a few Common Loons, Horned Grebes, Lesser Scaup, Red-breasted Mergansers, American Coots, gulls, and terns. On occasion there will be many ducks, and you might see Canvasbacks and perhaps Surf Scoters and a Common Goldeneye or a Greater Scaup. Ducks here can be rather tame and often approach shore closely. Occasionally you can get a really good look at a Greater Scaup here. Because you can bird from your car here, this is also a good place to bird on a rainy day, and during fierce northeasters something rare might show up.

At all seasons the village is typically rather birdy, and you can spot several species by driving up and down the streets. Look for several woodpeckers, often including a Pileated. From South Avenue, return to Wall Street and then turn

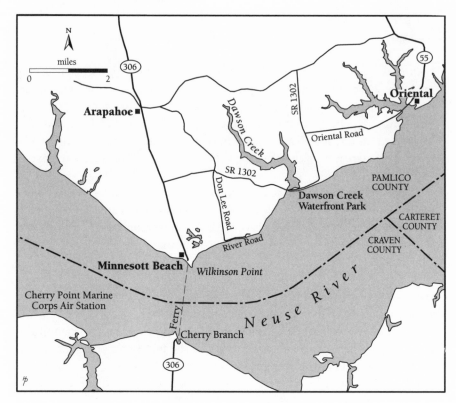

right along Factory Street. In winter, in the ponds on your left, you might spot a wild duck with the domesticated Mallards, and a Black-crowned Night-Heron is possible. From about November to February a few Rusty Blackbirds can often be seen walking about on the lawns, masquerading as Common Grackles. (Usually by late winter all such "grackles" are, unfortunately, real grackles.)

Return to NC 55, turn left, and continue across the bridge. (Across the bridge the highway becomes Oriental Road, SR 1308.) From May to July you will want to turn onto the first road to the left after you cross the bridge, and drive to the end, so that you can check out the swallows that nest beneath the bridge. Several Cliff Swallows are now nesting with the Barn Swallows. Pamlico County is the only county in coastal North Carolina where Cliffs are known to breed— they nest both at this site and at the Dawson Creek site.

Continue down Oriental Road until it ends, then turn left onto SR 1302. After 2.1 miles you will see **Dawson Creek Waterfront Park** on your left. This is another great place to check out the river from your car; you can often see a few diving ducks up close, and many rafts farther offshore. During low water levels (westerly winds) there will be sandy flats that may have several gulls.

At the adjacent bridge across Dawson Creek, Cliff Swallows nest from May to July.

Continue westward on SR 1302, watching for raptors, Eastern Bluebirds, and maybe a flock of American Pipits. After 2.1 miles turn left onto Don Lee Road and continue to the river (where the road becomes River Road). Here is yet another spot where you can bird from your car. Several diving ducks are often seen just offshore here, including Lesser Scaup, Ring-necked Ducks, and Ruddy Ducks.

Return to SR 1302 and turn left, toward NC 306. Turn left onto NC 306 and continue to Minnesott Beach. When you get to the entrance to the ferry terminal, continue past it to the end of the road. Look for a gap in the fence to your left. If you see one, walk through it and head toward the water. If not, walk back up the road, go through the entrance into Camp Seagull, and follow the fence down to the water. People do this on a regular basis, and the camp doesn't stop them.

The area before you is called **Wilkinson Point**. Except during high water levels, the point consists of a sand spit that extends out one hundred yards or more. This point, the last extensive sandy point that you encounter while moving up the river, is the sort of place that you will want to check every time you're in the vicinity, because vagrants stop here regularly, and there's always a chance something interesting will show up. American White Pelicans and Tundra Swans have been seen here, and a flock of Brant fed on the adjacent lawns during one severe cold spell.

Because the point is so small, however, its birdlife is chased away rather easily by a few people or dogs, and this spot is very popular with beachgoers. During the warmer months it is best to check this site first thing in the morning.

The point is often covered with loafing cormorants, Brown Pelicans, gulls, and terns. During much of the year you can find a Sanderling or two. This is probably the farthest point upriver where this species occurs regularly. In late summer you might find Least and Sandwich terns here.

In winter several diving ducks are almost always present just offshore. Numbers are variable, but several species are possible. Common Goldeneyes are seen here with some regularity, and Common Mergansers have been spotted on a couple of occasions. In the little bay formed by the point, look for Hooded Mergansers and maybe a dabbling duck or two. The pier beyond is often covered with gulls.

The low grassy dunes and weed-covered spoil site at the base of the spit and the adjacent lawn area are worth checking, especially during the migration periods and in winter. Several sparrows can usually be found in the weeds at the spoil site, and a Lark or Clay-colored sparrow might turn up during autumn. In late autumn and early winter the base of the spit and the adjacent lawns would seem to be good places to check for a Snow Bunting or Lapland Longspur.

Return north on NC 306. Just north of the ferry terminal you will see Country Club Drive to your left. Stay on this road until you reach the **Minnesott Beach Golf Course**. Just before the clubhouse, there is a pond on your right where you may see a duck or two. During uncrowded periods, ask for permission to bird the golf course grounds. Year-round residents here include Brown-headed Nuthatch, Eastern Bluebird, Pine Warbler, and Chipping Sparrow. In the breeding season this is a good area for Yellow-throated Warblers and Summer Tanagers.

From late April to early July, at dawn and dusk, you may hear Chuck-will's-widows along NC 306 from the north side of Minnesott Beach north for about a mile. Habitat for this species is also very good along 306 just north of Arapahoe (about 3 miles north of Minnesott Beach). These areas have native vegetation—longleaf pines with an understory of oaks. In many adjacent areas, where pine plantations predominate, you are more likely to hear Whip-poor-wills than Chuck-will's-widows.

NEUSE RIVER FERRY

On most days in winter, from about Thanksgiving to March, this ferry run is at least mildly entertaining, offering views of a few diving ducks. On occasion the birding here can be quite good, with large numbers of diving ducks and perhaps a rare gull. Taking the ferry can be an excellent rainy-day activity. All of the ferryboats on this run have enclosed and elevated passenger cabins, from which you will have a good view of the river.

The northern ferry terminal is at Minnesott Beach, and the southern terminal at Cherry Branch, east of Havelock. Each run takes about twenty minutes. The ferries run at convenient thirty-minute intervals throughout the daylight hours, so you never have long to wait. For the best lighting it is best to make this run from south to north. If you have the opportunity, try to take this ferry when the weather is calm so that you can spot ducks on the water more easily. Also, this run may be more interesting just after a severe northeaster has abated—there may be more ducks on this portion of the river then.

On most days in winter, look for a few Common Loons, Horned Grebes, Lesser Scaup, Buffleheads, and Red-breasted Mergansers. Less often you might spot a few Canvasbacks, Common Goldeneyes, Surf Scoters, and perhaps other divers.

Typically you can see several gulls following the ferry. For some reason one or two Laughing Gulls are often present throughout midwinter. A Glaucous Gull has been spotted behind the ferry on at least one occasion, and several Bonaparte's Gulls often feed over the turbulence created when the ferry turns around in the relatively shallow water of the Cherry Branch harbor. This also looks like a good spot to check for a Common Black-headed Gull.

Just out from the Minnesott Branch end of the run, watch for Wilkinson Point, a narrow sand spit that extends to the southeast. This spit often attracts a variety of birds. You might see one or two additional waterfowl species here—Common Mergansers have been spotted on a couple of occasions.

During the rest of the year this ferry run is much less interesting. Most of the time greedy Laughing Gulls predominate. Watch for a few Royal and Forster's terns. Again, be especially watchful as you pass Wilkinson Point: something of interest is always possible here.

At any season, birding at the ferry terminals while you wait can be mildly interesting. At the south terminal there are always a few chickadees, titmice, and Brown-headed Nuthatches. At the north terminal, look for Eastern Bluebirds, Chipping Sparrows, and Brown-headed Nuthatches along the nearby roadside. In late summer numerous Purple Martins and swallows may congregate around this terminal. Throughout the year, make a quick hike out to Wilkinson Point if you have time.

CEDAR ISLAND NATIONAL WILDLIFE REFUGE, CEDAR ISLAND AREA
MAP 21

Year after year, the following scenario no doubt occurs regularly: visiting birders heading up or down the coast by way of the Outer Banks notice the Cedar Island NWR on the highway map and stop by to check it out. But they see no waterfowl impoundments, no mud flats covered with shorebirds, few open-water vistas, and the wooded areas have just a handful of birds. There is an impressively large tract of salt marsh, but in full daylight and windy conditions—when most birders usually see it—the marsh appears almost totally devoid of birdlife. The visiting birders resume their trip, wondering why in the world this area was ever designated as a national wildlife refuge.

However, the refuge and adjacent areas definitely have some birding attractions, albeit subtle ones and/or ones that take place only during brief periods. The Cedar Island Marshes—the largest tract of unaltered, irregularly flooded salt marsh in North Carolina—harbor breeding Black, Clapper, and Virginia rails, as well as Seaside Sparrows and Marsh Wrens. The wooded areas within the refuge support a fairly good list of southern specialties, although the low density of birds means that you are likely to find most of the species only at the beginning of the nesting season, when singing is at its peak. Also, the whole Cedar Island area—near the ferry terminal, in particular—is a funnel for spring migrants, and you might see a rare species here, especially from late April until mid-May.

LOGISTICS. Unless you own a small boat or canoe, bird-watching in the Cedar Island Marshes is limited to what you can see from the 5-mile-long NC

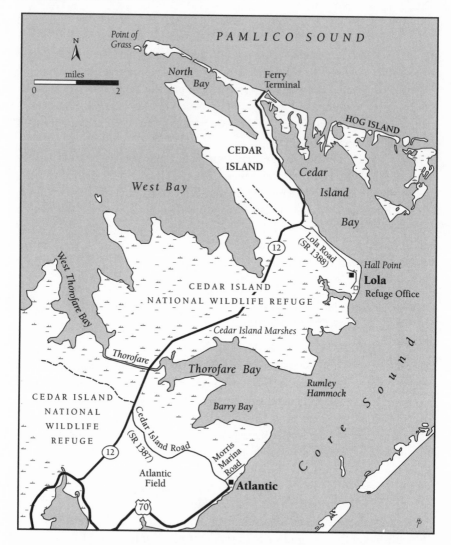

21. CEDAR ISLAND NATIONAL WILDLIFE REFUGE, CEDAR ISLAND AREA

12 causeway, which bisects them. On both sides the causeway is separated from the marshes by deep canals that can be easily crossed by canoe. Birding is a permitted activity; refuge signs barring entry for unpermitted activities do not apply. However, it is illegal to cross the canals into the refuge at night. The road shoulders along the causeway are wide enough for you to pull safely off the road. In the warmer months, during the calm nighttime and early morning hours—the best times to be here—mosquitoes can be terrible. Bring plenty of insect repellent.

The best time of year to bird these marshes is from about mid-April to mid-

June; early May is about the peak. The two best times of day are early morning, about sunrise, when it is calm or near calm; and after midnight when it is really, truly calm, preferably during a full moon. Sunrise is preferable if you want to see where you are and to see the birds you're hearing—including maybe, just maybe, a Black Rail. But if you would rather hear the sounds of the marsh and hear them well, including the "kik-kik-krrr" calls of dozens of Black Rails, then a late night visit is preferable. Of course, you can certainly combine late night and early morning visits, if you can survive the loss of sleep.

ON AN EARLY morning trip, start out at the Thorofare Bridge. From here drive toward Cedar Island about two hundred yards (or far enough so that you're not bothered by the sound of boat engines starting up at the nearby docks) for your first stop. For a good survey of the marshes, you will want to make several stops between here and the next bridge (about 3.5 miles from the Thorofare Bridge).

Beginning at the very first stop, you will hear the asthmatic "zhur-zeee's" of Seaside Sparrows, the reedy gurglings of Marsh Wrens, and the loud "witchity-wichity-witchity's" of Common Yellowthroats. The Seaside Sparrows are almost everywhere; you won't have any trouble seeing them. Look for the Yellow-throats in the patches of the tallest grass (big cordgrass) right next to the canals. The Marsh Wrens aren't quite so easy to see, but after you hear one, keep watching—you should see the singer eventually. Marsh Wrens respond readily to tapes of their song.

The rails call more sporadically, but you should hear a few loud "kak-kak-kak's" from Clapper Rails, a few low growly "kik-kik-krrr's" from Black Rails, and an occasional "kid-dik, kid-dik" or a descending grunting sound from a Virginia Rail. (The last sound is often made in response to a loud noise, such as hand-clapping.)

Alas, hearing rails is far easier than seeing them. However, if you patiently watch the edge of the canal bank as you drive along the causeway, there is a fairly good chance that you'll see a Clapper Rail. This is most likely to happen when water levels are low. (Water levels here are generally low during south-west winds, high during north and northeast winds; this area has essentially no lunar tide.) You might see a Black Rail or Virginia Rail in the same way, but don't count on it.

On the left side of the road, about 0.2 to 0.4 miles from the Thorofare Bridge, a few small, sparsely vegetated drains run up into the marsh. Check these drains closely, because you have a slight chance of seeing any of the rails here. If you hear a Virginia or Black Rail around these sparse areas, play a tape of several sequences of its song, then wait patiently and hope that the agitated bird will briefly walk into sight along the edge of an open area. Again, though, don't count on it.

Other marsh birds present in the breeding season are a few Least Bitterns and (rarely) American Bitterns. Look for either of these birds making a short flight across the marsh.

About 2 miles from the Thorofare Bridge, you will see on the left a large area dominated by a low-growing green grass (saltmeadow cordgrass). This is an especially good area for hearing Black Rails, but because of the thick, continuous cover, it is not good for seeing them.

Can you imagine thinking of a birding expedition as one of your most successful when in fact you didn't see a single bird? This could certainly be the case if you make a midnight birding trip to the Cedar Island Marshes between mid-April and mid-June, especially about early May. However, the night *must* be absolutely calm—"dead calm," as they say in eastern Carteret County. Even the slightest breeze can greatly inhibit the Black Rails' intensity of calling. A full moon is also desirable, because Marsh Wrens and Seaside Sparrows are more likely to be calling then, and even Black Rails may be more vocal then. (For all its reputation as a nocturnal bird, the Black Rail is in fact more crepuscular—that is, active during twilight—than nocturnal.)

Avoid making the trip within a few days of very heavy rains, unless you're also a herpetologist, because you may hear nothing but frogs. And again, don't forget the insect repellent.

If you hit it right, you should hear dozens of Black Rails and several Clapper and Virginia rails. Perhaps you'll hear a Black Rail calling close to the canal. If so, play a Black Rail tape, and you may draw the bird almost to the edge of the canal (though it probably won't walk into view). You may hear what was once considered "the ornithological mystery sound"—the "ki-ki-ki-QUEE-ah" now known to be a call of the Virginia Rail. If the moon is full, Marsh Wrens, Seaside Sparrows, and Common Yellowthroats will also be in song. Near the mainland and Cedar Island ends of the causeway, listen also for Barred and Great Horned owls, Chuck-will's-widows, and (rarely) a Whip-poor-will.

(Don't be surprised if at least one driver stops and asks if a car has gone into the canal. Just say no and look innocent—it's easier than trying to explain.)

Outside the breeding season the marshes are less interesting, but they still merit a visit. The best times to be here are at sunrise and sunset, and again, calm conditions are very important. The rails discussed above are present throughout the year; Virginia Rails become much more common during the cooler months, while Black Rails apparently become less common. One can occasionally induce Black Rails to call by playing a tape around sunset when the weather is calm and warm. They may even call in January. Soras are also present from autumn into spring but are more common during the migrations than in midwinter. Yellow Rails may also winter here.

Marsh Wrens winter in the marshes, and Sedge Wrens are also present from autumn into spring. Both call readily at sunset when it's calm. If you're on the causeway at twilight, scan the marshes for a Barn Owl or a Short-eared Owl. Both are seen occasionally.

For those avid life-listers who really want to add a Black Rail to their lists, I'm sorry that I can't be more encouraging. But the fact is that although there are many Black Rails here, this just isn't the best area to see one, especially if you don't have a canoe to cross the canals. However, one section of refuge marshes is accessible by foot, if you're willing to hike a little over a mile through an area thick with mosquitoes. From the intersection of NC 12 and SR 1388, go 0.1 miles south on NC 12. On your right you will see a dirt road. Walk this road about one-third mile, until you see a trail to the left. Take this trail and continue almost a mile until you reach the shore of West Bay. Follow the sandy, slightly elevated shoreline to your left. There are at least a few Black Rails in this section. There are also spots along the border of this strip where grass cover is either sparse or low. If you hear a Black Rail calling at one of these spots, you might be able either to get a glimpse of it by using tape-recorded calls or to flush it.

If you're lucky enough to be in the area at the right time, there's another way you might manage to see a Black Rail. The "right time" would be during a severe northeaster, with winds of thirty to forty miles per hour or more. These conditions do not occur frequently, but they do happen about once a year, typically around October-November or March–early April. Such weather can completely flood the marshes, pushing water (and rails) right up to the highway. Look along the piles of flotsam for a possible Black Rail. You might even see that other feathered mouse—a Yellow Rail. You should at least see Virginia and Clapper rails.

Keep in mind that playing around on the causeway when it's about to go underwater isn't the safest of games. The Cedar Island end of the causeway is lowest and floods first, so you might be wise to restrict your efforts to the mainland end of the causeway, landward of the Thorofare Bridge. This isn't the best area for rails, but it's the safest.

If you do encounter such conditions and you feel brave and energetic, this might be a good time to try the West Bay hike, though in this case much of the hike might be through shallow water. During such high wind tides you might be able to flush a few rails along the sandy beach. Actually, birds might appear here under conditions less severe than those required to force them onto the causeway—perhaps only twenty- to thirty-mile-an-hour winds.

For an enjoyable complement to an early May dawn on the causeway, work along SR 1388 to the **south end of Cedar Island**. Along this road you can see several breeding species and maybe a few migrants. Remember that the density of birds breeding on the island is low and that singing intensity drops off rapidly as the season progresses. You are not likely to have much success after mid- to late May.

Incidentally, if you get up early enough in the morning, you might want to visit this road before a dawn tour of the causeway. Chuck-will's-widows are easy to hear and see here.

About 0.1 miles from NC 12 you will drive through a small open area with young pines, surrounded by shrub-thicket vegetation. Listen here for White-eyed Vireos, Prairie Warblers, Common Yellowthroats, Rufous-sided Towhees, an Eastern Wood-Pewee, and maybe two or three Brown-headed Nuthatches.

Farther on, about 1.2 miles from NC 12, park at the small cemetery or the church and walk along the road here. Listen for Blue-gray Gnatcatchers, Pine Warblers, Yellow-throated Warblers, and Northern Parulas. Expect a migrant or two—a Blackpoll Warbler is likely. In the moist woods on the right you will hear a few Prothonotary Warblers, and maybe a Swainson's or a Black-throated Green as well.

If you want to go into the woods, there is a sand track that begins at 1.6 miles. However, you probably won't find anything here that can't be found from the highway.

At 1.8 miles look for the refuge headquarters on your right. Across the road is a large open area, with a maintenance building near the water. In this open area there are Purple Martin nest boxes, and Barn Swallows and Northern Rough-winged Swallows sometimes nest in and around the maintenance building and old radar structure. Expect Eastern Kingbirds, a few Indigo Buntings, and at least one pair of Blue Grosbeaks. Check this site carefully; it has the potential to attract rare migrants in the spring. A Scissor-tailed Flycatcher and a Lark Sparrow have been seen here between late April and mid-May.

In the moist woods behind the little pond next to the refuge headquarters, listen for Prothonotary Warblers and a Swainson's Warbler. A Swainson's is here virtually every spring.

Shortly beyond the refuge headquarters, the highway ends at a little bay. You will see a little sandbar that often has a few gulls and terns and maybe a few shorebirds. The shoreline here is often a flight line for wading birds headed to and from their nesting colonies. Look for both Glossy and White ibises.

SR 1388 is only marginally interesting outside the breeding season. After autumn cold fronts you may find a few migrants around the refuge headquarters. (Beware of mosquitoes!) During any season the headquarters area offers a scenic vista of the Core Sound and, beyond the sound, Core Banks. From about Thanksgiving to March, you can occasionally see a dark "cloud" far out over the sound—a vast flock of Redheads that has taken flight. Unfortunately, you are unlikely to see these birds at close range. On a calm full-moon night in November, you can often find two or three Whip-poor-wills along the road by using tape-recorded songs. They are unlikely to sing, but you may spot one as it flies in close.

Another area that you might want to check in the early morning is the section

of the refuge that lies on the mainland. This area is not as likely as Cedar Island to have migrants, but the breeding birds are more diverse. This area is also good through May and worth checking until mid-June. Brown-headed Nuthatches are regular here, and one or two Swainson's Warblers can often be found.

Check this area by walking a gated dirt road off NC 12. Look for this road on your right just after you head south from the marshes and just north of the convenience store on the east side of NC 12. Walking this road usually requires much insect repellent. Mosquitoes are usually bad, and biting flies can be ridiculously bad in May and June.

This road is about 3 miles long, but a walk of a mile or so will let you sample most of the types of habitats present. These habitats include moist shrubby areas, thick stands of pine trees, open stands of pine trees, swamp forests, and some areas where past fires have killed many of the trees.

Species you should find include Northern Bobwhite, Yellow-billed Cuckoo, Eastern Wood-Pewee, Eastern Kingbird, Great Crested Flycatcher, White-eyed Vireo, Prairie Warbler, and Orchard Oriole. Hairy Woodpeckers are seen occasionally; also, check the dead trees for a Red-headed Woodpecker or two. In the thick shrubby areas, listen for Yellow-breasted Chats. The Fish and Wildlife Service is planning to burn this area more frequently in the future, which should enhance the area for bobwhites and other species.

Near the beginning of the road you should be able to find a few Blue Grosbeaks. Brown-headed Nuthatches might occur anywhere along the road. About two-thirds of a mile from NC 12, there is a small borrow-pit pond on the right, and a swamp on both sides of the road just beyond the pond. Listen here for Prothonotary Warblers and maybe a Swainson's. About one-half mile past this swamp, the road passes close (within one hundred yards) to a section of swamp on the left. Walking over to this swamp may be easy or difficult, depending on how recently the intervening tract has been burned. Within the swamp listen for Acadian Flycatchers, Prothonotary and Hooded warblers, and maybe a Swainson's. Black-throated Green Warblers are also possible here, but they are not likely to be heard after early May.

Located at the end of NC 12 at Cedar Island, the **Cedar Island ferry terminal area** can be entertaining at any season but is especially worthy of attention from late April to mid-May during fair skies and rather brisk southwest or west winds. This area lies at the end of the line for land bird migrants (mostly diurnal migrants) headed northeastward through Carteret County. Relatively few spring-migrating land birds venture into Carteret County in the first place, but of those that do, a large percentage apparently get funneled along the narrow barrier beach that extends northwest from the ferry terminal. You'll probably never see more than a few dozen birds, but you're certain to be entertained, and you just might see something rare. Species that have been seen from late April to mid-May at the ferry terminal and along the barrier beach include Bald Eagle, Cooper's Hawk, Peregrine Falcon, Mississippi Kite, Cliff Swallow (locally rare), Yellow-headed Blackbird, and, my oh my, a Black-backed Wagtail, a species native to eastern Asia!

Occasionally your enjoyment of this area may be hindered considerably by military aircraft using the beach as an approach to a bombing range several miles to the west. These jets fly low and the noise is terrific. These flights are much less frequent on weekends. There's also a tiny air force here—don't forget the insect repellent.

After parking in the ferry terminal parking lot, make a quick survey of the grounds. Check all the fences and power lines. Eastern Kingbirds are common, and this would also seem to be a good spot for a Gray Kingbird or a Scissor-tailed Flycatcher.

Next, check the patches of trees and shrubs behind the motel. In addition to breeding species like Prairie Warbler, Common Yellowthroat, Carolina Wren, and Rufous-sided Towhee, you should find a few migrants. Look for Blackpoll and Yellow warblers.

You will notice a sand track that heads northwest, toward the beach. Follow it, checking all the power lines around the cottages. Although you're not really close to the marsh here, don't be surprised if you hear a "Black Rail." The abundance of Black Rails in the Cedar Island area is reflected in the repertoire of the local mockingbirds, thrashers, and catbirds, which often includes the rails' "kik-kik-krr."

After the sand track ends, continue up the barrier strand by walking along the beach and through the middle of the dune-shrub zone. The former is best for seeing a few shorebirds, the latter for finding a few more migrant land birds.

About a mile from the ferry terminal, the barrier beach becomes narrow enough that you can easily see all the birds flying along it. Get up on a dune that gives you good visibility and set up watch. Look for Blue Jays, swallows, an occasional hawk, and maybe a late flock of Cedar Waxwings. You might see all five species of swallows. This barrier beach is also a popular flight line for water birds. Look for gulls, terns, herons, egrets, and ibises—Glossies are most likely, but you might see Whites as well.

If you feel like exploring, you may want to continue to the tip of this barrier strand. To reach the end, you'll have to walk another mile and a half and wade two or three small inlets. These usually can be waded easily around their south-western ends. The rest of this barrier strand will give you more opportunities to watch for migrating land birds. If you make it to the last patch of shrubs, you will probably find a few warblers that have collected there, and maybe a thrush as well, perhaps waiting for night to resume their migrations. Near the end of this hike there are usually extensive flats where you will see several shorebirds. Watch for American Black Ducks and Gadwalls; this area approaches the Gadwalls' southern breeding limit. And you may well hear a Black Rail in the marshes adjacent to the barrier strip.

When you get back to the ferry terminal, check the power lines and fences again. Also, scope the little borrow-pit pond adjacent to the parking area, which usually has a few wading birds and shorebirds; White-rumped Sandpipers are regular in May. A few ducks are also possible—Fulvous Whistling-Ducks have been seen here in late April.

The ferry terminal area can be worth checking at other seasons as well. In winter the pond often has several ducks, and shorebirds are regular in late summer and autumn, when American Avocets and Buff-breasted Sandpipers have been seen. The adjacent shores usually have large numbers of gulls; Lesser Black-backed and Glaucous gulls have been spotted here in winter. Terns are common most of the year; in spring this is a good place to see breeding-plumaged Forster's Terns. Black Skimmers often congregate here in autumn. In winter scope the sound for Red-throated and Common loons, Horned Grebes, Red-breasted Mergansers, and other species. Common Eiders have been seen within the ferry harbor. In the breeding season look around the harbor for breeding Purple Martins, Barn Swallows, and Northern Rough-winged Swallows.

For further information: The Cedar Island NWR is staffed sporadically; phone 919-225-2511. The refuge is administered by the staff of Mattamuskeet NWR (Route 1, Box N-2, Swan Quarter, NC 27885; phone 919-926-4021).

DAVIS IMPOUNDMENT

Although this impoundment is privately owned and closed to the public, one corner of it lies right next to US 70 and can be checked out from the road shoulder. Bird activity here is extremely variable, but birders driving through the area would do well to make a brief stop to survey the site. At the community of Davis, US 70 makes a ninety-degree turn. From this point, drive west 1.3 miles. Here, pull off on the right-hand road shoulder (just before the bridge). You will see the impoundment off to the right.

Unfortunately, shrub vegetation growing on the impoundment's dikes greatly limits the view. However, by looking from different sites along the road shoulder, you can see most of the birds in this corner of the impoundment. The light here is best in the afternoon.

Again, bird activity here is quite variable. Usually you will see just a handful of ducks, most likely Mallards and American Black Ducks, and a couple of wading birds. But the birding can be quite good at times, although you're sure to be frustrated because of your limited view from the road shoulder. Birding here is typically best in late winter, when there may be numerous waterfowl, and during dry periods in summer.

The impoundment typically has few ducks during the hunting season, but a good number and variety are usually present later, from about late January to early March. (November, before the hunting season, is also good during some years.) Look especially for Mallards, American Black Ducks, Northern Pintails, American Wigeons, and Green-winged Teal. Check carefully for a drake Eurasian Wigeon; one has been spotted almost annually. Fulvous Whistling-Ducks are possible. A few diving ducks, including Redheads, are also possible.

During recent years this site has often provided a pleasant spectacle at sunset in mid- and late winter. Several hundred Tundra Swans, which feed in extensive farmlands a few miles to the north, fly to the impoundment in the evenings to roost. This is the southernmost site on the North Carolina coast where large flocks of swans can be seen.

The impoundment can also be plenty entertaining in summer if there is an extended period of dry weather, causing low water levels. When the water level first begins to recede, the impoundment may host large numbers of wading birds, including White and Glossy ibises. At such times there are often a few Black-necked Stilts.

If the weather is extremely dry, the impoundment may become attractive to shorebirds in July and August. Unfortunately, these birds are quite difficult to see well from the highway. Shorebirds found here include not only those species typical of intertidal habitats but also those more likely to be found at nontidal brackish pools, such as Lesser Yellowlegs, Pectoral Sandpiper, Stilt Sandpiper, and Long-billed Dowitcher. Rarer species seen here include American Avocet, Baird's Sandpiper, Ruff, and Wilson's Phalarope.

During such low water levels the impoundment is also attractive to Laughing Gulls, terns, and Black Skimmers. The terns you may see include Forster's, Least, Gull-billed and, in late summer, Caspian and Black.

Normal water levels during the warmer months typically offer dull birding, but even then you might see something of interest. There are always at least a few wading birds. Watch for Common Moorhens at the edges of the marsh vegetation, and hope for a Least Bittern to take flight.

At all seasons, in mid- to late morning on clear days, watch for raptors in the skies beyond the impoundment. Turkey Vultures are common, a Red-tailed Hawk will usually show up, and you might also see Black Vultures and a Red-shouldered Hawk. Ospreys are always in sight during the warmer months, and a Bald Eagle is possible at any season. In autumn and winter, watch for a Merlin.

NEW DRUM INLET

Although this Cape Lookout NS site can be one of the better birding spots along North Carolina's coastline, there are many years when it is not even seen by a bird-watcher, because it is quite difficult to get to. You don't visit here without some planning, effort, and expense.

During the migrations this is an excellent area for shorebirds, and occasionally something unusual shows up, such as a Long-billed Curlew. Wilson's and Piping plovers nest here, and there may also be colonies of Black Skimmers and Least, Common, and Gull-billed terns. In recent years this has been one of the most reliable sites in the state for Reddish Egrets; one or more have been present every summer.

By the way, the former Drum Inlet (now called Old Drum Inlet) filled in naturally during the 1960s. The present inlet, New Drum, is manmade: it was literally blasted open by the U.S. Army Corps of Engineers in December 1971. However, it too began filling in almost immediately and soon became too shallow to be used by fishing boats. There are now plans to dredge a new channel.

LOGISTICS. Not only is this area rather inaccessible—it is also split by the inlet into north and south sides. These two sections are both good birding areas, but they might as well be a hundred miles apart unless you have a boat. However, the south side is best, and unless I indicate otherwise, the description below refers to the south side.

The best way to visit this area is by means of a powerboat with a shallow draft; you can put in at the Texaco station on the waterfront (US 70) in Atlantic. Otherwise, the only access is by way of the Alger Willis ferry (phone 919-729-2791) from Davis to Core Banks. However, the ferry terminal is about 7 miles south of the inlet (although it gets a little closer every year as the inlet migrates southward). Thus, if you can't go by powerboat the only practical way to visit this site is to take a four-wheel-drive vehicle over on the ferry. The cost of transporting a vehicle is $60, plus $12 for each person. Obviously, this makes for an expensive trip, although it is more reasonable if there are several people to share the expense. If you do plan to bring a four-wheel-drive over, call the Cape Lookout NS Visitors Center (phone 919-728-2250) for general information and cautions regarding vehicle use in the seashore. Anyone going to the trouble and expense of visiting this site should consider combining it with a visit to Cape Lookout. Camping is allowed in the seashore (again, call the Park Service for cautions and general information). At the ferry terminal on Core Banks there are also several cabins for rent, run by Alger Willis Fishing Camps (phone 919-729-2791). These cabins are primitive, with no electricity. Nevertheless, they are usually filled up during the peak fall fishing season, October through November.

If you're long on enthusiasm and endurance, you might consider hiking to the inlet from the ferry terminal, especially during cooler weather. The ferry fee for a pedestrian is $12. Again, the distance is about 7 miles (and getting shorter every year). However, you will have to walk another 2 miles to bird the inlet area thoroughly. After you leave the cabin area, there is no drinking water. You can often hitch a ride along the beach, but don't bank on it.

The north side of the inlet is similarly inaccessible. It is about 6 miles from the inlet to the north Core Banks ferry terminal (but getting farther every year).

This ferry is run by Morris Marina, Kabin Kamps, and Ferry Service (phone 919-225-4261). This ferry charges the same fees for vehicle transportation, etc., as the Alger Willis ferry. If you plan to bring a vehicle to the north side of Drum Inlet, try to combine this visit with a trip to Portsmouth Island, an excellent shorebird area to the north. (You can drive from north Core Banks to Portsmouth Island; the inlets that formerly separated them filled in years ago.)

AGAIN, THIS DESCRIPTION refers to the south side of the inlet unless otherwise indicated.

New Drum Inlet is an important nesting area for Wilson's and Piping plovers, and there are usually colonies of Least Terns, and sometimes Common and Gull-billed terns and Black Skimmers as well. These nesting areas are restricted from public access; you will see several signs posted. Stay outside of these signs—you can see all the nesting species by working along the boundary of the area. To get to the shorebird flats beyond the nesting area, continue around the periphery of the signs. You can also get to the flats by cutting across the island farther south.

The Piping Plovers begin nesting here in April and may nest until July and August if eggs and young are lost to tides and predators. The Wilson's Plovers also nest from about April to July. Before and after the nesting period (and often during), both species can usually be found on the wetter tidal flats. Pipings can be fairly common here in migration (August to October), and a few sometimes overwinter. The Wilson's may also be fairly common on the flats in August, before they begin to migrate southward.

May is the major month for nesting activity by terns and skimmers. If they are successful, many birds may remain through June.

New Drum Inlet can be excellent for shorebirds during the migrations, especially from late April to late May and from about mid-July to October. At these times you can see most of those shorebird species that typically occur in intertidal habitats—species like Semipalmated Plover, Whimbrel, Western Sandpiper, Dunlin, and Short-billed Dowitcher. This site is especially attractive to Red Knots, which can usually be found during the migrations, and often occur during June and throughout winter as well. A few Marbled Godwits can usually be found here from July through autumn. In recent years a Long-billed Curlew has overwintered here; sightings of this species are most likely from late July to October.

Although intertidal habitats are not the best for finding rarer species of shorebirds, rarities are occasional here, undoubtedly because this is the best shorebird habitat for several miles. American Golden-Plovers have been seen here in autumn, American Avocets in late summer and autumn, and Wilson's Phalaropes in autumn. Remember that this area is seldom seen by birders; if it was visited regularly, it would probably boast a rather long list of rarities.

In addition to shorebirds, several species of terns can usually be seen resting on the flats. Sandwich Terns are regular here from April to November. This is one of the better sites in the state for seeing Black Terns. They are usually easy to find from late June (about a month earlier than most locations) to early September.

In the warmer months there is a fairly good variety of wading birds. From about mid-May to early October, one or more Reddish Egrets are almost the rule here.

Except for the inlet's water birds, the Core Banks area is not particularly interesting. However, there are a few resident Ring-necked Pheasants in the low shrub thickets. In autumn several hawks, including Peregrine Falcons, may sometimes be seen migrating down the barrier strand; in April and May, Swallow-tailed Kites have been spotted. Snow Buntings probably occur with some regularity on the higher portion of the inlet flats in November and December.

The north side of the inlet is similar, but the flats there are drier, and shore-birding is typically not rewarding. Wilson's and Piping plovers nest on the north side also.

For further information: For general information about the seashore, including a checklist of its birds, contact Cape Lookout NS, 131 Charles Street, Harkers Island, NC 28531; phone 919-728-2250. For information about access to south Core Banks and rental cabins there, contact Alger Willis Fishing Camps, P.O. Box 234, Davis, NC 28524; phone 919-729-2791. For information about access to north Core Banks and rental cabins, contact Morris Marina, Kabin Kamps, and Ferry Service, 1000 Morris Marina Road, Atlantic, NC 28511; phone 919-225-4261.

HARKERS ISLAND

This area is off the beaten path; birders are likely to visit it only when they use the island as an access point to parts of Cape Lookout NS. The island itself doesn't have much to offer birders, except that the two ends of the island can be good spots for seeing a variety of water birds in migration flights and flights to and from feeding and roosting areas.

The eastern tip of the island, called Shell Point, is especially intriguing. Visitors to the area are likely to end up here whether or not they are bird-watchers (many island residents make a brief visit here every day). The view overlooks water and sky to the northeast, southeast, and southwest. There is an unobstructed view of the sunrise every day of the year, and of sunsets from autumn to early spring.

Shell Point is located at the end of the main road (Island Road, SR 1335) that runs the length of the island. It adjoins the Cape Lookout NS Visitors Center, where adequate parking is available.

This site could be thought of as an inland cape. Here the orientation of the sounds' mainland shoreline changes from predominantly north-south to east-west. Birds moving up or down the coast by way of the sounds will often pass just off the tip of the island.

Perhaps the most reliable season for being thoroughly entertained here is the nesting season, from about late April to about early August. During this period several species of water birds nest on islands in the channel between here and Cape Lookout, and a good variety can always be seen from Shell Point.

For an especially entertaining time, get here a few minutes before sunrise. At that time wading birds will be heading out of the nesting colonies, and you can see most of the wading species that occur in the state, including White Ibises. Sunset is also good, but the evening flight is bit less impressive, because the birds return to the islands over a longer period of time.

To the south, toward the distant Cape Lookout Lighthouse, you will see a prominent sand island. This is a major nesting area for Royal and Sandwich terns. Not surprisingly, Shell Point is a great place to see Sandwich Terns during the nesting period, from about late April into July.

Shell Point can also be a good spot to set up watch during the migration periods. Of course, you shouldn't expect the numbers or variety that would pass a "real" cape—one on the ocean—but you're sure to be entertained, and occasionally you might see something out of the ordinary.

In springtime set up watch early in the morning, especially in March or April. The best weather is perhaps ahead of cold fronts, when the wind is light but is forecasted to increase from a southerly direction later in the day. Watch for loons, grebes, cormorants, a few ducks, shorebirds, gulls, and terns. Occasionally a few northbound scoters will take a shortcut across the sounds, so don't be surprised if you see a few of these fly by. Rarely, you might even see a jaeger.

Autumn is not as interesting on the average, but some days may provide an almost constant stream of southbound cormorants, gulls, and terns, with a few ducks. The best time seems to be early morning after cold fronts in October and November. If you see any scoters around early November, carefully check for a White-winged.

Wintertime birding here can range from dull to a lot of fun. Try to visit on a slick, calm morning, when it will be easy to spot several species on the water—Red-throated and Common loons, Horned Grebes, Red-breasted Mergansers, and Buffleheads. Occasionally you may see a goldeneye. Sometimes you might spot a distant "cloud" moving low over the water—a flock of several thousand Redheads. Unfortunately, these birds are virtually never seen at close range.

Because you can bird this area from your car, this is a good spot to check on a rainy day, or when it's bitterly cold, or, especially, during stormy weather. There are lee shores during both fierce northeasters and southwesters, so these may be particularly good occasions to check here. The Park Service building next to the road's end provides a good wind shelter.

The adjacent lawns and shrub thickets can occasionally be entertaining for land birding. If you're here at twilight from about late April to early July, you might hear a Chuck-will's-widow. After autumn cold fronts, passerines that have been pushed to the adjacent barrier islands during the previous night sometimes make daytime reorientation flights in which Shell Point is an important "mainland" arrival point; the best conditions are north winds in the morning following a night of northwest winds. Although the lawn area here is not extensive, it is nevertheless the largest expanse of such habitat around, and because of its geographically interesting location, it no doubt attracts unusual species occasionally—species like American Golden-Plover. On calm mornings in winter, the shrub thickets may be alive with Yellow-rumped Warblers, and you are sure to find one or two Orange-crowned Warblers as well.

The western tip of the island is generally much less interesting than Shell Point. However, at times the birding here is *more* interesting than at Shell Point, and you may see species here that you wouldn't see from Shell Point. This is another spot where most of what you see will be fly-bys, birds headed to and from feeding and roosting areas elsewhere. And it's a great place for sunsets most of the year.

To reach this site, begin at the bridges and causeway between the mainland and Harkers Island and drive toward Harkers Island. When you reach the end of the second bridge, at the Harkers Island shore, set your odometer at zero. Continue 0.8 miles, then turn right onto Branch Drive. Continue a short distance to the end, where there is a motel and marina. Drive to the far end of the marina's parking lot. (In midwinter the marina may be closed; this site would then be inaccessible.)

Most of the time this site will maintain your interest for no more than a few minutes. However, it can be fun about sunrise and sunset from late April to September, when wading birds are flying in and out of islands to the southwest, and around low tide—especially from late autumn to early spring, when shorebirds may be seen flying to and from feeding areas.

During their sunrise and sunset flights you may see most of the wading birds that occur in the state, including White and Glossy ibises. Around August and September, there are often impressive flights of Cattle Egrets. Although the nesting season is normally the most interesting, there may be flights of a handful of waders even in midwinter, especially during mild years.

Watches at low tide are most likely to be productive during fair weather and light or southwest winds. Northeast winds are unfavorable because the shorebird feeding areas upriver will not be exposed. Tidewise, the best time to be here is rather difficult to predict: it varies from about one hour after low tide on the oceanfront (when birds are beginning to fly upriver) to about five hours after low tide on the oceanfront (when birds are returning to inlet-area locations). Low tide watches can be especially productive and aesthetically pleasing at sunrise and sunset, although at sunset the light conditions are terrible for identifying fly-bys, most of which are rather distant.

During good conditions between late autumn and early spring, watch for flights of oystercatchers, Willets, Marbled Godwits, Western Sandpipers, Dunlins, and Short-billed Dowitchers. If you're lucky, you might also see something like a Long-billed Curlew. In autumn and early winter, if you're here at dusk, watch for the silhouettes of Black Skimmers feeding out over the river.

For further information: For information about Shell Point, contact Cape Lookout NS, 131 Charles Street, Harkers Island, NC 28531; phone 919-728-2250.

CAPE LOOKOUT
MAP 22

This site is rather inaccessible, and unless you have a four-wheel-drive vehicle, covering the area adequately requires a lot of walking. Nevertheless, there are certainly times when the birding rewards are high enough to make your effort worthwhile. Because woody vegetation is so limited, land bird migration can be very impressive here after autumn cold fronts. Searching for land bird migrants in spring can also be rewarding, although you'll find far fewer birds in spring than in autumn.

The point can be an excellent site for getting close views of gannets and scoters as they fly past from autumn until spring. Jaegers are also seen regularly here, and other pelagic species, such as Wilson's Storm-Petrels and shearwaters, are possible, especially if weather conditions are favorable. Several rare gulls and terns have been seen on the point itself, although Cape Lookout has received only limited birding activity. During some years there are nesting colonies, usually on the spit, and Wilson's and Piping plovers nest here.

Even at those times when the birding is not impressive, a visit to the cape can be truly enjoyable for most nature-oriented people. The area often provides a wonderful sense of isolation that is becoming increasingly hard to find on the barrier islands of our state. Standing at the tip of the point late in the afternoon, virtually surrounded by ocean, can be a memorable experience.

LOGISTICS. The primary means of access to Cape Lookout is by way of the pedestrian ferry (a Park Service concession) from Harkers Island. In recent years different concessionaires have run the ferry from different locations, and the schedules have frequently changed, so call the Cape Lookout NS Visitors Center (919-728-2250) for the most up-to-date information. The visitors center is located at the end of Island Road (the main road that runs down the island) at the eastern tip of the island.

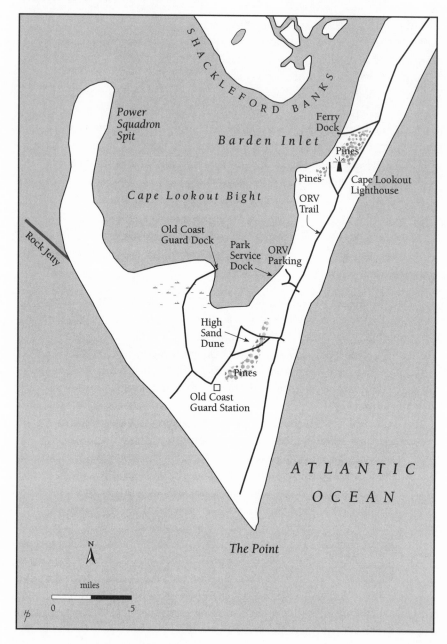

22. CAPE LOOKOUT

Currently the pedestrian ferry departs from Calico Jack's Marina (919-728-3575) on Harkers Island. The marina is located on Island Road, 0.2 miles from the Cape Lookout NS Visitors Center. The round-trip cost is $12 for adults. Also, a jitney service runs between the ferry dock at Cape Lookout and the point. This service is something a birder might consider using for part of the trip—for example, taking the jitney back from the point at the end of the day.

The ferry runs seasonally, from early April to Thanksgiving weekend, but large groups may be able to charter it during the off-season. Unfortunately, during most of the year the first run of the day is not until midmorning. However, 6 A.M. runs are available if enough people make reservations, and there are frequent 6 A.M. runs during the autumn fishing season (mid-September to November). Again, call for the latest information.

There are also concessionaires that use small boats (up to five or six passengers). Check with the Park Service for phone numbers of these concessionaires. This can be a good way to arrange an early morning run, and the cost per person is quite reasonable if you have a group of three or more.

There is no drinking water at the cape, so bring plenty to drink. Although vegetation is limited, the area usually supports a healthy mosquito population, so bring repellent as well. Restrooms are available at the lighthouse and just north of the point.

Because the average ferry trip doesn't enable you to be here early in the morning or late in the afternoon, you might consider camping out. Check with the Park Service to see what areas are currently off-limits. In this very exposed environment, be especially prepared for strong winds and changeable weather. And be warned that no-see-ums, or sand gnats, can cause pure misery on calm nights in the warmer months.

Groups interested in birding and learning about other types of barrier island natural history (especially dolphins and sea turtles) can inquire about the Cape Lookout Studies Program run by the North Carolina Maritime Museum in Beaufort (919-728-7317). These groups stay in the museum field station (the old coast guard station) at the cape. The field station may be reserved for a weekend or longer.

You can bring off-road vehicles to Cape Lookout by taking the small car ferry (a Park Service concession) from Davis to Core Banks and driving south (10-plus miles) down the barrier island. The ferry is run by Alger G. Willis Fishing Camps (919-729-2791) at Davis.

Again, much walking is required to cover this area, and because there is little habitat diversity, birding rewards can be rather limited relative to the amount of walking required. In general, the fall migration period is your best bet for a favorable ratio of good birding to amount of energy expended. However, for the best birding, it is essential that you visit after a good cold front—specifically, the morning after a night with brisk northwesterly winds. The most interesting period is from September until about October 15. Fronts later in the fall will still produce numerous migrants, but diversity drops off as the season progresses. Also, in late May pelagic species are seen with some regularity at the cape, and rarities can show up at any season.

THE FOLLOWING descriptions are based on a visit by way of the ferry, the primary means of access for most birders.

The **Cape Lookout ferry run** can often be plenty entertaining in itself. In late spring and early summer, one or more islands along the channel serve as nesting colonies for wading birds, gulls, terns, and skimmers. Expect to see large numbers of Royal and Sandwich terns. Look carefully—Sooty Terns are occasionally present, and other rarities are possible. In the cooler months the islands are used by roosting birds. Brown Pelicans are common all year, and Double-crested Cormorants are abundant from October to April.

During the migrations and in winter, large numbers of shorebirds may be seen along the southern portion of the ferry route, when water levels are low enough to expose the area's vast flats. (Tides along the ferry route lag about two to three hours behind those on the oceanfront, but water levels are strongly influenced by wind direction. In early autumn, water levels low enough to expose the flats may occur only rarely.) In the warmer months the borders of the flats often have numerous wading birds, including White Ibises. When the ferry runs near the southeastern tip of Shackleford Banks, watch the shoreline carefully. Several shorebirds often rest here, especially at high tide. Look for American Oystercatchers, Whimbrels, and others. Occasionally, in fall, a few Marbled Godwits and a Long-billed Curlew may be spotted here.

In the vicinity of the **ferry dock** at the cape, extending to just beyond the Cape Lookout Lighthouse, there is a small area of pine trees and shrub thickets. This area—the cape's northernmost stretch of relatively tall pines—can be one of the better spots after a cold front. Migrating land birds displaced during the previous night's winds may pile up here before deciding to head back toward the mainland. At the peak of migration Palm Warblers may be everywhere, and you should see several other warbler species as well. These pines can also be attractive to kinglets, woodpeckers, and other species. During some years you will see several Red-breasted Nuthatches.

If you come over on the early ferry in autumn, you may arrive here before sunrise. If so, wait a little while. When the sun begins to warm the eastern side of the vegetation (which is also the leeward side during a favorable northwest wind), birds will start to appear. By gradually working along this side of the vegetation, you can put together a good list, and the birds are typically very approachable if you stay quiet. (Squeaking may well be counterproductive in this situation.)

By the way, the pines and shrub thickets of the cape can also attract a few migrating land birds from April to the first week of June, after westerly winds associated with cold fronts. Typically you will find no more than a few individuals, but you do have a chance of getting good close looks at exhausted individuals in breeding plumage, including species like Northern Oriole, Scarlet Tanager, and Rose-breasted Grosbeak. And if you have the opportunity to bird the cape during northwesterly winds associated with a cool high pressure system between mid-May and early June, go for it! This is admittedly a rare situation, but it might bring very rare migrants, usually immatures. Some of my own best finds at the cape have been during such times and conditions.

From September to early spring, check the walls of the lighthouse carefully. Sometimes a Peregrine Falcon may be seen roosting here.

From the lighthouse you may want to continue down the cape by walking either the ocean beach, or the ORV trail that runs along the interior of the barrier strand, or perhaps along the shoreline of the bight. The ocean beach provides the easiest walking and the possibility of seeing a few shorebirds, often including Red Knots. The shoreline of the bight is easy to walk only at low tide; at this time of day this route may also produce a few shorebirds. When you reach a point south of the lighthouse, look out into the bight for two tall pilings. Each of these is typically topped with a Great Cormorant, even in the summer months. You will need a scope to see them well.

After a good cold front in autumn, you will probably want to walk the ORV trail. In the adjacent salt meadows you may flush a Bobolink or two, and you may find Marsh and Sedge wrens. If you walk actively through the meadows, you might flush a migrant rail, most likely a Virginia or a Sora.

Just south of the **parking area for ORVs**, and adjacent to a Park Service dock, look for a small structure and an adjacent patch of weedy vines and shrubs. This little patch of vegetation is rather isolated and can be a great place to check during the fall migration. Just stand quietly with the sun at your back and see what pops up.

From the ORV parking area walk southward using the ORV trail. When you get to the crossroads, turn right. Farther on, this trail forks to the left and right. Either way will take you into the "village"—the strip of cabins and the old coast guard station.

Just after the fork both trails pass through a long pine grove that stretches from north to south. This pine grove is similar to the one in the lighthouse area but is more extensive. In the breeding season Chuck-will's-widows can sometimes be found here. This pine grove can also be excellent after autumn cold fronts; there is sometimes a pile-up of birds in the northernmost section, north of the two ORV trails. This section is rather narrow, and by spreading out and walking abreast, three or more birders can effectively herd the birds along toward the north tip of the grove. This can be a good way to spot secretive species, such as cuckoos and thrushes. Occasionally you may flush a Barn Owl.

Adjacent to the village there is a rather extensive area of shrub thickets made up of wax myrtle, red cedar, red bay, and other species. Breeding birds here are generally commonplace species—Northern Mockingbird, Gray Catbird, Brown Thrasher, Mourning Dove, Common Yellowthroat, etc. Often one or two Yellow-billed Cuckoos can be seen. The habitat looks great for Painted Buntings, but for some reason they don't occur here. Let's hope that some invade in the future. Along the shoulders of the paved roadway running northwest from the old coast guard station, look carefully for Ring-necked Pheasants. A few were released several years ago, and a small population has become established.

The shrub thickets can also be excellent for migrant land birds after autumn cold fronts, although there don't seem to be any major funnel points and the birds are more difficult to see here than in the pine groves. Generally the best sites for getting good views of birds are the **old coast guard station**, the borders of the paved road that runs northwest from the station, and the cabin lawns and their borders. In addition to the numerous warblers, check these areas carefully for sparrows—Lark, White-crowned, and Clay-colored have been found. The old coast guard station is a good place to look for Western Kingbirds after fronts in October.

Immediately northwest of the station there is a small, open marshy area within the shrub thickets. In wet periods check here for a few wading birds and an occasional shorebird, like Spotted and Solitary sandpipers. The edges of this marshy area sometimes attract a Northern Waterthrush.

A little north of the old coast guard station, immediately north of a fork in the ORV trail, there is a relatively high sand dune. Climb this dune for a good overall view of the cape—the east beach, the southwest beach, and the bight. On clear days in fall, especially after cold fronts, this dune is a good observation post to use in watching for migrating hawks, swallows, and other species, sometimes including Great Blue Herons and other wading birds. Merlins and Peregrine Falcons are seen here regularly. Sharp-shinned Hawks are often common in October, and on good days one or two Cooper's Hawks may also be seen.

A paved road that runs northwest and north from the old coast guard station leads to the **old coast guard dock** at the edge of the Cape Lookout Bight. The station and the dock are almost a mile apart; the hike is most worthwhile when the birding is dull elsewhere. The marshes beside the bight will at least give you an opportunity to pad your daily list. A few wading birds and shorebirds are always around; shorebirds frequently roost on the sand banks adjacent to the dock at high tide.

A few Clapper Rails live in these marshes year-round. A Virginia Rail or Sora might be spotted during a good high tide in autumn, and such tides might also produce a few Seaside and Sharp-tailed sparrows. On one occasion a Black Rail was heard in July at the marshes' upper border, adjacent to the paved roadway—perhaps a few Blacks are summer residents here.

The dock is a good spot from which to scope the bight. You will see the two Great Cormorant perches mentioned above, but they are more distant from this site. In winter there are many Common Loons in the bight, and rarities such as Razorbills and Dovekies have also been spotted. Look carefully, especially in late May. Northward-migrating pelagic birds sometimes fly into the bight by mistake. Wilson's Storm-Petrel is the most likely pelagic, but others are possible—even a skua was found here once.

Near the base of the spit, on the ocean side, is a long **rock jetty**. Alas, this jetty is usually submerged, and no parts of it remain exposed during high tide, so it does not have as much potential for Purple Sandpipers and sea ducks as it otherwise might. A few Great Cormorants can often be seen feeding adjacent to the jetty during the cooler months; one or two immatures are typically present in summer. The few records of Harlequin Ducks and Common Eiders at the jetty have taken place mostly in late winter and early spring; presumably the jetty, on the west side of the cape, is spotted primarily by birds moving northward.

During the warmer months, eddies of Gulf Stream water occasionally move ashore in the Cape Lookout area, and several species of tropical fish can often be found around this jetty. One recent summer a Brown Booby spent a few days here.

Usually called "the Spit" or "the Hook," the **Power Squadron Spit** stretches for over a mile in length. Especially around its tip, the spit is often a favorite roosting area for pelicans, cormorants, gulls, terns, and shorebirds. During migration periods several species of shorebirds may be seen. In the dead of winter, gull flocks may blanket the spit during periods of heavy commercial fishing activity just offshore. These gull flocks tend to be unusually wary— definitely birds to scope. The ocean here is a major wintering area for Common Loons; interestingly, Red-throateds are scarce here. In the breeding season a few American Oystercatchers, Wilson's Plovers, and Piping Plovers nest. (Stay outside any roped-off areas—you still should be able to spot a few birds.) Some years a large nesting colony develops on the spit in May and June, and large numbers of terns—Least, Common, and Gull-billed—and Black Skimmers are present. Watch carefully—Sooty Terns have nested here, and Roseate Terns are also possible. (Again, stay out of any roped-off areas.) Outside of the nesting season, look for Wilson's and Piping plovers along the bight shoreline at the base of the spit, especially at low tide. Pipings are regular in migration and irregular in winter. Wilson's occur as early as March and as late as September. (Some of this shoreline may be posted in late summer to protect young Pipings.)

From the cape's **southwestern beach**, especially from the rock jetty southward, watch for migrating loons, gannets, and scoters during the spring migration, especially in the morning. Numbers of these birds frequently collide with the cape and get deflected southward along the southwestern beach. Perhaps because they are flying south when they want to be flying north, they approach the shore closely, sometimes flying within a few yards of the beach.

This situation may occur with a few pelagic species as well, especially after persistent northeasterly or easterly winds. Look especially for Wilson's Storm-Petrels from mid-May to mid-June; Pomarine and Parasitic jaegers from April to early June; and Sooty Shearwaters from mid-May to early June. Watch for Greater Shearwaters in mid- to late June. Audubon's Shearwaters are occasionally seen, mostly from mid-July to early August. Cory's Shearwaters might be seen from late spring through summer; they seem to be most likely in mid-summer.

Locally called "the Point," **Cape Lookout Point** can be the highlight of a visit to the cape, although at times—especially in summer—it may be almost bird-less. The number of birds you see will be influenced by several factors. Periodically the point builds seaward, and sometimes there is a narrow strip of land projecting up to half a mile into the ocean. Then the point is much more attractive to resting gulls and terns. Sometimes there is almost no such point, and the surf comes up almost to the dunes, providing little space for gulls and terns.

The point is generally more interesting during migrations and stormy weather—again, especially during northeasterly and easterly winds in spring. The number of fishermen present is very important; at times there is precious little room for birds. Fishing activity is most intense on weekends and in October. During much of the year there are very few fishermen at the point early in the morning and late in the afternoon, so you might well want to consider camping at the cape.

During most of the warmer months, you will find Royal, Sandwich, Least, and Common terns (though Leasts become scarce in September). This is an excellent site for Sandwich Terns, which may be seen reliably from early April to late November. Perhaps because this site is so maritime, in autumn Common Terns linger later here than along most of the state's coast; they are seen regularly through October. This is one of the better sites in the state, perhaps the best, for seeing Black Terns. One or two can often be found from mid-May into June, and several are always present from early July through mid-September.

Check the tern flocks carefully. Roseate Terns are found occasionally, especially about late May to July, and an Arctic Tern was once found here in late May after several days of strong easterly/northeasterly winds. Sooty Terns have been seen in summer, and on one August morning two Bridled Terns were seen flying by—a record all the more remarkable because it was not associated with a storm.

From autumn to spring you may spot a gull of interest. Lesser Black-backeds are being seen with increasing frequency; you might spot one even in the dead of summer. Look for Little Gulls in late winter and spring, when Bonaparte's Gulls are in northward migration. Glaucous and Iceland gulls have been found here in winter (one Iceland as early as mid-October).

From late October through April, Northern Gannets can be seen feeding just off the point and sometimes flying over it. This can also be a good site for getting great looks at scoters as they fly by; they are most likely during the migrations. Jaegers might be spotted just about any month of the year, although they are most likely in spring migration, and Black-legged Kittiwakes are possible in late autumn and winter. With luck you may have a jaeger or kittiwake fly right over your head.

During some years a tern nesting colony may develop on the point in May and June, enhancing your chances of finding a Roseate Tern, or an Arctic. In autumn, stormy weather and high tides often create a large shallow pool at the base of the point. This pool often attracts resting gulls, terns, and shorebirds. Look carefully here for American Golden-Plovers, phalaropes, or other rare shorebirds.

For further information: Write Cape Lookout NS, 131 Charles Street, Harkers Island, NC 28531; phone 919-728-2250. The visitors center is located at the eastern end of Harkers Island, and maps and a checklist of the area's birds are available.

EASTERN END OF SHACKLEFORD BANKS
MAP 23

Rather inaccessible and largely ignored by the public, this section of the Cape Lookout NS can be quite good for shorebirds and wading birds during the warmer months. This site is an excellent complement to nearby Cape Lookout; if you are planning a trip to Cape Lookout and hoping to see diverse waders and shorebirds, you would do well to visit this site instead.

East Shackleford has an expansive tract of mud flats that often attract large numbers and a fairly good variety of shorebirds—those typical of intertidal habitats—during the migrations, from late April to late May and from mid-July to October. During the autumn migration Marbled Godwits are fairly common, and occasionally a Long-billed Curlew is found. Wilson's Plovers are easy to find during the breeding season. The flats and associated tidal creeks also host a good variety of wading birds during the warmer months. White Ibises are common, and Yellow-crowned Night-Herons are regular in late summer.

Clapper Rails live in the adjacent marshes all year, and a few Seaside Sparrows are present from spring until autumn. A few Piping Plovers can often be found on the ocean side of the island, near the inlet, during the migrations.

If you're part of a group that includes nonbirders, you may be interested to know that the ocean beach at this end of Shackleford is often excellent for

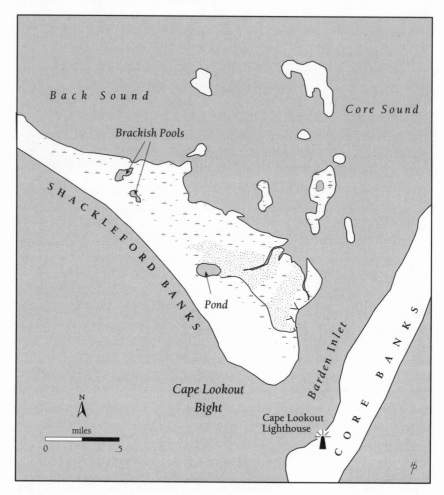

23. EASTERN END OF SHACKLEFORD BANKS

shelling because of current patterns. In fact, don't be surprised if you find a few coconuts from the tropics washed in along the beaches here.

Part of this area's appeal is its isolation and wonderful open, windswept, desolate appearance. You may see several boats along the ocean beach on weekends, but otherwise you will probably have the place pretty much to yourself. You can spend an entire day on the shorebird flats with no one around except the wild horses.

LOGISTICS. There is currently no regularly scheduled transportation to this site, but there are several people licensed to transport passengers to the island. Call the Park Service at 919-728-2250 for a list of these people as well as the latest access information.

Currently access is easiest to arrange from April through November. If you go during periods when the passenger boats are making frequent trips to Cape Lookout (during the summer months and on weekends), or if there are three or more people in your group, the charge per person is $12.

There is no drinking water in this area, so you will want to take plenty to drink. Sunscreen is also recommended. Mosquitoes and biting flies are not usually very bad here, but bring some repellent just in case. Despite the scarcity of woody vegetation, ticks are fairly common, but you won't be exposed to any unless you walk through the higher marshes (black needlerush marshes) and shrub areas. The mud flats are quite sticky, so wearing boots is rather tiring; it is best to wear tennis shoes and tolerate wet feet. If you spend any time shelling, keep in mind that one of the Park Service regulations is that no one may take live specimens or more than two gallons of seashells per day. If you come across the territories of any ground-nesting birds, such as Wilson's Plovers, please move on.

Camping is permitted here, but most people would not consider this a comfortable place to camp, and there is usually no advantage to being here first thing in the morning: tide level is the most important factor determining numbers of birds here. Also, mosquitoes and no-see-ums may be terrible at night.

Try to visit this site during the migration periods mentioned above. It is best to visit when high tide covers all the flats within the adjacent Back and Core sounds, forcing most of the shorebirds in the area onto the Shackleford flats. Low tide may have very few birds. The tide in the sounds behind Shackleford lags about two to three hours after that on the oceanfront. Because this area is so exposed, birding is best here when winds are light. Shorebirds are much more approachable during light wind conditions.

To thoroughly cover the major area of interest—the shorebird flats in the island's interior—be prepared to hike a total of about 2 miles. If you want to check some brackish pools farther west on the island, you will have to walk another mile and a half (round-trip). To cover the main area you should allow about four hours on the island. If you plan to visit the brackish pools, allow another couple of hours.

YOUR BOAT RIDE to the island will probably be along the channel from Harkers Island to Cape Lookout; read the Cape Lookout section to find out what you might expect to see on this trip. During high water levels some of the boat operators may take you across Back Sound farther west, which can also be interesting—you will pass by numerous small islands and shoals dotted with wading birds, shorebirds, and terns.

You will probably arrive on the island at the very eastern tip, next to Barden Inlet, where deep water lies beside the shore. From this shoreline the shorebird flats are becoming difficult to see, because much of the marshes around the flats are being invaded by shrubs. To find the flats, head north along the inlet shoreline until you come to a tidal creek, then follow the creek inland until you see the flats. At high tide this creek is deep; you will have to follow it almost to the pond before it becomes shallow enough to wade. Even here, there are some deeper spots—do not wade across unless you can see the bottom. You may want to walk around to the west side of the pond to get onto the flats.

The area referred to as "the pond" can be identified by the old telegraph pole still standing in it (a reminder of the days when telegraph poles ran all along most of the barrier islands, connecting the coast guard stations). You may prefer to find the flats by walking up the ocean beach until you see the pond and tele-graph pole. You may have to walk up on the dunes at intervals to spot the pond.

Again, this is a good area for shorebirds typical of intertidal habitats. Whim-brels are quite common here during their migration peaks. Marbled Godwits are being found with increasing frequency; they are now quite regular from late July into autumn and may be found at other seasons as well. This is one of the better sites in the state for Long-billed Curlews; one or two individuals are occasion-ally found from July into autumn, and sometimes throughout the winter. This is also a very good spot for Wilson's Plovers, although they may decline in the fu-ture as adjacent breeding habitat is invaded by vegetation. You should be able to find them from late March to mid-September; they are most common in August.

Although these flats are regularly flooded with tidal salt water, they are proba-bly often freshened by rainwater, and they regularly attract shorebirds that typi-cally shun intertidal flats, including American Avocet, Lesser Yellowlegs, White-rumped Sandpiper, Stilt Sandpiper, and Wilson's Phalarope. Red-necked and Red phalaropes have also been seen here during the spring migration period, and this would seem to be a likely spot for an American Golden-Plover in autumn.

This area has been visited by birders only a few times. If birders came here frequently, they would probably find rare shorebirds regularly, because this area is the best shorebird habitat for miles, and it lies next to a cape that projects far seaward. The site's best potential for rare shorebirds is probably in May, but July and August could also be good months.

There are always good numbers of wading birds here during the warmer months. You should see several White Ibises. Two or three Yellow-crowned Night-Herons usually show up from July (sometimes earlier) to September; you are most likely to see immatures.

Do not neglect the eastern section of the flats, which is somewhat hidden from the main area by a strip of high marsh. Pay special attention to this section during lower tide levels, when more birds will be found closer to the inlet. The strip of high marsh has a few breeding Seaside Sparrows from late March to August, and this is a good place to look for Seasides and Sharp-taileds during high tides in autumn.

Lying beside Barden Inlet is an area of regularly flooded marsh. A few Clapper Rails are resident here. During a rising tide you might see a few rails scurrying from these marshes across the open flats to the higher marshes west of here.

You will probably want to walk to the northeast corner of the flats, where you can overlook the adjacent islands and flats of Back Sound. At high tide the islands may be covered with resting birds. From May to September check the flats carefully for a Reddish Egret. This species has been seen in the area on a couple of occasions.

About half a mile northwest of the flats are some shallow brackish pools. These are largely nontidal but are flooded by higher-than-average tides, which are frequent in autumn. These pools are worth the extra hike primarily during dry weather in May, July, and August, when you are likely to find something different here. Look for species like Glossy Ibis, Lesser Yellowlegs, and Stilt, Pectoral, and White-rumped sandpipers. You can find these pools by hiking up the beach, occasionally checking from the dune crests.

Be sure to devote a little time to checking the island's ocean beach. As the Cape Lookout site description explains, northbound loons, gannets, scoters, and even pelagic species frequently collide with the cape. Some of these birds may enter the Cape Lookout Bight and be seen just off the beach here. Northbound jaegers have even been seen flying into Barden Inlet.

The same current patterns that often deposit seashells along this section of beach also frequently bring in the bodies of pelagic birds that have died at sea. From May to July you may want to look along the drift line of flotsam for such birds. A few Greater Shearwaters can usually be found around late June.

On the ocean side of Shackleford, not far from Barden Inlet, there is a wide sand flat at low tide. A few Piping Plovers are often seen here in March and April and from late July to October.

During the winter, access to this site is more difficult to arrange, and the birding then is usually rather dull, offering little variety. Actually, you may see large numbers of shorebirds, but the majority of them will be Black-bellied Plovers, Dunlins, and Western Sandpipers. A few Marbled Godwits can sometimes be found here in winter, and there might be a Long-billed Curlew as well. Also, one or two Whimbrels often overwinter at this site.

For further information: Write Cape Lookout NS, 131 Charles Street, Harkers Island, NC 28531; phone 919-728-2250. The visitors center is located at the eastern end of Harkers Island, and maps and a checklist of the area's birds are available.

WESTERN END OF SHACKLEFORD BANKS
MAP 24

The western end of Shackleford Banks, which is part of Cape Lookout NS, lies next to Beaufort Inlet and is about 2 miles south of the town of Beaufort. This island location is accessible only by boat.

This is not a major birding area. There is little habitat variety, and your

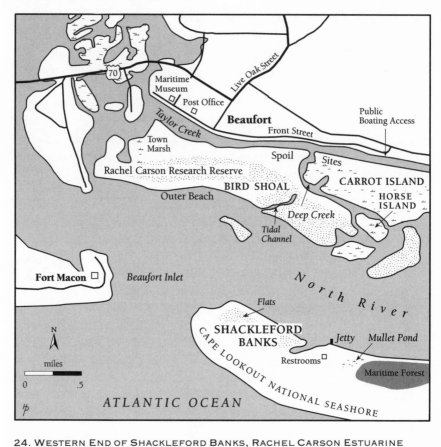

24. WESTERN END OF SHACKLEFORD BANKS, RACHEL CARSON ESTUARINE RESEARCH RESERVE

species list will typically be rather short. In fact, on some days the birding can be almost dull. However, Wilson's Plovers are common in the breeding season, and during the migrations you should see several species of shorebirds. Long-billed Curlews have been found here a few times. In winter the inlet shoreline may be covered with gulls, and you may see one of the rarer species. From late winter into spring, northbound loons, gannets, and other species may pass by just off the beach. You may also spot jaegers and other pelagic species during their respective migration periods. Shackleford is the sort of place where you may not see much, but you might find one bird that makes your day.

Even when the birding is dull, this area can be wonderfully appealing. If you can get out here in winter, or on a weekday in spring or autumn, you might have the whole place to yourself.

LOGISTICS. Currently there is no regularly scheduled ferry service to the island, but there are several transportation services that can be chartered.

These services run from Beaufort and Atlantic Beach. Call the Park Service at 919-728-2250 for a list of these services and for any updates about access to the island. The cost per person is quite reasonable (about $12) if a minimum number of passengers is met (the minimum varies from service to service, ranging from three to six people). Also, the Maritime Museum in Beaufort occasionally organizes field trips to the island; call the museum at 919-728-7317 for more information.

There are restrooms near the rock jetty, but there is no drinking water, so you will want to bring plenty to drink, especially in the warmer months. This open environment is conducive to bad sunburns; bring your sunscreen.

You are more likely to enjoy your trip if you avoid weekends from May to Labor Day. The sound shoreline can be surprisingly crowded. You will especially want to avoid Fourth of July weekends. Try to arrange a trip when winds are forecasted to be light.

THIS DESCRIPTION of the island involves a hike of 4 or 5 miles that will take you along or through the major habitats at the west end of the island. Passenger boats to the island usually unload near the small rock jetty, which is about a mile from the inlet, so the tour begins at the jetty.

During much of the year the jetty has a few Ruddy Turnstones and often a few other shorebirds. On rare occasions in winter a scoter may be spotted on the water nearby, and a King Eider was once found here.

From the jetty, head back into the interior of the island until you see some scattered shrub thickets of red cedar and wax myrtle. After autumn cold fronts these thickets may attract a minor pile-up of passerine migrants. From October into winter you might flush a Barn Owl here.

From the thickets walk eastward across the open dunes until you find an extensive cattail marsh. From about October until April, clap your hands; you might hear a Virginia Rail or Sora respond. In summer you might get lucky and see a Least Bittern. (Many locals still refer to this site as "Mullet Pond." At the turn of the century it lay beside the inlet shoreline, and a small channel connected it with the inlet.)

The edge of the woods from here eastward can sometimes be worth checking, especially during the winter months, when there is more varied birdlife, and when there are no ticks, which can be terrible during the warmer months. If you work along the woods with the dunes to your right, you will see wet areas alternating with slightly higher ridges, and occasional trails leading back into the woods. In winter the birding can be good but unpredictable. During windy conditions you may see almost nothing, but calm sunny mornings can be a lot of fun. Yellow-rumped Warblers will be everywhere, and you should also find House Wrens, both kinglets, a Solitary Vireo, several Orange-crowned Warblers, and others. Autumn migration can occasionally be good. In the breeding season there is little variety; look for Northern Cardinals, Carolina Wrens, Brown Thrashers, and Gray Catbirds. Strangely, Painted Buntings are scarce here, though the habitat is excellent.

From the woods to the ocean beach is a rather boring hike of almost half a mile through open dunes. In late spring and summer you might flush a Common Nighthawk in this area.

When you come to the beach, head to your right, toward the inlet. During much of the year you should see Sanderlings, Black-bellied Plovers, and Willets here. Whimbrels are frequent during the migrations. From here to the inlet, which is about a mile away, large numbers of gulls may congregate in winter. Lesser Black-backeds are seen regularly, and there are several records of Black-legged Kittiwakes along this stretch. Glaucous and Iceland gulls are also possible.

In winter check the ocean for Red-throated and Common loons and Northern Gannets. They often feed very close to shore here. Late winter and early spring can be good for northbound loons, gannets, scoters, gulls, and terns, which may pass by just off the beach. In April and May, especially during easterly winds, you may see Pomarine and Parasitic jaegers. During similar conditions you might also see Wilson's Storm-Petrels and Sooty Shearwaters around late May, Greater Shearwaters in mid- to late June, and Audubon's and Cory's shearwaters from mid-July to early August.

Just before the inlet, on the wide berm on your right, look for Wilson's Plovers (and occasionally a breeding colony of Least Terns) in spring and early summer, but stay out of the nesting area. From autumn to early spring a flock of Semipalmated Plovers often rests here at high tide. These may be joined by Piping Plovers and sometimes one or two Wilson's Plovers. In November and early December this spot would be worth checking for Snow Buntings.

From this point, at least from autumn to early spring, you might want to bypass the inlet shoreline and cut across the island through the moist grassland area. On rare occasions a Short-eared Owl has been flushed here.

After crossing the grassland you will come to the flats. Often these flats are the major birding attraction of this site, although numbers of shorebirds here are typically low and the birding is rather unpredictable. In general, high tide is best (but extremely high tides are not good). Overall, the best times to bird here are from April to May and from July to September; several species occur then, including the Whimbrel, which is often common. This is also a good spot for Red Knots. From mid-March through August you will have no trouble finding Wilson's Plovers. Piping Plovers are often found from August to April but are unpredictable. Marbled Godwits are also seen occasionally. You might even find a Long-billed Curlew; August is perhaps the best time to look.

If you're not exhausted after the long hike and you'd like to do some more exploring, hike down the sound shoreline to the east. Here you will find some small marshy inlets that often attract a few shorebirds and wading birds.

For further information: Contact Cape Lookout NS, 131 Charles Street, Harkers Island, NC 28531; phone 919-728-2250. The visitors center is located at the eastern end of Harkers Island, and maps and a checklist of the area's birds are available.

RACHEL CARSON ESTUARINE RESEARCH RESERVE, BEAUFORT TO NORTH RIVER AREA
MAPS 24, 25

The Beaufort region boasts one truly excellent birding area—the Rachel Carson Estuarine Research Reserve, which harbors a rich variety of shorebirds. This site is accessible only by boat. However, from Beaufort to North River there are numerous good birding areas that are accessible by car and foot. Together these sites offer a good variety of birds, including shorebirds and a long list of frequently sought-after species, including White Ibis, Marbled Godwit, Long-billed Dowitcher, Black Rail and other rails, rare gulls, Brown-headed Nuthatch, Swainson's Warbler, Painted Bunting, and Seaside and Sharp-tailed sparrows.

The **Rachel Carson Estuarine Research Reserve**, located just south of Beaufort across the channel called Taylor Creek, has an excellent variety of intertidal and other habitats—tidal creeks, sand flats, mud flats, oyster rocks, an inlet beach, salt marshes (some grazed by horses), bare spoil sites, and shrub thickets. Shorebirding is excellent here much of the year, and various water birds are represented as well. Plus, this is an area where rarities occur rather often.

The reserve is over 3 miles long and includes different sections: Town Marsh, Bird Shoal, Horse Island, Carrot Island, and numerous dredge disposal sites along Taylor Creek. Some visitors may wonder why the name "Carrot Island" refers to several separate islands and marshes, and how the term "Carrot" could apply to anything out here anyway. Actually, "Carrot Island" was originally "Cart Island," and the name applied to the high ground (shrub thickets) just north of Horse Island. Mapmakers later turned "Cart" into "Carrot" and applied the term to the larger area.

LOGISTICS. The average tidal range at the reserve is about three feet. The tide here lags about one hour behind that of the oceanfront; it is approximately the same as tides listed for Beaufort (Pivers Island).

The reserve is open to the public, but camping is not allowed. The nearest public boat ramp is at the east end of Front Street on the Beaufort waterfront. Because much of the water within the reserve is shallow, a canoe is a good way to visit the area. Canoes can also be put in at the downtown waterfront area, just west of the post office, at a couple of sites that are neither bulkheaded nor

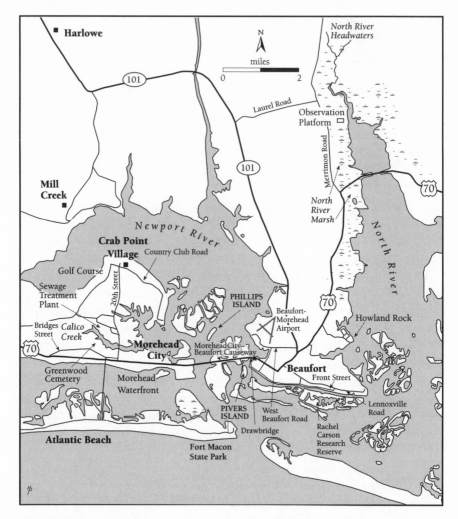

25. RACHEL CARSON ESTUARINE RESEARCH RESERVE (BEAUFORT TO NORTH RIVER AREA), MOREHEAD CITY AREA, MOREHEAD CITY–BEAUFORT CAUSEWAY

posted as private. Signs in this area say that parking is limited to two hours, but this law hasn't been enforced in the past during the cooler months, when plenty of parking is available.

Currently there are people licensed to take passengers from Beaufort to the reserve. For the latest information about access, check with the reserve manager at 919-728-2170 or the Maritime Museum at 919-728-7317.

If you do come over in your own boat or canoe, a good means of access into the area is by way of Deep Creek. This creek is close to the best birding sites, and having a boat here will enable you to cross some sections of water so that you can cover more ground during the middle and high tide periods. If you do bring a canoe or boat up the creek, watch out for oyster rocks. Also, note that Deep Creek is now largely filled in adjacent to the Bird Shoal, so there is no longer a continuous channel except at full high tide. For this reason you will want to have a canoe, kayak, or lightweight aluminum boat that you can carry or drag across short distances.

If someone is bringing you over to the reserve during the high tide period, you might try to arrange to be dropped off on the outer beach, or at least on the western side of the unnamed creek at Town Marsh at the reserve's western end. You can walk to the outer beach from here, although it's a long hike. During low tide, or if you don't mind getting your feet wet, you can also easily get to the outer beach by crossing the flats opposite Live Oak Street in Beaufort (also marked by tall range markers in Taylor Creek). This section of the flats is usually exposed; even during extremely high autumn tides, it is usually less than knee-deep.

Unfortunately, the outer beach is often crowded during the warmer months. From May to September, early morning and late afternoon visits are best, and weekends should be avoided. However, the flats adjacent to Horse Island are never crowded.

GIVING DIRECTIONS on how to bird here is somewhat difficult, because the area has changed much in recent years and continues to change. The outer beach has migrated landward, and much of Bird Shoal has become elevated to the point that it floods only at high tide. Some formerly subtidal areas have become intertidal, and some intertidal areas have become overgrown with marsh grass. These geographic changes have resulted in changes in bird use.

In former years the reserve was most attractive to shorebirds as a resting/roosting area, but some of the favored resting areas have become overgrown with marsh grasses, so some species go elsewhere at full high tide. Nevertheless, the largest numbers of birds still occur just before or after high tide, and the flats can be almost birdless during extremely low tides. In general, the best shorebirding here occurs during periods of brisk northerly winds and high water levels, when birds are forced away from other sites nearby.

Probably the best shorebirding strategies given current conditions are to start at the east end of the outer beach at high tide and work eastward while the tide falls, or to start on the flats near Horse Island about low tide and work westward while the tide rises, ending up at the eastern end of the outer beach around high tide. Thus, covering this area will take several hours. Note the small tidal channel just off the eastern end of the outer beach. During middle and low tides you can wade it easily, but you should avoid it at high tide. Again, it is good to bring a boat with a shallow draft.

This is an excellent area for shorebirds, at least for the species typically associated with intertidal habitats. Almost all year, a good to excellent variety of such species can be found. Species that can be found virtually all the time (except June, in some cases) are Black-bellied Plover, Semipalmated Plover, American Oystercatcher, Greater Yellowlegs, Willet, Ruddy Turnstone, Sanderling, Western Sandpiper, and Short-billed Dowitcher.

Wilson's Plovers are easy to find from late March to mid-September; you may see as many as a hundred in August and early September. About ten Piping Plovers overwinter each year. They are more common during the migrations, from March to April and from August to September. Whimbrels are common from April to May and from July to September, and one or two often linger through June and the winter. Marbled Godwits can be found from about July to April; there may be up to 150 birds in autumn and winter. (These birds sometimes rest on the oyster rocks where Deep Creek meets Taylor Creek.) During some years one or two Long-billed Curlews may be spotted with the godwits. Dunlins are abundant from late October to May. Least Sandpipers are common during the migrations, and a few overwinter. Look for them especially on the muddy flats and grazed marshes in the Horse Island area. Semipalmated Sandpipers are common in May but uncommon in the autumn migration, mostly around August. Red Knots are rather unpredictable. One or two might be found in any month; they are usually most predictable in May. They are fairly common during some winters.

Shorebirds that are primarily associated with fresh water or shallow brackish pools and impoundments rather than intertidal habitats are relatively scarce here. However, look for White-rumped Sandpipers in May and for occasional Lesser Yellowlegs and Pectoral and Stilt sandpipers during migration peaks. Surprisingly, one or two Long-billed Dowitchers are sometimes seen in winter. Look (and listen) for them on oyster rocks. Rare shorebirds that have been spotted here include American Golden-Plover, American Avocet, Upland Sandpiper (on a bare spoil site), Hudsonian Godwit, Curlew Sandpiper, and Red-necked and Wilson's phalaropes.

On the outer beach (or the shoals out in the inlet) you can often find resting Brown Pelicans, gulls, terns and, in autumn and winter, large numbers of Double-crested Cormorants. During the warmer months you should find a good variety of terns. Sandwich Terns are frequent from April to November. From September to November you will probably spot large flocks of Black Skimmers as they mass together prior to their southward migration (although a handful may remain throughout the winter). In autumn and winter, if all the shorebirds in the area get up at once and fly about, check the skies for a Peregrine.

In winter carefully walk the small area of dry flats and young dunes on the outer beach. One or two Savannah Sparrows of the Ipswich race (large and pale) may be spotted here, and Lapland Longspurs and Snow Buntings are also possible.

Both the tidal creek between Horse Island and Carrot Island and the flats nearby have numerous wading birds in the warmer months and a few in winter. Look for White Ibises at all seasons. One or two Yellow-crowned Night-Herons may be spotted here in mid- to late summer. In summer check the flats for a Reddish Egret. This rarity is being found in the state with increasing frequency, and habitat here appears to be optimal.

If you have your own boat, you may also want to bird along the tidal creek between Horse Island and Carrot Island at high tide. Several shorebirds, especially godwits and oystercatchers, often rest on Horse Island. The shrub hammocks on the south side of Carrot Island are frequently used by resting wading birds, including Black-crowned Night-Herons. Check the marshes of Horse Island and Carrot Island for Sharp-tailed and Seaside sparrows in autumn and for Sharp-taileds (with an occasional Seaside) throughout the winter.

If you have a boat, the spoil disposal sites along Taylor Creek east of Deep Creek are also worth checking. Many of these are covered with patches of shrub thickets that support a few species of common land birds, such as cardinals, towhees, and Boat-tailed Grackles. A few Painted Buntings breed in these thickets. In the shrub thickets near the menhaden processing plant (located at the east end of Front Street), there are usually large numbers of wading birds, and this is also an excellent place to see Black-crowned Night-Herons.

As you check out shrubby sites anywhere in the reserve during the fall and winter, you should be alert to the possibility of a roosting Barn Owl (Great Horned is also possible). And as you walk through grassy or high-marsh areas, you may on rare occasions flush a Short-eared Owl.

A **TOUR OF** the mainland from Beaufort to the North River area can begin at the small **drawbridge on US 70**. As you enter Beaufort from the west, pull off on your left just past this bridge. (See map 25.)

Just beyond the bridge there is a fish house. In winter this is a good spot to check for rare gulls. Both Iceland and Glaucous gulls have been seen here.

Continue east on US 70 to the first stoplight, and turn left on Turner Street. Drive 0.4 miles to the end of this street. Just before the stop sign, a drive to your left leads to a public boat ramp. The ramp area offers you a good point from which to survey the adjacent bay (Town Creek); many gulls may be here in winter.

At the end of Turner Street, turn left onto West Beaufort Road. To your right you will see the southern end of the **Beaufort-Morehead airport** (Michael J. Smith Field). From late July to early September a few Upland Sandpipers are usually present, and you might be able to spot one from the road, at least if the area has been recently mowed. (Uplands have also been seen from the airport terminal off NC 101.)

Just beyond the airport, you will pass an extensive area of shrub thickets on the right and a few weedy areas on the left. During the breeding season you should be able to find Indigo Buntings, Painted Buntings, and Blue Grosbeaks along this section of road. In winter one or two Orange-crowned Warblers can usually be found.

Take Turner Street back into Beaufort. Two blocks past US 70, turn left onto Ann Street. In the first block you will notice the **Old Burying Ground** on your left. The live oaks here are worth checking, primarily in early May, when you may find Blackpoll and Yellow warblers and possibly other migrants. A few migrants may be found here during the fall migration as well. Even if you don't see a single bird, you're sure to appreciate the quiet beauty of this spot.

Continue east on Ann Street. Turn right on the second street you come to—Queen Street. This street ends on Front Street, which runs along the Beaufort waterfront. Turn left on Front Street and drive 1.1 miles; here you will notice that the sand banks across the channel are broken by a tidal creek (Deep Creek), enabling you to see distant flats (Bird Shoal) and, beyond them, Beaufort Inlet. Park on the shoulder and check this area. At high tide oystercatchers often rest on the oyster rocks across the channel, and Marbled Godwits may join them in winter. Unfortunately, the light here is usually terrible, except early in the morning or late in the afternoon.

Continue 0.8 miles, until Front Street turns abruptly away from the water. Here there is a public boat ramp and parking area. Just to the east is a menhaden processing plant, and the adjacent channel can be one of the best spots around Beaufort to look for rare gulls in winter.

From the end of Front Street, turn left onto the Lennoxville Road and drive 1.5 miles to US 70. Turn right. After another 1.5 miles, just before you come to the city limit, look for Pinners Point Road (SR 1303). This road leads to **Howland Rock,** a site that can provide excellent shorebirding at times. Formerly the name "Howland Rock" referred to the site's oyster rocks; now the name is applied primarily to the nearby housing subdivision.

Howland Rock is most interesting from October to March. This is definitely a low tide birding spot; typically you will find almost nothing here at high tide. Furthermore, tidal levels here are strongly influenced by wind and other weather variables. Tides that are low enough to expose the flats and provide good shorebirding may not occur every day—particularly in autumn, when adequately low water levels may not occur for a week or more. In general, avoid stormy conditions or winds from the northeast, east, or southeast. Fair weather is best, with winds from the northwest, west, or southwest. Tides here lag about two to three hours after those on the oceanfront, or one to two hours after those listed for Beaufort (Pivers Island). More birds may actually arrive toward the end of the low tide period, as the tide begins to rise farther down the estuary.

To get to Howland Rock, drive down the Pinners Point Road about half a mile, until it becomes Howland Parkway. Shortly thereafter, turn left onto Locust Lane. Continue to the stop sign and turn right onto North Shore Road. Drive to the end of the road and park outside the gate for the private dock.

Walk a few feet along the left side of the mowed area until you see a footpath that runs out on a marshy spit. At the end of the spit there are several oyster rocks and, if the tide is right, a large mud flat north of the rocks.

From the end of the spit you can easily scope the entire area. If you want to get out onto the mud flat, though, you'll have to do some wading. Unfortunately, a narrow channel runs through the oyster rocks, and this channel is more than one foot deep at low tide. You can get around this channel by walking toward your left, into the shallow bay, which is about one foot deep here. If you take this option be careful to note your course so that you can return along the same route. In any case, the tidal amplitude here is typically less than two feet, and the tide does not rise rapidly.

The primary birding attraction of this site is the large flock of Marbled Godwits present each year from October to March. The flock sometimes numbers 150 or more. There is also a large flock of Willets, which numbers at least two or three hundred. Check through these birds carefully: the flock included a Long-billed Curlew one winter, an American Avocet another winter, and a Hudsonian Godwit one November.

Other shorebirds that are common in winter are Black-bellied Plover, Short-billed Dowitcher, Dunlin, and Western Sandpiper. Sometimes you may find a few Red Knots mixed in with the dowitchers. Among the oyster rocks there are always a few American Oystercatchers and Ruddy Turnstones.

The shallow bay usually has a few wading birds, often including White Ibises. Black Skimmers are frequent in autumn, and a few are sometimes present even in midwinter. Scope out over the river and toward the marshes to the east and southeast for Red-breasted Mergansers and Buffleheads, maybe a Common Goldeneye, and on rare occasions an Oldsquaw.

Although this is predominantly a low tide site, some of the godwits and Willets sometimes remain here during high tide to rest on the oyster rocks, especially during nice weather. In this case you will be able to see them rather closely, without doing any wading.

Although most birding at this site has been done during the autumn and winter, the birding would probably be enjoyable during the warmer months as well. Shorebirds are likely to use the site regularly then, especially during the migration periods, and wading birds and terns are undoubtedly common. (And wading will be less undesirable!)

Farther north up the North River estuary is a shorebirding site with very different habitat—the **North River Marsh**, which is largely nontidal. To get here, return to US 70 and turn right. Drive 3.5 miles, to where US 70 makes a ninety-degree turn to the right (at a stoplight). You will soon see the North River Marsh on your right. Park in the little pulloff on your right at the beginning of the causeway, 0.7 miles from the stoplight.

North River Marsh is a short-grass marsh (in part because of the presence of horses and cattle) with numerous shallow, brackish pools. This site can be good for several species of shorebirds that are scarce in intertidal areas, such as Common Snipe, Lesser Yellowlegs, and Stilt, Pectoral, and White-rumped sandpipers. However, the site is best in the spring migration; in late summer and autumn, water levels may not be adequate for shorebirds. During some years one or two pairs of Black-necked Stilts breed here. Seaside Sparrows breed here too, and Sharp-tailed Sparrows can be found from autumn to spring. North of the highway you can often flush a few rails, and Black Rails breed in this area. Marsh Wrens often breed here also.

The main area of interest—the area south of the highway—is sometimes posted against trespassing. However, any signs posted usually just say "No Hunting." And if the area is posted, you can still bird it to some extent from the river shoreline.

This area is at its best when water levels in the pools are fairly low; average tides do not flood most of the marsh. Rainy weather and extremely high tides may flood the marshes too deeply. Extremely high tides are most likely in autumn and in conjunction with strong northeast winds.

To get to the area south of the highway, walk along the shoreline until you come to a ditch. Wade out around the mouth of this ditch, walking carefully to avoid oysters and old post stumps. Farther from shore, the bottom is less muddy. The tide here lags about three to four hours after that on the oceanfront. At low tide the water here is only inches deep; at high tide it may be about one foot or, rarely, two feet deep.

The primary period to look for the shorebirds listed above is from the last few days of April until about May 10. Until about May 1 you may also find Long-billed Dowitchers. More widespread types of shorebirds, like Dunlins and Black-bellied Plovers, also occur.

The autumn shorebird migration is typically less interesting, in part because water levels are often high. But the early part of the migration, during July and August, is sometimes entertaining, and a Ruff was once seen here in late July.

Seaside Sparrows breed in the taller rushes around the pools, and occasionally you might flush a Least Bittern. Wading birds are often common in summer, especially during mid- to late summer, when the pools may begin to dry up and concentrate fish. White and Glossy ibises are usually present, and one or two

Yellow-crowned Night-Herons can often be found from July to September. Low pool levels in late summer can attract several terns, including Gull-billed Terns.

In fall migration, if water levels are too high for shorebirds, you might want to devote some effort to trying to flush secretive species. In the short-grass areas Sharp-tailed Sparrows are frequent. In the tall rushes around the pools you might find an American Bittern. In both areas you could flush Clapper and Virginia rails, Soras, and maybe something better if you're lucky.

The marshes are much less interesting in winter. There are always several snipe, and often a few other shorebirds, sometimes including Long-billed Dowitchers. Also look for a few ducks, especially American Black Ducks and Green-winged Teal.

From the parking area you can easily get to the marshes north of the road—there are no ditches here. However, where you first enter the marshes, watch out for one slightly lower, wetter strip (perhaps the remnant of a ditch).

Along the river there is a zone of short-grass marsh. Sharp-tailed Sparrows are usually easy to find from late October through April. Clapper and Virginia rails might be flushed here at any season, and Soras might be seen during migrations and in winter. The marshes are slightly higher close to the river, and rails are likely to concentrate in the clumps of taller rushes during extremely high autumnal tides. This may be an area where one can at least hope to flush a Yellow Rail.

In the zone of taller rushes farther from the river, Seaside Sparrows are common from April to August. Marsh Wrens are common in autumn and winter and sometimes breed here. Virginia and Black rails also breed. However, because of the noise from the nearby highway, this is not a good site for hearing rails.

You can sample more of the North River's marshes at another site farther to the north—the **Carteret Wildlife Club's observation platform**. This site is excellent for Virginia Rails and is quite reliable for Black Rails.

To get to the observation deck, return west on US 70 to the stoplight. Here, turn right onto Merrimon Road (SR 1300). At 1.9 miles from the stoplight, you will see a brick church on your right. Take the first right turn past this church, at 2.0 miles past the stoplight. You may worry that you have turned onto a private drive, but despite appearances this really is a public road. In fact, this was the first roadway that crossed the North River to the eastern part of the county.

During dry periods you may be able to drive all the way out to the marsh, although the narrow section at the culvert just past the last house can be tricky. But typically you will have to park just past the last house, at the culvert. Pull up far enough that you do not block the drive into this house. From here the marsh is a short walk down the roadway. You will see an elevated platform on your right.

The platform can be a great place to visit at sunrise or sunset during the breeding season, especially in April and May. It is important to be here when the weather is calm or nearly calm; avoid northeast winds, in particular. You will usually need lots of insect repellent. Get up on the platform and just watch and listen quietly.

Seaside Sparrows are common; there are usually a few Marsh Wrens as well, but you may have to walk closer to the river to find them. Where the marsh and shrubs come together around the observation deck, you may hear the dry, chattering song of a Sedge Wren in April and the first few days of May.

Listen for the various calls of Virginia Rails ("kid-dik, kid-dik," high-pitched "kek-kek-kek's," and low grunting sounds) and the low "ki-ki-krr" of one or two Black Rails. You should also hear a few Clapper Rails, which typically stay out toward the river. The Black Rails call mostly in April and May; calling becomes more sporadic as summer progresses. By the way, Black Rails have occasionally been seen from this overlook by birders who did nothing more aggressive than sit quietly and watch. On one occasion adults and chicks were seen walking around the base of the platform, sometimes walking out into the bare areas. On two occasions adults were seen flushing up from the marsh with Virginia Rails in pursuit!

As you listen, watch for a Northern Harrier coursing over the marshes (more likely in April than May). This is also a good spot for seeing a few migrants (mostly shorebirds) heading north, or a few wading birds on their way out to feeding areas or back to roost. In May you may hear a few Bobolinks overhead in the evening. Common Nighthawks are frequent, and if you are here at twilight you are almost certain to hear a Chuck-will's-widow.

You can walk out into the marshes closer to the river by following the bank of the ditch that parallels the roadway you came in on. In these marshes you will find more extensive short-grass areas and some shallow pools that often have a few shorebirds and wading birds.

Visits to this site can be almost as entertaining during other seasons. Again, the periods around sunrise and sunset are best, and calm conditions are even more important. (During calm conditions at sunset, you may need insect repellent most of the year, even in midwinter.)

Virginia Rails are more common during the cooler months, and Soras are present during the migrations and often in winter. Outside the breeding season Black Rails sometimes call on their own during calm conditions at sunset. They are least likely to call on their own in December and January, although they may respond to a tape then.

Marsh Wrens are also more common during the cooler months, and Sedge Wrens can be found in the upper portions of the marsh from late October to early May. During calm conditions at sunset, listen for their distinctive low, resonant call-notes. In these same months you should find Sharp-tailed Sparrows in the marshes adjacent to the river.

Northern Harriers are frequent in the cooler months, and if you scan the tops of the trees on the far side of the river, you might spot a Bald Eagle. Near sunset, watch for Turkey and Black vultures heading to roost.

At twilight in winter you will almost certainly hear, and sometimes you will see, Great Horned Owls. On rare occasions you may spot a Barn Owl feeding over the marsh.

From autumn to spring, during extremely high tides—two to three feet above normal—a visit to this site will probably be very productive. Tides of this height occur here about once a year, usually in autumn; they are extremely unlikely in winter and spring. If you do have the opportunity to be here during such a tide, try to come well before the water levels peak. (The tide here lags four hours or more after that on the oceanfront.) Get on the boardwalk, be still and quiet, and watch for rails moving inland. Or if you don't mind getting wet(ter), wade out to some of the isolated clumps of taller vegetation (needlerush); some rails may concentrate in these clumps. Either way, you should see several Virginia Rails, and you may see some of the other rails as well. Yellow Rails have been found here twice during such extreme tides, once in October and once in January. Again, tides high enough to enable you to see rails are very unusual events. If a tide does not completely cover the short-grass areas with water, you are not going to see anything.

Farther up the Merrimon Road, the **North River Headwaters** is another good birding spot that definitely merits a visit during the breeding season. The habitat here differs markedly from that of the previous sites on this tour of the Beaufort region.

To reach this site, return to the Merrimon Road (SR 1300) and drive north 2.2 miles, until you see a pulloff on your right. The woods on both sides of the road from here to the next pulloff can provide a good variety of land birds during the breeding season. (Both pulloffs are on the right, next to culverts that run beneath the highway.) Because the roadside ditches are deep, you will have to bird from the highway. Highway traffic can be noisy and, on weekdays, starts early in the day. Sunday mornings, which have little traffic, are best.

Breeding birds here include Yellow-billed Cuckoos, Acadian Flycatchers, White-eyed and Red-eyed vireos (and occasionally a Yellow-throated), and several warblers, including Prothonotary, Northern Parula, Hooded, Yellow-throated, and usually a Swainson's. Listen for Swainson's Warblers from mid- or late April to early July. One or two Black-throated Green Warblers may be heard here from late March to early May.

If you arrive here before daylight, you can hear both Chuck-will's-widows and Whip-poor-wills. This is also a good spot year-round for Barred Owls and Eastern Screech-Owls. (Great Horned Owls are also present but are unlikely to be heard during the summer.)

For further information: For information about the Rachel Carson Estuarine

Research Reserve, contact the Reserve Manager, North Carolina National Estuarine Research Reserve, P.O. Box 1040, Beaufort, NC 28516; phone 919-728-2170. The reserve office is located in the Watercraft Center across from the North Carolina Maritime Museum on Front Street. A checklist of the reserve's birds is available.

MOREHEAD CITY AREA, MOREHEAD CITY–BEAUFORT CAUSEWAY
MAP 25

This increasingly urbanized area has no prime birding spots, but there are several easily accessible sites that offer a pretty fair variety of birds. These include such species as Black-crowned Night-Heron, White Ibis, Clapper Rail, Painted Bunting, and Seaside and Sharp-tailed sparrows. Occasionally something unusual shows up, including rare gulls in winter.

A site that can be entertaining at any season is **Calico Creek**, at the Twentieth Street bridge. To reach this site, drive into Morehead City on US 70 (Arendell Street). When you reach Twentieth Street, turn north (left if you're coming into town from the west). Continue on through the stoplight and past a cemetery until you come to a small bridge that crosses a tidal creek. Parking is currently allowed on the west shoulder of the road, so this can be a good spot to check on a rainy day. If No Parking signs are posted in the future (as they were until recently), then you can park back up the road next to the cemetery.

This is a low tide site; high tide is typically very dull. Low tide here lags about two hours after that on the ocean. During most weather conditions, water levels low enough to produce good birding may last for a few hours. During northeast winds, though—particularly in autumn—adequately low water levels may be very brief, and sometimes they do not occur at all.

At all seasons wading birds are easy to find here; more are around during the warmer months. White Ibises are almost always present. Several shorebirds may occur during the migrations, and a few during other seasons as well. Most of the year you should be able to find a Greater Yellowlegs. A few American Oystercatchers can often be seen working on the clumps of oysters toward the east.

In winter there are always Hooded Mergansers and Green-winged Teal; Red-breasted Mergansers, Buffleheads, Mallards, and American Black Ducks often occur; and occasionally other species can be found, especially after severe cold. Check the male teal carefully; during two winters an individual of the Eurasian race was spotted here.

Boat-tailed Grackles are always present. You will probably hear Clapper Rails; seeing one is a bit more difficult, but if you patiently scan the edges of the marsh grass, you should eventually spot one skulking along. (This strategy is likely to be successful only when the tide is fully low.)

You can also survey the creek from the ends of several streets to the east, especially from Seventeenth, Thirteenth, Eleventh, and Seventh streets. These street ends offer views of piers that often harbor resting gulls and terns, especially in winter. These sites are also more likely to have American Oystercatchers and other shorebirds. Off Eleventh and Seventh streets you may sometimes see one or two Common Goldeneyes with the Buffleheads in winter.

Upstream from the Calico Creek bridge is the **Morehead City sewage treatment plant**. This small plant usually attracts few birds, but it provides an access point to another section of Calico Creek. Unlike the bridge area, the treatment plant site is often good at both high and low tides.

To get to the treatment plant, continue north (away from US 70) on Twentieth Street. After 0.4 miles, turn left onto Mayberry Loop Road and drive 0.4 miles. Just after a public housing project on your left, turn left onto Treatment Plant Road, which ends at the treatment plant.

Park outside the gate and walk toward your right. You will soon see the creek. A pipeline here often has several wading birds perched on it, especially at high tide. Continue to the end of the treatment plant. Here you will see an opening in the shrubbery to your right and a path that runs over to the creek. During the winter you may see Green-winged Teal and Hooded Mergansers where the outfall pipeline discharges; a Common Moorhen may also be spotted here on rare occasions.

At low tide Clapper Rails may be seen along the edge of the creek; at high tide you might flush one at the upper edges of the marsh. In the migration periods you might also flush a Sora, and you may see Marsh Wrens and occasionally Sharp-tailed Sparrows here in autumn and winter.

The shrubby areas around the treatment plant are also worth checking. In the breeding season Painted Buntings are sometimes seen here, and in winter look for a Solitary Vireo and an Orange-crowned Warbler with the Carolina Chickadees and Yellow-rumped Warblers.

If there are several gulls within the treatment plant, you might ask for permission to walk around within the facility. However, the plant is small enough that you can easily see all the birds within it from outside the gate. Check through the gulls carefully; a Common Black-headed Gull was found here during three straight winters.

Not far from the treatment plant is the **Morehead City Country Club golf course**. From the treatment plant, turn left onto Mayberry Loop Road. After 0.2 miles, turn left onto Tootle Road and continue to the stop sign. Turn right onto Country Club Road. After 0.3 miles, turn left onto the road to the clubhouse. Park here and ask for permission to bird in the area.

The golf course is often crowded; try to avoid peak periods. Early mornings on weekdays are best. If the course is crowded, you can at least check the marshes and mud flats behind the clubhouse.

At all seasons you should see chickadees, titmice, Pine Warblers, and Brown-headed Nuthatches. A few woodpeckers are always present, including Red-headed Woodpeckers in the warmer months; Hairy Woodpeckers are occasional at any season. In the breeding season listen for a few Yellow-throated Warblers and Summer Tanagers along the borders of the golf course.

In the marshes beside the clubhouse, Marsh Wrens are present all year but are most frequent in autumn and winter. The flats beyond the marshes can be very productive during a good low tide but, alas, are rather distant (you'll definitely need a scope) and are also largely obscured from view by the marshes. Low tide lags about two to three hours after that on the oceanfront; water levels low enough to produce good birding are most likely during high pressure systems and southwest, west, or northwest winds.

When water levels are adequate, the flats often have several wading birds, especially in the warmer months, and numerous shorebirds, especially during the migrations. In winter several ducks are usually present; Mallards, American Black Ducks, and Green-winged Teal are most frequent.

To get back to Morehead City, return the way you came, or turn left onto Country Club Road and continue until you see the Twentieth Street Extension on your right.

Another spot in Morehead that is often worth checking for small land birds is the **Greenwood Cemetery** area. To get here, turn west on Bridges Street (which parallels US 70 and lies one block to the north) from Twentieth Street. Continue several blocks, to the first stoplight, and turn right onto Barbour Road. Then turn right onto Myrtle Street. Continue until you see the cemetery on your left. Just ahead is a public works area. The borders of these two areas are thickly tangled with privet hedge and other shrubs. Look for Gray Catbirds, Brown Thrashers, and Northern Mockingbirds at all seasons. In the breeding season Painted Buntings are sometimes found. In winter White-throated, Swamp, and Song sparrows are common, and a few Orange-crowned Warblers can be found among the ubiquitous Yellow-rumpeds.

This would seem to be a good place to check for a few migrating land birds after cold fronts in autumn or during the peak of the spring migration. And if you play a screech-owl tape here on a calm night, you're almost certain to get a response.

To get to the **Morehead City waterfront**, drive back out to US 70 and continue east into downtown Morehead. At Eighth Street, turn right. The waterfront area runs from the end of Eighth Street east to the end of Fourth Street. The waterfront is most deserving of a stop during the winter, especially in midwinter, during severe cold. Gull numbers vary greatly according to fishing activity; when large numbers of gulls are present, you have a fairly good chance of finding a Lesser Black-backed, and you might also spot a Glaucous or Iceland. If few gulls are present, you might try throwing out some bread at the end of Fourth Street late in the afternoon, because large numbers of gulls frequently roost on top of the various structures at the state port nearby.

From the block between Fourth and Fifth streets, check the shrub thickets on the island across the channel. Wading birds frequently rest here, especially in the winter. Look for Great Blue Herons, White Ibises, and Black-crowned Night-Herons. In spring and early summer Painted Buntings breed in these shrub thickets; their songs can sometimes be heard drifting across the channel.

From the waterfront, drive back to US 70 and turn right. After crossing the railroad tracks, look for the **Morehead City Yacht Basin** on your left. Pull into the easternmost parking area (the one farthest from the building). From the shore look across the channel to the shrub thickets of an island. On sunny winter days this is a great place to see numerous Black-crowned Night-Herons and other wading birds resting in the sun.

Continue driving east on US 70, toward Beaufort. On late afternoons in fall or winter, you might pull off on the shoulder just before you start onto the high-rise bridge. From here check around the top of the upraised railroad bridge (next to the highway bridge) for a Peregrine Falcon. This is a favored roosting spot.

After crossing the high-rise bridge onto the Morehead City–Beaufort causeway, turn left onto the roadway that leads to the **Regional Public Beach Access area**. Park near the beginning of this roadway. On your right you will see a dredge disposal area. Sometimes dredging activity creates a large shallow pool within the diked area. This pool is typically not very productive, but sometimes it attracts a few shorebirds, especially in migration. On rare occasions species such as White-rumped Sandpiper, Wilson's Phalarope, and American Avocet have been found. During some years a few Least Terns still nest on this disposal site, and occasionally there is a pair of Wilson's Plovers as well. If nesting birds are present, do not enter the area—survey it from the dike.

A walk to the north dike of the spoil site is a good spot for surveying the adjacent marshes and the lower Newport River. Toward the north you will see an island with a chimney—Phillips Island, an Audubon Society sanctuary that holds a nesting colony of herons, egrets, and ibises. In mid- to late summer, impressive numbers of these birds can be seen flying to the island at sunset to roost.

The band of marshes on the east side of the spoil site is a good place to find Seaside and Sharp-tailed sparrows and Marsh Wrens. The best time to check for these species is at high tide (which lags about one to two hours after that on the oceanfront) during light wind conditions, especially in the early morning or late afternoon. Seaside Sparrows and Marsh Wrens breed here, and both can be found throughout the year (although Seasides may be scarce in midwinter). The Sharp-taileds can be found from October through April.

The rest of the causeway marshes can be checked from US 70. Wading birds are common in the warmer months; a few also occur in winter. White Ibises and Black-crowned Night-Herons are always present (look for the latter at dusk); in summer look for a few Yellow-crowned Night-Herons. Try walking along the border of these marshes at full high tide: you may flush a Clapper Rail at any season, and possibly a Sora or Virginia Rail during migration.

Within the marshes there are two bays that come up to the highway. At low tide these bays often have a few shorebirds, especially during migration. In winter look for Buffleheads, Hooded Mergansers, and Red-breasted Mergansers.

At the eastern end of the causeway marshes there are several shrub-thicket hammocks. Wading birds often roost here at high tide, although in recent winters Brown Pelicans have often usurped these sites.

At the eastern end of the causeway are several fish houses. This is often an excellent area to check for rare gulls in midwinter. Check the area from US 70, from the end of old US 70 (also marked as Old Causeway Road and SR 1205), or from the small bridge to Pivers Island (you can park at the small marina just north of the bridge). Throwing some bread out from this bridge during a rising tide is the quickest way to check out the gulls in the area. Also, the shrubs along old US 70 just west of the Pivers Island Road often have a pair of Painted Buntings in the breeding season.

BOGUE BANKS, FORT MACON STATE PARK, AND
THEODORE ROOSEVELT NATURAL AREA
MAP 26

This barrier island is rather densely developed and becomes even more so every year. Not surprisingly, the island is quite crowded during the warmer months. Fortunately, though, there are two state parks—Fort Macon SP and Theodore Roosevelt NA. These parks, plus the many ocean fishing piers and the tidal flats beside Bogue Inlet, can provide the opportunity for some good birding.

The fishing piers near the eastern end of the island are of special interest, because this east-west island intercepts and concentrates northward-migrating water birds from late winter through spring, and ocean bird-watching during this period can be quite entertaining, providing good looks at a variety of species, including gannets, scoters, jaegers, and sometimes storm-petrels and shearwaters. In addition, the parks and the Bogue Inlet flats together offer several sought-after species, such as White Ibis, Clapper Rail, Wilson's and Piping plovers, Sandwich Tern, Marsh Wren, Orange-crowned Warbler, Painted Bunting, and Seaside and Sharp-tailed sparrows.

THIS TOUR OF Bogue Banks runs from east to west, beginning at Fort Macon SP and ending at the tidal flats next to Bogue Inlet.

Fort Macon SP is located at the eastern end of Bogue Banks, just east of

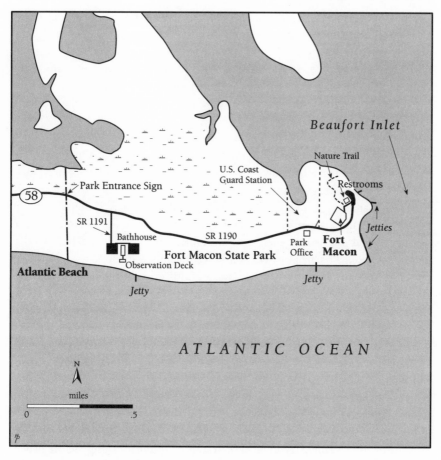

26. FORT MACON STATE PARK

Atlantic Beach. The park begins at the end of NC 58; at the park boundary the highway becomes SR 1190. The park opens at 8 A.M. Closing time varies seasonally; the park is generally open until sunset. The parking areas and beaches are typically very crowded (the parking areas sometimes fill up) during the summer months and on weekends in spring (beginning at Easter) and autumn (through October). At these times you should make an effort to be here early in the day, preferably right at opening time. (By the way, the parking areas often open a few minutes before 8 A.M.) Typically the most interesting section of the park is the fort and inlet area, which you can reach by driving to the parking lot at the end of SR 1190.

The inlet can be entertaining during every season. To scope it, walk onto the top of a dune beside the walkway that runs from the beginning of the parking lot. The inlet is the one section of the park that is often best checked late in the day, because the light is better then.

From midspring through summer you can expect a good variety of terns. Sandwich Terns can be seen here from April through November, although they may be scarce in June. In August, if you are here near sunset, you may see many Black Terns flying through the inlet to roost. In autumn, if you are here about sunset and it's calm, watch for Black Skimmers slicing the water.

Winter is potentially the best time to be here, although the birds' numbers vary widely then. If you can arrange it, come here just after stormy weather with strong northerly or northeasterly winds. Midtide may be best, because tide lines can develop then in the section of inlet just out from the park. On a good day, expect large numbers of Brown Pelicans, Double-crested Cormorants, Red-breasted Mergansers, gulls and terns, and several Common Loons. Occasionally Northern Gannets enter the inlet and feed just off the beach. If there is a lot of action, watch for a jaeger. Even Black-legged Kittiwakes enter the inlet on rare occasions, and one winter there was an impressive and inexplicable two-day invasion of Red Phalaropes, with birds feeding just off the shore. For some reason Great Cormorants are rather scarce at this inlet, but they are seen occasionally, so check the channel markers anyway.

Unfortunately, the rock jetties at the inlet do not offer nearly as much potential as in the past, when a few Purple Sandpipers were present every winter, and a Harlequin Duck or eider appeared almost every winter. In recent years the jetties have been largely buried by accreted sand; also, they no longer project into deep water. If the shoreline remains the same, birding possibilities will remain limited. However, a return to an erosional period could restore the habitat that was formerly available.

But even if the jetties remain as they are now, it is always worthwhile to check at least the longest one. Try to be here first thing in the morning, before fishermen arrive. Calm sea conditions are also desirable, because the end of the longest jetty is now almost in the surf zone—you are not likely to see anything here when it is rough. A few Ruddy Turnstones can be found much of the year. Currently your best chance of finding a Purple Sandpiper, although it's admittedly a slim chance, occurs in late winter and early spring, when a northbound migrant might stop here. Look especially near the end of the longest jetty. A scoter, Oldsquaw, eider, or Harlequin Duck may rarely be seen off the end of this jetty, although these birds are not likely to linger here as in the past. In winter and early spring a few Red-breasted Mergansers and Bonaparte's Gulls frequently feed in the eddies just off the tip of the longest jetty. In late winter, if large numbers of Bonaparte's Gulls are present, look carefully for a Little Gull.

The dense shrub thickets around the fort provide habitat for a good variety of land birds throughout the year. You will want to check the trail leading into the fort; the outer walls of the fort; the nature trail (Elliott Coues trail); and the cleared strips (septic drain field areas) beside the nature trail. The nature trail is short, perhaps just less than three hundred yards. It begins on the trail to the fort and ends on the inlet shoreline. From here you can walk back along the shore to the parking lot.

The trail is named for Elliott Coues, who has been called the father of modern American ornithology. Between 1869 and 1871 Coues served a stint as physician at the fort and kept records of the birds he observed here. The environment has changed drastically since that time; in the 1800s there was virtually no woody vegetation around the fort, which was often described as being at the end of a narrow sand spit.

Birds that can be found throughout the year include Boat-tailed Grackles (joined by Common Grackles in the breeding season), Carolina Wrens, Northern Cardinals, Rufous-sided Towhees, Gray Catbirds, and Brown Thrashers. In the breeding season you should also find a few Prairie Warblers and Orchard Orioles, as well as one or two Painted Buntings. Listen for the bunting's warbling song from late April until at least early July. If you don't find one along the trails, go back and check the shrub thickets near the parking area. From April through June you should find one or more nesting pairs of Northern Rough-winged Swallows inside the fort.

This east-west island is typically not very good for migrant passerines in autumn. Nevertheless, check the shrub thickets around the fort after strong cold fronts with north or northwest winds for at least a few migrants. Near the beginning of the nature trail, check out the first cleared strip on your left. Just off the nature trail there is an open weedy area that can be good for sparrows—in October, look for White-crowned and hope for Clay-colored. Closer to the inlet, the trail takes you beneath most of the vegetation. This can be a good place to stand quietly and watch for a few minutes. The grassy, cleared section of the outer wall of the fort (the section facing the inlet) can be good for Palm Warblers and sparrows.

From late September through October, after cold fronts with strong north to northwest winds, you will definitely want to climb to the top of the fort's south corner about midmorning. (This corner lies opposite the outer wall that has been cleared and planted in grass.) This is a great vantage point from which to check for migrating Tree Swallows and hawks. On good days there may be thousands of Tree Swallows, dozens of Sharp-shinned Hawks, and a few American Kestrels. Also look for Cooper's Hawks, Merlins, and Peregrine Falcons. Watch for birds crossing the inlet from the east (Shackleford Banks); the birds often fly directly over the fort.

Avoid windy days in winter, because this area is quite exposed. On calm mornings the shrub thickets may teem with Yellow-rumped Warblers. Listen for the crisp chip-note of an Orange-crowned Warbler, especially in midmorning. A particularly good area for them is along the cleared septic drain line near the beginning of the nature trail. A few Black-crowned Night-Herons and Great Blue Herons often roost in the shrub thickets beside the nature trail about halfway to the inlet. Typically you will hear them flush, but you will have difficulty seeing them.

Near the western end of the park is the bathhouse parking lot; turn in at SR 1191. Seaward of the bathhouse, an elevated rain shelter overlooks the ocean. In winter and on early mornings in spring this can be a good spot to set up a scope. The adjacent beaches often have a few shorebirds. Low tide is best, and you will need to be here when few people are present. During most of the year you may find Sanderlings, Ruddy Turnstones (around the little jetty), Black-bellied Plovers, and Willets. Red Knots may be common in May, and a few are often present in autumn and winter. Look for Whimbrels in spring and late summer.

You can bird some more shrub-thicket areas by walking along the entrance road and nearby highway. The highway is quite busy all year, but this area does offer another opportunity for finding Painted Buntings in the breeding season. In winter check all the chickadee flocks (usually two or three). You will usually find Orange-crowned Warblers, and maybe a lingering White-eyed Vireo or Black-and-white Warbler.

Just across from the park entrance sign is a relatively high dune from which you can scope the adjacent marshes and tidal creeks. A low or rising tide is probably best. (The tide here lags one or two hours after that on the ocean-front.) You should see several wading birds in the warmer months and a few in winter. A few White Ibises are always present. Look for oystercatchers, Greater Yellowlegs, and perhaps other shorebirds as well. In winter there may be Buffleheads and Hooded and Red-breasted mergansers.

At the park entrance it is easy to enter the park's marshes. From autumn to spring, if you are willing to do some wading (in a few inches of water), you can find Sharp-tailed Sparrows, Seaside Sparrows, and Marsh Wrens by working along the marshes' upper border at high tide. If you're lucky you might flush an American Bittern. If you don't want to wade, you might try working this strip an hour after high tide; it will be drier and the birds may still be present.

The easternmost fishing pier on the island, the **Triple S Pier**, is located just west of the state park. From the park entrance (and Atlantic Beach city limit), head west on NC 58 for 0.6 miles; turn left on Henderson Street and continue to the pier. This pier is usually open from March to early December and is often open all winter. In winter, or first thing in the morning in March and April, the pierhouse may be closed; if it is, drive around back on the east side to see if this gate to the pier is open.

This pier and the seven other ocean fishing piers on the island all project several hundred feet from shore and thus provide excellent points from which to survey the ocean for birds. The amount of parking available at the different piers varies, but parking is usually available during the most interesting birding periods. Few of the Bogue Banks piers charge sightseers for admission. Most of the piers are closed in winter; the exceptions are noted. The three easternmost piers—Triple S, Oceanana, and Sportsman's—all have rain shelters at their ends.

Ocean birding along Bogue Banks is generally most interesting from about February through May, when ocean birds like loons, gannets, scoters, gulls, and terns are migrating northward. Even jaegers are regularly spotted in April and May, and other pelagic species are possible from May into summer.

The reason Bogue Banks is relatively interesting during this period is that many of these northbound ocean birds, in order to avoid crossing land, head east just off the beaches when they encounter the island and thus become concentrated from west to east. Obviously, the easternmost piers will have the most birds. Triple S Pier is best, although the next two piers, just a mile to the west—Oceanana and Sportsman's—are probably about as good.

More birds seem to migrate ahead of approaching weather systems; overall, the best times are relatively calm mornings when winds are forecast to become southerly and to increase later in the day. In this situation many birds are moving while viewing conditions are good. However, to find the jaegers and other pelagic species you should look during steady northeast, east, or southeast winds. In general, the best time of day is just after sunrise. (With the jaegers and other pelagic species, there seems to be another peak of movement in late afternoon.)

Northern Gannets and Red-throated and Common loons can often be seen migrating north in February, especially if there has been a warming trend. During these late winter movements you may rarely spot a Black-legged Kittiwake. The scoter migration peaks in March and early April; look for Blacks and Surfs and an occasional White-winged. April mornings can offer a lot of variety; some mornings can have a steady procession of gannets, loons, shorebirds, gulls, and terns.

During April and May watch carefully for jaegers. Pomarines are regular throughout this period; Parasitics peak in May, especially late May. Very rarely a Long-tailed may be spotted in late May. From May to summer several other pelagic species are occasionally seen off the piers, including Wilson's Storm-Petrel and Sooty, Greater, Cory's, and Audubon's shearwaters. The Wilson's Storm-Petrel and Sooty Shearwater are most likely from mid-May to early June, the Greater Shearwater in mid- to late June, and the Cory's and Audubon's shearwaters in late July and early August. Again, northeast, east, or southeast winds enhance your chances of seeing these birds. Audubon's Shearwaters are most likely when mats of sargassum wash ashore.

Ocean birding along this island is generally less interesting at other seasons. The fall migration is relatively dull, because most southbound migrants bypass this east-west shoreline. Occasionally in December and January the ocean can be quite active during strong northeast or north winds, with gannets plunging just off the beaches and loons present in large numbers. Strong north or northwest winds in December and early January can also trigger impressive south-ward migrations of gulls—mostly Laughing Gulls—and other species. These flights typically pass just off the ends of the piers.

THE FOLLOWING description of Bogue Banks makes use of the mileposts along NC 58. Milepost 1 stands just west of the Triple S Pier.

Oceanana Pier, which is located opposite milepost 1.5, is closed in winter. However, you should check it from shore (or from the adjacent Sportsman's Pier), because in winter it occasionally attracts a scoter or Oldsquaw; Harlequin Ducks have also been found here a couple of times.

Sportsman's Pier is located opposite milepost 1.7. This pier is open all winter (as is the coffee shop in the pierhouse).

At milepost 4.7 you will see the Sheraton Motel on your left. The pier here is also open all winter.

At milepost 7.0, in Pine Knoll Shores, turn right at the stoplight onto Pine Knoll Boulevard. Go 0.15 miles and turn left onto Roosevelt Drive, which leads to the **North Carolina Aquarium**. Open seven days a week, the aquarium has many interesting underwater exhibits, with tanks simulating several different marine habitats.

Surrounding the aquarium is the **Theodore Roosevelt NA**. This state park protects the last significant tract of maritime forest left on the island. The park is more interesting botanically than ornithologically; nevertheless, the birding can be quite entertaining year-round, and you can find some breeding land bird species here that can't be found elsewhere on the island.

The gate to the aquarium and the park is open from 9 A.M. to 5 P.M. from Monday through Saturday and from 1 to 5 P.M. on Sunday. Actually, the gate usually opens earlier than the official time, often about 8 A.M. on weekdays. If you get here early, you can park at the pulloff just outside the gate and bird along the road.

The primary areas to check are the woods along the road into the aquarium (including the section outside the gate), the shrubby areas around the aquarium parking lot, and the nature trail (the Alice Hoffman Trail). The nature trail is about half a mile long. It skirts the edge of a marsh, then winds through the forest, with short boardwalks across a couple of swamp areas. It also has a spur that overlooks East Pond, a large brackish pond.

If you would like to explore a little in the interior of the park, go to the power pole just inside the gate, on the southwest side of Roosevelt Drive (left as you're driving into the aquarium). From here, work your way through the vines next to the road, then walk about a hundred yards directly away from the road, until you come to a prominent east-west ridge. You can follow this ridge several hundred yards westward to get more of a feel for this very special forest.

Even though this park is on an island, watch out for poisonous snakes. Timber rattlesnakes are now quite rare, but copperheads, usually small and quite docile, are seen here occasionally. Away from the roadway and parking lot, mosquitoes can be very bad, especially after wet weather.

Around the parking lot and along Roosevelt Drive, birds found throughout the year include Carolina Wren, Red-bellied Woodpecker, Gray Catbird, Northern Cardinal, and Rufous-sided Towhee. There are a few Carolina Chickadees; Tufted Titmice were formerly very rare visitors here on the island, but several have been seen in recent years, and they are apparently becoming established.

Most breeding species do not sing very late in the year on this barrier island. In general, you'll hear the most singing from late April to early June. Listen for Pine and Yellow-throated warblers around the aquarium. From Roosevelt Drive and the nature trail, listen for Great Crested Flycatchers, White-eyed and Red-eyed vireos, Prothonotary Warblers, and Northern Parulas. (These species can also be found from the ridge described above.) From late April to July you might find a pair of Painted Buntings around the parking lot.

Like Fort Macon, this site is somewhat mediocre for finding migrating land birds in fall. Nevertheless, cold fronts in late September and early October can provide an entertaining variety of warblers and other migrants. In general, your best bet is to concentrate on the low, thick growth around the parking lot or at the beginning of the nature trail. By walking quietly on the trail you could also find such species as Ovenbird and Northern Waterthrush; look for Ovenbirds in the upland areas and Northern Waterthrushes along the edges of the swamps.

Winter can be especially pleasant in this park. Visit early on a clear, crisp, calm morning if you can. Yellow-rumped Warblers are abundant, and you should have little trouble finding Golden-crowned and Ruby-crowned kinglets. Carefully check out the chickadee flocks—you should always find an Orange-crowned Warbler and a Solitary Vireo there. Just past the beginning of the nature trail—next to the septic drain field, in the weedy patch on your left—look for Fox Sparrows, along with White-throated Sparrows, House Wrens, and other species.

At any season, if you walk the nature trail, don't neglect to take the spur down to the East Pond. This spot is very scenic, and there are often a few wading birds here, especially in summer. In mid- to late summer you might see a Yellow-crowned Night-Heron. In winter you may see a few Hooded Mergansers or other ducks.

The **Iron Steamer Pier** is just off NC 58 at milepost 7.4. Red-throated Loons often greatly outnumber Commons here in winter, in contrast with the situation on the eastern end of the island, and this would probably be a better spot to hope for a rarity like a Red-necked Grebe. Unfortunately, this pier is usually closed in midwinter.

At milepost 10.4, in Salter Path, there is a **Regional Public Beach Access**, where you can check another section of ocean. Restrooms are available except in winter.

At the **Indian Beach Pier**, in Indian Beach at milepost 12.1, parking is limited. There is adequate parking at the **Emerald Isle Pier**, in Emerald Isle at milepost 14.9. Both of these piers are closed in winter.

To reach the **Bogue Inlet Pier**, turn left onto Bogue Inlet Drive at the stoplight at milepost 19.4 in Emerald Isle. This pier is probably a little more interesting in autumn than the piers to the east.

The **Bogue Inlet Point** area, including the flats at the inlet, offer additional birding possibilities. Painted Buntings breed in the shrub thickets near the end of the island, and these thickets can also be good for passerine migrants in autumn. The Bogue Inlet flats have a good variety of shorebirds most of the year, including breeding Wilson's Plovers. Unfortunately, there is little parking available here.

To reach this area, turn left onto Coast Guard Road at the stoplight at milepost 20.9. This road ends at a stop sign (at Inlet Drive) after 2.6 miles. Try to find a spot next to an undeveloped lot where there isn't a No Parking sign. Enforcement of these signs seems to be strictest during peak people periods, especially summer weekends. Transgressions in winter might be overlooked entirely. Perhaps a public parking area will soon be established around the point; until that happens, the parking situation will continue to get worse.

During mornings from late April into July, walk the various streets listening for Painted Buntings. Enough vegetation is being left around many of the cottages that buntings will probably persist here in the future.

In late September and October, after cold fronts with northwesterly winds, there is often a pile-up of migrant land birds here at the end of the island; birding can vary from mildly entertaining to excellent. Walk along all the streets and check all the shrub patches. Frequently many birds will pile up in the shrubs closest to the inlet. Palm Warblers are usually common, and several warbler species occur in late September and early October. In mid- to late October look for sparrows, including White-crowned, especially near the coast guard station. And check all the wires in the vicinity for Western Kingbirds, especially around mid-October.

To get to the flats, walk west down Inlet Drive for 0.3 miles from the end of Coast Guard Road. You will see an ORV ramp leading to the inlet. (ORVs can be driven out to the beach from September to May. Vehicles have to be registered with the town, and there is a registration fee.) After crossing the ramp, walk out to the inlet shoreline, then north along the shoreline. After a few hundred yards you will see the flats to your right. There are also small dunes and a developing salt marsh at the flats' border.

Expect several species of shorebirds here during the migrations and winter. A few Piping Plovers are to be expected, especially from March to April and August to September; a handful remain throughout the winter. The habitat is also good for Red Knots. They are most likely in May, but one or two might be found during any month. In the breeding season look for Willets, American Oystercatchers, and several Wilson's Plovers. The plovers are easy to find from late March to early September. (Stay out of any areas where birds are obviously nesting, whether the areas are posted or not.)

In the developing marsh look for Sharp-tailed and Seaside sparrows and Clapper Rails, at least during the fall migration. In the future, as the marsh increases in density, these birds are likely to be found during other seasons as well. In the bay beside the marsh look for several wading birds at low tide in the warmer months. Check the higher sand spits, those immediately adjacent to the inlet, for Snow Buntings after cold fronts in November and December.

Bogue Inlet is continually shifting back and forth. When it shifts westward, erosion occurs on the west side of the inlet, and accretion on the east side. Accretion results in the creation of habitat for shorebirds and certain other species. Over the years the open flats gradually become dunes and marshes, and habitat for shorebirds is lost. Then the inlet swings back again, washing away the dunes and marshes but creating new habitat on the opposite side of the inlet. In the future there will be periods when this site is underwater, periods when there are good shorebirding flats, and periods when there are marshes. So remember: if this side of the inlet doesn't have the habitat you're looking for, the opposite side (at Hammocks Beach SP) might.

For further information: For information about Fort Macon SP, write Fort Macon SP, P.O. Box 127, Atlantic Beach, NC 28512; phone 919-726-3775. The Theodore Roosevelt NA is administered by Fort Macon SP, but questions about access to this site should be addressed to the North Carolina Aquarium, P.O. Box 580, Atlantic Beach, NC 28512; phone 919-247-4004.

CROATAN NATIONAL FOREST (NORTH SECTION), NEW BERN AREA
MAP 27

The northern section of the Croatan NF offers very good birding most of the year. The area harbors a healthy population of Red-cockaded Woodpeckers, and a nice variety of land birds are present at all seasons. Spring and early summer are especially good; then you can find a long list of warblers, including Worm-eating, Yellow-throated, Black-throated Green, Kentucky, and Swainson's. The last can be found at several sites. Barred Owls are fairly common, and Chuck-will's-widows and Whip-poor-wills are easy to find in the breeding season.

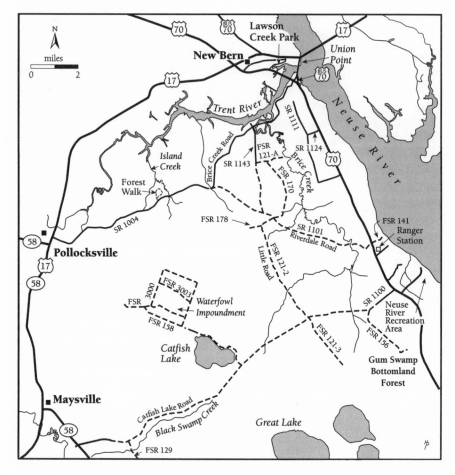

27. CROATAN NATIONAL FOREST (NORTH SECTION), NEW BERN AREA

In winter the adjacent Neuse River often hosts large rafts of Ruddy Ducks and sometimes other diving ducks. The national forest also has a waterfowl impoundment, which can be mildly interesting during the winter.

Even when birding is slow, this area can be appealing because of some significant natural areas. There are some high-quality tracts of longleaf pine, including a site that has never been logged. You can also see stands of Atlantic white cedar, a Piedmont-like near-climax area of upland hardwoods, and other interesting areas.

A CONVENIENT SPOT to begin a tour of the northern Croatan is in New Bern, at **Union Point Park**. The park lies at Union Point, where the Trent and Neuse rivers merge. You can reach this site from US 17 by turning south onto US 70 Business and pulling left into the park just before you get to the Trent River bridge. Or, from US 70 East, take the "East Front Street" exit. Just after crossing the Trent River bridge, turn right into the park.

This is a spot worth visiting primarily in winter. Check the gulls and scan the river for cormorants, Horned Grebes, and Forster's Terns. Brown Pelicans are now regular here, at least in late winter and early spring; formerly a sighting this far upriver would have been accidental. On a rainy day you can bird from your car here, and this is the sort of spot where you might spot something rare during severe weather.

From Union Point turn right onto US 70 Business, go one block, and turn left onto Pollock Street. Continue several blocks (you will pass Tryon Palace on your left). Turn left onto Queen Street. At the stop sign, turn left onto First Street/Pembroke Road. After the road curves sharply to the right, and before you get to US 70, turn left into **Lawson Creek Park**.

This park lies on a former landfill. It is certainly not a major birding area but is definitely worth checking in winter and during the migrations. Habitats present here are open ballfields, shrub thickets, and marshes, and you can look over a section of the Trent River from the parking area at the boat ramp.

In winter check the open fields for Killdeers and often a snipe or two. The shrub areas harbor White-throated, Song, and Swamp sparrows. Yellow-rumped Warblers are common, and you might find an Orange-crowned Warbler or a lingering gnatcatcher. Check the roadside ditches carefully—King Rails and American Bitterns have been spotted here.

During the migrations check the shrubs for a few passerines. A Sora might turn up along one of the ditches. Large flocks of swallows, mostly Trees, often congregate over the river. In spring and late summer you should find a few Banks, and maybe a Cliff or two, in these flocks.

Incidentally, Lawson Creek is named for John Lawson, who might be considered the first serious birdwatcher in North Carolina. Lawson lived in New Bern for several years during the early eighteenth century; an excellent naturalist, he described the flora and fauna of the state in *A New Voyage to Carolina*, first published in 1709. The nomenclature used by Lawson was in most cases very different from the nomenclature we use today, and in some cases it is impossible to know which birds he was referring to. In most cases, however, his descriptions are quite adequate. His book is fascinating, revealing many of the changes in birdlife that have taken place over almost three centuries.

From Lawson Creek Park, turn left, take the overpass across US 70, then turn right onto US 70 East. Once you merge into US 70, note your odometer. After 3.5 miles, turn right onto West Grantham Road (SR 1124). At the stop sign, turn right onto Old Airport Road (SR 1111). Where this road ends, turn right onto the unpaved road by an animal shelter. At the end of this road is a gate, and beyond the gate are several sewage lagoons. This area is usually open on week-days. These lagoons often have several ducks in winter. Ruddy Ducks and

Hooded Mergansers are most frequent, but several species of both dabblers and divers are possible. A Cooper's Hawk often overwinters in this area. During migrations you may see a few shorebirds.

Return to US 70 and turn right. After 5.1 miles look for a convenience store on your right and, on the median, a small sign denoting the Riverdale community. Here, turn left across the highway. Look for FSR 141, which continues one-half mile to the Neuse River. Breeding species along this road include Yellow-throated Warbler and Summer Tanager. At the end of the road is the **Fishers Landing Recreational Site**. You will want to walk down to the river in winter. From about Thanksgiving through at least March, a few thousand Ruddy Ducks are often present. This flock usually includes a few Lesser Scaup and Ring-necked Ducks, and occasionally you may spot one or two Canvasbacks, Redheads, and Black and Surf scoters. Also look for Red-breasted Mergansers and Horned Grebes.

Around the parking area there are mature hardwoods and pines, and a hardwood drain lies beside the parking area toward the south. Thus, there is habitat for a good variety of forest land birds. Breeding species include Wood Thrush, Yellow-throated Warbler, Ovenbird, and Summer Tanager. Carolina Chickadees, Tufted Titmice, and several woodpeckers can be found throughout the year.

Take FSR 141 back to US 70 and turn left. After 0.5 miles you will see the **Croatan Ranger Station** on your left. Stop here for visitor information and an excellent map of the Croatan. Pine Warblers and Brown-headed Nuthatches are common around the ranger station throughout the year, and there is also a pine with an artificially created Red-cockaded Woodpecker cavity. (Such artificially created cavities are being used to recover the forest's Red-cockaded Woodpecker population.) In the breeding season listen for Yellow-throated Warblers, Summer Tanagers, and Chipping Sparrows.

Keep heading east on US 70, and after 1.9 miles watch for a sign that says "National Forest Recreation Area." Turn left here onto Flanners Beach Road and drive to the **Neuse River Recreation Area** (also called Flanners Beach). The recreation area has a pleasant campground, which is open from about April through October.

During the breeding season you will want to explore around the campground and the parking and picnic areas, and along the edges of the swamp forest that parallels the road into the recreation area. There is also a short nature trail, with a boardwalk across a swamp and an overlook on the river. To reach this trail, follow a footpath that extends from the northwest end of the picnic area. Before this footpath ends at the river shore, watch for the nature trail loop on your left.

With its mature trees and its mixture of pines and hardwoods, upland and wetland habitats, and dense forest and open camping and picnic areas, this site offers a very good variety of land birds. Throughout the year you can expect to find Red-bellied, Downy, and Pileated woodpeckers, Carolina Chickadees, Tufted Titmice, and both White-breasted and Brown-headed nuthatches. Barred Owls may be heard from the road into the recreation area, and Eastern Screech-Owls are common around the parking areas and campground. (If you stay in the campground, you are almost certain to see a screech-owl, even if you do not use a tape-recorded call.)

During the breeding season the campground, the parking and picnic areas, and the woods edges around these sites should produce a good variety of species, including Red-headed Woodpecker, Eastern Wood-Pewee, Great Crested Fly-catcher, Blue-gray Gnatcatcher, Wood Thrush, Yellow-throated Vireo, Yellow-throated Warbler, and Summer Tanager. Check the nearby swamp forest by walking the road into the recreation area, which parallels it, and the nature trail. Species that can be found easily include Acadian Flycatcher, Red-eyed Vireo, Northern Parula, Prothonotary Warbler, Ovenbird, and Hooded Warbler. One or two Swainson's Warblers can often be found, and some years a Louisiana Water-thrush is present. (This site marks the current southeastern limit of the water-thrush's breeding range in the Croatan.) From late April to July Chuck-will's-widows can be heard around the recreation area and along the road into it. From April through June the eroding bluffs along the river shore provide nesting habitat for Rough-winged Swallows.

In winter the birding here can also be productive; flocks of kinglets and an occasional Brown Creeper join the permanent resident species. However, you should avoid days with strong north and northeast winds, which sweep off the river and greatly inhibit bird activity. This area often has the same flocks of waterfowl as the Fishers Landing Recreational Site, but scoters are slightly more likely to be seen here.

When you return to US 70, turn right and go 0.3 miles, then turn left onto Catfish Lake Road (SR 1100). Continue 1.4 miles, then turn left onto FSR 156. After 1.25 miles look for a small opening in the woods on your right and an obscure footpath that runs away from the road. This area, called the **Gum Swamp Bottomland Forest**, is a very special place. This "swamp" does not lie along a stream valley—the forest is nearly level. And the fact that this area is not very wet makes it noteworthy: in eastern North Carolina most such hardwood swamps on relatively dry soils were cleared off long ago and converted to agriculture or pine plantations. This site is also noteworthy for the relative maturity of the forest. You will see numerous trees with diameters of about two feet, and several with diameters of about three feet.

This area is most productive during the breeding season, especially in May and June. During the rest of the year birding here is not particularly rewarding, although the area is always worth a visit just for its aesthetic appeal. For a good survey of the area's breeding birds, walk about four hundred yards away from the road, where there are more pines and more undergrowth. The trail, which is obscure enough near the road, becomes practically nonexistent farther back. On cloudy days you will want to carry a compass—it is very easy to get turned around in this flat, featureless area. Common breeding species of this forest include Yellow-billed Cuckoo, Acadian Flycatcher, Red-eyed Vireo, Northern Parula, Ovenbird, and Hooded Warbler. This is a particularly good area for seeing Acadian Flycatchers. Kentucky Warblers are sometimes present, and farther back from the road you should listen for Black-and-white, Swainson's, and Black-throated Green warblers. The Black-and-white and Black-throated Green warblers are early singers, heard mainly in April; the Black-throated Green seldom sings here after early June. Swainson's are not present every year; they may be most likely at this site during wet years. They should be relatively easy to see, because the subcanopy and shrub layers are fairly open. Barred Owls are present throughout the year.

Return to SR 1100 and turn left. After 2.5 miles turn left onto the southern portion of **Little Road** (FSR 121-3). This road extends southward about 2.5 miles. (*Note*: The southern portion of Little Road may become impassable in wet weather, especially in winter.) Along the first 1.5 miles you will pass through several slightly elevated sites dominated by longleaf pine. Here there are permanent resident Brown-headed Nuthatches, Eastern Bluebirds, Pine Warblers, and Red-cockaded Woodpeckers. (Red-cockaded cavity trees are identified by blue paint.) In the breeding season you will also easily find Eastern Wood-Pewees and Great Crested Flycatchers. Along the last mile of road, wetter areas are more frequent; some sites are dominated by trees and some by shrubs. Along this section Gray Catbirds and Rufous-sided Towhees are common all year. In the breeding season common species include White-eyed Vireo, Prairie Warbler, Common Yellowthroat, and Yellow-breasted Chat. Listen for a few Prothonotary and Worm-eating warblers; usually you can find one or two Swainson's Warblers as well.

The 4.9-mile section of Little Road between Catfish Lake Road and Riverdale Road is FSR 121-2. It runs through the heart of the national forest's Red-cockaded Woodpecker population. You will see numerous cavity trees, marked with blue paint. If you make several stops along this road beginning at sunrise, you should have no trouble finding the woodpeckers at any season. During the peak of the nesting season, in May and early June, they are rather easy to find throughout the day. Bachman's Sparrows sometimes breed in this area but are not reliable—on average, one or two territorial males are found about every other year. Listen for them from April into August. They might turn up at any of the Red-cockaded Woodpecker colony sites north of the west prong of Brice Creek, but listen especially at 2.5 miles from Catfish Lake Road, and beside the power line at 4.2 miles.

At these Red-cockaded sites you can expect any of the species listed for the south section of the Little Road. In the breeding season look for Red-headed Woodpeckers and Summer Tanagers as well.

Other sites worth checking along FSR 121-2 are the bridge at Brice Creek, at 1.4 miles; the swamps on the left side of the road at 2.6 and 2.8 miles; and the little bridge at 3.5 miles. The Brice Creek site is good for Barred Owls, and you might also see Wood Ducks here. In the breeding season all three sites have Acadian Flycatchers and several warblers—Swainson's Warblers have been found at all three. For another potential Swainson's site, take FSR 178 on your left at 4.4 miles and drive to the end. (Some editions of the U.S. Forest Service map of the Croatan NF erroneously label this road as FSR 175.) The swamp here, with its thick ground cover of broadleaf evergreens, is excellent habitat for Swainson's Warblers.

Because this road is so quiet during the predawn hours (except during the deer hunting season, October to January 1), it is an excellent road for listening for owls, goatsuckers, and American Woodcocks. Both Chuck-will's-widows and Whip-poor-wills may be heard from April to July. Strangely, in recent years Whips have begun to predominate, and Chucks are getting more difficult to find. Great Horned Owls and Eastern Screech-Owls may be heard anywhere along the road; listen for Barred Owls at Brice Creek and where Little Road intersects with Riverdale Road. Listen for American Woodcocks from December to April, at twilight or during a full moon, especially when it is calm and warm. A good place to find this species is the power-line crossing at 4.2 miles.

At 4.9 miles FSR 121-2 ends at Riverdale Road (SR 1101). (By the way, during much of the year you will want to avoid using Riverdale Road if at all possible. It may be the very worst state-maintained road in North Carolina. In winter and during rainy periods it may be reduced to a strip of mud. In dry weather you will often encounter deep ruts with rock-hard sides.) Near the intersection you will see a little bridge where Riverdale Road crosses a swamp. In the breeding season check here for Acadian Flycatchers and a few warblers—Swainson's is possible. In winter this is a good spot for Winter Wrens, Hermit Thrushes, and Fox Sparrows.

Cross over Riverdale Road, reset your odometer, and continue on **Mill Branch Road** (FSR 170). Here the character of the forest changes from that farther south. On the upland sites, loblolly pine rather than longleaf is predominant, and hardwood trees are more common. White-breasted Nuthatches, which are scarce along the Little Road south of here, become frequent. This section of road is also quite good for Summer Tanagers in the breeding season. At 1.5 miles a small section of stream has been impounded; you might see Wood Ducks here.

At the end of FSR 170 turn right onto FSR 121-A. Just beyond this turn, FSR 610 begins on your left. FSR 610 is gated after a short distance, but foot traffic is permitted beyond the gate. This road runs through an area of fields and hedgerows maintained by the State Wildlife Resources Commission to provide habitat for small game. This area is not particularly birdy, but you should see several of the more common species. In winter expect White-throated, Song, and Field sparrows. In the breeding season look for Indigo Buntings and Blue Grosbeaks. Northern Bobwhites are frequent here; a few Wild Turkeys are sometimes seen from the end of the road.

At the end of FSR 121-A you will see a boat ramp and parking area at **Brice Creek**. This scenic spot can be quite good for land birds throughout the year. At any season this is a good area for Hairy and Pileated woodpeckers. In winter the chickadee-titmouse-kinglet flocks typically offer a good variety, including White-breasted Nuthatch, Brown Creeper, and Solitary Vireo. In the breeding season this site is excellent for gnatcatchers, Yellow-throated Warblers, and Northern Parulas. One or two Yellow-throated Vireos are usually present, and you might find a Swainson's Warbler in the low woods northwest of the boat ramp.

From Brice Creek drive back out FSR 121-A and turn right onto SR 1143. Continue to the stop sign and turn left onto Brice Creek Road (SR 1004). Continue 5.4 miles. Just past a small bridge you will see a small parking area on your right and a sign for the **Island Creek Forest Walk**. This is another very special area, one that contrasts greatly with most of the Croatan. Island Creek has steep banks with outcroppings of limestone, and during much of the year there is a relatively swift current (swift for the outer coastal plain). The area has an upland forest as well as a narrow swamp forest of bald cypresses and hardwoods along the stream. Much of the upland forest is in a near-climax state, dominated by a rich variety of mature hardwoods. Because of the maturity of the forest as well as the soil conditions provided by the presence of the limestone outcroppings, this site has several rare species and numerous species that are more typical of the Piedmont than the coastal plain. Needless to say, this site is well worth a visit even when birding is slow.

The nature trail runs through the forest for about half a mile. It follows the creek at the beginning but then loops back into the forest. If you would like to explore more of the stream than you see along the nature trail, look for a footpath that begins where the nature trail pulls away from the stream (just before the eighth interpretive marker). Even though this area is very reminiscent of the Piedmont, the stream is nevertheless a coastal plain stream—cottonmouths are often common here.

This area is always good for woodpeckers; Pileateds are always present, and you can often find one or two Hairies. Not surprisingly, this Piedmont-like area usually has one or more pairs of White-breasted Nuthatches. A few Wild Turkeys live here; on rare occasions you may spot one or two. If you walk the trail about sunset, you might be able to call up a Barred Owl. Also, a few Wood Ducks can often be found.

Island Creek is most interesting in the breeding season, from April to June. Along the creek watch for Acadian Flycatchers making sorties in pursuit of food, and listen for Prothonotary Warblers and Northern Parulas. If you walk along the creek far enough, you are almost certain to find one or more Louisiana Waterthrushes. In the upland areas listen for Wood Thrushes, Red-eyed Vireos, and Ovenbirds. One or more Kentucky Warblers are usually present. Along the latter half of the nature trail, listen for a Yellow-throated Vireo and for Summer Tanagers.

This area can often be entertaining in winter as well. Look through the chickadee-kinglet flocks for a Solitary Vireo and a Brown Creeper. Winter Wrens are frequent along the stream, and you might also flush a woodcock. On warm days in late winter you are sure to hear a Red-shouldered Hawk screaming overhead. During finch winters this area often attracts Pine Siskins, Purple Finches, and Evening Grosbeaks.

Farther down SR 1004, at 0.7 miles from the Forest Walk parking lot, note another Red-cockaded Woodpecker colony on your right. This site is also good for Brown-headed Nuthatches and Pine Warblers. From here to Pollocksville watch carefully for Black Vultures.

The final stops on this tour of the northern Croatan are in the Catfish Lake area. To get here, drive on down SR 1004 to US 17 at Pollocksville. Turn left and continue to Maysville. (US 17 is joined by NC 58 between Pollocksville and Maysville.) At Maysville turn left onto NC 58. After 2.2 miles turn left onto SR 1105. (*Note*: Old Forest Service maps indicate that you can drive directly from Pollocksville to the Catfish Lake Impoundment and Catfish Lake. However, this is *not* true now, because a road on private land has been closed to the public.)

On SR 1105, after you have gone 2.1 miles from NC 58, there is a culvert where the pavement ends. For one-quarter mile from this point you will want to check the woods on your left between April and June. In this area tall pines and hardwoods border a drain, and you may find several breeding species, including Acadian Flycatcher, Yellow-throated Vireo, Prothonotary Warbler, and Summer Tanager.

Just beyond these woods is FSR 129 on your right. This is a worthwhile side trip during the breeding season. Drive down this road 0.5 miles, until you come to a bridge across a scenic little stream (**Black Swamp Creek**). During the breeding season, birds found here include Acadian Flycatcher, Yellow-throated and Red-eyed vireos, Prothonotary Warbler, and Northern Parula. Louisiana Waterthrushes are found here some years, so this site marks another spot along the limit of their breeding range. Wood Ducks are occasionally seen here, and this is probably a good spot for Barred Owls. This stream can be checked at another site 0.2 miles farther. Here you will see a gate and trail on your left; follow the trail about four hundred yards to a little bluff that overlooks the stream.

Return to SR 1105 and turn right. At 5.7 miles turn left onto FSR 158 and reset your odometer to zero. At 0.5 miles you will see the northeast end of **Catfish Lake** on your left. This lake is acidic and generally devoid of birdlife but is picturesque. Note the abundance of Atlantic white cedar around the lake; this species is absent in most of the Croatan. For birders the lake is worth visiting primarily for its breeding land birds.

This area is rather exposed, and calm mornings are definitely preferable. Avoid southwesterly winds in particular. Mornings in early to mid-April can be nice, with the many dreamy, lispy songs of Black-throated Green and Prairie warblers, but the birdlife is most diverse from late April to early June.

You will want to check all along the road, from the northeast end of the lake to the last parking area. The most productive areas are the taller trees near the northeast end of the lake (from about 0.5 to 0.8 miles) and near the county line (from about 1.3 to 1.6 miles).

The first area offers more diversity, but the two areas are equally good for species frequently sought after by visiting birders, like Acadian Flycatcher and Black-throated Green, Prothonotary, Worm-eating, and Swainson's warblers. On a good morning you should be able to find several Swainson's Warblers.

In winter the birding can be good on calm sunny mornings. Species found here include Hermit Thrush, Winter Wren, and Solitary Vireo. In early July large numbers of Purple Martins may congregate here prior to their southward migration.

To reach the **Catfish Lake Waterfowl Impoundment**, drive to the end of FSR 158 and turn right onto FSR 3000. Shortly beyond this turn you will come to a gate and see the impoundment ahead.

In the past this impoundment has usually been quite dull, hardly worth a visit, partly because of the highly acidic soil conditions. But the impoundment is now being more intensively managed, and it is likely to get better in the future.

The impoundment most merits a visit between November and March. Often more birds use the impoundment for roosting than feeding, so a late afternoon visit is best. Duck hunting is allowed here, but only for a few days during the season.

Currently, only the first subimpoundment that you see is flooded deeply; it usually has the most birds, or at least the most visible birds. Look for a few dabbling ducks, including Wood Ducks, and Ring-necked Ducks, Hooded Mergansers, and maybe a few swans and geese. If numbers of birds are encouraging, or if you feel like exploring some more, follow the south dike (on your right). You will eventually come to the "moist soil" section of the impoundment. Watch for more dabbling ducks, maybe including American Wigeons and Northern Pintails. This vast open area provides a good opportunity to watch for Red-tailed and Red-shouldered hawks, Northern Harriers, and Turkey and Black vultures. Occasionally a Bald Eagle is seen here.

The other seasons are much less interesting. A few Wood Ducks are present all summer. Swallows sometimes congregate here during the migrations. When the deep subimpoundment is drawn down in summer, wading birds occasionally congregate. Rarely, you may find Anhingas at such times.

In the breeding season you will want to drive west on FSR 3000 to the Forest Service boundary. In the woods on both sides of the road you should find several warblers, including Hooded, Worm-eating, and Swainson's.

By the way, if the birding is dull you might like to hike about 1.5 miles to see a tract of virgin longleaf pines on the north side of the impoundment. Walk up FSR 3000, along the impoundment's west side, until you come to FSR 3003. Take this road until you come to a grove of longleaf pines. You will probably not be impressed by the size of these trees, but they are old. Some trees here, and on similar "islands" that you can see to the north, northeast, and southeast, date back to the Revolutionary War. They have never been logged because of the inaccessibility of the area.

For further information: For information about the Croatan NF, contact the U.S. Forest Service, Croatan Ranger District, 141 East Fisher Avenue, New Bern, NC 28560; phone 919-638-5628. The Forest Service offers a detailed map of the Croatan for a nominal fee. This map is highly recommended to visiting birders.

CROATAN NATIONAL FOREST (EAST SECTION)
MAP 28

This is the forgotten section of the Croatan, visited by few birders—partly because it is a bit out of the way for most travelers, but mostly because Red-cockaded Woodpeckers and Bachman's Sparrows are scarce here. Nevertheless, this area does offer a good variety of land birds at all seasons, especially the nesting season. There is a good variety of breeding warblers; Worm-eating Warblers are common, and Swainson's Warblers can be found fairly easily at numerous sites. The winter season can also be a lot of fun.

This section of the Croatan offers access to the Neuse River, where you might see several diving ducks, sometimes including Surf Scoters. There is also a road down to the lower Newport River estuary, where you can see wading birds and shorebirds and perhaps find Clapper Rails and other marsh birds. This area also features the Neusiok Trail, a hiking trail that runs about 15 miles from the Neuse River to the Newport River. Segments of this trail can be quite productive for birds.

THE TOUR DESCRIBED below covers more than 40 miles, including several side trips. The tour runs from Havelock east to Harlowe, then south to the Mill Creek area, and then west to Newport.

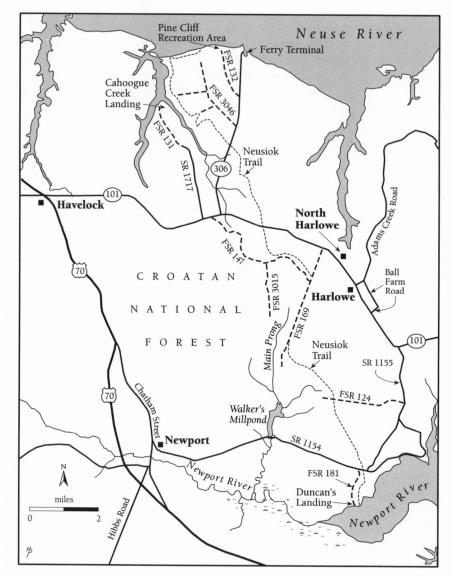

28. CROATAN NATIONAL FOREST (EAST SECTION)

From the intersection of US 70 and NC 101 in Havelock, take NC 101 east. After 4.7 miles, turn left on SR 1717, which is called Cahoogue (or Cahooque; the locals say "ka-HOO-kee") Road. Where the pavement ends (after 1.9 miles) bear left onto the Forest Service road. This road can be good for both Chuck-will's-widows and Whip-poor-wills during the breeding season. The end of the road, at **Cahoogue Creek Landing**, is a pleasant spot during the nesting season. Listen for Northern Parulas and Prothonotary and Yellow-throated warblers.

Return to NC 101 and turn left. After 0.5 miles, turn left onto NC 306. At 1.9 miles you will see the parking area for the **Neusiok Trail**. The northern section of the trail, on the left side of the road, is very pretty in areas and is worth hiking from late October to early June. It is about 5.5 miles from here to the end of the trail, at Pine Cliff Recreation Area; for the last mile and a half the trail follows the Neuse River shoreline. Much of the trail is very winding, and you should allow about six hours each way to walk the whole thing. (*Note*: Part or all of the 1.5-mile-long road into the recreation area is gated at night and in winter.)

Actually, you're not likely to find any species along the trail that can't be found easily from roadside areas, except perhaps for Wild Turkeys, which may be spotted occasionally. Also, the trail goes through some areas of soft mud hidden beneath leaf litter, and it is easy to sink up to your calves before you know it. The trail is marked by white paint and metal strips on trees. In places you may accidentally branch off the trail onto firelines and other pathways if you do not watch for the trail markers. Also, during northeast winds there may be little or no beach along the Neuse River shoreline, and hiking this section can be difficult then.

If you want to walk only part of this section, you could go as far as the first or second spur road off FSR 3046. (These two roads are gated, but both are less than a mile long.) You will see the first spur road at about 2 miles along the trail, and the second at about 3 miles. The trail passes within a few yards of where the second spur road ends, so this road can be easily seen from the trail. But the trail misses the end of the first spur road by a few hundred yards, so you will have to watch carefully for it. (A logging trail runs from the Neusiok Trail out to this road.) And a final warning: the noise from military aircraft can be terrific at times. However, Sundays are usually quiet.

During the breeding season, from around April 20 until early June, you should at least consider walking the first mile or so, beginning at NC 306. This section of the trail is perhaps the prettiest and has most of the birds. The trail runs for the first half mile through young trees but then, for about a quarter mile, through an area of fairly mature pines and hardwoods. This section parallels a swamp on your right. Between the uplands and the swamp there is a prominent slope. The ground here is covered with galax in spots, and the area is reminiscent of the Piedmont.

In the breeding season listen for Yellow-billed Cuckoos, Eastern Wood-Pewees, Great Crested Flycatchers, Blue-gray Gnatcatchers, Red-eyed and Yellow-throated vireos, Yellow-throated and Pine warblers, Ovenbirds, Summer Tanagers, and several other species. Brown-headed Nuthatches and several woodpeckers live here year-round, and hikes along this trail can also be fun in late autumn and winter. Check through the chickadees, titmice, and kinglets for a Solitary Vireo or Brown Creeper. Strangely, White-breasted Nuthatches have not been found here, although the habitat is excellent and they occur just 1 mile west at the Cherry Point air station.

After about a mile the trail crosses a wide swamp. In the breeding season you will easily find Acadian Flycatchers, Red-eyed Vireos, Prothonotary Warblers, and Northern Parulas. The trail is somewhat less interesting after this swamp, but you will have more chances for finding less common or secretive species if you keep walking. At all seasons you might spot a Barred Owl, a Red-shouldered Hawk, an American Woodcock (more likely in winter), a Hairy Woodpecker, or even a Wild Turkey. (Turkeys may sometimes be spotted by looking down the north end of FSR 3046, or the west ends of the two spur roads off 3046, about sunrise.)

Farther up NC 306, 1.3 miles north of the Neusiok Trail crossing, you will see FSR 132, which ends at the **Pine Cliff Recreation Area**. (*Note*: Part or all of this road is gated at night and during the winter.) In the nesting season this road can be good for both Whip-poor-wills and Chuck-will's-widows.

At the recreation area you will want to walk down the Neusiok Trail for a few hundred yards, to where a little bridge crosses a small wetland slough. To find the trail, walk into the picnic area; you will see the trail on your left. Follow it down to the river shore. Just before the trail reaches the shore, a little path branches off to the left and goes down to the wetland slough. By birding from the picnic area to the wetland slough, you can find a fairly good variety of resident land birds, including Acadian Flycatchers; Wood Thrushes; Red-eyed, Yellow-throated, and White-eyed vireos; Northern Parulas; Ovenbirds; Yellow-throated, Pine, and Prothonotary warblers; and Summer Tanagers. In winter the river often has a few diving ducks, sometimes including Surf Scoters.

Return to NC 306 and drive back to NC 101. Turn right, drive 0.3 miles, and turn left onto FSR 147 (**Billfinger Road**). From 2.3 to 3.0 miles, on your left, you will see several open stands of longleaf pines. These stands are good places to look for Brown-headed Nuthatches and several woodpeckers at all seasons. You might spot a Red-cockaded, but sadly, this species is now almost extirpated from this part of the Croatan. In the breeding season these sites have Eastern Wood-Pewees, Blue Grosbeaks, and Summer Tanagers.

In May you may see several goldenrods along the roadsides, or within the open pine stands if these have been recently burned. These are spring-flowering goldenrods, endemic to southeastern North Carolina and a few counties in northeastern South Carolina. They may actually be fairly common in such open stands of pine, but only where certain soil types occur. Look for them especially where shrub-sized sweet gums grow beneath longleaf pines.

At 3.9 miles, turn right onto FSR 169 and reset your odometer to zero. For the first mile or so you will pass through rather low-growing pocosin vegetation. Gray Catbirds and Rufous-sided Towhees are common here throughout the year. In the nesting season you will hear several White-eyed Vireos, Prairie

Warblers, and Common Yellowthroats. Also listen for a Yellow-breasted Chat or two and the low, buzzy song of a few Worm-eating Warblers.

Farther down the road the pines are taller, and there is a well-developed understory of broadleaf evergreen vegetation. From late April to June you will want to make several stops between 1.5 and 2.1 miles. Easy-to-find species include Yellow-billed Cuckoo, Acadian Flycatcher, Brown-headed Nuthatch, Ovenbird, and Yellow-throated, Hooded, and Worm-eating warblers. Worm-eating Warblers are especially common here; you might also find Black-and-white Warblers, Kentucky Warblers, and one or two Swainson's Warblers. This site also has a few Black-throated Greens, but they are seldom heard after early May. Listen for them especially from late March to late April.

In winter—early winter, at least—this section of road can be quite entertaining. However, avoid days with northerly or northeasterly winds, which blow down the road and greatly inhibit bird activity. If possible, be here about mid-morning on a clear calm day, when the sun is beginning to warm the vegetation and bring out a variety of birds. Look for large numbers of kinglets, chickadees, titmice, Brown-headed Nuthatches, and Yellow-rumped and Pine warblers; a couple of Solitary Vireos; and an Orange-crowned Warbler or two. Along the ditches look for House Wrens and Swamp Sparrows. This is also a good area for woodpeckers, including Pileated and Hairy. You might find a White-eyed Vireo, and on warm days you might hear one singing. Also look and listen for Red-shouldered Hawks and, as the day warms, Turkey and Black vultures.

If you would like to get off the road along this section, you might want to walk a little ways along the Neusiok Trail, which leaves the road at 2.0 miles.

The road ends at a gate 2.4 miles from FSR 147. During most of the year you will want to park here and walk one-quarter mile to the right, following the road to the **Main Prong** stream. This road follows the Forest Service boundary but is actually outside the boundary, on land leased by a hunt club. During most of the year this situation doesn't present any problem, but you should stay off this road during the deer hunting season (about late October to January 1), except on Sundays.

At the end of the road you will see a path that runs through the woods to the swamp forest. Head right—to the north—to stay on National Forest land. You will want to walk at least a few hundred yards. (Watch your step—cotton-mouths are fairly common here.) To your right, paralleling the swamp, is a strip of upland pine-oak woods. On the slope between the upland and the swamp, some patches of ground are covered with dwarf palmettos. This area can be good all year for Red-shouldered Hawks, and this is a very good area for seeing Pileated and Hairy woodpeckers. You may hear a Barred Owl call at any time of day.

Late April to June is the best time to be here. Acadian Flycatchers, Red-eyed Vireos, Prothonotary Warblers, and Northern Parulas are common. On the slope and upland woods to your right, listen for Wood Thrushes, Yellow-throated Vireos, Ovenbirds, Hooded Warblers, Summer Tanagers, and one or two Black-and-white Warblers. A Swainson's Warbler can be found here every year, undoubtedly attracted by the thick growth of palmettos. If you walk far enough—about four hundred yards—you will see an extensive growth of dog-hobble (a low-growing broadleaf evergreen shrub with serrate leaves) where you are almost certain to find a Kentucky Warbler.

Winter, from November to March, can also be enjoyable. Check the tree trunks for a Brown Creeper when a chickadee-titmouse flock passes through. Winter Wrens are easy to find among the fallen trees. Watch the treetops for goldfinches and possibly some winter finches. If you walk far enough, you might flush a woodcock—it's easier some years than others. In the thick growth along the adjacent slope, watch for Hermit Thrushes and Fox Sparrows.

Anhingas are apparently regular in this general area in spring and early summer. In the past they could often be seen soaring here in late morning, but unfortunately there are now no open areas where you can watch the skies. However, if any of the tree farm south of the road is clear-cut in the future, you might want to do some watching toward the southwest in late morning. You might not see Anhingas, but you should at least see Black and Turkey vultures and Red-shouldered Hawks.

FROM HERE, TURN around and head back up FSR 169. When you get to FSR 147, don't turn left, but go straight out to NC 101 and turn right.

In the **North Harlowe–Harlowe** area, watch for Turkey and Black vultures. (At Harlowe you might consider this short side trip: turn left onto Adams Creek Road. Just across the bridge, turn right onto Ball Farm Road. Park next to the extensive fields on your left and check for Turkey and Black vultures and Red-tailed and Red-shouldered hawks. Continue down Ball Farm Road, which leads back to NC 101.) Keep driving south on NC 101. After the highway bends to the left, just before the bridge across Harlowe Canal, turn right onto Old Winberry Road (SR 1155). After 1.3 miles you will see FSR 124 to your right. You might want to turn here and drive 1.8 miles, to where the Neusiok Trail crosses the road. From about April 20 to June, a short walk north (to the right) along the trail should produce several Worm-eating and Hooded warblers. You might also hear a Swainson's Warbler.

Continue down SR 1155 until it ends at the stop sign at Mill Creek community. Then turn right onto Mill Creek Road (SR 1154). Ahead you will see the Neusiok Trail and, just beyond the trail, a small recycling station. Park outside the station and walk the trail a short distance to the north. (A road behind the station intersects the trail.)

In these open pine woods look for Brown-headed Nuthatches, Eastern Bluebirds, Pine Warblers, and several woodpeckers, including Hairy Woodpeckers, at all seasons. Easy-to-find nesting species include Eastern Wood-Pewee, White-eyed Vireo, Yellow-throated Warbler, Prairie Warbler, Summer Tanager, and Blue Grosbeak. In winter you might find a Red-breasted Nuthatch here.

In the breeding season and in winter you might consider hiking the Neusiok Trail from here north to FSR 124. This section is about 2.5 miles long; you should allow about three hours each way for leisurely walking and birding. The first part of the trail here runs through upland areas of longleaf pine. Farther along there are extensive, wetter tracts of longleaf pine flatwoods, and the last part of the trail runs through pocosin vegetation. The first half also crosses several small drains. Although they are quite small, these drains may be quite wet during rainy periods, and after very rainy periods you may not be able to get through.

If you walk the whole trail, other species you may find include Yellow-billed Cuckoo, Acadian Flycatcher, Northern Parula, Prothonotary Warbler, Worm-eating Warbler, and Yellow-breasted Chat. You will probably hear one or more Swainson's Warblers.

After about a mile you will see a couple of sites where several trees are marked with blue paint. You might see a Red-cockaded Woodpecker here, but this is another area of the Croatan where the species has been virtually extirpated. However, these sites are good for Brown-headed Nuthatches; Pileated, Hairy, and Red-headed woodpeckers; and Eastern Bluebirds. Around the shrubby margins of these areas listen for a Swainson's Warbler or two. Between the last Red-cockaded site and FSR 124 you should hear Worm-eating Warblers as well. In winter this section of trail is good for flocks of chickadees, titmice, Brown-headed Nuthatches, Pine Warblers, and Eastern Bluebirds. Shrubby areas are good for Gray Catbirds, towhees, and House Wrens.

Just west of the recycling station, look for FSR 181, which runs south (to the left) about a mile to **Duncan's Landing** on the Newport River estuary. This road is very good for Chuck-will's-widows from mid-April to July. The flats on the estuary can be productive, but it is important to be here during low tide. The tide here lags about three hours after the oceanfront tide. During north and northeast winds, especially in autumn, the tide may not get low enough for birding to be productive. Unfortunately, lighting conditions are usually terrible, because you are looking south. If you can arrange it, be here at low tide near sunset. And bring a scope; many of the birds are rather distant.

Most of the year you will see several wading birds; the warmer months offer the most diversity. White Ibises are frequent. Shorebirds are common during the migrations. In August many Semipalmated Sandpipers may feed here, although they largely shun tidal flats farther downriver at this season. Shorebird numbers are lower in winter, but you should still see several Dunlins, with a few Greater Yellowlegs and Black-bellied Plovers.

In winter look for several Buffleheads and Hooded and Red-breasted mergansers out on the bay. Look around the net stakes for a possible goldeneye. On the flats across the bay you may be able to identify a few Mallards, Black Ducks, and Green-winged Teal.

From autumn to spring, follow the shoreline to the left, then walk out into the salt marsh beyond, where you can usually find a few Marsh Wrens and Sharp-tailed Sparrows (and Swamp Sparrows along the upper margins), and occasionally Sedge Wrens and Seaside Sparrows. These birds are easiest to find at high tide. On rare occasions you might kick up an American Bittern. At any season it is rather easy to find a Clapper Rail. (Marsh Wrens and Seaside Sparrows breed in the more extensive marshes to the southwest, but they are not likely to be seen around the landing.)

The woods at the landing can be birdy on calm sunny days in winter, especially about midmorning. Among the chickadees, titmice, and kinglets, you will easily find a few Solitary Vireos and Orange-crowned Warblers. Along the edge of the marsh look for a few Palm Warblers.

Return to Mill Creek Road and turn left. After 2.5 miles pull off the road next to the dam at a pretty little pond, called **Walker's Millpond**. Birding can be very good here from mid-April to June and during the winter. This is private land, and most of it is posted, so you are largely limited to birding from the road shoulders. For this reason you should aim for times with light traffic; early on a Sunday morning is best.

You will want to check the margins of the woods just north of the pulloff, the vegetation along the dam, and the edges of the woodlot on the west side of the pond. In the breeding season Prothonotary and Yellow-throated warblers and Northern Parulas are common. At the western end of the dam listen for a Yellow-throated Vireo. Worm-eating Warblers are regular in the woods north of the pulloff. From the dam you will be able to see two or more Osprey nests. About midmorning look toward the north end of the pond to check for soaring Turkey and Black vultures, Red-shouldered Hawks, and maybe, just maybe, an Anhinga.

Look for a small footpath that leads to the bottomland south of the pond, following the stream a short distance. If you take the footpath along the stream a little ways, you should be able to see an Acadian Flycatcher, and you might spot a Barred Owl. Listen here for a Swainson's Warbler—one is present virtually every year. In winter, walk into the bottomland and search out any flocks of chickadees, titmice, and kinglets. This is a good spot for a Brown Creeper, and you are likely to see a Pileated Woodpecker. Listen for the double call-note of a Winter Wren, and check the trees for a few Rusty Blackbirds.

CONTINUE WESTWARD on SR 1154 to the town of **Newport**. At 0.6 miles beyond the prison, turn left onto Walker Street and park at the church where the road turns right. From mid-April to June, walking down the railroad tracks to the Newport River (about 0.4 miles away) can be enjoyable. You are likely to have a Red-shouldered Hawk fly over here. As you walk along, the woods on your right gradually get wetter, so you will go from Wood Thrushes to Acadian Flycatchers and Prothonotary Warblers. About halfway to the bridge, listen carefully for a Swainson's Warbler.

Drive down Railroad Street to Main Street, then turn left. At the stop sign, turn left onto Chatham Street and go 0.5 miles. Then turn right onto Roberts Road, then immediately left onto Hibbs Road. Continue on across US 70, noting your mileage at the intersection.

From 0.3 to 0.7 miles past US 70 you will see an open stand of longleaf pines on the right. At all seasons this area is good for Brown-headed Nuthatches and Pine Warblers. You will see trees marked with blue paint, indicating that these are Red-cockaded Woodpecker cavity trees. Sadly, though, the birds are now apparently extirpated from this site. Listen here for Great Crested Flycatchers, Eastern Wood-Pewees, and Summer Tanagers in the breeding season. If the area has been recently burned, listen for Bachman's Sparrows from April to August.

For further information: For information about the Croatan NF, contact U.S. Forest Service, Croatan Ranger District, 141 East Fisher Avenue, New Bern, NC 28560; phone 919-638-5628. For a nominal fee the Forest Service offers a detailed map of the Croatan and adjacent areas. This map is highly recommended to visiting birders.

CROATAN NATIONAL FOREST (SOUTH SECTION)
MAP 29

This section of the Croatan NF is the one most birders think of when they hear the word "Croatan." This part of the forest has the largest area of open pine flatwoods (often called "savannas") and the northeasternmost sites in the United States where Bachman's Sparrows occur reliably, and there are several colonies of Red-cockaded Woodpeckers. Henslow's Sparrows sometimes overwinter at some of the same sites where Bachman's Sparrows breed.

This area hosts numerous other summer resident and permanent resident species that birders frequently seek, like Black Vulture, Barred Owl, Chuck-will's-widow, Whip-poor-will, Brown-headed Nuthatch, Summer Tanager, Blue Grosbeak, and Yellow-throated, Prothonotary, and Swainson's warblers. Although there is relatively little habitat diversity, most of the warblers that breed in coastal North Carolina can be found in this area.

Although this area is most interesting in the nesting season, the open pine lands can be plenty entertaining (and are typically most comfortable) during the winter months, with their resident Red-cockaded Woodpeckers, Brown-headed Nuthatches, Eastern Bluebirds, and Pine Warblers. Trying to find the supersecretive Bachman's and Henslow's sparrows can be a lot of fun.

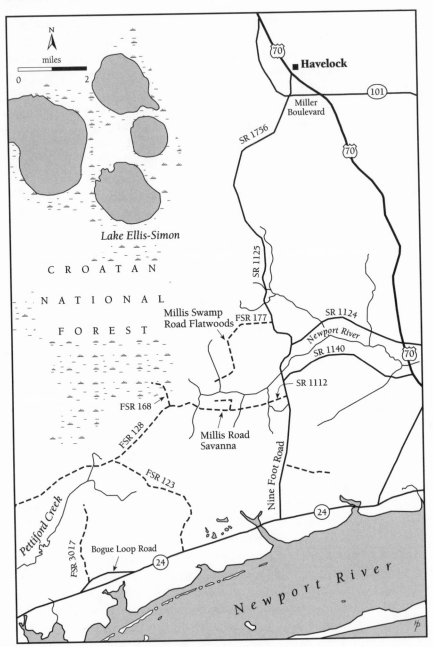

29. CROATAN NATIONAL FOREST (SOUTH SECTION)

Even when the birding is slow, most people will enjoy walking through the Millis Road Savanna. This site is burned regularly and is an excellent example of what much of the Southeast looked like until this century. There are numerous insectivorous plants, including a few Venus flytraps, and if there has been a fire recently, the displays of wildflowers can be impressive.

LOGISTICS. This area is most interesting during the breeding season. However, many of the swamps and streams in this area are quite small and tend to dry up, literally and figuratively, early in the season. A search for breeding species will be most successful from mid- or late April (depending on the species) to late May. Of course, many species can be found well into the summer—a few Swainson's Warblers can usually be found well into June—but this early period will provide the best overall birding. Likewise, because these swamps are so small, they are often almost silent by midmorning. Thus, you should try to bird this area quite early in the day, except when birds are first arriving in April.

THE TOUR DESCRIBED below covers approximately 15 to 20 miles, mostly along Forest Service roads. Unless I indicate otherwise, the descriptions refer to the nesting season.

The tour starts in Havelock at the stoplight where NC 101 meets US 70. From this point, head west on Miller Boulevard, which lies opposite NC 101. After 0.8 miles, at the railroad tracks, turn left onto Lake Road (SR 1756 in Craven County, SR 1125 in Carteret) and reset your odometer to zero.

Between 1.7 and 4.2 miles the areas beside the highway are private sylvicultural lands, mostly covered by pine plantations that are several years old, but there may also be some recently cleared and planted sites. In the older vegetation, listen for Ovenbirds and Worm-eating and Black-and-white warblers. Recently cleared sites with much herbaceous vegetation are more interesting. Look and listen here for Northern Bobwhites, Eastern Kingbirds, Prairie Warblers, Blue Grosbeaks, and Indigo Buntings. Although there are no records for Henslow's Sparrows, some years there has been suitable habitat for them.

Any clearings here can be great places to scan the skies year-round in mid- to late morning for soaring Black and Turkey vultures and Red-tailed and Red-shouldered hawks. If you are really lucky, you might spot an Anhinga (most likely in April and May). A few sometimes nest at a private lake a few miles west.

Between 4.2 and 4.8 miles the road is bordered by National Forest land. On the right toward the middle of this section there is a hardwood swamp bordered by wet pine woods with an understory of broadleaf evergreen vegetation. This is a good area for Acadian Flycatchers, Ovenbirds, and Yellow-throated, Prothonotary, Worm-eating, and Hooded warblers. Swainson's Warblers are occasional here. One or two Black-throated Green Warblers can often be heard; they are most likely from late March to mid-May.

Between 5.2 and 5.6 miles you will see an open pine woods on your right. This area has a few Red-cockaded Woodpeckers (their cavity trees are identified with blue paint) and is good for many species typical of open pine woods—Eastern Wood-Pewee, Brown-headed Nuthatch, Eastern Bluebird, Pine Warbler, and often Summer Tanager. It is not nearly as good as some of the sites below but is perhaps worthwhile if you want to restrict your birding to major roadways and don't want to venture down the Forest Service roads (for example, during the deer hunting season in autumn).

At 6.7 miles, turn right onto the Millis Swamp Road (FSR 177). After 0.8 miles, beginning at the bend in the road, you will see a nice expanse of open pine flatwoods, called the **Millis Swamp Road Flatwoods** (not to be confused with the Millis Road Savanna below). This is a very good area for Red-cockaded Woodpeckers and all the species typical of open pine woods. Virtually every year one or two Bachman's Sparrows can be heard here, from about mid-April to July. A Henslow's Sparrow was flushed here one winter following a growing-season fire.

Return to Lake Road, reset your odometer to zero, and turn right. At 0.9 miles, continue straight onto Nine Foot Road. At 1.7 miles, at the bridge across the Southwest Prong of the Newport River, you may want to stop and listen for Acadian Flycatchers, Prothonotary Warblers, and other swamp forest species, although highway traffic is always noisy here.

At 2.3 miles, turn right onto **Millis Road** (which begins as SR 1112 but soon becomes FSR 128) and reset your odometer. The road passes by a few residences, fields, and a stable. Look for Cattle Egrets, Blue Grosbeaks, Indigo Buntings, and Orchard Orioles.

If you like listening for sounds of the night, the Millis Road can be great fun at any time of year, but especially during the breeding season, from about mid-April to early July. Because many of the habitats along the road are quite open, calm conditions are very important. For a particularly interesting situation, begin driving the road about two hours before sunrise when there is a full moon or near-full moon. It is as if dawn begins particularly early. Along the first 2 or 3 miles of the road you should hear three species of owls and three species of goatsuckers—screech-owl, Great Horned Owl (which calls infrequently this time of year), and Barred Owl, and Common Nighthawk, Chuck-will's-widow, and Whip-poor-will. If the moon is bright enough, you may also hear Bachman's Sparrows. In winter listen for the three owls and the "peenting" of American Woodcocks.

At 1.3 miles the road crosses a small drain, **Peak Swamp**, which is definitely an early season spot. Listen here for White-eyed Vireos, Worm-eating Warblers, an Acadian Flycatcher, and maybe a Swainson's.

Just ahead on the right you will see a gated road (FSR 3019). This road, which is about one-half mile long, ends next to the headwaters of the **Southwest**

Prong of the Newport River. This is a good spot for Yellow-billed Cuckoos, Acadian Flycatchers, Red-eyed Vireos, Northern Parulas, and Prothonotary and Hooded warblers, with an occasional Swainson's.

On the left side of the Millis Road is the beginning of one of the most interesting sites in the Croatan NF, the **Millis Road Savanna**. This savanna (which would be more properly considered an open example of a wet pine flatwoods) stretches along the left side of the road for the next mile.

This site is the single most popular birding site in the Croatan. Not only does the savanna harbor several Red-cockaded Woodpeckers, but Bachman's Sparrows are almost always easy to find. Each year at least ten to fifteen territorial males can be heard along the savanna's length. The savanna would be a lot of fun even without these two specialties: it is easy to find most species typical of pine woods and open pine woods, including Eastern Wood-Pewee, Brown-headed Nuthatch, Eastern Bluebird, and Pine Warbler. This area has such an open aspect that it even has species like Common Nighthawk and Eastern Meadowlark. This is a very good area for Red-headed Woodpeckers (in the breeding season), and one or two Hairy Woodpeckers can often be found. Two other frequently sought-after species that occur here are Summer Tanager and Blue Grosbeak. Because it is burned frequently, this is still a good area for bobwhites.

The Forest Service burns this area every few years to maintain its natural ecology. The savanna is an excellent example of the way vast areas of the Southeast looked for thousands of years, until the twentieth century. The more recently it has been burned, the more interesting the area is. It is most interesting after a growing-season fire, which best mimics the natural fire regime. The area harbors a few Venus flytraps, although you are unlikely to see any (regrettably, poaching has greatly diminished their numbers). There are three species of pitcher plants as well as several other scarce or locally scarce savanna species.

The Red-cockadeds are rather easy to find about May and June, when they're nesting. Otherwise, look for them a few minutes after sunrise. During most years Bachman's Sparrows are summer residents only. They are easiest to find when they sing, and they sing most dependably from about mid-April to early August, sometimes later. In April their singing may be erratic, depending on the weather; calm and warm is best. Occasionally they sing as early as late March, and they have been heard as early as late February. Singing is of course most frequent early in the morning, but this species often sings vigorously in the heat of midday, often when virtually everything else is silent.

Sometimes there is a resurgence in singing activity about sunset, and the birds have also been heard at night during a full moon. After they quit singing in August, Bachman's Sparrows are more difficult to find, but with a little effort you can often flush one through early October.

Red-cockaded Woodpeckers are mostly restricted to the east end of the savanna, so this is the best area to check. It is also the part of the savanna that is easiest to walk through: a jeep trail that leaves the Millis Road at 1.4 miles runs right by several Red-cockaded cavity trees. This trail across the savanna is high and dry, except near the beginning, where it crosses a little drain that can become wet and muddy. Since the grass cover of the savanna can be thick at times, I should mention that pigmy rattlesnakes occur here. The eastern diamondback rattlesnake is also a remote possibility, though they are virtually extirpated this far north. (On a more reassuring note, I have never seen a poisonous snake here myself.)

The jeep trail eventually runs along next to a burned-over area of pocosin vegetation (on your left as you walk out the trail), where there are dead trees and thick shrubby ground cover. Look and listen here for Eastern Kingbirds, Great Crested Flycatchers, White-eyed Vireos, Prairie Warblers, Common Yellowthroats, and Yellow-breasted Chats. You should also find one or two House Wrens; in fact, this site typifies the species' nesting habitat in the North Carolina coastal area, which contrasts quite dramatically with their habitat farther inland.

On clear, crisp winter days with light winds, this site can also be thoroughly enjoyable. Look for small feeding flocks that include Red-cockadeds, Brown-headed Nuthatches, Eastern Bluebirds, and Pine Warblers. For a real challenge, try to flush a Henslow's Sparrow. Most years this is almost a lost cause, like finding a needle in a haystack. But if there has been a fire during the previous growing season, resulting in especially thick grass cover and abundant seeds, there may actually be several of these birds, and a few Bachman's Sparrows may also overwinter. The grass cover is thickest along the eastern border of the ridge that the jeep trail follows. If you have no idea what the term "ridge" means at this almost-flat site, stop on Millis Road at 1.5 miles, just past the beginning of the jeep trail, and turn toward the savanna. On the left is the ridge; on the right is a narrow swale covered with shrub vegetation. The savanna's thickest grass cover lies in a swath that parallels this line of shrub vegetation.

An excellent indicator for your probability of success of finding Henslow's or Bachman's sparrows is the number of Swamp Sparrows present. If you flush just an occasional Swamp, your chances of finding a Henslow's or Bachman's will be extremely slim. But if you see numerous Swamps, you have a fairly good chance. By the way, there's no need to inspect every sparrow that flushes. Wait for one that doesn't flush until you almost step on it.

At 2.4 miles Millis Road crosses the narrow **Millis Swamp**, where you might hear a Barred Owl at dawn. Listen for Worm-eating and Prothonotary warblers, and sometimes a Swainson's. Early in the season, you may hear one or two Black-throated Green Warblers. During some years there may be a territorial male American Redstart, which will almost certainly be a one-year-old male.

At 3.1 miles note FSR 168, which is bit less than a mile long, on your right. This road is usually terrible but is very tempting. It isn't too bad at the beginning, but very gradually gets worse, and there are almost no turnarounds. You may end up having to back all the way out, and as you are backing up it is very easy to slide off into one of the adjacent ditches. Actually, the best area on the road is only about two to three hundred yards in. Here the road runs through a wet woods with thick shrub cover, good for Worm-eating, Swainson's, and Hooded warblers. This is one of the most reliable sites in the Millis Road area for Swainson's Warblers. These birds may also be heard near the end of FSR 168.

Reset your odometer to zero and continue down the Millis Road for 2.6 miles, to a little bridge across **Pettiford Creek**, a scenic stream and a very good spot for Barred Owls. Listen here for Acadian Flycatchers, Northern Parulas, Ovenbirds, and Prothonotary and Yellow-throated warblers. Nearby, listen for Ovenbirds and maybe a Yellow-throated Vireo. A Kentucky Warbler is also possible.

Turn around and head back east on Millis Road. After 0.5 miles, turn right onto FSR 123, resetting your odometer to zero at the turn. From 1.3 to 2.1 miles you will pass through some very open flatwoods, where Bachman's Sparrows are present some years. The land between 2.7 and 3.0 miles is another good area for Red-cockaded Woodpeckers. This area is somewhat different from the Red-cockaded habitat you have seen previously, with drier soils and many young turkey oaks. Brown Thrashers are common in such landscapes.

The intersection of FSR 123 and NC 24 is a good spot to end the tour. If you would like to see still more good open pine woods habitats, though, head west on NC 24 for 1.4 miles and turn right on Bogue Loop Road. After going 1.1 miles, turn right on FSR 3017. From 0.7 to 1.2 miles this road passes through an area with several Red-cockaded Woodpeckers—you'll see the cavity trees. For an even nicer area, continue to the end of the road—half a mile farther—and then hike another mile through some especially attractive open pine stands, which harbor more Red-cockadeds, with an occasional Bachman's Sparrow.

For further information: Contact the U.S. Forest Service, Croatan Ranger District, 141 East Fisher Avenue, New Bern, NC 28560; phone 919-638-5628. The Forest Service offers a detailed map of the Croatan for a nominal fee. This map is highly recommended to visiting birders.

CROATAN NATIONAL FOREST
(SOUTHWEST SECTION)
MAP 30

This section of the Croatan offers a good variety of land birds, especially in the breeding season. A few Red-cockaded Woodpeckers can be found at all seasons, and other permanent resident species include Black Vulture, Barred Owl, and

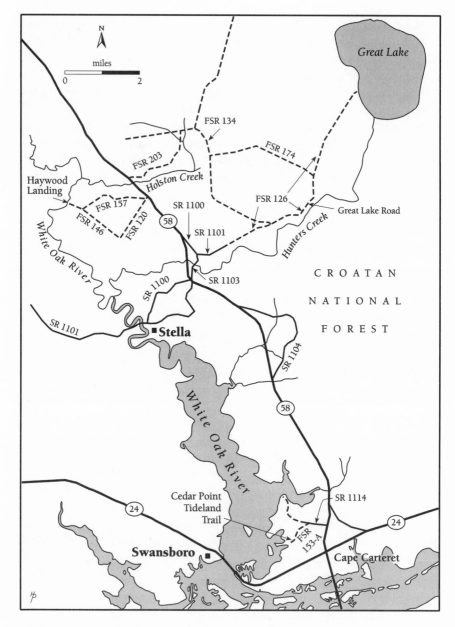

30. CROATAN NATIONAL FOREST (SOUTHWEST SECTION)

Brown-headed Nuthatch. Frequently sought breeders include Chuck-will's-widow, Acadian Flycatcher, Summer Tanager, and Yellow-throated, Prothonotary, and Swainson's warblers.

This section has a good variety of habitats. The Cedar Point Tideland Trail has boardwalks that cross sections of salt marshes. Along the Great Lake Road are open pine lands, small stream swamps, and pocosin vegetation. Great Lake is scenic, although the lake itself usually does not attract birds. Haywood Landing on the White Oak River features rich mixed woods of pine and hardwoods suggestive of the Piedmont.

The highlight of this section of the Croatan NF is Great Lake Road. An early morning drive along this road during the nesting season can be a lot of fun and is a good way to see most of the breeding birds of the Croatan.

THE TOUR DESCRIBED below covers about 20 miles and, unless otherwise indicated, refers to the nesting season.

The tour begins at Cape Carteret, at the intersection of NC 24 and NC 58. From this intersection, take NC 58 north for 0.7 miles. Then turn left on SR 1114. Go 0.5 miles, then turn left on FSR 153-A, which continues about a mile to a camping area (open most of the year), a boat ramp, and the tideland trail.

This road can be good for Chuck-will's-widows in the nesting season and screech-owls throughout the year. Most of the time the parking area and campground are better for land birds (especially for seeing them) than the nature trail; look here for Brown-headed Nuthatches and Pine Warblers at all seasons. Species you should be able to find during the nesting season include Yellow-throated Warbler (at this site they seldom sing after June 1), Red-headed Woodpecker, Blue-gray Gnatcatcher, and Summer Tanager.

Again, the Central Coast section is not very good for land birds migrating in autumn. However, this site, which is near the southwestern corner of the mainland of Carteret County, often has at least a few migrant warblers from August to October. In May both Swallow-tailed and Mississippi kites have been seen overhead here.

You might see a few wading birds around the little bay at the boat ramp, especially at low tide. The tide here lags about two hours after that on the oceanfront. Listen for Clapper Rails. On rare occasions, during a really low tide, you might see one venture down to the marsh edge.

The **Cedar Point Tideland Trail** is scenic, especially at sunset, but do not come here expecting to see many marsh birds. These marshes are just not very good for most marsh species, although occasionally you might see a Clapper Rail. During the warmer months you are likely to see several wading birds.

The trail forms a loop about 1 mile in length. You can make a shorter walk of about one-half mile by going left at the beginning, crossing one boardwalk, walking the short loop through low shrubby woods on an island, and then returning. However, you probably will want to walk the entire trail, especially in the nesting season, because the eastern portion runs through extensive wooded areas—mostly upland pine-oak woods, but there are also a couple of small drains.

For breeding land birds, the trail is at its best for a rather short period, from about late April to mid-May. By June many birds will already have quit singing. Begin the trail by turning right, and in the wooded area along the eastern half of the trail, look and listen for more Brown-headed Nuthatches and for species like Yellow-billed Cuckoo, Pileated Woodpecker, Eastern Wood-Pewee, and Summer Tanager. At the drains listen for Acadian Flycatchers, White-eyed Vireos, and Prothonotary Warblers.

In the low shrubby woods on the islands along the western half of the trail, look for Prairie Warblers. Painted Buntings should occur here at least occasionally. From August to October check through the little bands of chickadees for migrant warblers.

Return to NC 58, reset your odometer to zero, and turn left. After 4.0 miles, bear right onto Old Church Road (SR 1104). After 2.3 miles, you will see open longleaf pine woods on your left. This area has a few Red-cockaded Woodpeckers and is good all year for Brown-headed Nuthatches and Pine Warblers. In the breeding season listen for Eastern Wood-Pewees.

Continue on Old Church Road until it comes back to NC 58. Then continue north on NC 58 for 1.4 miles, to an intersection and store. (A side trip you might consider at this point is to the salt marshes along the White Oak River, about 2 miles westward. Turn left onto Stella Road [SR 1100] and continue 1.8 miles to SR 1101. Then turn right. Just beyond this intersection the highway crosses the White Oak River and adjoining marshes. Clapper Rails are resident here. King Rails might also occur, because the salinity is rather low. However, you are unlikely to see any rails except when they are forced onto the road during extremely high autumn tides. The tide here lags about three hours after that on the oceanfront.)

Just past the store, turn right onto SR 1103/SR 1100. After 0.7 miles, turn right on SR 1101 (**Great Lake Road**) and reset your odometer to zero. This road continues almost 7 miles to Great Lake. After 0.7 miles the road becomes an unpaved Forest Service road (FSR 126). At its beginning this road has a gravel surface and is good during all weather conditions, but after about 4 miles a few spots become impassable in wet weather.

An early morning drive along this road in the breeding season can be plenty rewarding. The peak time is from about April 15 (although some species arrive earlier, and a few arrive in late April) until about June 15.

If you work the road before dawn, you're likely to hear Eastern Screech-Owls and Barred Owls. Listen for the Barreds especially at the little bridges at 2.2 and 3.2 miles. Chuck-will's-widows are common from about 0.9 to 2.1 miles, and Whip-poor-wills are likely in the pine plantations at about 4.0 miles.

At 0.8 miles there is a little stream where you should listen for Wood Thrushes, Prothonotary Warblers, and Ovenbirds. Some years you might hear a Kentucky Warbler at this site. From here to 1.5 miles the road is bordered by a woodland dominated by pines, but with a hardwood understory in patches. Species you can find along this section include Eastern Wood-Pewee, Brown-headed Nuthatch, Yellow-throated Vireo, Yellow-throated Warbler, and Summer Tanager.

The little bridge across the swamp at 2.2 miles is a good spot to stop and listen for several species, including Pileated Woodpecker, Acadian Flycatcher, Red-eyed Vireo, Northern Parula, and Yellow-throated, Prothonotary, and Hooded warblers. During some years a Great Blue Heron nesting colony is located just downstream, and you may see birds flying to and from the colony. If you don't hear a Swainson's Warbler from the bridge, you can often hear one by walking down the gated roadway to the right at 2.1 miles. This roadway parallels the swamp. If you venture into the swamp, be careful: cottonmouths are fairly common here.

From 2.3 to 3.1 miles the road passes several recently logged areas on the right. These clearings provide opportunities for watching the skies above the headwaters of Hunters Creek. On clear days, about midmorning, you can usually see Turkey Vultures and a Red-shouldered Hawk or two. Less frequent, although seen regularly, are Black Vultures and Red-tailed Hawks. In spring, hope for an Anhinga.

Also stop and listen at the culvert at 2.6 miles, and especially at the bridge at 3.2 miles. At the latter site you should hear Northern Parulas and Yellow-throated and Prothonotary warblers, and a Swainson's Warbler is possible. One or two Black-throated Green Warblers can usually be heard at this bridge from late March until about mid-May.

From just beyond the bridge to FSR 174 on your left, at 4.1 miles, the road runs through pines with a fairly thick undergrowth of broadleaf evergreen vegetation. This is excellent habitat for Worm-eating Warblers.

After 5.3 miles the pocosin vegetation becomes more and more stunted. In this area listen for Gray Catbirds, Prairie Warblers, Common Yellowthroats, and Yellow-breasted Chats.

At the end of the road you will see the expansive **Great Lake**, lined with bald cypress. You can survey the lake more easily by taking the smaller roadway to the left that begins near the end of the main road. However, this acidic lake is typically almost birdless. Several Ospreys nest each year, and you might see a few Wood Ducks, but usually these birds will be rather distant. Anhingas have bred on the east side of the lake on a few occasions, but they are not likely to be seen from this side of the lake. Don't be surprised if you see a few alligators.

If you're feeling adventuresome, you might want to explore the south, southeast, and east shores of the lake. The extensive swamp forest here is dominated by mature sweet gums, grading into thicker pocosin vegetation away from the lake. (The area is relatively dry for a "swamp forest"—you can walk through it without getting your feet wet.) A visit to this area would require a trip by way of small boat or canoe across a mile or more of open water, which you should consider only when it is near calm or when there are light southerly winds.

(Don't get caught on this lake when winds are strong and northerly!) Such a trip would be most productive and comfortable early in the nesting season, about April 15 to 20. If you do consider such a trip, watch for cottonmouths. And be aware that if you get away from the lake on a cloudy day, it is easy to get turned around.

At least thirteen species of warblers nest here. Northern Parulas and Prothonotary Warblers are abundant, and Swainson's Warblers are easy to find along the borders of the swamp. This area also hosts one of the state's larger coastal nesting populations of Black-throated Green Warblers, and this is one of the southeasternmost sites in the state where American Redstarts breed. This wild area is the sort of place where one can dream of finding a Bachman's Warbler!

Return to the beginning of Great Lake Road and turn right on SR 1100, which leads back to NC 58. Bear right on 58 and continue 1.3 miles. Then turn left on FSR 120 and follow the signs 2.2 miles to **Haywood Landing** on the White Oak River. Park in the parking lot, explore around it, and walk back a ways along the road you drove in on. Species you should have little trouble finding include Acadian Flycatcher, Wood Thrush, Yellow-throated Vireo, Northern Parula, Summer Tanager, and Yellow-throated and Prothonotary warblers.

For further information: Contact the U.S. Forest Service, Croatan Ranger District, 141 East Fisher Avenue, New Bern, NC 28560; phone 919-638-5628.

HAMMOCKS BEACH STATE PARK
MAP 31

This state park, which occupies a whole barrier island (Bear Island), is not a major birding area, although the birding can be pretty good at times. Formerly, the east end of the island—next to Bogue Inlet—offered good numbers and a good variety of shorebirds. In recent years, however, the inlet has shifted westward, washing away most of the shorebird habitat. Nevertheless, you can always find at least a few shorebirds here as well as at the west end of the island and along the wide ocean beaches. A few Wilson's Plovers nest on the island, and there are Painted Buntings both on the island and at the park headquarters on the mainland. The eastern end of the island has an extensive salt marsh, with resident Clapper Rails and a few breeding Seaside Sparrows. During the fall migration these marshes can be good for both Seaside and Sharp-tailed sparrows.

Small ferries provide access to the island. The 2-mile ferry run through the extensive marshes between the mainland and island can be a pretty good birding excursion in itself; a nice variety of wading birds is usually present. If you're not interested in hiking the long distances required to bird the island thoroughly, you might at least consider taking the ferry over and back.

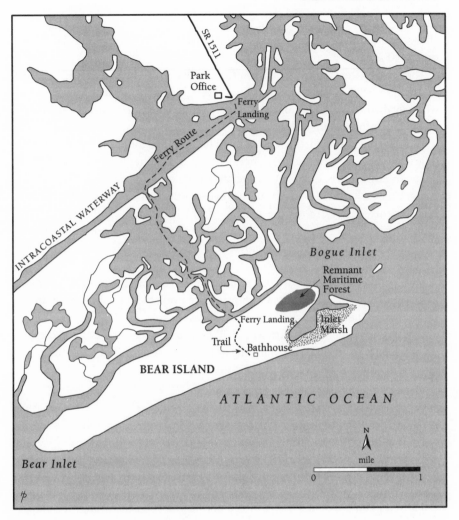

31. HAMMOCKS BEACH STATE PARK

Actually, you won't mind if the birding is only fair here. The island is always a joy to visit. It is unspoiled and almost never crowded (if you get away from the bathhouse area), with scenic dunes and a wide flat beach—the kind you rarely see on the state's developed beaches.

LOGISTICS. The park office and ferry dock are located on the mainland near Swansboro. From Swansboro, take NC 24 west, then turn left on Hammocks Beach Road (SR 1511). This road ends at the park; watch for the signs directing you there.

The ferry runs daily from June 1 through Labor Day and on weekends in May and September. There is a $2 fee for adults, $1 for children. The ferries run almost continuously during the day. Unfortunately, the first run of the day is not until 9:30 A.M.

There is usually a waiting line. You should plan to get here early and go over on the first ferry of the day. From June through August, arrange to visit on a weekday if you can; in May and September, opt for cool weekends. For the most up-to-date information, call the park at 910-326-4881.

To cover the island adequately, you will have to do a lot of hiking. It is half a mile from the ferry terminal to the ocean beach and 2 miles from the terminal to Bogue Inlet. So it is best to visit on a relatively cool, cloudy day. Fortunately, the flat ocean beach provides easy walking, except during the highest tides. Water, refreshments, and restrooms are available at the bathhouse. By the way, as you walk the island you may be surprised on a clear day to hear the continual sound of "thunder." This sound is actually from artillery fire at the nearby Camp Lejeune Marine Corps Base.

Most people fall in love with this island; in case you join their ranks, you may be interested to know that a few campsites are available on a first-come, first-served basis. These sites usually fill up on weekends.

There is now a concessionaire who will take passengers to the island during the off-season (or in the early morning and late afternoon). For a minimum of two people, the fee per person is $12. Call the park for details.

THE FOLLOWING DESCRIPTION is based on a visit to Hammocks Beach by way of the ferry and emphasizes the May to September period.

While you're waiting for the ferry in the morning, you can do a little birding in the shrubby areas around the parking lot. In the breeding season you should be able to find Indigo Buntings, Orchard Orioles, one or two Painted Buntings, and maybe Blue Grosbeaks. In May and September a few migrants are possible.

The ferry run only takes about fifteen minutes. If you can, arrange for one of your ferry crossings to be at low tide, which lags about one hour after that on the oceanfront. A good low tide with a full or new moon and westerly winds will expose many flats. Watch for a few Willets and American Oystercatchers and, during the migrations, other species of shorebirds. You should also see several herons and egrets, and maybe White Ibises. With luck you might spot a Clapper Rail along the marsh edges.

The other extreme—an above-average high tide, which frequently occurs during full and new moons in August and September—can also be productive. You can see small flocks of wading birds resting on the highest points in the marshes, and you might see a Clapper Rail in flight. Least Bitterns are also possible, although they seem to be getting scarcer each year.

Most of the time you will see one or more Ospreys. From mid-July into August you may see Barn Swallows, with a few other swallows mixed in, feeding and slowly working their way down the coast. In September watch for kestrels, and maybe a Merlin or Peregrine Falcon, especially toward the end of the month.

A half-mile-long gravel-asphalt trail leads from the ferry dock to the ocean beach and bathhouse. The habitat along this trail is open dunes with small patches of shrub thickets. A few species of land birds nest here, including Prairie Warbler and Painted Bunting. Listen for the buntings until about mid-July.

Unless it's high tide, you're sure to notice how wide and gently sloping the beach is. This sort of beach profile seems to be very attractive to shorebirds. If you come over on the first ferry and the tide is not too high, you should see several species of shorebirds in the migrations—during May and from late July on. Red Knots seem to be especially attracted to such beaches. About mid-May you may see hundreds of these birds in their colorful spring plumage. Such beaches also attract migrating Piping Plovers, and you could see two or three of these birds in August and September. Whimbrels are often common around August 1.

It is about 1.5 miles from the bathhouse to **Bogue Inlet** at the east end of the island. A few years ago this area was a rather good concentration point for resting shorebirds, gulls, and terns at high tide. More recently, though, Bogue Inlet has shifted westward, washing most of the flats away. Perhaps the inlet will soon shift east again, exposing new shorebird flats. Or perhaps the channel will continue as far as the prominent tide creek in the marshes at the island's west end before it begins shifting back east again. (By the way, this creek is actually a remnant of the inlet channel's 1949 location!)

In any event, you should still be able to find at least a few shorebirds here. A handful of Wilson's Plovers still nest along the marsh edges. Look for them from late March until early September. You should also see Willets and perhaps a pair of oystercatchers. (Don't disturb any birds that are obviously nesting.) The best time to be here is at high tide, when shorebirds have been forced here from nearby marshes. In May and from mid-July on you should see at least a handful of other species, such as Semipalmated Plover, Greater Yellowlegs, Semipalmated Sandpiper (spring migration), Western Sandpiper (fall migration), Dunlin (spring migration), and Short-billed Dowitcher.

Just west of the inlet shore is a rather extensive salt marsh. A few Clapper Rails are resident, and a few Seaside Sparrows usually breed here. The upper portions of this marsh have rather low-growing and sparse cover, with occasional small clumps of thicker cover, and the bottom here is sandy and easy to walk across. This is a perfect setup for flushing marsh birds during an abnormally high tide. During such a tide in September you might flush Clapper Rails, Seaside Sparrows, Sharp-tailed Sparrows (after mid-September), and Marsh Wrens, and maybe a Virginia Rail or Sora as well. Concentrate on the little patches of thicker growth; in this sort of place you could even hope for a Black or Yellow rail.

A 2-mile hike takes you from the bathhouse to the west end of the island, at **Bear Inlet**. This area is less interesting than the east end of the island. Actually, a fair number of shorebirds often rest here at high tide, but they stay on inlet flats a few hundred yards from Bear Island, too far for good viewing. The sandy flats of this inlet look great for a vagrant Reddish Egret in late summer. Aside from the birding, a hike to this end of the island is quite pleasant—you'll typically have the beach pretty much to yourself.

Now that there are concessionaires running to the island during the off-season, you have the opportunity to see Hammocks Beach on really uncrowded days, when you can have almost the whole island to yourself. Calm, warm days in winter can be particularly nice. At this season the ocean may be dotted with Red-throated and Common loons and Horned Grebes, and Northern Gannets may plunge for fish just beyond the breakers.

For further information: Contact Hammocks Beach SP, Route 2, Box 295, Swansboro, NC 28584; phone 910-326-4881. Although the ferry is operated only seasonally, the office is operated year-round.

THE SOUTH COAST SECTION

TOPSAIL ISLAND

Perhaps Topsail Island is most noteworthy for the large numbers of birds that can be seen off its northern end in winter. Much of the sea bottom just offshore consists of a rocky substrate—a rarity in North Carolina. Because of this biologically rich hard-bottom, these waters attract large numbers of loons, Horned Grebes, cormorants, and gannets throughout the winter. Although this area is birded rarely, Red-necked Grebes have been seen here on several occasions; in fact, Topsail may be one of the state's best spots for this species.

Topsail Island has numerous fishing piers and access points, allowing you to check many sections of the ocean. The southernmost piers can be especially good vantage points for watching southbound loons, scoters, and other species in late autumn and early winter.

There are also at least three examples of another distinctive habitat—pilings from former fishing piers that were largely destroyed by storms. These pilings attract several Great Cormorants each winter. Small flocks of Buffleheads frequently feed around these pilings, and a scoter or Oldsquaw, and on rare occasions a Harlequin Duck, will sometimes join them. Steady erosion along the island may bring about an increase in this type of habitat.

New River Inlet, at the north end of the island, has a few shorebirds during the migrations and in winter. You can find Seaside and Sharp-tailed sparrows and Marsh and Sedge wrens in the marshes here from autumn to spring; a few Seasides breed during some years. Clapper Rails can be found all year. Near this inlet there is a brackish pond where Common Moorhens overwinter.

New Topsail Inlet is fairly good for shorebirds during the migrations and in winter. Piping Plovers are regular here during the migrations, and one or two may overwinter. A few Wilson's Plovers breed here. Some years there is a nest-

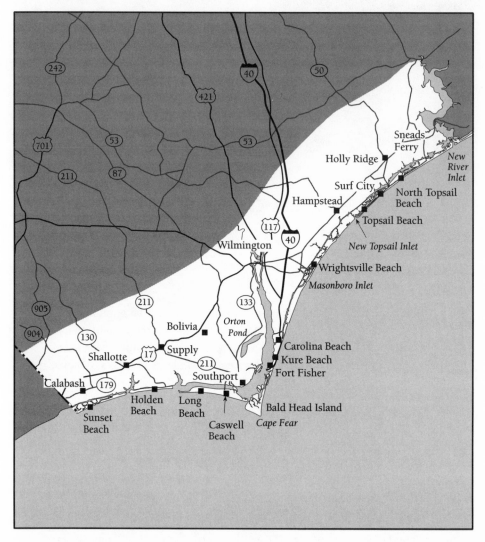

THE SOUTH COAST SECTION

ing colony near the inlet, with Least Terns, Black Skimmers, and sometimes Common and Gull-billed terns.

Painted Buntings breed at numerous sites here. And because the island is so narrow, it can be a fairly good place to watch southbound hawks during the autumn migration.

LOGISTICS. The island is about 20 miles long; it includes the communities of North Topsail Beach, Surf City, and Topsail Beach. This tour of the island begins at New River Inlet and heads south. As you will see, this island is undergoing constant erosion. Certain sections of road are now being relocated; others will undoubtedly have to be relocated in the near future. Keep in mind that as roads are rerouted, mileages given here may become inaccurate. Indeed, some of the sites mentioned may disappear. Nevertheless, the island's major birding attractions should persist for many years—the waters off the north end of the island will continue to attract water birds in winter, the eroding shoreline of the New River Inlet should remain good for marsh sparrows and wrens, and the accreting shoreline at New Topsail Inlet should still draw at least as many shorebirds. Much of the island is interesting only in winter; unless otherwise indicated, these descriptions refer to the winter months.

TO GET TO the island's north end, drive to the end of SR 1568. This road has many bends and turns and has several different names along its length, and portions of it are frequently being relocated. If you get confused, watch for the 1568 posted on stop signs. If you don't see it, just keep following what seems to be the major road.

Where SR 1568 ends, you will see a sign that says "End State Road." Turn left here onto **River Road**. Just ahead on the right you will see a brackish pond, which you can check from the road. Although surrounded by development, this pond usually attracts a pretty good variety of birds. From autumn to spring look for Swamp Sparrows in the cattails and for a few Pied-billed Grebes and American Coots on the pond. Usually you can spot two or three Common Moorhens weaving through the cattails at the pond's edge. During wet years the moorhens may also stay around in summer.

During low water levels in May to early June or in late summer to early autumn, you may see a few shorebirds. There will never be more than a few, but here you might see species that you probably won't find in nearby intertidal areas, such as Lesser Yellowlegs. In May and early June, White-rumped Sandpipers are possible; around August, hope for a Stilt Sandpiper.

Because this site has many power lines and is at the island's north end, a Gray Kingbird might be possible in late May. Farther along on River Road, listen for Painted Buntings in the shrubs from late April through July. Park where the pavement ends. To the right, toward the ocean, you may see a point of sand. (This point is steadily eroding, but sand is pumped here periodically.) During the cooler months there may be a flock of gulls here. Lesser Black-backeds are seen occasionally, and a Glaucous Gull is a possibility in winter. During the warmer months look for numerous terns, often including a few Sandwich Terns.

To the left of where you park, there is a cross section of wet habitats, beginning with shrubs and ending with extensive tidal marshes. From autumn to spring you can find Sedge and Marsh wrens and Swamp, Sharp-tailed, and Seaside sparrows in this area. Look for Swamp Sparrows in the shrubs and for Sedge Wrens in the narrow zone that mixes marsh and low shrubs. The other three species are easiest to find at full high tide, which here lags about one to two hours after that on the oceanfront. Then wade out and kick through the thicker patches of marsh. Also look for Clapper Rails. On the drier sites between the marshes and the inlet, expect to see several Savannah Sparrows. At least during some years a few Seaside Sparrows breed here; listen for them in the higher portions of the marshes, near the shrub zone. You might have to walk south a ways before you find any. This section of marsh also appears to be at least marginally suitable habitat for breeding season Black Rails.

This area can also be fairly good for wading birds during the warmer months, and you should see at least a few shorebirds during the migrations and in winter. Try to get here about middle tide and bird the area while the tide rises. Shorebirds here include primarily intertidal species, like Semipalmated Plover, Greater Yellowlegs, Western Sandpiper, Dunlin, and Short-billed Dowitcher. Least Sandpipers are common during the spring and autumn migrations, and Semipalmateds are common in May. In late spring and late summer you should see several Whimbrels. You may see one or two Wilson's Plovers during the breeding season.

Return to the state road and set your odometer to zero. In the following paragraphs I will point out four sites between here and NC 210 where you can easily get to the ocean. In winter you will want to try to get to the ocean at additional sites if possible.

At 1.3 miles you will see **Onslow County Beach Access #1**. From the oceanfront here you will see the remains of an old fishing pier to the right, about one-quarter mile away. (You may be able to find parking closer to this old pier.) The pilings here attract several Great Cormorants from mid-October through April. You will probably see birds in several different plumages. One or two Greats often stay throughout the summer as well. Unfortunately, the light is almost always terrible; the best light here, as on the rest of the island, is at sunset. In winter—especially if there is a flock of Buffleheads—look for a scoter or Oldsquaw and hope for a Harlequin Duck.

In the breeding season check the shrubs on the sound side of the parking lot for Painted Buntings. If you miss them here, watch the roadside wires as you drive south on the island. A bird might occur wherever there are extensive shrub thickets.

At 3.4 miles you will see **Salty's Fishing Pier**, where birders have seen Harlequin Ducks swimming around the pilings on a couple of occasions. The pier is open from around late March to mid-December. This pier seems to be almost private. If you ask to walk out on it, be sure to buy a snack first. This site is of particular interest because it lies near the ocean's productive hard-bottom areas. From around late November to early April you should scope this area carefully from either the pier or the parking lot; you will probably see numerous Red-throated and Common loons, Horned Grebes, cormorants, Northern Gannets, and Red-breasted Mergansers, with occasional flocks of scoters. Unfortunately, most birds are typically rather distant. One of the best times to be here is during a very strong northwest wind, when many birds will move in somewhat closer to shore. (The very best conditions may be when strong northwest winds follow a vicious northeaster.) Red-necked Grebes may be occasional here; watch for one especially around March. These waters are so productive that you might even spot a rarity like a Western Grebe or Razorbill.

During the winter you should also check the ocean from **Onslow County Beach Access #4**, at 4.4 miles, and at a pulloff beside the dumpsters, at 5.0 miles. (The latter site may not be accessible in the future.)

At 5.2 miles, during the warmer months, check the marshes on your right for wading birds. A Least Bittern is possible here. When you get to NC 210, reset your odometer to zero and turn left. The marshes on the right at 0.3 miles may harbor a few wading birds in dry weather during the warmer months.

At 1.5 miles, opposite the parking lot for a restaurant, there are more pilings left over from an old pier. The signs here say that parking is for restaurant customers only, but in winter you could probably make a quick survey of the pilings from the dune walkover without upsetting anyone. (However, the parking lot may be closed during part of the winter.) Great Cormorants are much less likely to be seen on these pilings than on the ones farther north, but Harlequin Ducks are perhaps as likely here as anywhere on the island.

Onslow County Beach Access #2 is at 4.0 miles. In the breeding season you might hear Painted Buntings in this area. In winter look for an Orange-crowned Warbler among the Yellow-rumpeds. The island is quite narrow here, so this is a good place to watch southbound swallows in late summer and hawks in autumn.

From here south into Surf City, there are **four fishing piers**—Ocean City, Scotch Bonnet, Barnacle Bill's, and Surf City. There are also numerous small access points (with parking for only a few cars), so you can check the ocean thoroughly in winter. At 7.4 miles, turn left onto Shell Drive and then left onto Dolphin Street to get to the oceanfront street (Shore Drive). Then follow this street southward. These piers are open until at least mid-December; one or two sometimes remain open all winter.

Typically, the farther south you go, the less productive the ocean is, with fewer and fewer loons and grebes on the water. However, the farther south you go, the more migrating birds you will see in late autumn and early winter. Late October to early November is the peak time for scoters. Watch for Blacks and Surfs and maybe a White-winged. After strong cold fronts from mid-November through December there are frequently impressive flights of loons, grebes, cormorants, mergansers, and gulls, with a few scoters and other ducks. During these flights watch for an occasional jaeger or kittiwake.

At the point where NC 50 merges into Shore Drive, reset your odometer to zero. At 3.5 miles, just before **Queen's Grant condominiums**, look for a dune crossover and parking spaces for two or three cars. Off this beach you'll see the remains of another former pier. On these pilings look for a few Great Cormorants with the Double-cresteds. There is always a flock of Buffleheads here; check through these birds for something more unusual.

At 5.1 miles, turn left onto Flake Avenue and then right onto the oceanfront road (Ocean Boulevard). On the left you will see the **Jolly Roger Fishing Pier**, the southernmost pier on the island. This is Topsail's best pier for watching southbound flights in late autumn and early winter.

Drive almost to the end of Ocean Boulevard. Just before you get to the Serenity Point condominiums, you will see several dune crossovers on the left and a strip where several cars can park. On weekends during the warmer months you probably won't find a parking place here unless you arrive first thing in the morning.

From here to the inlet is a hike of almost a mile; it gets farther every year as the inlet migrates southward. This walk can be entertaining year-round. During many years you will see a nesting colony of Least Terns and Black Skimmers in May and early summer. Sometimes there may also be a few Common and Gull-billed terns. Whether or not the colony is posted, do not walk through it; check it from the periphery instead, and stay away from any birds that are obviously nesting. A few American Oystercatchers and Wilson's Plovers also nest in the area. Look for the plovers from early April to mid-September.

During the migrations and in winter you may see several species of shorebirds if the beaches are uncrowded. The best time to be here is about one hour after high tide on the oceanfront—you should see several flocks of resting shorebirds then. You can usually find a few Piping Plovers from August to September and from March to early April; one or two sometimes overwinter here. This is a fairly good area for Red Knots. During the warmer months you will see several terns. Sandwiches are frequent in spring and autumn; Caspians are common in autumn.

HOLLY SHELTER GAME LAND
(NORTHWEST SECTION)
MAP 32

The Holly Shelter Game Land, located in Pender County, contains two excellent birding sites in two totally different habitats. In the northwestern section a dike along the Northeast Cape Fear River provides an excellent opportunity for seeing warblers and other swamp forest passerines during the breeding season. The game land's southeastern section, near US 17, harbors a few Red-cockaded Woodpeckers and is an excellent place to find breeding season Bachman's Sparrows and other species typical of open pine woods habitats.

The **dike along the Northeast Cape Fear** is a beginning birder's paradise, because the birds here are not always out of sight among the treetops. Many of the birds can be easily seen in the lower vegetation along the dike, so you can get great looks at Prothonotary Warblers, Northern Parulas, and several other species during the breeding season. Although this site can be enjoyable as early as the end of March, when gnatcatchers, Northern Parulas, and Yellow-throated Warblers have arrived, it is at its best from late April to June. In addition to the several species of passerines, this site is good for Red-shouldered Hawks, Barred Owls, and Chuck-will's-widows, and you might also see a few Wood Ducks.

LOGISTICS. To reach this area, take NC 210 east from Interstate 40. About 0.6 miles after you have crossed the Northeast Cape Fear, turn left onto Shaw Highway (SR 1520). Continue 7.3 miles until you see a Wildlife Resources Commission boating access sign. Turn left and drive to the boat ramp and parking area beside the river.

THE FOLLOWING DESCRIPTION pertains primarily to the peak period, from late April to June.

Some species that you should hear along the entrance road and around the parking lot are Red-headed Woodpecker, Eastern Wood-Pewee, Yellow-throated Warbler, Pine Warbler, and Summer Tanager. If you get here at dawn, you should hear Chuck-will's-widows and Barred Owls. (Chuck-will's-widows can also be heard along SR 1520.)

At the far corner of the parking lot you will see a gate and the beginning of the trail that runs along the dike. This trail leads to the corner of the game land, about a mile away; the trail is quite pleasant, with the river on one side and an extensive swamp forest on the other. (The swamp is actually a series of wooded impoundments created in part by the introduction of the dike.) Although most of the species here can be found in the first couple of hundred yards, you will probably want to walk the whole mile, because this area is so pleasant and because you may find additional species beyond the end of the dike.

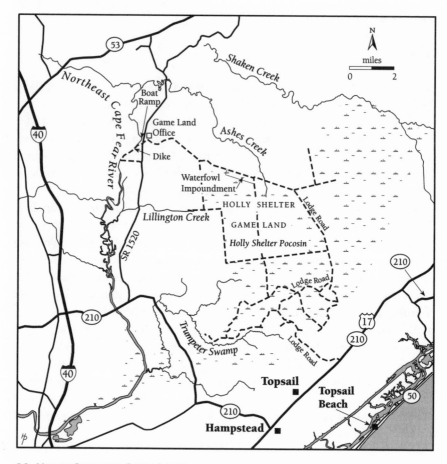

32. HOLLY SHELTER GAME LAND

Prothonotary Warblers and Northern Parulas are all over the place—you will have no trouble seeing several of both species. An especially good place for getting close looks at Prothonotaries is at the water control structure about three hundred yards down the trail: look on the left, just before the structure, for an obscure footpath that overlooks a small area of open water. (Watch for cottonmouths here.)

Other species you should have little trouble seeing include Yellow-billed Cuckoo, Pileated Woodpecker, Acadian Flycatcher, Blue-gray Gnatcatcher, White-eyed Vireo, Red-eyed Vireo, and Hooded Warbler. You might see a few Wood Ducks in the impoundments, and you might spot a Barred Owl. There are often a few White-breasted Nuthatches and Yellow-throated Vireos and one or two Hairy Woodpeckers. A Swainson's Warbler is possible, but much of the area is too wet for this species. During the migration period watch for a few other warblers, like Black-and-white, American Redstart, and Northern Waterthrush.

After about a mile the trail and game land boundary turn left, away from the river. You can walk the trail another quarter mile or so to explore some different habitat. Near another trail to the left, where the habitat is generally shrubby, listen for White-eyed Vireos and Hooded Warblers. If you walk down this spur trail a ways you might hear a Swainson's Warbler on your left.

Farther down the main trail you will see an open pine woods on the left and shrubby areas on the right. Look and listen here for Brown-headed Nuthatches, Pine Warblers, and Prairie Warblers. Unfortunately, you cannot follow the trail back out to SR 1520 because it crosses private land; instead you will have to retrace your steps to the parking lot.

From mid- to late morning the parking lot can be a great place to sit and eat a snack and watch the sky above the river. Turkey Vultures, Chimney Swifts, and swallows are common here. You can usually find Red-shouldered Hawks, and you might spot a Black Vulture. If you're really lucky, maybe a Swallow-tailed or Mississippi kite will fly by.

During the breeding season you may want to pad your warbler list by doing some roadside birding along SR 1520 from here north, to the bridge just south of Players (about 3.3 miles). This is sylvicultural land, so the habitat changes from year to year. Nevertheless, if you make several stops you should be able to hear Black-and-white and Worm-eating warblers, Ovenbirds, Summer Tanagers, and Blue Grosbeaks. In wetter areas you should be able to find one or more Swainson's Warblers.

You might also want to sample a little of the pocosin habitat by walking down **Lodge Road** a quarter mile or more. (This road is closed to vehicular traffic from March 1 to August 31.) Lodge Road begins on SR 1520, 0.2 miles north of the road into the boat ramp. Gray Catbirds, Prairie Warblers, Common Yellowthroats, and Rufous-sided Towhees are common, and you should find a few Yellow-breasted Chats. And don't be surprised if you see a bear.

Although the riverside dike is at its best from late April to June, and singing diminishes rapidly after June, you should be able to see most of the breeding birds listed above throughout the summer. Prothonotary Warblers can be seen reliably at least through August, and Acadian Flycatchers still call into early September. This location is also pretty good after cold fronts in September and early October, when American Redstarts may be everywhere. Winter is less interesting but can still be entertaining. Chickadees, titmice, and woodpeckers are always common. Given winter's lack of vegetation cover, you are more likely to spot Wood Ducks or a Barred Owl then. In winter you may also want to drive to a waterfowl impoundment 4.5 miles down Lodge Road. The soil here is very acidic, so the impoundment usually does not have many birds, but it is a winter roosting site for Wood Ducks.

For further information: Contact Holly Shelter Game Land, Route 1, Box 222,

Burgaw, NC 28425; phone 910-259-5555. The office is located on SR 1520 just north of the parking lot for the boat ramp.

HOLLY SHELTER GAME LAND
(SOUTHEAST SECTION)
MAP 32

This section of the game land features an impressively large expanse of pine savannas and flatwoods that can provide excellent birding in the nesting season, especially from mid-April to June. This is one of the state's best areas for Bachman's Sparrows. Red-cockaded Woodpeckers are easy to find here, and the area also supports other species typical of open pine woods habitats. A few Swainson's Warblers also breed in this area. Even when birding is poor, you may appreciate the area's aesthetic appeal—this may be the best place in North Carolina to see what most of the Southeast looked like for centuries. The display of savanna wildflowers is often impressive, and this is a good place to see Venus flytraps in their natural habitat. (Don't forget that the flytraps and other vegetation are protected by law. Poaching of Venus flytraps is a serious ongoing problem in this area, and you may well be checked by a state wildlife agent during your visit.)

To reach this area, begin at the intersection of NC 210 and US 17 in Hampstead. Drive north on US 17 for 4.4 miles. On the left, just past the Topsail Baptist Church, you will see the beginning of **Lodge Road** on your left (look for a Wildlife Commission sign at the gate). This gate is closed from March 1 to August 31; however, a hike of a little over a mile in is usually far enough for Bachman's Sparrows and Red-cockaded Woodpeckers. Do not block the gate when you park.

In late spring and summer, this open, sandy environment gets quite hot during the day. On most days you will want to start out at dawn so that you can finish your hike early in the day. If you start out early enough, you should hear Chuck-will's-widows and see one or more Common Nighthawks. Along the first mile of the road there are numerous low-growing turkey oaks, making this an especially good area for Summer Tanagers and Yellow-throated Warblers.

After about a mile the road begins a straight stretch about a mile long, oriented northwest to southeast. Around the middle of this stretch a power line crosses the road. From the beginning of this straight section to just beyond the power line, the open flatwoods on your right is an excellent place for Bachman's Sparrows; they sing reliably beginning in early April (sometimes earlier). This area also has a few Red-cockaded Woodpeckers; their cavity trees are marked with white. Other species you should be able to find here during the breeding season include Northern Bobwhite, Eastern Wood-Pewee, Great Crested Flycatcher, Eastern Kingbird, Brown-headed Nuthatch, Eastern Bluebird, Pine

Warbler, Common Yellowthroat, and Blue Grosbeak. This is also a fairly good area for Hairy Woodpeckers.

If you can handle a really long hike, continue to the next power line, which is about 2.5 miles from US 17. Just before the power line the road turns sharply to the right. Just before this turn you will see **Trumpeter Swamp** on your left, about a hundred yards from the road. You will hear Northern Parulas and Prothonotary and Hooded warblers in this area; Swainson's Warblers also occur fairly frequently.

In the half mile past the power line the road crosses three drains, all of which look good for Swainson's Warblers. By the way, both power-line corridors are good places to find Venus flytraps and other insectivorous plants.

As summer progresses, a walk along Lodge Road becomes less and less enjoyable. The birds get harder to find, and the heat and humidity get worse and worse. With a little effort you can find most of the birds of the open pine lands throughout the summer, but as the season progresses, it becomes even more important to be here first thing in the morning. The Bachman's Sparrows sing regularly until early August; thereafter, singing becomes more sporadic.

Outside the nesting season this area is less interesting, but from September 1 to February 28 you can drive in, so it's easier then to explore more of this exceptional area. Remember that this is a game land, open to hunting. During the hunting seasons in autumn and winter you should avoid hunting days (Mondays, Wednesdays, Saturdays, and holidays). In September and early October you can usually find one or more Bachman's Sparrows by kicking through the grass in the stretch of open flatwoods described above. In winter you'll see flocks made up of chickadees, titmice, Brown-headed Nuthatches, kinglets, and Pine Warblers. Beginning around mid-November, kick through the grass of the open flatwoods for a possible wintering Henslow's Sparrow. A wintering Bachman's is also possible; and if the weather is warm enough, on rare occasions Bachman's Sparrows may sing as early as the end of February.

For further information: Contact Holly Shelter Game Land, Route 1, Box 222, Burgaw, NC 28425; phone 910-259-5555. The office is located in the northwest section of the game land, on SR 1520 just north of the Northeast Cape Fear boat ramp.

WILMINGTON AREA

Although it is the most densely populated area in the coastal region, the Wilmington area offers several good birding spots. The New Hanover International Airport attracts Upland Sandpipers each year in late summer, and this is the coastal region's only reliable site for Grasshopper Sparrows. Occasionally something rare shows up here. Within Wilmington there are also several old cemeteries, some of which can attract migrant passerines.

Not far from downtown Wilmington is the thoroughly delightful Greenfield Lake, where one or two Anhingas often occur during the warmer months. You can find a few Wood Ducks here at any season, and other dabblers in winter. The trees bordering the lake host a good variety of land birds, including Brown-headed Nuthatches, throughout the year. Summer resident species include Yellow-throated and Prothonotary warblers and Northern Parula. This site can be quite good during the migrations and has attracted several rarities over the years.

Just across the Cape Fear River from downtown Wilmington is the USS North Carolina Battleship Memorial. The tidal fresh-water marshes at this site harbor King Rails throughout the year, and Virginia Rails and Soras during the cooler months. During the migrations large numbers of swallows often congregate here, and other interesting migrants are also possible.

North of town, off US 421, are Sutton Lake and the county landfill. The lake sometimes attracts waterfowl, especially in late winter. The landfill sometimes attracts gulls in winter, and there have been a few sightings of the rarer species.

THIS TOUR BEGINS at the **New Hanover International Airport**. To reach this site, take Twenty-third Street north from US 17 and follow the signs directing you to the airport. After you begin driving toward the main terminal, you will see large open areas to your left and right. The area to the left is usually more interesting. You can survey it rather thoroughly from the roads that circle it. If you want to walk the grounds, check first with airport security; many birders have walked the grounds without being questioned, but one or two have been stopped and told that the grounds were off-limits.

From about mid-July to early September you can often find a few migrant Upland Sandpipers here. The peak time is probably around early to mid-August, particularly when the grounds have just been mowed. After heavy rains in late summer and early autumn, Pectoral Sandpipers are also possible. Around September, after prolonged northeast winds or the passage of a hurricane or tropical storm, an American Golden-Plover or Buff-breasted Sandpiper would be possible.

Every year a few Grasshopper Sparrows occur here during the breeding season. Listen for their insectlike song from around May through August. Sometimes they sing from the ornamental shrubs along the entrance road, especially just after the grounds have been mowed. Horned Larks have shown up here on a few occasions. Lark sightings are most likely in winter, although a summer sighting is also possible. During many winters the coastal plain will occasionally get snow while the immediate coast gets rain; this sort of weather might bring American Pipits and Horned Larks, and maybe something unusual, to this site.

Three cemeteries on the north side of Wilmington are often good during the migrations and can be entertaining at other seasons. To reach these areas, return to Twenty-third Street and turn left. Continue to the first stoplight and turn right onto Princess Place Drive. After 0.3 miles you will see Bellevue Cemetery on your right. Continue down Princess Place Drive; turn right onto Sixteenth Street to reach Pine Forest Cemetery, and Fifteenth Street to reach Oakdale Cemetery. All three cemeteries offer the same types of habitat—a parklike setting with a few large trees and several shrubs or dogwoods. Burnt Mill Creek and its tributaries border the cemeteries. Thick privet hedges stand between the cemeteries and the creek. Oakdale is the largest of the cemeteries and has the least traffic noise.

Gray Catbirds and Brown Thrashers are easy to find year-round. Summer resident species include Yellow-billed Cuckoo, Great Crested Flycatcher, Blue-gray Gnatcatcher, Northern Parula, Indigo Bunting, and Orchard Oriole. At the little bridge between the main part of Oakdale and the annex, look for a Prothonotary Warbler. In winter check the privet thickets for Hermit Thrushes, Ruby-crowned Kinglets, and an Orange-crowned Warbler.

The best time to check these areas for migrant warblers and other passerines is after cold fronts in late September and early October. There won't be as many birds here as at barrier island sites, but there is often a good variety. In the privet borders you can often find Veeries and Swainson's Thrushes. These sites are often worth checking in late April and early May. Don't expect many migrants then, but you might find a few uncommon species in spring plumage. Because the Wilmington area lies farther west than much of the North Carolina coast, several of those species with more westerly migration routes—"trans-Gulf migrants"—are a bit more likely to be seen here, in both spring and autumn, than at many other coastal sites.

Birding around **Greenfield Lake** is almost always fun. Located within the city of Wilmington, this site is quite scenic and very appealing, especially in April, when the azaleas around the lake are in bloom. To reach this site from Oakdale Cemetery, return to Sixteenth Street and turn right. After a few blocks, Sixteenth Street becomes US 17. Continue through town until you see the T-intersection where US 17 meets US 421. Here, turn left onto 421. After seven blocks, turn left onto Greenfield Street, and then right onto Fourth Street. At the end of Fourth Street, park in the parking lot on the right. From the far end of the parking lot, walk over to the nearby canoe rental place, and check out the lower end of the lake. You should also check the lake from several sites (some are described below) along Lake Shore Drive, which winds about 5 miles around the lake.

From around early April to early October you can often find one or two Anhingas on the lake. Sightings are most frequent in late summer; on rare occasions an Anhinga shows up in winter. You might see one by itself or perched in a tree with cormorants.

Great Blue Herons and Great Egrets are present year-round. Green Herons are frequently attracted to this site, and one or two sometimes remain throughout the winter. Pied-billed Grebes are easy to find in the cooler months, and a few are often present in summer. There are several American Coots during the cooler months; a Common Moorhen might occur at any season. In summer you might even see a feeding Least or Gull-billed tern, looking very out of place at this tree-fringed fresh-water lake.

You should see at least a few Wood Ducks at any season, and you may see other ducks in winter, especially during colder years. One year birders found a male Cinnamon Teal.

The lake is surrounded by a bald-cypress fringe of varying width and by drier areas of pines and hardwoods. These drier sites contain many azaleas and are maintained as rather gardenlike habitat, but fortunately they are not maintained too well. There are plenty of brushy margins, so not surprisingly, this area can be good for land birds year-round.

Some land birds that live here throughout the year include Red-bellied and Downy woodpeckers, Brown-headed Nuthatches, Pine Warblers, and a few White-breasted Nuthatches. Boat-tailed Grackles are found "inland" at least to the dam. Summer resident species include Great Crested Flycatcher, Blue-gray Gnatcatcher, Wood Thrush, Northern Parula, Yellow-throated and Prothonotary warblers, and Orchard Oriole.

Winter can also be nice. The chickadee-kinglet flocks typically draw a good variety of associates, including Solitary Vireo and Orange-crowned Warbler, often a gnatcatcher, and sometimes a Black-and-white or Yellow-throated warbler. In fact, this area can be a good magnet for unusual lingerers and out-of-range species. A Wilson's Warbler and a Black-throated Gray Warbler have been found here in January.

This area can also produce a good variety of migrant passerines after cold fronts in September and early October. In contrast with many of the barrier island sites, birding here may be almost as good in the afternoon as in the morning.

In addition to surveying the lower lake from the boat rental area, you can also walk over to the dam, and the road around the lake—Lake Shore Drive—offers several good vantage points. There aren't any No Parking signs along this road, but at most sites parking on the street looks a bit risky. However, a few stretches of the road are wider and are adequate for parking. A paved walkway also circles the lake. To reach this road, drive out of the parking lot the way you came in. At the stop sign, turn right and drive to the next stop sign. Here, set your odometer to zero and turn right onto Lake Shore Drive. (You will notice mileposts along this route, but the mileages given below do *not* correspond to these mileposts.)

At 0.3 miles, look for a path on the right to a footbridge ("Lion's Bridge") across an arm of the lake. This spot offers an obstructed view of a large portion of the lake. Check this area for ducks in winter. In addition to Wood Ducks, look for American Wigeons, Gadwalls, and other dabblers. In the trees out in the middle of the lake, look for an Anhinga.

At 0.9 miles you will see picnic tables on the lake shore. In winter look for a few "real" ducks with the domesticated ones. The marsh to your left harbors Swamp Sparrows during the cooler months. This marsh often has a couple of moorhens as well, but they can be hard to see from where you're standing. During the cooler months, listen for a Virginia Rail.

At 2.0 miles there is a parking lot for a short boardwalk nature trail. Before you walk it, head back along the road shoulder, in the direction you just came from, for about three hundred yards, until you reach a little dock. From this dock you will have another view of the marsh you saw at the previous stop. If a moorhen is lurking along the edges there, you're more likely to see it from this location.

From the boardwalk nature trail you will often see Wood Ducks. In the breeding season this is a good spot for Prothonotary Warblers. About two hundred yards farther down Lake Shore Drive, on the right, you will see a pumping station and a cleared strip that runs down to the lake. The borders of this strip can be very good during the autumn migration.

At 2.3 miles there is a small parking area with a limited view of the south end of the lake. This south end is a good area to look for an Anhinga. Other good spots for checking the lake are the little dock at 3.2 miles (just past the "mile 3" marker) and the area beside the Greenfield Amphitheatre (at 3.5 miles).

To get to the **USS North Carolina Battleship Memorial**, return to US 421 and turn right. Continue across the Cape Fear River; you will then see signs directing you to the memorial.

The marshes beside the road you drove in on, as far down as the old gated roadway, harbor a few King Rails throughout the year. They often call at sunrise and sunset. If you play a taped call, you might get to see one. Low tide (which lags about three hours behind that on the oceanfront) is best. Watch for birds scurrying around the edges of little openings in the marsh. On rare occasions during extremely high tides, birders spot a rail feeding on the road shoulder. In recent years an occasional Clapper Rail has been seen at this upriver location; formerly they never appeared this far inland.

From September through April listen for Virginia Rails and Soras. You are especially likely to hear Soras during the migrations, in September and April. A Least Bittern is a possibility from mid-April to September. During the cooler months look for Marsh Wrens and Swamp Sparrows as well.

During the migrations you may see large flocks of swallows. Bank Swallows are much more frequent in this area than along most of the state's coast. In winter birders can usually find Tree Swallows also.

In late spring and summer, if you're here at dusk, you'll see several Common

Nighthawks. Some birders heard the calls of an Antillean Nighthawk one sum-mer, but they never reported the observation.

Opposite the parking lot you will see an unnamed, unnumbered road that runs south, paralleling the river. About a mile long, this road first crosses a swamp forest and then passes openings and weedy areas. It is worth checking, especially during the migrations, but the roadside property is privately owned, so you can only bird from the road. In the swamp, look for Prothonotary Warblers in the breeding season; Rusty Blackbirds are possible in late autumn and winter. Farther down the road, a variety of migrants are possible after autumn cold fronts. Check the weedy areas for sparrows after late autumn cold fronts and in winter. After October cold fronts check the wires for a Western Kingbird; a Gray Kingbird made an appearance in this area one May.

Return to US 421 and turn right. Drive 4.3 miles and turn left onto SR 2145. (Look for a sign that says "Sutton Lake.") At the end of this road you will see **Sutton Lake**, the cooling lake for the L. V. Sutton Electric Plant. This lake is often almost birdless but can be interesting at times. Sometimes in late winter there may be several dabbling ducks and Ring-necked Ducks. A Eurasian Wigeon once showed up. Check the treetops for a Bald Eagle.

Return to US 421 and turn left. After 2.1 miles, turn right onto the entrance road to the county landfill—**New Hanover County Solid Waste Disposal Site**. This landfill is open on weekdays and on Saturday mornings. You can usually get permission to drive in, but you will be instructed to stay on the main road. This is not a very "juicy" landfill and is not particularly attractive to gulls. However, in mid- and late winter—especially after cold weather—you might find several hundred birds. Lesser Black-backed Gulls appear occasionally, and there have been a few sightings of Iceland and Glaucous gulls. Turkey Vultures are common here, and a few Blacks are possible. You will often see Boat-tailed Grackles, which look rather out of place here. This site may be their inland limit along the Cape Fear.

WRIGHTSVILLE BEACH AREA

This area is most interesting from late autumn to early spring. Fortunately, during this time of year you will find readily available parking (and no parking meters). One of the fishing piers (Johnnie Mercer's) is open throughout the winter and can be a good place to watch loons and grebes. This island is also quite good for migrating water birds in late autumn and early winter.

Unfortunately, you'll need a boat in order to fully appreciate this area's most notable feature. At the south end of Wrightsville there is a jetty that projects half a mile into the sea. This jetty (along with the one on the other side of Mason-boro Inlet) harbors several Purple Sandpipers each winter, and it regularly attracts rarer species like eiders and Harlequin Duck. Unfortunately, the jetty doesn't extend to land—it starts about two hundred yards from the shore. So most sightings of the jetty specialties are distant and not very satisfying. However, Great Cormorants are easy to see here. You can usually see them on pilings just off the beach from autumn to spring.

From autumn to spring you can often find a few Seaside and Sharp-tailed sparrows in the island's marshes, and Clapper Rails are present all year. During the migration and in winter you may see several shorebirds at the north end of the island.

Airlie Gardens, near Wrightsville Beach, is a good spot for several species of breeding season land birds, including Northern Parula and Yellow-throated Warbler. A few Wood Ducks are often here as well.

Logistics. Wrightsville Beach's parking meters operate from about April 1 into October. At the south end of the island there are a few spots without meters, but you will have to arrive very early in the morning to get one.

This tour begins at the bridge across the Intracoastal Waterway (US 74/76). From here, continue toward the barrier island. Just ahead, where 74 and 76 separate, turn left and follow 74 toward the north end of the island. After you reach the island, 74 makes a ninety-degree turn to the left onto Lumina Avenue.

After a few blocks, bear left onto **Parmele Street**, drive to the end, and park just outside the water treatment plant. From autumn to spring this plant can be a good place to see Sharp-tailed and Seaside sparrows without even getting your feet wet. Come here at full high tide, which is about one hour after high tide on the oceanfront. Beside the road shoulder you will see a couple of higher spots at the edge of the marsh, where a few sparrows and often a Clapper Rail may be spotted.

From here return to Lumina Avenue and turn left, then drive a couple of miles to the parking lot at the end of the road. Here, at the border of the salt marshes, you will see a few slightly elevated sandy strips with sparse grass cover. At full high tide (about one hour after that on the oceanfront) you can often find a Clapper Rail lurking along the edges of these strips; from autumn to spring you should see several Sharp-tailed and Seaside sparrows.

Just to the north you will see **Mason Inlet**, which is migrating south at a rapid rate. In fact, this parking lot may be threatened in a few years. A sandy spit borders the inlet, extending back into the estuary. At high tide you may see a few flocks of shorebirds here during those precious few times when the spit is not overrun with people and their dogs—like early mornings on weekdays in winter. Look for a few oystercatchers, Semipalmated Plovers, Western Sandpipers, Dunlins, and Short-billed Dowitchers. Often there are more birds on the other side of the inlet, which you can check out with a scope. During the migrations, at low tide, you are sure to see a few Whimbrels if you wade back into the marshes. During the warmer months look for several species of terns, including Least and Sandwich.

Head back down Lumina Avenue to **Johnnie Mercer's Fishing Pier**, at the ninety-degree turn on US 74. This pier is always open; it is a great place to survey the ocean in winter. Calm mornings are especially nice, although the light is much better in the afternoon. From late November through March the waters are usually dotted with Red-throated and Common loons and, often, Horned Grebes. Sort through these birds carefully—Razorbills have occurred here on a few occasions. Once, during a late January storm, Red Phalaropes were seen right off the pier.

Because the coastline here is oriented almost north-south, ocean birding can be particularly entertaining during late autumn and early winter, when many species are southbound. The scoter migration peaks in late October and early November; look for frequent strings of scoters flying past, especially on mornings after strong cold fronts. And after strong cold fronts from mid-November into December there may be heavy flights of loons, cormorants, mergansers, gulls, and terns, with a smattering of other species. There may be an occasional Black-legged Kittiwake among these birds. From autumn through early winter, watch for an occasional Parasitic or Pomarine jaeger.

From the pier, drive south on Lumina Avenue. This street ends at the stoplight just before the bridge; turn left there onto US 76. Continue toward the south end of the island. At first the highway runs along the sound side of the island. The pilings and boat docks here usually host numerous gulls. On rare occasions during severe winters, something like a Glaucous Gull shows up. At dusk check these pilings for a few Black-crowned Night-Herons. Eared Grebes have visited the nearby channel on a few occasions in late winter and early spring.

Near the end of the road, at its final turn, you will see several parking spaces and a **Regional Public Beach Access** site. After you cross the dune, walk to your left through an area of developing dunes until you see the rock jetties—the north jetty ahead of you and the south jetty off to the right. Toward the north jetty you will see two tall pilings. This is one of the state's most reliable sites for Great Cormorants. You can usually see birds perched on the pilings from around mid-October to April; one or two immature birds often remain throughout the summer.

The jetties attract several Purple Sandpipers, and they probably have more potential for attracting rarities than any other jetties in the state. Unfortunately, from shore you can see only a fraction of the birds on or near the jetties, even with a scope. And birders check the jetties by boat only irregularly.

You could put a boat in nearby, at the public boat ramp on NC 74/76 on the Wrightsville Beach side of the Intracoastal Waterway. A small group of birders might be able to hire someone at one of the area's numerous marinas to take them out along the jetties, especially on calm days. If you can get to Masonboro Island (which also requires a boat ride), you can get a somewhat better look at the south jetty, but these jetties are not made for walking on; the best way to check them is from a boat.

Several Purple Sandpipers overwinter on the jetties each year, from around mid-November to late April. Least Sandpipers and Red Knots—a very strange combination for most birders—frequently associate with the wintering Purples. During the winter one or two scoters (Black or Surf) or an Oldsquaw often hang around the jetties. Almost every winter, birders find at least one eider or Harlequin Duck here. Undoubtedly there would be more records of these birds if the jetties were checked by boat more often. On one Christmas count, after extreme weather, birders found one Common Eider, one King Eider, and four Harlequin Ducks at the same time. Razorbills have been seen here a couple of times; look for them especially during stormy weather. This site produced North Carolina's most exciting jetty sighting to date: a Black Guillemot showed up one April!

If you plan to survey the jetties from shore, remember that the late afternoon sun is best. Sea ducks are probably more likely to be seen from shore around high tide. The best time to see something good from shore would probably be during a really severe northeaster. During such conditions any sea ducks in the area might concentrate along the south side of the north jetty and move farther inside the inlet, closer to shore. This might be your best opportunity for spotting a Razorbill or other alcid.

Located on the mainland opposite Wrightsville Beach, **Airlie Gardens** can be good for land birds. Spring is especially nice here. Blue-gray Gnatcatchers, Northern Parulas, and Yellow-throated Warblers are common. You'll have to pay an admission fee ($6 in March and April, $5 the rest of the year, children free), and all species present here can be found easily at nearby areas. However, this site is worth visiting just for its beautiful Deep South scenery, including massive live oaks draped with Spanish moss.

To reach the gardens, drive toward the mainland on NC 74/76. When you get to the bridge across the Intracoastal Waterway, slow down—your turn lies just past the bridge. Take Airlie Road, the first left after the bridge. After 1.3 miles you will see the entrance to the gardens on your left. Airlie is open from March 1 through September. It is open at 8 A.M. in March and April, but not until 9 A.M. during the rest of the year. Closing time is at 5 P.M.

This site always has at least a fairly good variety of land birds. Springtime arrives early here; by late March gnatcatchers are everywhere, and the songs of Northern Parulas and Yellow-throated Warblers fill the air. Late April is probably the best time to be here; look for a few migrants then. From about April 20 to August, look and listen for a few Painted Buntings. Red-bellied and Pileated woodpeckers live here year-round, and Red-headeds are present at least during the breeding season. This site is probably pretty good for migrants after cold fronts in September.

Airlie Gardens has a large pond that usually hosts a few Wood Ducks, especially in March and September. Hooded Mergansers and a few dabbling ducks, especially Northern Pintails, overwinter here. These birds typically linger until around early April. Blue-winged Teal may occur during the migration periods.

Many of the area's land birds can actually be seen from Airlie Road, so you could bird this road first thing in the morning, or in winter, when the gardens are closed. However, there are no parking spots along much of the road. You may be able to park where the road bends away from the Intracoastal Waterway, but you might find No Parking signs here. If you do park here, use caution. If you park at one of the restaurants closer to US 74/76, you will have to hike over half a mile to get to the good birding spots, and the road shoulders near the gardens are narrow. Be cautious in this area, as there is much traffic along the road.

If you can ignore the traffic, birding along this road can be pleasant on a winter morning. You will see Golden-crowned and Ruby-crowned kinglets and should have no trouble finding a couple of Solitary Vireos and Orange-crowned Warblers. Also look and listen for one or two gnatcatchers, and maybe a Black-and-white or Yellow-throated warbler.

For further information: For more information about Airlie Gardens, you can call 910-763-4646.

MASONBORO ISLAND
MAP 33

Between the beach developments of Wrightsville Beach and Carolina Beach lies a completely undeveloped 8-mile-long barrier island called Masonboro Island. It is administered by the state as the Masonboro Island Estuarine Research Reserve. Most of this island is extremely narrow: for the most part, a zone of low dunes only a few feet wide separates the ocean from the extensive salt marshes of the estuary. This narrow strip of sand is continually being overwashed and is retreating into the marshes.

Birding on Masonboro Island can be very enjoyable, but every species that can be found here can also be found at nearby sites that are much more easily accessible. Wilson's Plovers nest here, and Dick Bay near the island's south end is good for a variety of shorebirds during the migrations and in winter. This is a good place to find Marbled Godwits, and a Piping Plover is usually present.

Carolina Beach Inlet, at the island's south end, is good for terns during the warmer months. At the north end of the island you'll see the south jetty of Masonboro Inlet. The jetty is very difficult to get out on, but from shore you

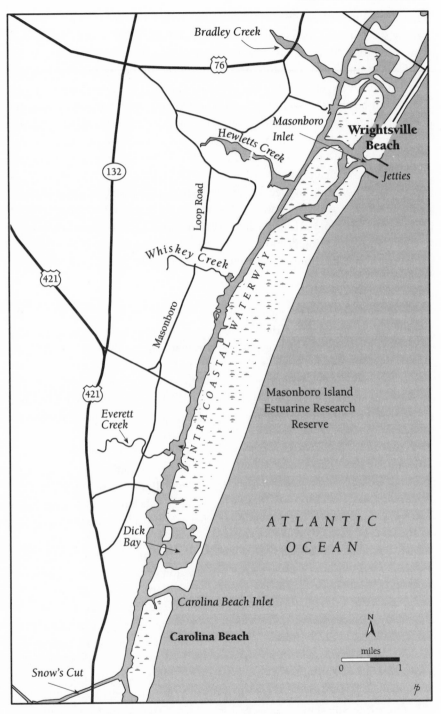

Bradley Creek

76

Masonboro
Inlet

**Wrightsville
Beach**

Hewletts Creek

Jetties

132

Loop Road

Whiskey Creek

421

INTRACOASTAL WATERWAY

Masonboro

Masonboro Island
Estuarine Research
Reserve

Everett
Creek

421

ATLANTIC

OCEAN

Dick
Bay

Carolina Beach Inlet

N

Carolina Beach

miles

0   1

Snow's Cut

33. MASONBORO ISLAND

should see Purple Sandpipers and maybe a sea duck in winter. From autumn to spring the salt marshes harbor large numbers of Sharp-tailed and Seaside sparrows, and these birds are easy to see at high tide.

If you're interested in visiting the island primarily just to see what it's like, you should try to get out here during the late autumn or winter on a clear, calm day. You'll be able to cover a lot more of the island comfortably. In winter the ocean is often alive with loons, cormorants, gannets, and other species.

LOGISTICS. Transportation to the island is currently by private boat only. There are public boat ramps off US 74/76 on the Intracoastal Waterway at Wrightsville Beach and at Snows Cut at the north end of Carolina Beach. In the future, transportation to the island from Wrightsville Beach or Carolina Beach will probably be available. Call the North Carolina National Estuarine Research Reserve at 910-256-3721 for the latest information.

Don't forget to bring drinking water, especially during the warmer months. Insects are not generally a problem, but you'll probably want to bring sunscreen.

THE NORTH AND SOUTH ends of the island are the most accessible areas. At the **north tip of the island** is the south jetty of Masonboro Inlet. You probably shouldn't try to get out on this jetty, but by checking its south side from shore, and by climbing onto the jetty to scan along its north side, you can probably see a few Purple Sandpipers from around mid-November to late April. You will also have an unobstructed view of the south side of the north jetty, which you could check with a scope. The Wrightsville Beach site guide lists some of the species you should look for near the jetties.

Along the north end of the island is a quarter-mile-wide area of dunes and developing dunes. In winter you should see several Savannah Sparrows in this area. In the past, visitors occasionally found Snow Buntings, but these sightings have become more infrequent as most of the open flats have given way to dunes. In the breeding season you may also see a few Wilson's Plovers in this area. (Stay away from any ground-nesting species that are obviously nesting.)

About a mile south of the jetty lies a wide expanse of salt marshes. These marshes support good populations of migrant and wintering Seaside and Sharp-tailed sparrows; the Seasides arrive in August and the Sharp-taileds around late September. If you check the upper borders of the marshes at full high tide (which lags about one hour after that on the oceanfront), you should have no trouble finding several of both species. From autumn to spring you should also see a few Marsh Wrens. A few Clapper Rails live here year-round. An American Bittern is possible during the migrations, a Least Bittern in late summer.

From around mid-July to May, if you walk along the beach an hour or two after high tide, you should see several shorebirds that have been forced out of the marshes. These birds feed on the beach for a couple of hours until the tide is low enough for them to head back to the marshes. During the cooler months you should see several Black-bellied Plovers, oystercatchers, Willets, turnstones, Sanderlings, Western Sandpipers, and Short-billed Dowitchers. Whimbrels are common during their migrations; one sometimes occurs here in winter.

On winter days with calm conditions or westerly winds, you may be impressed by the numbers of loons just offshore. Check through any Horned Grebes for a possible Red-necked. Gannets often plunge just beyond the surf.

If you come to the **south end of the island**, your visit will probably begin on the shoreline along or near the inland waterway. Walk along the inlet shoreline to the ocean beach, then walk north along the island.

The inlet shoreline is constantly changing. Sometimes peat deposits are exposed by erosion, and these deposits can attract Ruddy Turnstones, Red Knots, and other shorebirds. During the warmer months numerous terns will be feeding over the inlet. Sandwich Terns regularly linger here until about December 15. Extensive salt marshes border the inlet. These marshes can be good for the same marsh birds listed above.

Sometimes a spit forms next to the inlet; spits like this can attract resting shorebirds at high tide. During the migrations and in winter check any such spit for Semipalmated and Piping plovers. Breeding-season Wilson's Plovers are frequent in this area.

Once you reach the ocean beach, walk north for a little over half a mile; on the left you will see **Dick Bay**, which at low tide is an expanse of mud flats, at full high tide a bay that reaches almost to the ocean. From around mid-July until May this area can offer good numbers of shorebirds typical of intertidal habitats. This area is best during the rising tide; get here about an hour after low tide and work the area for a couple of hours. Whimbrels are common during the migrations. You should find several Marbled Godwits from around late August to early April. From late summer to May this area usually has several Semipalmated Plovers. You can often find one or two Piping Plovers between August and early April.

For further information: Contact the North Carolina National Estuarine Research Reserve, 7205 Wrightsville Avenue, Wilmington, NC 28403; phone 910-256-3721.

FORT FISHER–CAROLINA BEACH AREA
MAPS 34, 35

The local chamber of commerce touts this area as "Pleasure Island," and the area can certainly provide some pleasurable birding. In general, the best birding takes place during the migrations—especially in autumn, when large numbers of migrants, both water and land birds, are funneled down this peninsula; rarities are frequent then. However, this area is also outstanding in winter,

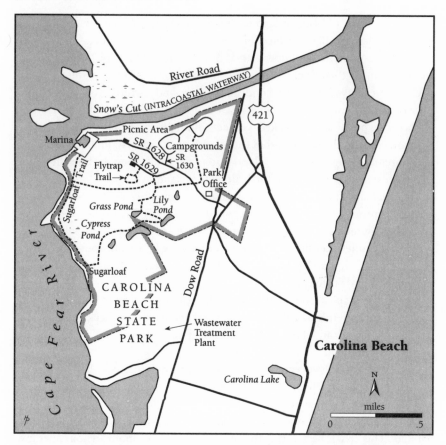

34. Fort Fisher–Carolina Beach Area (Carolina Beach State Park)

which also offers the possibility of rarities and an excellent variety of shorebirds and other water birds. Furthermore, there are many sites where you can bird from your car during rainy or stormy weather. The breeding season is also entertaining. Frequently sought-after breeding species include Wilson's Plover, Chuck-will's-widow, Prothonotary Warbler, Summer Tanager, Blue Grosbeak, and Painted Bunting. Most years one or more Swainson's Warblers make appearances.

The Fort Fisher–Carolina Beach area can be especially good for a "mixed family"—one with both rabid birders and rabid nonbirders. Several sites in the area can simultaneously entertain such a family, whether the nonbirders would rather fish, swim, tour historic sites, or visit the North Carolina Aquarium.

Rare species that have been found in this area include Northern Fulmar, Roseate Spoonbill, Razorbill, White-tailed Kite, and Red-necked, Western, and Eared grebes. The list would no doubt be longer if the area were birded more heavily, especially in the autumn. Ironically, this southern area is one of the

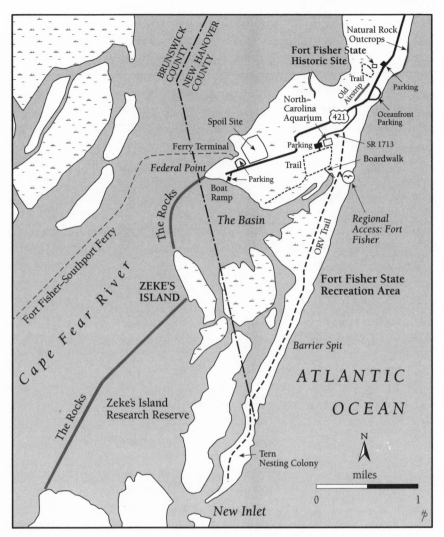

Natural Rock Outcrops

Fort Fisher State Historic Site

Trail

Old Airstrip

Parking

BRUNSWICK COUNTY

NEW HANOVER COUNTY

North-Carolina Aquarium

421

Oceanfront Parking

Spoil Site

Parking

SR 1713

Ferry Terminal

Trail

Boardwalk

Federal Point

Parking

Regional Access: Fort Fisher

Boat Ramp

The Basin

ORV Trail

The Rocks

Fort Fisher–Southport Ferry

Fort Fisher State Recreation Area

ZEKE'S ISLAND

C a p e   F e a r   R i v e r

Barrier Spit

A T L A N T I C

O C E A N

The Rocks

Zeke's Island Research Reserve

N

Tern Nesting Colony

miles

0   1

New Inlet

35. FORT FISHER–CAROLINA BEACH AREA (FORT FISHER AREA)

state's best places for northern species such as Red-necked Grebe and Razorbill, undoubtedly because of the biologically rich hard-bottom areas just offshore.

ACCESS TO PLEASURE ISLAND is primarily via US 421 from Wilmington. After you cross the bridge over the inland waterway (Snow's Cut), take the first right, onto Dow Road. After 0.3 miles you will see the entrance to Carolina Beach SP on your right.

The park is most interesting during the breeding season, from about late April to early June, and after cold fronts in September and October. Wintertime can be at least mildly interesting. The park is a pleasant spot to camp, especially from autumn to spring. Camping may be inconvenient: you cannot leave the park until 8 A.M. (park opening time) and you must be back in the park early in the evening (closing time varies seasonally). But if you mainly want to look for the park's land birds early in the morning, especially during the breeding season, you will probably want to stay at the campground. Being here at twilight and night will also give you the chance to hear Chuck-will's-widows.

The main road through the park is SR 1628. From early April to late June Chuck-will's-widows can almost always be heard calling at dusk along this road, from the park office to the campground; on the nearby portion of SR 1629; and beside the campground.

Species that occur in the breeding season around the campground, along SR 1628, and around the picnic area include Pine and Yellow-throated warblers, Summer Tanager, and Blue Grosbeak. Brown-headed Nuthatches can be found year-round. This area can also be good after cold fronts in September and October, but many birders don't work these woods until late morning, after they have thoroughly worked the better land-birding sites at Fort Fisher and Federal Point. Then they check these woods to add such species as Veery and other migrant thrushes to their daily lists. If you're looking for thrushes, park next to the campground entrance road (SR 1630) and walk left along the campground loop road. In the woods on your left you will see a thick growth of privet shrubs where birders frequently find thrushes. During the autumn migration walk the overflow camping area (campground number 2) as well.

On calm winter mornings the chickadee-titmouse-kinglet flocks here can attract Brown-headed Nuthatches, Solitary Vireos, and Pine and Orange-crowned warblers. Gray Catbirds and Hermit Thrushes are also common in this area.

On SR 1628, 0.2 miles from the campground entrance, check the moist woods on both sides of the road during the breeding season. Listen for one or two Yellow-billed Cuckoos, Acadian Flycatchers, Red-eyed Vireos, Northern Parulas, and Prothonotary Warblers. A Swainson's Warbler is heard here some years.

At any season it is worth visiting the marina to scan the river. The light will be best in the early morning. Look for pelicans, gulls, and terns year-round. In winter there may be a few ducks, rarely including Canvasbacks. Ospreys are common from March to October, and one or two remain throughout the winter. In the breeding season look for Painted Buntings in the shrubbery around the parking lot.

In general, the park's many nature trails do not hold much promise for birders. The **Sugarloaf Trail**, which runs south along the river shore for about a mile, from the marina to a high promontory known as "the Sugarloaf," offers the most appeal. The low shrubs along much of this trail harbor Painted Buntings and Blue Grosbeaks during the breeding season. After autumn cold fronts migrant passerines may work their way northward along the shore, and the river hosts many water birds year-round.

At the end of SR 1629, near the parking lot for the **Flytrap Nature Trail**, look for a trail through an area of moist woods. Swainson's Warblers have also been heard in this area. You can see flytraps and several other insectivorous plants along the Flytrap Nature Trail, a half-mile loop.

On Dow Road, 0.9 miles south of the park entrance, you will see the entrance to the **Carolina Beach Wastewater Treatment Plant**. This site is typically most interesting in winter but is often productive during migrations; a rarity might turn up at this sort of place after a storm. This facility is open from 7:30 A.M. to 3:30 P.M. on weekdays. The staff members are friendly and let birders in readily. If you visit the plant, check in with them and make every effort to follow their instructions, especially regarding when to leave. Please don't do anything that would jeopardize the birding freedom of others.

During winter these ponds host several ducks; scaup and Buffleheads are the most frequent, but other species occur as well. Check the gulls carefully—a Common Black-headed Gull showed up here two straight winters. The ponds may also harbor shorebirds during stormy weather and unusually high tides. In the warmer months there are usually several herons, egrets, and ibises, and during the migrations you may see a few shorebirds around the pools.

The shrubbery along the borders of the plant can attract many warblers in fall. Also, take note of this special situation: there is a "pond site" reserved for overflow. It lies between the two main lines of ponds. In autumn this site can be overgrown with herbaceous vegetation, and it probably attracts an occasional rail. If you happen to be at the plant when they begin piping overflow water into this pond site, you might see one or more rails being flushed out.

The **barrier spit** at the north end of Carolina Beach is often worth checking. Unfortunately, a beach nourishment project has created a massive sand pile, and sand from this pile has blown over and buried much of the adjacent marsh. ORV traffic also tends to be heavy here. Nevertheless, this site is still appealing, because the spit is narrow enough that you can bird marshes, flats, and the ocean all at the same time. During much of the year you can see several species of wading birds and shorebirds with relative ease. Wilson's Plovers nest here, Clapper Rails are common, and from autumn to spring Seaside and Sharp-tailed sparrows are easy to find.

To reach the spit, turn west (left if you're entering town) off US 421 onto Carl Winner Avenue, drive to the oceanfront street (Carolina Beach Avenue), turn left, and continue to the end of the road. There are only a few parking spaces here; you might not want to visit this site on summer weekends and other peak periods.

There is a fishing pier here. If you see a flock of Buffleheads around the pier's pilings in winter, study them carefully—Harlequin Ducks have occurred here a few times. This is also a good spot to see gannets and flocks of scoters.

The entire spit, to Carolina Beach Inlet, is over a mile long. However, you only need to walk a short distance to see wading birds and shorebirds. The best time to visit here is low to middle tide. Tides in the estuary lag about one to two hours behind those on the ocean. Most of the time you can find a few White Ibises. During the migrations and in winter you will see Dunlins, Short-billed Dowitchers, Western Sandpipers, and often a few Marbled Godwits. Whimbrels are frequent in migration.

Currently there is a large tern and skimmer colony near the end of the spit, on the dredged material. Look for Least and Common terns, Black Skimmers, and Wilson's Plovers, but stay outside any roped-off areas.

If the expanse of flats beside the inlet is large enough (its size varies from year to year), check at high tide for flocks of gulls, terns, and shorebirds, especially in winter, when fewer people are present. When the tide is falling, you may notice a prominent tide line where the brown water from the Cape Fear River meets the bluer sea water. This line typically attracts many feeding pelicans, gulls, and terns year-round.

Carolina Lake, a small, shallow fresh-water lake, lies within Carolina Beach next to US 421. Typically the lake attracts few birds, but it's worth checking, especially during the migrations and during stormy weather in winter. In winter there may be a few coots and ducks; during winter storms check the gull flocks carefully—Lesser Black-backed Gulls occur occasionally. Especially during the migrations you may want to walk around the pond, checking all the marshy borders along the southwest side. Look for migrant land birds and for species like Least Bittern and Common Moorhen. In late spring a Purple Gallinule is a possibility.

All of the oceanfront area from Carolina Beach to Fort Fisher is worth checking, although the Fort Fisher area is usually best. The fishing piers at Carolina Beach and Kure Beach can be excellent vantage points for checking southbound gannets and scoters from mid-October into December. The many beach access points in the Kure Beach area, as well as the oceanfront parking area beside the Kure Beach pier, can be great spots for birding from your car on rainy winter days. In winter sort carefully through the Buffleheads near the Kure Beach Pier—this is another potentially good spot for Harlequin Ducks.

Approximately 4 miles south of Carolina Beach there is an excellent birding area that also has much historical significance—the **Fort Fisher State Historic Site**. This site centers around the remnants of a primarily earthen Civil War fort where major battles were fought in December 1864 and January 1865. This is an excellent place for a birder with a history-buff spouse. You can park either in the museum parking lot or just to the south in a parking area that overlooks the ocean.

Especially during the autumn migration, a survey of the Fort Fisher museum area can yield a long list of birds in a short time and with relatively little walking. Within a small area there are shrub thickets and a live oak forest, an excellent view of the ocean, and a trail/boardwalk that runs along a salt marsh and beside the Cape Fear River.

The **oceanfront parking area** is several feet above sea level and is an excellent place to survey the ocean. Any season can be entertaining, but the most productive birding takes place in the winter and after strong cold fronts in late autumn.

These waters are very productive, apparently because of the many submerged rock outcroppings just offshore. In winter look for Northern Gannets, Horned Grebes, scoters, large numbers of Red-throated Loons, and one or two Oldsquaws. Look hard for species like Red-necked Grebe and Razorbill. The best time to survey the ocean here is not during a strong northeaster, as might be expected, but during a westerly wind: such winds apparently cause some upwelling, which attracts more birds, and the smooth ocean surface westerly winds create makes the birds easier to see. At this site you can see a lot on a stormy winter day while staying cozy in your car.

This north-south coastline is excellent for southbound birds in autumn. After strong cold fronts from mid-October into December look for strings of Northern Gannets and all three types of scoters, as well as cormorants, gulls, and terns. With luck you might spot something like a kittiwake, or maybe even a fulmar.

Especially in winter you might want to walk northward along the beach a short distance. In addition to the rocks that have been placed here to prevent erosion of the historic site, you will see two or three areas of flat, soft rock formations. These outcrops are coquina rock, and this is the only naturally rocky area on the state's coastline. These rock outcrops seem to be very attractive to shorebirds, especially in winter; shorebirds often feed here hungrily while totally ignoring the rocks introduced for erosion control. This is often a good spot for Red Knots, a species that most birders do not associate with rocky coastlines. On rare occasions a Purple Sandpiper shows up here; sightings are most likely in November. You can virtually always see one or more small flocks of Buffleheads just out from the rock outcrops, and an Oldsquaw or a scoter or two will often be with them. Harlequin Ducks have been spotted here once or twice.

Near the museum there is an excellent variety of habitat for land birds—from scattered trees (south of the museum) to open ground and shrub thickets to a live oak forest (behind the museum). Thus, the area hosts a good variety of land birds year-round and an excellent assortment during the fall migration.

Species you can find throughout the year include cardinals, chickadees, and titmice. In the breeding season look for Painted Buntings, especially in the shrub thickets along the abandoned runway. Winter can also be nice; in addition to the thousands of Yellow-rumped Warblers you may see Palm and Orange-crowned warblers, Solitary Vireos, and often a few gnatcatchers. This may be the northernmost site on the Atlantic coast where you can reasonably expect to see a seaside winter gnatcatcher.

The presence of several different habitats in close proximity can make for some excellent birding during fall migration, especially in September and October after strong cold fronts with northwest to north winds. You can tally quite a long list here then, and several rarities have made appearances. At this time of year be sure to check the loop trail that runs south and west of the museum. Often you will find the most birds near the trail's beginning, in the trees on your right. The trail also has a good overlook (on one of the mounds associated with the former fort) and a boardwalk that runs across an arm of salt marsh. This is a good spot to see a Marsh Wren and to hear Clapper Rails. In fall migration you should also work along the power-line clearing along the west side of the museum parking lot.

Just south of the Fort Fisher SHS, look for SR 1713. This road leads to a beach access area, to the beginning of an ORV roadway that follows the barrier spit to New Inlet, and to the **North Carolina Aquarium**.

The aquarium is another good spot for a family with both birders and non-birders. It has excellent marine and estuarine exhibits, and the surrounding shrub thickets and the northern extension of a tidal bay ("**the Basin**") can provide some pretty good birding. The shrub thickets host a few Painted Buntings in the breeding season and are very reliable for Orange-crowned Warblers in winter. At dusk in winter you might spot a Barn Owl working the area. A boardwalk crosses the northern extension of the Basin, which includes both open water and salt marshes. At any season, but especially during the warmer months, you should see several wading birds—a Roseate Spoonbill was once seen here. At low tide watch the marsh edges for one of the abundant Clapper Rails. Surprisingly, the tide here lags about three hours behind that on the oceanfront, which is only a few hundred yards away. You should have little trouble finding Seaside and Sharp-tailed sparrows from autumn to spring.

As you walk toward the aquarium from the parking lot, look for a trail on your left. From this trail you will see a bird feeder next to the building. From mid-April to October you might spot a Painted Bunting at this feeder. Nearby you will see an open grassy area. The borders of this area can be very good for sparrows during the fall migration.

From the south side of the aquarium parking lot, look for the beginning of a hiking trail. This loop trail, which is almost a mile long, ends at the aquarium building. The first quarter mile of the trail, which runs beneath young live oaks, can be worth walking during the fall migration. Here you can get good close looks at many birds. Walk at least as far as the border between the shrub thickets and marsh, about one-quarter mile from the parking lot, an especially good area after fall cold fronts.

A tour of the **barrier spit** south to New Inlet (sometimes called Corncake Inlet by the locals) will be most appealing if you have a four-wheel-drive vehicle. Otherwise, it's a very long hike—about 3 miles one-way. Along the first mile of this ORV trail you will travel along extensive salt marshes. If the tide is high, you should be able to flush Clapper Rails year-round and Seaside and Sharp-tailed sparrows from autumn to spring. During the migrations you might be able to flush other rail species as well.

Farther south the spit's estuarine shoreline becomes more open, and you will probably see several shorebirds, usually including Marbled Godwits, and maybe a Long-billed Curlew. Check the Basin for loons, grebes, and ducks in winter, and for gulls and terns throughout the year.

At any season the flats beside the inlet will offer the barrier spit's best birding. In spring and early summer there is a tern and skimmer nesting colony, which you can survey from outside the ropes. American Oystercatchers also nest here. So do Wilson's Plovers; this is one of the state's better areas for them. In recent summers one or more Reddish Egrets' have been spotted on the tidal flats just inside the inlet.

In late autumn and winter you should thoroughly cover all the dry flats and dunes in the tern colony area. On the open flats watch for possible Lapland Longspurs and Snow Buntings. Some birders have flushed Short-eared Owls from the vegetation among the larger dunes.

The inlet is typically at its best during the colder months, when there are fewer beachgoers. Try to be here at high tide, when gulls, terns, and shorebirds that have been chased off the nearby tidal flats congregate here. You can usually expect large numbers of Dunlins, Western Sandpipers, and Short-billed Dowitchers. Look for Piping Plovers as well; a few are likely from March to mid-April and from August to early October, and one or two sometimes remain throughout the winter.

The ocean off the spit usually doesn't offer any species that can't be seen more easily elsewhere. However, in winter you might want to check it anyway on the chance of seeing a rarity, which this area certainly could produce.

Near the end of US 421, on the right, you will see the Fort Fisher ferry terminal. The open areas beside the terminal can be excellent for sparrows during the fall migration. Possibilities include White-crowned, Lincoln's, Clay-colored, and Lark.

At the very end of US 421 lies **Federal Point**. Extending from the point is perhaps the most unique birding area in the state—"the Rocks," a 3-mile-long rock breakwater that runs southward between the Basin and the river. This rich area is part of the Zeke's Island Estuarine Research Reserve.

The Federal Point parking area, at the end of US 421, consists of a marl-paved section (to the left) and an unimproved area (to the right). The area to the right may look wet, because it's often covered by high tides. Park here with care; by the way, high tide here lags about two hours after that on the oceanfront.

After fall cold fronts the area right around the parking lot—including the shrub thickets just back up the road—can host a pile-up of migrants. This is often the first area that local birders check on the morning after a cold front; they may start here and work back up toward Fort Fisher.

At low tide during the migrations and in winter, you can sometimes see several shorebirds from the nearby boat ramp. Look for Marbled Godwits and a Long-billed Curlew. In winter you might also see loons, grebes, and a few ducks here, and you can sometimes see a nice variety from your car on a rainy day. This could be a very good spot to check during a severe winter northeaster. A Red-necked Grebe was seen here once.

The breakwater begins near the parking area. Before you start out on it, check out the prominent dune to your right. This dune is actually what remains of **Battery Buchanan**, part of Fort Fisher's defense system. This site provides an excellent overlook for the river and a great vantage point for watching south-bound hawks after fall cold fronts.

The Rocks can be excellent for birding, but please remember that this site can be treacherous. You should avoid it whenever the breakwater might be getting wet, whether because of high tide, rain, or strong winds. These rocks can be awash or even completely underwater during the highest tides. The upper surface of the breakwater provides decent footing during dry conditions, but even a little moisture makes the thin layer of algae very slippery. And if you begin to slide, there's nothing to stop you until you reach the border of razor-sharp oysters at the bottom. Also, the rock breakwater's elevation is not the same throughout its length. On a section just north of Zeke's Island, some of the upper paved surface has eroded away. The elevation also declines gradually as you head south from Zeke's Island, and there is one major break here that you probably won't be able to cross under any conditions.

But don't be scared off entirely; during dry conditions the walking is reason-ably safe—actually, very smooth sailing most of the way. To be safe, though, visit the area on a dry, sunny day, and head out only during a falling tide. If you become more familiar with the area, you might become more confident about staying out closer to high tide, which often offers the best birding.

To get the most out of this area, be prepared to hike at least beyond **Zeke's Island**—about 1.5 miles one-way. For the best birding conditions (but not the safest), get here during the beginning of the rising tide and bird leisurely while the tide rises. As the water level gets higher, many shorebirds head to the Rocks to rest. Just be sure not to get trapped out here during high water levels. If you do get caught, seek refuge at Zeke's Island until the tide recedes to a safe level.

Any season can be interesting here, but winter is the best because then waterfowl join the gulls, terns, and shorebirds.

As you start out on the Rocks you will notice a small salt marsh on your left. From autumn to spring you can expect to find Seaside and Sharp-tailed sparrows here. Farther along, you will experience the special appeal of a walk on the Rocks—the condition of being virtually surrounded by water, with the tidal basin on one side and the vast expanse of the lower Cape Fear on the other. At all seasons you will see plenty of pelicans, gulls, and terns. In winter you will also see Common Loons and Horned Grebes, especially in the Basin.

Before you get to Zeke's Island, you will notice several tall range markers to your right, out in the river. From October through April these markers are favored loafing spots for several Great Cormorants. In fact, there are typically only Greats here, no Double-cresteds. Beginning in February, look for the white flank patches on the adult cormorants. Ironically, this southern site has the state's largest population of this northern species. One or two immature/subadult Greats often remain here throughout the summer.

Zeke's Island has shrub thickets, which can be worth checking for stray autumn migrants, and small patches of bordering marshes, which are good places to find Seaside and Sharp-tailed sparrows.

The birding is typically best beyond Zeke's Island. During low and changing tides the open water, oyster rocks, and mud flats on the east side of the Rocks usually host an excellent variety of gulls, terns, and shorebirds. Late afternoon provides the best light. Oystercatchers are always present, and you should also see several Marbled Godwits (a colorful sight in low winter sun), except perhaps in late spring and early summer. A Long-billed Curlew usually joins the godwits. Western Sandpipers and Short-billed Dowitchers are common during most of the year.

In winter check the river for Common Loons, Horned Grebes, scaup, and goldeneyes. There is usually a flock of up to twenty Common Goldeneyes; this is the South Coast section's only reliable spot for this species. Some winters there may be a Brant or two as well.

During migrations you are very likely to see Peregrine Falcons and Merlins, and a member of each species often overwinters.

Look for Ruddy Turnstones and Least Sandpipers feeding on the breakwater almost year-round. The presence of Least Sandpipers, which are common in winter, is noteworthy: this species is not typically associated with rock structures. Even more surprising, in winter a few Long-billed Dowitchers sometimes feed along the algae on the breakwater's slopes.

During high tides the shorebirds that typically feed on the mud flats often head to the rock breakwater to rest, and at times—especially in winter, when there are few fishermen—the Rocks may be almost covered with oystercatchers, dowitchers, knots, Sanderlings, sandpipers, and other birds. You could safely witness this spectacle by spending a whole high tide near Zeke's Island. Or if you have a small boat with a shallow draft, you could put in at the Federal Point ramp and survey the Rocks from offshore.

The **Fort Fisher to Southport ferry** probably won't offer you any species you can't see in the Fort Fisher–Federal Point area. However, it will take you past a few nesting islands in the breeding season, and in winter you might see a few waterfowl. The ferry is another option for rainy days, when you can get up in the passenger section and search through the windows. In general, a run at low tide is likely to be more interesting. Low tide here lags about one or two hours after that on the oceanfront.

There are several runs a day, especially during the summer months. The current cost (one-way) for a regular-sized vehicle is $3. See a current state highway map for the latest schedule and fee information. (During the summer the ferries may run more frequently than the official schedule indicates.)

At any season you will see numerous pelicans, gulls, and terns, especially if there are prominent tide lines during your run. Most of the year there will also be many cormorants. Don't be surprised if you see an American White Pelican—they make occasional appearances here.

The particular islands suitable for nesting birds will vary from year to year, but the ferry route currently passes right next to several nesting islands. You may see young pelicans and terns at fairly close range. Look carefully—Sooty Terns have nested in this area once or twice, and one year a beautiful adult Masked Booby summered at one of the nesting islands. Undoubtedly, seabirds like gannets and scoters occasionally head northward up the river during the spring migration. You might even see a jaeger. One May a birder saw a frigate-bird soaring here.

For further information: For information about Carolina Beach SP, contact Carolina Beach SP, P.O. Box 475, Carolina Beach, NC 28428; phone 910-428-8206. For information about Fort Fisher SHS, contact Fort Fisher SHS, P.O. Box 68, Kure Beach, NC 28449; phone 910-458-5538. For information about the North Carolina Aquarium, contact North Carolina Aquarium, P.O. Box 130, Kure Beach, NC 28449; phone 910-458-8257. For information about Zeke's Island Estuarine Research Reserve, contact North Carolina National Estuarine Research Reserve, 7205 Wrightsville Avenue, Wilmington, NC 28403; phone 910-256-3721.

ORTON POND, ORTON PLANTATION, BRUNSWICK
TOWN STATE HISTORIC SITE, AND NEARBY AREAS
MAP 36

This area features some excellent birding along with beautiful Deep South scenery—the cypress-fringed Orton Pond, the live oak–shaded drive into Orton Plantation, and the old rice fields between the plantation and the Cape Fear River. Even when birding is slow, a visit to this area can be entertaining. The Orton Plantation gardens are spectacular in the spring, and the area is rich in history. The lower Cape Fear River was once the northern limit of the South Atlantic states' rice culture, and the old rice fields at Orton are a reminder of that era. Brunswick Town SHS marks the site of the region's first English settlement. The site encompasses the remains of the old church, unearthed remains of the foundations of several residences, and the earthworks of a Civil War fort built by the Confederates.

This area can be entertaining at any season, but it is best during the breeding season, from mid-April into June. Breeding land birds that are easy to find here include Chuck-will's-widow, Acadian Flycatcher, Northern Parula, Yellow-throated and Prothonotary warblers, Summer Tanager, Blue Grosbeak, and Painted Bunting. Black Vultures, Barred Owls, and Brown-headed Nuthatches are year-round residents.

Wood Ducks are easy to find at Orton Pond throughout the year. Anhingas occur regularly here during the warmer months, and sometimes in winter. From autumn to spring you can often find an adult Bald Eagle at the pond.

King Rails are resident in the marshes at and near Orton Plantation and are sometimes spotted from NC 133 and along the causeway into the plantation. Virginia Rails and Soras also winter in these marshes.

A few miles northwest of Orton Plantation, public roads cross streams that are excellent for land birds during the breeding season. These sites are very good places to find Swainson's Warblers.

LOGISTICS. Orton Plantation is private; there is an admission fee of $7. This site is open from March through November and closed in winter. Opening time is 8 A.M.; closing time is 6 P.M. in spring and summer and 5 P.M. in autumn. Hours for the Brunswick Town SHS vary seasonally. From April 1 through October 31 it is open from 9 A.M. to 5 P.M. (1 to 5 P.M. on Sunday). From November 1 through March 31, it is open from 10 A.M. to 4 P.M. (1 to 4 P.M. on Sunday) but is closed on Mondays.

THIS TOUR BEGINS at the dam at **Orton Pond**. To get to this site, watch for signs on NC 133 directing you to Orton Plantation. If you're driving in from the north, turn onto Plantation Road and drive by the plantation entrance. If you're

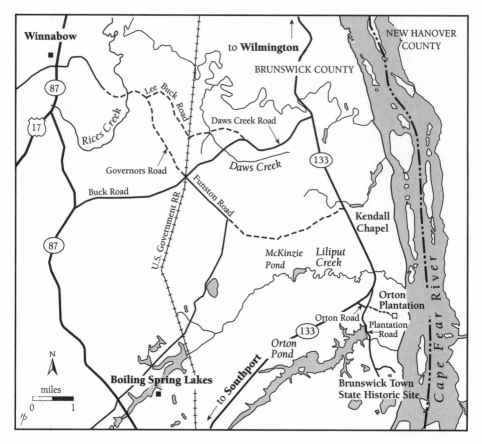

36. ORTON POND, ORTON PLANTATION, BRUNSWICK TOWN STATE HISTORIC
SITE, AND NEARBY AREAS

driving in from the south, turn right onto Orton Road and then right onto
Plantation Road, almost across from the plantation entrance. About one-half
mile south of this entrance you will see Orton Pond on your right, west and
southwest of the road. This is all private land and is heavily posted, so your
birding will be limited to the road shoulders. The light here is best in the early
morning, terrible in the afternoon.

To see this spot at its best, be here at dawn during the breeding season, from
about mid-April to June. If you get here early enough, you are sure to hear
Barred Owls and Chuck-will's-widows. A little later, the dawn chorus includes
Yellow-throated and Prothonotary warblers and Northern Parulas (and Acadian
Flycatchers from late April on). Great Blue Herons fly to and from the pond,
Wood Ducks dabble about the edges, and Ospreys exclaim their displeasure at
your presence.

The pond is a great place for seeing Wood Ducks at any season; they are most common during the winter months, when Ring-necked Ducks and a few other ducks may also be present. You can usually spot a few Common Moorhens along the pond's edges from autumn to spring; they are less frequent in summer.

Anhingas are rather reliable at this site from April to early October, but you may have to watch very patiently to spot one. They are easiest to find from midmorning on, when you might see them perched in the open, spreading their wings to dry. During low water levels, carefully check the stumps in the pond. Otherwise, check the tops of the lower trees around the pond. In mid- to late morning on clear days watch for soaring birds. One or two Anhingas sometimes overwinter here, especially during milder years.

Each year, from around September to spring, you can often see one or two adult Bald Eagles from the dam. Check for them in all the treetops.

In mid- to late morning on clear days year-round you can usually see several Turkey Vultures soaring above the pond, and a few Black Vultures and a Red-shouldered Hawk may join them.

Beyond Orton Pond, Plantation Road continues about a mile to the **Brunswick Town SHS**. The road runs through open woods of longleaf pines and oaks. Brown-headed Nuthatches live here throughout the year. Easy-to-find species in the nesting season include Chuck-will's-widow, Summer Tanager, and Blue Grosbeak.

In terms of birding, the Brunswick Town SHS is entertaining during the breeding season but is only mildly interesting at other times. Most of the species here can also be found easily along the roadside outside the site—something to keep in mind, because this site does not open early in the day.

Recently, much of the historic site has been cleared, so it is now a rather open, parklike setting of pines and oaks, and the birds here are quite easy to spot. However, this open setting can make for rather dull birding when it's windy or hot. Get here as early as you can in the morning. The historic site itself is actually rather small; plan to bird around the parking lot, along all the pathways through the site of the old town, and along the earthworks of the old fort.

This area is at its best from around mid-April (late April for some species) to June. From the pathways through the town site and along the earthworks of the old fort, you should easily find species like Eastern Wood-Pewee, Northern Parula, Yellow-throated Warbler, Blue Grosbeak, and Painted Bunting. The Blue Grosbeak and Painted Bunting sing into August. Look for the buntings next to the river. They sometimes sing from the oaks beside the fort's earthworks; from the path on the top of the earthworks you can get excellent, almost eye-level views.

Brown-headed Nuthatches are easy to find at any season. This open, parklike habitat is also good for woodpeckers: Pileateds are here year-round, and Red-headeds are frequent during the warmer months.

Summer Tanagers are easy to find around the parking lot and picnic area from mid-April to August, and they can often be found in September as well. If you miss them here, watch for them along the road to Russellborough, at the north end of the historic site.

Brunswick Town is less rewarding outside the breeding season. The open habitat offers good views of migrants during the autumn migration; unfortunately, few migrants travel along this side of the river. Calm mornings in winter can be quite enjoyable. This is a good area for finding Solitary Vireos and Orange-crowned Warblers among the flocks of chickadees, titmice, kinglets, and Yellow-rumped Warblers. You may even see a gnatcatcher, Black-and-white Warbler, or Yellow-throated Warbler.

From Brunswick Town SHS, return to **Orton Plantation**. Like Brunswick Town, this site is most interesting from mid- to late April into June. For the most enjoyable birding come right at opening time and avoid weekends during the peak flower period (in April).

People who birded this site in the 1970s and earlier generally find present-day Orton disappointing. The open marshes along the causeway into the gardens, which once hosted Anhingas, Least Bitterns, rails, and Purple Gallinules, are growing up into a rather birdless shrub swamp. And the old rice fields that were once managed for waterfowl have grown up in thick reeds and are also quite birdless, although there are tentative plans to restore them so that they will begin to attract waterfowl again.

You can still find a few rails along the causeway, and the gardens are quite good for land birds. Beginning birders will especially enjoy the gardens. Many of the birds here are quite tame, so you can get great leisurely looks at a wide range of species.

The beginning of the road into Orton Plantation is bordered by live oaks covered with Spanish moss. The causeway lies just ahead. Do not stop and bird the causeway before you have paid your ticket to the gardens—this makes the management angry. Go pay and then drive or walk back. Again, this formerly superlative birding site has deteriorated greatly. Nevertheless, a few King Rails persist and can be heard throughout the year. You might hear a Least Bittern here between April and August, but your chances of seeing one are slight. From autumn to spring the marshes also harbor a few Virginia Rails and Soras. Occasionally you might spot an Anhinga soaring overhead.

Beyond the causeway, the road curves right into the ticket office and then left into the gardens. Plan to walk all the trails through the gardens; the total distance is less than half a mile. (A map of the gardens is available from the ticket office.) Species that you should have little trouble seeing in the breeding season include Ruby-throated Hummingbird, Great Crested Flycatcher, Blue-gray Gnatcatcher, Northern Parula, Yellow-throated Warbler, Summer Tanager, Blue Grosbeak, Painted Bunting, and Orchard Oriole. The Blue Grosbeak and Painted Bunting are reliable from late April into August. If you have trouble finding the buntings, look especially at the north end of the gardens, near the colonial-period cemetery. The gardens almost always offer good close looks at Pileated Woodpeckers, as well as Red-bellieds and Downies. Red-headeds can usually be seen from April to October.

Be alert around any of the ponds. Anhingas are occasional, and a Purple Gallinule might show up in spring. You should at least see a few alligators.

In autumn migration the gardens are great for getting good looks at migrants. Again, though, relatively few migrants occur along this side of the river.

Return to Plantation Road and turn right, then turn right onto NC 133. Just ahead are the Liliput Creek Marshes, where you might see a King Rail, although highway traffic is always bad. The best times to look for the rails are at low tide or during the sort of extremely high tide that often occurs in September and October. The tide here lags about three hours after that on the oceanfront. At low tide look down the creek channel on both sides of the road, especially on the east side; you might see a bird lurking along the bank. During extreme high tides, birds can be forced up to the highway shoulders.

During much of the year you will want to stop your tour of the area at this point. However, from mid-April to June you should drive a few miles farther to check three swamp forest sites. These are on private land, so your birding will be limited to the road shoulders, but highway traffic is light at all three sites.

Continue north on NC 133 for 4.1 miles, then turn left onto Daws Creek Road. After 2.0 miles, bear right onto Lee Buck Road. After 1.0 miles this road crosses **Daws Creek**, a good spot for Acadian Flycatcher, Northern Parula, and Prothonotary and Hooded warblers. A Swainson's Warbler is also possible.

From here, continue to Governors Road and turn right. A short distance beyond the turn you will see a little bridge across **Rices Creek**. Swamp borders the road for almost half a mile in this area, and a very good variety of species can be found here. Species you should be able to find include Red-shouldered Hawk; Yellow-billed Cuckoo; Pileated Woodpecker; Acadian Flycatcher; Red-eyed, Yellow-throated, and White-eyed vireos; Northern Parulas; and Prothonotary, Hooded, and Swainson's warblers. Swainson's Warblers at this site probably sing regularly into July.

Turn around and drive back to the intersection with Daws Creek Road. The pine plantations along this section of Governors Road are good for both Chuck-will's-widows and Whip-poor-wills during the breeding season.

At Daws Creek Road, turn left. After 1.3 miles, beyond a pasture that may be almost covered with Cattle Egrets, you will see **Daws Creek**. The swamp here is rather scruffy, but the dense growth of cane here is a good place to find Swainson's Warblers.

From this site you can continue on Daws Creek Road to NC 133 or take Governors Road to NC 17.

For further information: For information about Brunswick Town SHS, contact Brunswick Town SHS, Route 1, Box 55, Winnabow, NC 28479; phone 910-371-6613. For information about Orton Plantation, contact Orton Plantation Gardens, Route 1, Winnabow, NC 28479; phone 910-371-6851.

SOUTHPORT AREA

The Southport area can be a lot of fun at any season. From the waterfront area and city pier you can always see a variety of water birds. You can look out over the river from your car, so this is a great place to check on a rainy or stormy day. From this vantage point you can see large numbers of wading birds flying to and from the nearby Battery Island heronry during the breeding season; you might also spot a Black-crowned or Yellow-crowned night-heron or maybe even a rarity. An entertaining variety of birds fly by during the migrations.

At the Southport city dock you can always find Clapper Rails. Black Vultures live in the Southport area year-round, and Summer Tanagers and Painted Buntings occur in the breeding season.

The Carolina Power and Light Company plant just outside Southport has a holding pond that attracts a variety of water birds. This pond, which you can visit only during business hours on weekdays, is sometimes almost filled with very tame and approachable wading birds; this is a great place for a beginning birder to learn the field marks of many of these birds. This pond also attracts gulls, terns, and a few ducks and shorebirds, and rarities no doubt appear regularly.

TO BEGIN THIS TOUR, take NC 211 into downtown Southport. One block from the water, where NC 211 turns to the left, continue straight ahead and turn left onto Bay Street. Here on the Southport waterfront you will see many parking spaces—some right next to the river—and the **Southport City Pier**. Birding here is always entertaining; often you can compile a long list without even moving. Because you can bird from your car, this is a great place to bird on a rainy or stormy day—especially a stormy one, which offers a good chance for a rarity.

On the lawns and parking areas there are always several Boat-tailed Grackles and gulls—mostly Laughings in the warmer months, Ring-billeds the rest of the year. From late autumn to early spring check the gulls for a rarity, like a Black-headed Gull. If you scope from the pier at low tide, you can usually see several oystercatchers on the oyster rocks off to the southwest. (The tide here lags about one hour after that on the oceanfront.)

Tide lines frequently form just offshore here; they attract numerous pelicans, gulls, and terns year-round. From autumn to spring they may also draw many Double-crested Cormorants. Nesting-season terns include Sandwich and Least. In winter look for Royals and Forster's. From midwinter to early spring you can often see many Bonaparte's Gulls.

In winter you should also see numerous Red-breasted Mergansers and a few Horned Grebes and Buffleheads on the water; also, watch for scaup and other ducks flying by. From around October to March an American White Pelican is a possibility.

This spot might be thought of as an inland cape, where the mainland shoreline changes from predominantly north-south to predominantly east-west. Primarily because the nearby barrier beaches both to the northeast and southwest are so low, many birds migrating through the region abandon their typical barrier beach routes and instead make a shortcut right by this inland cape. On good days you can tally a good variety of migrant water and land birds without walking a step. Typically you will see more birds in the early morning, although shorebird flights can also be good late in the day, when the light is better.

The shorebird migrations peak between mid-April and May and between mid-July and August. Whimbrels are frequent in both the spring and late summer flights. In May most of the sandpipers flying by are Semipalmateds; in late summer Westerns usually predominate.

In late winter watch for several migrating ducks—mostly scaup and Red-breasted Mergansers, but you should see a few other species as well. In April, around sunrise, watch for Common Loons, usually flying high.

On many August mornings you will see good numbers of swallows flying south, and you might see all the swallow species that occur in the state. After autumn cold fronts watch for hawks, including occasional Peregrine Falcons and Merlins.

So many birds pass by here that a rarity is always possible. In late spring you can hope for a Swallow-tailed or Mississippi kite. On a few occasions in summer, birders have seen frigatebirds soaring overhead.

About half a mile to the southeast, across the river, you will see a low shrub-covered island called **Battery Island**. Each year thousands of wading birds, mostly White Ibises, nest on the island, which is protected by the National Audubon Society. From April to August the dawn and sunset flights to and from the island can be spectacular, especially in late summer. Most of these birds fly past the Southport waterfront. These flights may give you views of every type of wading bird that nests in the state except for Great Blue Heron. You will see fewer birds during the rest of the day, although the daylight hours offer better light for picking out the less common species—Glossy Ibis and Black-crowned and Yellow-crowned night-herons. Watch carefully—a Roseate Spoonbill was a frequent visitor to the island one year, and Reddish Egrets may use the island for roosting on rare occasions in late summer.

From the waterfront, drive down Bay Street until it comes back out to NC 211 (Moore Street). Then turn right and continue to the **Southport–Fort Fisher ferry terminal**. In the breeding season listen for Summer Tanagers near the entrance to the terminal and Painted Buntings toward the water. Near the ferry dock you will see a salt marsh on your left. You can hear Clapper Rails here most of the time; at low tide watch for rails at openings in the marsh.

At the stop sign on your way out of the terminal, turn right onto the Moore Street extension (SR 1528). After 0.3 miles you will cross **Price Creek**. Here you can occasionally see roosting vultures, both Black and Turkey.

After 0.6 miles you will see Leonard Road to your left. From this point on, much of the remainder of SR 1528—as well as SR 1534 (Shepard Road), to the right—is bordered by shrubs and weedy patches. This is private land, so you can only bird from the roadside. After late autumn cold fronts and in winter you should see a good variety of sparrows and other small land birds. In the breeding season look for Painted Buntings. In mid- to late morning, especially in the warmer months, you might spot an Anhinga soaring overhead.

Take SR 1528 and NC 211 back into Southport. Before you get to where NC 211 turns right, look for the **Old Smithville Burying Ground** on your right. Covered with live oak trees, this site is worth walking through even when the birding is slow. It can be good for warblers after cold fronts in September and early October.

Where NC 211 turns right, turn left and return to Bay Street. Here, turn right and follow the waterfront along Bay Street, Yacht Basin Street, and Brunswick Street. After you turn left onto Brunswick Street, look for the **Southport City Dock**, a long L-shaped dock. (On the shore by this dock you will see a sign that says "Parking for Loading and Unloading between Yellow Lines Only.") You may not be able to park here; if not, drive on to the Southport Boat Harbor and walk back to this dock. From the city dock, at low tide you are almost certain to see one or more Clapper Rails feeding along the edge of the marsh. At dusk this is also a good spot for Black-crowned Night-Herons. To get back to NC 211 from the boat harbor parking lot, drive to the stop sign and turn right onto West Street.

During weekday business hours (8 A.M. to 4:30 P.M.), you can also check out the holding pond at the **Carolina Power and Light plant**. To get here, take NC 211 out of Southport, then turn right onto NC 87. Drive 1.1 miles, then turn right at the sign that says "Carolina Power and Light Brunswick Plant." After 1.0 miles you will come to a Yield sign. Here, turn right, drive to the administration building, and notify the plant's security personnel of your intention to visit the holding pond at the biology lab. From the administration building, return to the Yield sign; at this intersection, continue straight ahead and follow the main road around the plant, until there is once again a canal on your right and you see a sign that says "Bio Lab." Continue to the end of the road, where you will see the biology lab on your left. Remember to follow any instructions that you have been given, and please do not try to visit this pond at other times. In short, do not do anything that might jeopardize birders' future bird-watching privileges at this interesting site.

During most of the year you can see many different wading birds at close range here. The numbers of birds can be especially impressive during colder-than-normal weather in autumn and spring. In the winter months there are often several Hooded Mergansers, and during the migrations a few shorebirds are usually present. At all seasons you will see several gulls. Forster's Terns are common during the cooler months. Rarities and out-of-season birds no doubt occur at this site regularly. A Wood Stork once appeared in summer, and Black-necked Stilts have shown up in late March. This would be a good place to look for a rare gull, especially a Common Black-headed.

BALD HEAD ISLAND
MAP 37

This island has received little attention from birders, which is perhaps to be expected. It is relatively expensive to visit the island, especially if you rent a golf cart, which you will need to do if you plan to make a really thorough tour (the island is 3 miles long). You get to the island by ferry; the first run of the day doesn't arrive until after 8:30 A.M. Actually, during most of the year you will not see much variety in the birdlife. Even when the island is most interesting, it is overshadowed by nearby areas. For instance, the island can be very good for land bird migrants in autumn, but it is not nearly as good as nearby Fort Fisher, where you can arrive at dawn.

Nevertheless, this island does have some strong points that can make for at least a pleasant (and sometimes an exciting) day of birding. The ferry ride alone can be a rewarding experience: the ferry route goes right by the state's largest heronry, where you can see most of the wading birds that occur in North Carolina. Again, the island can be very good for land bird migrants, and fortunately, the northwest end of the island—the end near the ferry terminal—is best.

Cape Fear and the waters off the cape can be quite good. During the cooler months this is a good spot for seeing birds like Northern Gannets and scoters; jaegers are seen with some regularity too. The island's wooded areas can be quite entertaining on calm, clear winter days. Among the myriad Yellow-rumped Warblers you are likely to find Orange-crowned Warblers and Solitary Vireos, some half-hardy species, and maybe a bona fide rarity.

Painted Buntings are common summer residents in the shrub thickets and along the borders of the maritime forest. A few Wilson's Plovers occur during the warmer months, although they may become more difficult to find in future years.

Your perspective on Bald Head's birding rewards is likely to be very different if you're vacationing on the island (and thus can be birding at dawn) and have access to a golf cart. Rental cottages are available.

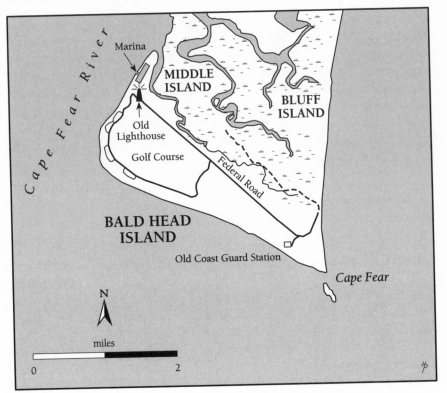

37. BALD HEAD ISLAND

Even when the birding is slow, this site is worth visiting. Cape Fear is North Carolina's southernmost point of land, and Bald Head Island is a bit unlike anywhere else in the state. Cabbage palmettos are common—this is their northern limit—and you're likely to feel like you're in South Carolina rather than North Carolina. Yet, standing at the tip of Cape Fear during the cooler months, you can't help but experience some of the wildness typical of the barrier islands farther north.

The island also features a scenic old lighthouse called Old Baldy—the state's oldest standing lighthouse. Near the southeast end of the island there is a state-owned maritime forest preserve, which is to be left in its natural state. This tract can be viewed from Federal Road, which runs the length of the island. This maritime forest is noteworthy for its cabbage palmettos and its abundance of broadleaf evergreen vegetation. Such vegetation is dominant in all maritime forests from Cape Hatteras south, but especially in this forest. The abundance of Carolina laurel-cherry (usually called "cherry-laurel") is also noteworthy.

Walking about on this island, especially in the forest, can be hot, boring, and buggy in the summer. If you're more interested in just seeing the area than in looking for any particular species, you would probably most enjoy a visit between November and April on a clear day with light wind.

LOGISTICS. Except for the state-owned maritime forest area, Bald Head Island is a privately owned island, but anyone may ride over on the ferry and walk the beaches and various roadways. The ferry to the island (which is only a passenger ferry) leaves from Indigo Plantation at Southport—watch for signs as you drive in to Southport on NC 211. The ferry runs hourly; the first run leaves Southport at 8 A.M. and the last leaves Bald Head at 7 P.M. The ferry crossing takes about thirty minutes, and the round-trip cost is $15. No automobiles are allowed on the island. You can rent a golf cart for $30 a day. You may want to bring a bicycle over; it costs $10 to transport a bicycle on the ferry.

THIS TOUR BEGINS at the ferry terminal on the mainland. The first part of the ferry run is along the Intracoastal Waterway—most interesting at low tide, when you should see a few wading birds and oystercatchers at all seasons.

When you reach the Cape Fear River, the ferry will turn toward the right. After this turn look for **Battery Island**, a shrub-covered island on your left. This island is almost covered with nesting herons, egrets, and ibises during the nesting season. White Ibises are common, and if you're lucky, you might see a Glossy Ibis or a Black-crowned or Yellow-crowned night-heron fly by. Some years a Bald Eagle (always an immature) shows up on the island, harassing the wading birds and being harassed by Red-winged Blackbirds, Boat-tailed Grackles, and Fish Crows. If you return on the last ferry of the day in July or August, you should witness a spectacle—vast numbers of waders flying to the island to roost.

South of the island you should see an exposed shoal at low tide. This shoal often hosts several shorebirds. During the cooler months look for a few Marbled Godwits.

The mouth of the Cape Fear is wide, and you will feel like you're in the ocean before you reach Bald Head. If there are tide lines, you may see many gulls (including Bonaparte's Gulls in winter and early spring) and terns. Be alert in this area—jaegers have sometimes entered the inlet in spring, and frigatebirds have been seen soaring overhead here in late spring and summer.

As you approach Bald Head, watch for a sand spit just north of the marina. If there are many birds here, you may want to walk down to it after you arrive on the island. It is a favored loafing site for gulls, terns, and shorebirds, especially at high tide. In the marshes next to the marina you will always see a few wading birds. Clapper Rails are common. Watch for them along the marsh edges at full high tide.

Bald Head Island can be very good for land bird migrants after autumn cold fronts. September and early October (until around October 10) offer the best potential for a good variety; unfortunately, though, strong fronts are rare during this period. They are more likely in mid- to late October, and good numbers of migrants can still be seen then, although there is little overall variety, especially of warblers. However, these late fronts are good for sparrows and for over-wintering species like kinglets, and for a possible Western Kingbird. Try to visit after fronts with northwest or north winds; northeast winds can be very unproductive.

Fortunately, the island's best site for migrants is the area of scattered shrubs and trees around the lighthouse, just a few hundred yards from the marina. Especially during northwest winds, large numbers of birds may pile up here, hesitant to cross the Cape Fear. If you come over on the first ferry of the day, you can be birding here by 9 A.M.—not the crack of dawn, but still early enough for rewarding birding. Sometimes pile-ups don't develop until a couple of hours after dawn anyway.

If you are fortunate enough to be here during a good wave of autumn migrants, patiently check all the little niches around the lighthouse and chapel, as well as the corner of the golf course. Often the isolated trees at the lighthouse provide the best views of warblers. Stand a little distance away and wait for birds to occasionally pop into the open. The edge of the golf course would probably be a good spot to check for a Western Kingbird around mid-October.

The golf course ponds usually have few birds but could always attract something interesting, especially during the migrations. From autumn to spring look for a few coots and moorhens.

Only a few land birds nest on Bald Head, but one nesting species is the Painted Bunting. Listen for these birds from mid-April to around early August. You might find them at the lighthouse, in shrub thickets, and along the maritime forest anywhere on the island.

From here on, this description assumes that you have a golf cart or bicycle or that you're prepared for a long hike. Fortunately, Federal Road, which runs the length of the island, is easy to walk.

As you proceed down Federal Road from the lighthouse, you will first pass through areas of maritime forest where roads are being introduced and houses built. This edge effect makes for good birding (although not as good as at the island's northwest end) after autumn cold fronts and in winter, especially on clear, calm winter mornings. In addition to the Yellow-rumped Warblers, which may be almost everywhere, you should have no trouble finding several Orange-crowned Warblers and at least a few Solitary Vireos. You should also find one or more half-hardy species, like Blue-gray Gnatcatcher, White-eyed Vireo, and Black-and-white Warbler. In this semitropical-looking setting, you might even hope for something more unusual.

About a mile and a half down Federal Road, you will see the maritime forest preserve. The roadside here can be good for wintertime birding, but the forest itself is much more interesting botanically than ornithologically. By the way, much of the forest's canopy was destroyed by a hurricane in 1984.

Near the east end of the island, to your right, you will see a road to an old coast guard station called Captain Charlie's. Wilson's Plovers nest along the edges of the dunes here. From Captain Charlie's you can walk along the ocean beach to the **point of Cape Fear**, almost half a mile away.

During much of the year this is the most interesting site on the island. Get here as early in the morning as you can; late afternoon can also be good.

Like all capes, this one is constantly changing. Sometimes the beach lies close to the dunes, but often there is a distinct barren point projecting at least a couple of hundred yards. There may be tide pools at the base of this point. Frequently one or more shoals develop just off the point, and sometimes these shoals are close enough that terns and gulls resting on them can be seen well.

The point attracts a good variety of gulls and/or terns during most of the year. It is especially good for terns when there are shoals and a well-defined point. Royal Terns are common throughout the year. Look for Sandwich Terns from late March until early or mid-December. As at the other capes, a few Common Terns may linger here well into autumn. This is the sort of place where Roseate Terns sometimes make appearances; there is a mid-July record for this site. During the cooler months look for a Lesser Black-backed Gull. Any tide pools in the area can attract a few shorebirds.

Ocean birding is most entertaining at this site during the cooler months, especially from around late October to mid-November and late February to early April. During these periods migrating scoters are especially likely to come close by the point; they may occasionally fly nearby throughout the winter. From late October to mid-April Northern Gannets often feed just off the point.

During the migration periods Pomarine and Parasitic jaegers occasionally fly by the point, and they have even been sighted in midwinter. This would be a good site for a kittiwake around late November. Around late July look for an Audubon's Shearwater.

The beaches from here north can be fairly good for migrating hawks in autumn. Around late September and early October you are likely to see one or more Peregrine Falcons.

For further information: For ferry reservations and further information, call Bald Head Island Management, Inc., at 800-443-6305.

CASWELL BEACH TO LONG BEACH

Despite the area's dense development, a drive along this section of barrier beach—often called Oak Island—can be entertaining at any season. A visit here is often most enjoyable from autumn to spring, when parking is more readily available and you can also drive through the Fort Caswell retreat/camp.

Ocean birding along much of the island can be good for loons, Horned Grebes, and Northern Gannets in winter. The island's eastern end, especially the

Yaupon Beach Fishing Pier, can be good in late winter and early spring for northbound water birds; also, the outfall of cooling water from the nuclear plant at Southport lies one-half mile from the shore here. This outfall often attracts good numbers of gulls and terns, although the distance make these birds difficult to see well.

On weekdays from September to May you can drive the main road through the Fort Caswell camp. This road ends at the mouth of the Cape Fear River, where large numbers of birds often feed over the tide lines.

A fresh-water marsh beside the ocean at Long Beach has several Common Moorhens each winter. There are often a few ducks here then, and a few Virginia Rails and Soras are resident during the cooler months.

At the west end of the island is Lockwoods Folly Inlet, where you can usually find several species of shorebirds during the migrations and in winter. This is a good place to find Wilson's Plovers from April to early September, and Piping Plovers show up regularly during the migrations. Clapper Rails live here year-round, and Seaside and Sharp-tailed sparrows are easy to find from autumn to spring.

THE TOUR STARTS at the end of NC 133 in Yaupon Beach. Here, at the stop-light, continue straight onto Caswell Beach Road (SR 1100). Follow this road about 3 miles, until the state road ends.

The land beyond this point is the **Fort Caswell** retreat/summer camp, owned by the North Carolina Baptist Assembly. From Memorial Day to Labor Day this site is closed to visitors, but during the rest of the year you can drive along the main road during business hours on weekdays (8 A.M. to 4:30 P.M.). From Monday through Thursday, for a $2 fee (to cover insurance), you can also walk over to the remnants of the old fort or walk out on the fishing pier at the inlet.

A drive along the main road, which is almost a mile long, can be worthwhile at any season. Just after you enter the retreat, check the lawns along the road-side for shorebirds at high tide, especially during stormy and rainy weather. (The tide here lags about an hour after that on the oceanfront.) After autumn northeasters this would be a good spot to check for a golden-plover. Most of the retreat consists of lawns with scattered trees—good habitat for stray Western Kingbirds in autumn. Because the retreat is at the island's east end, it would also be a likely spot for a Gray Kingbird to show up around late May.

The road passes salt marshes and a tidal bay. During the warmer months you should see several wading birds. White Ibises are always present; in September look for one or two Yellow-crowned Night-Herons. In spring listen for the reedy song of a Marsh Wren. At low tide, along the margins of the tidal bay, you might spot a Clapper Rail year-round; shorebirds may also appear at low tide, espe-cially during the migrations.

The end of the road overlooks the mouth of the Cape Fear River. Well-defined tide lines occur commonly here, attracting numerous pelicans, gulls, and terns throughout the year. Look for Royal Terns at any season; from early April to late November you can usually see Sandwich Terns as well. This could be a very good spot to check during a fierce southwest wind, when you might spot something of interest just off this lee shore.

At any season you will want to check the ocean at the **public beach access** on Caswell Beach Road, 1.5 miles west of the entrance into Fort Caswell. On calm days you will probably be able to discern, about one-half mile offshore, an area of slightly turbulent water. This turbulence marks the outfall for water used to cool the nuclear power plant at Southport. You may see many gulls and terns feeding in this area year-round. It is unfortunate that the outfall is so distant, because it probably attracts rarities regularly. Species that might be expected to occur here in winter include Black-legged Kittiwake and Little and Black-headed gulls. During the migrations, the flocks of feeding gulls and terns no doubt attract jaegers regularly. The best light for checking this area occurs around sunrise.

During times when few people are here—in winter, and at sunrise in spring and autumn—there is often a flock of gulls and terns on the beach, and you can sort through these birds from the dune walkover. In winter look for Royal and Forster's terns and Bonaparte's Gulls. You might even spot one of the rarer gulls. From early April to late November this can be a good place to get good looks at Sandwich Terns.

About a mile farther west on Caswell Beach Road you will see the entrance to the **Oak Island Golf Club**. During the autumn migration you can either ask for permission to walk the borders of the fairways or walk the streets that border the golf course. The shrub margins can be good for passerine migrants after autumn cold fronts. From late April to early August this is a good area for Painted Buntings.

Return to the stoplight at the end of NC 133 and turn left onto Yaupon Drive (SR 1104). Then turn left onto McGlamery Street and continue to Ocean Drive, which runs along the oceanfront. You will see access to the ocean at many of the side streets off Ocean Drive. Parking is limited but adequate during the better birding period, autumn to spring.

The **Yaupon Beach Fishing Pier** is located on Ocean Drive. This pier is open at least from late March to early December, and you can often walk out on it in midwinter. Lying just a few miles west of Cape Fear, this is a good spot to set up watch from late winter into spring, when many water birds are northbound. Watch for migrating loons, grebes, gannets, cormorants, scoters, mergansers, gulls, and terns. In April and May watch for an occasional jaeger, especially after northeast and east winds. Some years, you might spot a Sooty Shearwater or Wilson's Storm-Petrel around late May.

At the west end of Ocean Drive, turn right onto Seventy-ninth Street and return to SR 1004 (this section is named Oak Island Drive), and turn left. At Sixty-fourth Street, turn left and continue toward the ocean. You will see a fresh-water marsh, with an open pond on the left. (You can check other sections of this marsh from other side streets to the east and west.) This marsh is constantly changing. It gets narrower almost every year due to overwash from the beach. Real estate development is also encroaching upon it; yet it is still interesting. From autumn to spring there are always numerous American Coots and Common Moorhens. Occasionally you can find one or two moorhens in summer. From autumn to spring, if water levels are not too high and you watch the marsh edges patiently enough, you might see a Sora or Virginia Rail. Especially in the warmer months, look for a few wading birds. In winter a few dabbling ducks and Ring-necked Ducks are often at the pond, and other diving ducks are possible. On average the pond is most interesting in late winter, from February to March, because northbound birds are more likely to spot it. Given its location right next to the ocean, this site has some potential for rarities during severe weather.

Return to Oak Island Drive and turn left. At Fifty-eighth Street, turn left and continue to Beach Drive—the oceanfront street—and turn right. Drive to Nineteenth Place, turn right, and continue to the end. Here you will see a boardwalk that crosses a salt marsh and a canal. At low tide (which lags about an hour after that on the oceanfront) you might be able to spot a Clapper Rail here year-round by patiently watching a marsh opening or the edge of the canal. During the migrations a Virginia Rail or Sora would also be possible. This spot could also attract passerine migrants after cold fronts in autumn. From late April to early August listen for Painted Buntings. If you miss them here, take an early morning drive along nearby streets that border shrub thickets, watching for buntings in the tops of shrubs or on power lines.

Farther west on Beach Drive, you will see the **Ocean Crest Fishing Pier** and the **Long Beach Fishing Pier**. The Long Beach pier claims to be—and looks like—the longest fishing pier in North Carolina. Both piers have shelters at the end and are often open all winter, offering great observation points for loons, Horned Grebes, Northern Gannets, and occasional flocks of scoters.

Continue west on Beach Drive. Near the end of the island, 1.7 miles past the Long Beach pier, bear right onto Kings Lynn Road (SR 1828), which ends right next to the estuary near **Lockwoods Folly Inlet**. This spot can be crowded during the warmer months, so you should check it first thing in the morning, preferably on a weekday. During uncrowded periods you can often see several birds from your car, so this can be a good spot to check on a rainy or stormy day.

From the end of Kings Lynn Road, at low or middle tide, watch for a Clapper Rail along the edges of the marshy patch just across the tidal creek. Just back up the road, where the marshes meet high ground, look for Seaside and Sharp-tailed sparrows at high tide from autumn to spring.

Between the end of the road and the ocean you will see a large open sand and shell area—a dredged material disposal site. In late spring and early summer a few American Oystercatchers and Wilson's Plovers nest here. (In late summer you are more likely to see Wilson's Plovers along the shore of the estuary.) Do not disturb nesting birds—watch them from the edge of the area for a brief time, then move away. Least Terns and Black Skimmers also nest here some years. All of these ground-nesting species may decline in the future: the spoil material that provided a short-term bonanza may lead to a long-term bust, because extensive dunes will probably form as a result of the spoil deposition. This open habitat may sometimes attract Snow Buntings or longspurs in late autumn and winter.

The sand and mud flats between the road end and the inlet are best checked during a rising tide. During the warmer months watch for a few wading birds. A Reddish Egret is a possibility in late summer. During the migrations and in winter look for shorebirds, including Black-bellied and Semipalmated plovers, Greater Yellowlegs, Willet, Western Sandpiper, Dunlin, and Short-billed Dowitcher. During the migrations this is a good area for Whimbrels. A few Marbled Godwits sometimes occur during the cooler months. A Long-billed Curlew is possible in late summer or autumn. During the migrations—from August to September and from March to early April—you can often find one or two Piping Plovers; these birds sometimes overwinter.

At any season you should see several gulls and terns around the inlet. During the cooler months look for a Lesser Black-backed Gull. Look for Sandwich Terns from April to November, especially during the migrations. Black Skimmers often congregate in autumn. In winter look for Forster's, Royal, and Caspian terns.

For further information: For information about the North Carolina Baptist Assembly retreat at Fort Caswell, contact North Carolina Baptist Assembly, Oak Island, NC 28465; phone 910-278-9501.

GREEN SWAMP AREA
MAP 38

Most people who take the public roads through the area called Green Swamp may wonder why they didn't see any "swamps." Most of the wetland habitats in this area are not what the average person thinks of as swampland. In addition, most of these wetlands have been converted to pine plantations, which will probably form the casual visitor's dominant impression of the area.

The original Green Swamp covered a vast area—about 200,000 acres. Most of

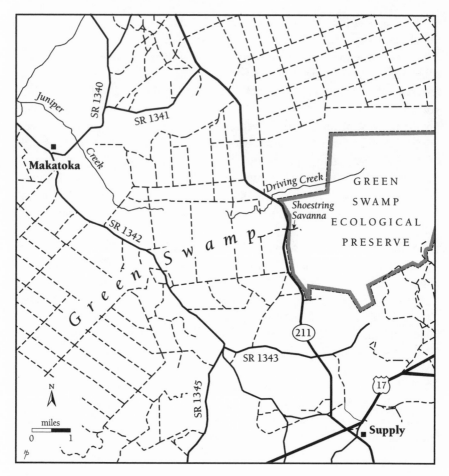

38. GREEN SWAMP AREA

this area has been or is being converted to pine plantations. Fortunately, the Nature Conservancy has acquired about 16,000 acres; this tract, called the Green Swamp Ecological Preserve, lies mostly on the east side of NC 211 and protects pocosins, pine savannas, Atlantic white cedar forests, and bay forests.

This area harbors a good variety of permanent resident and summer resident species, including several frequently sought-after birds. A few Red-cockaded Woodpeckers live at some of the savanna sites. Bachman's Sparrows are easy to find in the breeding season, and a few certainly overwinter, although they can be very difficult to find then. The Green Swamp area is one of the state's best locations for Swainson's Warblers.

Brown-headed Nuthatches and Pine Warblers are easy to find in the pine savannas throughout the year, and in the breeding season both Chuck-will's-widows and Whip-poor-wills are easy to hear along the roads at night. Some other permanent and summer resident species in this area include Black Vulture, Barred Owl, Red-headed and Hairy woodpeckers, Acadian Flycatcher, Yellow-throated Vireo, Summer Tanager, Blue Grosbeak, and Black-throated Green, Yellow-throated, Prothonotary, and Worm-eating warblers. All of the warbler species that breed in coastal North Carolina have been found in the Green Swamp area. This is the southernmost area along the Atlantic coast where nesting Worm-eating Warblers occur in large numbers. Just to the south, in coastal South Carolina, the geology and plant communities change abruptly, and as a result there are very few Worm-eatings there.

One of the area's specialties, the Henslow's Sparrow, occurs primarily in man-made habitat—in young pine plantations. They are found only in the youngest plantations, when the vegetation is primarily herbaceous. After the pines grow a few feet tall, the birds abandon the site. These birds apparently occur primarily in the breeding season, or at least they are easier to find then, when they are uttering their pathetic attempts at song. In winter they also occur to some extent in natural pine savannas, but they are very difficult to find then. In this county—the southernmost in the state—Bachman's Sparrows seem to have less narrow habitat requirements than they do farther north. Birders can not only find them in the natural pine savannas but can also hear them in the open pine plantations.

Birding aside, this area is interesting because it contains several exemplary plant communities. The most interesting of these is the pine savanna. The Green Swamp has some of the highest-quality wet pine savannas in the Southeast. These open pine lands may appear to lack diversity, but that is definitely not true. Some Green Swamp sites contain as much diversity of ground flora as any place in North America. Several species of orchids and insectivorous plants grow here.

LOGISTICS. Unfortunately, most of this interesting area is off-limits or inaccessible. The Nature Conservancy land is not a public park; the savanna habitats are quite fragile, so most are off-limits to the general public. However, a mile-long trail across the Shoestring Savanna is open to the public, and Red-cockaded Woodpeckers, Bachman's Sparrows, and other species typical of open pine habitats occur there. Other savanna sites lie next to NC 211, and roadside birding can be pretty good at these areas, although the highway traffic is irritating. Most land in the area is private forestry land. Some of this private land is posted, some is not. Even on unposted lands, it is probably best not to walk more than a few feet away from the road. Deer hunting is very popular in the Green Swamp, and from mid-October to January 1 you would do well to visit here only on Sundays. The Nature Conservancy land is also open to hunting.

Only a tiny fraction of the Green Swamp area can even be seen from public roadways, but many private logging roads crisscross the area. Most of these currently are open to the public; however, most of these roads are terrible during the cooler months or after rainy weather. A four-wheel-drive vehicle is the best way to explore them, although during dry weather you may consider driving in for short distances in a regular car, especially if you're searching for Henslow's Sparrows. (The numerous private logging roads are shown in the *North Carolina Atlas and Gazetteer* as well as on map 38.)

However, you can see a good variety of habitats and most of the area's birdlife along the 25-mile tour described below. This tour follows public roads—NC 211 bordering the Nature Conservancy property (including the Shoestring Savanna trail), SR 1343, SR 1342, SR 1340, and SR 1341. The last three of these roads are unpaved and usually have little traffic. SR 1342 can be rather messy during rainy weather but is always passable.

The most interesting time to go birding in this area is during the breeding season, from mid-April (late April for some species) to June. This environment gets quite hot on most days from late spring through summer. For good birding, it is important to be here very early in the morning.

UNLESS OTHERWISE INDICATED, the descriptions below refer to the breeding season.

This tour starts at the bridge over Driving Creek (sometimes incorrectly called Juniper Creek) on NC 211, at the northwest corner of the Nature Conservancy property. The bridge is 6.6 miles north of the NC 211/US 17 intersection and 4.2 miles south of the SR 1341/NC 211 junction.

Species you should hear at the bridge include White-eyed Vireo and Hooded, Black-throated Green, and Swainson's warblers. This is a very good site for Swainson's Warblers; you can usually find one or two here. In the Green Swamp area these birds begin to sing about April 15; they sing reliably until early July and are sometimes heard as late as early August. Black-throated Green Warblers arrive in late March; they sing most readily in early April. By early June you'll hear their song only occasionally.

At Driving Creek, set your odometer to zero and head south toward Supply. In the early morning you will want to stop several times between 0.2 and 2.8 miles to check the open pine habitats of the Nature Conservancy lands. Concentrate on the more open areas between 0.2 and 1.7 miles. From around mid-April through July you are certain to hear several Bachman's Sparrows. They may sing as early as late February, but this early in the season their singing is more sporadic, usually spurred by abnormally warm weather.

At any season you should have little trouble finding Brown-headed Nuthatches, Eastern Bluebirds, and Pine Warblers. Listen for Red-cockaded Woodpeckers, especially at 1.2 miles. In the breeding season listen for Eastern Wood-Pewees, Eastern Kingbirds, Yellow-throated and Prairie warblers, and Summer Tanagers. The towhees here are probably the "whitest-eyed" of any in North Carolina. These Nature Conservancy lands will certainly become even more interesting in the future, as areas are burned over more frequently and pine plantations are reconverted to pine savannas.

In the breeding season you should walk at least the first half of the mile-long trail across **Shoestring Savanna**, part of the Nature Conservancy land. As you drive south, this site is on your left, 0.8 miles from the Driving Creek bridge. Look for a pulloff just past a borrow-pit pond. Pull in here and walk along the main trail beside the pond.

At the fork near the end of the pond, bear right onto the main trail. For the next few hundred yards the trail passes through pine plantations. When you reach a wet shrub area, look carefully—the trail is easy to lose here. Look for a small boardwalk across the wet area; the boardwalk and trail may be almost hidden from view by the thick shrub growth.

Beyond this point the trail crosses two more drains (without boardwalks) and three areas of savanna before gradually tapering down to nothing. The first savanna is the largest and best for birding. Look for a few Red-cockaded Wood-pecker cavity trees. The birds are easiest to find in May and June, when they are nesting, but you can usually find them at other seasons as well.

In the breeding season listen for a few Bachman's Sparrows. Listen for one or two Red-headed and Hairy woodpeckers too. In the wet shrubby areas that border the savannas, listen for White-eyed Vireo, Common Yellowthroat, and Prairie, Hooded, and Prothonotary warblers. Worm-eating and Swainson's warblers are also possible.

On clear winter mornings when winds are light, this trail can offer a lot of variety, with none of the heat, humidity, and insects that you must put up with in summer. Look for little bands that include kinglets, Brown-headed Nuthatches, bluebirds, Pine Warblers, and a few Red-cockaded Woodpeckers. Inspect any birds that flush from the ground cover—you're most likely to see House Wrens and Swamp Sparrows, but a Bachman's or Henslow's sparrow is also possible. Ruby-crowned Kinglets, Hermit Thrushes, and Gray Catbirds are common in the wet shrub areas. Solitary Vireos are easy to find, and on a warm day you might hear the song of a White-eyed Vireo.

At 4.4 miles south of the Driving Creek bridge, turn right onto Little Macedonia Road (SR 1343). In late autumn and winter watch for possible Vesper Sparrows in the fields along this road.

At the end of Little Macedonia Road, turn right onto Makatoka Road (SR 1342) and set your odometer to zero. Virtually all of the land beside this road is sylvicultural land. Mostly you will see young pine plantations, with an occasional clear-cut. At clear-cut areas listen for Blue Grosbeaks and watch for bobwhites running across the roads. Clear-cuts are good spots for checking the sky. In mid- to late morning watch for Turkey and Black vultures and Red-shouldered and Red-tailed hawks. At any really large and wet clear-cut, listen for Henslow's Sparrows. You will see several logging roads cutting off from the

Makatoka Road. If these roads are not posted, you might want to explore them a little ways—especially if you have a four-wheel-drive vehicle—to look for large clear-cuts and listen for Henslow's Sparrows.

Many of the pine plantations are quite boring, but the older plantations with thick undergrowths of broadleaf evergreen vegetation, harbor many of the same birds that are found in the area's natural pocosins and bay forests. Worm-eating Warblers are easy to find, and you might hear a few Ovenbirds and Black-and-white Warblers.

At 4.5 miles down the Makatoka Road you will come to a bridge over **Muddy Branch**. You will want to park here and walk a few hundred yards along the road past the bridge, and a few hundred yards down the logging road you just passed to the right, if it is not posted. This is a good place to hear a Barred Owl. From the state road, look and listen for Pileated Woodpeckers, Acadian Flycatchers, Northern Parulas, Red-eyed and Yellow-throated vireos, and Prothonotary, Hooded, and Black-throated Green warblers. Walking down the logging road will increase your chances of hearing a Swainson's Warbler, and you might hear a Worm-eating here as well.

By driving Makatoka Road and other nearby roads before dawn you can find several nocturnal species—Great Horned Owl, Barred Owl, Eastern Screech-Owl, Chuck-will's-widow, and Whip-poor-will. In this area the two goatsuckers begin calling around early April. The number of Whip-poor-wills here has increased dramatically in recent years; at most sites they now greatly outnumber the Chucks. You are more likely to hear Chuck-will's-widows in the more natural habitat on Nature Conservancy land along NC 211, but traffic noise is quite bothersome there.

By the way, both Bachman's and Henslow's sparrows are known to sing at night, at least occasionally, during a full moon. A calm night could be a good time to listen for the weak song of a Henslow's; highway traffic would be light then.

At the end of the Makatoka Road, at the community of Makatoka, turn right onto Camp Branch Road (SR 1340) and reset your odometer to zero. At 0.8 miles you will come to the bridge across scenic **Juniper Creek**. Park here and walk the road for a few hundred yards past the bridge.

Occasionally you might see Wood Ducks flying by. This is another good spot for Yellow-billed Cuckoo, Acadian Flycatcher, Northern Parula, Prothonotary Warbler, and Red-eyed and Yellow-throated vireos. You will usually hear a Swainson's Warbler as well.

At 2.0 miles—just before Egypt Road, to your right—you will see a small drain. Check here for Acadian Flycatcher and Black-throated Green and Swainson's warblers. Turn onto Egypt Road (SR 1341), which will take you back to NC 211. When you get to 211, turn right. After 1 mile you will see a bridge—another good spot for Prothonotary, Black-throated Green, and Swainson's warblers.

You will often find some of the best habitat for breeding Henslow's Sparrows along several miles of NC 211, from the Driving Creek bridge north. Look for especially large clear-cuts and for pine plantations in which the trees are no more than a few feet high. If you see unposted logging roads off 211 you may want to explore them a little ways. Clear-cut spots with especially thick grass cover can be good for wintering Henslow's Sparrows. Again, though, you should not walk in more than a few feet from the roads, and you should stay out of the area entirely during the deer hunting season.

For further information: For information about the Green Swamp Ecological Preserve, contact Nature Conservancy—North Carolina Chapter, Carr Mill Mall, Suite D-12, Carrboro, NC 27510; phone 919-967-7007.

HOLDEN BEACH

Unfortunately, the most interesting spot on this island is quite difficult to get to, requiring a round-trip hike of about 5 miles. The flats beside Shallotte Inlet, at the island's western end, can be good for a variety of shorebirds during the migrations and in winter. Wilson's and Piping plovers nest here, and Piping Plovers stay here throughout the year.

A much more easily accessible spot is the eastern end of the island, where you can find a few gulls, terns, and shorebirds. The nearby shrub thickets have Painted Buntings during the breeding season.

The Holden Beach Fishing Pier can be good for ocean birding in winter and spring, especially in late winter and early spring, when many birds are north-bound. The island also features three open marsh areas where a few gulls, terns, and shorebirds may congregate during high tides and stormy weather. You can also see rails and marsh sparrows here during extremely high tides in autumn.

Holden Beach is a very quiet, family-oriented beach that is seldom crowded. However, there is little parking for the general public. During the summer it is best to avoid weekends and to get here at dawn.

AFTER YOU TAKE the NC 130 bridge across the Intracoastal Waterway onto the island, turn left on Ocean Boulevard. After 0.9 miles, at Avenue A, you will see the first of several public beach accessways, each with a few parking spaces. There is also limited parking at the end of the road, next to **Lockwoods Folly Inlet**. This shore of the inlet, which is rapidly eroding, is typically not very interesting, but you can always find a few gulls, terns, and shorebirds. Try to visit this site at low or middle tides; at high tide there is usually no beach to walk along.

At low tide there are usually exposed shoals in the inlet, and these are often covered with gulls and terns, especially Royal Terns. You may see a few Least Terns around the inlet in spring and summer, and Sandwich Terns during the migrations. Never expect to see more than a few shorebirds along this eroding shoreline; the migrations are your best bet.

Beside the inlet you will see shrub thickets, which host Gray Catbirds, Northern Cardinals, and Rufous-sided Towhees year-round. In the breeding season listen for White-eyed Vireos and Prairie Warblers and one or two Painted Buntings. If the inlet has created any steep sand banks by cutting into the dunes, check these banks for Northern Rough-winged Swallows and their nesting burrows from April to June.

Turn around and head west on Ocean Boulevard. When you get to the end of the NC 130 bridge, set your odometer to zero. At 1.6 miles you will see the **Holden Beach Fishing Pier** on your left. This has a rain/wind shelter at its end. It is usually open as early as March and as late as December, and you can sometimes walk out on it in midwinter. It can be a good place to watch for Horned Grebes, gannets, both loons, and occasional flocks of scoters. This east-west coastline is most entertaining from late winter into spring, when birds are northbound. On early mornings from late February to mid-April—especially calm mornings ahead of cold fronts—you can see a variety of migrants stream by.

Farther west along Ocean Boulevard, on the right, you will notice three distinctive open areas. From the bridge, these areas are located at 1.8 to 2.1 miles; 2.3 to 3.6 miles; and 4.0 to 4.3 miles. These marshy areas, which receive limited tidal exchange, contain a few patches of barren flats, larger areas of sparsely vegetated flats, and some thicker marsh vegetation. These areas are flooded only by the highest tides. You cannot park along Ocean Boulevard, but you can park along the side roads that border these marshy areas. Park on the side of the road that does not have any cottages; pull over as far as you can, but don't get stuck.

These open marsh areas are usually almost birdless, but they can be interesting at times. Gulls and terns sometimes flock here during stormy weather and high tides. In late summer look for a few Black Terns. These areas are always good feeding habitat for Gull-billed Terns; watch for them from April until August.

During stormy weather and high tides look for a few shorebirds, especially during the migrations. Almost all shorebirds here will be typical intertidal species—e.g., Black-bellied and Semipalmated plovers, Willet, Whimbrel, Western Sandpiper, and Short-billed Dowitcher—that have been forced here by higher than usual tides. However, this habitat might also attract some of the rarer species, especially after rainy weather. Buff-breasted Sandpipers may sometimes turn up here in August and September; after intense northeasters in autumn these areas might attract a golden-plover.

Much of the marsh vegetation is rather sparse, so these areas can be good places to see rails and marsh sparrows during extremely high tides in autumn.

(The tide here lags one to two hours after that on the oceanfront.) There are several slightly elevated spots within the marshes. When water floods everything except these spots, you have an excellent opportunity to see Clapper Rails and Sharp-tailed and Seaside sparrows, and maybe a Virginia Rail or Sora, or perhaps something even more unusual.

The flats at the island's western end, next to **Shallotte Inlet**, can be good for shorebirds most of the year. Wilson's Plovers are easy to find during the nesting season, and one or two pairs of Piping Plovers have nested here in recent years. However, you'll have to hike about 2.5 miles (one-way) to get to this site, as the western end of the island (except the beach) is closed to the public.

Perhaps its relative inaccessibility is one reason that this site has nesting Wilson's and Piping plovers (although the presence of prime nesting habitat is probably more important). The beach here certainly has its share of people during the nesting season, though, and on weekends dozens of people may come here by boat; so I decided that including the area in this book would not attract enough additional visitors to disturb the nesting birds. It would be best not to come here during the nesting season (April through July), but if you do, stay on the immediate beach—at the high water mark or below—whether or not you see any signs denoting the nesting areas. Do not walk through any dry sand/shell areas. For a nonbirder to disturb nesting birds is bad; for a birder to do so is outrageous.

The nearest public dune walkover to this site is between 1017 and 1019 Ocean Boulevard West, 4.4 miles from the bridge; the closest parking lot to this walkover is along Sailfish Drive, at 4.0 miles. The walk will be easiest if you do not make it at full high tide, but the beach here is gently sloping and never difficult to walk. This wide beach attracts many Red Knots during the spring migration.

From late March to early September Wilson's Plovers are easy to find on the flats beside the inlet. The few Piping Plovers nest from around April to July. These birds have very strict requirements for nesting habitat: they need newly accreted areas with little dune development and little or no vegetation. In a few years they will probably quit nesting in this area; however, the area will probably remain fairly good for migrating and wintering Pipings for many years.

From mid-July to mid-May you can usually find a good variety of intertidal shorebirds here. In winter look for several Semipalmated Plovers, Sanderlings, Western Sandpipers, Dunlins, and Short-billed Dowitchers. Whimbrels are common in late spring and late summer. A few Marbled Godwits show up occasionally, especially in late summer and autumn. Although they are most likely to be seen in spring, Red Knots are also regular here in autumn and winter.

There is a large dredged-material island nearby, so these flats usually have several Least Terns in spring and early summer. In late summer look for a good variety of terns, including Sandwich and Black. Caspian Terns are most common in autumn, but one or two may occur at any season. In late summer and autumn there is often a small flock of Black Skimmers, and a handful of these birds often overwinter.

As the developing salt marsh here gets bigger, Clapper Rails will become easier to find. Look for a few wading birds, especially during the warmer months. In late summer a Reddish Egret is a possibility.

CALABASH, SUNSET BEACH, BIRD ISLAND AREA
MAP 39

Calabash, Sunset Beach, and Bird Island lie in the southwest corner of Brunswick County, on the South Carolina border. Indeed, for those who don't mind getting their feet wet, this tour sneaks across the border into South Carolina. This area features some fresh-water ponds that can be entertaining at any season, some fairly good shorebird flats, a wadeable inlet and, if you're willing to wade the inlet, a walk along the beach of an uninhabited island and at least a peek at the half-mile long jetties at Little River Inlet.

The fresh-water ponds, located on the mainland portion of Sunset Beach, have long attracted North Carolina birders who wanted to see Wood Storks. Each year, in late summer, a small flock spends some time here, making this the state's only location where you can regularly find this species. These ponds also attract other wading birds. White Ibises are common at all seasons, and a few Yellow-crowned Night-Herons occur during the warmer months. Anhingas are also frequent during the warmer months.

The area's salt marshes host a good population of Clapper Rails, and you can often find Seaside and Sharp-tailed sparrows as well.

The tidal flats at the west end of the barrier island portion of Sunset Beach attract a Reddish Egret almost every summer. These flats are fairly good for shorebirds. Wilson's Plovers are easy to find during the warmer months, and a few Pipings usually show up during the migrations and sometimes in winter.

The wide, gently sloping beaches of Sunset Beach and Bird Island may be covered with Red Knots during the spring migration. Because they are difficult to get to, the jetties at Little River Inlet have received almost no attention from birders. However, they harbor Purple Sandpipers and a few Great Cormorants each winter, and they probably attract a few sea ducks regularly.

Birding aside, this area is a delightful place to visit. The beach portion of Sunset Beach has resisted high-density development and high-rises; you know that you're entering a special place when you have to wait in line for the old single-lane pontoon bridge across the Intracoastal Waterway. On weekdays from autumn to spring, the beaches are uncrowded; if you wade across to Bird Island, you will have that beach pretty much to yourself.

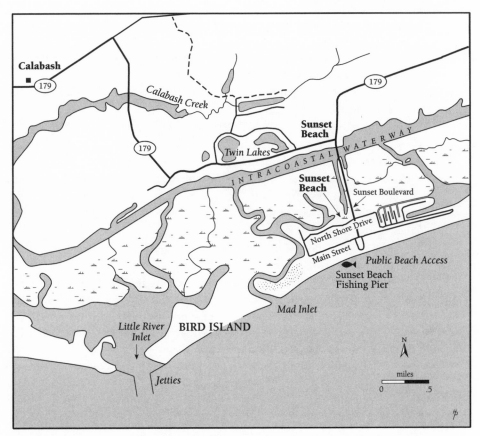

39. Calabash, Sunset Beach, Bird Island Area

Compared to most of the North Carolina coast, this area seems less maritime. There are no wide bays or sounds over which biting winds blow in winter. Instead, the coast here is nestled up against the mainland, and winter windchill values are almost always benign. Even during the coldest winter weather, this area is usually comfortable, at least when the sun is shining.

Incidentally, most people assume that the point where the North Carolina–South Carolina line intersects the coast (on Bird Island) is the southernmost point on the North Carolina coast; actually, Cape Fear on Bald Head Island projects slightly farther south. Instead, this is the coast's westernmost point: in fact, the state line here lies about 175 miles west of Cape Hatteras.

This tour starts in the community of Calabash, at the junction of NC 179 and River Road (currently the town's only intersection with a stoplight). From here, drive down River Road. Where this road ends on the waterfront, turn right onto Nance Street and continue to **Capt. Jim's Marina.**

The little open marsh next to the marina's parking lot is worth checking at low tide (the tide here lags about one hour after that on the oceanfront). At any season you may get excellent views of Clapper Rails as they weave in and out of the marsh edge. In mid- to late summer there may be one or two supertame Yellow-crowned Night-Herons (usually immatures) munching on fiddler crabs only a few feet away.

Return to NC 179, set your odometer to zero, and turn right. At 1.8 miles you will see **Calabash Creek**, a broad tidal creek with oyster rocks, salt marshes, and extensive mud flats. Pull off on the right just before the bridge.

This site is most entertaining at low tide during the warmer months; you will see numerous wading birds then. Late afternoon is usually best, because there are often more birds east of the bridge. Expect White Ibises and look for a few Yellow-crowned Night-Herons, especially in late summer. At all seasons you should be able to spot a Clapper Rail without much trouble. Scan the marsh edges to your left as you face up the creek (east).

Continue down NC 179. At 3.4 miles you will see the first of two large freshwater ponds on your left; the second pond lies next to the road at 4.0 miles. These ponds were created when tidal marshes were dammed up during the construction of the highway, and the area has traditionally been called **Twin Lakes**.

Unfortunately, the land around the ponds is privately owned, so your birding here is mostly limited to the road shoulder. At the first pond the roadside vegetation greatly limits your view of the pond. You can see a lot more here if you find the pond overflow drain, work through the vegetation, and wade out calf-deep (cautiously—the bottom gets very soft a little farther out). At the second pond you can walk out a few feet onto the edge of the golf course and look back along the marsh edge.

Some patience is necessary here. Perhaps because you can only glimpse part of the ponds' shorelines, the birdlife within them may seem to be constantly changing. You might check the ponds one hour and not see an Anhinga, then come back an hour later and see one immediately.

Lake Shore Drive circles around the north shores of the ponds; from this road you can glimpse other sections of the ponds across yards and undeveloped lots. The light is usually bad, though.

Overall, these ponds are best first thing in the morning. However, if you're looking for wading birds—including Wood Storks—it is best to be here at high tide, when the birds are forced in from the salt marshes. A high tide at sunrise or sunset is especially nice.

You are most likely to see the Wood Storks from around mid-July to late August, but birders have seen them as early as mid-June and at least as late as late September. At all seasons you can expect to see other waders, including White Ibises. A few Yellow-crowned Night-Herons are reliable from July to

September; you might see them as early as April and as late as October. This is also a good spot for Black-crowned Night-Herons; you may spot a few year-round. The first pond is often a better place than the second to find night-herons: wade out and look toward your left.

Anhingas are also seen regularly at the ponds. They are most frequent in late summer, but you might see them from April to October and on rare occasions in winter. Common Moorhens can always be found at the ponds, but they are most common during the cooler months. Adult Purple Gallinules probably show up here on rare occasions in late April and May, and immature birds have showed up in autumn.

From late autumn to spring there are many Pied-billed Grebes and American Coots and usually a few dabbling ducks, Ring-necked Ducks, and scaup. One winter a Eurasian Wigeon made an appearance.

At both sites you should check the salt marshes on the south side of the highway. Wood Storks and night-herons are sometimes spotted here at low tide. Clapper Rails are common; you are most likely to see them at low tide, around the edges of any openings in the marshes. From autumn to spring look for Seaside and Sharp-tailed sparrows during very high tides, especially across from the second pond.

Farther north, in the residential development, there are two other ponds you will probably want to check. These ponds are generally less interesting than the Twin Lakes, but they often have more wading birds and are usually better for Anhingas. To reach these ponds, turn around and head west on NC 179. Just past the westernmost pond, turn right onto Lake Shore Drive. After going 0.4 miles, turn left onto Sunset Lakes Boulevard. Shortly beyond this turn, on your right, you will see a long narrow pond stretching to the east. In the trees at the pond's far end you should see numerous waders, especially White Ibises, at high tide. (If you want to try to get closer to these birds, drive to the end of Medcalf Drive—the road to the right just before you get to the pond. From the end of this road, walk along the corner of the golf course.)

Just beyond this pond, bear left onto Pearl Boulevard, where on your right you will see another pond that often has a few Anhingas. The dead trees at the far end of the pond may be covered with wading birds at high tide.

Return to NC 179 and turn left. Shortly past the second pond you will come to a stop sign where 179 turns to the left. Here, turn right onto Sunset Boulevard, which leads to the barrier island. Beyond the bridge the road runs along a half-mile-long causeway that crosses extensive salt marshes. Near the beginning of the causeway there are a couple of spots on the right where you can pull off the road.

These marshes are most interesting at low tide during the warmer months, when there are many wading birds. A low tide at sunrise is especially nice.

Wood Storks are seen here occasionally in late summer. Watch year-round for

Clapper Rails skulking along the marsh edges. These marshes harbor Seaside Sparrows most of the year (they may be absent or scarce from April to July) and Sharp-tailed Sparrows from autumn to spring. Listen for their call-notes during calm conditions early and late in the day, or watch for birds pushed up to the edge of the causeway during high tides.

After you reach the barrier island, continue to the stop sign on Main Street. The public beach access area ahead, next to the fishing pier, usually has adequate parking.

To reach the shorebird flats at the island's west end, you may have to park here and hike almost a mile down the beach. You might want to first see whether any parking spaces are available at the west end of Main Street. Turn right onto Main Street and drive to its end (about one-half mile); there are only six parking spaces here, but you can often find vacant ones on weekdays from autumn to spring, and if you get here early enough you might even find a space on a summer weekend. If you can park here, look for a walkway across the dunes to the beach. If you can't, quickly scan the flats and tidal creek (Reddish Egrets have been seen here), then return to the public beach access area.

Even a walk from the beach access site is not a bad hike; this beach is easy to walk even at high tide. During the spring migration, from late April to early June, Red Knots are often common along these beaches.

At the west end of Sunset Beach you will come to a long spit where dunes are developing, and beyond these dunes you will see **Mad Inlet** and intertidal sand flats. These flats may deteriorate in the future—the Mad Inlet area may fill in as nearby Little River Inlet increasingly becomes predominant.

Currently these flats are one of the state's best sites for Reddish Egrets. One is found almost annually, usually between July and September. Immature dark-morph birds are most likely. From late March to September you should also be able to find a few Wilson's Plovers.

This is quite a small inlet, so you will probably never see more than a few hundred shorebirds, but you should be able to find a fairly good variety of intertidal species from about mid-July to late May. Try to either be here at full high tide, when shorebirds are forced onto the flats from the salt marshes and ocean beaches, or arrive at high tide and work the area as the tide begins to fall.

These sand flats usually host a few Piping Plovers during the migrations, and one or two of these birds may overwinter. You might spot one or two Marbled Godwits at any season, but they are most likely in autumn. You should see a good variety of loafing terns during the warmer months. Look for Gull-billeds from April to August; Sandwich Terns are most common in spring and autumn.

If it's warm and you're feeling adventuresome, you might want to wade across the inlet to **Bird Island**, which is currently uninhabited. As you will see, Mad Inlet is hardly imposing; it is best considered a tidal creek that flows into the ocean. However, inlets and tidal creeks are always changing; you should *not* wade across if you can't see the bottom. You may want to hold off unless you see others also wading over, so that you can cross at the same spot—most people wade over right beside the ocean. It is best to wade over at midtide when the tide is falling, so that you can spend three hours on Bird Island and return to the inlet about full low tide, allowing plenty of margin for error.

Bird Island is privately owned, but you will not be trespassing if you stay below the mean high water line. Like those of Sunset Beach, the beaches here are wide and attract many shorebirds. In summer, if the wind is light, you can hear Painted Buntings singing in the shrub thickets of the island. Because it lies so far west, in late summer and autumn this island is probably as good for migrating swallows as any island on North Carolina's coast. It should also be a good place to find hawks in autumn.

Bird Island is about a mile long; its western tip lies in South Carolina. About halfway down the island, if you see a mailbox at the edge of the dunes, look inside: it should contain a logbook in which you can record your experiences for posterity. Near the end of the island you will see a state boundary marker.

At the end of the island you will see a jetty that extends almost one-half mile offshore. There is also a jetty on the other side of the inlet. These jetties have a lot of potential for attracting interesting species, but they have received almost no attention from birders, because they are even more inaccessible from the inlet's South Carolina side.

Unfortunately, there is no paved surface on top of the jetty, and getting out on it even a short distance is very laborious and rather unsafe, so you are pretty much limited to what you can see from shore. Purple Sandpipers regularly winter here from November through April, but you would be lucky to glimpse one. At low tide they are not likely to be close to shore. You are more likely to see Great Cormorants, although they will be distant—most likely sitting on the channel markers off the ends of the jetties. A few are usually here from October to April, and one or two are possible throughout the summer.

The jetty makes an obvious turn to the left about halfway out. During the winter months, especially during brisk westerly winds, a few Red-breasted Mergansers and Buffleheads may gather in the slight bay formed by this bend. Look carefully for a scoter or Oldsquaw or, if you're lucky, an eider.

It is indeed regrettable that birders virtually never see these jetties; because they extend so far into the ocean, they have good potential for birds like eiders, Harlequin Ducks, or maybe even an alcid. A birder with access to a boat might find a winter survey of these jetties quite rewarding.

CHAPTER 9

PELAGIC TRIPS

At least in terms of variety, North Carolina offers the most exciting pelagic birding along the East Coast. Because the Gulf Stream lies not far offshore, many species are much easier to see off North Carolina than off states farther north, including Audubon's Shearwater, Masked Booby, Bridled Tern, and Sooty Tern. On the other hand, northern species like Northern Fulmar, Manx Shearwater, and Great Skua are regular visitors off our coast each year. Even some of the alcid species may occur quite regularly off our northern coast, although this speculation has yet to be proven.

Several noteworthy species are far easier to find off North Carolina than anywhere else in the United States. (At least some of these birds probably occur just as frequently off South Carolina and Georgia, but birding trips to the Gulf Stream are seldom run from those coasts because of the almost prohibitive distances involved.) The two best examples of such species are the Black-capped Petrel and Band-rumped Storm-Petrel, deep-water species that are seen regularly on chartered birding trips out of Oregon and Hatteras inlets. Although harder to come by, the White-tailed Tropicbird is as likely to be seen off our coast as anywhere else in the United States. The rare, eagerly sought-after White-faced Storm-Petrel is seen about as often off our coast as anywhere in North America. As leaders and planners of pelagic birding trips become increasingly knowledgeable, birders' chances to see this species may become a little more reliable in the future.

Much of the reason for North Carolina's pelagic birding appeal is the proximity of Oregon and Hatteras inlets to deep water. The Black-capped Petrels and Band-rumped Storm-Petrels are usually found in waters of a hundred fathoms or deeper. Increasingly, chartered trips are going out into deeper and deeper waters—500 to 1,000 fathoms and more—which have produced other exciting species. It is now apparent that Herald Petrel and Soft-plumaged Petrel are regular in these waters, and other species, such as Bulwer's Petrel, may also be possible.

In the future, chartered pelagic trips may get even better, as new ideas regarding microdistribution are investigated. Although birders now spend a lot of time either following the Gulf Stream edge or going out into the deeper 500- to 1,000-fathom waters, we have devoted little time to exploring the *combination* of Gulf Stream edge and 500- to 1,000-fathom water, which occurs where the Gulf Stream bends eastward. The future might also hold occasional chartered trips into the bird-rich Gulf Stream eddies that sometimes form well off the state's South Coast; satellite data can reveal these eddies' locations. In the past there have been only a handful of winter pelagic trips. Such trips will certainly become more frequent in the future. Some are now being planned for the waters near the Virginia border, where some of the alcids may prove to be regular visitors.

Birding aside, a trip to the Gulf Stream on a nice day can be a wonderful experience. The clear, deep blue waters are enchanting. Dolphins frequently surf alongside the boat, and on most trips you will see a few whales. You never know what else you might see. Just below the boat, easily visible through the clear water, the striking profile of a hammerhead shark might appear. Occasionally you might get to closely inspect an ocean sunfish, a really odd creature.

After all this talk of exciting rarities and of fun, a cautionary note is in order. Although many trips are heavenly, many are something less than that. Some trips are uncomfortable; some are incredibly boring. Although exciting species can occur in the offshore waters, the density of birdlife there is actually quite low; at times you can go for long periods with just an occasional sighting of a distant bird. And although chartered birding trips don't go out during really bad conditions, it is sometimes rough enough that you really can't use binoculars. Even on the calmest days, don't expect pelagic bird-watching to be anything like birding on land. The boat is always rocking enough that it is difficult to keep birds in binocular view. Many sightings will be of birds that only the leaders feel comfortable identifying—and there may well be disagreement among them! So if you like to get really close, leisurely views of birds before you feel confident identifying them, be prepared for frustrations.

GENERAL ADVICE

On offshore trips at any season you will need sunscreen. It is very easy to get badly burned. During the cooler months you will want to dress warmly, with several layers; windchills offshore can be vicious. During the warmest months— June through September—it may feel cool at dawn on the way out, but be prepared for steamy conditions, especially if you're heading for the Gulf Stream, where the water is in the eighty-degree range during much of this period. Some people are most susceptible to seasickness when it gets hot. Although a jacket and long pants are best for the ride out, you will want to have the option of stripping down to very lightweight clothes later. (Shorts are fine, but don't forget the sunscreen). It is good to bring some extra clothes in case there are rain showers or you get doused with spray.

The bane of pelagic birding is seasickness. Some people are never affected by this problem, while some are always affected—sometimes before the boat even reaches the inlet! Most people are not bothered by average sea conditions but may get sick when it's really rough. Generally, make sure that you eat some breakfast, but eat light. Sometimes people don't get sick unless they lie down; if you feel bad, stand and look at the horizon. Some birders chew on soda crackers and sip ginger ale. Probably the best advice is to get a good night's sleep before your trip.

Medications such as Dramamine can be helpful, but they make most people drowsy. Boat captains have noticed that relatively few people using Scopolamine ear patches get sick. This medication, which requires a prescription, seldom causes drowsiness. Any drug can cause a negative reaction. If you are trying out a new medication, test it at home first—don't wait until you get offshore!

The waves will always cause the boat to rock at least a little. A scope is of course useless, and even binoculars are difficult to use. Lightweight, lower-power binoculars (7×) are actually best. Indeed, you might best learn to identify seabirds by doing lots of watching with no binoculars at all, concentrating on the birds' general shapes and flight patterns. This is the primary method of identifying pelagic birds anyway; many of the more subtle markings are really almost impossible to see during at-sea conditions.

For information about how and when to see the various pelagic species, refer to part 3 and the appendix. For beginning birders, "pelagic species" refers to species that occur primarily over the offshore waters—fulmar, petrels, storm-petrels, shearwaters, tropicbirds, boobies, phalaropes, jaegers, skuas, Black-legged Kittiwake, Sabine's Gull, Brown Noddy, the alcids, and Roseate, Arctic, Bridled, and Sooty terns.

CHARTERED BIRDING TRIPS

Birders planning to head offshore in search of pelagic birds have two main options: either to take one of the chartered birding trips, which almost always run out of Oregon and Hatteras inlets, or to go out on one of the fishing headboats that run out of a few different sites. The first option is by far the best. Only on these chartered trips will you actually get to the Gulf Stream edge and the deeper waters far offshore, where many of the specialties are to be found. There will be many pairs of eyes aboard, including those of several leaders

experienced in seabird identification. And on these trips the boat belongs to the birders. If you see something of interest, you can alter your course and check it out. You will also run right along tide lines and bits of flotsam, allowing you to get close looks at some birds. From the headboats, on the other hand, you'll get good looks only at those occasional birds that fly close to the boat. Furthermore, the headboats usually fish at basically the same spot all day. If that spot happens to be dull, it can be a long day indeed.

Chartered birding trips are organized regularly by four different birding tour groups, which are listed at the end of this section. Chances are good that these groups will continue to organize pelagic trips off North Carolina's coast for several years, although some may quit and others may take their place. For more up-to-date information, look for ads in the American Birding Association newsletter or sometimes in the Carolina Bird Club newsletter. The cost of these chartered trips is about $100; expect this figure to go up in the future, especially as trips go farther offshore.

Virtually all chartered birding trips take place between mid-May and mid-September. This period offers the most variety and, overall, the best chance for many of the more eagerly sought-after species. This also tends to be the period when weather is least likely to interfere with the trips. (On average, winter has precious few days when you would want to be on a small boat in the Gulf Stream.) Between mid-May and mid-September there are many organized trips, and the number has been increasing as interest in offshore birding has grown.

Most trips begin about 6 A.M. and return to dock at 5 P.M. Most trips follow the same general plan: You head offshore quickly through the bird-poor inshore waters, then work along the edge of the Gulf Stream for a while, checking out prominent seaweed lines for species like Audubon's Shearwater, phalaropes, jaegers, and Bridled Tern. Then you head farther out in search of deep-water species, like Black-capped Petrel, Band-rumped Storm-Petrel, or something even more exciting. Particular trips may emphasize either the Gulf Stream edge or the deeper waters. Also, trips may be designed around the weather. Brisk northeast winds will usually rule out any deep-water plans.

These are the four birding tour groups that currently organize pelagic trips off the North Carolina coast:

Brian Patteson
P.O. Box 1135
Amherst, VA 24521
804-933-8687

OBServ
3901 Trimble Road
Nashville, TN 37215
615-292-2739

Focus on Nature Tours
P.O. Box 9021
Wilmington, DE 19809
302-529-1876

Pterodroma Ptours
303 Dunhagen Place
Cary, NC 27511
919-460-0338

BIRDING FROM FISHING HEADBOATS

Birders can also ride along on one of the fishing headboats that run out of Hatteras Village, Morehead City–Atlantic Beach, and Carolina Beach. These boats are listed at the end of this section. By the way, the term "headboat" refers to boats that infrequently run chartered fishing trips but more often run trips that are open to anyone who shows up and pays the fee—thus they charge people "by the head." Overall, your opportunities for good birding from the headboats are much more limited. These boats concentrate almost totally on bottom fishing. Thus, although they may go well offshore, they stay where the water is no more than about three hundred feet deep. These boats also want to avoid current as much as possible, so they avoid the Gulf Stream. However, birding from a headboat does have some advantages. For nonfishing sightseers, most trips only cost about $20, and you can wait for perfect weather before deciding to go out.

The headboats are fairly large and comfortable—up to one hundred feet long. Seasickness-prone individuals are less likely to get sick on these boats. All of them have large upper decks that are great for spotting birds. Although the birding is on average much less exciting than on chartered birding trips, it can be quite good at times. Over the years, headboat trips have produced some exciting records, including an accidental Red-billed Tropicbird. The White-tailed Tropicbird is one specialty species that is almost as likely to be seen from a headboat as from a chartered trip. The best time of year to go out on a headboat is in mid- to late May. At that time, when many species are northbound and approach shore a little more closely than usual, headboat birding can be almost as good as birding from a chartered trip.

Another positive feature of the headboats is that many of them go out at any season. The boats at Carolina Beach and Hatteras run from around early April to late November. The boats at Morehead City–Atlantic Beach run fairly often throughout the winter. Of course, many of these winter trips are canceled because of weather. Also, several of these winter trips are overnight trips. I have made one of these trips, and I wouldn't recommend them. It is almost impossible to sleep on the boat, and if the birding is dull, you will experience the longest twenty hours of your life.

Pelagic birding options in the state expanded in 1993, when a new headboat, the "Miss Hatteras," began running out of Hatteras Village. This boat has the positive features of the other headboats, but it is not limited to bottom fishing. It often does some fishing along the edge of the Gulf Stream. Even when it is not actually in the Stream it gets close enough to it, so it offers a pretty good chance of seeing a good variety of birds.

Of the boats in the Morehead City area, the "Captain Stacy" is your best bet. If the weather is benign, this boat often goes east of Cape Lookout, where the birding is often fairly good. Before you sign up for a trip out of Morehead City–Atlantic Beach, you might ask the captain if he knows which way he's going that day. (Usually he will be noncommittal.) Beware of trips to the southwest, which are typically quite boring. Because Carolina Beach lies relatively far to the west and distant from the Gulf Stream, trips from there are generally the least interesting, although even these trips have produced some goodies.

Here are the docking sites and phone numbers of current headboats, arranged from north to south:

"Miss Hatteras"
Oden Docks
Hatteras
919-986-2365

"Carolina Princess"
South Eighth Street
Morehead City
919-726-5479

"Continental Shelf"
South Sixth Street
Morehead City
919-726-7454

"Captain Stacy"
Atlantic Beach causeway
Atlantic Beach
919-726-4675

"Pirate Queen"
Carl Winner Avenue
Carolina Beach
910-458-5626

"Winner Queen"
Carl Winner Avenue
Carolina Beach
910-458-5356

BRIEF SEASONAL SURVEY

December through February
The few chartered trips to the Gulf Stream that have been made during this period have not been very interesting. However, Black-capped Petrels are known to occur throughout the winter, and Black-legged Kittiwakes are fairly easy to find. Sometimes there are good numbers of Red Phalaropes. Most trips scheduled during this period have been canceled because of the weather. In the future there will probably be occasional trips to the waters near the Virginia line, primarily to look for alcids. These trips may depart from Oregon Inlet or Virginia Beach. Because these trips stay well inshore of the Gulf Stream, the weather is less likely to interfere with them.

During this period you might consider going out on one of the headboats out of Morehead City–Atlantic Beach. On most days you will see little or nothing, but in this area Black-legged Kittiwakes are most likely to be seen in December. You might see Red Phalaropes, and toward the end of February you could hope for a fulmar, Manx Shearwater, or Great Skua.

March and April

Currently no chartered trips are run during this period. Let's hope that some are organized in the future, because Northern Fulmars often occur in large numbers then off the Outer Banks. Red Phalaropes are often common in April, and March may be the best month to see a Manx Shearwater. The peak time for fulmars might also be the best time to look for a Great Skua.

The "Miss Hatteras" headboat begins its runs out of Hatteras Village in April. Probably many of these trips will be canceled because of weather, but a trip then might be interesting. You would have a pretty good chance of seeing fulmars and Red Phalaropes, and the possibility of a Manx Shearwater or Great Skua.

There are many opportunities to get offshore from Morehead City–Atlantic Beach during this period, although the birding potential from here is not as good. Red Phalaropes and Pomarine Jaegers are seen on most trips in April. Trips that run east or southeast offer the best chances for something interesting. In these waters you might see a Northern Fulmar, Manx Shearwater, or even a Great Skua in March or at the beginning of April.

May

Chartered trips out of Oregon and Hatteras inlets begin in mid-May. The mid- to late May period is certainly the high point of the pelagic birding season off the North Carolina coast. In addition to the permanent resident Black-capped Petrels, you may see most of the summer resident/visitor species, which have arrived or are arriving at this time—species like Cory's, Greater, and Audubon's shearwaters; Wilson's and Leach's storm-petrels; and Bridled Tern. This is also the peak time for many migrating species—Sooty Shearwater, Red-necked Phalarope, jaegers, South Polar Skua, and Arctic Tern. On a good day you might see all three species of jaeger and a South Polar Skua. In late May a Sabine's Gull is possible, and this seems to be one of the peak times for White-tailed Tropicbird. A few Band-rumped Storm-Petrels begin showing up at the end of May, and there have been sightings of both Herald and Soft-plumaged petrels at that time.

Because many of these northward-moving birds are following the Gulf Stream edge, on a good day you could probably see most of these species by going out on the "Miss Hatteras" during this mid- to late May peak. The headboats farther south can also be pretty good during this period, although you shouldn't expect to see any of the deeper-water species.

June and July

Although variety gradually declines during these months, chartered trips remain interesting. Actually, during the first few days of June you may see several of the migrant species that primarily pass through in May. Some of the summer resident species gradually increase during this period, like Bridled Tern. Greater

Shearwater numbers often peak in late June and early July. The weather in June and July is often very calm, allowing comfortable rides well into the deeper waters, where Black-capped Petrels are often common and Leach's and Band-rumped storm-petrels rather easy to find. In June a Soft-plumaged Petrel is possible in these waters. There's always the possibility of a tropicbird or South Polar Skua, and sightings of the rare Masked Booby become somewhat more likely in July.

Trips on the "Miss Hatteras" might produce many of the same species as chartered trips, especially at the beginning of June. However, on the headboat you would be much less likely to see some of the deeper-water species, like Band-rumped and Leach's storm-petrels. The headboats farther south can be pretty good during the first few days of June; they gradually become less interesting as summer progresses, although you never know what might fly by. Between mid-July and mid-August, White-tailed Tropicbirds are occasionally sighted from headboats out of Morehead City–Atlantic Beach on trips to the east and southeast.

August and September

August is "deep summer" for the offshore waters; temperatures in the Gulf Stream may climb into the upper eighties. At the end of August and in September, northeasters become somewhat more likely, and weather suitable for trips well offshore is a bit less dependable. Yet these months can also offer some of the most tranquil weather of the year. Few chartered trips are run after mid-September.

Several of the summer resident species, like Greater Shearwater and Wilson's, Leach's, and Band-rumped storm-petrels, gradually decline during the period, although large numbers of Wilson's Storm-Petrels and a few Leach's Storm-Petrels remain well into September to the northeast of Oregon Inlet. On the other hand, Audubon's Shearwaters and Bridled Terns peak during this period, and Sooty Terns often become fairly common in August and early September. The autumn migration of Red-necked Phalaropes peaks in August. Birders often see several jaegers on trips during these months, but many of these birds are in plumages that make specific identification difficult. A full adult Long-tailed is sighted on rare occasions. Two specialties that birders hope to see during this period are Herald Petrel and White-faced Storm-Petrel. The Herald is apparently occasional during August in the deeper offshore waters; the White-faced apparently peaks around mid- to late August but is still rare then. White-tailed Tropicbirds and South Polar Skuas remain occasional until early September. September is probably the best month to look for the very rare Sabine's Gull.

During this period the most interesting headboat by far is the "Miss Hatteras," which could allow you to see many of the above species. Farther south, headboat trips can be very dull, although trips out of Morehead City–Atlantic Beach that run east and southeast of Cape Lookout can be pretty good.

October and November
Only rarely are chartered trips run during this period. The variety of birds over the Gulf Stream steadily declines as autumn progresses. A small number of Northern Fulmars apparently move through the area during these months; these birds are most frequent about November 1. Both Red Phalaropes and Black-legged Kittiwakes increase during November, becoming fairly common by the end of the month.

A trip on the "Miss Hatteras" about November 1 could be interesting. You might see all three of the above species. Black-legged Kittiwakes are sighted regularly from the headboats farther south in November, and sightings of Red Phalaropes become more frequent during that month. As with trips farther north, you might find a fulmar by heading east out of Morehead City–Atlantic Beach about November 1.

PART 3

BIRDS OF
SPECIAL
INTEREST

THIS SECTION GIVES more detailed information on finding birds that are often sought after because they are scarce, local, or secretive, or often puzzled over because they are difficult to identify. Each species account lists the best sites, times, and conditions for finding the species. Seasonal information is intended to supplement the bar graphs.

Although this book was not meant to be an identification guide, some species accounts in this chapter also include information on identification. This information is provided primarily for beginning birders and is given mostly for those species for which the same identification errors show up repeatedly.

RED-THROATED LOON

This generally common winter resident is listed here because there are a few sites where it is rather scarce, and beginning birders might be puzzled if they have trouble finding a bird described as common.

Red-throateds occur primarily from November to April. They are found almost exclusively on the ocean and the more expansive saltwater estuaries: the Pamlico and Core sounds and the lower Pamlico and Neuse rivers.

Particularly good areas for seeing Red-throateds are the Outer Banks, from Nags Head to Cape Hatteras; off any of the barrier beaches from Topsail Island south to Fort Fisher; and from the Pamlico Sound ferries. The Fort Fisher area in particular always has large numbers of this species from Thanksgiving through February. From the Pamlico Sound ferries, Red-throateds are seen primarily during the middle of the runs, in the deeper waters; Common Loons, on the other hand, are predominantly seen in the shallower waters.

From mid-March to mid-April you're most likely to see Red-throateds off the northern beaches, from Cape Hatteras north, although large numbers sometimes congregate on Pamlico Sound during this period. Also, Red-throateds are frequently seen migrating north in the early mornings during this period, off the south-facing beaches at Cape Hatteras and between Cape Lookout and eastern Bogue Banks.

RED-NECKED GREBE

This large grebe is a rare winter visitor, at least at favored sites. Red-neckeds are most likely to occur between late November and mid-March. Almost all sightings have been on the ocean, although a few have been on Pamlico Sound. On average, there are a couple of sightings each winter, although during exceptional years there may be several. Nevertheless, the species is typically quite difficult to find. And when you do find a Red-necked Grebe, it is likely to be some distance out from shore, giving you a less-than-satisfactory sighting.

Most sightings of Red-necked Grebes have been made along the beaches from Nags Head to Cape Hatteras. Farther south, there have been several sightings near the north end of Topsail Island and at Fort Fisher. Interestingly, the latter two sites have extensive hard-bottom areas just offshore. Your chances of finding a Red-necked Grebe may be best when large numbers of Horned Grebes (and perhaps Red-throated Loons) are present. In the Pea Island–Rodanthe area, during calm conditions, a prominent tide line sometimes develops and may come all the way into shore; such tide lines can attract Red-necked Grebes and other rarities, such as alcids. At all sites, smooth sea conditions—the result of an absence of wind or an offshore wind—will greatly enhance your chances of spotting one of these birds. Strong offshore winds can also cause a little upwelling near shore, bringing feeding loons and grebes in close to the beaches.

On very rare occasions Red-necked Grebes have been seen from the Cedar Island–Ocracoke ferry, and although there are no records, sightings from the Ocracoke–Swan Quarter ferry would be at least as likely. Unfortunately, a sighting from these ferries is likely to be very brief and unsatisfactory, leaving you scratching your head and wondering.

The Red-necked Grebe seems to be reported more often than it is actually seen. Certainly some reports of Red-neckeds have actually been of Horned Grebes. Under typical viewing conditions (i.e., a distant bird on the water, seen through a scope, with heat waves and distortion), a Horned Grebe can do a great Red-necked imitation. The bird can appear to have quite a long neck, and the neck's dark color contrasts with a white cheek patch. And some Horned Grebes actually do have somewhat dusky forenecks. To be certain that you've seen a Red-necked, get a good size and shape comparison with a nearby Horned Grebe or loon, or better yet, find a Red-necked close enough that you can be absolutely certain of the bill length and color. Easier said than done, of course.

EARED GREBE

This small grebe was formerly a very rare winter visitor in coastal North Carolina. Since the late 1980s, though, it has been found with increasing frequency. Eared Grebes are now rare winter residents/visitors from November to March and are occasional at a few favored locales. Considering the rate of increase in recent years, they may merit an occasional/uncommon designation in the near future. In coastal North Carolina, this species has been found in various habitats, including the ocean, sheltered waters of estuaries, and on fresh water. However, a majority of the sightings have occurred at fresh-water and brackish sites such as impoundments, so on average this species appears to favor different habitats from those favored by Horned Grebes, which look similar to Eareds.

For the best chance of finding one of these birds and getting a good look at it, check the impoundments at Pea Island NWR, the impoundment next to the Entrance Road at Mattamuskeet NWR, or the Salt Pond at Cape Hatteras. November and December are perhaps the best months. The Basin near Fort Fisher looks like an area where Eared Grebes should occur somewhat regularly; March and early April may be the best months at this site. Although no sightings have been made there, the Carolina Beach Wastewater Treatment Plant is another likely-looking site for this species, and here a bird could be seen at close range. October to December is probably the most likely period for an Eared Grebe to show up here.

Virtually all Eared Grebe sightings in coastal North Carolina have been of birds in winter plumage. There has been a moderate amount of variation in the appearance of many of these birds. However, Eared Grebes always have thinner bills, thinner necks, and more peaked crowns than Horned Grebes do. You should always be suspicious of any "Horned Grebe" seen on fresh- or brackish-water ponds or impoundments, and the smaller the body of water is, the more suspicious you should be—especially around October.

NORTHERN FULMAR

This rather gull-like tubenose is strictly pelagic. It is very rarely seen from land in North Carolina. Fulmars have been seen in the offshore waters from October to May. Occurring primarily during the spring, they are fairly common—sometimes common—off the north Outer Banks (from Cape Hatteras north) in March and April. They are found mainly along the edge of the Gulf Stream but are sometimes seen closer to shore.

Unfortunately, they are absent or nearly absent during the period when most chartered birding trips to the Gulf Stream out of Oregon and Hatteras inlets are scheduled, although there have been rare mid-May sightings. Perhaps in the future some trips will be organized for early spring. You might also see a Northern Fulmar by taking the fishing headboat out of Hatteras in April. Although this boat does not normally go to the edge of the Gulf Stream, you would have at least a fairly good chance of seeing a fulmar. Fulmars are also seen occasionally from headboats out of the Morehead City–Atlantic Beach area. Here they are most likely to be seen in March and early April.

Attempting to see this bird from land will almost certainly be a waste of time, but perhaps your best bet would be to watch from the south beaches of Cape Hatteras during an intense northeaster in March or April.

SOFT-PLUMAGED PETREL

One of the most exciting birding discoveries in coastal North Carolina in recent years has been the discovery that a few of these rare gadfly-petrels apparently occur off our coast with some regularity. The Gulf Stream area off North Carolina's coast is the only United States location where a birder might reasonably expect to see this petrel.

The few sightings recorded have taken place between late May and late June, and the species is best considered very rare during this period. It remains to be seen whether any of these petrels will make appearances later in the summer or at other seasons. In general, these birds are found where Black-capped Petrels occur, over and near the Gulf Stream where the water is deep, usually a hundred fathoms and deeper.

The only way you'll have the slightest chance of seeing a Soft-plumaged Petrel is to go on one of the chartered trips out of Oregon Inlet or Hatteras Inlet during the late May–late June period; late May–early June may be best. Do not be too optimistic; many birders have made numerous trips during this period without seeing one.

Consult *A Field Guide to Seabirds of the World* and *Seabirds: An Identification Guide*, both by Peter Harrison, for help in identifying these birds. Most or all of the Soft-plumaged Petrels that occur off North Carolina probably belong to the subspecies that breeds in the eastern North Atlantic. (This population, named "Cape Verde Petrel," may actually be a separate species.) Birds of this population have breast bands that are incomplete or totally absent. The birds sighted in North Carolina have had a discernible "W" pattern on the upper wings but not the underwings (unlike the photograph in *A Field Guide to Seabirds of the World*).

HERALD PETREL

Birding trips off Oregon and Hatteras inlets have been increasingly frequent in the last few years, and these trips have revealed that this gadfly-petrel, like the Soft-plumaged Petrel, occurs regularly off North Carolina's coast. In contrast with the Soft-plumaged Petrel, however, you have an almost reasonable chance of seeing a Herald. This is the only location in the United States where a birder can reasonably expect to see this species.

Based on current records, it appears that this species is very rare in late May–early June and occasional in August. As pelagic trips are made more often, perhaps sightings will also take place in late June and July. These birds are most likely to be seen over the same waters where Black-capped Petrels are regular—the deep Gulf Stream waters, usually a hundred fathoms or deeper.

For a chance of seeing this bird, go on one of the chartered trips out of Oregon Inlet or Hatteras Inlet during the month of August.

Consult *A Field Guide to Seabirds of the World* and *Seabirds: An Identification Guide*, both by Peter Harrison, for help in identifying these birds. Light-morph, intermediate-morph, and dark-morph individuals have been observed off North Carolina's coast. In terms of plumage, these petrels are somewhat reminiscent of jaegers; however, their manner of flight is quite different. Dark-morph individuals are suggestive of Sooty Shearwaters. In light wind conditions, their flight patterns may not be very different, but during brisk winds the petrel exhibits the roller-coaster flight pattern typical of *Pterodroma* petrels.

BLACK-CAPPED PETREL

This species is one of the main reasons that pelagic birding trips out of Oregon and Hatteras inlets are so popular: Black-capped Petrels are found more easily over the deep Gulf Stream waters off North Carolina than anywhere else in the United States. This species is fairly common (often common) in the offshore waters all year but is strictly pelagic, limited largely to those waters over about a hundred fathoms in depth.

Black-cappeds are seen on most of the chartered trips out of Oregon and Hatteras inlets, although they have been missed on occasion. Unless you take one of these trips, you're almost certain *not* to find one. You might see one occasionally from the headboat out of Hatteras and they have been seen occasionally from headboats out of Morehead City–Atlantic Beach, but only on those rare trips that go far toward the southeast. This species has never been seen from land in the state—except in the eye of a hurricane!

At a distance where no details can be seen, Black-capped Petrels can usually be picked out by their very characteristic flight, with graceful arcs that are quite exaggerated vertically. At the apex of each arc, they hold their wings perpendicular to the water. Actually, it sometimes seems that the bird is on the verge of flying upside-down.

CORY'S SHEARWATER

This species is pelagic, but not very strictly pelagic; birds have been seen frequently in near-shore waters and occasionally from land. Cory's Shearwaters have been found off the North Carolina coast from April to late November and are common from late May to early October.

Chartered trips out of Oregon and Hatteras inlets are certain to encounter this species; the headboat out of Hatteras Inlet is also a good way to dependably find this species. Elsewhere, birders aboard headboats traveling out of Morehead City–Atlantic Beach and Carolina Beach will usually find this species between late May and early October.

The best spot to look for this species from land is at Cape Hatteras. Here they are seen regularly in late May and the first few days of June, especially when there are northeast and east winds. Otherwise, from mid-June to October they are occasional. In the Cape Lookout area these birds are most likely to be seen between mid-July and early August, when they are occasional during invasions of Audubon's Shearwaters.

GREATER SHEARWATER

Like Cory's Shearwater, this pelagic species is seen from land with some regularity, at least when conditions are right. Greaters have been found in the state's offshore waters from April to early December, but they occur primarily from mid-June to early July, when they are common off the Outer Banks and fairly common elsewhere. Numbers in late summer are rather variable, but on average Greaters are fairly common off the Outer Banks. Elsewhere, they are uncommon to occasional during this period.

Between mid-June and early July you will usually see this species whether you take a chartered birding trip or go out on one of the headboats. The birds are especially likely after steady northeast or east winds. In late summer and early autumn you are unlikely to see this species unless you go on a chartered trip out of Oregon or Hatteras inlets.

After northeast to east winds, Greaters are frequently seen at Cape Hatteras Point from late May to early July; from south of here to Bogue Banks they are occasional from mid-June to early July.

Some Cory's Shearwaters show a faint light rump band and can thus be misidentified as Greaters. To be certain you've got a Greater, look for the black bill, the blackish crown contrasting with white cheeks, and the dark smudge across the belly.

SOOTY SHEARWATER

This is a "pelagic species that isn't." In other words, although this species is actually pelagic, your best chances of seeing this bird in North Carolina are when birds heading north between mid-May and early June concentrate along shorelines due to geography and weather. During some years, when there are steady northeast or east winds, birds are seen regularly from Bodie Island to Bogue Banks; at these times they are fairly common at Cape Hatteras and uncommon elsewhere. During other years, sightings are only occasional.

Outside of the peak, between mid-May and early June, your chances of finding a Sooty are slight. Strangely, as summer progresses, they are more likely to be seen on offshore birding trips to the Gulf Stream than from shore. However, the chances of finding one after late June are very slight.

MANX SHEARWATER

This primarily cold- or cool-water pelagic bird has been recorded in the state's offshore waters in winter and spring. The population seems to peak about late February and March, when they are uncommon off the northern Outer Banks and perhaps occasional elsewhere.

Unfortunately, they are absent or nearly so during the period when chartered birding trips run out of Oregon and Hatteras inlets. You might see one by going out on the headboat out of Hatteras in April. Manx Shearwaters are also occasionally seen from headboats out of Morehead City–Atlantic Beach from late February through March. The species has also been seen from land on the Outer Banks in midwinter, but finding one this way would be a fluke. Strangely, in recent years a few birds have been spotted moving past Cape Hatteras Point in late May during major flights of pelagic species. Be aware, however, that a few Audubon's Shearwaters, which look quite similar to Manxes, have also been seen in these flights.

The exact status of the species off our coast has been clouded by its resemblance to the Audubon's Shearwater. Formerly Audubon's was thought to be absent in midwinter, so any small black-and-white shearwater at that season was automatically considered to be a Manx. Now, however, we know that Audubon's Shearwaters do occur regularly in winter.

When you see a real Manx, you will momentarily consider the possibility of a larger shearwater, such as a Greater, because of the Manx's silhouette and manner of flight. In contrast, when you see the long-tailed silhouette and fluttery flight of an Audubon's, you will probably think only of Audubon's.

AUDUBON'S SHEARWATER

This small warm-water-loving tubenose occurs off our coast throughout the year, although it is scarce in midwinter, when it is limited to the Gulf Stream. Audubon's Shearwaters are common in the offshore waters from midsummer into autumn, and from about mid-July to early August they often occur rather close to shore.

Between May and October, you are almost certain to see them if you take one of the chartered birding trips out of Oregon and Hatteras inlets between May and October, and you can usually see them if you take the headboat out of Hatteras. From July to September, you can usually see them from headboats out of Morehead City–Atlantic Beach, especially from mid-July to mid-August.

These birds are seen from shore with some regularity along the south-facing beaches from Cape Lookout to Bogue Banks between mid-July and early August. Look for them especially when easterly winds and certain current conditions bring in large amounts of sargassum and Portuguese man-o'-war jellyfish. At Cape Hatteras, they might occur at any time from May to October (they've even been seen here in winter), but the only time you can reasonably expect to see one is during either the midsummer period or a slight peak that takes place in late May.

The small-bodied, long-tailed silhouette and fluttery flight of this species are characteristic. You are unlikely to confuse an Audubon's Shearwater with anything else.

WILSON'S STORM-PETREL

This species is found offshore from April to autumn. They are most common from May to July, with good numbers remaining until September from Cape Hatteras north.

If you take one of the chartered birding trips out of Oregon and Hatteras inlets between May and October, or the headboat out of Hatteras between May and early September, you are certain to see this species. Between mid-May and early July you are also certain to see this species from headboats out of Morehead City–Atlantic Beach and Carolina Beach. However, in this area they are more difficult to find as summer progresses.

Wilson's Storm-Petrels are seen regularly at Cape Hatteras Point from about mid-May to early August, and they can be fairly common here between mid-May and early June. From Bodie Island to Bogue Banks, they are seen regularly between mid-May and mid-June, especially during steady winds from the northeast and east.

WHITE-FACED STORM-PETREL

On chartered birding trips out of Oregon and Hatteras inlets, this species is eagerly sought after but seldom seen. White-faceds are very rare to rare offshore from Cape Hatteras north between early August and early October, with most records in late August (perhaps simply because that is when most trips searching for the species are made). They are assumed to be most likely in the cooler offshore waters from Oregon Inlet north, although this assumption has been questioned.

The only way you can even hope to see this species off North Carolina's coast is to take one of the chartered birding trips out of Oregon or Hatteras inlets. There is one record from land, in connection with a late September hurricane.

LEACH'S STORM-PETREL

This species is largely restricted to the waters far offshore; it is usually seen over water about a hundred fathoms and deeper. Leach's Storm-Petrels have been reported off the North Carolina coast from April to December, but most records are from June to August. They are most likely from Cape Hatteras north. In this area, although never reliable, they are sometimes found in double-digit numbers from late June to August. Overall, they seem to be most common from late June through July.

You are likely to find this species in North Carolina only on one of the chartered trips out of Oregon or Hatteras inlets. If you can arrange it, take a trip in late June or July. On trips that get far into the offshore waters and encounter conditions smooth enough to allow good visibility, you are fairly likely to see a few birds. These deep-water birds are virtually never seen from land in the state. However, there have been a handful of sightings from Cape Hatteras Point in late May and June.

The erratic nighthawklike flight of this species is very characteristic and sets the bird apart at some distance. A cautionary note: Wilson's Storm-Petrels migrating along shorelines in spring and early summer may fly rather directly, without any of the slow, aimless feeding activity that is so characteristic of the species. Sometimes beginning birders mistake such a bird for a Leach's.

BAND-RUMPED STORM-PETREL

This species is another reason that pelagic birding trips out of Oregon and Hatteras inlets are so popular. North Carolina's offshore waters are the only area in North America where birders can reasonably expect to see the Band-rumped Storm-Petrel, which nests in the eastern Atlantic.

The Band-rumped is a bird of the deep Gulf Stream waters, at least a hundred fathoms deep, and has been reported from late May to early September, with an apparent peak of abundance in late June and July. Even during this period, the species is generally uncommon.

Don't expect to see this bird except on one of the pelagic birding trips out of

Oregon or Hatteras inlets. For the best chance of seeing one, line up a trip in late June or July. Band-rumpeds are most likely to be seen during conditions that also attract large numbers of Wilson's Storm-Petrels. Actually, on trips that get into the deeper waters and encounter sea conditions smooth enough to allow good visibility, chances are rather good that you will find a few Band-rumpeds.

Understandably, many birders come back from the offshore trips thinking to themselves, "I believe I saw one—but did I really?" Band-rumped Storm-Petrels are not a conspicuously different bird; they look a lot like Wilson's Storm-Petrels. And they are rather shy, typically staying away from boats and unfortunately not often coming in to chum. Furthermore, with this species birders usually get few opportunities to study flight differences at close range. Birders often spot Band-rumped Storm-Petrels as they are being flushed from the water with Wilson's Storm-Petrels, and these species fly pretty much the same when they are being chased.

However, a Band-rumped is definitely bigger than a Wilson's—it weighs about one-third more. When the two species are flushed together from the water, this difference in size is readily apparent. A notable behavioral difference is that Band-rumpeds will often be the first in a flock of storm-petrels to fly when the boat is approaching. However, don't make the mistake of assuming that all storm-petrels that flush readily are Band-rumpeds.

WHITE-TAILED TROPICBIRD

The tropicbird is one of those hard-to-find species that birders hope for—but don't really expect to see—when they register for pelagic birding trips. Once you find them, however, tropicbirds can put on a pretty good show, flying around the boat for a minute or two and allowing everyone really good views and photographs. They are not easy to come by, but they are found as frequently off North Carolina's coast as anywhere in the United States.

The White-tailed is strictly a pelagic species. Most records are from May to September. They are generally rare but are occasional during two peaks—in late May and from mid-July to early September. They seem to be most frequent along the edge of the Gulf Stream, but many records are from waters somewhat closer to shore.

Your best chance of finding this bird is by taking one of the birding trips out of Oregon or Hatteras inlets in late May or between mid-July and early September. Because this species is not restricted to the Gulf Stream or deeper waters, it is almost as likely to be seen from one of the headboats out of Morehead City–Atlantic Beach (the peak time from here seems to be mid-July to mid-August) and Hatteras.

You could easily go a lifetime without seeing a tropicbird from land in North Carolina. However, there are two records from land: one for Cape Hatteras, one for Cape Lookout.

If you do see a tropicbird, you will want to rule out the possibility that it is a Red-billed, which is accidental. This is especially true if you see a tropicbird in May or early June. Carry a camera along: if you do have a tropicbird, you will likely have the opportunity to photograph it, and you can use the photograph later, on terra firma, to critique your field identification.

MASKED BOOBY

This tropical sulid has been found in the state's offshore waters from June to early October. However, most records are from late June to the beginning of September; during this period, boobies are rare. Most recorded sightings have taken place along the edge of the Gulf Stream. The species has been seen from land only in extremely rare cases. However, one year an individual summered in a pelican colony on the lower Cape Fear River near Fort Fisher.

Your only hope of seeing this species is to take one of the chartered birding trips out of Oregon or Hatteras inlets. The best time for this species may be around late June and early July, when boat captains have reported several of these birds during "tuna blitzes." You might try for this species by taking the headboat out of Hatteras during this late June–early July period.

Identifying an adult Masked Booby is easy at close range, but be careful when identifying distant individuals—Northern Gannets, which look similar, have been found throughout the summer. Generally, a summer sulid close to shore is most likely to be a gannet, while a summer sulid along the Gulf Stream edge is most likely to be a booby. However, off Cape Hatteras, the Gulf Stream is often only a few miles from shore, and near its edge, gannets are frequent in May, not too unlikely in June, and possible in late summer.

NORTHERN GANNET

This species is a common winter resident and migrant in the near-shore waters; Northern Gannets are frequently seen just off the beaches. They are included in this list because at times they may be slightly difficult to see, at least closely.

During the winter, they are rather easy to see anywhere from the Outer Banks southward; the Outer Banks may be the most consistently good area for seeing them well. For a really good look at one, go out to Cape Hatteras Point. Here you can see gannets in spectacular plunges just a few yards away. From about Thanksgiving to February, the oceanfront parking area at Fort Fisher is another great place to watch feeding gannets at close range (even while you sit in your car).

During the southward migration, from October into December, gannets are seen most easily from the east-facing beaches—anywhere from Cape Hatteras north, at Cape Lookout, and from Wrightsville Beach south to Cape Fear. During the northward migration, from about March to May, they are most likely to be seen from the south-facing beaches at and near the three capes.

AMERICAN WHITE PELICAN

Along most of our coast, this species is a rare year-round visitor, except in autumn, when it is occasional. Along the Outer Banks, White Pelicans are occasional throughout the year. In all areas, they have been increasing steadily.

White Pelicans are most widespread and easiest to find in autumn, about October and November. Then you might see one anywhere along the coast, although the impoundments at Pea Island NWR are probably your best bet. For many years an individual has summered on the Brown Pelican nesting islands at Ocracoke Inlet. On rare occasions this bird can be seen from the Cedar Island–Ocracoke ferry or the Swan Quarter–Ocracoke ferry. For the last few years, one or more birds have also summered on Brown Pelican nesting islands at Oregon Inlet (Bodie Island). You might spot one from the marina at Oregon Inlet. In winter, it has become almost the rule that a White Pelican can be spotted on one of the islands along the Hatteras Inlet ferry route. White Pelicans are also spotted during some winters from the Fort Fisher–Southport ferry.

If you get a good view, a White Pelican is impossible to confuse with any other bird. However, it is not unusual to see Brown Pelicans that appear rather bleached out, and beginning birders sometimes call such birds White Pelicans.

GREAT CORMORANT

On the 1970 Bodie–Pea Island Christmas Bird Count, great excitement resulted from the report of a super-rarity, a bird previously unknown in North Carolina— a Great Cormorant! Since that year this species has increased steadily in coastal North Carolina. Today it is an uncommon winter resident, although locally Great Cormorants are impossible to miss.

Great Cormorants occur mainly from October to April. Occasionally, one or more immatures will remain all summer at one of the more favored localities. Largely restricted to the ocean and inlets, Great Cormorants feed primarily over hard-bottom areas and are often found near jetties and shipwrecks.

The current hot spot for seeing these cormorants—and seeing them well, and with several birds in various plumages—is at Zeke's Island, along the rock breakwater (the Rocks) south of Fort Fisher. This site involves a long and sometimes potentially dangerous hike. However, the birds are also seen frequently where the rock breakwater begins, at Federal Point, and they may be seen flying or feeding in the ocean just off the oceanfront parking area at Fort Fisher. Masonboro Inlet at Wrightsville Beach is another reliable (and easily accessible) site. Other sites where Greats are regular include: the Oregon Inlet bridge, especially on the range markers inside the inlet (although this site is rather distant); Pea Island, from the beach opposite the south end of North Pond (watch for a bird feeding around the shipwreck); off the Hatteras Island Fishing Pier at Rodanthe (watch for a feeding bird at the nearby shipwreck at low tide); just outside the village of Ocracoke, along the ferry route to Cedar Island and Swan Quarter (check the smokestack of the sunken dredge); and Cape Lookout (either at the jetty or on pilings in the bight). An excellent, although transitory, situation that often attracts roosting Greats is where an ocean fishing pier has been damaged by a storm to the point that nothing but pilings remain. Such sites now exist on Topsail Island.

Pay special attention to the choicest, highest cormorant perches, for these will often be claimed by the Greats. The higher sites often accentuate their larger sizes—in a mixed flock of cormorants, the Greats will often stand out as men among boys.

In first-winter and adult plumages, the identification of Great Cormorants is straightforward. Perhaps the most difficult identification problem is that posed by the occasional summering individuals, which are most likely to be immatures or subadults. In these cases, the faded plumage presents few clincher field marks.

ANHINGA

Historically, the status of the Anhinga has waxed and waned in North Carolina. Currently, we are in a definite waxing phase, with birds breeding as far north as the Alligator River NWR. Nevertheless, Anhingas are still difficult to find along most of the coast. Many of the better sites for the species are off-limits or are very difficult to get to.

Anhingas occur primarily in the South Coast section. Here they are uncommon from April to early summer, becoming fairly common from about late June to mid-September. They decline during autumn, becoming rare in midwinter. North of this section, Anhingas are occasional and very local, occurring primarily from April to August.

Two sites where these birds can usually be found are Orton Pond and Twin Lakes (on the mainland at Sunset Beach). Somewhat less dependable is Greenfield Lake in Wilmington. Farther north, there are no dependable and easily accessible sites. Anhingas are seen rather often on the east side of Great Lake in the Croatan NF (southwest section) in mid- to late summer, but this site is undependable and requires a boat trip.

Anhingas are easy to identify: they are snakier and have much larger tails than cormorants. Nevertheless, beginning birders sometimes assume that cormorants don't occur in fresh water and thus that any cormorant-like bird seen in fresh water, especially in summer, must be an Anhinga. This mistake is sometimes made during the summer at the impoundments at Pea Island NWR.

MAGNIFICENT FRIGATEBIRD

Frigatebirds are very rare to rare spring and summer visitors along the state's coast. Most recorded sightings have taken place between mid-May and early July, from Cape Lookout southward. Despite their rarity, looking for frigatebirds is not always a waste of time. They have vast wingspans and often follow shorelines, so it is easy to watch for them. And they often show up in connection with certain weather conditions, so there is some predictability to their occurrences.

Many of the May and June sightings have taken place during periods of fair weather. However, from late June to early September, most records have occurred during periods of unstable tropical air masses with strong southerly winds—the kind of weather that produces waterspouts. Watch for frigatebirds especially when such weather is associated with a tropical storm or hurricane that has gone ashore farther south and is moving northward across the inland Carolinas.

Most sightings have been of birds in flight up or down the coast. However, Beaufort Inlet is notable as a site where birds sometimes linger, putting on a day-long show. Perhaps vagrants moving north become confused when they encounter a shoreline that begins to bend southward.

AMERICAN BITTERN

This secretive marsh species is primarily a migrant and winter resident. During migration it is uncommon; in winter it is occasional. This species is definitely declining; it is seen much less frequently than a few years ago. In the breeding season, American Bitterns are generally absent, but they apparently breed locally.

During migration and in winter, Pea Island NWR and Bodie Island are probably the best areas for finding this species. If you check enough marsh edges at the ponds and impoundments and along ditches, you will eventually find one. They can also usually be found at Mattamuskeet NWR and Mackay Island NWR during the migrations.

In autumn, American Bitterns are encountered regularly at the edges of salt marshes along the southern part of the coast. Check near tidal guts, where the grass is thick, especially at high tide.

During spring migration and in the breeding season, listen for the bittern's unique, booming "oonk-a-tsoonk"—like a pile being driven into mud. You're most likely to hear this at dawn.

During the breeding season, bitterns are perhaps most likely to be found at Mattamuskeet NWR. They might also be spotted at Mackay Island NWR, Bodie Island, and Cedar Island NWR.

American Bitterns are easy to identify, but beginning birders sometimes misidentify immature night-herons as bitterns. Note that American Bitterns almost never perch in shrubs and trees like night-herons do.

LEAST BITTERN

This small, brightly colored bittern is fairly common along much of the state's coast, although secretive and difficult to find, during the spring migration and summer. They occur in salt, brackish, and fresh marshes. Strangely, they are scarce along most of the Outer Banks, despite the abundance of habitat.

The highway causeway at Mackay Island NWR is one of the best places in the state for this species and is also easily accessible. Be here at dawn. You are almost certain to hear their cuckoo-like calls and to see one or two birds making short flights.

The Pamlico Point Impoundment area can be good but is quite inaccessible. Likewise, sites where birds may be found at Mattamuskeet NWR are unpredictable and require long hikes. You might also find Least Bitterns at Bodie Island, at Cedar Island NWR, and at the USS North Carolina Battleship Memorial at Wilmington.

From Beaufort south, Least Bitterns are often fairly common in tidal marshes in late summer. Wade out during abnormally high tides, checking thicker stands of grasses along the tidal creeks, and you will probably see one or more.

REDDISH EGRET

This species is currently a rare visitor from late spring to early autumn; Reddish Egrets are occasional at a few sites from July to September. Formerly extremely rare, they have increased significantly in recent years. If this trend continues, the "rare to occasional" designation will no longer be appropriate.

Almost all records have occurred at or near the ocean inlets. Significantly, most records have occurred at inlets with extensive sandy tidal flats.

Currently the most reliable and accessible spot for this species is at New Inlet south of Fort Fisher. New Drum Inlet at Cape Lookout NS is equally good but much harder to get to. Other sites worth checking are Oregon Inlet (Bodie Island), Portsmouth Island, and Mad Inlet (at the west end of Sunset Beach).

Most Reddish Egrets recorded in North Carolina have been dark-phase birds, and most have been subadults. These birds have a more subtle plumage than adults do. Beginning birders sometimes identify adult Little Blue Herons and immature Tricolored Herons as Reddish Egrets, because both have more reddish color on their heads and necks than is depicted in most field guides. Also, Tricoloreds can feed in a rather frenzied manner, not unlike Reddish Egrets. Note that the Reddish Egret is noticeably larger than the Tricolored and Little Blue herons.

BLACK-CROWNED NIGHT-HERON

This bulky, short-legged, mostly nocturnal heron is a fairly common permanent resident along our coast, but it varies greatly in abundance from area to area. In some locales it is scarce and rather hard to find, while in others it is one of the most common heron species, especially in winter.

In the Outer Banks section, Black-crowneds can usually be found at Bodie Island, Oregon Inlet Fishing Center, Pea Island NWR, and Ocracoke Island. On Bodie Island, look for them along the canals at North Bodie. At the Oregon Inlet

Fishing Center, watch for birds feeding from the pilings at dusk or night. At Pea Island, a few birds can usually be found roosting in the northwest corner of North Pond. On Ocracoke Island, look for birds in the marshes adjacent to the jeep trail to South Point, especially during the nesting season.

In the Central Coast section, Black-crowneds can be found readily in the Morehead City–Beaufort area. On the Morehead and Beaufort waterfronts, watch for birds feeding from pilings at night. Especially during the colder months, Black-crowneds are frequent scavengers; watch for them around the fish houses at Beaufort, especially near the menhaden processing plant on Front Street.

In the South Coast section, Black-crowneds can usually be found at Twin Lakes in Sunset Beach.

In adult plumage, Black-crowneds would never be misidentified. In immature plumage, however, they are sometimes called Yellow-crowned Night-Herons and even American Bitterns. A major source of confusion seems to be the fact that nonadult plumages of Black-crowneds often predominate, and you can often see numerous birds without a single adult being present. Beginning birders often reason that these birds can't be Black-crowned Night-Herons, because there couldn't be so many immature birds around without any adults, so they must be bitterns.

YELLOW-CROWNED NIGHT-HERON

The Yellow-crowned Night-Heron is primarily a summer resident, generally uncommon but fairly common locally, found primarily from April through September. These birds are generally absent in winter, although there are a handful of records, mostly from the South Coast section. In North Carolina at least, the Yellow-crowned Night-Heron is much less nocturnal than the Black-crowned.

In the Outer Banks section, you can usually find Yellow-crowneds easily at the lighthouse pond on Bodie Island, at Pea Island NWR, and on Ocracoke Island. At Pea Island, look for them along the west side of North Pond and the west side of South Pond. (The latter site is open to the public only during scheduled bird walks.) On Ocracoke Island, Yellow-crowneds nest in the pines next to NC 12 near the Park Service campground. Look for them here, at the nearby Hammock Hills Nature Trail overlook, or from the jeep trail to South Point. (Yellow-crowneds may not arrive in numbers in the Outer Banks section until about May 1.)

In the South Coast section, look for Yellow-crowneds at the Basin near Fort Fisher and at Twin Lakes in Sunset Beach. From April to August, watch for flybys from the city pier at Southport.

Adult Yellow-crowned Night-Herons are unmistakable, but the immatures do present identification problems—mainly confusion with Black-crowned Night-Herons. However, while immature Black-crowneds are called Yellow-crowneds with some frequency, the converse is rather rare. One might imagine that the legs of a Black-crowned are long enough that the bird could be a Yellow-crowned, but the opposite is not likely to happen. Yellow-crowneds have long legs that trail well beyond the tail when the bird is at flight, so here's a good rule of thumb: if the flying bird's silhouette momentarily reminds you of a Little Blue Heron or Tricolored Heron, then you've got a real Yellow-crowned. Yellow-crowneds have relatively large bills and heads that contrast greatly with their slender necks. Immature birds have all-dark bills, unlike immature Black-crowneds.

WHITE IBIS

During the first half of the twentieth century, the White Ibis was known here only as a scarce postbreeding dispersant; but now the White Ibis is a permanent resident along the state's coast from Bodie Island south. However, their abundance varies greatly from site to site—they are common to very common locally, especially in the vicinity of nesting islands, but uncommon in many areas.

White Ibises currently can be seen reliably throughout the year in the Fort Fisher–Southport area and at Bodie Island, Pea Island NWR, the marshes near Ocracoke Village, the marshes in the Morehead City–Beaufort area, and Twin Lakes at Sunset Beach. From the city pier at Southport, you can see an almost steady stream of ibises flying in and out of the Battery Island nesting colony between April and August.

WOOD STORK

It is an understatement to say that the boundary of this species' normal range in the state is clear-cut. At Twin Lakes in Sunset Beach, just over a mile from the South Carolina line, storks are annual summer residents, uncommon from late June to mid-September. But elsewhere—including sites a few miles north and east—storks are always very rare.

If you want to see this species in the state, visit Twin Lakes between late June and mid-September. These birds are easiest to find from mid-July through August.

FULVOUS WHISTLING-DUCK

This primarily southwestern species is generally rare along North Carolina's coast. However, every few years there is an invasion, and several birds are reported from one or more sites. These invasions occur mostly in late autumn and early winter; during some years, at least when it is mild, the birds may linger on throughout the winter. There may also be lesser invasions in the spring, especially April. Nonbreeding birds have even lingered into midsummer.

When Fulvous Whistling-Ducks do appear, sites where they seem to be most frequent are Bodie Island, Pea Island NWR, Mattamuskeet NWR, ponds in the Cape Hatteras area, and the Pamlico Point Impoundment. On Bodie and Pea islands, you will want to check the logbook at the Pea Island NWR visitors center to see if any have been reported. At Cape Hatteras, check the logbook at the Cape Hatteras ranger station. At Mattamuskeet NWR, check with the refuge personnel.

Whistling-Ducks look very distinctive and are easy to identify. Standing Whistling-Ducks have a noticeable long-necked profile, and flying ones have a peculiar hunchbacked look and whitish rump band; in these cases the birds are difficult to overlook. However, distant swimming birds do not always stand out so easily. Note that the length measurement in most field guides reflects their long neck, so the birds are not as large as one might assume—much slighter than the larger dabblers.

GREATER WHITE-FRONTED GOOSE

Overall, this species is an extremely rare winter visitor in North Carolina. However, every couple of years or so one turns up at Pea Island NWR or Mattamuskeet NWR (and adjacent areas). They often feed in fields with Canada Geese, so you won't have trouble finding Greater White-fronteds if they're in the neighborhood.

At both areas, this species is probably most likely from November to January. At Pea Island, look for them at New Field. At Mattamuskeet, check with refuge personnel to see if they have been sighted in the area.

ROSS' GOOSE

There is only one site in the state where this species occurs regularly. At Pea Island NWR, one (rarely more) shows up almost every year, from about mid-October to early February. Sightings are most frequent from about October 15 to Thanksgiving, and if you look hard enough you might be able to find one every year during that period.

If you want to see a Ross' Goose, sort through the Snow Geese carefully during the peak period. If you see flocks next to the highway at New Field, stay in your car while you scrutinize them. Look for a bird much smaller than the Snow Geese, with no grin patch and a very white head (not muddied like the heads of the Snows). If you don't see one, check the logbook at the visitors center to find out if one has been sighted.

At close range, the Ross' Goose is distinctly different and easy to identify. However, on one occasion a hybrid Snow-Ross' was found here.

You're not likely to find this species away from Pea Island NWR (or adjacent Bodie Island). However, there are records for two other sites—Pungo Lake and Lake Phelps—and the species might also occur at Mattamuskeet NWR and Mackay Island NWR.

BRANT

The status of this species has waxed and waned (actually waned and waxed) considerably during this century. Currently it is increasing and is a fairly common winter resident. However, Brants are very local and can be found dependably in only two areas—Hatteras and Ocracoke inlets. They are most likely from mid-November to early April. Their numbers can vary dramatically from year to year according to the severity of the winter. During more severe winters, they will be found easily, often to late April, sometimes later. During milder winters, they may be scarce, with most individuals migrating north after early winter.

To see Brants, take the Hatteras Inlet ferry or either of the two ferries to Ocracoke Village (from Cedar Island or Swan Quarter). On the last two ferries, look for the birds just out from the village. On the flats, even at a great distance, Brants can be picked out easily by their distinctive silhouettes—short necks and small heads.

Elsewhere, Brants are usually quite difficult to find. They are uncommon around Oregon Inlet; you might see a few from the Oregon Inlet Fishing Center. Farther south, Brants are sometimes seen from the Cape Lookout ferry in November. A few sometimes show up in the Fort Fisher area, and you might see these birds from the rock breakwater (the Rocks). During severe winters, Brants may turn up in many areas.

EURASIAN WIGEON

To find a male Eurasian Wigeon, the instructions are quite simple: find a large number of American Wigeons and scan through them for a "drake Redhead." Eurasian Wigeons commonly associate with American Wigeons, and a drake Eurasian Wigeon's coloration resembles a drake Redhead's.

Eurasian Wigeons have been found in coastal North Carolina from late September to April. They are very rare in most areas but are regular at Bodie Island, Pea Island NWR, and Mattamuskeet NWR. At the first two sites, they occur most frequently from late October through November, when they are uncommon. They become less frequent as winter progresses. This pattern also holds true at Mattamuskeet NWR, although birds are always less frequent there. They are occasional during the peak period, in November. Check the lighthouse pond and the smaller roadside ponds at Bodie Island, and North Pond at Pea Island. (The South Pond, which is usually off-limits, is equally good.) At Mattamuskeet, ask the refuge personnel about the locations of any recent sightings.

Elsewhere in the state, Eurasian Wigeons are much harder to come by. They are probably regular at the relatively inaccessible Pamlico Point Impoundment. In recent years, there have been several sightings at Davis Impoundment in the Central Coast section. This impoundment is private and off-limits, but birds are occasionally seen from US 70, which runs adjacent to one corner of the impoundment. At this site you are most likely to see a bird in February and early March.

Female Eurasian Wigeons are much less easy to pick out. Usually they are more rusty-headed than female Americans. Consult one of the more advanced field guides.

GREATER SCAUP

It may be that no bird that occurs as regularly in the state as the Greater Scaup is as poorly understood in terms of temporal and ecological status. This situation occurs because the Greater closely resembles the more common Lesser Scaup and because ducks are typically difficult to get close to for inspection of fine details.

Greater Scaup are winter residents that occur primarily just off the ocean beaches (usually as fly-bys) and on the larger sounds, mostly from late November through March. During this period, they are uncommon, becoming more common in midwinter if there has been extreme cold.

Typical birders want not just to see Greater Scaup but to see them very well. At Pea Island NWR, these birds sometimes occur on the impoundments where they can be seen rather closely. Similarly, one or two of them are sometimes seen along the causeway across Lake Mattamuskeet.

Also watch off the beaches of the Outer Banks, especially in midwinter. If you can, get out on one of the ocean fishing piers at Nags Head, Rodanthe, or Avon in the afternoon when the light is good. If you do see a Greater Scaup flying by, you might get a good look at the bold white stripe extending out onto the primaries. Farther south, the oceanfront parking area at Fort Fisher is another relatively good spot for this species. Again, the afternoon light is best. Nearby, the fishing pier at Kure Beach is sometimes open in winter. Here you could get a relatively good look at a fly-by.

By the way, don't assume that ocean scaup have to be Greaters. They are actually most likely to be Lessers, and this is especially true during the migrations.

The two scaup species cannot be reliably distinguished based on the head color of males. If you see a bird on the water, look closely at its head shape: the Greater Scaup has a smoothly rounded head. Consult one of the newer field guides.

COMMON EIDER

This species is a winter visitor/resident along our coast. Common Eiders occur primarily from late November to early March, when they are rare, except occasional on the Outer Banks. Sometimes individuals may linger well into the summer. They are largely restricted to the ocean and inlets and are most likely to be found around rock jetties and similar structures.

Eiders will probably become somewhat regular near the recently constructed groin at Oregon Inlet, which can be seen from Pea Island NWR. Other Outer Banks sites to check include Pea Island NWR (the shipwreck opposite the south end of North Pond) and off the Hatteras Island Fishing Pier at Rodanthe. Eiders are sometimes spotted from the Hatteras Inlet ferry as well.

South of the Outer Banks, sightings of Common Eiders are much less frequent. However, look for them at the jetties at Fort Macon SP. You may also see them at Wrightsville Beach, but you will rarely have the opportunity to get a close look at one here unless you own a boat.

Note that adult males are extremely rare in this region. Virtually all sightings are of females and immature males.

KING EIDER

Most of the preceding statements about the status of the Common Eider also hold true for the King Eider. Look for them at the same sites. However, King Eiders are much less likely to linger in the spring, and there are no summer records.

HARLEQUIN DUCK

This is another northern seacoast species found with increasing frequency in North Carolina. Harlequin Ducks are winter visitors/residents, found primarily from early December to early March. Then they are occasional on the Outer Banks, especially at Oregon Inlet, but rare elsewhere. On occasion they have lingered in spring as late as May. Harlequins are found primarily near rock jetties and similar structures on the oceanfront and around the inlets. They have been found along the western side of Pamlico Sound, but this location is extremely unusual.

In recent years Harlequins have been found more and more frequently at the bridge across Oregon Inlet, especially around the supports near the south end of the bridge. With the recent construction of a groin nearby, Harlequins may become even more regular at this location. Elsewhere on the Outer Banks, watch for Harlequins under the fishing piers at Kitty Hawk, Kill Devil Hills, Nags Head, and Rodanthe. They are sometimes spotted off the groins at the Cape Hatteras Lighthouse.

Farther south, Harlequin Ducks are rare but regular. Watch for them at the jetties at Fort Macon and Wrightsville Beach, and off the natural rock outcrops on the beach at Fort Fisher. At Wrightsville Beach, though, you're not likely to see one unless you own a boat. In the South Coast section, Harlequins may also occur wherever pilings remain from piers damaged or destroyed by storms; Topsail Island currently offers such sites. In the South Coast section, Harlequin Ducks frequently associate with Buffleheads.

If you get a good look, an adult male Harlequin Duck is impossible to misidentify, but the plumage of females is more subtle and requires a better view. Most of the birds that show up in our waters are immature males. In early winter, these often appear very similar to females.

OLDSQUAW

This winter visitor/resident occurs (rather locally) along the oceanfront and on the larger sounds, mostly from about mid-November to March. In most areas,

Oldsquaws are only occasional, but on Pamlico Sound within and adjacent to Swanquarter NWR, they are common. At this site they are found regularly into April.

If you really want to see an Oldsquaw in North Carolina, take the Swan Quarter–Ocracoke ferry between late November and early April. The period from mid-February through March is especially good. The second most reliable site for this species is, curiously, in the South Coast section. One or more individuals can often be seen off the natural rock outcrops on the beach at Fort Fisher, with the Buffleheads. If you miss them here, walk the rock breakwater (the Rocks) at the end of US 421. They are occasionally seen here as well. At these two sites Oldsquaws are most likely from late November to February. Oldsquaws also occur regularly at Oregon Inlet and will likely become more regular here in the future due to the construction of a new groin.

Elsewhere, check the groins at Cape Hatteras Lighthouse, the jetties at Fort Macon and Wrightsville Beach, and fishing piers in all sections. Oldsquaws might be seen as fly-bys anywhere along the ocean beaches, especially after severe cold.

BLACK SCOTER

Both Black and Surf scoters are fairly common winter residents in North Carolina, and both are common at certain times. But beginning birders often become frustrated trying to get good looks at them, because they are sea ducks, seen most often as ocean fly-bys—often at some distance.

The Black Scoter is fairly common off the ocean beaches in winter and is common during the peak migration periods—late October to early November and late March to early April. These scoters also occur on Pamlico Sound and the lower Pamlico and Neuse rivers. On western Pamlico Sound and the lower Pamlico River, they are also fairly common, sometimes common. Individuals sometimes linger into the summer.

For an excellent chance not only of seeing Black Scoters but of getting good looks at them, take the Swan Quarter–Ocracoke ferry in winter, scheduling the trip so that you have the sun at your back. Also try watching for southbound scoters in late October and early November, after cold fronts, from east-facing ocean beaches, especially from Cape Hatteras north. Afternoon, when the light is favorable, is the best time. Or watch for northbound scoters from the south-facing beaches in late March and early April. Early morning has the biggest flights of birds and the best lighting.

In winter, Black Scoters are also seen somewhat regularly from the Cedar Island–Ocracoke ferry and the Pamlico River ferry. Along the ocean beaches, they may be spotted at any site with rock jetties or similar structures. One or two are often seen off the natural rock outcrop at Fort Fisher (mostly in early winter), and they should become regular near the new groin at Oregon Inlet.

If you get a good view, the adult male Black Scoter is unmistakable. However, beginning birders sometimes misidentify females and immature males as Ruddy Ducks. In North Carolina, though, Ruddy Ducks are virtually never seen on the ocean.

SURF SCOTER

Much of the information about Black Scoters is also applicable to Surf Scoters, but there are some noteworthy differences. Surf Scoters are more common than Blacks on the Pamlico Sound and the lower Pamlico and Neuse rivers. They are seen commonly from the Swan Quarter–Ocracoke ferry and are seen on most trips on the Pamlico River ferry and the Cedar Island–Ocracoke ferry. Surf Scoters are most common during severely cold winters. They are less likely than Black Scoters to linger into summer.

Like Black Scoters, Surf Scoters are regularly found at rock jetties and similar structures. In early winter, the natural rock outcrop at Fort Fisher may have one or two Surf Scoters.

WHITE-WINGED SCOTER

In North Carolina, the White-winged is the least common scoter. It is a winter visitor/resident, found primarily from November to early April. Overall, White-winged Scoters are uncommon from Cape Hatteras north and occasional farther south. However, they may become fairly common south to the Outer Banks during severe cold. They are found primarily on the ocean but are occasional on Pamlico Sound and the lower Pamlico River. White-winged Scoters are slightly more common (uncommon in all sections) during their migrations—early November, roughly, and late March–early April. They are most widespread around early November, when they might even be seen on fresh water.

Again, this species occurs at rock jetties and similar structures and may become regular in the future at the new Oregon Inlet groin. Otherwise, watch for migrating White-wingeds as you would for Blacks. White-winged Scoters are also occasionally seen from the Swan Quarter–Ocracoke ferry, especially in late February and March.

COMMON GOLDENEYE

In North Carolina, the Common Goldeneye is an uncommon and local winter resident, occurring mostly from late November to late March. These birds are largely restricted to the sounds, although they are sometimes seen as ocean fly-bys. They are often found at sites favored by Buffleheads.

Probably the most reliable spot for this species is along the rock breakwater (the Rocks) that begins at the south end of US 421 south of Fort Fisher. Birders often find several birds at this location. However, you will often have to make a long hike to find these birds. A more accessible and fairly reliable area for this species is the northern end of Roanoke Island. Watch from the shoreline at the

Fort Raleigh NHS or from the end of Morrison Grove Road. Finding a bird will be easier when the water is smooth; avoid strong northerly winds. Goldeneyes are also seen fairly often along the Swan Quarter end of the Swan Quarter–Ocracoke ferry and are occasional near Ocracoke on the Swan Quarter–Ocracoke and Cedar Island–Ocracoke ferries.

In all areas, adult males are seen rather infrequently. Most birds are females or immature males.

COMMON MERGANSER

Most recorded sightings of this winter visitor have taken place between early December and mid-March. During this period the species is rare on average, but there is a lot of variation from year to year. During many winters birders have found no mergansers at all, while during other winters, after extreme cold, there have been several sightings recorded. In our area Common Mergansers are perhaps most likely on fresh water, but they have also been found on brackish and salt water.

Even during severe winters, no areas are consistently good for this species. However, some areas to check are the impoundments at Pea Island NWR; Lake Phelps; Lake Mattamuskeet; the Salt Pond at Cape Hatteras Point; and the Basin south of Fort Fisher. At the last two sites, birds have sometimes shown up even during mild winters.

Almost all Common Mergansers found in coastal North Carolina are females. You will need a good close view to satisfy yourself that you are indeed seeing this rare merganser. At close range you will be able to see the well-defined white chin and the crisp, well-defined line of demarcation on the neck.

BLACK VULTURE

Overall, the Black Vulture is much less common and widespread than its larger cousin, the Turkey Vulture. However, Black Vultures are fairly common locally. Some of the more reliable sites for this species are the Lake Phelps area; Pocosin Lakes NWR (Pungo unit); the Lake Mattamuskeet area; Croatan NF (east and south sections); Holly Shelter Game Land (northwest section); the Orton Pond area; and the Green Swamp area.

AMERICAN SWALLOW-TAILED KITE

Birders in North Carolina can feel lucky that this beautiful and graceful creature of the Deep South at least wanders northward into our area each spring, although it doesn't nest here. Swallow-tailed Kites are most likely from mid-April through May. During this period they are rare along the immediate coast as far north as Oregon Inlet, but occasional from Cape Hatteras to Portsmouth Island. Birds are usually seen in flight following the barrier islands or shorelines of the adjacent mainland. They may be seen heading north or returning south. However, birds reaching the Buxton Woods at Cape Hatteras—a relatively large island of habitat—sometimes linger for several days, perhaps weeks, before returning south.

If you really want to see this species in North Carolina, go to the Cape Hatteras area between mid-April and June 1. Drive along the highway to Cape Hatteras Point and from Cape Hatteras to Frisco, watching the sky as much as possible. Even better, go to the Park Service campground near Frisco and set up watch on one of the tall dunes that overlook the forest. Mid- to late morning on a clear day is best.

During this same period, on days with clear skies and southwest winds, you might also try a mid- to late morning watch near the north end of Ocracoke Island. Watch from one of the dunes where the island is narrow. If a kite does fly by, you will be sure to see it.

Elsewhere along the coast, Swallow-taileds might be sighted anywhere along the barrier islands or along the shoreline of the adjacent mainland from Carteret County south. Look especially in places where potential migration pathways are squeezed into a very narrow corridor.

MISSISSIPPI KITE

Until a few years ago, this species was extremely rare on the North Carolina coast. However, during recent years it has been found with increasing regularity as a spring migrant. Mississippi Kites are rare during their peak period of occurrence, in May and early June. There are also a handful of records in early to mid-October.

If this species continues to increase at the rate it has in recent years, it may soon be of occasional status along the immediate coast in May and early June. In general, watch for it at the same types of places where Swallow-tailed Kites occur. However, although most records of Swallow-taileds have come from the barrier islands, about half of the records for this species have come from the shoreline of the mainland (from Carteret County south). It remains to be seen whether this pattern will continue as more records accumulate. In October, sightings are perhaps most likely on the barrier islands of the South Coast section.

So far, most springtime Mississippi Kites seen along North Carolina's coast have been in subadult plumage. These are similar enough to adults that no one should have any trouble identifying them.

BALD EAGLE

The status of our national bird in coastal North Carolina, in comparison with many coastal areas of the United States, is quite poor. At most sites eagles are found only occasionally. However, they are increasing very gradually.

For by far the best chance of seeing a Bald Eagle in this area, go to Matta-muskeet NWR anytime from late October into February. You are almost certain to see birds from the causeway or at the lake near the refuge office. During the rest of the year, eagles are not as reliable, but you might spot one. In late autumn and early winter, one or two birds can usually be found at Pocosin Lakes NWR (Pungo unit). This site may become even more reliable in future years. At the dam at Orton Pond, an adult can usually be found from autumn to spring.

In late spring and summer, immature and subadult eagles sometimes take up residence near heron colonies. On Ocracoke Island, watch the skies carefully near the Pony Pasture and along the ORV trail to South Point.

Adult Bald Eagles are easy to identify, but beginning birders usually have trouble identifying immature eagles and sometimes identify Red-tailed Hawks as eagles, because of their size. Remember that it is impossible to judge the size of a soaring bird unless there are other birds around for direct comparison. However, the wing-flapping of an eagle is noticeably heavy and labored.

COOPER'S HAWK

Most beginning birders at first have no trouble seeing Cooper's Hawks—because they think every female Sharp-shinned is a Cooper's. However, as birders become more skilled, they begin to realize that Cooper's Hawks are indeed rather scarce in coastal North Carolina and that they probably haven't seen a real one yet.

In general, this species is occasional in winter and rare in summer, but uncommon during the autumn migration, mostly after cold fronts from late September through October. They are slowly but steadily increasing in autumn and winter, and at some sites they are now uncommon throughout winter.

If you want to see a real Cooper's Hawk, and to see it well, then head for the barrier islands in October, particularly when there are clear skies and north-westerly winds. Set up watch at sites where migrating raptors are funneled through a narrow corridor and you are at the same elevation as the passing hawks. Two such areas are the dune ridge on the west side of Jockey's Ridge SP and Battery Buchanan south of Fort Fisher. Consult one of the newer field guides for all the ways to distinguish between Cooper's and Sharp-shinned hawks. Your high perch will provide you with a good view for seeing one of the most obvious differences: Cooper's Hawks have much longer tails than Sharp-shinneds. A side view will make this difference most visible.

In winter, Cooper's Hawks are becoming regular at sites where birdlife is abundant, such as impoundments. Look for them at Alligator River NWR (north section), at Mattamuskeet NWR, at Pocosin Lakes NWR (Pungo unit), along the west side of North Pond at Pea Island NWR, and similar areas. The Pungo Lake area is especially reliable; you will usually see a couple of birds in a morning.

GOLDEN EAGLE

This species is an extremely rare winter visitor in most of our area. However, Golden Eagles are found every couple of years or so at Pocosin Lakes NWR

(Pungo unit) and Mattamuskeet NWR; they are most likely from mid-November to mid-February.

If you want to try for this species, head for Pungo or Mattamuskeet. At Pungo, go to the observation tower and check the treetops around the lake with a scope. Unfortunately, a sighting here is likely to be distant and unsatisfying. At Mattamuskeet you are most likely to see one at the east end of the lake. Here an immature bird once flew directly over the heads of a startled ornithology class. At both refuges, check with refuge personnel to see if there have been any recent sightings.

Beginning birders should be aware that immature Bald Eagles can have fairly well-defined areas of white in the wings. Such birds are sometimes called Golden Eagles by the unwary. Consult one of the more advanced field guides.

MERLIN

This is another raptor species that beginning birders usually have trouble identifying. Frequently such birders call female American Kestrels Merlins, remarking, "That bird had to be a Merlin; it was definitely too big for a kestrel."

The Merlin is most common as an autumn migrant. Merlins are fairly common during the peak of migration, from late September to late October. In winter they are uncommon and rather local.

If you want to get a good look at a Merlin, head for the Outer Banks or any potentially good hawk-watching site on the other barrier islands, such as Battery Buchanan near Fort Fisher. During the winter months, Pea Island NWR and Bodie Island are perhaps the best areas to look, but Merlins are also seen regularly at several sites where the habitat is open and large numbers of birds are present—such as waterfowl impoundments and flats adjacent to inlets.

At a distance, perhaps because most of them are rather dark, Merlins do not look very big. Often a Merlin looks no bigger than a kestrel; it may even look smaller. Look for a small, dark, rapidly flying falcon. This bird doesn't exhibit any of the buoyant hesitancy typical of a Kestrel. Only at very close range will the larger bulk of a Merlin become apparent to you.

PEREGRINE FALCON

This species is often what beginning birders are looking for when they visit the Outer Banks in autumn. And not even the most jaded longtime birder tires of seeing a Peregrine.

The Peregrine Falcon has increased steadily during the last twenty years. In autumn it is an uncommon migrant along the barrier islands, mostly from late September to late October, and is even fairly common from Bodie Island to Cape Hatteras. A few Peregrines linger throughout the winter, when they are uncommon along the Outer Banks and occasional along the other barrier islands.

For an excellent chance of seeing a Peregrine and seeing it well, set up watch at one of the observation platforms at the North Pond of Pea Island NWR during the autumn migration period, especially around the first week in October. If one does come into view it might put on a good display, chasing shorebirds and waterfowl or getting into a real aerial dogfight with a harrier or other hawk.

In winter, Bodie Island, Pea Island NWR, and Cape Hatteras Point are the best areas for finding Peregrines. An individual that usually winters in the Morehead City–Beaufort area can often be seen late in the afternoon, resting on the raised portion of the railroad bridge adjacent to the high-rise bridge between Morehead and Beaufort. In the Fort Fisher area, an individual often overwinters near Zeke's Island. Walk the Rocks—the rock breakwater that begins at the south end of US 421—and watch for the bird in flight or perched on one of the range or channel markers in the river.

Whenever you notice flocks of gulls, terns, shorebirds, and small waterfowl taking flight in panic for no apparent reason, search the skies. You will probably spot a Peregrine. (Similarly, small shorebirds take flight when a Merlin is in the area.)

RING-NECKED PHEASANT

For years this introduced species occurred in good numbers on all the barrier islands from Oregon Inlet south to Hatteras Inlet. Pheasants were especially common at Pea Island NWR—an automatic find at New Field. Lately, though, this status has changed dramatically. Throughout this area the birds have decreased noticeably, and they are completely absent from some areas, although a few seem to be hanging on at Pea Island. Curiously, Ocracoke Island is now the best area on the Outer Banks to look for them, although they became established here only a few years ago.

Elsewhere there are also established populations on Portsmouth Island and on Core Banks south to Cape Lookout. However, these populations are reportedly supplemented with introduced birds, brought over from time to time (illegally) by hunters.

From late winter to spring, you can find pheasants easily by listening for the male's territorial call. Listen for a loud "kok-kak."

WILD TURKEY

Coastal North Carolina is certainly not one of the better areas in the country for seeing this wary species. Populations here are widely scattered, and the numbers of birds are low in most areas. However, turkeys are increasing and may be easier to find in the future.

Perhaps the best population within coastal North Carolina is at the Camp Lejeune Marine Corps Base. This area is off-limits except to drive-through traffic along NC 172. If you drive this highway through the base at dawn, you might get lucky and glimpse a turkey, but don't bet on it. Elsewhere, birds might be spotted at the western end of the Mattamuskeet NWR, along the Island

Creek Forest Walk in the Croatan NF (north section), or along the northern part of the Neusiok Trail in the Croatan NF (east section).

In spring, listen for the male's loud gobbling call. Turkeys often give this call in response to some disturbance, such as the calls of Barred Owls and Pileated Woodpeckers or the slamming of a car door.

NORTHERN BOBWHITE

Most North Carolina birders probably saw a bobwhite before they ever became seriously interested in birds. However, visiting birders from the North and the West often want to find this species.

Bobwhites are fairly common permanent residents in most mainland areas and are readily found in the breeding season, when they are loudly vocal and rather easily seen. However, during the rest of the year they can be very difficult to see, especially during very cold weather. Unfortunately, this species is declining steadily in the state. In the future they will probably become increasingly difficult to see, especially during the nonbreeding season.

During the nonbreeding season, a particularly good site for this species is along the Wildlife Drive at the Mattamuskeet NWR. The Wildlife Drive at Pocosin Lakes NWR (Pungo unit) is also fairly good during this season.

In the spring and early summer, bobwhites can be located easily by their loud "bob-white" calls. During the cooler months, you can often hear their "hoy" call-notes at dusk and dawn, especially when the weather is calm. Listen especially in large areas with thick ground cover, such as recent clear-cuts.

YELLOW RAIL

Ah yes, one of the mice. The yellow one. The one that doesn't call.

Coastal North Carolina has both of the feathered mice, the Yellow Rail and the Black Rail. Birders eagerly search for both but very seldom see them. The Black Rail is easier to find because it breeds here and thus calls regularly. But the Yellow Rail is virtually silent during its North Carolina months, making it particularly hard to locate.

The Yellow Rail is apparently (or unapparently!) a regular, perhaps uncommon, autumn migrant and winter resident, occurring primarily from early October to late March, perhaps later. They are probably most common and widespread during the autumn migration, about October. In winter they are known to occur in irregularly flooded salt marshes, salt meadows, and clear-cut pocosin areas with thick herbaceous cover. These habitats are all moist but are rarely flooded with more than a couple of inches of water. During the autumn migration they have also been found along the borders of regularly flooded salt marshes.

If you would like to try to see a Yellow Rail in North Carolina, I should warn you that your efforts will probably be futile, but you might try to get to one of the following areas during a combination of stormy weather and high lunar tides between early October and early November: the marshes at Oregon Inlet (highest water level occurs with strong west or southwest winds behind intense low pressure plus high lunar tide); the salt meadows at Cape Hatteras Point (extremely high tides and heavy rainfall); the small area of marshes near the Hatteras Inlet ferry terminal on Ocracoke Island (high lunar tide plus strong northwesterly winds behind an intense low pressure storm); the salt meadows at the south end of Ocracoke Island (strong northwesterly winds behind intense low pressure plus high lunar tide); the Cedar Island Marshes (strong northeasterly winds); and the marshes along the barrier spit south of Fort Fisher (extreme lunar tide and strong low pressure).

I should stress that winds strong enough to produce adequately high water levels should be at least thirty miles per hour, sustained. Some of these sites are definitely not prime Yellow Rail habitat, but the birds undoubtedly occur here at least as autumn migrants, and high tide conditions might force them out into the open.

At the Cedar Island Marshes, drive slowly back and forth along the causeway, watching for rails huddled along its edge. (Please note: during extreme wind tides, parts of the highway may be flooded.) At the other sites, concentrate on the edges, where the marshes are bordered by relatively sparse dune vegetation. If birds are driven up into this zone, you will have a chance of spotting one.

Trying to find the birds in winter is probably even more of a lost cause. On one occasion, participants in the Cape Hatteras Christmas Bird Count successfully coaxed a bird into view at the salt meadows near the Cape Point campground by clicking two rocks together. Try this technique here or at similar sites—the marshes at the south end of Ocracoke Island, for instance—at night, or perhaps at dawn or sunset. You might get lucky.

Presumably wintering birds sometimes call before they depart in the spring; they've been heard in other southern states. So during that period (March, perhaps April) you might try to coax one into view by clicking rocks or playing a tape at night, dawn, or sunset.

BLACK RAIL

The other mouse. The blackish one. The one that's relatively easy to find in the state. Fortunately, Black Rails call in North Carolina, so birders here do have a reasonable chance of finding one—at least in the breeding season—and a slight chance of seeing one.

Black Rails are permanent residents in at least a few marshes in our area. They seem to prefer irregularly flooded salt marshes, vegetated with a mixture of black needlerush and saltmeadow cordgrass and/or salt grass. Such marshes are usually moist but are seldom flooded with more than an inch or two of water. This type of marsh occurs most commonly in the Pamlico Sound region. Furthermore, Black Rails are much more likely to be found in extensive marshes.

The birds seem to be, and probably are, more common in summer than in winter. It's difficult to make comparisons, though, because the birds are more vocal during the breeding season.

Numbers of wintering birds are almost certainly influenced by the severity of the weather. However, in winter birds may occur in some types of marshes they would ignore in summer. Black Rails are probably most widespread in autumn migration. I believe that Black Rails that call in winter are almost certain to be permanent resident individuals. If this is true, rails may be present in some additional habitats in winter, but they are not likely to be heard in these areas.

Much has been written about this bird's tendency to give its "ki-ki-krr" call only in the middle of the night, and some people even suggest that the bird is nocturnal. However, my experience in coastal North Carolina suggests that the Black Rail is predominantly *not* a nocturnal species. True, there are some calm nights in the breeding season when it seems that every rail in a marsh is calling, but nevertheless, the birds are predominantly diurnal. They are most likely to respond to a tape during the late afternoon, about sunset. However, a very efficient way to find out if Black Rails inhabit an area is to do some nighttime listening. After midnight, during calm—really calm—conditions and when human-generated noise is at a minimum, you might hear a Black Rail call half a mile away across the marshes. By the way, in my experience, nighttime calling is more frequent during full-moon conditions. However, most Black Rail enthusiasts claim that the opposite is true.

There are only a handful of sites where Black Rails have been found frequently. These are the marshes at the south end of Roanoke Island, near Wanchese; the Cedar Island Marshes, in Cedar Island NWR; and the North River Marsh (Carteret Wildlife Club site), near Beaufort. Other sites where birds are heard regularly are the salt meadows at the south end of Ocracoke Island, and the Pungo River Marshes, next to US 264, on the border between Beaufort and Hyde counties. Birds are occasionally heard at Pea Island NWR and Bodie Island.

If you would like to try to see a Black Rail, take a tape recorder and a tape of Black Rail calls out into one of these areas, perhaps about an hour before sunset (depending on how long you're willing to tolerate the mosquitoes). Birds are likely to respond to a taped call from April to about September. They are especially responsive from mid-April into May.

Play your tape occasionally and do lots of listening. If you don't get any responses, move around and try different sites. And be very, very still. Think about it—to a Black Rail, the foot shifting of a human probably feels similar to what the foot shifting of a Tyrannosaurus rex would feel like to us. When you do get a bird to respond, try this novel approach: stay as still as possible, continuing to play the tape occasionally, for as long as you can tolerate it. (A lightweight lawn chair is a nice item to bring along.) Eventually, the bird may briefly walk into view. More active measures—such as rushing the bird—are almost invariably futile at the dense grass-covered sites where the birds are found. The bird is more likely to be stomped on than to be flushed. If there are some openings or sparsely vegetated patches in the vicinity, a group of several people might be able to walk a bird out into the open by walking very slowly and close together.

At night birds are more likely to flush, but you are not likely to get a good view. More than likely, you'll have no idea whether it's really a rail, much less which species of rail it is. However, if surrounded by several people and then slowly approached, a night-calling rail will occasionally climb up into the marsh grass and freeze there, allowing excellent flashlight views at close range.

At most of the areas listed above (except the Pungo River Marshes), Black Rails will sometimes respond to tapes in the winter. During this season calm conditions are even more important, and the warmer it is, the better.

You might also look for Black Rails during high tides in autumn and in March and April, at the same sites and during the same conditions listed for Yellow Rails.

CLAPPER RAIL

Compared to its more mousy kin, the Clapper Rail is indeed easy to find and see. This permanent resident species is especially representative of the regularly flooded salt marshes from Morehead City southward. Here Clapper Rails are common throughout the year. Clappers are also found in the limited areas of regularly flooded salt marshes and in the more extensive tracts of irregularly flooded salt marshes along the barrier islands north to Bodie Island, and along the shorelines of the Pamlico Sound. In these more northern areas, birds are fairly common to common from spring until autumn but are generally uncommon in winter.

This species is particularly easy to find in the South Coast section. With patient watching, you should have little trouble spotting one wherever there are extensive stands of marshes. Curiously, the two best times for seeing birds are at full low tide and at full high tide. At high tide, watch for birds that are making short flights or walking along the marsh edges. At low tide, watch for birds skulking down from marsh cover to the edge of the water. Birds are more likely to be seen early in the morning or late in the afternoon. Like other rails, Clappers can be called in readily by tape-recorded calls. Although many areas are good, a specific site worth mentioning is the barrier spit south of Fort Fisher (including the elevated boardwalk at the North Carolina Aquarium). Watch for birds from the boardwalk at low tide. Farther down the spit, look for birds during full high tides.

Elsewhere, birds can usually be found at Calico Creek in Morehead City and along the Morehead City–Beaufort causeway. At Cedar Island NWR, a few birds can often be spotted along the banks of the canals along the NC 12 causeway during low water levels (after west and southwest winds) in the warmer months.

On the Outer Banks, watch for Clapper Rails from the observation platform at Bodie Island Lighthouse Pond or go to Oregon Inlet adjacent to the fishing center. At the lighthouse pond, you're most likely to be successful during the warmer months. Check this location late in the afternoon (for best lighting) during low water levels (which are unpredictable here but generally follow dry weather). Here you may see Clapper Rails, King Rails, or "Cling Rails"—birds that appear to be in between the two. At Oregon Inlet, wade out from the south end of the marina, across a little slough, and walk through the marshes. High tide is best, but the slough may be thigh-deep then. Even at low tide, if you walk long enough you can find Clapper Rails here at any season. If you don't want to get your feet wet, walk out on the pedestrian walkway on the side of the bridge and watch the slough area patiently during low water levels (low lunar tide and north or northeast winds), especially early or late in the day.

KING RAIL

This attractive species replaces the Clapper Rail in fresh-water marshes. In North Carolina it is a rather local permanent resident. King Rails are generally uncommon but are fairly common in a few areas. Although these rails are largely restricted to fresh marshes, a few are seen in brackish and irregularly flooded salt marshes, especially in winter.

Because Kings and Clappers are known to hybridize in many areas, some authorities consider them to be one species, and the two species may be lumped together in the future. In some brackish marsh areas you may indeed see birds that look intermediate to the figures shown in the field guides for the two species. In fact, "Cling Rail" is a common term in birder jargon. Even if the two species are combined in the future, the birds of the fresh-water marshes will always be worth looking for because they're so attractive, with their rich reddish-brown coloration, well-marked upper parts, and strongly barred flanks.

You can easily call King Rails into view with a tape recording, especially during the breeding season, when the most effective tape is the "kik-brr" call of an unmated female. Or if water levels are low, you should eventually see a bird by patiently watching small, open flats within the marshes. Like all rails, they are most likely to be seen around dawn and sunset. Avoid windy weather.

King Rails with typical plumage are found easily at Mackay Island NWR, along the highway causeway; along the causeway to Church Island (Waterlily); and at the USS North Carolina Battleship Memorial at Wilmington. Mattamuskeet NWR can be good, but the best sites here can be transitory due to changing water levels, and getting to the best sites often requires long hikes. Orton Plantation is fairly good, but birds can be difficult to see here.

On the Outer Banks, Pea Island NWR and Bodie Island can also be fairly good for King Rails, but birds seen here are often "Cling Rails." At North Bodie, watch along the edges of all ponds. The observation platform at the Bodie Island Lighthouse Pond, at sunset and when water levels are low, is especially good. At Pea Island NWR, watch from the observation deck at the southeast corner of North Pond.

VIRGINIA RAIL

This species, which occurs primarily as a migrant and winter resident, is found in fresh, brackish, and irregularly flooded salt marshes. Especially common in brackish and irregularly flooded salt marshes in the Pamlico Sound region, Virginia Rails are common from mid-September to mid-April. During the breeding season, they are found primarily northward from the North River in Carteret County and are fairly common locally.

Virginia Rails are very curious and aggressive and respond readily to tape-recorded calls, usually walking into view within seconds. Often they seem to be plenty responsive to tapes of other rail species as well, especially to Sora calls. The quickest way to find out if Virginia Rails are in a marsh is to clap your hands and listen for their "grunting" response.

Some of the better areas for seeing Virginia Rails are Mackay Island NWR, along the highway causeway (good at least from autumn to spring); Bodie Island, along the paths to the duck blinds at North Bodie (at least from autumn to spring); the Roanoke Island Marshes near Wanchese (all year); and the North River Marsh (Carteret Wildlife Club site) near Beaufort (all year). The Cedar Island NWR has large numbers of Virginia Rails all year, but you will need a canoe (or a long hike) to get into the marshes here. The Bodie Island Lighthouse Pond can be good but is undependable, because there is no way to predict when the water will drop to a low enough level. However, you might get a great view of a rail here at sunset without even getting your feet wet. Autumn to spring is best here, but birds are occasionally seen in the nesting season. You might even see an adult with chicks. Farther south, Virginia Rails are rather dependable at the USS North Carolina Battleship Memorial in Wilmington from October to mid-April.

SORA

The Sora is fairly common during the migrations—in April and from late August to mid-October. In winter they are generally uncommon and local, although they may be fairly common at a few sites. Wintering Soras seem to be rather sensitive to severe cold; they are much easier to find during mild years. Even taking weather into account, wintering Soras are rather sporadic. A site with several birds one year might have none the next and then several again the next. Soras occur mostly in fresh and brackish marshes, often in cattails. During the migrations they frequently occur along the borders of regularly flooded salt marshes, and they occasionally overwinter in irregularly flooded salt marshes.

Soras often respond readily to the sound of hands clapping or a rock thrown into the marsh. Listen for a sharp "keek" or their characteristic whinnying call. (Virginia Rails also have an alarm note similar to the "keek" call.) Soras are inquisitive and will frequently come into view when a tape of their calls is played, although they are not as aggressive as Virginia Rails.

During the migration periods, Soras might show up anywhere. Some good areas are Mackay Island NWR, along the highway causeway; Bodie Island; Mattamuskeet NWR; and the USS North Carolina Battleship Memorial in Wilmington. During high tides, kick along the edges of salt marshes. You might flush a Sora in addition to the more common Clapper Rails.

In winter the Battleship Memorial is a fairly reliable site for this species. The fresh-water pond at Long Beach (Sixty-fourth Street) and Twin Lakes at Sunset Beach are two other areas where these birds might be spotted.

PURPLE GALLINULE

This beautiful, primarily tropical species was formerly a regular summer resident in the South Coast section. One or two could almost always be found at Orton Plantation. However, in recent years this species has declined noticeably. Currently, in the South Coast section it is only a rare summer resident or visitor. Sightings are somewhat more frequent from late April through May; presumably many of these records are overshoots. Farther north, Purple Gallinules are very rare summer visitors, except rare during the period from late April through May.

Currently, your best chance of finding this species is to check ponds in the South Coast section between late April and May. The farther south you look, the more likely you are to find a bird. Two sites worth checking are the fresh-water pond at Long Beach (Sixty-fourth Street) and Twin Lakes at Sunset Beach.

COMMON MOORHEN

This species, which is generally a permanent resident, is found in ponds with marshy edges or in large marshes with patches of open water. It is found primarily in fresh water but is also frequent in brackish impoundments. Northward, moorhens are fairly common during the warmer months but uncommon in winter, and they may become scarce after severe cold. In the South Coast section, they are fairly common all year; at some sites, they are most common in winter. Although moorhens can retire into the marsh and be quite secretive, they frequently swim out onto open water as well, especially early in the morning.

Some of the better sites for seeing moorhens are the East Pool impoundment at Mackay Island NWR (better during the warmer months); Mattamuskeet NWR (better during the warmer months; ask refuge personnel for locations of recent sightings); North Pond and South Pond at Pea Island NWR (better during the warmer months); the fresh-water pond at Long Beach (Sixty-fourth Street; better in winter); and Twin Lakes at Sunset Beach (good all year).

At North Pond at Pea Island NWR, watch from the observation deck at the southeast corner of the impoundment or walk to the northwest side of the impoundment. The west side of South Pond is also very good, but this area is off-limits unless you visit as part of a tour led by refuge personnel.

AMERICAN GOLDEN-PLOVER

This plover is predominantly an autumn migrant. On the Outer Banks, golden-plovers are occasional from late August to early November; elsewhere, they are rare during the autumn peak, in September. Golden-plovers are very rare throughout coastal North Carolina during the spring migration and are also very rare vagrants on the Outer Banks in early summer. These plovers are quite infrequent in tidal habitats where the similar Black-bellied Plover is common. They are more likely to be found on drier flats and either dry or wet short-grass areas.

You are most likely to find this species by visiting Cape Hatteras Point from late September through October, especially after prolonged periods of northeasterly winds. Check the sparsely vegetated sand flats south of the Salt Pond. Other Outer Banks sites worth checking for this species, during the same period and with the same weather conditions, are the salt flats at Pea Island; along the ORV trail to South Point at Ocracoke Island; and perhaps the Wright Brothers Memorial at Kitty Hawk, if the weather is really nasty.

Elsewhere, look for golden-plovers on the barrier islands, especially in September. Again, prolonged periods of northeast winds are best. Check expansive, relatively dry flats at the ends of the islands where such habitat is available.

In all plumages, golden-plovers are easily distinguished from Black-bellied Plovers, because they lack the Black-bellieds' black axillars and light rump. In all plumages, golden-plovers stand out as small, dark birds in comparison with Black-bellieds. Some beginning birders mistakenly assume that any plover in winter plumage that is not decidedly gray is a golden-plover; but winter-plumaged Black-bellieds frequently look more brown than gray, especially when seen at a distance.

WILSON'S PLOVER

This southern plover is a summer resident, occurring primarily from late March to early September. From Portsmouth Island south, Wilson's Plovers are fairly common locally. A few birds also nest sporadically on Ocracoke Island and at Hatteras Spit on Hatteras Island; however, sightings in these areas are decreasing. Wilson's Plovers formerly nested at Oregon Inlet, but there haven't been any records there in years. Wilson's Plovers are found primarily on the updrift side of inlets, at the accreting ends of the barrier islands, where there is suitable nesting habitat: above-tidal flats with little dune and vegetation development. Such habitats are becoming increasingly rare as human beings stabilize the barrier islands. Sparsely vegetated spoil islands are also good nesting habitat for this species, but such sites are also becoming increasingly rare.

Sites where this species can be reliably found, and where suitable habitat should be present in the future, are the flats at Portsmouth Island; the spit (hook) at Cape Lookout; all of Shackleford Banks; Rachel Carson Estuarine Research Reserve; Hammocks Beach SP; Masonboro Island; the barrier spit south of Fort Fisher; and the west end of Holden Beach. Note that all these sites require a boat ride and/or very long hikes. Three sites that require shorter hikes, but where parking is usually limited, are Bogue Inlet Point (Bogue Banks), the barrier spit at the north end of Carolina Beach, and the west end of Sunset Beach. On the Outer Banks, you might be able to spot one or two birds at Hatteras Spit on Hatteras Island or at the north or south ends of Ocracoke Island. Both these sites involve very long hikes if you don't have an ORV. At all sites, stay away from any birds that are obviously nesting, and don't enter any areas that are posted to protect the birds.

This plover is quite easy to identify. Look for the long and large all-black bill and the pinkish-beige legs.

PIPING PLOVER

This small, pale-colored plover, which is officially recognized as "threatened," is a permanent resident, generally uncommon. Piping Plovers are very local breeders, mostly in Cape Hatteras NS and Cape Lookout NS. In portions of the Cape Lookout NS, they are fairly common during the nesting season. Their preferred habitat is extensive sand flats with little vegetation and dune development. Such habitat is found adjacent to inlets and at similar sites. In winter Piping Plovers are found primarily on tidal flats at the inlets, mostly from Beaufort Inlet south. However, several birds may winter farther north during mild winters. Piping Plovers are most widespread during the migrations, especially from mid-March to mid-April and from August to October. During these periods they are frequently seen on the ocean beaches.

To look for this species in the breeding season, go to Cape Hatteras Point, Hatteras Spit, Portsmouth Island, or the spit (hook) at Cape Lookout. Do not go into any posted areas!

Better yet, look for the birds during migrations or in winter. During the migrations, you can usually find at least one or two birds at any of the inlets where extensive flats are present, such as Oregon Inlet (Bodie Island), Portsmouth Island, Rachel Carson Estuarine Research Reserve, Bogue Inlet Point (Bogue Banks), the southern end of Topsail Island, the barrier spit south of Fort Fisher, the west end of Holden Beach, and the west end of Sunset Beach. Also watch along the ocean beaches, especially where they are wide. In winter, currently reliable sites are Rachel Carson Estuarine Research Reserve, Bogue Inlet Point, and the west end of Holden Beach.

BLACK-NECKED STILT

This ridiculously long-legged, strikingly black-and-white shorebird is a summer resident, largely restricted to Pea Island NWR and Bodie Island. From mid-

April through August stilts are fairly common here and uncommon elsewhere. They are found at brackish nontidal pools and similar sites, such as drawn-down impoundments and pools at dredging sites. Away from the Bodie Island–Pea Island area, suitable habitat for this species is seldom present for long periods. For instance, an impoundment that is drawn down for one summer may attract birds during that period.

To see a Black-necked Stilt, go to the observation deck at Bodie Island Lighthouse Pond or walk the dikes at the impoundments at Pea Island NWR. You should have little trouble finding one here. Also, several birds are often present at the rather inaccessible Pamlico Point Impoundment. Elsewhere, you are most likely to see birds during mid- to late summer at drawn-down impoundments or dredge spoil sites.

AMERICAN AVOCET

Like the Black-necked Stilt, this predominantly western species is typical of brackish nontidal pools and similar sites, although it may also be found on tidal flats, especially in migration. It is by far most common at the Bodie Island–Pea Island area, where it is a fairly common autumn migrant, mostly from August to mid-November. During many years several birds remain all winter, although there may be few to none after extremely severe cold. A few avocets linger throughout the summer as well; strangely, there is a breeding record for Pea Island. Elsewhere, avocets are most likely to be found during the autumn migration; they are occasional from late July to mid-November.

To find this species reliably, go to Pea Island NWR and Bodie Island in autumn. If you don't spot any birds, check out the logbook at the Pea Island NWR visitors center for locations of recent sightings. Elsewhere, an avocet might show up anywhere during the autumn period, especially at drawn-down impoundments and dredging sites.

UPLAND SANDPIPER

As its name indicates, this shorebird is found primarily in relatively dry upland habitats. Upland Sandpipers are frequently found in areas with short-grass cover, such as airports. In North Carolina they are also found on dry, sandy, sparsely vegetated flats, like those at Cape Hatteras Point. This species is found almost exclusively during the autumn migration period, mostly between mid-July and early September. During this period they are occasional in most areas but uncommon at a few sites. They are very rare during the spring migration; most records are from mid-April to mid-May.

To find this species most reliably, go to the New Hanover County airport in Wilmington during the autumn migration period. The Dare County airport on Roanoke Island is also rather reliable. Birds also occur regularly at the Beaufort-Morehead airport, but you will usually not be able to see them from the public roadways. This species is not easy to find on the Outer Banks, but you might see one or two birds at the Wright Brothers National Memorial (best during rainy and windy weather), the Park Service campground at Salvo, and Cape Hatteras Point and the nearby campground. You are fortunate indeed if you find a bird at the campground areas, because there you can drive up close to them for excellent views.

If you get a good look, Uplands are very easy to identify, with their yellow legs, small heads, and large eyes. If you see them at a distance, note their stiff-winged flight and distinctive call.

LONG-BILLED CURLEW

The Long-billed Curlew, our largest shorebird, is found primarily on tidal flats. These curlews typically occur at sites also favored by large flocks of Marbled Godwits. Long-billeds winter at two or three sites along our coast. Usually no more than one bird is found; rarely there will be two or three. These wintering birds are found primarily from mid-July to mid-April. Otherwise Long-billeds are most likely to be spotted during the autumn migration period, from July to November, when they are rare.

Currently the most reliable and accessible site for this species is at the Basin south of Fort Fisher. An individual has overwintered here for several years. Watch for it from the barrier spit or the rock breakwater (the Rocks). Sometimes at low tide, especially during rainy weather and northeast winds, this bird feeds right next to the boat ramp at the end of US 421. One or two birds often winter in the Portsmouth Island area, coming in to the flats primarily during stormy weather and high water levels. Individuals also sometimes overwinter at New Drum Inlet, the east end of Shackleford Banks, and the Rachel Carson Estuarine Research Reserve at Beaufort.

Elsewhere, watch for Long-billeds at any of the inlets, especially between July and November. Sites where birds have been found in recent years include Oregon Inlet (Bodie Island), the north end of Ocracoke Island, the south end of Ocracoke Island, and the west end of Shackleford Banks.

If you get a fairly close look, most Long-billed Curlews are easy to identify. They have ridiculously long curved bills that set them apart at once. However, bill lengths vary among shorebirds, and beginning birders sometimes try to turn longer-billed Whimbrels into Long-billed Curlews. Note that Whimbrels have conspicuous head-striping; Long-billeds do not. At close range you can see the definitive cinnamon wing linings of the Long-billed. The general coloration of a Long-billed Curlew is more like that of a Marbled Godwit than that of a Whimbrel. Also, Long-billed Curlews are always as big or bigger than Marbled Godwits—a helpful fact, because the two species frequently associate.

HUDSONIAN GODWIT

In our area, this godwit is rarely found on tidal flats, preferring shallow, brackish, nontidal areas. It is almost exclusively an autumn migrant. Hudsonian

Godwits are virtually restricted to the Outer Banks, particularly Bodie and Pea islands. During the peak migration, in September and October, they are uncommon here and rare from Cape Hatteras Point to Portsmouth Island. Elsewhere there have been only a handful of sightings. There are a couple of spring records (late May) at Bodie Island.

For the best chance of seeing this species, go to Bodie and Pea islands in September and October. If you can, go after a period of sustained northeast winds. Carefully check Bodie Island Lighthouse Pond and the North Pond impoundment at Pea Island. If you don't see any birds, check the logbook at the Pea Island NWR visitors center for locations of any recent sightings. Elsewhere your chances of seeing this bird are remote. Your next best chance of finding one is at the Salt Pond at Cape Hatteras Point.

Some of the birds seen in our area still have traces of breeding plumage and are quite easy to pick out because of the chestnut color of their underparts. However, in winter plumage the birds are not so conspicuous. At a distance they might be overlooked in a flock of Willets because the two species look similar. Look for the Hudsonian's long, slightly upturned bill. Also, when a Hudsonian Godwit flies, its white tailband (white upper-tail coverts) makes it quite conspicuous. You should always make sure that you are not seeing a Black-tailed Godwit, which has been found at Bodie Island on at least one occasion. The Black-tailed has a bold white wing stripe, suggestive of a Willet; its underwing linings are white, while the Hudsonian's are blackish.

MARBLED GODWIT

This godwit is found primarily on tidal flats. However, Marbled Godwits also occur frequently on the ponds and impoundments at Bodie and Pea islands. Marbleds are most common and widespread during the autumn migration, from August to November, when they are uncommon to locally fairly common. However, this species is also a very local winter resident, with numerous birds overwintering at a handful of sites. At these sites a few birds are sometimes seen throughout the early summer.

Sites where good numbers of godwits overwinter and where birds can usually be seen from late July through March are the Portsmouth Island flats, the Rachel Carson Estuarine Research Reserve, Masonboro Island (Dick Bay area), and the Basin south of Fort Fisher. The last site is most reliable and easiest to get to. Birds can be seen from the barrier spit or the rock breakwater (the Rocks), and often, at low tide, several birds can be seen from the boat ramp at the end of US 421. At Portsmouth Island, the numbers of birds are variable. You are most likely to see these birds during high water levels; at other times they fly out to distant shoals in Pamlico Sound. The Rachel Carson site requires a boat trip, but several godwits can sometimes be seen from Front Street in Beaufort at high tide. These birds also regularly feed at Howland Rock north of

Beaufort, which is accessible by car. Masonboro Island is accessible only by boat, but a few birds from this flock frequently feed at the north end of Carolina Beach.

Apart from these wintering sites, godwits are most likely to be seen during the autumn migration period. Watch for them at Oregon Inlet (Bodie Island); Bodie Island Lighthouse Pond; the impoundments at Pea Island NWR; Hatteras Inlet; the south end of Ocracoke Island; New Drum Inlet; the east end of Shackleford Banks; the west end of Holden Beach; and the west end of Sunset Beach.

RED KNOT

Knots are found primarily on ocean beaches and on sand flats adjacent to inlets, although they occur in other habitats as well, especially during the peak of spring migration. Surprisingly, wintering birds often feed on rock jetties and similar structures in the South Coast section. Knots are most common during the spring migration, which peaks in mid- to late May. They are less common during the rather protracted autumn migration, primarily from August to mid-November. During this period they are fairly common on the Outer Banks and on some of the east-facing beaches but uncommon elsewhere. Knots overwinter to some extent—their status at this season is quite variable. Some years they may be found at only a few sites; during other (usually mild) years, they may be widespread.

During the peak of spring migration, Knots can be found easily on most of the ocean beaches or on extensive flats next to inlets. They seem to prefer beaches that are gently sloping, like Hammocks Beach SP, Holden Beach, and Sunset Beach. During the autumn migration period, Cape Hatteras Point is probably the most reliable site for this species. Sites where birds overwinter every year are the Portsmouth Island flats, the Rachel Carson Estuarine Research Reserve, and the Fort Fisher area. At the last site, a few Knots can usually be found at low tide feeding on the natural rock outcrops near the Fort Fisher SHS. In early summer, Knots can be found most reliably on the Portsmouth flats.

Breeding-plumaged Knots are easy to identify and are never overlooked. In winter plumage, though, Knots are very nondescript, with no obvious field marks. They are often identified primarily by elimination. Knots are about the same size as dowitchers, with which they sometimes associate, but they have shorter bills. On ocean beaches you usually get the chance to compare them with Sanderlings: Knots are obviously bigger. Perhaps the Knot's most distinctive field characteristic is its light (but not white) rump. Feeding flocks on ocean beaches often stand out at a distance because the flocks are tightly packed. Summering birds (those sighted in late June and early July) are usually in winter plumage.

WHITE-RUMPED SANDPIPER

This is definitely a pool-type shorebird, one typically found at shallow brackish nontidal pools, including drawn-down impoundments and dredging sites. However, during the peak of the spring migration it regularly occurs on tidal flats as well. White-rumpeds occur mainly during the spring migration, mostly in May, when they are fairly common on the Outer Banks and uncommon elsewhere. The spring migration continues into June, and birds may be seen as late as late June and early July. During their autumn migration, which peaks from mid-August through October, they are uncommon on the Outer Banks and occasional elsewhere.

To see a White-rumped Sandpiper, go to Bodie Island or Pea Island NWR in May, especially mid-May. You should have little trouble finding a few birds in the ponds and impoundments. These are also the best areas in autumn, and you are unlikely to see the birds elsewhere.

This species is slightly, but noticeably, larger than Semipalmated and Western sandpipers. Its silhouette is long and attenuated. The bird has a conspicuous white rump when flushed, and its very high, thin call is very distinctive.

BAIRD'S SANDPIPER

Quite scarce here, this species is one of the "grasspipers"—shorebirds primarily associated with short-grass habitats. In North Carolina it is also found at dried-up pools, the relatively dry margins of impoundments and dredging sites, and dry, sparsely vegetated sand flats. This species is strictly an autumn migrant; most recorded sightings have taken place between mid-August and early October. Even then, it is rare in most areas, but occasional at better sites on the Outer Banks.

Currently the best site for this species is the dry, sparsely vegetated flats south of the Salt Pond at Cape Hatteras. Look especially from early September to early October. (There may actually be two peaks, one in early September and one in early October.) Other areas worth checking are the Wright Brothers National Memorial, if the weather has been stormy; the salt flats at Pea Island NWR; and the pools and impoundments at Bodie and Pea islands if drought conditions have occurred.

This species is rather difficult to identify. In size and silhouette, it is very much like a White-rumped Sandpiper. Thus, look for a sandpiper slightly larger than Semipalmateds and Westerns. However, the Baird's does not have the white rump of the White-rumped, and its call-note is a raspy "kreep." It is buffy in all plumages.

PURPLE SANDPIPER

In the early part of the twentieth century, this "rockpiper" was a rare vagrant south of natural rocky seacoast areas in New England. Today, though, the species uses the jetties and groins that have been constructed along the ocean beaches and at ocean inlets and has become a regular winter resident along North Carolina's coast. However, because jetties and groins are widely scattered along our ocean shorelines, and because some of these structures are not large enough to provide roosting sites at high tide, Purple Sandpipers are still very local in this area, found regularly at only two or three sites. Purples are easiest to find from mid-November to late March. They sometimes linger into May.

Currently the only reliable and easily accessible site for this species is the south end of Oregon Inlet (Pea Island NWR), either at the base of the bridge supports or on the nearby groin. Usually about five birds can be found here. The jetties at Masonboro Inlet (Wrightsville Beach) harbor a dozen or more birds each winter, but they are difficult to see here unless you own a boat. Sometimes you can spot birds with a scope from the south end of Wrightsville Beach, but these sightings are usually not satisfactory. The jetties at the inlet at Fort Macon SP have traditionally been a reliable spot for getting good looks at Purple Sandpipers. In recent years, however, the beach has built out, burying large parts of the jetties, and these sandpipers have thus become unreliable. In the future there will probably be periods of erosion and accretion, with birds becoming more or less reliable accordingly. Elsewhere, Purple Sandpipers are seen only rarely, sometimes showing up at sites like the rock outcrops at Fort Fisher (mostly in November) or the groins at the Cape Hatteras Lighthouse.

Winter-plumaged Purple Sandpipers, with their distinctive slaty color, are easy to identify if you get a good look. However, remember that other shorebirds—such as Sanderlings, Dunlins, Red Knots, and Ruddy Turnstones—also frequently feed on rock jetties. Strange as it might seem, Knots in winter plumage have been called Purple Sandpipers. To a birder used to seeing Purple Sandpipers only in winter plumage, a first sighting in late April or May may initially cause confusion: the birds are then largely brownish rather than slaty and are thus less distinctive.

CURLEW SANDPIPER

In the birding world, the North Carolina coast is somewhat famous for this primarily Eurasian species. For several years the north end of Portsmouth Island has been one of the more reliable spots in the United States for seeing a Curlew Sandpiper, and many birders have made the boat trip over from Ocracoke Island so that they could add this species to their life lists.

On the North Carolina coast there have been few sightings on flats that are flooded by regular lunar tides. The Portsmouth Island flats, where most sightings have occurred, are flooded irregularly, primarily by rain and wind tides. Furthermore, many of the sightings here have been at shallow, largely nontidal pools adjacent to the inlet. Elsewhere along this coast, most sightings have been at brackish nontidal sites like drawn-down impoundments and dredging sites. For the coast overall, this species is a very rare spring and autumn migrant. However, these sandpipers are rare in May and occasional in July and early August at Portsmouth Island and at Pea Island NWR during low water levels.

Your best bet for finding a Curlew Sandpiper is to visit the Portsmouth Island flats between mid-July and the first week of August. If possible, schedule your trip a day or two after heavy rains or a strong northeaster. When the impoundments at Pea Island NWR are drawn down, they can be almost as good, and they don't require a long boat ride. However, remember that only North Pond impoundment is regularly open to the public; South Pond is accessible only through specially arranged tours. Elsewhere, your chances of finding this species are slim, but you might watch for them at the ponds on Bodie Island, the Salt Pond at Cape Hatteras Point, and drawn-down impoundments, dredging sites, and similar areas.

Breeding-plumaged birds, with their curved bills and cinnamon color, are hard to miss. Fortunately, birds seen in July and August usually have enough cinnamon color that they are easy to pick out. However, birds seen in September and October are much trickier. Look for a white-rumped bird with a silhouette somewhere in between a Dunlin's and a Stilt Sandpiper's. Consult one of the more advanced field guides.

BUFF-BREASTED SANDPIPER

This is another one of the "grasspipers"—shorebirds typically associated with upland, short-grass habitats. However, in North Carolina they are more likely to be seen on sparsely vegetated sandy flats and around the borders of drawn-down impoundments and dried-up pools. On exceptional occasions, particularly during the peak of autumn migration—around early September—they may even be found on the berm of ocean beaches and inlets.

This species is strictly an autumn migrant, occurring primarily on the Outer Banks. Here they are occasional from mid-August to mid-October. Elsewhere, this species is rare, with most recorded sightings in September.

Currently, the best spot for this species is the sparsely vegetated sand flats south of the Salt Pond at Cape Hatteras Point. Elsewhere on the Outer Banks, check the salt flats at Pea Island NWR; the impoundments and ponds at Bodie Island and Pea Island NWR during drought conditions; the Wright Brothers National Memorial during stormy weather; and perhaps the Park Service campground at Salvo. Away from the Outer Banks, no sites stand out as particularly good; however, you're most likely to spot a bird during the first few days of September.

The habitat in which it occurs will help you identify this species, but the bird's appearance is also rather distinctive. Look for a thin-necked, small-headed shorebird with all-white underwings.

RUFF

In North Carolina vagrants of this primarily Eurasian species are most likely to be spotted at brackish nontidal pools and similar sites. They are virtually never seen on tidal flats. Ruffs (the females are called Reeves) are very rare during the spring migration, mostly from late April to late May. During the autumn migration they are very rare to rare; most recorded sightings have taken place from early July to early September.

Based on past records, there doesn't seem to be any particular site where this species is most likely to be found. The ponds and impoundments at Bodie Island and Pea Island NWR and the Salt Pond at Cape Hatteras Point are perhaps your best bets. Elsewhere, check at drawn-down impoundments and dredging sites. In all areas, mid- to late July seems to be the best time to look for this bird.

Unfortunately, most Ruffs sighted in North Carolina have not been in breeding plumage. Consult one of the more advanced field guides. In general, look for a bird with a posture and silhouette intermediate between those of yellow-legs and Pectoral Sandpipers. Many (perhaps most) of the birds seen in our area have had orangish legs and a black bill, with a small but conspicuous area of white feathering at the base of the bill. Also look for white underwings. The U-shaped white band on the rump is distinctive but can be difficult to see well.

LONG-BILLED DOWITCHER

It cannot be overstressed that, in North Carolina at least, this dowitcher is found primarily in brackish, nontidal habitats, such as pools, impoundments, and dredging sites. In general, it avoids tidal flats. In contrast, the more common and widely distributed Short-billed Dowitcher is commonly found in both tidal and nontidal areas. However, Long-billeds do not avoid tidal flats entirely. In winter they are sometimes seen on the flats just inside Oregon Inlet, perhaps forced there from nearby ponds and impoundments by ice or high water levels. Some years, several wintering Long-billeds can be found along the algae-covered rock breakwater (the Rocks) south of Fort Fisher.

The Long-billed Dowitcher is most widespread during the autumn migration, from about early August to early December. During this time they are fairly common at Bodie Island and at Pea Island NWR but generally uncommon elsewhere. Long-billeds also overwinter very locally: the largest population is at Bodie and Pea islands, although the numbers vary widely according to the severity of the weather. Wintering birds (or perhaps spring migrants) can usually be found until late April, occasionally early May.

For the best chance of finding this species, visit Bodie Island and Pea Island NWR during the autumn migration. A few birds can usually be found at the Bodie Island Lighthouse Pond throughout the winter, except after severe cold. Also, if water levels are low, look for Long-billeds at Mattamuskeet NWR during the autumn migration (sometimes in winter). From late autumn to April, a few birds can usually be found at the North River Marsh near Beaufort. Again, Long-billeds are sometimes seen at the rock breakwater south of Fort Fisher, at least from late autumn through winter. At this location, though, Long-billeds will always be outnumbered by Short-billeds.

On average, Long-billed Dowitchers do have longer bills than Short-billeds do, but there is some overlap. The longest-billed individuals, though, can usually be picked out rather easily—they are suggestive of little godwits. The most reliable way of identifying a Long-billed Dowitcher is by voice. Long-billeds frequently give a sharp "keek" call that is completely different from the soft "tu-tu" of a Short-billed. Fortunately, Long-billeds are very vocal, typically giving their "keek" call at the slightest alarm. (Dowitchers that have to be flushed several times before they call are almost invariably Short-billeds.) Sometimes when a Long-billed is flushed it gives not the "keek" call but a hurried multi-syllabic call that sounds like the call made by some Short-billeds when they flush. Be alert to this possibility.

WILSON'S PHALAROPE

Unlike the Red and Red-necked phalaropes, this bird is not pelagic. In fact, Wilson's Phalaropes are rarely seen in tidal habitats; they are most likely at shallow brackish pools and similar sites. They are very rare during the spring migration, with most records from early May to early June. The autumn migration extends from about early July to mid-October, peaking from late July to early September, when these birds are uncommon at Bodie Island and Pea Island NWR and occasional elsewhere.

For the best chance of finding this species, check the ponds and impoundments at Bodie and Pea islands from late July to early September. Birds are also seen regularly at the Salt Pond at Cape Hatteras Point during this period. Elsewhere along the coast, check drawn-down impoundments and dredging sites when these habitats are available.

Most Wilson's Phalaropes seen in North Carolina are in nonbreeding plumage, but the birds are still rather easy to pick out. They are often first noticed because they feed so actively. The overall shape of this bird is distinctive: the head is relatively small and the body quite dumpy. The long, needlelike bill and light upper tail coverts are also noteworthy.

RED-NECKED PHALAROPE

This phalarope is definitely a pelagic species. However, Red-necked Phalaropes are seen with some regularity from shore at Cape Hatteras and Cape Lookout and are occasionally seen on land, usually at ponds and impoundments on the Outer Banks. Red-neckeds are fairly common to common migrants in the off-shore waters from early May to early June and from early August to mid-October. They are found mostly along the edge of the Gulf Stream and at other sites where bottom features result in the mixing of water masses—for example, over the shoals several miles off the capes.

For the best chance of finding this bird, take one of the chartered birding trips out of Oregon Inlet or Hatteras Inlet during the peak migration periods, especially mid-May and mid- to late August. Your next best bet is to take the "Miss Hatteras" out of Hatteras Village. This species is also seen regularly from the headboats out of Morehead City–Atlantic Beach, but only on trips to the east and southeast, which go by the Cape Lookout shoals. Birds can probably be seen occasionally from the headboats out of Carolina Beach. During strong northeast or east winds, you might be able to find a few of these birds at Cape Hatteras Point, especially from mid-May to early June and from mid-August to early September. Watch for birds flying over the ocean, and if there are any tidal pools at the point, check them closely. Also, check the impoundments and ponds anywhere on the Outer Banks. You are most likely to find birds in mid- and late May and around early September. Records at such sites are more frequent during stormy weather. However, many such sightings—especially in spring—have occurred during fair weather with light winds.

On pelagic trips it is often frustratingly difficult to see phalaropes well, especially from one of the fishing headboats. However, on chartered birding trips you can sometimes get fairly good views of birds swimming along grass lines. For a really satisfying look at a Red-necked Phalarope, go to Cape Hatteras Point or check the ponds and impoundments elsewhere on the Outer Banks in mid- to late May.

Although breeding-plumaged Red-necked and Red phalaropes are readily identifiable, distinguishing between the two from a boat when they are in nonbreeding plumage is tricky. Consult a field guide. In North Carolina there is relatively little overlap in the two species' seasonal occurrence: most Red Phalaropes leave before the Red-neckeds in spring and arrive later in autumn. Note that the Red-necked Phalarope has a much thinner bill than the Red's, and that Red Phalaropes in nonbreeding plumage frequently have all-dark bills—a fact some field guides do not mention.

RED PHALAROPE

Slightly larger and bulkier than the Red-necked, this phalarope is strongly pelagic, rarely seen on land or even from land, although many thousands often occur in the offshore waters in April. Nevertheless, there is an interesting aberrant record: thousands of these birds once came into the waters just off the beaches and even into the inlets along Bogue Banks in early February, and this sort of occurrence could happen again. In North Carolina the species is a migrant and winter resident; most recorded sightings have taken place from about mid-September to early May. Red Phalaropes are common during the migration peaks—in December, roughly, and in April. They are apparently fairly common in midwinter, but there is little information available for this period. This species seems to be most common over shoals several miles off the capes and along the edge of the Gulf Stream.

Currently, this species is seldom seen on chartered birding trips out of Oregon Inlet and Hatteras Inlet because these trips usually run outside of the species' period of occurrence. However, you might see a few birds in mid-September. In April, during the peak spring migration, Red Phalaropes are seen on most of the headboat runs out of Morehead City–Atlantic Beach; during this period they probably could be seen as reliably from the headboat out of Carolina Beach or more reliably, I would presume, from the new headboat at Hatteras Village. From about late February through March, they are seen on about half of the Morehead City–Atlantic Beach headboat runs that go to the southeast or east, i.e., those that go past the Cape Lookout shoals. Spotting a Red Phalarope on land or from land is quite a feat. Your best bet would be to go to Cape Hatteras Point during a severe northeaster in April and check any tide pools there. Strangely, after the peak of migration, in May, birds are sometimes found on the ponds and impoundments of the Outer Banks and elsewhere. Such sightings are very rare, but keep them in mind, because they offer the opportunity to get good looks at birds in breeding plumage. Also, many of these May records occur during fair weather. Reds also very rarely turn up on ponds and impoundments of the Outer Banks from late September into November.

See the discussion of Red-necked Phalaropes for comments about field identification. Note that many or most of the Red Phalaropes seen in our waters in mid-April are still in nonbreeding plumage.

POMARINE JAEGER

This jaeger, like the others, is primarily pelagic. However, this species is frequently found in the near-shore waters and is occasionally seen from land, especially when conditions are right. Pomarine Jaegers occur off our coast during every month of the year, but they are most frequent during the migration periods, especially from early April through May and from late July to early November. During these periods they are fairly common along the edge of the Gulf Stream. During the peaks of migration, about late April to late May and late September to early November, they are seen from land regularly—especially along the Outer Banks, where they are uncommon.

You may get a very good look at one of these birds by taking a chartered birding trip out of Oregon or Hatteras inlets during the migration periods, especially in spring. Occasionally a bird will fly in quite close to the boat while checking out a chum slick or harassing other seabirds. Good views are also sometimes possible from the headboats, as a bird comes in close to pick up bait from the water. The "Miss Hatteras" out of Hatteras Village is your best bet, but

Pomarine Jaegers are also seen regularly from headboats out of Morehead City–Atlantic Beach and Carolina Beach. Again, spring is the best time.

During the spring migration period, watch for these birds from the south-facing beaches in the Cape Hatteras area and from Cape Lookout to Atlantic Beach. During periods of northeast and easterly winds, patient watching will almost always be rewarded with a sighting or two; on rare occasions numerous birds will be seen moving past Cape Hatteras Point. In autumn you might also see birds by watching from east-facing beaches, especially from Bodie Island to Cape Hatteras (again, northeast and east winds are best). Although many of the birds seen from shore are distant fly-bys, individuals sometimes fly directly over the tips of the capes. Rarely, an individual will actually rest on the sand at Cape Hatteras Point.

Identification of jaegers, especially immatures and subadults, is a rather arcane science (or art). Refer to the more advanced field guides. Spring is the best time for beginning birders to try identifying their first jaegers, because most birds seen then are adults in breeding plumage, with the fully developed central tail feathers by which the different species can easily be recognized. The Pomarine Jaeger can usually be picked out at some distance by its large size and powerful flight, rather like that of a large gull. However, there is some overlap between the largest Parasitics and the smallest Pomarines, and birds within this overlap zone will be difficult to pick out based on flight. Also, the powerful flight of this species is a helpful characteristic only during normal winds. As wind speeds increase, differences in flight between this species and the smaller jaegers decrease.

PARASITIC JAEGER

This jaeger is also of regular occurrence off our coast. However, Parasitics largely shun the deeper offshore waters; most migration apparently occurs within a few miles of land. These birds are seen from shore occasionally, especially during certain weather conditions. Parasitics have been reported throughout most of the year but are virtually absent in midsummer. Most frequent during the migration periods, they are uncommon to fairly common from late April to early June and uncommon from late August to early November. From about late April to early June and late September to early November, they are seen from shore with some regularity, especially along the Outer Banks.

This species is seen less frequently than the Pomarine on chartered birding trips out of Oregon and Hatteras inlets. However, at least one or two will usually be seen on trips in mid- to late May. Like Pomarines, Parasitic Jaegers frequently come in close for excellent views. Birds may also be seen from the headboats during the same period. During the autumn migration period, Parasitics are seen less frequently, with only occasional close sightings, and are usually in difficult-to-identify plumages.

The tips given for finding Pomarine Jaegers from land are also applicable for Parasitics. In spring, though, Parasitics are most likely to be seen in mid- and late May.

On average, this jaeger is noticeably less robust than a Pomarine Jaeger, and its flight is reminiscent of a falcon's. The immature and subadult birds are notoriously difficult to identify; consult one of the more advanced field guides.

LONG-TAILED JAEGER

This is our scarcest jaeger and, I believe most would agree, our classiest—at least, the adults with the long "streamer" central tail feathers are classy. Long-taileds are highly pelagic and are only rarely seen from land in North Carolina. Virtually all records are for the migration periods. Most spring records have occurred in mid- to late May, when the birds are occasional to uncommon. In autumn Long-taileds are apparently rare from mid-August to early November. However, their exact status is clouded by the fact that most jaegers seen during this time are not adults, so identification is more tentative. Long-taileds may actually be occasional during at least part of the autumn migration.

Because nonadult Long-tailed and Parasitic jaegers look rather similar, especially when seen from a distance at sea, most birders will not be satisfied until they have seen an adult Long-tailed with fully developed central tail feathers. For a possible sighting of one of these exquisite creatures, take a chartered birding trip out of Oregon or Hatteras inlets in late May. During this period, you have about a one-in-three chance of seeing a Long-tailed. In late May birds are also occasionally sighted from the headboats. The "Miss Hatteras" probably presents the best headboat opportunity, although birds are sometimes spotted from the boats off Morehead City–Atlantic Beach. Long-taileds are also sometimes seen on chartered birding trips out of Oregon and Hatteras inlets during the autumn migration period; sightings are typically less than satisfactory, however, usually of immature and subadult birds. However, adults with full streamers have been seen on rare occasions in August and September.

Rarely, in late May birds have been spotted from land at Cape Hatteras Point— even flying directly over the tip of the point. Such sightings are most likely after several days of northeast or east winds. During such conditions, birds have also been spotted from Cape Lookout to Atlantic Beach, but these sightings are even more unusual.

Although adults with full streamer tail feathers are very easy to identify, Long-tailed Jaegers in other plumages can be difficult to differentiate from Parasitics. Consult the more advanced field guides; note that this is the smallest, most buoyant jaeger, with a rather tern-like flight.

GREAT SKUA

There are only a handful of records, ranging from early December to early April, for this primarily Arctic and near-Arctic pelagic species. However, there is very little birding activity in the offshore waters in winter, and the species may prove to be at least rare in the offshore waters from the Central Coast section northward.

Since there are currently no chartered offshore birding trips in the state in winter, your chances of finding this species are slim indeed. However, if you get really lucky, you might spot one from a headboat out of Morehead City–Atlantic Beach. The best time to try may be from about late February to early April. (For some reason, more interesting "winter birds" are seen from these boats during the late winter–early spring period.) You might also try the "Miss Hatteras" out of Hatteras Village at the beginning of its season, in early April. On calm days, dramatic tide lines sometimes develop in the Pea Island–Rodanthe area, and these can be extremely attractive to birds. If you are lucky enough to witness such an event during the winter, you might consider settling in for some serious scoping, because a Great Skua is one of the rarities you could at least hope for. A skua was seen from shore in this area one February. Although there are no records from Cape Hatteras Point, this is another site you might check for a Great Skua; a vicious northeaster in March or early April might be a good time to try.

SOUTH POLAR SKUA

This skua breeds in the Antarctic and "winters" in the North Atlantic during our summer months. Off our coast South Polar Skuas have been found from May to September. There is a peak in late May when they are uncommon; after this peak they are occasional throughout the summer. This species is pelagic, largely restricted to the Gulf Stream and its edge. However, during the late May peak, birds are occasionally seen over the near-shore waters and very rarely seen from land, primarily at Cape Hatteras Point.

You are most likely to see this species by taking a chartered birding trip out of Oregon Inlet or Hatteras Inlet in late May; you will have about a one-in-three chance. South Polar Skuas are also occasionally spotted on these trips during the summer months, and during the late May peak they are occasionally sighted from the headboats out of Morehead City–Atlantic Beach. Some of these sightings have been at close range, with birds coming right up to the boats to pluck bait from the water. The new headboat out of Hatteras Village offers another possible way to see this species, especially in late May. You would not be as likely to see a skua on this headboat trip as on a chartered birding trip, but you would be more likely to see one from this boat than from one of the Morehead City–Atlantic Beach headboats. You will probably never see this species from land in the state, although birds have been spotted at Cape Hatteras and Cape Lookout in late May. In fact, birds have flown right over the tip of Cape Hatteras Point. If you would like to try to see one of these birds from land, visit Cape Hatteras Point in late May after several days of northeast and east winds.

At a distance, South Polar Skuas are reminiscent of first-year Herring Gulls, but with striking white patches at the bases of the primaries. Occasionally an overly enthusiastic birder will try to call a Pomarine Jaeger a skua, because Pomarines (especially some individuals) are large and bulky. A general rule of thumb is that if you have any doubt about a bird, it's a jaeger. When you see a real skua, you'll have no doubt. Be aware that Great Skuas might sometimes linger until May, so there could be a slight overlap in these two species' seasonal occurrence; as in spring, individuals seen in autumn might belong to either species. Consult one of the more advanced field guides.

FRANKLIN'S GULL

This is the "non-sea seagull," which breeds on the prairies and migrates primarily through the middle of the continent. In North Carolina this species is a very rare autumn migrant on the Outer Banks, with a handful of records from early October to early November. There are also single sightings for spring (Currituck County) and for summer (also Outer Banks).

To try to find a Franklin's Gull, visit the Outer Banks in autumn and check the ponds and impoundments at Bodie Island, Pea Island NWR, and Cape Hatteras Point. If you do find a bird, it will probably be an immature and will most likely be associated with Laughing Gulls, so consult one of the more advanced field guides for identification help. Note that all Franklin's Gulls are definitely smaller than Laughing Gulls, with smaller and slimmer bills. When you first see one, you may for a second think you have a Bonaparte's Gull. Although there is only one summer record, this species might be expected to occur along the Outer Banks with some regularity during June and July, based on records in states to our north. Check the ponds and impoundments. Franklin's Gulls seen at this season will almost certainly be one-year-olds, which are the trickiest to identify. Again, consult one of the more advanced field guides and remember that you are looking for a smaller bird with a smaller and slimmer bill.

Occasionally, beginning birders seeing their first fully breeding-plumaged Laughing Gull in April and May will mistakenly call it a Franklin's. Some Laughing Gulls at this season have reddish legs (unlike the blackish legs shown in the field guides). In addition, the white eye crescents are conspicuous, and the mantle color is or appears to be lighter in color than later in the season. Also, adult Laughing Gulls often have a little bit of whitish color at the tips of the outermost primaries (again, unlike the all-dark primaries shown in many field guides).

LITTLE GULL

This gull, our smallest, is seen primarily over the ocean or on ocean beaches, although there are also a few records at ponds and impoundments. Once found exclusively in the Old World, this species was not recorded in coastal North Carolina until the early 1970s. From then until the late 1980s, the frequency of sightings increased greatly. The growing frequency of sightings probably reflects not only an actual population increase but also our increased ability to find these birds.

Ecologically and temporally, this species is very much a Bonaparte's Gull. Little Gulls are seen primarily where Bonaparte's Gulls are most common—at the same sites and times and during the same conditions.

This species is primarily a winter resident. Although Little Gulls have been seen as early as August and as late as May, the great majority of sightings have taken place between late December and early April. During this period, the birds are occasional (to uncommon in midwinter) in the North Coast and Outer Banks sections and rare in the Central Coast section.

For the best chance of finding a Little Gull, go to the Outer Banks from late January to early March. Make numerous stops all along the oceanfront and search for large feeding groups of Bonaparte's Gulls. In general, these groups will be found primarily where there are brisk offshore winds. Thus, during southwest winds, work along the coastline from Cape Hatteras north, and during north and northeast winds, check the south-facing beaches at Cape Hatteras. If you find an aggregation of a thousand or more Bonaparte's Gulls, you should be able to find a Little. During really blustery winds—roughly thirty miles per hour or more—you should also be able to find a few Little Gulls resting at Cape Hatteras Point. Interestingly, in the Central Coast section, early April is one of the best times to look for this species, because Bonaparte's Gulls are then in northward migration. Watch from the piers at the eastern end of Atlantic Beach or at Cape Lookout. On mornings when hundreds of Bonaparte's Gulls are streaming by, you have a fair chance of spotting a Little.

Little Gulls are definitely smaller and daintier than Bonaparte's Gulls, with more rounded wing tips. By far the most Little Gulls sighted will be feeding out over the ocean at some distance. Under these conditions the first-winter birds are usually easier to pick out than the adults, because the younger birds' pronounced "W" pattern across the wings shows up for a good distance. To pick out an adult, you really need good lighting conditions while you're searching. The blackish underwing of the Little is an excellent field mark, but with poor light, the underwing of the Bonaparte's can appear to be blackish also. Just as important: on the Little, look for the absence both of black-tipped primaries and of the white wedge on the upper wing surface. The lack of black-tipped primaries is also a good field mark to watch for as you scan through flocks of Bonaparte's Gulls on shore. However, be aware that at a glance, the little bit of the blackish underwing exposed when a Little Gull is at rest might be passed off as black on the upper surface of the primaries. Don't overlook a Little by making this mistake.

COMMON BLACK-HEADED GULL

This is another species formerly restricted to the Eastern Hemisphere that is now increasing and becoming established in the Western Hemisphere. In North

Carolina, it is still rare and occurs much less predictably than the Little Gull. However, it does seem to be increasing slowly.

Black-headed Gulls are very rare to rare from mid-October to late April; most records fall between late October and late March. Most sightings have been on the barrier islands or on the adjacent mainland; there are few records from farther inland. So far, many or most records have taken place at sewage treatment plants and brackish nontidal pools and similar sites. However, these birds have also been seen on ocean beaches and at parking areas, fish houses, and other sites that attract large numbers of gulls. In North Carolina, Black-headed Gulls are frequently seen in company with Bonaparte's Gulls, although they have been seen with other species as well, especially Laughing and Ring-billed gulls.

This is one rare species for which it is difficult to plan a successful search. In the Outer Banks region, search out all areas that have large numbers of gulls. You could also check primarily at pools and impoundments, such as at Bodie Island, Pea Island, Cape Hatteras Point, and the northeast end of Ocracoke Island. Don't necessarily limit your searches to the peak period mentioned above—migrating Black-headeds should occur on the Outer Banks more frequently than the records indicate. Remember to check the logbooks at Pea Island NWR and the Cape Hatteras ranger station. Elsewhere, check at sewage treatment plants and recently active spoil disposal sites, particularly those that attract Bonaparte's Gulls, especially from late October to late March. On average, the sewage treatment plant at Carolina Beach may be the best area to check.

Fortunately, most sightings of this species are at close range, and the birds are usually in close association with Bonaparte's Gulls (or Laughings or Ring-billeds), allowing excellent evaluations of size. A Common Black-headed Gull is definitely larger than a Bonaparte's Gull—about the size of a Laughing Gull—with a much longer and stouter bill than a Bonaparte's. In adults, the red bill is an excellent field mark, as is the blackish area on the underside of the primaries. Plumage differences between immature Black-headeds and Bonaparte's Gulls are more subtle, but the size differences are very noticeable, and the Black-headed has a two-toned bill (often reddish by midwinter). Consult one of the more advanced field guides.

THAYER'S GULL

This is indeed a controversial bird. Some authorities consider it a well-marked race of the Iceland Gull, and the two will probably be lumped together as one species in the future. Whatever its taxonomic status, it is true that the Thayer's Gull does occur in North Carolina and that most individuals can be identified. Even if the Thayer's and the Iceland are considered one species in the future, birders will still search for Thayer's Gulls, challenged by the fact that these birds are quite rare and difficult to identify.

This species was not reliably recorded along our coast until the 1980s, and there are still only a few records, but sightings are becoming more frequent. The increased frequency of sightings undoubtedly reflects in part our increased ability to pick these birds out, but there has probably also been an increase in their population, as is the case with most of the gulls. Based on current information, one would have to consider this species very rare from about mid-December to early March. However, the species might actually rate a "rare" designation in the Cape Hatteras area in midwinter.

This is a bird of the near-shore ocean waters, beaches, and inlets, sometimes found at landfills, fish houses, and similar sites. In short, you might find it just about anywhere you find Herring Gulls. Realistically, though, you're probably not going to have a reasonable chance of finding a Thayer's Gull unless you sort through a lot of Herring Gulls. A site that has a Thayer's Gull will probably have at least a few thousand Herring Gulls.

Cape Hatteras Point is the site where you're most likely to find one of these gulls. However, don't even imagine that you might spot one unless you visit during the conditions, meteorological and otherwise, that force vast numbers of Herring Gulls onto the point—for example, an intense storm or a fish kill. Other sites where you might watch for Thayer's Gulls are the harbors at Wanchese (Roanoke Island) and Hatteras Village and the fish houses in the Morehead City–Beaufort area. You're really not very likely to find a Thayer's at these sites, but you might, especially in midwinter during times when many fish are being brought in.

Both adult and first-winter Thayer's Gulls have been recorded in North Carolina. Overall, first-winter birds are perhaps most likely. However, if you find a Thayer's at a site where most of the Herring Gulls are adults, then the Thayer's will also most likely be an adult. (The probability of finding a second- or third-winter Thayer's Gull is extremely low.)

Field identification of Thayer's Gulls is a rather esoteric science, and you should consult the newer, more advanced field guides. A general rule of thumb for both first-winter and adult birds is to look for a bird that can be safely considered neither a Herring Gull nor an Iceland Gull. Most first-winter birds are initially called Iceland Gulls, because they are somewhat pale; however, the wing tips are as dark as the rest of the wing (or a little darker). A general rule of thumb for an adult Thayer's is that you are looking for a bird that looks like a Herring Gull while at rest but an Iceland Gull while in flight. With gulls one should always be alert to the possibility of leucistic and hybrid birds. If a bird's plumage is obviously worn and frayed and the soft parts (bill and legs) colors are apparently aberrant, move on. In regard to hybrids, beware of birds that are the "wrong size," especially those with wrong-sized bills, and of birds with "wrong-colored" soft parts.

ICELAND GULL

This attractive northern white-winged gull is another species being found with increasing frequency in North Carolina. To some extent, this increase must stem from growing observer awareness, but certainly the actual population of the birds has been increasing as well. Iceland Gulls occur over the near-shore ocean waters and along the barrier islands, especially at capes and inlets. They are attracted to fish houses and landfills that are not more than a few miles away from the coast.

This winter resident has been found as early as mid-October and as late as late April. However, most records are from late December to early March. During this period Iceland Gulls are occasional south to about Morehead City and rare farther south.

In many respects, searching for this bird is a lot like searching for a Thayer's Gull. To find an Iceland, visit sites that can produce large numbers of Herring Gulls, and go during conditions when gull numbers are likely to be near peak levels. During stormy weather, Cape Hatteras Point is the best site for this bird. Probably the second-best site is the harbor at Hatteras Village, where an Iceland can often be found during midwinter periods when large quantities of fish are being landed. Other areas worth checking are the harbor at Wanchese (Roanoke Island) and the fish houses in the Morehead City–Beaufort area.

Most records of this species are of first-winter birds, although adults are also encountered regularly. Second- and third-winter birds are quite rare. If you find an Iceland at a site where most of the Herring Gulls are adults, the Iceland will most likely also be an adult.

To identify Iceland Gulls, take along one of the newer, more advanced field guides. The others just are not helpful and in some cases are actually misleading. Be aware that both adult and immature birds are typically much more conspicuous while in flight, when the large area of white or whitish in the wing tips is exposed. Resting birds can be quite inconspicuous. Most Iceland Gulls are definitely smaller in bulk than Herring Gulls, with a decidedly smaller bill.

Note that there is much variation in the overall body color of first-winter birds. The darkest individuals are easy to overlook until they take flight. In our area, most first-winter birds have all-black or almost all-black bills. Adults have a lighter mantle color than adult Herring Gulls do, and usually you can discern the differences between the bill and leg colors: the bill is more greenish yellow, while a Herring Gull's bill is orangish yellow, and the legs are a duskier, deeper pink, while a Herring Gull's legs are a pinkish beige.

LESSER BLACK-BACKED GULL

Today it seems amazing that this species, which was formerly restricted to the Eastern Hemisphere, was not recorded in coastal North Carolina until 1968.

Since that first sighting, Lesser Black-backeds have increased steadily, and they continue to increase. This species is now primarily a winter resident, found mostly from November through March. However, a few sightings are now occurring throughout the summer. During the peak winter period, Lesser Black-backed Gulls are uncommon on the Outer Banks (fairly common at Cape Hatteras) and occasional elsewhere. In summer they are now rare on the Outer Banks and very rare elsewhere. Ecologically, this species is very much a Herring Gull. Look for them along the barrier islands, especially at capes and inlets, and at fish houses and landfills.

You can be almost certain of finding this species if you head to Cape Hatteras Point during severe weather in winter, when thousands of gulls are present. Other sites to check for this species are the Dare County landfill adjacent to Alligator River NWR; the harbor at Wanchese (Roanoke Island); Oregon Inlet (Bodie Island); the harbor at Hatteras Village; Hatteras Inlet; the fish houses at Morehead City and Beaufort; and the New Hanover County landfill near Wilmington.

Especially when Lesser Black-backed Gulls were first found on our coast, birders often searched among Great Black-backed Gulls for smaller birds with slightly lighter mantles. Some of these birders no doubt sorted through a flock of Great Black-backeds until they found a ratty-looking subadult that also happened to be a bit on the small side, then happily checked off "Lesser Black-backed Gull" on their life lists. Don't do this! You should not be looking for a small, relatively light-backed Great Black-backed; you should be looking for a slightly small, dark-backed Herring Gull.

Although there is some slight overlap, a Lesser Black-backed Gull among Herrings will usually be noticeably smaller and slimmer. The bill is noticeably smaller as well. Of course, yellow legs clinch the identification of an adult Lesser Black-backed. The legs of second- and third-winter birds are frequently yellow (or yellowish) as well. Second- and third-winter birds are usually fairly easy to pick out because at least part of their mantle is colored like the adults'. Traditionally, identification of first-winter birds has been considered virtually impossible, but at least for those who study gulls regularly, this task is not really that difficult. Consult one of the more advanced field guides to see the wing pattern of first-winter birds. Also noteworthy are the bill, which remains all black well into or throughout the winter, and the relatively strong contrast (compared to a first-year Herring Gull) between the light rump and the rest of the upper parts.

GLAUCOUS GULL

This is the big white-winged gull—some individuals are the size of Great Black-backeds. Glaucous Gulls are found mostly along the barrier islands, especially at capes and inlets, and at fish houses and landfills. Although they are seldom found far from the ocean, they have been recorded along the western shores of Pamlico Sound.

This northern species is found primarily from late December to early March. However, individuals sometimes linger into spring, and there have even been a few sightings in summer. During the peak period, Glaucous Gulls are occasional as far south as Morehead City and rare farther south.

You are most likely to find this species by visiting Cape Hatteras Point in stormy weather between late December and early March. Other sites worth checking are the harbor at Wanchese (Roanoke Island); Oregon Inlet (Bodie Island); the harbor at Hatteras Village; and the fish houses at Morehead City and Beaufort. Although this species has been found about as often in the state as the Iceland Gull, it is somewhat less predictable. On a day when thousands of Herring Gulls are present at Cape Hatteras, you are more likely to find an Iceland there than a Glaucous. On the other hand, Glaucous Gulls are perhaps more likely to show up on an ocean beach nowhere close to a cape or inlet, in a flock of only a few gulls.

In coastal North Carolina, virtually all records of this species are of first-winter birds. Adults and second- and third-year birds are very rarely seen. Formerly most North Carolina records described "second-winter" birds, but now we know that most of these whitish Glaucous Gulls were actually first-winter birds. Only rarely will a first-winter bird look as dark as the "typical first-winter" bird pictured in some of the older field guides. First-winter birds that are largely whitish are much more likely. Fortunately, these large, whitish birds are quite conspicuous within a flock of gulls. Occasionally a birder will come across a Glaucous Gull that is almost as small as a Herring Gull. Such birds are frequently misidentified as Iceland Gulls. If you aren't sure, check the bill carefully. Even the smallest Glaucous Gull has a larger bill than a Herring Gull's.

BLACK-LEGGED KITTIWAKE

This buoyantly flying pelagic species is a winter resident off the state's coast. Black-legged Kittiwakes seem to occur primarily in the near-shore waters and are sometimes seen from land. Kittiwakes are most common from mid-November to early February, when they are fairly common off the North Coast and Outer Banks and uncommon farther south. Although this species is fairly common off much of North Carolina's coast, they are nevertheless somewhat difficult to find here, because there are no chartered birding trips during the peak period of occurrence. Kittiwakes are seen on about half the headboat trips out of Morehead City–Atlantic Beach in November. Curiously, this seems to be the best month in this area; birds are seen less frequently later in the winter. If the new headboat out of Hatteras Village runs as late as November, it will provide an even more reliable means of finding this species.

You're most likely to spot this species from land by going to Cape Hatteras in late November or December, especially during stormy weather. Birds are occasionally seen flying past the point during this period, although typically the birds sighted are rather distant fly-bys. Although Cape Hatteras Point is the best site, fly-bys may also be seen from any of the other north-south beaches in late November and December, especially along the Outer Banks north to Bodie Island. Sometimes an individual, probably an immature, will be found resting on the beach. Such sightings are most likely at Cape Hatteras Point but might occur anywhere. In late winter, around February, watch for northbound kittiwakes from the south-facing beaches at and near Cape Hatteras and Cape Lookout. Your efforts are likely to be unsuccessful, but you might get lucky.

In flight at a distance, immature birds—with the striking dark "W" pattern across the upper surface of their wings—are much easier to pick out than adults. At close range, the adults' unmarked bills and black legs make them easy to identify. At a distance, however, they have no striking field marks. Their flight is typically buoyant and wheeling; they look like they would be at home in a stormy world. Although none of the other gulls really looks like a kittiwake, beginning birders sometimes call second-winter Ring-billed Gulls kittiwakes, because their wing tips may be all black, with no white mixed in.

Sabine's Gull

Unfortunately, this striking gull is found only as a very rare migrant in North Carolina. It is a pelagic species, probably most likely to occur along the edge of the Gulf Stream. It has been found on land on a few occasions; most of these records are from the Outer Banks. Most spring sightings of this species have been during late May; most autumn sightings have been from late August to early October.

A search for this species here is almost certain to be futile, but if you would like to try anyway, your best bet is to take one of the offshore birding trips out of Oregon or Hatteras inlets in late May or in September. You're even less likely to see one of these birds on land or from land. However, look from Cape Hatteras Point in late May, especially after persistent northeast or east winds. During the autumn migration period, check the Salt Pond at Cape Hatteras Point.

Both the adult and juvenile plumages are so striking that Sabine's Gulls are unlikely to be confused with anything else. However, an overly enthusiastic birder might try to turn a first-winter kittiwake into a juvenile Sabine's.

Gull-billed Tern

This species is a locally fairly common summer resident, found mostly from mid-April to mid-August. Gull-billed Terns are found primarily on the barrier islands and adjacent mainland from Bodie Island south. Although these terns are distinctive in appearance and behavior, beginning birders often tend to misidentify other terns as Gull-billeds.

To find a Gull-billed Tern, do not look out over the water, expecting to see them fishing with the other terns. Look for them patrolling over the swash zone of the ocean beaches and over salt marshes, sand flats, dunes, shrub thickets, roadsides, and even fields. They feed on a variety of nonfish food, including mole crabs on the ocean beach, fiddler crabs on the marshes and sand flats, and insects and even larger terrestrial fare elsewhere. And when a Gull-billed Tern spots its prey, it does not dive headfirst; it swoops down and plucks the prey up.

Very early autumn migrants, Gull-billeds are quite difficult to find after early September. They are most widespread in early and mid-August, after the nesting season. During the nesting season they are most likely to be seen in areas near nesting colonies. Areas that should continue to have colonies in the future are the national seashores—especially near the inlets—and the lower Cape Fear River region.

SANDWICH TERN

This species is seen more often than it is identified. Sandwich Terns are fairly common to common along most of our coast from early April to mid-November. They are seen over the ocean, especially around the inlets and at the capes, and over the adjacent estuaries. Sandwich Terns are usually closely associated with Royal Terns. In an area with many Royal Terns, you should be able to find Sandwich Terns as well (although Sandwich Terns do not occur as far up the estuaries as Royals do).

From April to early May and from mid-July to mid-November, Sandwich Terns are widespread and can be found along most oceanfront areas south of Oregon Inlet. However, while nesting—roughly mid-May to early July—they are much more local, largely restricted to the vicinity of their nesting islands. Sites where the birds currently nest and where there will probably be nesting habitat in future years are Oregon, Hatteras, and Ocracoke inlets; the Cape Lookout area; and the lower Cape Fear River.

There seem to be two main reasons why beginning birders frequently overlook this bird: 1) they believe that Sandwich Terns are scarce; 2) the birds' yellow bill tip is frequently hard to see—in immature birds it may be very limited in extent or even altogether absent. At a distance this yellow bill tip fades into the background, and birders may then identify these birds as Gull-billed Terns, even though the two species are not at all similar. Helpful field marks for Sandwich Terns are the presence of considerable black or blackish around the back of the head when the birds are in winter plumage (beginning in July) and the loud "kir-rick" call, which is somewhat similar to a Royal Tern's but is distinctly two-syllabled.

ROSEATE TERN

When birders first see this bird, some descriptions that instantly come to mind are highly subjective ones, like "sleek," "graceful," "ethereal," "elegant," "aristocratic." If you review some of the older ornithological literature, you will see that this creature has apparently always created such impressions. In North Carolina this species apparently occurs largely in the offshore waters, although there are only a couple of records from offshore. Most of our records have come from the southern Outer Banks, especially Cape Hatteras, where the birds come in to rest. This species is a migrant and a summer visitor. Overall, Roseate Terns are very rare to rare, except occasional in the southern Outer Banks in late May and from mid- to late summer. Perhaps birds seen in summer are of Caribbean rather than northeastern origin. At least one pair has nested in the state (near Cape Lookout in 1973), and future nesting is certainly possible, most likely at Common Tern colonies adjacent or close to the ocean in the Outer Banks area.

Currently you're most likely to find this species by going to Cape Hatteras Point in late May and from late June to about mid-August. You will need to spend much of the day checking the tern colony, because a Roseate may spend much of its time feeding offshore, coming into the colony area only briefly. Late afternoon may be the best time to look. You will definitely want to check any terns resting at any small pools between the colony and the tip of the point. During at least some years, migrant Roseates are occasional along the south Outer Banks from Portsmouth Island to Cape Hatteras in late May. There are also several records for Cape Lookout Point between late May and July. Sightings may be occasional here during times when a tern colony is present. This species is apparently very rare to rare during the autumn migration; perhaps the best sites to check are Cape Hatteras and Cape Lookout points.

A birder seeing his or her first fully breeding-plumaged Forster's Tern often concludes immediately that the bird has to be a Roseate Tern because it looks so white and has a long tail. But Forster's Terns' primaries are lighter than the rest of their wing, while Roseates' are not. And although the Forster's Tern has a very long tail, its wings are also relatively long, so that when a Forster's is at rest, the tail doesn't project as far beyond the wing tips as it does in the Roseate. Roseates don't call very frequently here, but listen for a two-syllable plover-like call that is totally unlike the calls of any of the other terns. Forster's Terns are absent (or nearly so) at the capes in early summer.

I can't resist bringing up another potential point of confusion. At Pea Island one spring, at sites where Common and Forster's terns were breeding side by side, I saw two or three birds (in breeding plumage) that appeared to be Common/Forster's hybrids. I even heard the "diagnostic" call, which in this case was clearly intermediate between the "ki-yrrr" of the Common and the "zruur" of the Forster's. In some ways these assumed hybrids were similar to Roseate Terns. Although their plumage was quite light, their primaries were not conspicuously lighter than the rest of the wing. Also, the bases of their bills were not truly orange, as in Forster's, but duskier.

ARCTIC TERN

In North Carolina this tern is definitely a pelagic species. Arctic Terns are largely limited to the deeper waters well offshore (Gulf Stream and beyond) and occur primarily during the spring migration. During their peak, about mid- to late May, they are uncommon well offshore of the Outer Banks and North Coast and probably occasional farther south. The autumn status of this species is open to question. There are several records, but no definitive records, i.e., specimens or photographs. The Carolina Bird Club Records Committee has reexamined one photograph of an autumn "Arctic" and determined that the bird was actually a Common Tern. At best, the species is very rare in autumn. On land, this species is very rare. There have been late May sightings at Cape Hatteras and Cape Lookout points. There are also a few autumn reports from Cape Hatteras Point, but none of these birds were photographed.

On land, separating Arctic from Common terns is rather difficult; offshore, where the birds are almost always seen in flight at a distance, the task often involves mostly guesswork. Keep in mind that Common Terns occur frequently in the deep offshore waters and are rather common in migration, always greatly outnumbering Arctic Terns. A "Comic Tern" seen on an offshore trip is far more likely to be a Common than an Arctic.

You're likely to see this bird in North Carolina only by going out on one of the chartered birding trips out of Oregon Inlet or Hatteras Inlet during the spring migration peak. Beginning birders are almost certain not to get a really satisfying view of one. However, on rare occasions a bird might be seen resting on flotsam, allowing an almost reasonable view.

Sightings of this species from fishing headboats out of Hatteras Village and Morehead City–Atlantic Beach are even more likely to be unsatisfying. Because these are fishing trips, you will not get to inspect any birds perched on flotsam. Your best chance of finding this species on land is to check Cape Hatteras Point during strong northeast to east winds in mid- to late May.

Consult one of the more advanced field guides regarding identification of this species. Unfortunately, many of the field marks traditionally used to separate this species from the Common Tern are variable and of a subjective nature. For instance, Common Terns sometimes have all-red bills; more important, on an offshore trip they frequently look like they do when they don't. Also, the classic Arctic field mark—the white cheek patch—is certainly present, albeit more subtle and diffuse, in a breeding-plumaged Common. You should concentrate on the general silhouette of an Arctic (much more short-legged, short-billed, and short-necked) and the generally uniform color of the upper surface of the wings (but beware: in the offshore waters a bright sun can make the upper surface of a Common Tern's wing look uniform). Another potential problem in autumn is that some Common Terns retain their breeding plumage longer than others (this difference is very noticeable at Cape Hatteras Point, where some late-breeding birds are usually mixed in with others). On spotting one of these late-breeding terns—a bird much grayer than the others—some birders may believe they have found an Arctic.

BRIDLED TERN

This pelagic species is a summer resident off our coast. Bridled Terns are found primarily along the edge of the Gulf Stream, where they are fairly common from mid-June to mid-September. Actually, they vary rather considerably in abundance; they are most common when there are prominent grass (sargassum) lines along the edge of the Gulf Stream. During most years they are common in late summer.

You will probably see at least a few of these birds if you take one of the chartered birding trips out of Oregon or Hatteras inlets during the summer period, and during August and early September you are likely to see several. Trips in mid- and late May are not so reliable, but you have a fairly good chance of seeing a bird then too. On these chartered trips you will usually see one or more birds perched on flotsam, allowing some really close views. Bridled Terns are also seen regularly from the headboats out of Morehead City–Atlantic Beach (mostly on trips to the east and southeast) and Hatteras Village, but you probably won't have the opportunity for any really close looks unless a bird flies right by the boat. In spite of this bird's status offshore, including its occasional occurrence in the near-shore waters, it is virtually never seen from land. However, there is one fair-weather record for Cape Lookout Point (in addition to several records associated with hurricanes and tropical storms).

Consult one of the more advanced field guides for assistance with identifying all the plumages of this species. Many of the birds in North Carolina waters are in subadult plumage, which looks quite different from any plumage of the Sooty Tern. In adult plumage, identification is somewhat more problematic, because the Bridled Terns look rather similar to adult Sooty Terns. The upper parts of a Bridled are more brown, while those of a Sooty look more blackish, but judging this difference in bright sunlight can be tricky. A better field mark for the Bridled is the white collar area behind the dark cap. Be advised that Black Terns are frequent in the offshore waters in late summer. Beginning birders sometimes misidentify these—especially the juveniles—as Bridleds.

SOOTY TERN

This is another pelagic species that probably occurs primarily over the Gulf Stream. The Sooty Tern is a summer resident, generally uncommon, but fairly common from about mid-August to early September. In recent years a few of these birds have regularly visited tern colonies lying immediately adjacent to or within a couple of miles of the ocean, such as the colony at Cape Hatteras Point, where Sooties now rate an "uncommon" designation. There have even been several nestings, but so far these have all been unsuccessful: apparently no eggs have hatched.

Currently you are most likely to see a Sooty Tern (and to get a really good look) by visiting Cape Hatteras Point from about late May to early August. (You might want to check at the ranger station logbook to see whether one has been recorded; if so, carefully note at what point in the colony it was seen.) Be prepared to spend several hours scoping for a bird within the colony or watching for one to fly in or out. There have also been several nestings on islands along the channel between Harkers Island and Cape Lookout, and birds have been seen from the passenger ferry that runs between these points. Sooty Terns have also been seen from the Hatteras Inlet ferry.

If you'd like to look for a Sooty the good old-fashioned way—by making a pelagic trip—your best bet is to sign up for one of the chartered trips out of Oregon or Hatteras inlets during the late summer peak. You are quite likely to see Sooties then, but you're not as likely to get as good a view as on land at Cape Hatteras Point. The major identification problem is the fact that at a distance adult Sooties look much like Bridleds. However, during the late summer peak, the Sooties you see will likely be made up of pairs or small groups that usually include a few juveniles, which are dark all over. The presence of these juveniles will help in your identification. Sooty Terns are also occasionally seen from headboats out of Hatteras Village and Morehead City–Atlantic Beach during the late summer peak.

DOVEKIE

Historically, flocks of this northern pelagic species sometimes came southward to our coast (and even appeared inland on rare occasions) during sporadic "invasions," usually about November. However, there has not been a major invasion since 1966. Dovekies are now rare winter visitors, although they might be occasional off the North Coast section.

You are not likely to find this bird in North Carolina. A pelagic trip off the Outer Banks or farther north in winter might produce a few, but such trips are not currently made. Very rarely, one or more are spotted from the beaches between Bodie Island and Cape Hatteras Point, and injured birds sometimes come ashore. Sightings have ranged from November to early March.

RAZORBILL

This large alcid is generally a rare winter visitor along our coast. However, Razorbills may be occasional in the offshore waters off the North Coast and northern Outer Banks. Most of the recorded sightings have taken place between mid-November and mid-March.

This species might also be found with more regularity in our state if there were regular winter pelagic trips. Spotting a Razorbill from shore is not easy, but at least one is sighted almost every year. The new groin at Oregon Inlet may prove to be a site where this species is found occasionally, especially during foggy or stormy weather. Another possible site for this species is the Pea Island–Rodanthe area. Here, look for the prominent tide line (best seen in calm weather) that sometimes develops here. This tide line shifts position continually, sometimes moving south to Rodanthe, sometimes north to Pea Island. At times it becomes extremely well defined, with many birds feeding along it. Razorbills have been spotted on such occasions. Several sightings have also been made in the Cape Hatteras area, especially at the point, where fly-bys have been seen within a hundred yards of land. Strangely, another one of the "better" areas for this species is at and around Fort Fisher. Here the offshore bottom is rocky, with a relative abundance of sealife, and Razorbills have been seen in the area on several occasions.

COMMON GROUND-DOVE

The status of this species in the state has varied greatly since 1900. Early in the century, it was apparently scarce but regular on the barrier islands from about Fort Fisher southward. In the 1960s and 1970s, there was a northward explosion: ground-doves became resident all the way to Fort Macon SP, although they were still limited to the barrier islands. Then, beginning about 1980, ground-doves began declining rapidly. Today there are apparently no longer any resident birds in the state. In most of the region, sightings are now very rare, mostly taking place in late summer and autumn. However, on the south Brunswick County barrier islands, from Holden Beach westward, sightings are slightly more frequent. There visitors are rare during most of the year but occasional from late August through autumn. Your best chance of finding a ground-dove in North Carolina is to walk the west end of Holden Beach or drive the streets of Sunset Beach during this late summer–autumn period.

BARN OWL

Barn Owls feed largely over open areas—marshes, fields, and dunes. In North Carolina this species occurs primarily as an uncommon winter resident, from about early October to late March, mostly on the barrier islands and adjacent mainland. During the warmer months these owls are scarce and very local. Unfortunately, Barn Owls have decreased noticeably in the last twenty years. They are now scarce or absent at many sites where they could once be found easily. There seems to be a strong correlation between absence/scarcity of this species and presence of Great Horned Owls.

If you would like to see a Barn Owl, go to the Outer Banks during the winter months. The best area now seems to be Ocracoke Island. Areas that are not as good but usually have a few birds are Bodie Island, Pea Island NWR, the highway between Avon and Buxton, and the highway between Frisco and Hatteras Village. Farther south, you might see a bird or two at Fort Macon SP and at Fort Fisher.

The best way to see a Barn Owl is to scan the sky at twilight, looking toward the sunrise or sunset. A full moon can also produce enough light to scan for them. Watch for the owl's rather mothlike flight and its distinctive heart-shaped face. Occasionally you might see one in your headlights. In cold weather, birds at Ocracoke Island have been seen feeding half an hour before sunset. Barn Owls can be "squeaked in" rather readily, especially on calm nights.

BARRED OWL

This species is a locally fairly common permanent resident throughout most sections of the mainland. Barred Owls may be found at Great Dismal Swamp NWR, Merchant's Millpond SP, Chowan Swamp Game Land, Alligator River NWR (both sections), Pettigrew SP, Mattamuskeet NWR, Goose Creek SP, Croatan NF (all sections), Holly Shelter Game Land (northwest section), the Orton Pond area, and the Green Swamp area.

Barred Owls are quite vocal throughout the year and can be readily called in with imitations of their calls. They are most responsive around twilight. But in the larger swamps, where it is rather shady, they can frequently be called in up to a couple of hours after sunrise or before sunset.

SHORT-EARED OWL

Like the Barn Owl, this species is typical of open habitats. It is a winter resident, found mostly from mid-November to mid-March. Short-eared Owls are generally occasional but are sometimes more common locally. Short-eareds are most likely in damp or wet areas, such as marshes and wet fields. Although a few sites are annually reliable for this species, to some extent these birds seem rather opportunistic: several may overwinter at a site that has an abundant food supply one year, and none may show up the next year.

Traditionally, two of the most regular sites for Short-eared Owls—although you're more likely to miss them than see them—are over the marshes along north Bodie Island and at the campground at Cape Hatteras Point. At both sites, search the skies after sunset. Watch for the Short-eared's distinctive night-hawklike flight. Unlike the Barn Owl, this species cannot usually be squeaked in. In recent years a few birds have also been found near the end of the barrier spit south of Fort Fisher, and this may prove to be a reliable site. Note that this area requires a long hike if you don't have a four-wheel-drive vehicle. However, apparently the birds usually roost on the spit, so you might be able to flush them and see them in daylight.

Another area that is currently good for Short-eareds is the farmland west of Lake Phelps, in and adjacent to the Pocosin Lakes NWR. Short-eareds should also occur in the Pungo unit of Pocosin Lakes. Elsewhere, this species might be expected anywhere with large field complexes that are wet and have many weedy fallow areas. An area with a particularly high density of Northern Harriers is an area that you'll want to check at twilight for Short-eareds. Occasionally, grassy dredged-material islands along the inland waterway in the Central and South Coast sections will attract two or three wintering owls, and you might flush one in the daylight.

In your search for Short-eareds, don't forget that in most areas, the Barn Owl is more likely than the Short-eared to be spotted over marshes.

NORTHERN SAW-WHET OWL

This winter resident is apparently rare on North Carolina's coast; most records fall between early November and late February. However, it is very difficult to assess this owl's status, because it virtually never calls in our area, and like other owls it rarely appears in daytime. It might be somewhat more regular than the records indicate, perhaps occasional on the Outer Banks.

An effort to find this bird will almost certainly be unsuccessful. However, especially on the Outer Banks, you might try driving slowly at night through areas where your headlights will illuminate shrub thicket borders—for example, along the road to Cape Hatteras Point. Also, while playing tapes of this owl, check all the vegetation around you with a flashlight, because if you do attract a bird, it will probably remain silent. Saw-whets have been heard on a couple of occasions in our area. In the Outer Banks area, sightings have taken place in several different types of wooded habitats, but note that some of the records have come from low-growth shrub thickets, including sites where screech-owls are scarce or absent.

CHUCK-WILL'S-WIDOW

Long considered to be *the* southern goatsucker, the Chuck-will's-widow is common throughout rural sections of the mainland from about late April through August. In the Albemarle-Pamlico and Central Coast sections, these birds seem to be most common where wooded areas adjoin the coastal marshes. In the South Coast section, they are especially common in dry areas with broadleaf vegetation.

Chucks are found most easily from late April to about early July. Later in the summer, they call less frequently, although their calling may pick up slightly toward the end of August. Chucks call most frequently during twilight or during a full moon and can be completely silent on a black night. They can often be called in rather closely with a tape of their song; however, you may not get to see much more than a bird's silhouette as it flutters overhead. Occasionally you might spot one on a sandy road and be able to drive up close enough that you see it well in your headlights.

Some very good areas for this species are Gull Rock Game Land, Goose Creek SP, Croatan NF (all sections), Holly Shelter Game Land (both sections), Carolina Beach SP and the Fort Fisher area, and the Orton Pond area.

The Outer Banks section is not so reliable for this species, but a few birds can usually be found on Roanoke Island, at Bodie Island Lighthouse, and at Cape Hatteras.

WHIP-POOR-WILL

For most of this century, the Whip-poor-will was *the* northern goatsucker. In North Carolina it was most likely to be found in autumn, with a few sightings recorded in winter. Today, though, it is a locally fairly common breeder from mid-April through August. Whip-poor-wills are most common in the dense stands of loblolly pines found on sylvicultural lands.

Some areas where this species can usually be found are Merchants Millpond SP, Goose Creek SP, Croatan NF (all sections), Governors Road near Orton Pond, and the Green Swamp area. Like the Chuck-will's-widow, this species calls most often at twilight or during a full moon. They may also be attracted with a tape of their call.

This species seems to be fairly regular and widespread during the autumn migration, about November. Although they don't call then, they will often flutter about in response to taped calls, uttering a low "whit." They are most likely to be called up at twilight, or during a full moon, when it is calm and warm. They seem to be most frequent where shrub thickets occur in proximity to extensive marshes—for example, along the road to the south end of Cedar Island. Another likely-looking area is at Fort Fisher.

RED-COCKADED WOODPECKER

One of the species most sought after by out-of-state birders, the Red-cockaded is a very local permanent resident in pine woodlands. Key habitat requirements are an open aspect (with very little shrub and subcanopy vegetation) and old-growth trees. Red-cockadeds nest only in live pines. In North Carolina the birds nest primarily in longleaf pines, but they frequently use loblolly and pond pines also. Of course, the bird's favored habitat is not the sort favored by modern-day sylviculture, and that is why the bird is an endangered species. Red-cockadeds are now virtually limited to public lands, where the birds' required habitat is maintained by fire management and where some trees are allowed to grow old enough to be suitable as cavity trees.

Regrettably, these birds are now virtually extirpated from the North Coast and Albemarle-Pamlico sections. There are a few birds at Alligator River NWR, but these are inaccessible. Farther south, Red-cockadeds are still fairly easy to find in the Croatan NF (north and south sections), Holly Shelter Game Land (southeast section), and the Green Swamp area.

To find Red-cockaded Woodpeckers, first find their cavity trees. These trees are distinctive, with resin all around the tree, near the cavity. This resin flows from small holes pecked by the birds. At a distance these trees look whitish. If a cavity tree is currently being used, there will also be some fresh resin, which is clear. Furthermore, most cavity trees are marked with paint; the color of the paint varies from one jurisdiction to another. Birds are easiest to find in May and June, when they are nesting. Set up watch then near an active cavity tree and wait for a changing of the guard (during incubation) or for a bird to bring food to the young. Please don't stand close to the trees or disturb the birds.

Outside the nesting season, the birds are more difficult to find. You're most likely to find them by being near the cavity trees about an hour before sunset or, better, about sunrise.

Red-cockadeds are quite vocal and are easily located by their harsh, frequent calls. Even their feeding actions tend to be noisy. In winter they often move through the woods in little bands made up of chickadees, Brown-headed Nuthatches, Pine Warblers, bluebirds, and other species.

WESTERN KINGBIRD

This primarily western species occurs regularly along the barrier islands and adjacent mainland each autumn, from September to November. Rarely one will linger into winter, especially during milder years. There is also one record of a June vagrant. Sightings are most frequent in October, when the species is uncommon on the Outer Banks and occasional elsewhere.

To see a Western Kingbird most reliably, try to get to the Outer Banks in October, especially mid-October, on the morning after a good cold front with a west to northwest wind. The migrant trap on the south side of Oregon Inlet (Pea Island NWR) may be your best bet, but you might spot one on power lines anywhere.

Ocracoke Island also seems to be a good spot for this species. Because some Westerns often linger in the area for several days, remember to check the logbooks at Pea Island NWR and Cape Hatteras NS ranger station. Some other areas worth checking are Currituck Banks, Cape Lookout, and Fort Fisher.

Western Kingbirds are easy to identify, but you should always scrutinize possible Westerns carefully so as not to overlook an even rarer flycatcher/kingbird. This is particularly true if you encounter a "Western" outside the usual autumn months.

GRAY KINGBIRD

One of these primarily tropical birds shows up almost every year in May or June; birders should always be on the watch at this time of year. Gray Kingbirds are rare from mid-May to early June along the barrier islands (sometimes on the adjacent mainland) from Bodie Island southward. Based on the records, the species is very rare from mid-June to early October. Within this period, however, sightings are probably somewhat more likely in September and early October.

If you'd like to see one of these birds, be especially watchful on trips to the barrier islands from Bodie Island south between mid-May and early June. Based on the records, no sites really stand out as better than others, although the southern Outer Banks may be the most promising area in general. It would seem that sites with the most potential would offer a combination of good habitat—open habitats with utility wires for perches—and a barrier of inhospitable habitat, especially water, to the north and northeast. Some sites with these characteristics are the old coast guard station at Pea Island NWR; the east and northeast sides of Buxton; the ferry terminal at the northeast end of Ocracoke Island; Portsmouth Village; the Cedar Island ferry terminal (although this site is a bit far "inland"); the coast guard station area at Fort Macon SP; and Fort Caswell (adjacent to Caswell Beach).

Scissor-tailed Flycatcher

Records of this very rare but highly conspicuous species do not fit any into well-defined seasonal pattern—they are scattered from late April to early December. Most birds have been found on the barrier islands or soundside areas of the adjacent mainland.

You are not likely to find these flycatchers in North Carolina. However, they are perhaps most likely to be spotted on the Outer Banks between late May and mid-June and in October. If you do encounter a long-tailed flycatcher, you will want to rule out the accidental Fork-tailed Flycatcher, which is also a possibility.

Brown-headed Nuthatch

On average, this bird of pine and mixed woods is fairly common. Brown-headed Nuthatches are common in areas dominated by longleaf pine in the South and Central Coast sections. They are also frequently found where pine-dominated woods abut coastal marshes in the Albemarle-Pamlico and Central Coast sections. Such areas typically have numerous snags that provide nesting habitat. Over most of the North Coast and Albemarle-Pamlico sections, Brown-headeds are uncommon because of the lack of suitable habitat.

Some good to excellent sites for this species are listed below. At the more northern sites you can usually find the birds after some effort; from the Croatan NF south, they are almost impossible to miss. Check Merchant's Millpond SP, Alligator River NWR (both sections), Mattamuskeet NWR, Goose Creek SP, Roanoke Island, Goose Creek Game Land, the Minnesott Beach area, Croatan NF (all sections), Holly Shelter Game Land (both sections), Carolina Beach SP, the Orton Pond area, and Green Swamp.

To find this species, listen for its nasal calls, which have been likened to the cries some toy dolls make when you squeeze them. Especially considering its size, this bird makes a pretty good racket when it's feeding; one might think there's a woodpecker up in the trees. During the nonnesting season, the nuthatches are frequent in feeding flocks that also include chickadees, titmice, and other species.

SEDGE WREN

Although inconspicuous, this species is a common winter resident except after extreme cold. Sedge Wrens occur primarily from October to April. There are a few records of singing birds in August, and it is possible that this species may rarely nest in our area. Sedge Wrens are most typical of the upper borders of extensive marshes—usually salt or brackish—where there are a few low-growing shrubs. Such areas are often not very wet, merely moist. They are also found in moist, recently clear-cut areas with thick grassy cover.

Some of the better areas for this species are the Roanoke Island Marshes near Wanchese; Bodie Island; New Field at Pea Island NWR; Ocracoke Island (especially the salt meadows beside the ORV trail to South Point); the Cedar Island Marshes; the North River Marsh (Carteret Wildlife Club site) near Beaufort; and Topsail Island adjacent to New River Inlet.

Like many marsh birds, Sedge Wrens can be very secretive and inconspicuous. The best time to look for them is at sunrise (sunset is almost as good) when it is calm. Walk into their habitat then, moving from site to site, and listen carefully. They frequently give a distinctive call—a low, resonant note. They can be very inquisitive at this time of day, perhaps wondering what sort of predator has invaded their roosting area, and they often come out into the open. Sedge Wrens may sing very actively before they leave in spring, often throughout the day. Their song is low and chattering. Listen for this song in April and the first few days of May.

MARSH WREN

This locally common permanent resident occurs in wetter portions of the marshes than the Sedge Wren does. Typically Marsh Wrens are found at sites that have a few inches of water and a dense growth of grasses, rushes, sedges, or cattails. In general they are more common but also more local in the breeding season; in the cooler months they are less common but more widespread.

Some sites that are good for Marsh Wrens at all seasons are the NC 615 causeway at Mackay Island NWR; the Roanoke Island Marshes near Wanchese; the Pungo River Marshes; Pea Island NWR; the marshes near Hobucken; the Cedar Island Marshes; and the North River Marsh (Carteret Wildlife Club site) near Beaufort. Some sites that are good except during the breeding season are Bodie Island, Fort Fisher area, and the USS North Carolina Battleship Memorial at Wilmington.

ORANGE-CROWNED WARBLER

This blandly plumaged warbler is certainly seen more often than it is recognized. In North Carolina it is mostly an uncommon (locally fairly common) winter resident, found primarily from November to early April. Orange-crowned Warblers are found primarily in dense shrub thickets on the barrier islands and nearby mainland from Bodie Island southward, although they are most common from Cape Hatteras south.

The best site for this species is Buxton Woods at Cape Hatteras; birds are found more readily here than on barrier islands farther to the south. Two sites that are almost as good are Fort Fisher and relatively inaccessible Bald Head Island. Strangely, the causeway at Lake Mattamuskeet is very reliable for this species, at least early in the winter, though it is rather far inland.

You will find this bird most easily by listening for it. Especially on sunny, calm days, about midmorning, listen for its crisp chip-note, which is reminiscent of a cardinal's. This note is readily distinguished from the flat call-notes of the omnipresent Yellow-rumped Warblers. Orange-crowneds feed very actively and usually stay within the foliage, so they might be passed off as Ruby-crowned Kinglets. When you get a bird in view, note the yellow undertail coverts and the absence of wing bars.

PROTHONOTARY WARBLER

This brilliantly colored bird is a common and widespread summer resident that can be found in all mainland swamps except those that are very small and isolated. They are found primarily from mid-April to August. Although most common in swamps, they are also frequent in moist woods that are never flooded. Actually, the presence of some dead trees may be their primary nesting requirement, because they are cavity nesters. In fact, you can find Prothonotaries at impoundments that have dead trees but virtually no green vegetation.

Some very good areas for this species are Mackay Island NWR, Great Dismal Swamp NWR, Merchants Millpond SP, Chowan Swamp Game Land, Alligator River NWR (both sections), Pettigrew SP, Mattamuskeet NWR, Goose Creek SP, Goose Creek Game Land, Croatan NF (all sections), Holly Shelter Game Land (northwest section), the Orton Pond area, and Green Swamp.

These birds are most easily located from April to about early July, when singing their loud "sweet-sweet-sweet." However, they are also found fairly readily later in the season, thanks to their bright plumage, and they seem to remain in good numbers later than some breeders. However, they may move out of many of the smaller swamps late in the season (late July to early September). Two sites that are particularly good for finding Prothonotaries late in the season are the Great Dismal Swamp NWR and Holly Shelter Game Land (northwest section).

WORM-EATING WARBLER

Most out-of-state birders would never guess that coastal North Carolina is a good area for seeing this species. Indeed, most field guides do not acknowledge that it occurs here during the nesting season. Actually, the Worm-eating is a locally fairly common summer resident throughout much of the coastal area.

Breeding birds arrive about mid-April and probably stay until about August. (The species is also an occasional autumn migrant.) In North Carolina this bird's primary natural nesting habitat is what may be referred to as pond pine woodland—areas where a moderate stand of pines overtops an approximately ten- to twenty-foot-high growth of thick vegetation made up primarily of broadleaf evergreens. Pine plantations with similar habitat characteristics may also harbor Worm-eating Warblers.

Some good areas for Worm-eatings are Alligator River NWR (both sections), Goose Creek Game Land, Croatan NF (all sections), SR 1520 adjacent to the northwest section of Holly Shelter Game Land, and the Green Swamp area.

This bird is best located by song; unfortunately many people can't hear this song, because it is quite high-pitched. The song is much like that of a Pine Warbler but faster and "drier" (not as musical). The two species commonly occur in the same areas, but the Pine Warblers typically sing from higher sites, up in the pines. The Worm-eatings usually remain in the lower, thicker growth, and they sing until about early July. As summer progresses they become increasingly difficult to find.

SWAINSON'S WARBLER

This is one of the species most eagerly sought by out-of-state birders. It is a generally uncommon and local summer resident, occurring roughly from mid-April to August, although one isn't likely to find Swainson's Warblers after they quit singing, around early July (later in some areas). These warblers occur in habitats that are moist to wet and have thick shrub-level vegetation. Overall, they seem to be most frequent along streams lined with thick growths of cane or broadleaf evergreen shrubs.

Some of the better areas for this species are Great Dismal Swamp NWR (especially along Jericho Lane), Chowan Swamp Game Land, Alligator River NWR (south section), Gull Rock Game Land, Croatan NF (all sections), and the Green Swamp area. At very small streams in the Croatan NF, there may be little singing after early June. At Great Dismal Swamp NWR, singing is frequent until at least mid-July. Less dependable sites are Alligator River NWR (north section), Goose Creek Game Land, Cedar Island NWR, the North River headwaters north of Beaufort, Holly Shelter Game Land (both sections), Carolina Beach SP, and Daws and Rices creeks in the Orton Plantation area.

You can find this bird by listening for its loud, ringing "wheel-wheel-wheel-WHAT-cha-tell." Hooded Warblers often sing a virtually identical song, but the Hooded's song is not so loud and ringing.

Often a Swainson's sings so persistently and obliviously that you might be able to eventually spot the singer, provided you are patient and the vegetation is not impenetrable. Note that these birds seem to be ventriloquists: you should look all around, not just in the apparent direction of the song. Swainson's

Warblers are almost totally unresponsive to squeaking. However, they are usually extremely aggressive toward a taped recording of their song. Please don't abuse this responsiveness by playing the tape for a long period, especially at sites where many birders are likely to visit. If you can, try to spot the bird without using a tape. In many areas it really isn't that difficult.

LOUISIANA WATERTHRUSH

Out-of-state birders often assume that this species is a common and widespread breeder in North Carolina, but that is definitely not the case. This waterthrush is fairly common in the Great Dismal Swamp NWR and uncommon elsewhere in the western half of the North Coast section. Farther south, though, they are very local in occurrence, found here and there along the inland border of the region. These more southern birds are very restricted in habitat use; they live almost exclusively where there are streams with steep banks and a noticeable current. This is one of the earliest warblers to arrive in the spring—you might hear one in late March. They are seldom heard in song after about mid-May (somewhat later in the Great Dismal Swamp). At least some are present until about August, but they become increasingly scarce and difficult to find as summer progresses.

By far the best site for this species is the Great Dismal Swamp NWR, where birds may be spotted from any of the roadways into the swamp. Watch for them along the canals. A few also breed at Merchants Millpond SP. Farther south, one or two can usually be found at the Island Creek Forest Walk in the Croatan NF (north section).

Of course this bird is most easily found during its peak singing period, about early April to early May (to mid-June in the Great Dismal Swamp). After singing has ceased you might still be able to spot one by watching carefully along the streams and ditches of the above areas. However, these birds are very early autumn migrants; by August you'll have little chance of finding one. Be aware that a waterthrush seen in late summer is far more likely to be a Northern. Migration of Northerns is well under way in August, and there is even a record as early as mid-July.

SUMMER TANAGER

This species is a common summer resident throughout much of the region, especially from the Croatan NF south. Summer Tanagers are most typical of mixed woods that are somewhat open in aspect. They are especially common in oak-pine woods on dry sites in the Central and South Coast sections. Summer Tanagers begin arriving about mid-April. Breeding birds presumably stay until August or September. There is also a noticeable autumn migration on the barrier islands.

Some good sites for this species during the breeding season are Great Dismal Swamp NWR (in the refuge office area), Merchants Millpond SP, Goose Creek

SP, Goose Creek Game Land, the Minnesott Beach area, Croatan NF (all sections), Holly Shelter Game Land (both sections), Carolina Beach SP, and the area around Brunswick Town SHS. In autumn, Carolina Beach SP and the Brunswick Town area are the best sites.

This species is most easily found when the male is singing its robin-like song, until July. Later in the season they're still rather easy to find, because of their frequently given and distinctive "pi-tuk-i-tuk" call.

BLUE GROSBEAK

This species is sometimes sought after by birders from northern states. It is a common summer resident. Blue Grosbeaks are found in open brushy habitats, such as abandoned fields and clearings, and in hedgerows in agricultural areas, but they also occur in open woodlands. They arrive in numbers about the end of April and remain common throughout most of the summer. There is evidently an autumn migration as well, especially on the barrier islands.

These birds can be found easily along roadsides in most agricultural areas. Some specific sites on public lands include Alligator River NWR (north section), fields around Lake Mattamuskeet, Goose Creek Game Land, Cedar Island NWR, Croatan NF (all sections), Holly Shelter Game Land (southeast section), and Brunswick Town SHS. At Alligator River NWR birds may not be present until late May. At Cedar Island NWR they may be gone by late summer.

The loud finch-like warble of this species is very different from the Indigo Bunting's song. Fortunately, Blue Grosbeaks often sing vigorously in the middle of the day, and they sing well into August.

PAINTED BUNTING

This is one of the most frequently sought-after species in North Carolina, probably in part because the northeastern limit of this subtropical finch lies within our region. Also, no one ever tires of seeing the gaudily colored males.

In North Carolina the Painted Bunting is essentially limited to the barrier islands and a very narrow strip of the adjacent mainland, from Marshallberg and Fort Macon SP in Carteret County southward. (Remarkably, though, their northern limit is actually on the mainland, and they are scarce on Shackleford Banks and unrecorded at Cape Lookout.) Painted Buntings are found primarily in dense shrub thickets, typically vine-covered and impenetrable, although they sometimes occur in well-wooded residential areas. They are locally fairly common from late April through July, gradually decreasing through August, September, and October. They overwinter rarely, most often at feeders.

Some good sites are West Beaufort Road near the Beaufort-Morehead airport, Fort Macon SP, Hammocks Beach SP (both mainland and barrier island), Carolina Beach SP, Fort Fisher, Orton Plantation, Brunswick Town SHS, and Bald Head Island.

These birds are rather persistent singers from their arrival until about mid-

July north and early August south. The song is a scratchy warble. Be advised that first-year males, which look like females, also sing. After they quit singing, Painted Buntings are more difficult to spot, but with a little patience you can usually find them through August. In autumn the best sites to check are Fort Fisher and the nearby North Carolina Aquarium (especially its bird feeder).

Adult males are of course unmistakable, but beginning birders often puzzle over females/immature males. Remember that no other birds have both the greenish coloration and the finch bill.

BACHMAN'S SPARROW

Coastal North Carolina is the northeasternmost area where this species is found regularly. For this reason, and because it occurs quite locally, it is one of our most sought-after species. For all its popularity, it is really a plain little bird. Actually, to many birders a Bachman's Sparrow is memorable primarily for its clear distinctive song and characteristic habitat. At the handful of sites where it is regular, this sparrow is a fairly common summer resident, present mostly from about March to early October. In winter Bachman's Sparrows are generally rare, but they may be occasional in Brunswick County and sometimes farther north when habitat is suitable.

In coastal North Carolina this species is very local, found at only a few sites from the Croatan NF south. North of the Croatan, records are very unusual and will probably become accidental in the near future. In virtually all of our area, Bachman's Sparrows are extremely selective about habitat. They are found primarily in savannas and open pine woodlands that have a thick grass cover and virtually no subcanopy or shrub vegetation. Such habitats are maintained by frequent fire management, so the birds are now virtually restricted to public and Nature Conservancy lands. In our southernmost county—Brunswick—the birds are perhaps a bit less choosy. There they have been found in some open pine plantations and woodlands where ground cover is not so thick. Even in Brunswick County, though, birds will probably be largely limited to public and Nature Conservancy lands in a few years. Wintering birds are most likely at sites that were burned over during the previous growing season.

The best sites for this species are Millis Road Savanna in the Croatan NF (south section), Holly Shelter Game Land (southeast section), and NC 211 through the Green Swamp. These sites are all burned regularly and should remain reliable for Bachman's Sparrows in the future.

By far the best way to find this species is to listen for its loud "seee-SLIP-SLIP-SLIP." This song recalls that of a Field Sparrow, which doesn't nest in these areas. Singing normally begins about late March or early April, but on rare occasions begins as early as late February at sites where birds have overwintered. Singing continues until about early August, sometimes later. Although Bachman's Sparrows sing most vigorously early in the morning, they often sing in the heat of midday. Singing sometimes picks up again late in the afternoon, and birds have also been heard during a full moon.

Once you've heard a Bachman's singing, you can usually find it with a little patience. However, these birds often seem to be ventriloquists. Check all the saplings and the lower branches of trees in the vicinity of where the bird seems to be. These birds often stick to the same singing site for long periods. If you're quiet, you can often study them with a scope. Bachman's often respond well to tapes of their song.

After the singing season, birds become increasingly difficult to find. However, through September and early October you can usually flush one after a little effort. This is a bird that doesn't flush until you're about to step on it. When you do flush one, freeze. The bird may stop in a shrub to examine you, allowing you a chance to examine it. Don't waste this opportunity. After repeated flushings, the birds get more and more wary.

Birds are especially difficult to find from November to February. They are most likely at sites that have been burned over during the previous growing season. Wintering birds are perhaps occasional at the Green Swamp preserve, but except for the nature trail, this Nature Conservancy preserve is off-limits (in order to protect rare plants). Wintering birds might also be found at Holly Shelter Game Land (southeast section). However, all fire management is currently limited to the winter months, decreasing the probability that birds over-winter here. At this time there is little chance of finding these birds in the Croatan NF in winter; but the U.S. Forest Service is carrying out more prescribed burns during the growing season (to mimic the natural system), so overwintering may become more likely in the future at sites like Millis Road Savanna.

The Bachman's is a large sparrow, with a flat forehead and long rounded tail. During the warmer months, it is the only sparrow likely to be seen at the above sites. From November to about early April, other sparrows—especially Swamp Sparrows—are much more likely. However, the only other sparrow that doesn't flush until it's almost stepped on is the Henslow's, which looks very different.

CLAY-COLORED SPARROW

This primarily western species is a regular autumn migrant in our area. Clay-colored Sparrows are most likely to be found from late September to late October, when they are occasional on the Outer Banks and Fort Fisher and rare elsewhere on the barrier islands. They are found primarily along the borders of shrub thickets. A few sometimes linger into winter, when they are very rare.

To find this bird, head to Pea Island NWR or Fort Fisher during the autumn peak, especially after cold fronts with northwest or west winds. At Pea Island, check at the north end of the island (near the old coast guard station) and the north and south dikes of North Pond. At Fort Fisher, check the borders of the shrub thickets near the museum, the borders of the open grassy area at the North Carolina Aquarium, and around the ferry terminal.

In most Clay-colored Sparrows the distinctive face pattern is apparent. Immature Chipping Sparrows are sometimes called Clay-coloreds, but in real Clay-coloreds, the color of the rump does not contrast with the back.

LARK SPARROW

Like the Clay-colored Sparrow, this is a primarily western species that regularly occurs in our area each autumn. Lark Sparrows are most likely to be found from mid-August to early October, when they are occasional on the Outer Banks and rare elsewhere on the barrier islands. They are found primarily along the borders of shrub thickets. Lark Sparrows are very rare in winter and spring.

For the best chance of finding this bird, visit Pea Island NWR during the autumn peak. Cold fronts with northwest or west winds are probably best, although there are few such fronts in August and early September. Check around the old coast guard station at the north end of the island, and along north and south dikes at North Pond. Other sites worth checking are the Wright Brothers National Memorial, the Bodie Island Lighthouse area, and the Fort Fisher area.

Even immature Lark Sparrows are easy to identify. In addition to the distinctive face pattern and relatively large size, note the white outer tail feathers.

HENSLOW'S SPARROW

This attractive and very secretive little sparrow is generally rare at all seasons in the coastal area. However, during times when good habitat becomes temporarily available, you have a reasonable chance of finding one.

Henslow's Sparrows occasionally breed along the western periphery of the coastal area. Thus far, virtually all breeding records have been in pocosin regions within extensive clear-cuts that have been replanted with young pines. Apparently it is essential that a tract be very moist or wet, with thick grass cover.

Keep in mind that this type of habitat is transitory. After the pines grow a few feet tall and the invading shrubs become dense, the birds will abandon an area; thus, sites probably are suitable for no more than a few years. Areas suitable for breeding Henslow's Sparrows are most likely to be created on a regular basis in Washington, Beaufort, Craven, Pender, and Brunswick counties, where there are both potential habitat and intense sylvicultural activity. In Washington, Beaufort, and Craven counties, though, you're not likely to see any good habitat adjacent to public roadways, and most logging roads that run through potential habitat are closed. These birds have been heard from NC 50 near Maple Hill in Pender County, and they are heard with some regularity along NC 211 and adjacent logging roads in the Green Swamp, but there is no assurance that these logging roads will be open in the future. Breeding birds are not likely to be found on any public lands, although there is one breeding season record for the Croatan NF.

To find a Henslow's during the breeding season, listen for its weak, insectlike "ti-slick." They probably sing primarily from late April to July, although they may be heard in August. They frequently sing from the tops of young pines and shrubs, often so persistently that you can set up a scope and get an excellent view.

Wintering birds sometimes are found (from November to about early April) either in clear-cut areas like those described above or in moist or wet pine savannas. In clear-cuts that have especially thick grass cover, birds are sometimes occasional. In pine savannas—found from the Croatan NF south—Henslow's are generally rare, but they are probably occasional in the Green Swamp area. They can be uncommon in all areas when habitat is optimal: that is, when there is very thick grass cover following a fire the previous summer. This is admittedly a rare situation, although prescribed burns during the growing season are being carried out increasingly by the U.S. and state forest services and other agencies.

Wintering Henslow's Sparrows are probably most likely in the Green Swamp preserve; except for the nature trail, though, this Nature Conservancy preserve is off-limits (in order to protect rare plants). Birds might sometimes be found in the Holly Shelter Game Land (southeast section), although this area receives only winter burns. Birds will probably become regular at this site if the state's Wildlife Resources Commission begins a growing-season burn policy. In the Croatan NF wintering birds are sometimes found at Millis Road Savanna. Most years they are absent or quite scarce, but during at least one winter, following a growing-season burn, they were actually fairly common. The U.S. Forest Service is carrying out more growing season prescribed burns, and wintering Henslow's Sparrows may become even more regular at this site (and perhaps at sites nearby).

To find a winter Henslow's, work your way through the above areas, kicking around in the thicker tufts of grass. This activity is good for a group of birders; try sweeping through the area with everyone abreast of each other, about five feet apart. If the habitat is indeed suitable, you will flush several Swamp Sparrows—large and dark sparrows with long tails. You may eventually have a small short-tailed sparrow flush almost at your feet, flutter a short distance, and then fall back into the grass awkwardly. That's the bird! If you're lucky, it might fly into a low shrub, where you can study it for several minutes before it flies. If a Henslow's lands on the ground, a group can often surround it, close in on it, and get ridiculously close looks before it finally flies or runs away.

Seen at close range, the Henslow's is indeed a colorful, attractive sparrow. Note the striped crown and olive head.

SHARP-TAILED SPARROW

This sparrow is found primarily in regularly flooded salt marshes, especially near inlets. It is a winter resident, fairly common to common from late September through April. Sharp-tailed Sparrows are common from Beaufort Inlet south and are fairly common near inlets farther north. They are most widespread during the autumn migration (mid-October through November). During this time they are often easier to find along the Outer Banks than later in the winter; they are also regular then along the borders of irregularly flooded salt marshes, including those along the western shores of Pamlico Sound.

During average conditions, the marsh sparrows can often be difficult to see well. It is important to search for these birds when there is no wind or only a light wind. Check out potential areas around sunrise or sunset; birds can often be squeaked into view readily at these times. The marsh sparrows are also best searched for during high tides—the higher the better—when birds become concentrated along the upper borders of the marshes. In autumn, and in the South Coast section in winter, you will usually have the opportunity to study Sharp-taileds and Seasides together. But in winter, if you are north of the South Coast section, you may look through a lot of Sharp-taileds before you see a Seaside. Before they leave in spring, Sharp-taileds sometimes give their gasping little song, which doesn't carry very far. You are most likely to hear this song in May.

Some good marshes to check for this species are those at the marina at Oregon Inlet (autumn to spring); those opposite the south end of North Pond at Pea Island NWR (autumn to spring); those near the Hatteras Inlet ferry terminal on Ocracoke Island (best in autumn); and those on the barrier spit south of Fort Fisher and at the end of US 421 (autumn to spring). Good sites requiring long hikes or four-wheel-drive vehicles are the Hatteras Spit (autumn to spring) and the South Point road at Ocracoke Island (autumn to spring). The short-grass marshes adjacent to US 70 at North River Marsh near Beaufort are reliable for Sharp-taileds in early and mid-May.

SEASIDE SPARROW

In most areas, "Seaside Sparrow" is definitely a misnomer: these marsh sparrows are seldom found by the seaside. The Seaside Sparrow is a permanent resident in our area, but there is a pronounced shift in the populations of these birds from summer to winter, both geographically and ecologically. In the breeding season—from about late March to August—Seasides are found primarily in irregularly flooded salt marshes, and they are most common where such marshes are extensive, as in the Central Coast section. In winter the birds are largely restricted to regularly flooded salt marshes, especially near inlets. Then they are common in the South Coast section but generally uncommon farther north, where they are quite local. The birds are most widespread during the autumn migration period, from about late August through October.

In the breeding season some of the better and easily accessible sites for this species are the marshes opposite the south end of North Pond at Pea Island NWR; the marshes near the Hatteras Inlet ferry terminal on Ocracoke Island;

the salt meadows along the South Point road at Ocracoke Island; the Cedar Island Marshes; North River Marsh near Beaufort (Carteret Wildlife Club site); and the marshes along SR 1228 near Hobucken. Other sites worth checking are the Roanoke Island Marshes near Wanchese and the marshes on the north side of Oregon Inlet. A few birds—"real" Seaside Sparrows—nest in the saltmeadow cordgrass along the lower slopes of the dunes at Portsmouth Island. During the autumn migration, birds can be found in most regularly flooded salt marshes along the coast. From November to early March, they are most easily found in the marshes of the South Coast section. They are especially common at Masonboro Island and the barrier spit and end of US 421 near Fort Fisher. Farther north, a few birds can usually be found near the marina at Oregon Inlet; opposite the south end of North Pond at Pea Island NWR; Hatteras Spit; and the Morehead City–Beaufort causeway.

When Seasides are singing, about late March to July, you can easily locate them by listening for their asthmatic "zhir-zee" songs. In August, they can usually be found rather easily in their nesting areas, even though the birds rarely sing then. During the other seasons, follow the same advice suggested for Sharp-taileds.

LINCOLN'S SPARROW

This pretty little sparrow is rather scarce in our area and very secretive. It is also rather difficult to identify—many beginning birders have sorted through Song Sparrow after Song Sparrow wondering, "Is this one a Lincoln's? Maybe this one."

Traditionally this species has been considered a rare winter resident in our area. However, in recent years they have been found to be occasional from about late October through March in the Albemarle-Pamlico section. Preferred habitat (or possibly just the habitat in which they are easiest to find) is the sort of long brushpile created after clearing operations, usually in moist or wet situations. Birds seem to be most likely a couple of years after the piles are created, when weedy growth on them is the lushest. This habitat is transitory, of course, and is seldom found on public lands; also, this type of habitat will become rarer in the future. Birds certainly also occur in other habitats, especially moist thickets, but the probability of finding one in such areas is slight.

During the autumn migration Lincoln's Sparrows also turn up on the barrier islands. They are most likely on the Outer Banks and at Fort Fisher, where they are occasional during October.

Again, good habitat in the Albemarle-Pamlico section is not likely to be found on public lands. By driving around in the area you might find suitable habitat close enough to a road that you can check it from the road shoulder. Birds are sometimes seen in less-than-prime habitat—wet thickets—around Lake Mattamuskeet. After October cold fronts, check the thickets at Pea Island

NWR and at Fort Fisher. At Pea Island work the north end of the island and the dikes.

Wintering birds are easiest to find during calm conditions early and late in the day, when they are a little more likely to pop into the open. Although these birds are sometimes squeaked into view, you may see them most easily by being quiet.

Identification of this bird isn't that difficult if you really see one. If you're questioning whether the bird you're looking at is a Song or Lincoln's sparrow, you're probably looking at a Song. When you see a real Lincoln's, you will immediately be impressed by its slim build and "clean" look. These birds are noticeably buffy, and their buffy eye ring is quite distinctive.

WHITE-CROWNED SPARROW

In most of coastal North Carolina this large, attractive sparrow is an occasional autumn migrant (in October) and rare winter visitor. On the Outer Banks, however, White-crowneds are uncommon to fairly common from early October to late November. In recent years they have also been found to be an uncommon winter resident in weedy areas of recently cleared farmland just west of Lake Phelps, but the habitat in which they occur is transitory, and birds will probably become scarce at this site in the future.

Winter habitat of this species is very different from that of the White-throated Sparrow. The White-crowned is found in hedgerows, weedy sites, and low thickets in predominantly open areas.

After cold fronts in mid- and late October, you are almost certain to find this species at Pea Island NWR. Check at the north end of the island and along the dikes at North Pond. White-crowneds are also seen regularly in the scrub growth next to the Cape Hatteras Lighthouse. Away from the Outer Banks section, two good sites for this species are Cape Lookout and Fort Fisher. Again, try to go after cold fronts in mid- to late October.

In winter look for White-crowneds in the scrub growth just west of Lake Phelps, next to Shore Drive (SR 1183), in the Pocosin Lakes NWR. However, the number of sightings here will probably decline in the future. These sparrows are sometimes seen in the scrub growth at the Cape Hatteras Lighthouse and at Fort Fisher in winter.

This sparrow is easy to identify. Note the pinkish bill, which is present in all plumages.

LAPLAND LONGSPUR

In North Carolina this Arctic nester has much in common with the Snow Bunting. They are both winter residents/visitors and often occur in the same habitats and at the same sites, although they are virtually never seen together.

Traditionally this species has been found primarily on the Outer Banks, mainly from mid-October to early February, when it is occasional. In most other parts of the region Laplands are very rare; most records have come from the barrier islands. In recent years, though, wintering flocks have been found on the vast agricultural lands just west of Lake Phelps, and the species here has an average status of uncommon, although the numbers of birds and the ease with which they are found vary from year to year.

On the Outer Banks and other barrier islands, most sightings are of small flocks, and there are several records of single birds. Flocks are larger near Lake Phelps; one record describes a flock of almost one hundred birds. On the barrier islands, longspurs are found primarily in the same type of habitat as Snow Buntings—dry, expansive, sparsely vegetated sand flats. The habitat near Lake Phelps is vast barren fields.

In the Outer Banks area the best sites to check for this species are the Oregon Inlet flats (Bodie Island), Cape Hatteras Point, and Hatteras Spit. Sightings seem to be most frequent from late October to early December. West of Lake Phelps, drive the road through Tyson Farms. Although this road is private, it is not currently closed to the public. At this site birds seem to arrive later and remain later than elsewhere—about late November to late February. Only at the Outer Banks and Tyson Farms are you likely to find this bird. However, one site worth mentioning is the barrier spit south of Fort Fisher. Birds are sighted here every two or three years, and occurrences may actually be almost annual. Furthermore, suitable habitat should be available here for years.

Their flocking habits and tendency to occur in open habitats will help you identify these birds. At sites on the Outer Banks they can often be approached quite closely. When the birds fly, listen for their distinctive dry rattle. If you see a longspur on the barrier islands in autumn, scrutinize it carefully to rule out the possibility of other longspur species—although such a sighting would be accidental.

SNOW BUNTING

On a windy, bitterly cold winter day, the sight of a flock of Snow Buntings on some barren flats on the Outer Banks seems most appropriate. This Arctic nester is a winter resident/visitor along our state's coast. Snow Buntings are found primarily from Cape Lookout north, where they are occasional from early November to mid-February. Farther south, they are rare during this period, although they may be occasional after strong cold fronts from mid-November to mid-December. In North Carolina these birds usually occur in small flocks, and sometimes single birds are seen.

Almost all recorded sightings of this species in our area have taken place on the barrier islands, although there are also a few sightings from the adjacent mainland. Many birders have the mistaken impression that this bird occurs in well-vegetated dunes. Actually, they are found primarily on dry, open, sparsely vegetated flats, like those that often occur on the updrift side of inlets, although they have been sighted on wide berms seaward of the dunes as well.

Cape Hatteras Point, Hatteras Spit, and the Oregon Inlet flats (Bodie Island) are three good sites for this species. The wide berm along Currituck Banks north of Corolla is currently quite good but may be less reliable in the future as real estate development continues. South of the Outer Banks, these birds might be seen adjacent to any of the inlets. The barrier spit south of Fort Fisher has very good habitat for this species, and good habitat should be present in the future as well.

Identification of these birds is easy, aided by their occurrence in flocks and in open habitats. They can often be approached quite closely. Note the large white wing patches on buntings in flight.

YELLOW-HEADED BLACKBIRD

This blackbird is regular enough as an autumn migrant on the Outer Banks that persistent birders have a reasonable chance of finding one. Yellow-headeds are rare in this section from late August to early October, except for a peak of occurrence in early September, when they are occasional. Elsewhere along the coast, the birds are very rare to rare during this migration period. This blackbird is also a very rare winter and spring visitor, when it is most likely to be found around livestock in extensive agricultural areas.

For the best chance of finding this bird, head to the Outer Banks in early September. Pea Island NWR and Cape Hatteras Point seem to be the best sites. In winter you have a slight chance of finding this bird in the Lake Mattamuskeet area; mid- and late winter seem to be best. Drive the secondary roads on the northeast and southeast sides of the lake, searching out flocks of blackbirds associating with livestock.

The majority of birds seen in our area are females and immature males. Although these are not as conspicuous as adult males, they are easy to identify if you see them well. Yellow-headeds are not likely to be confused with anything else, although overly enthusiastic birders have, at least momentarily, identified female Boat-tailed Grackles as Yellow-headed Blackbirds.

RUSTY BLACKBIRD

Beginning birders often search unsuccessfully for this generally uncommon winter resident. These birders may sort through large flocks of grackles, Red-winged Blackbirds, and cowbirds, wondering if Rusties don't really occur in the area or if they are merely overlooking them.

Rusty Blackbirds are uncommon from mid-November to late March, although they are fairly common locally. In most areas they are not seen out in fields with other blackbirds but instead are typical of swampy habitats. They are often very easy to find in wet areas adjacent to pig farms, although the best such sites are off-limits to the public. In the Albemarle-Pamlico region, they may be seen in wet fields with other blackbirds, and they are frequent in Oriental, where they walk about in yards like Common Grackles. About late October and early November, they occur regularly at some barrier island sites after cold fronts.

The Lake Mattamuskeet area and Oriental are two of the best sites for finding Rusties. At both places the birds are easiest to find in late autumn and early winter. At Mattamuskeet, check either along the Wildlife Drive past the refuge headquarters or around livestock on the north side of the lake. During the autumn migration two good sites for Rusties are the north end of Pea Island and Fort Fisher, but birds are likely to be seen during a rather short period, mostly in late October and early November.

To identify this bird, look for a pale-eyed blackbird about the same size as a Red-winged. By late November at least some of the males match the plumage of "spring males" shown in some field guides—that is, they are largely blackish, not rusty. In good light the plumage of these male birds has a noticeable greenish cast. Don't mistake such birds for Brewer's Blackbirds.

SHINY COWBIRD

Although not recorded in North Carolina until 1989, this rapidly increasing species is already a rare year-round visitor. It is quite likely that Shiny Cowbirds will be occasional within a few years, at least at certain seasons and in certain places.

Many beginning birders will ask, "What is a Shiny Cowbird?" Because it has only recently been found in the United States, this cowbird is not included in any of the current field guides. Shiny Cowbirds have been spreading northward from South America through the Caribbean since the beginning of this century and were first recorded in the Florida keys in 1985. Most birders have mixed feelings about the immigration of this species into our country. The male Shiny is quite attractive, and it is always fun to see a new species, but these cowbirds may parasitize some birds that are rarely bothered by Brown-headeds.

It is too early to predict with any certainty exactly what this bird's status may become. They may prove to be most common as a summer visitor, found primarily on the barrier islands and adjacent mainland. All Shiny Cowbirds seen so far in this state have been with Brown-headeds.

The Fort Fisher SHS, where a flock of cowbirds is usually present, may turn out to be a good spot to look for Shiny Cowbirds in future years. One site where birds have been observed is the Wild Birds Unlimited store at Cedar Point, just east of Swansboro. This store has several bird feeders just outside the windows; if a Shiny Cowbird is present, you'll get some close leisurely views.

Seen at close range, and with Brown-headeds for comparison, the male Shiny Cowbird is quite easy to pick out. It is about the same length as a Brown-headed but is obviously slimmer, with a flatter forehead and longer, thinner bill. It does not have a brown head. The bird's plumage is generally blackish, but in good light you will see the purple iridescence on the head, breast, and upper back. The female is much more difficult to identify. The plumage is very similar to that of a female Brown-headed Cowbird. When you see the Shiny with Brown-headeds, however, their different body, head, and bill shape is obvious.

Birds of Coastal
North Carolina
Frequency Graphs

All regularly occurring (i.e., nonaccidental) species are included in these frequency graphs, which are to be used in conjunction with the Birds of Coastal North Carolina annotated list (chapter 3). Refer to that section for definitions of the particular frequency levels. Note that the seasonal frequency levels "extremely rare" and "accidental" are not shown on the graphs.

Frequency graphs can be very useful; they give a reasonable picture of seasonal abundance that can be assimilated in an instant. In reality, though, the status of a species within a large region cannot be described entirely accurately using a bar-graph format. Statuses of some species vary greatly from site to site, making generalizations difficult. For each species, note any qualifiers included with the bar graph. If the qualifier mentions a locally different status for a season, it refers to the peak seasonal status.

For many species, the dates at which they arrive or depart, or become more or less common, may vary appreciably from north to south. In general, the dates shown on the bar graphs are averages. Allow about a week's deviation for North Coast and South Coast sites. More extreme variations are mentioned in the graph notes.

Please take into account that the information presented is for an average year. Extremely severe winter weather can lead to decreases in wading birds, shorebirds, and many small land birds, and increases in waterfowl. During mild winters, many species of waterfowl will be scarce. Abnormal weather in spring may hasten or delay the arrival of summer residents and the departure of winter residents.

Statuses given for many waterfowl species refer to wildlife refuges and other major sites.

Accidental species are listed at the end of chapter 3.

	January	February	March	April	May	June	July	August	September	October	November	December
RED-THROATED LOON locally less common												
PACIFIC LOON												
COMMON LOON												
PIED-BILLED GREBE very local in breeding season												
HORNED GREBE												
RED-NECKED GREBE status at favored sites												
EARED GREBE												
NORTHERN FULMAR status off northern Outer Banks; less common elsewhere												
SOFT-PLUMAGED PETREL												

HERALD PETREL

BLACK-CAPPED PETREL

CORY'S SHEARWATER

GREATER SHEARWATER
status off Outer Banks; less common farther south, especially after June; numbers widely variable in late summer

SOOTY SHEARWATER
spring peak status is for Cape Hatteras; less common elsewhere; extremely rare in autumn

MANX SHEARWATER
off northern Outer Banks; less common elsewhere

AUDUBON'S SHEARWATER

WILSON'S STORM-PETREL
midsummer to autumn status is for Cape Hatteras north; less common in south

= common   = fairly common   = uncommon   = occasional   = rare   = very rare

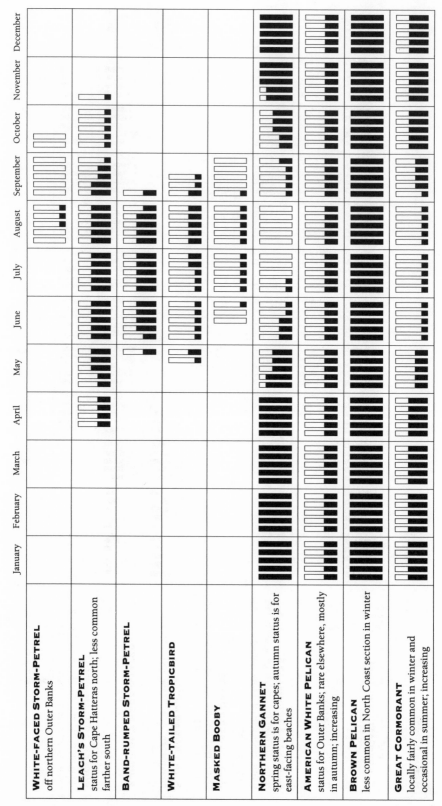

	January	February	March	April	May	June	July	August	September	October	November	December
WHITE-FACED STORM-PETREL off northern Outer Banks												
LEACH'S STORM-PETREL status for Cape Hatteras north; less common farther south												
BAND-RUMPED STORM-PETREL												
WHITE-TAILED TROPICBIRD												
MASKED BOOBY												
NORTHERN GANNET spring status is for capes; autumn status is for east-facing beaches												
AMERICAN WHITE PELICAN status for Outer Banks; rare elsewhere, mostly in autumn; increasing												
BROWN PELICAN less common in North Coast section in winter												
GREAT CORMORANT locally fairly common in winter and occasional in summer; increasing												

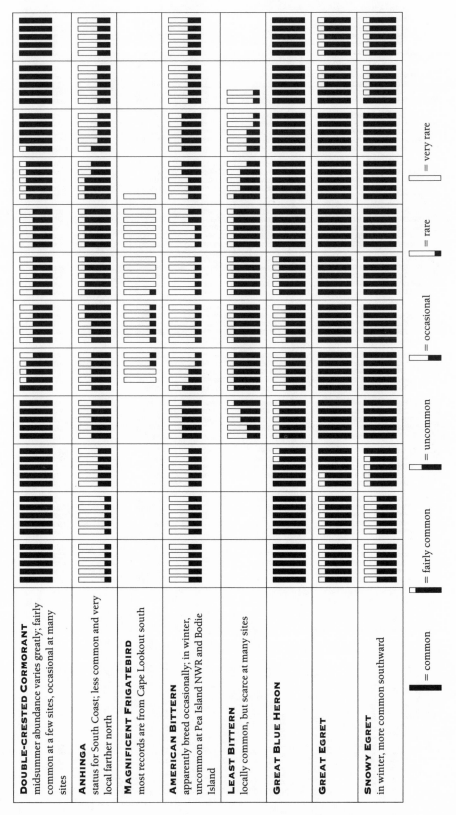

DOUBLE-CRESTED CORMORANT
midsummer abundance varies greatly; fairly common at a few sites, occasional at many sites

ANHINGA
status for South Coast; less common and very local farther north

MAGNIFICENT FRIGATEBIRD
most records are from Cape Lookout south

AMERICAN BITTERN
apparently breed occasionally; in winter, uncommon at Pea Island NWR and Bodie Island

LEAST BITTERN
locally common, but scarce at many sites

GREAT BLUE HERON

GREAT EGRET

SNOWY EGRET
in winter, more common southward

■ = common   ■ = fairly common   ▮ = uncommon   ▯ = occasional   ▢ = rare   ▯ = very rare

	January	February	March	April	May	June	July	August	September	October	November	December

LITTLE BLUE HERON
rather local; in winter, more common southward

TRICOLORED HERON
in winter, more common southward

REDDISH EGRET
occasional from July to September at a few sites; increasing

CATTLE EGRET
rather local, primarily in vicinity of breeding colonies; occasional throughout milder winters at favored sites

GREEN HERON
locally common; in South Coast section, arrive earlier in spring and are occasional throughout winter

BLACK-CROWNED NIGHT-HERON
average status; common at several sites, but uncommon in most areas

YELLOW-CROWNED NIGHT-HERON
locally fairly common; in South Coast section, arrive earlier in spring and may be very rare in winter.

WHITE IBIS
local; most widespread in late summer

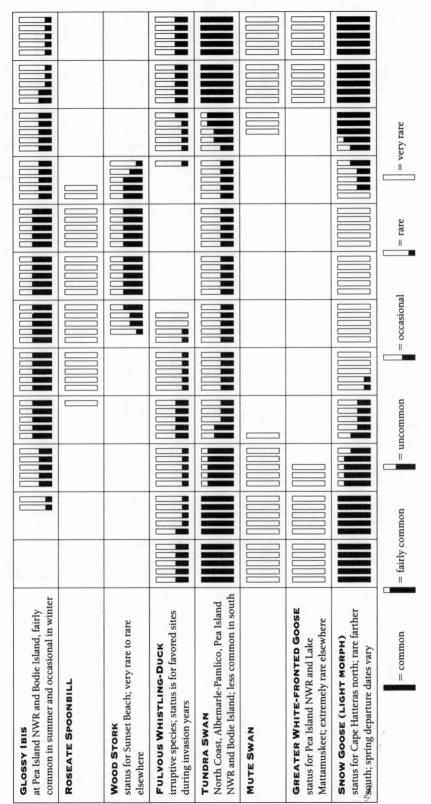

GLOSSY IBIS
at Pea Island NWR and Bodie Island, fairly common in summer and occasional in winter

ROSEATE SPOONBILL

WOOD STORK
status for Sunset Beach; very rare to rare elsewhere

FULVOUS WHISTLING-DUCK
irruptive species; status is for favored sites during invasion years

TUNDRA SWAN
North Coast, Albemarle-Pamlico, Pea Island NWR and Bodie Island; less common in south

MUTE SWAN

GREATER WHITE-FRONTED GOOSE
status for Pea Island NWR and Lake Mattamuskeet; extremely rare elsewhere

SNOW GOOSE (LIGHT MORPH)
status for Cape Hatteras north; rare farther south; spring departure dates vary

= common   = fairly common   = uncommon   = occasional   = rare   = very rare

484

	January	February	March	April	May	June	July	August	September	October	November	December

SNOW GOOSE (DARK MORPH)
status for Lake Mattamuskeet; less common at other refuges; rare in Central Coast and South Coast sections

ROSS' GOOSE
status for Pea Island NWR

BRANT
mostly restricted to Hatteras and Ocracoke inlets; generally rare south of Cape Lookout

CANADA GOOSE
less common in south

WOOD DUCK
locally common

GREEN-WINGED TEAL

"COMMON TEAL"
status for Pea Island NWR and Bodie Island; apparently extremely rare elsewhere

AMERICAN BLACK DUCK
less common southward; breeding status is for Outer Banks

MALLARD
less common southward; local in breeding season, but increasing

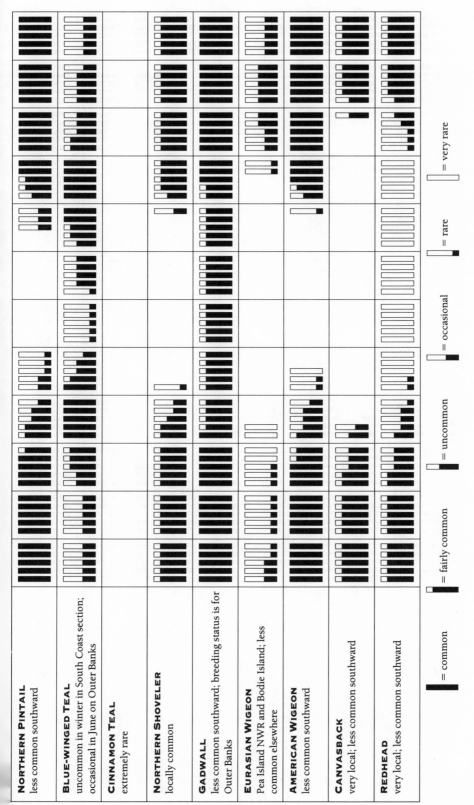

NORTHERN PINTAIL
less common southward

BLUE-WINGED TEAL
uncommon in winter in South Coast section;
occasional in June on Outer Banks

CINNAMON TEAL
extremely rare

NORTHERN SHOVELER
locally common

GADWALL
less common southward; breeding status is for
Outer Banks

EURASIAN WIGEON
Pea Island NWR and Bodie Island; less
common elsewhere

AMERICAN WIGEON
less common southward

CANVASBACK
very local; less common southward

REDHEAD
very local; less common southward

■ = common   ■ = fairly common   ■ = uncommon   ■ = occasional   ▯ = rare | = very rare

	January	February	March	April	May	June	July	August	September	October	November	December

RING-NECKED DUCK
local

GREATER SCAUP
primarily Outer Banks

LESSER SCAUP

COMMON EIDER
status for Outer Banks; less common
elsewhere; extremely rare in summer

KING EIDER
status for Outer Banks; less common
elsewhere

HARLEQUIN DUCK
status for Outer Banks; less common
elsewhere

OLDSQUAW
uncommon at a few sites; common on sound
near Swan Quarter

BLACK SCOTER
sometimes common in winter on western
Pamlico Sound

SURF SCOTER
common in winter on western Pamlico Sound

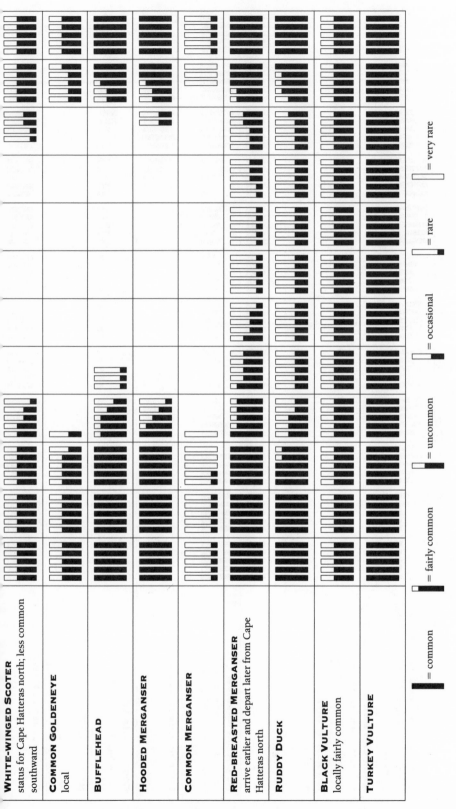

WHITE-WINGED SCOTER
status for Cape Hatteras north; less common southward

COMMON GOLDENEYE
local

BUFFLEHEAD

HOODED MERGANSER

COMMON MERGANSER

RED-BREASTED MERGANSER
arrive earlier and depart later from Cape Hatteras north

RUDDY DUCK

BLACK VULTURE
locally fairly common

TURKEY VULTURE

= common   = fairly common   = uncommon   = occasional   = rare   = very rare

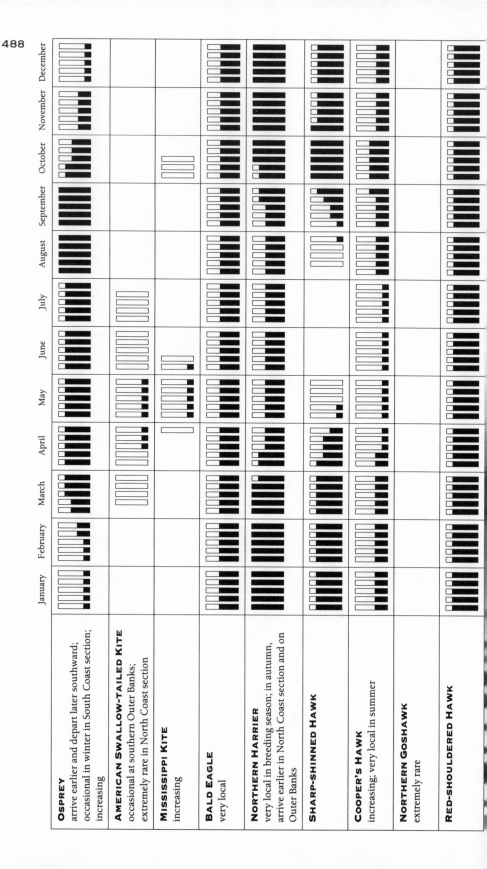

January February March April May June July August September October November December

OSPREY
arrive earlier and depart later southward;
occasional in winter in South Coast section;
increasing

AMERICAN SWALLOW-TAILED KITE
occasional at southern Outer Banks;
extremely rare in North Coast section

MISSISSIPPI KITE
increasing

BALD EAGLE
very local

NORTHERN HARRIER
very local in breeding season; in autumn,
arrive earlier in North Coast section and on
Outer Banks

SHARP-SHINNED HAWK

COOPER'S HAWK
increasing; very local in summer

NORTHERN GOSHAWK
extremely rare

RED-SHOULDERED HAWK

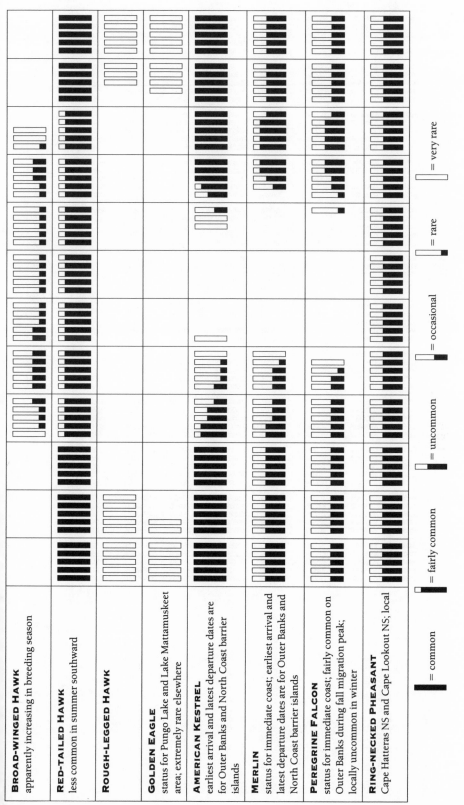

BROAD-WINGED HAWK
apparently increasing in breeding season

RED-TAILED HAWK
less common in summer southward

ROUGH-LEGGED HAWK

GOLDEN EAGLE
status for Pungo Lake and Lake Mattamuskeet area; extremely rare elsewhere

AMERICAN KESTREL
earliest arrival and latest departure dates are for Outer Banks and North Coast barrier islands

MERLIN
status for immediate coast; earliest arrival and latest departure dates are for Outer Banks and North Coast barrier islands

PEREGRINE FALCON
status for immediate coast; fairly common on Outer Banks during fall migration peak; locally uncommon in winter

RING-NECKED PHEASANT
Cape Hatteras NS and Cape Lookout NS; local

■ = common

▯■ = fairly common

▯ = uncommon

▯■ = occasional

▮ = rare

▯ = very rare

	January	February	March	April	May	June	July	August	September	October	November	December

WILD TURKEY
very local

NORTHERN BOBWHITE
common in some areas; decreasing; may be difficult to find outside of breeding season

YELLOW RAIL
assumed status

BLACK RAIL
locally fairly common to common during breeding season

CLAPPER RAIL
less common in winter north of Beaufort Inlet

KING RAIL
fairly common at a few sites

VIRGINIA RAIL
status from North River, Carteret County north; rare in summer farther south

SORA

PURPLE GALLINULE
status for South Coast section; elsewhere, very rare, except rare from late April through May

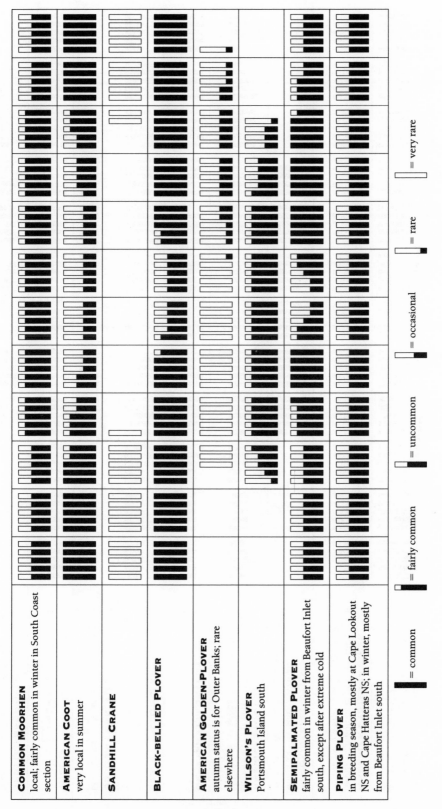

COMMON MOORHEN
local; fairly common in winter in South Coast section

AMERICAN COOT
very local in summer

SANDHILL CRANE

BLACK-BELLIED PLOVER

AMERICAN GOLDEN-PLOVER
autumn status is for Outer Banks; rare elsewhere

WILSON'S PLOVER
Portsmouth Island south

SEMIPALMATED PLOVER
fairly common in winter from Beaufort Inlet south, except after extreme cold

PIPING PLOVER
in breeding season, mostly at Cape Lookout NS and Cape Hatteras NS; in winter, mostly from Beaufort Inlet south

| | = common | | = fairly common | | = uncommon | | = occasional | | = rare | | = very rare |

	January	February	March	April	May	June	July	August	September	October	November	December

KILLDEER
local in breeding season

AMERICAN OYSTERCATCHER
locally common from Beaufort Inlet south, especially in winter; north of Beaufort Inlet, occasional in winter

BLACK-NECKED STILT
status for Pea Island NWR and Bodie Island; elsewhere, very local and uncommon

AMERICAN AVOCET
status for Pea Island NWR and Bodie Island; elsewhere, occasional from late July to mid-November

GREATER YELLOWLEGS

LESSER YELLOWLEGS
local, especially in winter; seldom seen in tidal areas

SOLITARY SANDPIPER
fairly common in South Coast section

WILLET
in winter, less common north of Beaufort Inlet

SPOTTED SANDPIPER
occasional throughout winter in South Coast section

UPLAND SANDPIPER
uncommon autumn migrant at a few sites

WHIMBREL
occasional throughout winter at a few sites

LONG-BILLED CURLEW
status for a few sites; elsewhere, rare, mostly from July to November

HUDSONIAN GODWIT
status for Pea Island NWR and Bodie Island; generally very rare elsewhere

MARBLED GODWIT
status at a few sites; elsewhere, uncommon to fairly common in autumn, occasional in winter, and rare in early summer

RUDDY TURNSTONE
in winter, common south, uncommon north of Beaufort Inlet

RED KNOT
autumn status is for Outer Banks and east-facing beaches; uncommon elsewhere; winter numbers highly variable

SANDERLING

= common   = fairly common   = uncommon   = occasional   = rare   = very rare

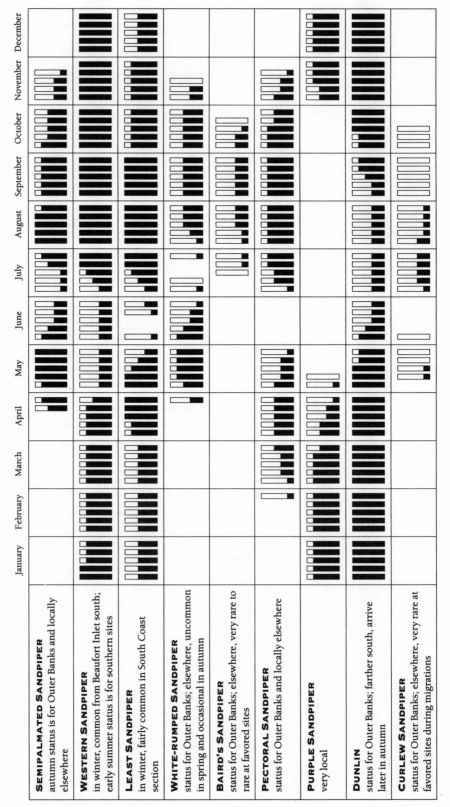

SEMIPALMATED SANDPIPER
autumn status is for Outer Banks and locally elsewhere

WESTERN SANDPIPER
in winter, common from Beaufort Inlet south; early summer status is for southern sites

LEAST SANDPIPER
in winter, fairly common in South Coast section

WHITE-RUMPED SANDPIPER
status for Outer Banks; elsewhere, uncommon in spring and occasional in autumn

BAIRD'S SANDPIPER
status for Outer Banks; elsewhere, very rare to rare at favored sites

PECTORAL SANDPIPER
status for Outer Banks and locally elsewhere

PURPLE SANDPIPER
very local

DUNLIN
status for Outer Banks; farther south, arrive later in autumn

CURLEW SANDPIPER
status for Outer Banks; elsewhere, very rare at favored sites during migrations

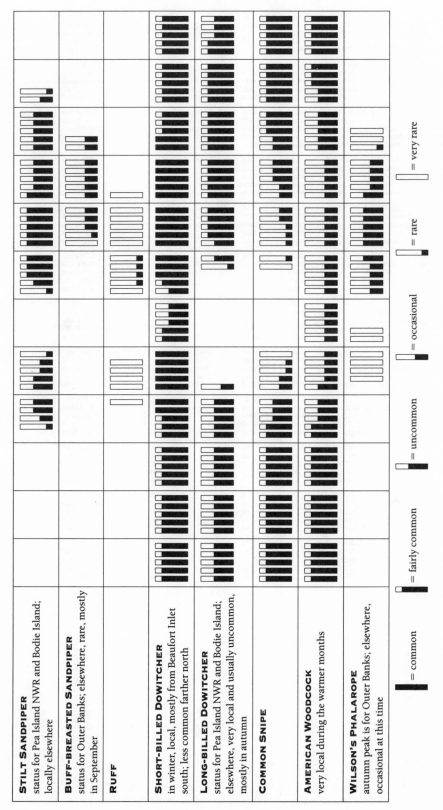

STILT SANDPIPER
status for Pea Island NWR and Bodie Island; locally elsewhere

BUFF-BREASTED SANDPIPER
status for Outer Banks; elsewhere, rare, mostly in September

RUFF

SHORT-BILLED DOWITCHER
in winter, local, mostly from Beaufort Inlet south; less common farther north

LONG-BILLED DOWITCHER
status for Pea Island NWR and Bodie Island; elsewhere, very local and usually uncommon, mostly in autumn

COMMON SNIPE

AMERICAN WOODCOCK
very local during the warmer months

WILSON'S PHALAROPE
autumn peak is for Outer Banks; elsewhere, occasional at this time

■ = common   ☐■ = fairly common   ☐■ = uncommon   ☐ = occasional   ☐■ = rare   ☐ = very rare

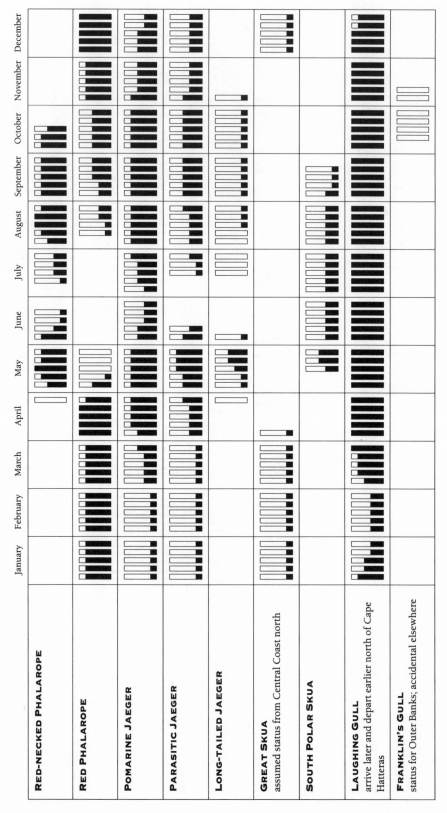

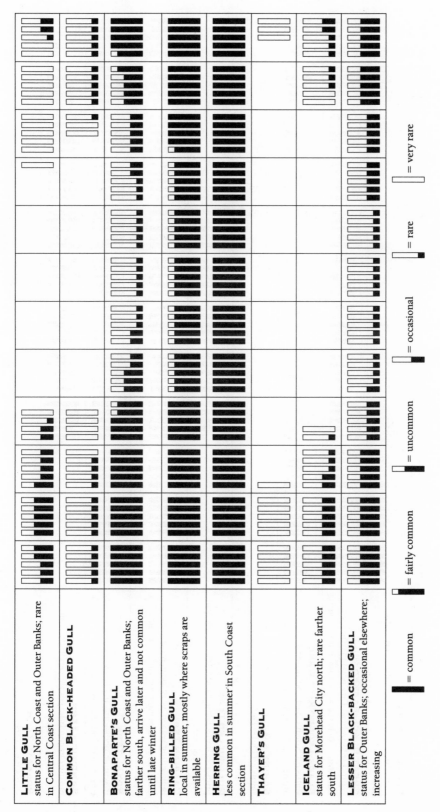

497

LITTLE GULL
status for North Coast and Outer Banks; rare in Central Coast section

COMMON BLACK-HEADED GULL

BONAPARTE'S GULL
status for North Coast and Outer Banks; farther south, arrive later and not common until late winter

RING-BILLED GULL
local in summer, mostly where scraps are available

HERRING GULL
less common in summer in South Coast section

THAYER'S GULL

ICELAND GULL
status for Morehead City north; rare farther south

LESSER BLACK-BACKED GULL
status for Outer Banks; occasional elsewhere; increasing

■ = common   □■ = fairly common   □■ = uncommon   □■ = occasional   □■ = rare   □ = very rare

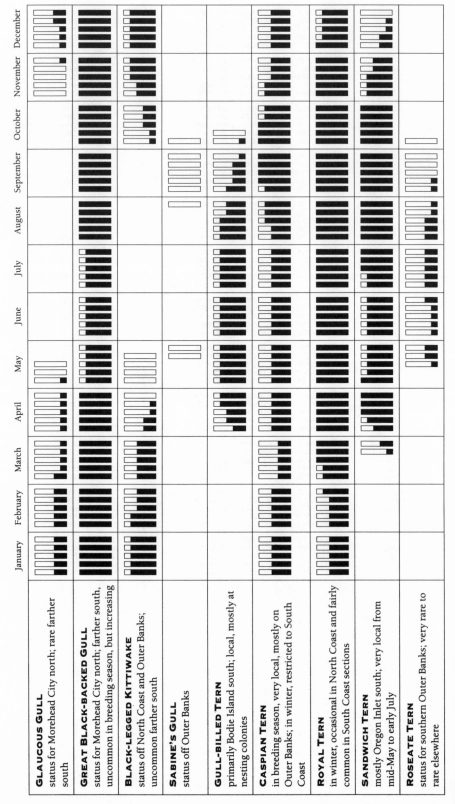

	January	February	March	April	May	June	July	August	September	October	November	December

GLAUCOUS GULL
status for Morehead City north; rare farther south

GREAT BLACK-BACKED GULL
status for Morehead City north; farther south, uncommon in breeding season, but increasing

BLACK-LEGGED KITTIWAKE
status off North Coast and Outer Banks; uncommon farther south

SABINE'S GULL
status off Outer Banks

GULL-BILLED TERN
primarily Bodie Island south; local, mostly at nesting colonies

CASPIAN TERN
in breeding season, very local, mostly on Outer Banks; in winter, restricted to South Coast

ROYAL TERN
in winter, occasional in North Coast and fairly common in South Coast sections

SANDWICH TERN
mostly Oregon Inlet south; very local from mid-May to early July

ROSEATE TERN
status for southern Outer Banks; very rare to rare elsewhere

COMMON TERN
in summer, local in South Coast section; autumn status is for a few favored sites, mostly at capes

ARCTIC TERN
spring status off North Coast and Outer Banks; less common farther south; autumn status open to question

FORSTER'S TERN
uncommon in North Coast section in midwinter; uncommon south of Beaufort Inlet in breeding season

LEAST TERN

BRIDLED TERN
numbers quite variable; often common in late summer

SOOTY TERN
early summer status is for Cape Hatteras; late summer peak is for offshore waters

BLACK TERN

BROWN NODDY
extremely rare

= common = fairly common = uncommon = occasional = rare = very rare

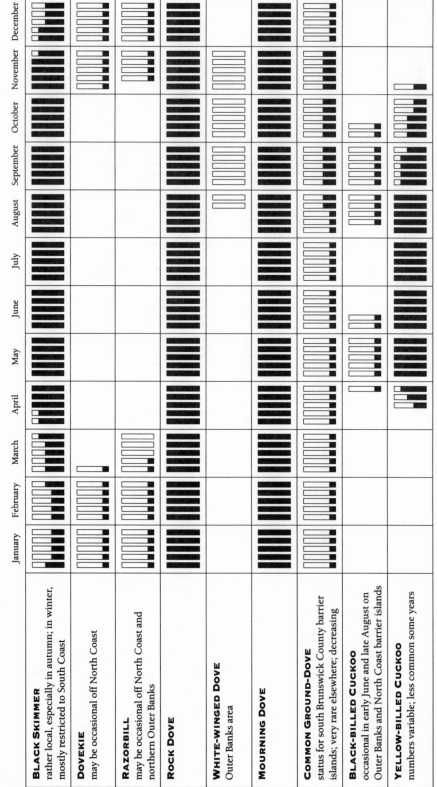

	January	February	March	April	May	June	July	August	September	October	November	December

BLACK SKIMMER
rather local, especially in autumn; in winter, mostly restricted to South Coast

DOVEKIE
may be occasional off North Coast

RAZORBILL
may be occasional off North Coast and northern Outer Banks

ROCK DOVE

WHITE-WINGED DOVE
Outer Banks area

MOURNING DOVE

COMMON GROUND-DOVE
status for south Brunswick County barrier islands; very rare elsewhere; decreasing

BLACK-BILLED CUCKOO
occasional in early June and late August on Outer Banks and North Coast barrier islands

YELLOW-BILLED CUCKOO
numbers variable; less common some years

BARN OWL
local; decreasing

EASTERN SCREECH-OWL

GREAT HORNED OWL
detected less frequently during warmer
months, when they call infrequently

SNOWY OWL
extremely rare

BARRED OWL

SHORT-EARED OWL
locally uncommon

NORTHERN SAW-WHET OWL
status for barrier islands from Cape Hatteras
north; very rare elsewhere

COMMON NIGHTHAWK
rather local; more common in autumn in
South Coast section

CHUCK-WILL'S-WIDOW
arrive earlier in South Coast section; call
infrequently after mid-July

| ▮ = common | ▯ = fairly common | ▯ = uncommon | ▯ = occasional | ▯ = rare | ▯ = very rare |

	January	February	March	April	May	June	July	August	September	October	November	December

WHIP-POOR-WILL
local but increasing; very rare in South Coast section in midwinter

CHIMNEY SWIFT
arrive earlier and depart later in South Coast section

RUBY-THROATED HUMMINGBIRD

RUFOUS HUMMINGBIRD

BELTED KINGFISHER
local during breeding season

RED-HEADED WOODPECKER
locally common in breeding season; locally uncommon in winter

RED-BELLIED WOODPECKER

YELLOW-BELLIED SAPSUCKER

DOWNY WOODPECKER

HAIRY WOODPECKER

RED-COCKADED WOODPECKER
very local

NORTHERN FLICKER

PILEATED WOODPECKER
locally common

OLIVE-SIDED FLYCATCHER

EASTERN WOOD-PEWEE

YELLOW-BELLIED FLYCATCHER

ACADIAN FLYCATCHER

ALDER FLYCATCHER
assumed to be a fall migrant, but no definitive
records

| = common | = fairly common | = uncommon | = occasional | = rare | = very rare |

	January	February	March	April	May	June	July	August	September	October	November	December

WILLOW FLYCATCHER
autumn status conjectural

LEAST FLYCATCHER
uncommon on Outer Banks and North Coast barrier islands

EASTERN PHOEBE
in winter, common southward; in summer, uncommon inland within North Coast section

GREAT CRESTED FLYCATCHER

WESTERN KINGBIRD
status for Outer Banks; occasional elsewhere

EASTERN KINGBIRD

GRAY KINGBIRD

SCISSOR-TAILED FLYCATCHER

HORNED LARK
occasional in Albemarle-Pamlico area; might turn up during any month along western border of region

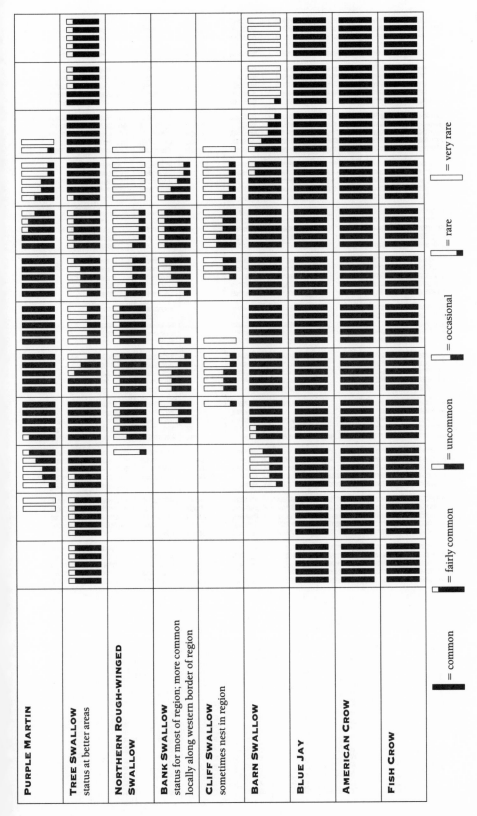

PURPLE MARTIN

TREE SWALLOW
status at better areas

NORTHERN ROUGH-WINGED
SWALLOW

BANK SWALLOW
status for most of region; more common
locally along western border of region

CLIFF SWALLOW
sometimes nest in region

BARN SWALLOW

BLUE JAY

AMERICAN CROW

FISH CROW

■ = common   ▮ = fairly common   ▯ = uncommon   ▯ = occasional   ▯ = rare   ▯ = very rare

	January	February	March	April	May	June	July	August	September	October	November	December

CAROLINA CHICKADEE

TUFTED TITMOUSE

RED-BREASTED NUTHATCH
irruptive species; status for invasion years

WHITE-BREASTED NUTHATCH
very local

BROWN-HEADED NUTHATCH
more common southward, less common northward

BROWN CREEPER
fairly common on Outer Banks in October

CAROLINA WREN

HOUSE WREN
in midwinter, less common northward; local in breeding season

WINTER WREN

SEDGE WREN

MARSH WREN

GOLDEN-CROWNED KINGLET
in spring, sometimes later in North Coast section

RUBY-CROWNED KINGLET

BLUE-GRAY GNATCATCHER
in South Coast section, arrive earlier in spring, more common in autumn, and occasional throughout milder winters

EASTERN BLUEBIRD

VEERY
spring status is for a few favored sites; rare elsewhere; autumn status is for South Coast; rare to occasional elsewhere

GRAY-CHEEKED THRUSH

= common　= fairly common　= uncommon　= occasional　= rare　= very rare

	January	February	March	April	May	June	July	August	September	October	November	December
SWAINSON'S THRUSH												
HERMIT THRUSH												
WOOD THRUSH more common in autumn in South Coast section												
AMERICAN ROBIN more widespread during cooler months												
GRAY CATBIRD less common southward during breeding season												
NORTHERN MOCKINGBIRD												
BROWN THRASHER												
AMERICAN PIPIT												
CEDAR WAXWING occasional all summer in North Coast section; in autumn, more common on Outer Banks												

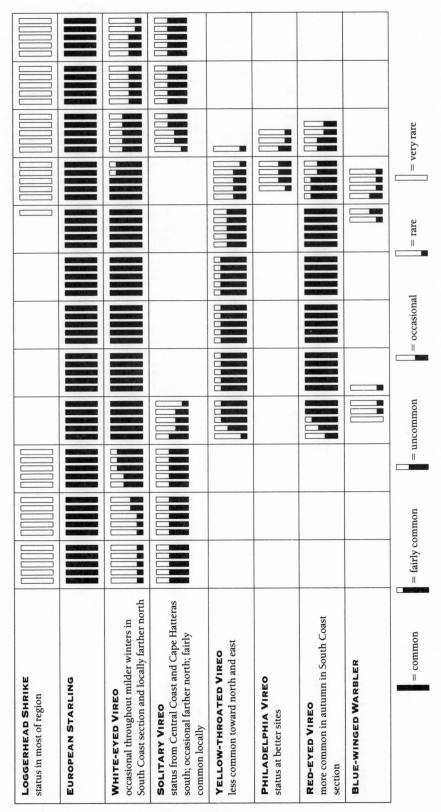

LOGGERHEAD SHRIKE
status in most of region

EUROPEAN STARLING

WHITE-EYED VIREO
occasional throughout milder winters in
South Coast section and locally farther north

SOLITARY VIREO
status from Central Coast and Cape Hatteras
south; occasional farther north; fairly
common locally

YELLOW-THROATED VIREO
less common toward north and east

PHILADELPHIA VIREO
status at better sites

RED-EYED VIREO
more common in autumn in South Coast
section

BLUE-WINGED WARBLER

= common   = fairly common   = uncommon   = occasional   = rare   = very rare

	January	February	March	April	May	June	July	August	September	October	November	December

GOLDEN-WINGED WARBLER

TENNESSEE WARBLER

ORANGE-CROWNED WARBLER
fairly common locally

NASHVILLE WARBLER

NORTHERN PARULA
in South Coast section, more common in autumn and very rare to late December

YELLOW WARBLER
very local breeder on barrier islands from Cape Hatteras north; fairly common through September in South Coast section

CHESTNUT-SIDED WARBLER

MAGNOLIA WARBLER

CAPE MAY WARBLER
autumn status for North Coast barrier islands and Outer Banks; uncommon to fairly common farther south

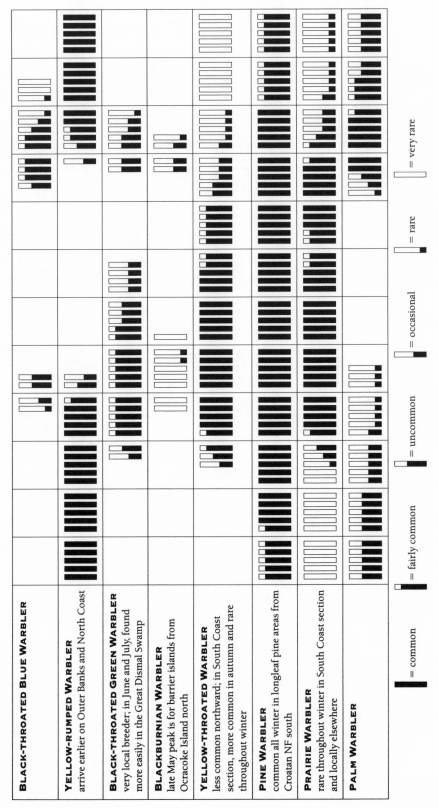

BLACK-THROATED BLUE WARBLER

YELLOW-RUMPED WARBLER
arrive earlier on Outer Banks and North Coast

BLACK-THROATED GREEN WARBLER
very local breeder; in June and July, found
more easily in the Great Dismal Swamp

BLACKBURNIAN WARBLER
late May peak is for barrier islands from
Ocracoke Island north

YELLOW-THROATED WARBLER
less common northward; in South Coast
section, more common in autumn and rare
throughout winter

PINE WARBLER
common all winter in longleaf pine areas from
Croatan NF south

PRAIRIE WARBLER
rare throughout winter in South Coast section
and locally elsewhere

PALM WARBLER

▮ = common ▯▮ = fairly common ▯▮ = uncommon ▯▮ = occasional ▯▯ = rare ▯ = very rare

	January	February	March	April	May	June	July	August	September	October	November	December
BAY-BREASTED WARBLER spring status for Outer Banks					▯▯▯				▮▮▮▮	▮▮		
BLACKPOLL WARBLER autumn status for North Coast barrier islands and Outer Banks; uncommon south and inland				▮	▮▮▮▮▮				▮	▮▮▮▮	▯	
CERULEAN WARBLER				▯				▮	▯▯▯▯▯	▯▯		
BLACK-AND-WHITE WARBLER in breeding season, more common northward and less common southward; occasional throughout winter in South Coast section	▮▮▮▮▮	▮▮▮▮▮	▮▮▮▮▮	▮▮▮▮▮	▮▮▮▮▮	▮▮▮▮▮	▮▮▮▮▮	▮▮▮▮▮	▮▮▮▮▮	▮▮▮▮▮	▮▮▮▮▮	▮▮▮▮▮
AMERICAN REDSTART in breeding season, very local, more common northward and less common southward				▮▮▮▮▮	▮▮▮▮▮	▮▮▮▮▮	▮▮▮▮▮	▮▮▮▮▮	▮▮▮▮▮	▮▮▮	▮	
PROTHONOTARY WARBLER arrive earlier in South Coast section; in late summer, found mostly in more extensive swamps				▮▮▮▮▮	▮▮▮▮▮	▮▮▮▮▮	▮▮▮▮▮	▮▮▮	▮▮			
WORM-EATING WARBLER locally common				▮▮▮▮	▮▮▮▮▮	▮▮▮▮▮	▮▮▮▮▮	▮▮▮▮	▯▯▯▯▯	▯		
SWAINSON'S WARBLER local; fairly common in some areas				▮▮▮▮	▮▮▮▮▮	▮▮▮▮▮	▮▮▮▮	▮▮▮▮▮				

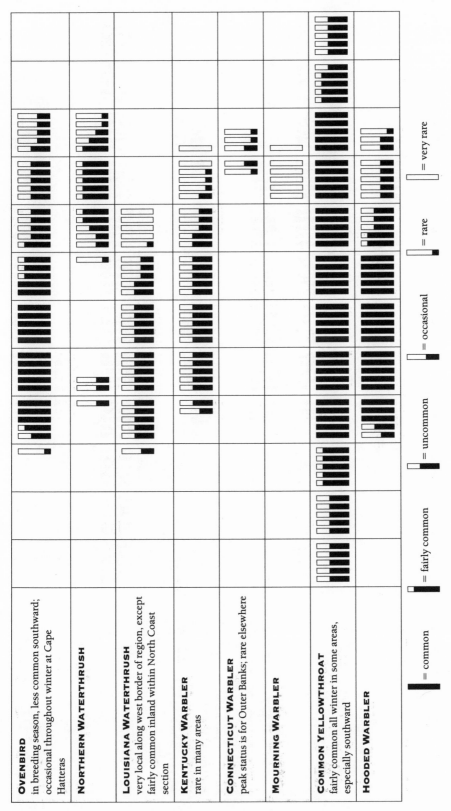

OVENBIRD
in breeding season, less common southward; occasional throughout winter at Cape Hatteras

NORTHERN WATERTHRUSH

LOUISIANA WATERTHRUSH
very local along west border of region, except fairly common inland within North Coast section

KENTUCKY WARBLER
rare in many areas

CONNECTICUT WARBLER
peak status is for Outer Banks; rare elsewhere

MOURNING WARBLER

COMMON YELLOWTHROAT
fairly common all winter in some areas, especially southward

HOODED WARBLER

= common   = fairly common   = uncommon   = occasional   = rare   = very rare

	January	February	March	April	May	June	July	August	September	October	November	December

WILSON'S WARBLER

CANADA WARBLER

YELLOW-BREASTED CHAT
common in many areas

SUMMER TANAGER
breeding status is for Croatan NF south; less common northward; more common in autumn in South Coast section

SCARLET TANAGER
uncommon breeder inland within North Coast section

WESTERN TANAGER

NORTHERN CARDINAL

ROSE-BREASTED GROSBEAK

BLUE GROSBEAK
less common in some areas

515

INDIGO BUNTING
in autumn, more common in South Coast section

PAINTED BUNTING
Carteret County south; local

DICKCISSEL
autumn status on Outer Banks and at Fort Fisher; rarer elsewhere; extremely rare in summer

RUFOUS-SIDED TOWHEE

BACHMAN'S SPARROW
extremely local

CHIPPING SPARROW
in summer, locally common, especially west and north

CLAY-COLORED SPARROW
status for Outer Banks and Fort Fisher; rarer elsewhere

FIELD SPARROW
in summer, very local over most of region, but fairly common on North Coast barrier islands and northern Outer Banks

= common   = fairly common   = uncommon   = occasional   = rare   = very rare

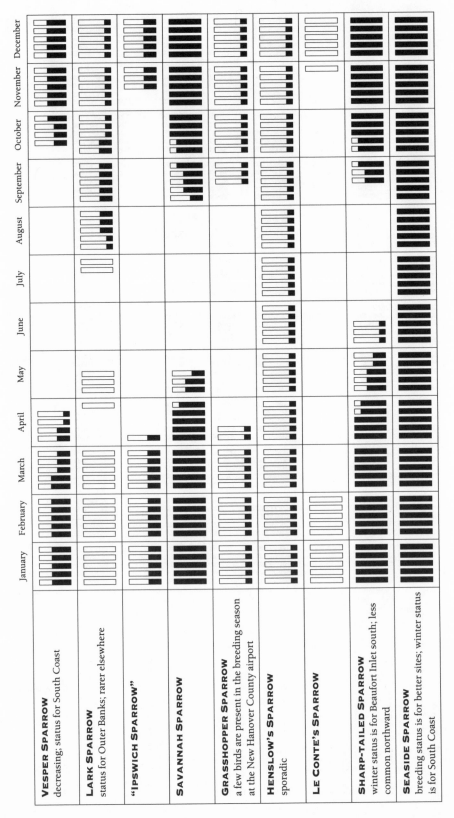

	January	February	March	April	May	June	July	August	September	October	November	December

VESPER SPARROW
decreasing; status for South Coast

LARK SPARROW
status for Outer Banks; rarer elsewhere

"IPSWICH SPARROW"

SAVANNAH SPARROW

GRASSHOPPER SPARROW
a few birds are present in the breeding season
at the New Hanover County airport

HENSLOW'S SPARROW
sporadic

LE CONTE'S SPARROW

SHARP-TAILED SPARROW
winter status is for Beaufort Inlet south; less
common northward

SEASIDE SPARROW
breeding status is for better sites; winter status
is for South Coast

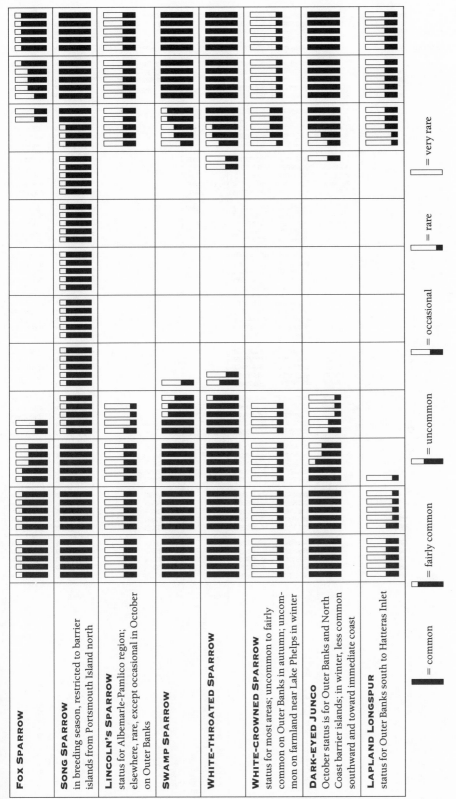

FOX SPARROW

SONG SPARROW
in breeding season, restricted to barrier islands from Portsmouth Island north

LINCOLN'S SPARROW
status for Albemarle-Pamlico region; elsewhere, rare, except occasional in October on Outer Banks

SWAMP SPARROW

WHITE-THROATED SPARROW

WHITE-CROWNED SPARROW
status for most areas; uncommon to fairly common on Outer Banks in autumn; uncommon on farmland near Lake Phelps in winter

DARK-EYED JUNCO
October status is for Outer Banks and North Coast barrier islands; in winter, less common southward and toward immediate coast

LAPLAND LONGSPUR
status for Outer Banks south to Hatteras Inlet

= common   = fairly common   = uncommon   = occasional   = rare   = very rare

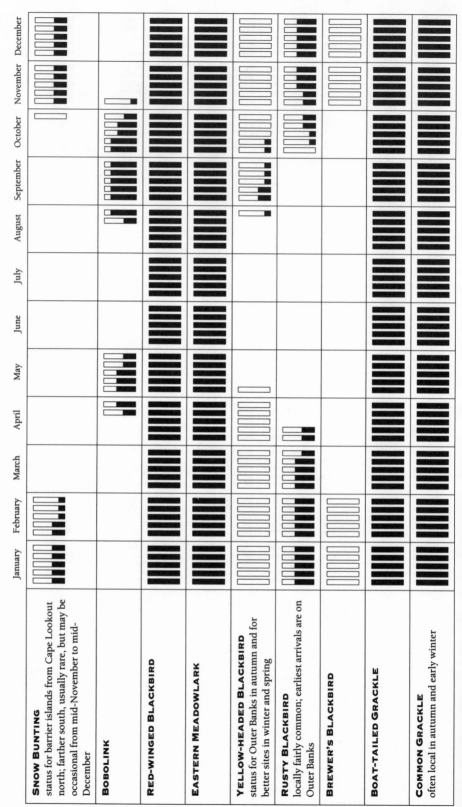

	January	February	March	April	May	June	July	August	September	October	November	December

SNOW BUNTING
status for barrier islands from Cape Lookout north; farther south, usually rare, but may be occasional from mid-November to mid-December

BOBOLINK

RED-WINGED BLACKBIRD

EASTERN MEADOWLARK

YELLOW-HEADED BLACKBIRD
status for Outer Banks in autumn and for better sites in winter and spring

RUSTY BLACKBIRD
locally fairly common; earliest arrivals are on Outer Banks

BREWER'S BLACKBIRD

BOAT-TAILED GRACKLE

COMMON GRACKLE
often local in autumn and early winter

SHINY COWBIRD
increasing

BROWN-HEADED COWBIRD
often local in autumn and early winter

ORCHARD ORIOLE

NORTHERN (BALTIMORE) ORIOLE
wintering birds are very local at feeders

PURPLE FINCH
irruptive species; status is for invasion years, which are becoming rare

HOUSE FINCH
less common in South Coast section during breeding season, but increasing

RED CROSSBILL

COMMON REDPOLL

PINE SISKIN
irruptive species; status is for invasion years, which are becoming rare

= common = fairly common = uncommon = occasional = rare = very rare

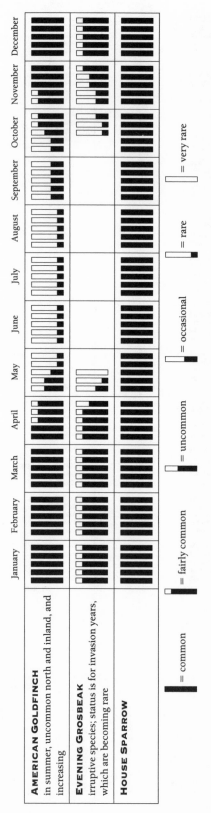

Page numbers in italics refer to status listings in chapter 3; page numbers in boldface refer to frequency graphs.